Jacques Blanc-Talon   Don Bone
Wilfried Philips   Dan Popescu
Paul Scheunders (Eds.)

Advanced Concepts for Intelligent Vision Systems

12th International Conference, ACIVS 2010
Sydney, Australia, December 13-16, 2010
Proceedings, Part I

 Springer

Volume Editors

Jacques Blanc-Talon
DGA/D4S/MRIS
94114 Arcueil, France
E-mail: jacques.blanc-talon@dga.defense.gouv.fr

Don Bone
Canon Information Systems Research Australia
Sydney, NSW 2113, Australia
E-mail: don.bone@cisra.canon.com.au

Wilfried Philips
Ghent University
B9000 Ghent, Belgium
E-mail: philips@telin.UGent.be

Dan Popescu
CSIRO ICT Centre
Epping, NSW 1710, Sydney, Australia
E-mail: dan.popescu@csiro.au

Paul Scheunders
University of Antwerp
2610 Wilrijk, Belgium
E-mail: Paul.Scheunders@ua.ac.be

Library of Congress Control Number: 2010940504

CR Subject Classification (1998): I.4, I.5, C.2, I.2, I.2.10, H.4

LNCS Sublibrary: SL 6 – Image Processing, Computer Vision, Pattern Recognition, and Graphics

ISSN   0302-9743
ISBN-10   3-642-17687-9 Springer Berlin Heidelberg New York
ISBN-13   978-3-642-17687-6 Springer Berlin Heidelberg New York

springer.com

© Springer-Verlag Berlin Heidelberg 2010
Printed in Germany

Typesetting: Camera-ready by author, data conversion by Scientific Publishing Services, Chennai, India
Printed on acid-free paper   06/3180

Lecture Notes in Computer Science 6474

Commenced Publication in 1973
Founding and Former Series Editors:
Gerhard Goos, Juris Hartmanis, and Jan van Leeuwen

Preface

This volume collects the papers accepted for presentation at the 12th International Conference on "Advanced Concepts for Intelligent Vision Systems" (ACIVS 2010). Following the first meeting in Baden-Baden (Germany) in 1999, which was part of a large multiconference, the ACIVS conference then developed into an independent scientific event and has ever since maintained the tradition of being a single track conference. ACIVS 2010 attracted computer scientists from 29 different countries, mostly from Europe, Australia, and the USA, but also from Asia.

Although ACIVS is a conference on all areas of image and video processing, submissions tend to gather within certain major fields of interest. This year 3D and depth processing and computer vision and surveillance were popular topics. Noteworthy are the growing number of papers related to theoretical developments. We would like to thank the invited speakers Mubarak Shah (University of Central Florida), Richard Kleihorst (VITO, Belgium), Richard Hartley (Australian National University), and David Suter (Adelaide University) for their valuable contributions.

A conference like ACIVS would not be feasible without the concerted effort of many people and support of various institutions. The paper submission and review procedure was carried out electronically and a minimum of two reviewers were assigned to each paper. From 144 submissions, 39 were selected for oral presentation and 39 as posters. A large and energetic Program Committee, helped by additional referees (111 people in total) – listed on the following pages – completed the long and demanding review process. We would like to thank all of them for their timely and high-quality reviews. Also, we would like to thank our sponsors, CSIRO, Ghent University, CiSRA, NICTA, Antwerp University, Philips Research, Barco, and DSP-Valley for their valuable support.

Last but not least, we would like to thank all the participants who trusted in our ability to organize this conference for the 12th time. We hope they attended a stimulating scientific event and enjoyed the atmosphere of the ACIVS social events in the city of Sydney.

September 2010

J. Blanc-Talon
D. Bone
D. Popescu
W. Philips
P. Scheunders

Organization

ACIVS 2010 was organized by CSIRO and Ghent University.

Steering Committee

Jacques Blanc-Talon	DGA, France
Wilfried Philips	Ghent University - IBBT, Belgium
Dan Popescu	CSIRO, Australia
Paul Scheunders	University of Antwerp, Belgium

Organizing Committee

Don Bone	Canon Information Systems Research Australia, Australia
Russell Connally	Macquarie University, Australia
Dan Popescu	CSIRO, Australia

Sponsors

ACIVS 2010 was sponsored by the following organizations:

- CSIRO
- Ghent University
- CiSRA
- NICTA
- Philips Research
- Barco
- DSP Valley
- Antwerp University

Program Committee

Hamid Aghajan	Stanford University, USA
Marc Antonini	Université de Nice Sophia Antipolis, France
Laure Blanc-Feraud	INRIA, France
Philippe Bolon	University of Savoie, France
Salah Bourennane	Ecole Centrale de Marseille, France
Dumitru Burdescu	University of Craiova, Romania
Umberto Castellani	Università degli Studi di Verona, Italy
Jocelyn Chanussot	INPG, France
Pamela Cosman	University of California at San Diego, USA
Yves D'Asseler	Ghent University, Belgium
Jennifer Davidson	Iowa State University, USA
Arturo de la Escalera Hueso	Universidad Carlos III de Madrid, Spain
Touradj Ebrahimi	Ecole Polytechnique Fédérale de Lausanne, Switzerland
Christine Fernandez-Maloigne	Université de Poitiers, France
Don Fraser	Australian Defence Force Academy, Australia
Jerome Gilles	UCLA, USA
Georgy Gimel'farb	The University of Auckland, New Zealand
Markku Hauta-Kasari	University of Eastern Finland, Finland
Mark Hedley	CSIRO ICT Centre, Australia
Dimitris Iakovidis	University of Athens, Greece
Tianzi Jiang	The Chinese Academy of Sciences, China
Arto Kaarna	Lappeenranta University of Technology, Finland
Andrzej Kasinski	Poznan University of Technology, Poland
Richard Kleihorst	VITO, Belgium
Nikos Komodakis	University of Crete, Crete
Murat Kunt	EPFL, Switzerland
Hideo Kuroda	FPT University, Vietnam
Olivier Laligant	IUT Le Creusot, France
Kenneth Lam	The Hong Kong Polytechnic University, China
Peter Lambert	Ghent University, Belgium
Alessandro Ledda	Artesis University College, Belgium
Maylor Leung	Nanyang Technological University, Singapore
Yue Li	CSIRO ICT Centre, Australia
Brian Lovell	University of Queensland, Australia
Guojun Lu	Monash University, Australia
Anthony Maeder	University of Western Sydney, Australia
Xavier Maldague	Université de Laval, Canada
Joseph Mariani	Université Paris VI, Paris XI, France
Gérard Medioni	USC/IRIS, USA

Fabrice Mériaudeau	IUT Le Creusot, France
Alfred Mertins	Universität zu Lübeck, Germany
Jean Meunier	Université de Montréal, Canada
Amar Mitiche	INRS, Canada
Rafael Molina	Universidad de Granada, Spain
Adrian Munteanu	Vrije Universiteit Brussel, Belgium
Frank Nielsen	Ecole Polytechnique - Sony CSL, France
Fernando Pereira	Instituto Superior Técnico, Portugal
Stuart Perry	Canon Information Systems Research Australia, Australia
Massimo Piccardi	University of Technology Sydney, Australia
Aleksandra Pizurica	Ghent University - IBBT, Belgium
William Puech	LIRMM, France
Gianni Ramponi	Trieste University, Italy
Paolo Remagnino	Kingston University, UK
Luis Salgado Alvarez de Sotomayor	Universidad Politécnica de Madrid, Spain
Guna Seetharaman	AFRL, USA
Andrzej Sluzek	Nanyang Technological University, Singapore
Changming Sun	CSIRO, CMIS, Australia
Hugues Talbot	ESIEE, France
Frederic Truchetet	Université de Bourgogne, France
Marc Van Droogenbroeck	University of Liège, Belgium
Peter Veelaert	University College Ghent, Belgium
Gerald Zauner	Fachhochschule Oberösterreich, Austria
Pavel Zemcik	Brno University of Technology, Czech Republic
Djemel Ziou	Sherbrooke University, Canada

Reviewers

Hamid Aghajan	Stanford University, USA
Marc Antonini	Université de Nice Sophia Antipolis, France
Sileye Ba	Telecom Bretagne, France
Etienne Baudrier	University of Strasbourg, France
Rik Bellens	Ghent University, Belgium
Jacques Blanc-Talon	DGA, France
Philippe Bolon	University of Savoie, France
Don Bone	Canon Information Systems Research Australia, Australia
Patrick Bonnin	Université de Versailles Saint Quentin, France
Alberto Borghese	University of Milan, Italy
Salah Bourennane	Ecole Centrale de Marseille, France
Dumitru Burdescu	University of Craiova, Romania
Alice Caplier	Université de Grenoble, France

Table of Contents – Part I

Image Processing and Analysis

Segmentation and Edge Detection

3D and Depth

Algorithms and Optimisations

Table of Contents – Part II

Video Processing

Surveillance and Camera Networks

Machine Vision

Remote Sensing

Recognition, Classification and Tracking

A Criterion of Noisy Images Quality

Sergey V. Sai, Ilya S. Sai, and Nikolay Yu. Sorokin

Pacific National University, Tikhookeanskaya str. 136,
Khabarovsk, Russia, 680035
sai@evm.khstu.ru

Abstract. This work describes an objective criterion of quality estimation of fine details in the noisy images in the normalized equal color space. Comparison with the standard PSNR criterion is presented for noisy images.

Keywords: Image analysis, fine details, filtering.

1 Introduction

The peak signal-to-noise ratio (PSNR) is considered nowadays the most popular criterion of noisy images [1]. According to this criterion the normalized root-mean-square deviation of color coordinates is calculated and the averaging is carried out at all pixels of the image. The ratio of the maximal amplitude (A) of the signal to the root-mean-square deviation in logarithmic scale defines PSNR value:

$$PSNR = 20 \lg \frac{A}{\sqrt{\frac{1}{N_x \cdot N_y} \sum_{i=1}^{N_x} \sum_{j=1}^{N_y} \Delta C_{i,j}}} \tag{1}$$

where $\Delta C_{i,j} = (R_{i,j} - \tilde{R}_{i,j})^2 + (G_{i,j} - \tilde{G}_{i,j})^2 + (B_{i,j} - \tilde{B}_{i,j})^2$, R,G,B – are the color signals without noise, $\tilde{R},\tilde{G},\tilde{B}$ – are the color signals with noise and $N_x \cdot N_y$ is the number of pixels in the image.

Thus, the closer the noisy image to the original, the bigger the PSNR value and therefore the better its quality we have. However this and other similar metrics allow for estimating only root-mean-square difference between images, therefore the best results from the metrics point of view are not always correspond to the best visual perception. For instance, the noisy image containing fine details with low contrast can have high PSNR value even when the details are not visible on the background noise.

Filtering algorithms of noisy images are well investigated and described in literature, e.g. [2]. They are usually specialize on suppression of a particular kind of noise. Meanwhile there are no universal filters, that could detect and suppress all kinds of noise. However many kinds of noise can be rather well approximated using model of Gaussian noise. And therefore the majority of algorithms are focused on suppression of this kind of noise. The basic problem at noise filtering is not to spoil sharpness of details borders of the image, and also not to lose the fine details that are comparable on amplitude with noise [3].

J. Blanc-Talon et al. (Eds.): ACIVS 2010, Part I, LNCS 6474, pp. 1–9, 2010.

One more complication is the rating of noise suppression quality. As a rule, the quality is estimated as follows: the artificial noise is imposed on the original image, and then the resulted image is filtered with the help of the chosen algorithm and compared to the initial image with the help of the chosen metrics. Thus, the closer the filtered image to the original, the bigger PSNR value (1) is obtained and that is considered the quality of the filtering algorithm. As it has been pointed above, the PSNR value allows for estimating only the root-mean-square difference between images, and therefore the best results from the point of view of the metrics (also other than PSNR) do not always correspond to the best visual perception [4].

As it was mentioned above, the PSNR value allows for estimating the root-mean-square difference between images. Therefore, the bigger PSNR values are not always correspond to better visual perception of fine details.

Works [5,6] present the search algorithm and the distortion analysis of fine details of real images after JPEG, JPEG-2000 and MPEG-4 compression. Results, presented in the current work are the development in the field of objective criterions of image quality.

2 Criterion of Quality Estimation of the Noisy Images

Lets consider an alternative algorithm and criterion of quality estimation of fine details in the noisy images.

The main idea of the algorithm is the transformation from the primary color space RGB into the equal color space, e.g., $W^*U^*V^*$. Color coordinates of the pixel in the Wyszecki system [7] are defined as follows:

$$W^* = 25Y^{1/3} - 17$$
$$U^* = 13W^*(u - u_0)$$
$$V^* = 13W^*(v - v_0),$$

where Y is the luminance, W^* is the brightness index, U^* and V^* are the chromaticity indices, u and v are the chromaticity coordinates in Mac-Adam diagram [8]; $u_0 = 0.201$ and $v_0 = 0.307$ are the chromaticity coordinates of basic white color.

This transformation into the equal color space allows for estimating the color differences of the big image details using the minimum perceptible color difference (MPCD). These values are almost equal through the whole color space [9]. Here the error of the color rendering is determined by the MPCD value using the following equation:

$$\varepsilon = 3\sqrt{(\Delta W^*)^2 + (\Delta U^*)^2 + (\Delta V^*)^2} \qquad (2)$$

where ΔW^*, ΔU^* and ΔV^* are difference values of color coordinates of two images. Formula (2) can be used for estimation of the color contrast of a big detail relative to the background.

Threshold values on brightness and chromaticity indices depend on the size of image details, background color coordinates, time period of object presentation and noise level. Therefore the formula (2) will not be objective for the analysis of color transfer distortions of fine details.

Works [6,10] propose to use the normalized value of the color contrast for estimating the color transfer distortions of fine details:

$$\Delta \overline{K} = 3\sqrt{(\Delta \overline{W}^*)^2 + (\Delta \overline{U}^*)^2 + (\Delta \overline{V}^*)^2} \tag{3}$$

where $\Delta \overline{W}^* = (W^*_{max} - W^*_{min})/\Delta W^*_{th}$, $\Delta \overline{U}^* = (U^*_{max} - U^*_{min})/\Delta U^*_{th}$, $\Delta \overline{V}^* = (V^*_{max} - V^*_{min})/\Delta V^*_{th}$ are the normalized to the thresholds contrast values of the image with fine details and ΔW^*_{th}, ΔU^*_{th}, ΔV^*_{th} are the thresholds according to brightness and chromaticity indices for fine details.

These threshold values are obtained experimentally [10] for fine details with sizes not exceeding one pixel. From the experimental data, for fine details of the test table located on a grey background threshold values are approximately $\Delta W^*_{th} \approx 6MPCD$ and $\Delta U^*_{th} \approx V^*_{th} \approx 72MPCD$.

Search algorithm [5] of fine details divides the image into the blocks of size 3×3. After this, the recognition of the image blocks using special binary masks is performed. These masks have the following attributes: a "dot object", a "thin line", a "texture fragment".

For recognition of those attributes the image of the block will be transformed to the binary form as follows. At first, the following condition is checked for each pixel of the block:

$$\sqrt{\left(\frac{\Delta W^*_i}{\Delta W^*_{th}}\right)^2 + \left(\frac{\Delta U^*_i}{\Delta U^*_{th}}\right)^2 + \left(\frac{\Delta V^*_i}{\Delta V^*_{th}}\right)^2} < 1 \tag{4}$$

where $\Delta W^*_i = 3(W^*_i - W^*_{min})$, $\Delta U^*_i = 3(U^*_i - U^*_{min})$, $\Delta V^*_i = 3(V^*_i - V^*_{min})$ – are the differences of the coordinates for the comparison of pixels color coordinates with the minimal value; or $\Delta W^*_i = 3(W^*_i - W^*_{max})$, $\Delta U^*_i = 3(U^*_i - U^*_{max})$, $\Delta V^*_i = 3(V^*_i - V^*_{max})$ – are the differences of the coordinates for the comparison of pixels color coordinates with the maximal value. If the condition (4) is fulfilled the decision on membership of the pixel to the minimal or to the maximal value is taken. The level of one is assigned to the maximal values and level of zero to the minimal values, accordingly.

After that, the binary block of the image is compared to the binary images of the masks for the identification of this block. If the image block is not equal to any mask the decision is made that this block does not contain the fine details. Also this block is then excluded from the analysis. Together with this, we exclude the image blocks with very high and very low contrast, i.e. when the condition $1 \le \Delta \overline{K} \le 4$ for these blocks is fullfilled.

Next for each found j-th block the deviation of the maximal value of color coordinates is computed:

$$\tilde{\varepsilon}_j = \max_N \left(3\sqrt{(\Delta \tilde{W}^*_{ij})^2 + (\Delta \tilde{U}^*_{ij})^2 + (\Delta \tilde{V}^*_{ij})^2}\right) \tag{5}$$

where $i = 1 \ldots N$, $N = 9$ and

$$\Delta \tilde{W}_{ij}^* = (W_{ij}^* - \tilde{W}_{ij}^*)/W_{th}^*$$
$$\Delta \tilde{U}_{ij}^* = (U_{ij}^* - \tilde{U}_{ij}^*)/U_{th}^*$$
$$\Delta \tilde{V}_{ij}^* = (V_{ij}^* - \tilde{V}_{ij}^*)/V_{th}^*$$

are deviations on brightness and on chromaticity normalized to the corresponding thresholds.

An average value of deviation for all M selected blocks of the image is computed as:

$$\bar{\varepsilon} = \frac{1}{M} \sum_{j=0}^{M-1} \bar{\varepsilon}_j. \tag{6}$$

Finally the degree of noise in the image is described by the average deviation value from equation (6).

A ten-point scale of quality, used in Adobe Photoshop 5.0 system, during the realization of JPEG compression algorithm is chosen [6]. Here we show experimentally that for the high image quality ($R \geq 7$) the mean error value must satisfy

$$\bar{\varepsilon} \leq 1. \tag{7}$$

Experimental results have shown very high correspondence between the criterion (7) and the subjective quality estimations. This was shown not only for the JPEG compression but for other lossy image compression algorithms.

Lets consider the features of the proposed criterion for the quality estimation of fine details in the noisy images. At the beginning the search algorithm of fine details is performed using on the images without noise. In difference to the described above algorithm the search condition is: if the normalized contrast satisfies

$$\Delta \overline{K} > 1 \tag{8}$$

for blocks 3×3, then the decision is made that the fine details or the border elements of big details are present in the image block.

In order to analyze the noise influence on the image definition reduction the following assumptions are used: 1) Interaction of signals and noise is additive. 2) Density distribution law of stationary noise probabilities is close to the normal law. 3) Noise in RGB signals of the decoded image is not correlative. Such assumptions are widely used in the engineering computations of noise-immune TV systems. They allow to simplify the analysis with the admissible errors.

Noise in the system results in "diffusion" of both objects color coordinates and background in the decoded image. Thus a point in RGB space is transformed into ellipsoid with semi axis. Their values are proportional to root-mean-square noise levels ($\sigma_R, \sigma_G, \sigma_B$). During the transformation $\{R_i G_i B_i\} \rightarrow \{W_i^* U_i^* V_i^*\}$ the values of equal color space coordinates become random variables with root-mean-square deviations ($\sigma_{W^*}, \sigma_{U^*}, \sigma_{V^*}$). Works [6,10] present the probability analysis of such transformation and obtain a criterion that describes when the fine detail will be recognized against the background noise.

This criterion is formulated as

$$\Delta\overline{K} \geq 3\sqrt{(\overline{\sigma}_{W*})^2 + (\overline{\sigma}_{U*})^2 + (\overline{\sigma}_{V*})^2} \tag{9}$$

where $\Delta\overline{K}$ is normalized contrast (3) of the block with fine details; $\overline{\sigma}_{W*}$, $\overline{\sigma}_{U*}$ and $\overline{\sigma}_{V*}$ are normalized to visual perception thresholds root-mean-square noise values. Note, that this criterion uses a simple "three sigma" rule [11].

Let's define criterion when the image noise will be imperceptible or hardly noticeable for an eye during the observation of fine details with the lowest contrast $\Delta\overline{K} \approx 1$:

$$\overline{\sigma}_\Sigma = \sqrt{(\overline{\sigma}_{W*})^2 + (\overline{\sigma}_{U*})^2 + (\overline{\sigma}_{V*})^2} \leq 1/3 \tag{10}$$

where $\overline{\sigma}_\Sigma$ is a total root-mean-square value computed for all image blocks that contain fine details. Values $\overline{\sigma}_{W*}$, $\overline{\sigma}_{U*}$ and $\overline{\sigma}_{V*}$ are computed as, e.g. for brightness:

$$\overline{\sigma}_{W*} = \max_M \left(\frac{1}{W_{th}^* \cdot N} \sum_{i=0}^{N-1} |W_{ij}^* - \tilde{W}_{ij}^*| \right) \tag{11}$$

where $N = 9$ – number of elements in the block, $j = 1 \ldots M$ and M is the number of blocks. Values $\overline{\sigma}_{U*}$ and $\overline{\sigma}_{V*}$ are computed similar to (11). Note, that in contrast to formulas (5) and (6) in (11), at first, we compute the mean value of the noise in the block and then select the maximum.

Thus, for estimating the noisiness of the fine details we should search for these details and then estimate the value $\overline{\sigma}_\Sigma$ using criterion (10). If this criterion is fulfilled the decision is made that:

- for the fine details the contrast change is imperceptible for an eye, and
- the presence of noise in the RGB channels does not impair the image quality.

3   Results of Comparison with PSNR Criterion

Main differences of the new criterion (10) from the PSNR (1) and from the well-known Structural Similarity (SSIM) index, described in [4], are:

- new algorithm analyzes distortions over the part of the image: it covers only image fragments that contain the fine details;
- root-mean-square difference between the source and noisy images is defined by the value $\overline{\sigma}_\Sigma$ which is estimated by the number of normalized thresholds of an eye.

Therefore, the proposed criterion (10) is more objective because it takes into account the features of the visual perception of the contrast distortions of fine details.

A program analyzer is implemented in order to investigate the efficiency of the quality estimation of fine details representation. As an additive noise models the fluctuation Gaussian noise and impulsive noise were selected.

Figures 1 and 2 show examples of the test images "Lena" and "Barbara" with different levels of the impulsive noise.

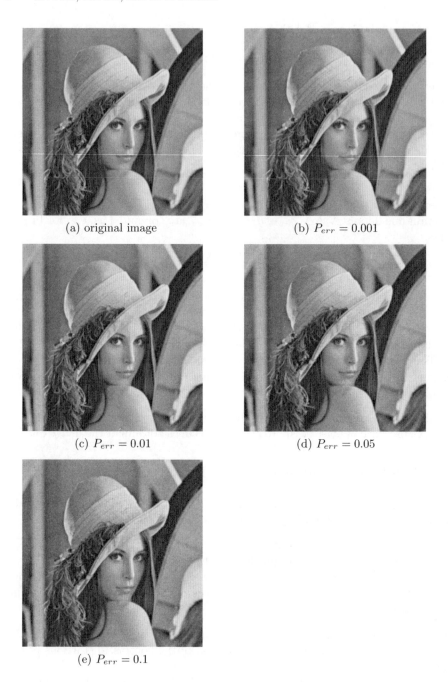

(a) original image

(b) $P_{err} = 0.001$

(c) $P_{err} = 0.01$

(d) $P_{err} = 0.05$

(e) $P_{err} = 0.1$

Fig. 1. Test image "Lena" with impulsive noise

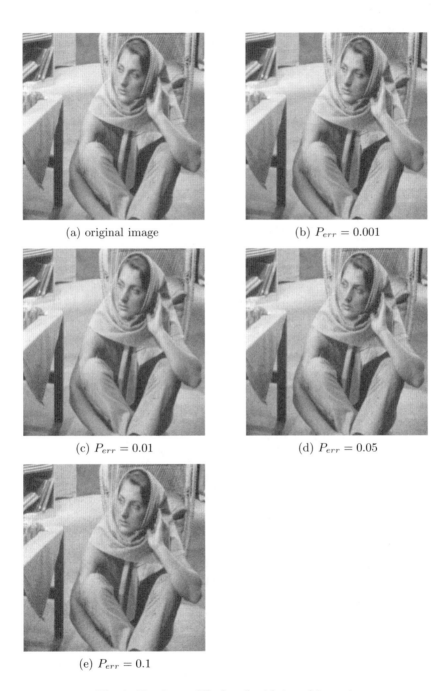

(a) original image   (b) $P_{err} = 0.001$

(c) $P_{err} = 0.01$ (d) $P_{err} = 0.05$

(e) $P_{err} = 0.1$

Fig. 2. Test image "Barbara" with impulsive noise

Table 1 contains the experimental dependencies of $\overline{\sigma}_\Sigma$ and PSNR from root-mean-square noise value (σ) for the test images "Lena" and "Barbara", accordingly. Here the root-mean-square value of the Gaussian noise was set as a ratio to the maximum amplitude (A) of the signal. The following assumption was used: $\sigma \approx \sigma_R \approx \sigma_G \approx \sigma_B$.

Table 1. Dependencies of $\overline{\sigma}_\Sigma$ and PSNR (in dB) from σ (in %) for two test images "Lena" and "Barbara"

σ	$\overline{\sigma}_{\Sigma\,Lena}$	$PSNR_{Lena}$	$\overline{\sigma}_{\Sigma\,Barbara}$	$PSNR_{Barbara}$
0.5	0.11	46.7	0.09	46.7
1.0	0.15	43.9	0.15	43.9
1.5	0.23	42.3	0.21	42.3
2.0	0.31	41.0	0.30	41.0
3.0	0.47	39.3	0.43	39.3

Table 2 presents the experimental dependencies of $\overline{\sigma}_\Sigma$ and PSNR from the error probability value P_{err} of the image transfer. The value P_{err} was set as a ratio of the number of error bytes to the whole number of bytes in the image when the impulsive noise was modeled.

Table 2. Dependencies of $\overline{\sigma}_\Sigma$ and PSNR (in dB) from P_{err} for two test images "Lena" and "Barbara"

P_{err}	$\overline{\sigma}_{\Sigma\,Lena}$	$PSNR_{Lena}$	$\overline{\sigma}_{\Sigma\,Barbara}$	$PSNR_{Barbara}$
0.001	0.36	61.3	0.38	60.3
0.005	0.54	54.1	0.44	54.2
0.01	0.69	51.2	0.62	50.7
0.05	0.91	44.0	0.90	43.9
0.1	1.09	41.0	1.16	41.0

Experimental results of the quality analysis of the noisy images have shown that the PSNR estimation gives different values for fluctuation and impulsive noise. Data from Tables 1 and 2 together with the subjective estimations show that the "good" image quality is: for Gaussian noise with PSNR>40 dB, and for impulsive noise with PSNR>60 dB. Therefore, the PSNR criterion is not objective for quality analysis of the images with different types of noise.

Proposed criterion (10) is more objective and gives adequate results compared to the subjective estimations independently from types of the noise. This is confirmed with the experimental results.

4   Conclusion

In conclusion it is necessary to note that the developed criterion can be used not only for the distortion analysis of fine details in images. It can be also used for the estimation of visibility of the noise on the image fragments with the constant brightness. In this case the fragments that contain the fine details should be excluded and the following criterion should be used: the noise in the image is invisible for an eye if $\sigma_\Sigma < 10$ MPCD, where σ_Σ – unnormalized additive value of the noise, computed for all image fragments with constant brightness.

The high quality reproduction of fine details of images is an important task for design of vision systems in various applications. The authors hope that the criterion offered in this work will help designers of vision systems to solve this task more efficiently.

References

1. Pratt, W.K.: Digital Image Processing. Wiley, Chichester (2001)
2. Gonzalez, R.S., Woods, R.E.: Digital Image Processing. Prentice Hall, New Jersey (2002)
3. Ben Hamza, A., Krim, H., Unal, G.B.: Unifying Probabilistic and Variational Estimation. IEEE Signal Processing Magazine 19(5), 37–47 (2002)
4. Wang, Z., Bovik, A.C., Sheikh, H.R., Simoncelli, E.P.: Image quality assessment: From error measurement to structural similarity. IEEE Transactios on Image Processing 13(4), 600–612 (2004)
5. Sai, S.V., Sorokin, N.Y.: Search Algorithm and the Distortion Analysis of Fine Details of Real Images. Pattern Recognition and Image Analysis 19(2), 257–261 (2009)
6. Sai, S.V.: Methods of the Definition Analysis of Fine Details of Images. In: Obinata, G., Dutta, A. (eds.) Vision Systems: Applications, pp. 279–296. I-Tech Education and Publishing, Vienna (2007)
7. Wyszecki, G.: Uniform Color Scales: CIE 1964 U*V*W* Conversion of OSA Committee Selection. In: JOSA, vol. 65, pp. 456–460 (1975)
8. Mac Adam, D.L.: Uniform Color Scales. In: JOSA, vol. 64, pp. 1691–1702 (1974)
9. Novakovsky, S.V.: Color in Color TV. Radio and communication, Moscow (1988)
10. Sai, S.V.: The Quality of Transmission and Reproduction of Fine Details in Color Television Images. Dalnauka, Vladivostok (2003)
11. Ventzel, E.S., Ovtharov, L.A.: Probability Theory and its Engineering Application. Higher school, Moscow (2000)

Subjective Evaluation of Image Quality Measures for White Noise Distorted Images

Atif Bin Mansoor and Adeel Anwar

College of Aeronautical Engineering,
National University of Sciences and Technology, Pakistan
atif-cae@nust.edu.pk, adeel_anwar88@hotmail.com

Abstract. Image Quality Assessment has diverse applications. A number of Image Quality measures are proposed, but none is proved to be true representative of human perception of image quality. We have subjectively investigated spectral distance based and human visual system based image quality measures for their effectiveness in representing the human perception for images corrupted with white noise. Each of the 160 images with various degrees of white noise is subjectively evaluated by 50 human subjects, resulting in 8000 human judgments. On the basis of evaluations, image independent human perception values are calculated. The perception values are plotted against spectral distance based and human visual system based image quality measures. The performance of quality measures is determined by graphical observations and polynomial curve fitting, resulting in best performance by Human Visual System Absolute norm.

1 Introduction

The aim of image quality assessment (IQA) is to provide human independent image quality assessment. Image quality assessment has vital usage in various image processing applications. Any image or video acquisition system can use quality measure to automatically optimize itself for capturing better quality images/video. Further, it can find its usage in the places where human subjective evaluation is not possible. It can be used for bench marking and optimizing image processing techniques like image enhancement, image restoration and image compression etc. However, devising a quantitative quality metric that follows the human subjective evaluation of images irrespective of noise type, noise strength and image contents is a difficult task [1]. Due to its wide applications, image quality assessment is an active research area, and many Image Quality Measures, IQMs have been proposed [2].Mean square error (MSE) has often been used to assess the image quality, but Guo and Meng have discussed the limitations of MSE and concluded that MSE alone can't provide reliable quality assessment [3]. Miyahara et al. proposed picture quality scale (PQS) for objective image quality assessment that is dependent upon structure, location and amount of error [4]. Wang et al. gave a new idea for IQA using

J. Blanc-Talon et al. (Eds.): ACIVS 2010, Part I, LNCS 6474, pp. 10–17, 2010.

structural approach and suggested that a measure based on structural similarity is closer to human perception [5]. Sheikh et al. compared 10 different IQA algorithms on the basis of judgment by different human subjects. They concluded that Visual Information Fidelity (VIF) measure performs best among them [6]. Avcibas et al. evaluated 26 Image quality measures statistically [7]. These IQMs are grouped into six categories based upon information they used i.e. pixel difference based, correlation based, edge based, spectral distance based, context based and human visual system based measures. The mutual relationship between these measures is found by plotting them via Kohonen's Self Organizing Map (SOM) algorithm. Based upon clustering results of SOM, Analysis of Variance ANOVA and subjective Mean Opinion Score, it was concluded that five IQMs i.e. Spectral Phase-Magnitude Error (S2), Block Spectral Phase-Magnitude Error (S5), Human Visual System Absolute norm (H1), Human Visual System L2 norm (H2), Edge Stability Measure (E2) are most discriminating. In this paper, we have investigated subjectively the performance of these quality measures for White noise corrupted images. The experimentation is used to check the independence of these measures from the image contents.

2 Approach

2.1 Selected Image Quality Measures

In our experiments, we selected four image quality measures. Among them, H1 and H2 are human visual system based while S2, S5 are spectral based IQMs. E2 was dropped due to its close proximity to H2 in self organizing map (SOM) [7].

HVS Modified Spectral Distortion. The human visual system is modeled by a band pass filter with its transfer function in the polar coordinates as [8]:

$$H(\rho) = \begin{cases} 0.05 e^{\rho^{0.554}} & \rho < 7 \\ e^{-9[|log_{10}\rho - log_{10}9|]^{2.3}} & \rho \geq 7 \end{cases} \tag{1}$$

where $\rho = \sqrt{\mu^2 + \nu^2}$. Taking inverse discrete cosine transform of an image processed by the above filter can be expressed via the U$\{.\}$ operator i.e.

$$U\{C(i,j)\} = DCT^{-1} H(\sqrt{\mu^2 + \nu^2}) \Omega(\mu, \nu) \tag{2}$$

where $\Omega(\mu, \nu)$ is the 2D DCT of the image and DCT^{-1} is the 2D inverse DCT. Two metrics for the Kth component multispectral image are normalized absolute error [9], [10]:

$$H1 = \frac{1}{K} \sum_{k=1}^{K} \frac{\sum_{i,j=0}^{N-1} |U\{C_k(i,j)\} - U\{\hat{C}_k(i,j)\}|}{\sum_{i,j=0}^{N-1} U\{C_k(i,j)\}} \tag{3}$$

and L2 norm:

$$H2 = \frac{1}{K} \sum_{k=1}^{K} [\frac{1}{N^2} \sum_{i,j=0}^{N-1} |U\{C_k(i,j)\} - U\{\hat{C}_k(i,j)\}|^2]^{1/2} \qquad (4)$$

Spectral Distance Measure. In spectral distance measures, the complex Fourier of the images is taken to give the distortion penalty functions [11], [12]. Considering the discrete Fourier transform of kth band of the original and coded images by $\Gamma_k(\mu, \nu)$ and $\hat{\Gamma}_k(\mu, \nu)$ respectively. The spectra are defined as:

$$\Gamma_k(\mu, \nu) = \sum_{m,n=0}^{N-1} C_k(m,n)e^{-2\pi i m \frac{u}{N}}.e^{-2\pi i m \frac{v}{N}}, \qquad k = 1, 2......K \qquad (5)$$

Spectral distortion measures, using difference metrics can be extended to multispectral images. Considering the phase and magnitude spectra:

$$\varphi(\mu, \nu) = tan^{-1}\Gamma(\mu, \nu) \qquad (6)$$

$$M(\mu, \nu) = |\Gamma(\mu, \nu)| \qquad (7)$$

The distortion in the phase and the magnitude spectra can be calculated and weighted separately. Thus spectral magnitude distortion can be defined as:

$$S = \frac{1}{N^2} \sum_{\mu,\nu=0}^{N-1} |M(\mu, \nu) - \hat{M}(\mu, \nu)|^2 \qquad (8)$$

The spectral phase distortion is:

$$S1 = \frac{1}{N^2} \sum_{\mu,\nu=0}^{N-1} |\varphi(\mu, \nu) - \hat{\varphi}(\mu, \nu)|^2 \qquad (9)$$

The weighted spectral distortion is defined as:

$$S2 = \frac{1}{N}(\lambda \sum_{\mu,\nu=0}^{N-1} |\varphi(\mu, \nu) - \hat{\varphi}(\mu, \nu)|^2) + (1 - \lambda) \sum_{\mu,\nu=0}^{N-1} |M(\mu, \nu) - \hat{M}(\mu, \nu)|^2) \qquad (10)$$

where 'λ' is chosen to give required weight to the phase and magnitude terms. The details about S5, Block spectral phase-magnitude error are given in [7].

2.2   Experimental Setup

Test images were taken from LIVE image quality assessment database that is being used as a standard by many image quality researchers [13]. The database consists of images with wide variation in their contents. In database for white noise distortion type, white noise of standard deviation sigma is added to RGB components of the images. In our subjective evaluation, 160 test images were used. The tests were conducted as per the guidelines described in the ITU-Recommendations for subjective assessment of quality for television pictures [14].Three identical workstations with 17-inch CRT displays were used for the test. To minimize external effects, all the tests were conducted in the same indoor environment. We used Double stimulus quality scale method, keeping in view its more precise image quality assessments. A Matlab based graphical user interface was designed to show human subjects a pair of pictures i.e. original and degraded ones. Human subjects selected for the test were male and female undergraduate students with no knowledge of image quality assessment. Human subjects were trained as per ITU-Recommendations [14], and a small training session was conducted before the test using images other than the actual test images.

The 160 images were rated using a five point quality scale; excellent, good, fair, poor and bad. The corresponding ratings were scaled upon a 1-100 score. Each image was rated by 50 humans, resulting in total 8000 human judgments. Individual scores of all 50 people for a particular image were averaged and a single human perception value (HPV) was formed, removing any human bias factor.

3   Results

3.1   Subjective Evaluation of White Noise

Figure 1 shows human perception value versus white noise. The graph is formed from 8000 human judgments of 160 images corrupted with varying amount of white noise according to procedure explained in previous paragraph. The graph

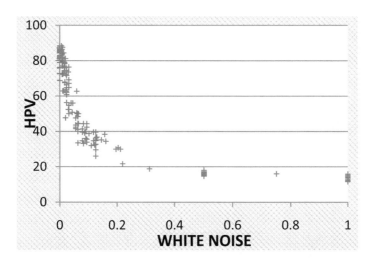

Fig. 1. Human Perception Value versus White Noise

shows an inverse relation between amount of noise and human subjective image quality perception. HPV decreases sharply with even small variation in white noise, depicting significant human sensitiveness to this type of distortion. The subjective results show that (a) For good human perception of an image quality even slight amount of white noise is not acceptable. (b) The respective HPVs for different images with the particular value of white noise are in close proximity, which indicates that human response to white noise depends upon the noise level and not upon the image contents.

3.2   Human Perception versus Selected Image Quality Measures

Figures 2, 3, 4 and 5 show human perception of white noise corrupted images against Spectral Phase-Magnitude Error (S2), Block Spectral Phase-Magnitude Error (S5), Human Visual System Absolute norm (H1) and Human Visual System L2 norm (H2) respectively. For every image, HPV is calculated by the procedure discussed earlier and corresponding quality metric value is calculated using respective image quality metric formula.

Following observations are made from these graphs:

– Figures 2 and 3 depict that for particular values of Spectral Phase-Magnitude Error (S2) and Block Spectral Phase-Magnitude Error (S5), the respective human perception values of different images are not in close proximity. This shows that though quality metrics S2 and S5 are responsive to white noise, they also dependent on image contents.
– In Figure 4, it is observed that as H1 increases there is a continuous decrease in human perception value. Further, the respective human perception values of different images for any value of H1 are in close proximity. This shows that variation in H1 does not depend on image contents but on the noise level.

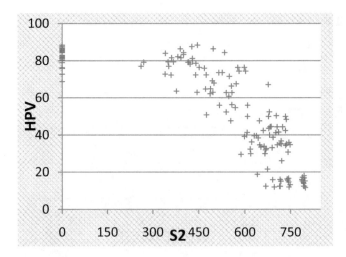

Fig. 2. Human Perception Value versus Spectral Phase-Magnitude Error

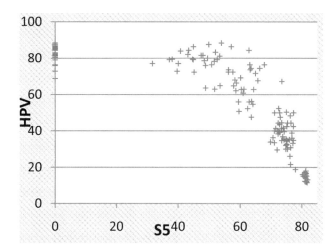

Fig. 3. Human Perception Value versus Block Spectral Phase-Magnitude Error

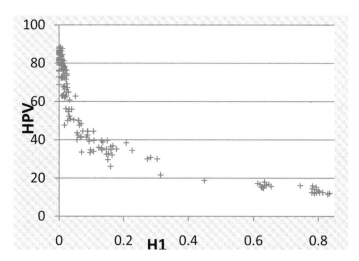

Fig. 4. Human Perception Value versus Human Visual System Absolute Norm

- In Figure 5, we observe that for a small variation in H2 there is a large variation in human perception values till value 30 on vertical axis, indicating H2 is less responsive to white noise in this range. After this limit, the graph exhibits effectiveness of H2 as quality measure for white noise.

Statistical analysis was performed on the human perception against selected image quality measures by fitting N-degree polynomials to validate the drawn inferences. Table 1 shows Root Mean Square Error (RMSE) and correlation coefficient (R^2) of best fitted polynomial against respective image quality measure.

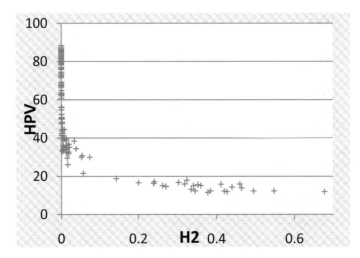

Fig. 5. Human Perception Value versus Human Visual System L2 Norm

Table 1. Polynomial fitting results against image quality measures

IQM	RMSE	R^2
Spectral Phase-Magnitude Error (S2)	10.42	0.836
Block Spectral Phase-Magnitude Error (S5)	7.58	0.912
Human Visual System Absolute norm(H1)	5.375	0.957
Human Visual System L2 norm (H2)	11.43	0.797

A low RMSE and high R^2 depict better functional relation between human perception curve and respective image quality measure.

On the basis of observations and polynomial fitting on the graphs, following results are drawn:

- Low RMSE and high correlation coefficient show that Human Visual System Absolute norm (H1) mathematically models the human perception better than other three measures for white noise.
- H2 is less responsive to changes in human perception, and therefore does not qualify as a good quality metric for images with white noise.
- The quality measure that is dependent on noise as well as image contents doesn't qualify as a good measure. H1, S2 and S5 all are responsive to white noise but S2 and S5 also depend upon image contents. Therefore, H1 is a better quality metric than S2 and S5.

On the basis of above results we conclude that Human Visual System Absolute norm (H1) is a better image quality measure for images with white noise distortion.

4 Conclusion

We present a subjective evaluation of spectral distance based and Human Visual system based quality measures. It is subjectively determined that in case of images distorted with white noise, Human Visual System Absolute norm (H1), Spectral Phase-Magnitude Error (S2) and Block Spectral Phase-Magnitude Error (S5) all are responsive to white noise, but S2 and S5 are not image contents independent. Further, Human Visual System L2 norm (H2) is less responsive to changes in human perception, and therefore does not qualify as a good quality metric for white noise distorted images. Human Visual System Absolute norm (H1) proves to be the best among these measures.

References

1. Wang, Z., Bovik, A.C., Lu, L.: Why is image quality assessment so difficult. In: IEEE International Conference on Acoustics, Speech and Signal Processing, vol. 4, pp. 3313–3316 (2002)
2. Eskicioglu, A.M.: Quality measurement for monochrome compressed images in the past 25 years. In: IEEE International Conference on Acoustics, Speech and Signal Processing, vol. 4, pp. 1907–1910 (2000)
3. Guo, L., Meng, Y.: What is wrong and right with MSE. In: Eighth IASTED International Conference on Signal and Image Processing, IASTED, pp. 212–215 (2006)
4. Miyahara, M., Kotani, K., Algazi, V.R.: Objective picture quality scale (PQS) for image coding. IEEE Transaction on Communications 9, 1215–1225 (1998)
5. Wang, Z., Bovik, A.C., Sheikh, H.R., Simoncelli, E.P.: Image quality assessment: From error measurement to structural similarity. IEEE Transaction on Image Processing 13 (January 2004)
6. Sheikh, H.R., Sabir, M.F., Bovik, A.C.: A statistical evaluation of recent full reference image quality assessment algorithm. IEEE Transaction on Image Processing 15, 3440–3451 (2006)
7. Avcibas, I., Sankur, B., Sayood, K.: Statistical evaluation of image quality measures. Journal of Electronic Imaging 11, 206–223 (2002)
8. Nill, N.B.: A visual model weighted cosine transform for image compression and quality assessment. IEEE Transactions on Communications 33(6), 551–557 (1985)
9. Eskicioglu, A.M., Fisher, P.S.: Image quality measures and their performance. IEEE Transactions on Communications 43(12), 2959–2965 (1995)
10. Avcibas, I., Sankur, B.: Statistical analysis of image quality measures. In: European Signal Processing Conf. EUSIPCO 2000, Tampere, Finland, pp. 2181–2184 (2000)
11. Nill, N.B., Bouzas, B.H.: Objective image quality measures derived from digital image power spectra. Optical Engineering 31(4), 813–825 (1992)
12. Lohmann, A.W., Mendelovic, D., Shabtay, G.: Significance of phase and amplitude in the Fourier domain. Journal of Optical Society of America A 14, 2901–2904 (1997)
13. Sheikh, H.R., Wang, Z., Cormack, L., Bovik, A.C.: Live image quality assessment database, http://www.live.ece.utrxas.edu/research/quality
14. ITU-R Recommendation BT. 500-11, Methodology for the subjective assessment of the quality for television pictures

Real-Time Retrieval of Near-Duplicate
Fragments in Images and Video-Clips

Andrzej Śluzek[1,2,*] and Mariusz Paradowski[3]

[1] Nanyang Technological University, Singapore
[2] Nicolaus Copernicus University, Toruń, Poland
[3] Wroclaw University of Technology, Poland
assluzek@ntu.edu.sg,
assluzek@fizyka.umk.pl,
mariusz.paradowski@pwr.wroc.pl

Abstract. Detection and localization of unspecified similar fragments in random images is one of the most challenging problems in CBVIR (classic techniques focusing on full-image or sub-image retrieval usually fail in such a problem). We propose a new method for near-duplicate image fragment matching using a *topology-based* framework. The method works on visual data only, i.e. no semantics or a'priori knowledge is assumed. Near-duplicity of image fragments is modeled by topological constraints on sets of matched keypoints (instead of geometric constrains typically used in image matching). The paper reports a time-efficient (i.e. capable of working in real time with a video input) implementation of the proposed method. The application can be run using a mid-range personal computer and a medium-quality video camera.

Keywords: CBVIR, near-duplicate fragments, keypoint matching, topological constrains, real-time application, video stream.

1 Introduction

The objective of content-based image retrieval is to determine whether the retrieved images share similar contents ("similarity" is often defined in a semantic or functional context, and visual appearances may play only a secondary role, see [1]). In the reported work, however, we address only a purely visual approach, i.e. we do not consider any similarities based on semantics or other non-visual information. Moreover, our notion of image similarity is more general than typical approaches of image retrieval (where whole images are matched) or object detection. Note that *object detection* is often almost equivalently referred to as *sub-image retrieval* because the content of the query image (object) is matched against parts of other images. Our objective is to determine if the matched

* The research presented in this paper is a part of A*STAR Science & Engineering Research Council grant 072 134 0052 (principal investigator: Dr A.Śluzek). The financial support of SERC is gratefully acknowledged.

J. Blanc-Talon et al. (Eds.): ACIVS 2010, Part I, LNCS 6474, pp. 18–29, 2010.

images contain any visually similar (near-duplicate) fragments without any prior knowledge on how many such fragments (if any) exist.

The problem can be specified as follows: **Given two random images $\mathcal{I}$ and $\mathcal{J}$, identify in them pairs of near-duplicate image fragments. The term "near-duplicate fragments" refers to unspecified fragments of (almost) identical objects. However, the visual appearances of those objects may differ because of different scene and camera settings, photometric conditions, digitization parameters and possibly because of certain natural deformations.**

Image matching based on local features (*keypoints* are the most typical example of such features) is a popular approach. The keypoint-based techniques usually combine local results (matching individual keypoints) and global geometry (e.g. mappings that relate the spatial coordinates in matched images). Typical geometric models used in state-of-the-art solutions of purely visual image matching include: similarity [2], affine [3,4,5,6], projective [7,8], epipolar [9] or non-linear [10] transformations.

Nevertheless, there are very few solutions reported on *image fragment matching*. To the best of our knowledge, there is only one non-semantic, local approach named *pattern entropy* [11], based on similarity transformations. Other solutions that can be mentioned include [12] (the concept of *key-places*) and [13]. However, they violate our main assumption regarding no *a'priori* information because *visual words* and/or *latent topics* precomputed from representative image or video-frames are used.

The major problem with near-duplicate fragment matching is that *RANSAC*-based methods [14] (which attempt to reject outliers using the statistical approach) in general fail if the number of correct matches is insignificant compared to the number of all matches. *Image co-segmentation* is another prospectively useful methodology. Its main goal is to separate foreground (consisting of similar objects) from background (e.g. [15,16]) which is expected to be different in the matched images. However, this method works on global image data (i.e. color and texture histograms) and is, therefore, sensitive to photometric changes.

The results presented in the paper are a continuation of our previous works on image fragment matching. We have already presented two geometric approaches based on matching triangles of keypoints [17] and matching elliptical keyregions [18,17]. However, both approaches are affine-based so that they are able to detect only near-duplicate fragments which are approximately planar. The proposed method is based on topological constraints. Additionally, we focus on the real-time implementation (and the corresponding issues of computational complexity).

2   Topological Near-Duplicate Fragments

In geometrically constrained matching, we identify (nearly) planar similar fragments by determining an affine transformation between keypoints belonging to these fragments. Alternatively, the topological approach consists in determining groups of matched keypoints that satisfy certain *topological constraints*. Pairs of keypoints satifying the constraints form a *topologically constrained graph*. A node in such a graph represents a pair of matched keypoint, while an edge between two nodes indicates that the corresponding keypoint pairs are topologically consistent. Fully connected sub-graphs indicate topologically-similar fragments of the matched images.

The method can work with practically any keypoint detectors and descriptors. We have tested several detectors (i.e. *Harris-Affine* [19], *Hessian-Affine* and *MSER* [20]) and descriptors (e.g. *SIFT* [5], *GLOH* [21], *SURF* [22] and *Moment invariants* [21]). Although the *Harris-Affine + SIFT* combination has been found the most successful in terms of performances, it is not the best choice for real-time applications. Instead, we have selected *SURF* detector/descriptor for which a highly efficient implementation is publicly available[1].

2.1 Keypoint Matching

Keypoints extracted from a pair of images are matched based on the similarity between their descriptors. We actually use two matching schemes. The first one is *one-to-one* (O2O) approach where two keypoints are matched if they are mutual nearest neighbors. This approach returns only the most reliable matches and the upper bound for the number of matched keypoint pairs is $min(n_I, n_J)$ (the lower bound is 0).

The second scheme is the *nearest neighbor* (NN) approach, which is as a special case of *many-to-many* (M2M) approach. This method matches all nearest-neighbor keypoint pairs (they do not have to be mutual nearest neighbours). The matches are slightly less reliable, but more keypoint pairs are returned; the upper bound is equal to $n_I + n_J$, the lower bound is $max(n_I, n_J)$. In the real-time implementation we select the second approach because the number of keypoints used for matching is limited (see Section 3) so that more keypoint pairs might be needed. Moreover, the NN scheme (or any other M2M scheme) can better handle images containing multiple copies of similar objects.

2.2 Topological Constraints

Pairs of matched keypoints represent local visual similarities between a pair of images. However, most of such similarities are incorrect in a wider context of both images. Usually, only a very small fraction of matched keypoint pairs represents the actual near-duplicates in the images. Those correctly matched keypoint pairs should be identified.

Several approaches exist for outliers rejection in image (and sub-image) matching. Those approaches are often based on the *RANSAC* paradigm. However, there are very few methods for detecting an unspecified number of similar fragments in a pair of images (e.g. [13]). Our previous approaches [18,17] model local relations between matched keypoints using local affine geometry. However, such

---

[1] Freeware OpenCV vision library provides an efficient implementation of SURF.

a solution is not flexible enough to handle deformed objects. Thus, we propose to relate pairs of matched keypoint using topology. Nevertheless, we again employ the local approach, i.e. pairs of matched keypoints are analyzed topologically within neighborhoods of a limited size only so that the image geometry still plays a certain role.

If matched keypoint pairs belong to similar fragments in the matched images, the keypoint neighbors should be similarly distributed in both images (even though the exact geometry can be different). Therefore, we propose a heuristic topological constraint representing such similar distributions. The constraint is based on the orientation of vectors connecting a given keypoint to its matched neighbors. An illustrative example is given in Fig. 1.

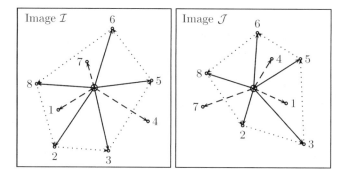

Fig. 1. For each pair of matched keypoints, the largest subset of orientation-ordered neighbors is found. An exemplary subset of size 5 is shown.

When we order the vectors in the first image, a similarly ordered sequence of the corresponding vectors is generally expected in the other image. However, if two keypoints are falsely matched, vectors are usually ordered very differently. Thus, to determine if a selected keypoint pair is correctly matched, we simply calculate how many such vectors are ordered in the same sequence in both images. If most of them do, the pair of keypoints is assumed matched correctly.

Given a pair of matched keypoints, we build the vectors in both images using only the closest m pairs of matched keypoints (i.e. the size of the neighborhood is not fixed geometrically because that would limit the scale invariance). By using a predefined number of neighbors we can predict the computational efficiency of the method. Unfortunately, certain keypoint detectors tend to generate dense clusters of (almost the same) keypoints. Such clusters could dominate the neighborhoods and eventually produce spurious artifacts. Therefore, we setup a minimum ϵ distance (5 pixels experimentally determined for images of resolutions above 640×480) for the neighborhood scan.

After the largest subset of consistently ordered vectors is found in both images for the currently processed keypoint pair $\langle s, t \rangle$, the acceptance criterion is applied. The pair is considered a correct match if the percentage of identically ordered vectors is large enough (i.e. exceeding a threshold value T). Additionally, the pair $\langle s, t \rangle$ is assumed topologically consistent with all its neighbors that form the identically ordered vectors.

Subsequently, we can build a *topological graph* based on the data generated in the previous step. The topological graph is a directed graph in which nodes are pairs of matched keypoints. Edges represent the topological consistencies between pairs of matched keypoints. To merge pairs of matched keypoints into near-duplicate fragments in both images, we simply group keypoint pairs (i.e. graph nodes) into topologically consistent clusters by finding fully connected sub-graphs of the *topological graph*. Sub-graphs which contain at least three nodes (keypoint pairs) define near-duplicate fragments in the matched images.

To exemplify performances of the topology-based near-duplicate detection (and to compare it to the geometry-based approach) Figs 2 and 3 are shown.

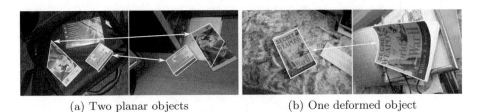

(a) Two planar objects   (b) One deformed object

Fig. 2. Manually outlined examples of planar and non-planar near-duplicate fragments. Test cases for geometric and topological approaches.

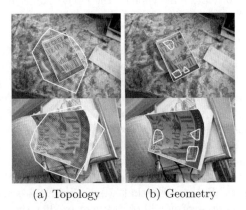

(a) Topology   (b) Geometry

Fig. 3. The geometric method is accurate but not flexible, the topological method is less accurate but more flexible

2.3   Computational Complexity

Our ultimate objective is to develop a retrieval system detecting near-duplicate fragments in real time (e.g. in a video input). Thus, the computational complexity analysis is an important step to identify any prospective weaknesses and/or bottlenecks of the algorithm.

Keypoints are identified in images by means of *SURF* detector/descriptor. *SURF* has been actually designed for real-time implementations and several such implementations are known, e.g. [23].

Given two images $\mathcal{I}$ and $\mathcal{J}$, we assume they contain correspondingly n_I and n_J keypoints described by feature vectors of f dimensionality. Thus, both O2O and NN keypoint matching methods require $f n_I n_J$ operations. Assuming that $n = max(n_I, n_J)$, the computational complexity of keypoint matching is $O(f n^2)$.

Subsequently, the topological consistency of keypoint pairs is verified. For each matched keypoint pair, the algorithm of neighborhood building and analysis has the complexity $O(n + m^3)$ (if m neighbors are used). Of course, we have to apply the algorithm to all matched keypoint pairs so that the overall complexity of the topological consistency verification is equal to $O(n^2 + n m^3)$.

The last step is grouping keypoint pairs (sub-graph detection in the topological graph). We employ the *union-find* algorithm, which has the computational complexity of $O(log^* n)$ for a set of size n. There are total nm neighbors for n keypoint pairs so that the overall complexity of the *union-find* algorithm is $O(mn log^* n)$.

Altogether, assuming that $log^* n < f$ and $log^* n < m$ (which is generally true) the computational complexity of the topology-based near-duplicate fragment detection in a pair of images is not larger than

$$O(f n^2) + O(n^2 + n m^3) + O(f n^2 + n m^2) = O(f n^2 + n m^3) \qquad (1)$$

The first component ($O(f n^2)$) of the complexity estimate is related to keypoint matching, while the second one $O(n m^3)$) corresponds to the analysis of topological consistencies. For a real-time implementation (see Section 3) the values of n and m should be optimized.

2.4   Matching Performances and Parameter Tuning

Performances of the proposed algorithm can be estimated using popular quality measures, i.e. *precision*, *recall* and their combination *f-measure*. However, there are two different aspects of the performances, i.e. we can first assess whether all near-duplicate fragments are detected and, secondly, we can estimate how accurately the shapes of near-duplicates are extracted. Therefore, the quality measures have to be differently defined in the contexts of these two aspects.

To measure how many similar fragments are found, we simply check if the algorithm matched *any* parts of the fragments from both images. Thus, for a single near-duplicate existing in both images, the value of matching quality is binary (found or not).

To measure how accurately the shapes of similar fragments are matched, we use the method described in [17]. First, we note that the ground-truth shape of near-duplicate fragments is not an intrinsic property of images. Since matching is not possible if no keypoints are detected within the relevant image fragments, the ground-truth shape should somehow incorporate the collection of keypoints detected within a fragment. Thus, after the shapes of similar fragments are manually outlined (see Fig. 2) the convex hull of all keypoints detected within the outlines is used as the *ground-truth shape* of the underlying fragment. Similarly, the convex hull of keypoints clusted by the algorithm is considered the *extracted shape* of a fragment. Then, we can measure how accurately (in terms of the overlapping areas) the shapes of matches near-duplicates have been estimated (more details in [17]).

Thus, we use six quality measures altogether, i.e. *precision*, *recall* and *f-measure* in the *object* aspect, and the same three measures in the *area* aspect.

The topology-based image fragment matching has two parameters determining its computational complexity (see Eq. 1) i.e. n – the number of matched keypoint pairs and m, which is the number of neighbors of a given keypoint pair that are tested for the topological consistency. If m is too small, we loose to a certain extent the scale invariance and, additionally, the quality degrades because of insufficient amounts of data available. On the other hand, too large neighborhoods dramatically increase the computational costs due to $O(nm^3)$ factor in the computational complexity.

The second important parameter is the keypoint pair acceptance threshold T (see Sub-section 2.2). The value of this parameter defines how many vectors, i.e. what percentage of m, have to be identically ordered in both images (see Fig. 1). The higher value of the parameter, the less is the chance for *false positives*. However, if the value of T is too high, the risk of *false negatives* also increases. Actually, th value of parameter T is related to the value of parameter m; they should be configured simultaneously. Based on extensive test with numerous images and different keypoint detectors, the recommended parameter values are: $m = 30$ and $T = 45\%$.

2.5 Topology *versus* Geometry – The Experimental Verification

To compare the topological algorithm to its affine counterpart, we have used a database of 100 diversified images captured under various lighting conditions. Within the ten thousand image pairs, over one thousand pairs contain similar objects. In the experiments, we used these images pairs and, additionally,

Table 1. Average precision (P), recall (R) and f-measure (FM) for our dataset by using *Harris-Affine* detector with *SIFT* descriptor and *SURF* detector/descriptor

Measure	P(obj.)	R(obj.)	FM(obj.)	P(area)	R(area)	FM(area)
Det./desc.	Geometrical method					
HarAff/SIFT	0.97	0.81	0.88	0.96	0.64	0.77
SURF/SURF	0.98	0.61	0.75	0.90	0.49	0.63
Det./desc.	Topological method					
HarAff/SIFT	0.98	0.92	0.95	0.64	0.79	0.71
SURF/SURF	0.97	0.79	0.87	0.50	0.70	0.59

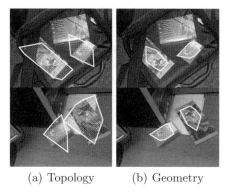

(a) Topology   (b) Geometry

Fig. 4. Both methods correctly match planar surfaces. The geometric approach captures only parts of objects; the topological approach captures objects with some background.

Fig. 5. Near-duplicates matched using the topological approach (Harris-Affine detector and SIFT descriptor applied)

randomly selected 1000 distracting image pairs (without similar objects). The database and the method are made publicly available[2].

As mentioned in Section 1, we have identified only one approach that can provide functionalities similar to our algorithm, i.e. the *entropy-based* approach [11].

---

[2] Database and the algorithm: http://www.ii.pwr.wroc.pl/~visible

The approach has been tested on our database using publicly available executables[3]. However, the achieved results are rather poor since the method is able to find only a few from over a thousand correct matches.

Because of lack of other alternatives, we have used our affine-based methods, [18,17], as the references. These methods have high *precision* (both in terms of the *area* and *object* aspects) but their *recall* is lower. They can find planar (or nearly planar) surfaces, but they are not designed to handle deformable or highly non-planar objects. The geometry-based methods usually find only the *interiors* of the similar fragments, because keypoints outside the fragments do not fit into affine transformations which are used to model the local image-to-image distortions (see the explanations in Section 2.4). These interiors are large sections of the actual similar objects, but some parts remain undetected so that *recall* is lower (in particular in the *area* aspect).

The topological method has been designed to more robustly handle object deformations. Thus, we expect higher *recall* values. However, some background fragments around the actual objects are often also captured (they satisfy the topological constrains) and, thus, the *area precision* is reduced. The *object precision* remains very high which means that the number of false positives has not changed (see Table 1). Apart form examples shown in Fig. 3, further examples of performances are shown in Figs 4 and 5.

3   Real-Time Implementation

The overall structure of the implemented real-time solution is shown in Fig. 6. The operations are practically identical for both database images and for on-line captured images (video frames). We use a standard keypoint detector/descriptor (*SURF*) which provides variable numbers of keypoints, depending on the image complexity. Therefore, in case of too many keypoints detected, some of them are ignored. We filter out the smallest (in terms of the circle or ellipse area) keypoints because they are considered the least exact. In most cases, however, the number of detected keypoints in a frame(image) is lower than the threshold and no keypoints are removed.

Because of a limited number of keypoints, we use the NN (i.e. a variant of *many-to-many*) approach to get a higher number of keypoint matches. M2M is more tolerant to a certain number of matching mistakes even though the overall average reliability of matching may be lower. It should be mentioned, nevertheless, that in poor quality video frames the number of extracted keypoints changes significantly from frame to frame, even if there is no physical movement.

Subsequently, we limit the number of keypoint pairs to obtain predictable timing characteristics of the application. We simply sort all keypoint pairs according to their similarity measure and select the best ones. The maximum number of matched keypoint pairs is $n = 250$ to effectively run the algorithm on the reference hardware. However, this parameter can be controlled by the user and larger

---

[3] Entropy method: http://www.cs.cityu.edu.hk/~wzhao2/lip-vireo.htm

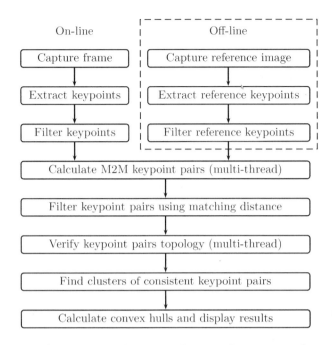

Fig. 6. Structure of a real-time solution matching a video stream and a query image(s)

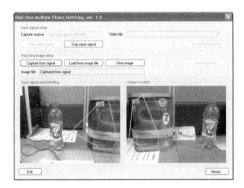

Fig. 7. A screenshot of a real-time implementation

values can be chosen for faster machines (e.g. personal computers equipped with multi-core CPU's).

The software is implemented using *.NET* platform together with *OpenCV* 2.0 library (including *SURF* detector provided there). Fig. 7 presents a screenshot captured during a real-time matching process. The software is publicly available at `http://www.ii.pwr.wroc.pl/~visible`.

The software has been tested using a variety of low- and medium-class webcams. The capturing resolutions is 640×480 (the recommended option) or 320×240. In the latter case, the quality of images is very poor and matching is far from perfect, but nevertheless still possible.

4 Conclusions

In the paper we have outlined a topology-based approach to image fragment matching in real time. In earlier papers, [24], we have suggested applications of the proposed method in assisting visually handicapped people and autonomous agents navigating in unknown and unexplored environments. The presented solution makes such systems feasible.

Currently, the implemented solution is able to match captured video frames with just a few reference images. Other applications may require detection of near-duplicate fragments in thousands/millions of database images, also in real-time. We have recently developed a *pre-retrieval* technique which is able to select a small subset of candidate images from a large database which are subsequently matched with the incoming video frames. The results will be reported in future papers.

References

1. Wang, J.Z., Li, J., Wiederhold, G.: Simplicity: Semantics-sensitive integrated matching for picture libraries. IEEE Transactions on Pattern Analysis and Machine Intelligence 23, 947–963 (2001)
2. Islam, M., Sluzek, A.: Relative scale method to locate an object in cluttered environment. Image and Vision Computing 26, 259–274 (2008)
3. Lowe, D.: Object recognition from local scale-invariant features. In: ICCV 1999, vol. 2, pp. 1150–1157 (1999)
4. Xiao, J., Shah, M.: Two-frame wide baseline matching. In: ICCV 2003, vol. 1, pp. 603–609. IEEE, Los Alamitos (2003)
5. Lowe, D.: Distinctive image features from scale-invariant keypoints. Int. J. Comput. Vis. 60, 91–110 (2004)
6. Chiu, H.P., Lozano-Perez, T.: Matching interest points using affine invariant concentric circles. In: Proceedings of the 18th International Conference on Pattern Recognition, vol. 2, pp. 167–170 (2006)
7. Mudigonda, P.K., Jawahar, C.V., Narayanan, P.J.: Geometric structure computation from conics. In: Fourth Indian Conference on Computer Vision, Graphics and Image Processing (2004)
8. Kannala, J., Salo, M., Heikkila, J.: Algorithms for computing a planar homography from conics in correspondence. In: British Machine Vision Conference (2006)
9. Tuytelaars, T., Gool, L.V.: Wide baseline stereo matching based on local, affinely invariant regions. In: Proc. of British Machine Vision Conference BMVC 2000, pp. 412–425 (2000)
10. Yang, D., Sluzek, A.: A low-dimensional local descriptor incorporating tps warping for image matching. Image and Vision Computing 28(8), 1184–1195 (2010)
11. Zhao, W.L., Ngo, C.W.: Scale-rotation invariant pattern entropy for keypoint-based near-duplicate detection. IEEE Transactions on Image Processing 18, 412–423 (2009)
12. Heritier, M., Foucher, S., Gagnon, L.: Key-places detection and clustering in movies using latent aspects. In: Proc. 14th IEEE Int. Conf. Image Processing, vol. 2, pp. II.225–II.228 (2007)

13. Chum, O., Perdoch, M., Matas, J.: Geometric min-hashing: Finding a (thick) needle in a haystack. In: Proc. of IEEE Conf. CVPR 2009, pp. 17–24 (2009)
14. Fischler, M., Bolles, R.: Random sample consensus: a paradigm for model fitting with applications to image analysis and automated cartography. In: Buxton, B.F., Cipolla, R. (eds.) ECCV 1996. LNCS, vol. 1064, pp. 683–695. Springer, Heidelberg (1996)
15. Rother, C., Kolmogorov, V., Minka, T., Blake, A.: Cosegmentation of image pairs by histogram matching – incorporating a global constraint into mrfs. In: Proc. IEEE Computer Society Conference on Computer Vision and Pattern Recognition, pp. 993–1000 (2006)
16. Mukherjee, L., Singh, V., Dyer, C.: R.: Half-integrality based algorithms for cosegmentation of images. In: Proc. of IEEE Conf. CVPR 2009, pp. 2028–2035 (2009)
17. Paradowski, M., Śluzek, A.: Local keypoints and global affine geometry: triangles and ellipses for image fragment matching. In: Kwasnicka, H., Jain, L. (eds.) Innovations in Intelligent Image Analysis. Springer, Heidelberg (in print, 2010)
18. Paradowski, M., Śluzek, A.: Detection of image fragments related by affine transforms: Matching triangles and ellipses. In: Proc. of ICISA 2010, Seul (2010)
19. Mikolajczyk, K., Schmid, C.: Scale and affine invariant interest point detectors. Int. J. Comput. Vision 60, 63–86 (2004)
20. Matas, J., Schum, O., Urban, M., Pajdla, T.: Robust wide-baseline stereo from maximally stable extremal regions. In: British Machine Vision Conference, pp. 384–393 (2002)
21. Mikolajczyk, K., Schmid, C.: A performance evaluation of local descriptors. IEEE Trans. PAMI 27, 1615–1630 (2005)
22. Bay, H., Ess, A., Tuytelaars, T., Van Gool, L.: Speeded-up robust features (surf). Computer Vision and Image Understanding 110, 346–359 (2008)
23. Cornelis, N., Gool, L.V.: Fast scale invariant feature detection and matching on programmable graphics hardware. In: CVPR 2008 Workshop (2008)
24. Śluzek, A., Paradowski, M.: A vision-based technique for assisting visually impaired people and autonomous agents. In: Proc. 3rd Int. Conf. Human System Interaction HSI 2010, Rzeszow (2010)

Toward the Detection of Urban Infrastructure's Edge Shadows

Cesar Isaza[1], Joaquin Salas[1,2,*], and Bogdan Raducanu[3]

[1] CICATA Queretaro, Instituto Politecnico Nacional, Mexico
[2] Visiting Scientist, Computer Science Department, Duke University
[3] Computer Vision Center, Barcelona, Spain

Abstract. In this paper, we propose a novel technique to detect the shadows cast by urban infrastructure, such as buildings, billboards, and traffic signs, using a sequence of images taken from a fixed camera. In our approach, we compute two different background models in parallel: one for the edges and one for the reflected light intensity. An algorithm is proposed to train the system to distinguish between moving edges in general and edges that belong to static objects, creating an edge background model. Then, during operation, a background intensity model allow us to separate between moving and static objects. Those edges included in the moving objects and those that belong to the edge background model are subtracted from the current image edges. The remaining edges are the ones cast by urban infrastructure. Our method is tested on a typical crossroad scene and the results show that the approach is sound and promising.

Keywords: background modelling, edge detection, shadow segmentation.

1 Introduction

During the automatic analysis of visual sequences, shadows become a nuisance that we have to deal with. In most cases, shadows need to be segregated from the objects being analyzed in order to characterize, recognize and measure their parameters with enough accuracy. The main difficulty arises from the fact that the objects' appearance is affected by their own shadows. Thus, depending on the illumination conditions, the camera viewpoint, and the objects translucency, the presence of shadows represent a significant challenge for computer vision based object analysis.

Our research focusses on the analysis of vehicle traffic scenes. In this context, we distinguish two different types of shadow: those cast by moving objects, such as vehicles and people, and those cast by urban infrastructure, such as buildings, billboards, street lights, etc. Vehicles' shadows can be detected using case analysis, as in [13]. Nonetheless, the possible range of interpretations for

---

* This research was partially supported with grants from CONACYT (CB-2005-01-51005), SIP-IPN (20101526) and the Fulbright Scholarship Board.

J. Blanc-Talon et al. (Eds.): ACIVS 2010, Part I, LNCS 6474, pp. 30–37, 2010.

urban infrastructure may be considerably wider. A survey of different approaches can be found in [7]. Much work has been done in the analysis of aerial images to estimate changes [11], segment [12], or recognize [8] buildings. In these cases, there is the significant difficulty that images are captured from different positions and different times, thus making it harder to use the simplification provided by the use of a fixed camera.

In this article, we propose a method to distinguish slow moving shadows cast by urban infrastructure, from fast moving ones, cast for instance by cars or people. In our approach, we compute two different background models in parallel: One for the edges and one for the reflected light intensity (see Fig. 1). The edge background model, which is similar to the one proposed by Jain et al.[4], is updated in periods that include a whole day of observation. The light intensity model, which is based on the mixture of Gaussians, proposed by Stauffer and Grimson in [9], gives us the objects that, at a specific moment, are considered foreground objects. Our method consists of subtracting the edges from the foreground objects, computed with the light intensity model, from the edges that are not part of the Background Edge Model.

The rest of the paper is organized as follow. In §2, we describe how the Background Edge Model is computed. Then, in §3, we present our method to detect the shadows casted by urban infrastructure. Next, in §4, we show some experimental results. Finally, we summarize our contributions and conclude our article.

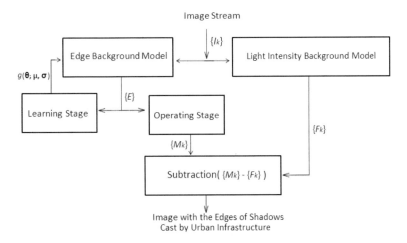

Fig. 1. Processing Diagram. Starting from the image stream $\{I_k\}$, two processes run in parallel. In one of them, the edge background model E is used to compute the moving edges $\{M_k\}$. In the second one, the light intensity background model $\{B_k\}$ and its derived foreground model $\{F_k\}$ are obtained. The edges that are part of the urban infrastructure are obtained subtracting the edges that are in the foreground objects $\{F_k\}$ from the moving edges $\{M_k\}$.

2   Edge Background Model

In our approach, we use fixed cameras. This means that their position, orientation, and optical parameters remain the same for a very extended period of time. Under these circumstances, it makes much sense to take advantage of the long-term acquired data, since the camera is exactly in the same operating condition. But, at this point, we face a problem. During the day, there may be large variations in light intensity. There has been a considerable research effort aimed to cope with these variations (see for instance [2,3,9,10]). Although the main goal of the mixture of distributions is to cope with these variations, we have managed to use the edges as our visual primitives, similarly to Jain *et al.* [4].

Let $I_k(\mathbf{x})$ be the k-th image in a sequence. The spatio-temporal variations along space identify points at which image brightness has discontinuities. Canny [1] introduced the concept of non-maximum suppression for edge images, points where the gradient of the magnitude assumes a local maximum in the gradient direction. For any single observation, the gradient in one specific point has an orientation $\theta(\mathbf{x})$. However, because of the intensity variations for a given pixel across the sequence, the angular orientation $\theta_k(\mathbf{x})$ of the gradient along the image sequence is a random variable with a Cauchy distribution (see Papoulis *et al.*[6]) of the form

$$f(\theta; \theta_0, \gamma) = \frac{1}{\pi}\left[\frac{\gamma}{(\theta - \theta_0)^2 + \gamma^2}\right],\tag{1}$$

where θ_0 is the location parameter, specifying the location of the peak of the distribution, and γ specifies the half-width at half-maximum [5]. Nonetheless, for simplicity, we have used a Gaussian model to fit the set of observations, as

$$g(\theta; \mu, \sigma) = ae^{-\frac{1}{2}\left(\frac{\theta - \mu}{\sigma}\right)^2},\tag{2}$$

where μ and σ are the distribution mean and standard deviation, respectively. We fit the logarithm of the data with a quadratic curve $f(x) = p_x^2 + p_2 x + p_3$, which coefficients are related to the Gaussian by

$$\sigma = \sqrt{\frac{-1}{2p_1}}, \mu = p_2\sigma^2, a = p_3 + \left(\frac{\mu}{\sigma}\right)^2.\tag{3}$$

During operation, when a new orientation of the gradient for a given pixel becomes available, it is compared with the edge background model just described. Whenever it is a significant difference between what is being computed and the model, the edge pixel is described as a moving one, otherwise, it belongs to the background.

3   Detecting the Shadows of Urban Infrastructure

Our objective is to distinguish the shadows cast by urban infrastructure, such as buildings, billboards, traffic signals and other alike. We assume that the Sun

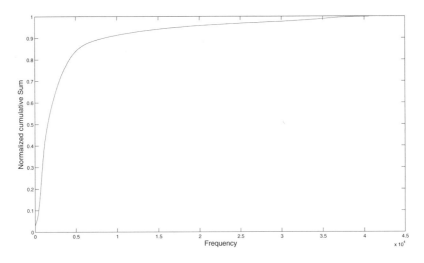

Fig. 2. Normalized accumulated histogram for the occurrence of edge pixels. This graph shows the normalized number of edge pixels that appear along the sequence. In this particular sequence, most of the pixels appear only for a few frames. We keep as background edge pixels those that show up for a considerable number of frames relatively to all the rest.

is the only source of illumination. Urban infrastructure has the distinctive feature that the shadows they cast not only move slower than most moving objects but with a consistent and systematic pattern provided by the Earth's motion. Without taking into account this information, shadows cast by urban infrastructure can easily be confused with the background. Our method is divided in two stages that run in parallel. One has the objective of computing the moving edges, while the second one has the objective of computing the moving objects. To compute the shadows cast by urban infrastructure, we subtract the edges of moving objects and the shadows in the edge background model from the edges of the current image.

During operation (see Fig. 1), an incoming intensity image $I_k(\mathbf{x})$ is processed using an edge detector filter. The orientation $\hat{\theta}_k(\mathbf{x})$ of each edge pixel is compared against the edge background model $E(\mathbf{x})$, previously computed using Eq. (1). Whenever there is a statistical difference in the observed orientation between the edge pixels in the current frame and the model, the edge pixel is considered part of a moving object $M_k(\mathbf{x})$.

In parallel runs a regular process, based on a mixture of Gaussians model[9], to compute the intensity background model $B_k(\mathbf{x})$. The incoming image $I_k(\mathbf{x})$ is subtracted from the background model to obtain the foreground or moving objects $F_k(\mathbf{x})$. Then, the edge image from $I_k(\mathbf{x})$ contained in $F_k(\mathbf{x})$ is subtracted from $M_k(\mathbf{x})$ to obtain the edges that are part of the shadows cast by the urban infrastructure.

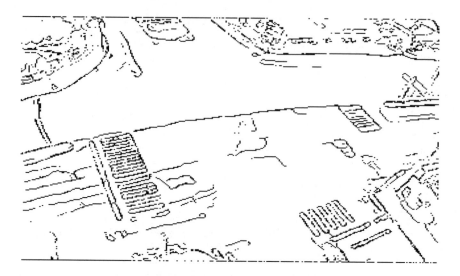

Fig. 3. Illustration of the constant edges map for our test image sequence. This is the result of analyzing the occurrence of edge pixels all along the image sequence. The ones illustrated here appeared in a number of frames above a certain predefined threshold. Fig. 4 shows the two images of the scene where this result has been obtained from.

4   Experimental Results

To test our method, we considered a sequence of images recorded at a typical crossroad scenario (see Fig. 4). In the interval between 8:00am to 4:00pm, we recorded about 41,000 frames at a rate of about 1.5 frames per second. The images were taken from the top of a 28m tower. Each image has a resolution of 480×640 pixels (width x height). Besides very mild vibrations, the camera's optical and positional parameters remained fixed.

The first task was to construct the edge background model. Starting from the edge image, computed using the Canny's edge detector[1] on the incoming image stream $\{I_k(\mathbf{x})\}$, we estimate the image gradient $\nabla I_k(\mathbf{x})$ of every edge pixel. After the whole sequence has been processed, a histogram of frequency is computed (see Fig. 2). Let $h(n)$ be an ordered set containing the number of frames that a given edge pixel in $\mathbf{x}$ shows up in the test sequence. The edge pixels that are part of the edge background model $E(\mathbf{x})$ are the ones that show up many times. For our method, we ruled out as background edges, all the edge pixels that appeared a number of times below a predefined threshold τ. In our case, we have chosen $\tau = 90\%$. This results in the edge background model depicted in Fig. 3. This illustration shows the edge pixels that remain for an extended period of time. It includes crosswalks, sidewalks, buildings, traffic signs, and other elements of the urban infrastructure. This procedure has the additional advantage that, for every edge pixel, it results an estimation of the Gaussian distribution of its orientation.

From the image sequence, we computed the intensity background model $B_k(\mathbf{x})$ using a mixture of Gaussians model [9]. After a suitable model of the intensity

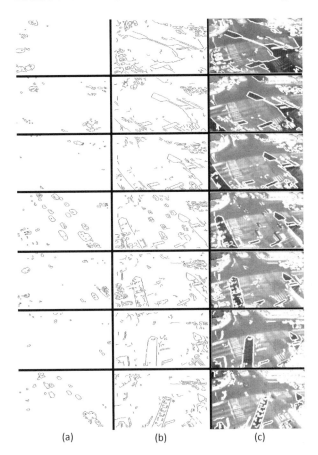

(a)   (b)   (c)

Fig. 4. Experimental results. (a) Edges of the moving objects computed with the mixture of Gaussians algorithm, (b) moving edges map, (c) Overlay of the detected urban infrastructure shadows on the gray-scale image. The shadows casted by fast moving objects are filtered out.

background has been computed, the foreground objects are detected using background subtraction, a technique where incoming frames are subtracted from the background model to detect moving objects. In parallel, the edge map for the current intensity image $I(\mathbf{x})$ is computed. This edge map is filtered using the moving objects just detected. The resulting edge pixels are subtracted from the moving edges previously detected. Fig. 4 shows the urban infrastructure shadows superimposed to its corresponding intensity map.

In the Table 1, we present some interesting measures about the performance of the system, specially related to Fig. 4. Note how, despite apparent low true positive and high false negative rates, TRP and FPR respectively, the algorithm gives good visual results. In particular, it has been observed that high frequency detail is easily missed during smoothing, previous to edge detection, taking out a large amounts of urban infrastructure edge shadows.

Table 1. Values of sensitivity and specificity. It has been noted that the low true positive and high false negative rates, TRP and FPR respectively, are due to the smoothing stage of the edge detection stage, which removes a considerable amount of detail related to the edges of interest.

Image	True Positive Rate (TPR)	False Positive Rate (FPR)	False Negative Rate (FNR)	True Negative Rate (TNR)
00170	0.1136	0.0193	0.8864	0.9807
05080	0.1778	0.0147	0.8222	0.9853
20070	0.153	0.0144	0.847	0.9856
25100	0.1294	0.0122	0.8706	0.9878
30160	0.0957	0.0125	0.9043	0.9875
35070	0.0997	0.0138	0.9003	0.9862
40080	0.1231	0.0104	0.8769	0.9896

5   Conclusion

In this paper, we have presented a strategy to detect the shadows cast by urban infrastructure such as buildings, traffic signs, towers, light poles, and large billboards. The strategy is sound, as it allows to segregate these shadows from others, cast by moving objects, such as vehicles and people. This result is important since shadows are pervasive and they tend to degrade the performance of computer vision systems. On the other hand, they could be a valuable source of information regarding the structure of the environment, including the position of the light sources.

Future work will focus upon the use of different projections obtained at extended periods of observation to gain understanding about the 3-D properties of the structures casting the shadows.

References

1. Canny, J.: A Computational Approach to Edge Detection. IEEE Transactions on Pattern Analysis and Machine Intelligence 8(6), 679–698 (1986)
2. Elgammal, A., Harwood, D., Davis, L.: Non-Parametric Model for Background Subtraction. In: Vernon, D. (ed.) ECCV 2000. LNCS, vol. 1843, pp. 751–767. Springer, Heidelberg (2000)
3. Horprasert, T., Harwood, D., Davis, L.: A Statistical Approach for Real-Time Robust Background Subtraction and Shadow Detection. In: IEEE International Conference on Computer Vision (1999)

4. Jain, V., Kimia, B., Mundy, J.: Background Modeling based on Subpixel Edges. In: IEEE International Conference on Image Processing, ICIP 2007, vol. 6 (2007)
5. Merran, E., Hastings, N., Peacock, B.: Statistical Distributions. Wiley, New York (2000)
6. Papoulis, A., Pillai, S.U., Unnikrishna, S.: Probability, random variables, and stochastic processes. McGraw-Hill, New York (2002)
7. Prati, A., Mikic, I., Trivedi, M.M., Cucchiara, R.: Detecting Moving Shadows: Algorithms and Evaluation. IEEE Transactions on Pattern Analysis and Machine Intelligence 25(7), 918–923 (2003)
8. Ren, K., Sun, H., Jia, Q., Shi, J.: Building recognition from aerial images combining segmentation and shadow. In: IEEE International Conference on Intelligent Computing and Intelligent Systems, pp. 578–582 (2009)
9. Stauffer, C., Grimson, E.: Learning Patterns of Activity using Real-Time Tracking. IEEE Transactions on Pattern Analysis and Machine Intelligence 22(8), 747–757 (2000)
10. Toyama, K., Krumm, J., Brumitt, B., Meyers, B.: Wallflower: Principles and Practice of Background Maintenance. In: IEEE International Conference on Computer Vision, p. 255 (1999)
11. Watanabe, S., Miyajima, K., Mukawa, N.: Detecting Changes of Buildings from Aerial Images using Shadow and Shading Model. In: International Conference on Pattern Recognition, vol. 2 (1998)
12. Wei, Y., Zhao, Z., Song, J.: Urban building extraction from high-resolution satellite panchromatic image using clustering and edge detection. In: IEEE International Geoscience and Remote Sensing Symposium, vol. 3 (2004)
13. Yang, Y., Ming, Y., Yongchao, M.: A Strategy to Detect the Moving Vehicle Shadows Based on Gray-Scale Information. In: International Conference on Intelligent Networks and Intelligent Systems, pp. 358–361 (2009)

Neural Image Thresholding Using SIFT:
A Comparative Study

Ahmed A. Othman[1] and Hamid R. Tizhoosh[2]

[1] Department of Systems Design Engineering,
University of Waterloo, Ontario, Canada
a4abdelr@uwaterloo.ca
[2] Department of Systems Design Engineering,
University of Waterloo, Ontario, Canada
tizhoosh@uwaterloo.ca

Abstract. The task of image thresholding mainly classifies the image data into two regions, a necessary step in many image analysis and recognition applications. Different images, however, possess different characteristics making the thresholding by one single algorithm very difficult if not impossible. Hence, to optimally binarize a single image, one must usually try more than one threshold in order to obtain maximum segmentation accuracy. This approach could be very complex and time-consuming especially when a large number of images should be segmented in real time. Generally the challenge arises because any thresholding method may perform well for a certain image class but not for all images. In this paper, a supervised neural network is used to "dynamically" threshold images by learning the suitable threshold for each image type. The thresholds generated by the neural network can be used to binarize the images in two different ways. In the first approach, the scale-invariant feature transform (SIFT) method is used to assign a number of key points to the whole image. In the second approach, the SIFT is used to assign a number of key points within a rectangle around the region of interest. The results of each test are compared with the Otsu algorithm, active shape models (ASM), and level sets technique (LS). The neural network is trained using a set of features extracted from medical images randomly selected form a sample set and then tested using the remaining images. This process is repeated multiple times to verify the generalization ability of the network. The average of segmentation accuracy is calculated by comparing every segmented image with corresponding gold standard images.

1 Introduction

As a bivalent pixel classification scheme, image thresholding can be viewed as the simplest technique for image segmentation. However, due to great differences in the image characteristics, different thresholds are required to segment different images. Therefore, if we use a *static* thresholding scheme to segment a set of different images, we may achieve accurate segmentation for some images and low

J. Blanc-Talon et al. (Eds.): ACIVS 2010, Part I, LNCS 6474, pp. 38–49, 2010.
© Springer-Verlag Berlin Heidelberg 2010

accuracy for others. Under "static" we understand techniques with no learning abilities. To receive higher segmentation accuracies, we must employ a *dynamic* approach with more flexibility in adjusting the threshold for every single image. Under "dynamic" we understand techniques with some learning capabilities.

In this paper, a supervised neural network is used to assign a different threshold to different images based on a set of image features extracted from a set of key points in the image using the SIFT method. The threshold assigned by the neural network is then used to segment the image. The neural network is trained using a set of simple features extracted from images along with their optimal threshold as a target value of the network. This paper is organized as: In section 2, a survey of some segmentation techniques, neural networks, active shape models (ASM) and level set segmentation techniques is provided. In section 3, the proposed technique is introduced and discussed. In section 4, medical images are used to test the proposed technique. In section 5, the paper is summarized and concluded.

2   Background

2.1   Gray-Level Segmentation

There are many methods to threshold gray-level images. The Otsu technique is considered as one of the most commonly used image thresholding techniques. For sake of comparison, we only focus on a comparison with Otsu algorithm, and hence briefly review the corresponding literature.

The Otsu method uses the image histogram to assign a threshold to the image [1]. It divides the image into two different classes of gray levels and assigns a threshold to the image where the variance of these two level is minimal [2]. Liu et al. [3] made a comparison between Otsu segmentation technique and K-means method. Zhu et al. [4] try to reduce the long search time of 2D Otsu method by proposing a new algorithm that improves the histogram usage. Fengjie et al. [5] propose a new algorithm combining the 2D Otsu segmentation technique with genetic algorithms to segment images of cables covered with ice from their background. Zhang et al. [6] propose a new algorithm that uses 2D histogram from 1D histogram to obtain optimal threshold from the Otsu algorithm by using fast wavelet transform algorithm. Lang et al. [7] propose a fast algorithm to overcome the high computational complexity of the 2D Otsu algorithm.

2.2   Neural Networks Segmentation

Due to the large number of different neural architectures on one hand, and different learning schemes on the other hand, it is difficult to provide an in-depth review of all neural approaches to image segmentation. Hence, we will summarize only those works that may be related to our approach.

Bahandar et al. [8] discuss the advantages of a hierarchical self-organizing neural network for image segmentation over the traditional (single-layer) self-organizing feature neural network. Ahmed et al. [9] present a two-stage neural network for volume segmentation of medical images to segment CT and MRI brain slices using feature extraction and unsupervised clustering. Chang et al. [10] used a three dimensional architecture of contextual constraint-based Hopfield with implementation of pixel classification on its third dimension neural to segment medical images. Faith et al. [11] provide a survey of the image segmentation by relaxation using constraint satisfaction neural network. Nunez et al. [12] introduce an algorithm for segmenting astronomical image using self-organizing neural networks and wavelets.

Kurnaz [13] presents an incremental neural network for the segmentation of tissues in ultrasound images. The approach uses discrete Fourier transform (DFT) and discrete cosine transform (DCT) to form elements of the feature vectors. Whereas the aforementioned works, and many others not mentioned here, propose sophisticated neural approaches for complex segmentation tasks, a simple and efficient neural approach to image thresholding seems to be still missing. Specially a fast and trainable threshold selection is still necessary for many practical applications.

2.3   Active Shape Models (ASM)

Cootes et al. [14] proposed a new statistical technique termed active shape models (ASM), which iteratively adapt to refine estimates of the pose, scale and shape of models of image objects. The ASM technique trains a set of examples to drive a set of flexible models that represent the objects as a set of contour points. After being trained, the ASM approach provides an initial guess of the location of the object in any new image. Moreover, the technique moves each point to a better position within the image and tries to adjust the shape and location of the model to fit the new object in the new image using an iterative procedure. Cootes et al. [15] propose a method to generate a model of shape and appearance of 2D images objects. They apply their method on medical images and state that it can be easily extended to deal with 3D images. Ghassan et al. [16] present a review of different techniques that model the difference appearance of objects in images generated because of natural shape variations, varying lighting conditions, 3D pose and other factors.

Rafeef et al. [17] propose a new approach that solves the problem of using Point Distribution Model to find an instance of the object class in an image not previously trained. They provide an iterative algorithm to force initial shape, or model template to deform to achieve a best match between data and model. Zhao et al. [18] propose a new method to overcome the problem of 3D active shape models caused when the number of training data in 3D applications is low. They use a partitioned representation of active shape model to solve the problem of limited training data which makes the region of interest represented by small number of eigenvectors that could not capture the full range of shape variability. Hodge et al. [19] propose a new algorithm that use 2D active shape models to segment the prostate boundary from ultrasound images. Lim et al. [20] propose a method to segment objects in 3D medical images using active shape models. The algorithm consist of two parts: generation method to create shape models in 3-D images and segmentation method that uses a scale model to segment objects in 3-D medical images.

The main disadvantages of ASM approach, from this paper's perspective, is its low accuracy when trained with small number of images, and the computational expense.

2.4 Scale-Invariant Feature Transform (SIFT)

Scale-Invariant Feature Transform (SIFT) is an algorithm mainly used to detect and describe local features for object recognition, image stitching, 3D modeling, gesture recognition, video tracking, and match moving. SIFT was published by Lowe [21] who uses a staged filtering approach that identifies stable points in scale space to detect the features. Moreover, SIFT creates image keys which represent blurred image gradients in multiple orientation planes and at multiple scales to allow for local geometric deformations. SIFT uses the image keys to identify candidate object matches and to verify each match by finding a low-residual least-square solution for the unknown model parameters. These features are invariant to image scaling, translation, and rotation, and partially invariant to illumination changes and affine or 3D projection.

Lindeberg [22] proposes a systematic methodology for dealing with the problem of how to select appropriate local scales for further analysis, not discussed in traditional scale-space theories. Bicego et al. [23] propose a model that uses SIFT in face authentication. They designed several matching schemes to ensure the real potential and applicability of the method. Yun et al. [24] use SIFT to present a self-calibration strategy to estimate intrinsic and extrinsic camera parameters. Lopez et al. [25] present a new feature matching algorithm that integrates SIFT local descriptors in the Iterative Closest Point (ICP) scheme to find the appropriate match between repetitive patterns that appear in man-made scenes. Tang et al. [26] propose a modification to SIFT algorithm to produce better invariant feature points for image matching under noise. In this paper we use SIFT to extract features to train a neural network.

2.5 Level Set Segmentation Technique (LS)

In traditional level sets [27] a common numerical scheme is used to initialize the function ϕ as a signed distance function before the evolution to overcome the problems of sharp and/or flat shape generated during the evolution. This scheme reshapes (or re-initializes) the function ϕ to be a signed distance function periodically during the evolution. Therefore the reinitialization process is crucial and cannot be avoided in traditional level set methods. The standard re-initialization method is to solve the following equation [28]:

$$\frac{\partial \phi}{\partial t} = \text{sign}(\phi_0)(1 - |V\phi|) \tag{1}$$

where ϕ_0 is the function to be re-initialized and $sign(\phi)$ is the sign function. Li et al. [29] completely eliminate the need for the re-initialization procedure by forcing the level set function to be close to a signed distance function. They present a new variational formulation for geometric active contours. Yan et al. [30] use a level-set framework to develop a new hybrid medical image segmentation method. liu et al. [31] propose a novel level set-based model to segment breast in ultrasound images. They use the differences between the actual and estimated probability densities of the intensities in different regions to develop an energy function.

3   Proposed Approach

The proposed algorithm uses a trained neural network to segment the images directly by generating a threshold $T \in [0, 255]$; the neural network estimates the suitable threshold based on the image characteristics. From a set of randomly selected images, the approach starts with extracting features from a set of points assigned by SIFT either for the whole image or within a rectangle around the region of interest. The Otsu method is used to deliver the initial threshold and then we find the best threshold via trial and error within the neighboring values to come up with the optimal threshold for every training image. These optimal values can be used as target values for the neural network. The proposed technique uses the randomly selected images along with their optimal thresholds to train a backpropagation neural network. After being trained, the neural network is used to generate a suitable threshold for a set of new images.

3.1   Detecting Algorithm

Training images are processed by a detection algorithm which calculates the position of the first seed point inside the region of interest. This point is calculated by tracing a 10×10 mask over the image and calculating the sum and the standard deviation of every mask and the correlation between the mask and its neighbors. Based on empirical knowledge about the test images, the region of interest has low gray-level intensities and generally a low standard deviation. Moreover, to be sure that the minimum sum and the minimum standard deviation are indeed from inside the region of interest, the correlation coefficients between each 10×10 mask and its preceding and following masks are calculated. Hence, for every 10×10 part of the image the minimum sum, standard deviation and correlation are considered to mark the position of a seed point inside the region of interest.

3.2   Feature Extraction

As the lack of sufficient number of training images is a general obstacle to any approach using neural learning, we use multiple seed points inside the region of interest for training image such that every sample image can be used multiple times. The proposed technique starts with extracting a set of features from every image and uses these features to assign best thresholds to different images. The process of extratcing features is performed using two different approaches:

1. Extracting features from the whole image.
   The training images are not passed through the detection algorithm as the whole images I is processed by SIFT to return n points.
2. Extracting features from a rectangle around the region of interest.

   (a) for every training image, the image is passed through the detection algorithm to obtain the seed point $P = (x, y)$ inside the region of interest. The algorithm proceeds by drawing a rectangle around the region of interest using the point P as the center of the rectangle. Based on the empirical knowledge used in the detection algorithm about the test images, the algorithm starts by finding a region around P as a small window around the point P (e.g. 10×10) and incrementally enlarges the window (e.g. up to 20×20). This process stops when the standard deviation of one region becomes grater than or less than the standard deviation of the previous region by a certain limit (e.g. 20%) and the last window is considered the retcangle region around the region of interest R.
   (b) The rectangle around the region of interest R is provided to the SIFT which then returns a set of key points within the rectangle R.

Now, we have n points generated via SIFT either in for whole image or inside the rectangle R. A 20×20 rectangle is generated around each point and features are calculated within this rectangle. Moreover, for each image, the optimal threshold is calculated in order to be used for supervised learning. We use simple features that can be calculated fast:

- The mean gray level μ_S for each 20×20 rectangle S around the seed point. The average gray level of a sub-image is an indication of its darkness/brightness.
- The standard deviation σ_S for each 20×20 rectangle S around the seed point. The intensity variation captured by the standard deviation quantifies our confidence in darkness/brightness of the sub-image.
- The distance $d_S = \max S - \min S$ between the maximum and the minimum of each 20×20 rectangle S around the seed point. This distance provides additional information to distinguish between different variation levels captured by standard deviation.

For $n = 50$, and $F = 3$ features, we will have $n \times F = 150$ features from every image. Whereas increasing F (i.e. more features) needs additional analysis and is only justified if it helps to increase the recognition ability of the network, the number of seed points n can be widely set with respect to computational constraints.

3.3   Training the Neural Network

A feed-forward backpropagation neural network is used to learn the set of sample images. The network consists of one input layer with 50 nodes (as many as we have seed points) and one hidden layer with 30 nodes and the output layer with one output (=the estimated threshold). For every training set, five different

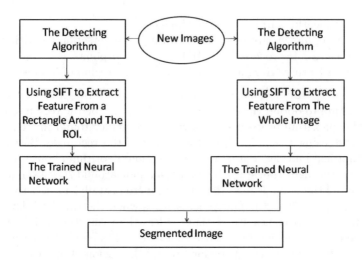

Fig. 1. Recalling the trained network to threshold new images

sample images are randomly selected from a larger database to train the neural network. The optimal thresholds for these five images are assigned as the target of the neural network. The network is trained using Matlab *trainrp* function with desired error set to $\epsilon = 0.000001$ to be achieved within maximum $N_E = 100000$ epochs.

3.4   Testing the Neural Network

After training, the neural network can threshold new images. We make two different tests for every new image I. In the first test, we take the whole image I as input for the SIFT which returns a set of key points N_1 inside I. In the second test, we pass I through the detecion algorithm (note that the seed point detection is a customized solution for our test case and can be replaced by a more reliable algorithm or by user input) to obtain a point inside the region of interest and then generate the rectangle R around the region of interest as previously described. The rectangle R is forwarded to the SIFT which returns a set of key points N_2 inside R. The set of pre-described features are now calculated from each point in the two sets N_1 and N_2. The extracted features form every point are the inputs for the neural network which assigns a suitable threshold to each image based on its features. The image is then segmented using the threshold based on two different approaches (Fig. 1):

- First Approach (NN$_I$): Taking the average of thresholds assigned by the neural network to each point $n_i \in N_1$:
  $$T^* = \frac{1}{|N_1|} \sum_{i=1}^{|N_1|} T_i$$
- Second Approach (NN$_R$): Taking the average of thresholds assigned by the neural network to each point $n_i \in N_2$:
  $$T^* = \frac{1}{|N_2|} \sum_{i=1}^{|N_2|} T_i$$

4   Experiments and Results

In this section, a set of 20 medical images are employed to train and test the proposed technique. These 20 images are quite difficult to segment. If we run every image individually and find the optimum threshold to every image via brute force, the maximum achievable segmentation accuracy is 84% (maximum achievable accuracy via pure thresholding).

The proposed approach randomly selects five of the images as a training set and the remaining 15 images are used for testing. This process is repeated 4 times to generate different training sets and investigate the generalization ability of the network. All results are calculated and recorded in the Tables 1, 2,3 and 4. The purpose of this experiment is to compare the results from the proposed technique with the whole image average thresholds (NN_I) and the rectangle around the region of interest thresholds (NN_R) and comparing them with the results by Otsu technique, active shape models (ASM) and level set technique (LS) via accuracy calculation using the gold standard images.

The following metrics have been employed to verify the performance of the techniques under investigation:

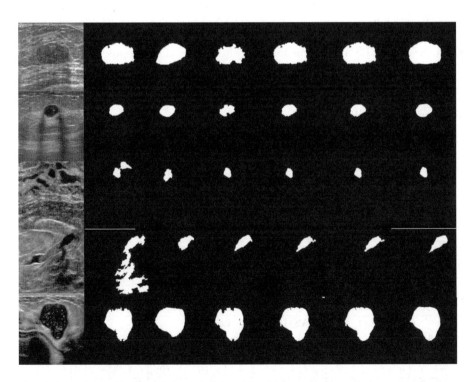

Fig. 2. Sample results (from left to right): original image, results of Otsu method,results of ASM method,results of LS method, results of first approach (NN_I), results of second approach (NN_R), and the gold standard image

1. The average of segmentation accuracy J is calculated using the area overlap (also called Jaccard Index)

$$J(A,B) = \frac{|A \cap B|}{|A \cup B|} \tag{2}$$

where A is the binary image and B is the gold standard image.
2. The standard deviation σ of the average of accuracy,
3. The 95% confidence interval (CI) of J.
4. The Hamming-based similarity η.
5. The Housdorff distance HD.

The results of different medical images segmented using the four algorithms are shown in Figure 2. It is obvious that both proposed algorithms, NN_I and NN_R, perform more accurately compared to the Otsu, ASM and LS methods. The results of the four training sets are presented in Tables 1, 2,3 and 4. Table 5 summarizes the results of all experiments. For Otsu thresholding and level set method, the algorithms are applied on the 20 images but we divide them into trained images (images that have been used to train the network) and tested images (images used for testing the proposed system) for a better comparison.

Generally, it is obvious from Tables 1, 2,3 and 4 that the proposed algorithm in both implementations - whole image (NN_I) and rectangle around the region of interest thresholds (NN_R) - has the highest accuracies compared with the Otsu, ASM and LS algorithms for all training sets. The proposed approach has

Table 1. Results of the first training set: The Jaccard Index J and its standard deviation σ, the 95%-confidence interval CI of J, the Hamming-based similarity η, and the Housdorff distance HD

Metric	Otsu		ASM		LS		NN_I		NN_R	
	Train	Test	Train	Test	Train	Test	Train	Test	Train	Test
J	70%	73%	76%	75%	76%	81%	82%	81%	79%	82%
σ	± 31%	± 18%	± 9%	± 13%	± 17%	± 12%	± 8%	± 9%	± 12%	± 11%
CI (%)	31-100	63-83	65-88	68-83	55-98	74-88	72-92	75-85	64-93	76-88
η	92%	98%	97%	99%	98%	99%	99%	99%	98%	99%
HD	7.7	6.8	7.2	6.2	5.9	5.8	5.6	5.4	5.8	5.2

Table 2. Results of the second training set: The Jaccard Index J and its standard deviation σ, the 95%-confidence interval CI of J, the Hamming-based similarity η, and the Housdorff distance HD

Metric	Otsu		ASM		LS		NN_I		NN_R	
	Train	Test	Train	Test	Train	Test	Train	Test	Train	Test
J	70%	73%	78%	74%	78%	80%	82%	80%	81%	82%
σ	± 30%	± 18%	± 8%	± 13%	± 8%	± 15%	± 10%	± 14%	± 11%	± 10%
CI (%)	30-100	63-83	78-88	67-82	68- 88	72-89	69-95	72-88	67-93	76-88
η	92%	97%	99%	98%	98%	99%	98%	99%	98%	99%
HD	7.8	6.7	5.6	6.7	6.4	5.6	6.2	5.6	6	5.1

Table 3. Results of the third training set: The Jaccard Index J and its standard deviation σ, the 95%-confidence interval CI of J, the Hamming-based similarity η, and the Housdorff distance HD

Metric	Otsu		ASM		LS		NN_I		NN_R	
	Train	Test	Train	Test	Train	Test	Train	Test	Train	Test
J	65%	75%	77%	75%	81%	79%	82%	82%	82%	84%
σ	± 28%	± 19%	± 9%	± 13%	± 8%	± 12%	± 12%	± 10%	± 11%	± 10%
CI (%)	29-99	64-85	67-88	67-82	59-100	72-86	67-96	76-87	67-95	78-90
η	90%	96%	98%	98%	99%	98%	99%	99%	98%	99%
HD	7.5	6.8	6.3	6.9	6.2	6	6.4	5.8	6	5.6

Table 4. Results of the fourth training set: The Jaccard Index J and its standard deviation σ, the 95%-confidence interval CI of J, the Hamming-based similarity η, and the Housdorff distance HD

Metric	Otsu		ASM		LS		NN_I		NN_R	
	Train	Test	Train	Test	Train	Test	Train	Test	Train	Test
J	75%	72%	75%	76%	81%	79%	84%	79%	80%	83%
σ	± 20%	± 22%	± 14%	± 12%	± 11%	± 14%	± 5%	± 11%	± 13%	± 10%
CI (%)	49-99	59-84	57-93	69-82	67-95	70-86	77-90	74-86	64-95	77-89
η	89%	98%	99%	98%	98%	98%	98%	98%	98%	99%
HD	9	6.3	6.4	6.5	6.3	6.2	6.1	5.7	5.5	5.8

Table 5. Summary of the results for the accuracy J and its 95%-confidence interval CI

Method	1st set		2nd set		3rd Set		4th Set	
	J	CI	J	CI	J	CI	J	CI
Otsu	73%	68% – 83%	73%	63%-83%	75%	64%-85%	72%	59%-84%
ASM	75%	68%-83%	74%	67%-82%	75%	67%-82%	76%	69%-82%
LS	81%	72% -88%	80%	72% -89%	79%	72% -86%	79%	70% -86%
NN_I	81%	75%-85%	80%	72%-88%	82%	76%-87%	82%	74%-86%
NN_R	82%	76%-88%	82%	76%-88%	84%	78%-90%	83%	77%-89%

the highest average segmentation accuracy and the lowest standard deviation for all cases.

Table 5 shows a summary of the results of the four training sets with focusing on the average of segmentation accuracy J and the 95% confidence interval CI. It can be seen that the proposed approach has the highest average segmentation accuracy and the shortest confidence intervals as well, which means that the proposed approach can provide more accurate and more consistent results. For example, in the third training set, the average accuracy of the proposed system using whole image (NN_I) raised from 75% (Otsu) and 75% (ASM) and 79% (LS) to 82% and to 84% with (NN_R) approach. Moreover, the confidence interval of the first approach (NN_I) is pushed higher from 64%–85% (Otsu), 67%–82% (ASM) and 72%–86% (LS) to 76%–87% and to 78%–90% for the second approach(NN_R) which means that the proposed approaches are more consistent. The housdorf distance is reduced from 6.8 (Otsu) , 6.9 (ASM) and 6 (LS) to 5.8 for the first approach (NN_I) and to 5.6 for the second approach(NN_R).

5 Conclusions

Image thresholding as the simplest form of segmentation is a critical process in image analysis. In most cases, the threshold generated by thresholding algorithms should be adjusted in order to obtain the maximum segmentation accuracy. Intelligent segmentation by training a neural network to generate the threshold for unseen images seems to be a viable alternative. This process extracts features from each image using SIFT algorithm either by extracing features from the whole image or from a rectangle around the region of interest. The extracted features are then used to train a feed-forward backpropagation neural network along with their optimal thresholds as target values for the network. The neural network could provide a threshold for new images resulting in higher accuracies compared to another intelligent technique (ASM), level set segmentation technique and a "static" technique such as Otsu method. This solution seems to increase the average accuracy of segmentation and also improves the confidence interval which means that the segmentation process becomes more consistent as well.

The emphasis of this work was to design a simple and practical approach for "dynamic" thresholding. The future work should investigate different and invariant features, and corresponding network architecture. A larger set of data should be employed as well to produce results of higher statistical significance.

References

1. Sezgin, M., Sankur, B.: Survey over image thresholding techniques and quantitative performance evaluation. Journal of Electronic Imaging 13, 146–165 (2004)
2. Otsu, N.: A threshold selection method from gray-level histograms, pp. 62–66. IEEE, Los Alamitos (1979)
3. Liu, D., Yu, J.: Otsu method and K-means. In: HIS 2009, pp. 344–349 (2009)
4. Zhu, N., Wang, G., Yang, G.: A Fast 2D Otsu Thresholding Algorithm Based on Improved Histogram. IEEE, Los Alamitos (2009)
5. Fengjie, S., He, W., Jieqing, F.: 2D Otsu Segmentation Algorithm Based on Simulated Annealing Genetic Algorithm for Iced-cable Images. In: IFITA 2009, pp. 600–602 (2009)
6. Zhang, J., Hu, J.: Image Segmentation Based on 2D Otsu Method with Histogram Analysis. In: CSSE 2008, pp. 105–108 (2008)
7. Lang, X., Zhu, F., Hao, Y.: Integral Image Based Fast Algorithm for Two-dimensional Otsu Thresholding. In: Congress on Image and Signal Processing, 677–681 (2008)
8. Bhandar, S.M., Koh, J., Suk, M.: A hierarchical neural network and its application to image segmentation. Mathematics and Computers in Simulation 41, 337–355 (1996)
9. Ahmed, M.N., Farag, A.A.: Two-stage neural network for volume segmentation of medical images. Pattern Recognition Letters 18, 1143–1151 (1997)

10. Chang, C.-Y., Chung, P.-C.: medical image segmentation using a contextual-constraint-based Hopfield neural cube. Image and Vision Computing 19, 669–678 (2001)
11. Kurugollu, F., Sankur, B., Harmanci, E.: Image segmentation by relaxation using constraint satisfaction neural network. Image and Vision Computing 20, 483–497 (2002)
12. Nuneza, J., Llacer, J.: Astronomical image segmentation by self-organizing neural networks and wavelets. Neural Networks 16 (2003)
13. Kurnaz, M.N., Dokur, Z., Olmez, T.: An incremental neural network for tissue segmentation in ultrasound images. Computer Methods and Programs in Biomedicine 85, 187–195 (2007)
14. Cootes, T.F., Taylor, C.J.: Active Shape Models - 'Smart Snakes'. pp. 265-275
15. Cootes, T.F., Hill, A., Haslam, J., Taylor, C.J.: The use of active shape models for locating structure in medical images. Image and Vision Computing 12(6), 355–366 (1994)
16. Hamarneh,G., Abu-Gharbieg, R., Gustavsson, T.: Review Active Shape Models - Part I: Modeling Shape and Gray Level Variations. In: SSAB (1998)
17. Abu-Gharbieg, R., Hamameh, G., Gustavasson, T.: Review Active Shape Models - Part II: Image Search and Classification. In: SSAB (1998)
18. Zhao, Z., Teoh, E.K.: Robust MR Image Segmentation Using 3D Partitioned Active Shape Models. In: ICARCV (2006)
19. Hodge, A.C., Fenster, A., Downey, D.B., Ladak, H.M.: Prostate boundary segmentation from ultrasound images using 2D active shape models: Optimisation and extension to 3D. Computer Methods and Programs in Biomedicine 84, 99–113 (2006)
20. Lim, S.-J., Ho, Y.S.: 3-D Active Shape Image Segmentation Using a Scale Model. In: ISSPIT, pp. 168–173 (2006)
21. Lowe, D.: Object recognition from local scale-invariant features. In: IEEE International Conference on Computer Vision, vol. 2, pp. 1150–1157 (1999)
22. Lindeberg, T.: Feature Detection with Automatic Scale Selection. IJCV 30(2), 79–116 (1998)
23. Bicego, M., Lagorio, A., Grosso, E., Tistarelli, M.: On the use of SIFT features for face authentication. In: Computer Vision and Pattern Recognition Workshops, art.1640475 (2006)
24. Yun, J., Park, R.: Self-calibration with two views using the scale-invariant feature transform. LNCS - I, pp. 589–598 (2006)
25. Lopez, R., Estrada, M.: Iterative closest SIFT formulation for robust feature matching. LNCS - II, pp. 502–513 (2006)
26. Tang, C., Wu, Y., Hor, M., Wang, W.: Modified SIFT descriptor for image matching under interference. In: ICMLC, Vol. 6, pp. 3294–3300 (2008)
27. Caselles, V., Kimmel, R., Sapiro, G.: Geodesic active contours. IJCV 22, 61–79 (1997)
28. Osher, S., Sethian, J.A.: Fronts propagating with curvature dependent speed: Algorithms based on Hamilton-Jacobi formulations. Phys. 79, 12–49 (1998)
29. Li, C., Xu, C., Gui, C., Fox, M.D.: Level Set Evolution Without Re-initialization: A New Variational Formulation. In: Computer Vision and Pattern Recognition, CVPR 2005 (2005)
30. Zhang, Y., Matuszewski, B.J., Shark, L.-K., Moore, C.J.: Medical image segmentation using new hybrid level-set method. In: Medivis 2008, pp. 71–76 (2008)
31. Liu, B., Cheng, H.D., Huang, J., Tian, J., Tang, X., Liu, J.: Probability density difference-based active contour for ultrasound image segmentation. Pattern Recognition 43, 2028–2042 (2010)

Statistical Rail Surface Classification Based on 2D and $2^1/_2$D Image Analysis⋆

Reinhold Huber-Mörk[1], Michael Nölle[1],
Andreas Oberhauser[2], and Edgar Fischmeister[1]

[1] Safety & Security Department
AIT Austrian Institute of Technology GmbH
{reinhold.huber, michael.noelle}@ait.ac.at
[2] Abteilung Bahnbau
Wiener Linien GmbH & Co KG
{andreas.oberhauser,edgar.fischmeister}@wienerlinien.at

Abstract. We present an approach to high-resolution rail surface analysis combining 2D image texture classification and $2^1/_2$D analysis of surface disruptions. Detailed analysis of images of rail surfaces is used to observe the condition of rails and, as a precaution, to avoid rail breaks and further damage. Single rails are observed by a color line scan camera at high resolution of approximately 0.2 millimeters and under special illumination in order to enable $2^1/_2$D image analysis. Gabor filter banks are used for 2D texture description and classes are modeled by Gaussian mixtures. A Bayesian classifier, which also incorporates background knowledge, is used to differentiate between surface texture classes. Classes which can be related to surface disruptions are derived from the analysis of the anti-correlation properties between two color channels. Images are illuminated by two light sources mounted at different position and operating at different wavelengths. Results for data gathered in the Vienna metro system are presented.

1 Introduction

In order to avoid severe accidents a frequent and adequate inspection of rails in railway networks is a necessary precaution. Traditionally, rail inspection was done by visual means, e.g. in combination with hammer sounding, and later automated inspection methods, e.g. ultrasonic or magnetic sensors, X-ray etc., were used. Although some problems are not detected by visual means, automated visual inspection offers additional information and a denser coverage when compared to established methods. Especially the analysis of rail wear resulting from rolling contact fatigue (RCF) [4] is well suited to high-resolution visual inspection of the rail head. So called spallings and headchecks result from small break outs on the rail surface and are often related to RCF [23]. Spallings typically occur in the center area of the rail head, whereas headchecks occur on the gauge side of the rail. Fig. 1 shows regions and typical surface characteristics as observed by a top down-view of a rail head.

⋆ This work is supported by the Austrian Federal Ministry for Transport, Innovation and Technology BMVIT, program line I2V "Intermodalität und Interoperabilität von Verkehrssystemen", project fractINSPECT.

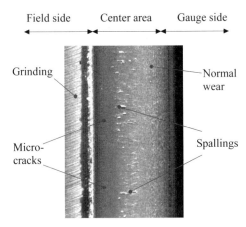

Fig. 1. Surface regions observed from a top-down view of the rail head surface and manual classification

Spallings and headchecks are commonly regarded to be preliminary stages of cracks and even rail breaks. Furthermore, preliminary stages of spallings and headchecks are the so called microcracks. Microcracks originate from plastic flow and wear away of the rail and show a characteristic appearance. In the studied data, microcracks become visible for resolutions better than 0.25 millimeters. Grinding is a measure to restore rail profile and remove distortions in order to avoid further damage. The application of grinding wheels results in a very specific surface texture. When the rail is run again after grinding the grinding texture disappears in the center and gauge regions and remains visible only at the field side. Apart from the already mentioned surface classes, classes describing non critical surface conditions and other typical surface appearances are observed on rails.

A number of surface classes describing the condition of rails are summarized in a hierarchical surface class repository, see Fig. 2. Classes of major interest are microcracks, grinding marks, headchecks, spallings and cracks. Grouping of classes was performed in our work, especially all non-critical classes were collected into a single class.

Our approach to high-resolution rail surface analysis combines 2D image texture classification with $2^1/_2$D analysis of surface disruptions. The data is acquired from a monitoring car using a color line scan camera and application specific placement of lighting. The resolution of the system is approximately 0.2 millimeters and special illumination is used to enable $2^1/_2$D image analysis. Features for 2D texture description are selected from Gabor filter banks and classes are modeled by Gaussian mixtures. A Bayesian classifier, which also incorporates background knowledge, is used to differentiate between surface texture classes. Classes which can be related to surface disruption are derived from the analysis of the so called anti-correlation properties between two color channels.

This paper is organized as follows: Section 2 provides an overview to related work in the field of rail inspection and approaches to similar problems in image analysis.

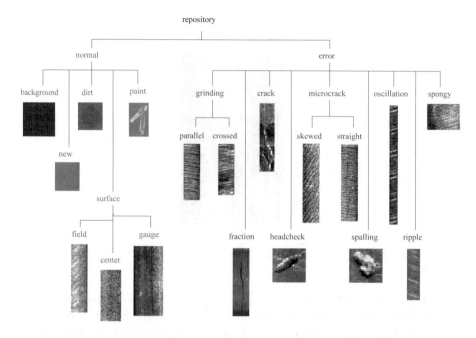

Fig. 2. Repository of rail head surface classes: normal or non-critical surface conditions are shown in the left branch, erroneous surface classes are shown in the right branch

Modeling of Gabor filter responses using Gaussian mixtures and incorporation of background knowledge is summarized in Sec. 3. The setup and detection strategy in $2^1/_2$D analysis is presented in Sec. 4. Feature selection, fusion of 2D and $2^1/_2$D information, as well as with background knowledge, and rejection of uncertain results is shown in Sec. 5. Results for data gathered in the Vienna metro system are presented in Sec. 6 and Sec. 7 concludes the paper.

2   Related Work

Various work in the field of maintenance systems for different components of the railroad system, e.g. sleepers, rails, overhead contact lines, was published. Methods for rail surface inspection based on other sensors include ultrasonic rail inspection and eddy-current-testing [10]. A vision based system for image based inspection of clips holding the rail track was presented in [20] and image based detection of general rail defects is described in [11].

When compared to our approach, the most similar work is a paper describing a system to detect rail corrugation which occurs mainly in high-speed trains [14]. The presence or absence of rail corrugation was detected correctly with a rate of 99.25 % for a sample of 200 positive and 200 negative images. The presented method used Gabor-filters, a wavelet filter bank and the so called Gabor wavelet transform together with nearest neighbor and support vector machine classifiers. Corrugation is a phenomenon showing undulation in the images at a relatively coarse scale, therefore a resolution of 2 millimeters was found sufficient for this task. Apart from the higher resolution, our approach is different to [14] with respect to a larger number of classes, a larger sample, a different classification method and fusion with additional sources of information.

No work dealing with much finer structures, e.g. microcracks, was published so far. Our work on 2D texture analysis investigates structures on this scale, thus requiring a much finer resolution on the order of magnitude of 0.2 millimeters.

Analysis of textured surfaces from images was approached by several methods, with the analysis of local statistical properties and the use of filter banks being the most prominent classes of algorithms [21]. For textures, which can be characterized by some directional and/or periodic appearance, filter based methods are well suited [17]. Gabor filter banks, which are well located in frequency and space, were frequently used in the field of texture classification [5].

The principle of analysis of reflection properties in the presented $2^1/_2$D analysis is related to the shape from shading (SFS) and photometric stereo (PS) methods. SFS deals with the determination of three-dimensional shape from a single image irradiance, whereas in PS the shading based reconstruction is based on two or more images [12]. Recently, a method similar to our approach of $2^1/_2$D analysis was used for solder paste inspection appeared [15]. An experimental study on specular refection from metallic surfaces and application to coin classification is discussed in [7].

3   Approach to 2D Analysis

For texture description we use two dimensional Gabor filters defined by [6]

$$g_{f\theta}(x,y) = \exp\left(-\frac{x'^2 + \nu^2 y'^2}{2\sigma^2}\right) \cos\left(2\pi \frac{x'}{\lambda} + \phi\right) \tag{1}$$

with

$$x' = x\cos\theta + y\sin\theta,$$
$$y' = -x\sin\theta + y\cos\theta. \tag{2}$$

Filter orientation is determined by θ. The parameter $\psi = 0$ results in a symmetric filter mask, whereas $\psi = -\pi/2$ is the asymmetric filter mask. The Gaussian envelope of the filter is specified by σ and the spatial aspect ratio ν. Commonly, a symmetric and an asymmetric filter mask are allocated into the real and imaginary parts of a complex function, thus forming a quadrature image filter [8].

Invariance to illumination change, in our case mainly induced by the curvature of the rail head, is obtained by image normalization. Pixel-based normalization to zero mean and unit standard deviation with respect to a local window was applied. Similar procedures, e.g. normalization to zero mean and L_1-norm [22], are commonly used.

The selection of orientation and scales mainly depends on the application. In order to cover the frequency of the observed ondulations of the textures of interest, namely microcrack and grinding texture, on the considered images the scales with wavelength $\lambda = 3, 6, 12$ and orientations of $\theta = 0, \pi/6, \pi/3, \pi/2, 2\pi/3, 5\pi/6$ were chosen.

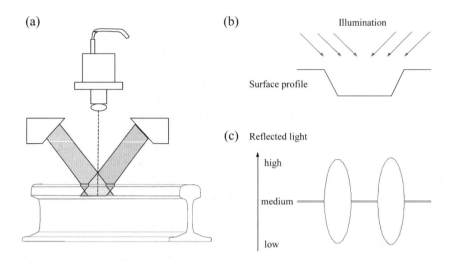

Fig. 3. Acquisition setup and model of reflection properties: (a) top-down view of the head head surface using a line camera and illumination by different line light sources under oblique angles, (b) distorted surface profile into driving direction and direction of sources of illumination, (c) model of reflectance for a distorted surface profile

The class conditional likelihoods for classes $C \in \{1, \ldots, \Omega\}$ are expressed by a Gaussian mixture model (GMM) [1]

$$p(\boldsymbol{x}|C) = \sum_{k=1}^{N_C} \alpha_k p_k(\boldsymbol{x}|C), \tag{3}$$

where $p_k(\boldsymbol{x}|C)$ is the Gaussian density with mean vector $\boldsymbol{\mu}_k$ and full covariance matrix Σ_k. The N_C is the number of components used to model class C. The maximum likelihood estimate for mixture models leads to the evaluation of a logarithm of sums and no closed form solution exists. Therefore, the Expectation Maximization (EM) algorithm was used [3]. A Bayes classifier determines class probabilities through $P(C|\boldsymbol{x}) = p(\boldsymbol{x}|C)P(C)$, where background knowledge might be represented by the class prior $P(C)$.

4   Approach to $2^1/_2$D Analysis

The same acquisition setup as for 2D images is used for $2^1/_2$D analysis. On the contrary to 2D analysis, where a single grayscale image is used, $2^1/_2$D analysis used the red and the blue channel of a color line scan camera image. Illuminating line light sources are placed parallel to the line scan camera. The lights and the camera itself are mounted on a railway vehicle and oriented orthogonal to the rail direction. The setup is shown in Fig. 3(a). The setup is based on a dark-field illumination principle, i.e. for undistorted surface patches only a small amount of light is reflected towards the sensor, whereas surface disruptions typically cause reflections.

One light source, e.g. a red one, is placed in front and another light source, e.g. the blue one, is placed behind the line camera with respect to the driving direction. The angle of specular reflection from undistorted rail surfaces into the camera is avoided [7] and strong reflections and shadows are observed in cases of surface disruptions only. The expected reflection properties due to a surface distortion, i.e. a spalling, is shown Fig. 3 (b). Light from two spectral channels, e.g. from a blue light source at the left and a red light source on the right, approach the object surface at oblique angles. The shown surface profile is a taken along the rail direction. Due to the dominating specular reflection on metal surfaces, light in the red channel is typically strongly reflected back to the camera when hitting the left edge of the surface disruption, see Fig. 3 (c). On the other hand, no specular reflection happens in the red channel on the edge on the right. The blue channel shows an opposite behavior when compared to the red channel, this property is termed anti-correlation.

The identification of surface disruptions is formulated similar to a target detection problem, i.e. a target T is identified if it is sufficiently different from its background B statistics. The context of target detection this is expressed by the ratio of maximum posteriori probabilities (MAPs) $P(T|s)/P(B|s) > 1$ for target and background, with s being the observed feature. Application of Bayes rule and Neyman-Pearson theory results in the likelihood test $P(s|T)/P(s|B) > t$, where t is a threshold [18].

In our case, a procedure in involving four target detectors of the form $s/\bar{s} > t_s$ and $s/\bar{s} < 1/t_s$, where s is a measurement corresponding to a potential target and the $\bar{s}$ is the estimated background, is proposed. Referring to Fig. 3(c), let the position for which detection is performed be in the middle of the surface profile. With $s = \{r, b\}$, where r and b are red and blue light received by the camera, the four target detection equations become

$$r_1/\bar{r} < 1/t_r, \quad r_{-1}/\bar{r} > t_r,$$
$$b_{-1}/\bar{b} < 1/t_b, \quad b_1/\bar{b} > t_b. \tag{4}$$

The subscript -1 indicate the position left, e.g. at one pixel distance, with respect to the detection position and position $+1$ is located right to the detection position. The r_i, b_i are the red and blue values for the pixel at position i and $\bar{r}, \bar{b}$ are background estimated by local smoothing. Two different thresholds t_r, t_b, related to the different color channels, are maintained. The combination of the four target detectors is done by taking into account the anti-correlation property, i.e. the presence of a target is assumed only if all four detectors coincide in their decision for a target.

5   Texture Feature Selection, Information Fusion and Rejection Option

Once the classes of interest are determined and training examples are chosen the Gabor filter bank is applied and pruned by selection of specific features. After an initial run of the classifier based on Gabor features it is possible to revise the result through background knowledge. The initial run provides parameters for the suggested model for background knowledge. Combination with information derived from $2^1/_2$D analysis is simply done by overriding the 2D results at those points. This is reasonable as the two sources of information are independent and the latter one is regarded to more critical from the point of application.

5.1   Feature Selection

Feature selection is the process of selecting a subset of features, i.e. filters, that perform best under some classification system [9]. Sequential backward selection (SBS) starts with the full set of features and iteratively shrinks the set of features. In each step the reduced set of features with smallest increase, or even the highest decrease, of the misclassification risk is retained. Due to its ease of implementation we decided to use SBS, although it was reported that SBS is not the best performing feature selection algorithm, especially when compared to floating search methods [16]. Therefore, we compared some of our results obtained with SBS to exhaustive search and found that for the considered rather large sample and low dimensional data set similar results are obtained.

The evaluation of a subset, i.e. the estimation of the misclassification risk, can either be based on some distance or divergence measure, e.g. the Kullback-Leibler distance [16], or cross-validation [13]. Cross-validation using the mean error rate r, evaluated on the hold-out set, was used

$$r = \frac{1}{N_h} \sum_{i=1}^{N_h} \delta(L(\boldsymbol{x}_i), \mathrm{argmax}_k\{p(C_k, \boldsymbol{x}_i)\}) \tag{5}$$

where N_h is the size of the hold-out set, $L(\boldsymbol{x}_i)$ is the class label associated with feature vector $\boldsymbol{x}_i$ and $\delta()$ is the discrete Kronecker delta function. Hold-out sets were generated by random partitioning the set of labeled data into training and hold-out sets of equal size. The presented error rates were obtained from the average mean error rates evaluated over 10 runs of SBS (10-fold cross validation). Fig. 4 shows the mean error rates for 10 runs of SBS.

Exhaustive search for 9 features obtained a mean error rate of 0.2195, whereas SBS delivered a rate of 0.2323. Using all features, the best error rate was found to be 0.198. Interestingly, the retained features when cutting the number of features to 50 percent, i.e. 9 features instead of 18, are concentrated at fine scales. Exhaustive search for 9 features retained Gabor features for

$$\lambda = 3 : \theta = 0, \pi/3, \pi/2, 2\pi/3, 5\pi/6$$
$$\lambda = 6 : \theta = 2\pi/3$$
$$\lambda = 12 : \theta = 0, \pi/6, 5\pi/6$$

(where $\theta = 0$ is the across rail direction and $\theta = \pi/2$ is the driving direction). Different runs of SBS delivered slightly different subsets of features; the best set of 9 features found by SBS consisted of Gabor features for

$$\lambda = 3 : \theta = \pi/6, \pi/3, \pi/2, 2\pi/3, 5\pi/6$$
$$\lambda = 6 : \theta = \pi/2$$
$$\lambda = 12 : \theta = 0, \pi/6, 5\pi/6.$$

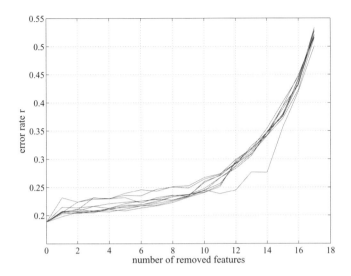

Fig. 4. Sequential backward selection: error rate depending on the number of discarded features for 10-fold cross validation

The difference of the features sets obtained by SBS and exhaustive search is only in two features, which are derived from the same scale, but different only at adjacent orientation.

5.2 Fusion with Background Knowledge

The posterior probability $P(C|y)$ for a class C conditioned on the position y in the direction perpendicular to the direction of travel is

$$P(C|y) = \sum_{k=1}^{M_C} \alpha_k p_k(y|C) P(C),$$ (6)

where y is the across track pixel position and M_C the number of mixture components used. Again, the EM algorithm is used to obtain the conditional likelihoods $p(y|C)$ modeled by GMMs.

For the estimation of $p(y|C)$ histograms of observed class frequency, after an initial step of classification without background knowledge, are extracted.

$$h(C, y) = \sum_{x=x_s}^{x_e} \delta(L(x, y), C),$$ (7)

where L is the label image $L \in \{1, \ldots, \Omega\}$, and x_s, x_e with $x_e > x_s$ are the along track coordinates.

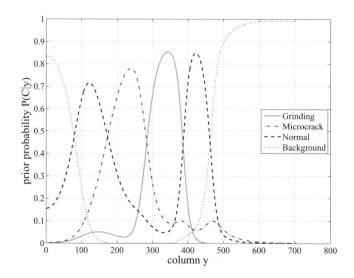

Fig. 5. Representation of background knowledge expressed by prior class probabilities for all classes of interest and conditioned on image columns. The gauge side of the rail head is found on the left and field side is located on the right.

Fig. 5 shows estimated $P(C|y)$ depending on the across track position y, e.g. the image column coordinates. For small y, which is the gauge side of the rail, and large y, background is most likely. In the gauge to central region of the rail normal conditions are most likely, in the central region microcracks are likely to be found and in the central to field region grinding is commonly observed and on the field side normal condition is most likely again.

5.3   Rejection of Uncertain Decisions

At spatial positions were class membership is very uncertain, it might happen that the classification result is also quite vague. Therefore we use a reject option on the posterior probabilities in 2D analysis [2]. A reject threshold $\theta_r = 0.5$, which ensures that the posterior probability for the selected class is always more certain than the sum of posterior probabilities taken over all other classes, was chosen.

5.4   Fusion of Results from 2D Texture and $2^{1}/_{2}$D Analysis

Features considered in 2D and $2^{1}/_{2}$D analysis could be considered conditionally independent. Therefore Bayes fusion of the results of separately analyzed features becomes admissible [19]. However, different classes are analyzed by the employed methods. The classes analyzed by 2D are well described by features characterizing image areas, whereas the classes studied by $2^{1}/_{2}$D analysis are related to small distortions in the image.

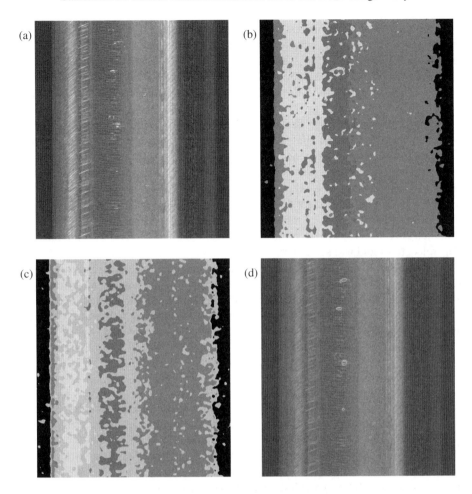

Fig. 6. Results of rail head surface classification: (a) Image acquired in red channel, (b) 2D classification, (c) 2D classification with rejection, (d) $2^1/_2$D classification overlaid on color image. Legend for (b) and (c): background ... black, normal rail surface ... blue, grinding area ... yellow, microcrack area ... red, no decision (rejection) ... gray. In (d) spallings are shown by enclosing polygons drawn in green color.

6   Results

The parameters for the Gabor filter bank were initially set by observing the periodicity of the main classes of interest, e.g. the microcracks and grinding structure, orthogonal to their orientation. e.g. into track direction. Fine tuning was done mainly in setting the parameters for the local energy function [17], where a symmetric Gaussian smoothing with window size 11×11 pixel and a $\sigma = 3$ applied to the magnitude of the complex Gabor filter response was found appropriate.

After initial experiments using the full class repository shown in Fig. 2 it was decided to reduce the number of classes to the most interesting ones. In 2D analysis microcracks and grinding are of major interest from the railway management point of view. Classes were grouped and feature selection was performed for the 2D analysis task. It was experimentally found, that it is appropriate to use $N_C = 15$ components with full covariance matrix in the GMM representation given in Eq. 3. The EM procedure was initialized by 5 iterations of k-nearest neighbor (k-NN with $k = N_C$) and the number of iterations in EM was set to 15.

Fig. 6(a) shows the image obtained in the red channel and Fig. 6(b) shows the results of a classification including fusion with background knowledge. The background knowledge was obtained from the evaluation of histogram taken over 5000 across track lines and prior probabilities are estimated using EM for the GMM given in Eq. 6 with $M_C = 3$ components for each class. The EM procedures is also initialized by kNN with $k = M_C$ and iterated for 15 steps. In a series of images taken along track the prior probabilities are updated repeatedly, e.g. whenever an acquisition of 5000 lines is complete. Fig. 6(c) shows the result with a reject option on the posterior probabilities. The reject threshold was set to 0.5.

The result of $2^1/_2$D analysis are overlaid onto a color image in Fig. 6(d). Due to different characteristics of illumination and color filters on the camera and different gain settings for the individual color channels different thresholds for red and blue channel $t_r = 1.2, t_b = 1.175$ were found experimentally. The detection of a surface disruption is only accepted if all four detectors given in Eq. 4 deliver a detection.

7   Conclusion

We have presented a statistical approach to feature selection, classification, detection and fusion applied to high-resolution analysis of rail head images in the Vienna metropolitan railroad network. Whereas the data is acquired in real-time, the processing is done off-line and presents valuable insight into the condition of rails for railway operators. The results appear to be reasonable for human observers. Due to the lack of ground truth it is not possible to provide detailed quantitative results. The approach could be extended to conventional rail networks, although materials and charges are different when compared to metropolitan networks. Future work includes analysis of time series of repeatedly taken rail sections, thus enabling analysis of the evolution of possible damage. Manual ground truth generation and quantitative assessment of the results is under investigation.

References

1. Bishop, C.M.: Neural Networks for Pattern Recognition, ch. 2.6: Mixture models, pp. 59–73. Oxford Univerity Press, Oxford (1995)
2. Bishop, C.M.: Pattern Recognition and Machine Learning, ch. 1.5: Decision theory, pp. 38–48. Springer, Heidelberg (2006)
3. Dempster, A., Laird, N., Rubin, D.: Maximum-likelihood from incomplete data via the EM algorithm. Journal of the Royal Statistical Society, Series B (Methodological) 39, 1–38 (1977)
4. Doherty, A., Clark, S., Care, R., Dembowsky, M.: Why rails crack. Ingenia 23, 23–28 (2005)

5. Field, D.J.: Relations between the statistics of natural images and the response properties of cortical cells. J. Optical Soc. Am. A 12, 2379–2394 (1987)
6. Grigorescu, S.E., Petkov, N., Kruizinga, P.: Comparison of texture features based on Gabor filters. IEEE Transactions on Image Processing 11(10), 1160–1167 (2002)
7. Hoßfeld, M., Chu, W., Adameck, M., Eich, M.: Fast 3D-vision system to classify metallic coins by their embossed topography. Electronic Letters on Computer Vision and Image Analysis 5(4), 47–63 (2006)
8. Jähne, B.: Digitale Bildverarbeitung, ch. 13.4.5: Quadraturfilter, 5th edn., pp. 383–384. Springer, Heidelberg (2002)
9. Jain, A., Zongker, D.: Feature selection: Evaluation, application and small sample performance. IEEE Transactions on Pattern Analysis and Machine Intelligence 19(2), 153–158 (1997)
10. Jarmulak, J., Kerckhoff, E.J.H., van't Veen, P.P.: Case-based reasoning for interpretation of data from non-destructive testing. Engineering Applications of Artificial Intelligence 14(4), 401–417 (2001)
11. Khandogin, I., Kummert, A., Maiwald, D.: Nonlinear image processing for automatic inspection of railroad lines. In: Proceedings of IEEE Workshop on Nonlinear Signal and Image Processing, vol. 1 (1997)
12. Klette, R., Schlüns, K., Koschan, A.: Computer Vision: Three-Dimensional Data from Images, ch. 7: Shape from Shading, pp. 263–300. Springer, Heidelberg (1998)
13. Kohavi, R.: A study of cross-validation and bootstrap for accuracy estimation and model selection. In: Proceedings of International Joint Conference on Artificial Intelligence, vol. 2, pp. 1137–1143 (1995)
14. Mandriota, C., Nitti, M., Ancona, N., Stella, E., Distante, A.: Filter-based feature selection for rail defect detection. Machine Vision and Applications 15, 179–185 (2004)
15. Pang, G.K., Chu, M.H.: Automated optical inspection of solder paste based on 2.5D visual images. In: Proceedings of International Conference on Mechatronics and Automation, pp. 982–987 (2009)
16. Pudil, P., Novovičová, J.: Novel methods for subset selection with respect to problem knowledge. IEEE Intelligent Systems 13(2), 66–72 (1998)
17. Randen, T., Husøy, J.H.: Filtering for texture classification: A comparative study. IEEE Trans. Pattern Anal. Mach. Intell. 21, 291–310 (1999)
18. Samson, V., Champagnat, F., Giovannelli, J.F.: Detection of point objects with random subpixel location and unknown amplitude. Applied Optics 43(2), 257–263 (2004)
19. Shi, X., Manduchi, R.: A study on Bayes feature fusion for image classification. In: Proc. of Conference on Computer Vision and Pattern Recognition Workshop (2003)
20. Singh, M., Singh, S., Jaiswal, J., Hempshall, J.: Autonomous rail track inspection using vision based system. In: Proceedings of International Conference on Computational Intelligence for Homeland Security and Personal Safety, pp. 56–59 (2006)
21. Tuceryan, M., Jain, A.K.: 2.1: Texture analysis. In: Chen, C.H., Pau, L.F., Wang, P.S.P. (eds.) Handbook of Pattern Recognition and Computer Vision, 2nd edn., pp. 207–248. World Scientific Publishing Co., Singapore (1998)
22. Varma, M., Zisserman, A.: A statistical approach to texture classification from single images. International Journal of Computer Vision 62(1-2), 61–81 (2005)
23. Zacher, M., Baumann, G., Le, R.: Modelle zur Prognose von Rollkontaktermüdungsschäden an Schienen. EI - Der Eisenbahningenieur 60(7), 44–52 (2009)

Salient-SIFT for Image Retrieval

Zhen Liang[1,*], Hong Fu[1,2], Zheru Chi[1], and Dagan Feng[1,3]

[1] Centre for Multimedia Signal Processing,
Department of Electronic and Information Engineering
The Hong Kong Polytechnic University, Hong Kong, China
zhenliang@eie.polyu.edu.hk, enzheru@inet.polyu.edu.hk
[2] Department of Computer Science, Chu Hai College of Higher Education, Hong Kong
enhongfu@inet.polyu.edu.hk
[3] School of Information Technologies, The University of Sydney, Sydney, Australia
enfeng@polyu.edu.hk

Abstract. Local descriptors have been wildly explored and utilized in image retrieval because of their transformation invariance. In this paper, we propose an improved set of features extarcted from local descriptors for more effective and efficient image retrieval. We propose a salient region selection method to detect human's Region Of Interest (hROI) from an image, which incorporates the Canny edge algorithm and the convex hull method into Itti's saliency model for obtaining hROI's. Our approach is a purely bottom-up process with better robustness. The salient region is used as a window to select the most distinctive features out of the Scale-Invariant Feature Transform (SIFT) features. Our proposed SIFT local descriptors is termed as salient-SIFT features. Experiment results show that the salient-SIFT features can characterize the human perception well and achieve better image retrieval performance than the original SIFT descriptors while the computational complexity is greatly reduced.

1 Introduction

Feature extraction and selection has always played an important role in image matching and object classification [1, 2]. How to efficiently extract local descriptors becomes a hot topic. The main focus of related research is to extract the descriptors which are invariant to image transformations, e.g. rotation, translation, scaling, and illumination changing. In the past decade, many invariant region detectors have been proposed [3, 4, 5, 6]. Furthermore, Mikolajczyk and Schmid in [7] evaluated the performance of a number of local detectors in terms of robustness, distinctiveness and invariance and concluded that the Scale-Invariant Feature Transform (SIFT) descriptor [4] is one of the best local descriptors which can successfully characterize the regions in most cases.

SIFT is a set of distinctive invariant local features extracted from images. For each key point, the features are extracted by sampling the gradient magnitudes and orientations (8 directions) of the 4 x 4 local regions around the key point. In total, there are 4 x 4 x 8 = 128 elements for each feature vector that characterizes a key point. The features are invariant to image transformations (scale, translation, and

---

* Corresponding author.

J. Blanc-Talon et al. (Eds.): ACIVS 2010, Part I, LNCS 6474, pp. 62–71, 2010.

rotation) and perform stably in image matching application. There are four major stages in SIFT feature extraction process. After candidate interesting points are detected in a series of difference-of-Gaussian (DoG) images, the unstable candidate points that have low contrast or are poorly localized along edge are removed. This is followed by assigning the dominant orientations to each key point in each local patch and constructing a local image descriptor for each key point based on the image gradient in the corresponding local neighborhood. The standard key point descriptor used by SIFT is 128-dimensional feature vector and about 2000 stable key points could be extracted from a typical image of 500×500 pixels (except for image size, the image content and parameters used also affect the detection results).

To encode a more compact and distinctive local descriptors, a concept of PCA-based local descriptors (termed PCA-SIFT) was proposed [5]. In this algorithm, the fourth stage in the standard SIFT algorithm was improved by using Principal Components Analysis (PCA) to normalize local gradient patches and the dimensionality of the feature vector was reduced to 20 with good matching results. It was shown in the paper that PCA-SIFT is both more distinctive and more compact leading to significant an improvement in matching accuracy and speed when compared with the standard SIFT.

However, in the PCA-SIFT algorithm, since an eigenspace to express the gradient images of local patches is created based on the all local descriptors in the provided image database, it should be recomputed once the database changes or the extraction parameters alter. In this paper, based on the standard SIFT algorithm, a salient-SIFT algorithm is proposed for a better image retrieval performance. Our approach can extract more distinctive and compact local descriptors to represent images without a need in recreating the eigenspace each time.

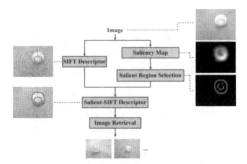

Fig. 1. The flowchart of our proposed algorithm

Fig. 1 depicts the main idea proposed in this paper. Firstly, Itti's saliency model [8] is applied to produce the corresponding saliency map of a color image. The process can successfully approximate the ROIs from the image by imitating the bottom-up visual attention procedure. Since the produced saliency map is a blur map that could not provide the exact contour about the extracted ROIs, the Canny detector is applied to extract the edges from the corresponding saliency map and the convex hull technique is adopted to form the contour based on a set of small and unconnected edge information. After this process, the image content within the formed contour is considered as a salient region. On the other hand, the standard SIFT algorithm is also utilized here to extract the local descriptors from the corresponding grayscale image. Since the extracted SIFT descriptors scatter the whole image, the salient region can help to select the SIFT descriptors which have a high salient value and to reduce the number of local descriptors. The selected SIFT descriptors are represented in an optimal dimensional space to form the salient-SIFT descriptors.

The paper is organized as follows. The salient region selection algorithm is explained in Section 2. Section 3 describes the concept of the salient-SIFT descriptors based on the standard SIFT, the selected salient region, and the locally linear reduction (LLE) algorithm. Experimental results with discussion are presented in Section 4. Finally, a conclusion is drawn in Section 5.

2 Salient Region Selection

Stable key points could be extracted from a typical image of 500×500 pixels but not all the extracted key points are necessary for image representation in image retrieval. In this paper, a concept of salient regions is proposed to select ROIs from the original color image and only the descriptors in the ROIs are considered as salient ones and used in the image retrieval. Our idea was inspired from the work [9]. However, we try to generate the salient object contour instead of using a rectangle shape, which can improve the description of a salient object and facilitate the selection of the most disctictive SIFT key points.

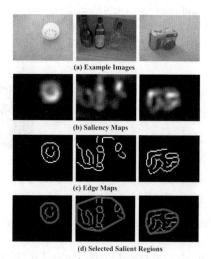

(a) Example Images

(b) Saliency Maps

(c) Edge Maps

(d) Selected Salient Regions

Fig. 2. Example images and their saliency maps, edge maps, and salient regions. (a) The original images; (b) saliency maps; (c) edge maps; (d) salient regions extracted.

Based on the bottom-up computational attention model proposed in [10], Itti et al proposed a multi-resolution and multi-feature visual attention model to mimic biological vision [8]. In this model, saliency regions (differing from surroundings in terms of intensity, color or orientation properties) in an image are detected and represented in a saliency map. Fig. 2(a) shows example images from the database used in our experiments. Fig. 2(b) shows the corresponding saliency maps of the representative images based on Itti's model. However, the produced saliency map of an image is a blur map, which lacks object edge information. The Canny detector is utilized on the produced saliency maps to extract edges and a set of short lines and curves can be obtained (see Fig. 2 (c)). To construct the contour of the object in the image, Delaunay's triangulation based convex hull technique is applied here to form the smallest convex polygon in 2-D space which contains all the detected edge points. Fig. 2 (d) shows the convex hull of edge groups where the red line represents convex hull and the blue-white dots stand for all the points in the extracted edges. The region encircled by the convex hull is treated as a salient region which will be further used to facilitate salient-SIFT key points extraction. In this paper, we consider only one dominant object in each image.

3 Salient-SIFT

In the original proposed SIFT algorithm [4], there could be about thousands of stable key points extracted from each image. As shown in Fig. 3(a), many key points (magenta arrows) have been extracted from the background but not from the object which should be more important for image retrieval.

Fig. 3. (a) SIFT key points; (b) salient-SIFT key points

In our approach, only the key points extracted from the object are used in image retrieval. We term these key points retained as salient-SIFT key points. Three steps are taken to obtain the salient-SIFT key points. Firstly, the SIFT algorithm is applied on the gray-scale image to extract the standard SIFT key points. Secondly, the salient region selection algorithm discussed in Section 2 is applied on the original color image to encircle the dominant object. Thirdly, to produce the salient-SIFT key points, we only retain the standard SIFT key points in the selected salient region. The example images with salient-SIFT key points (magenta arrows) are shown in Fig. 3(b) where the red polygon indicates the boundary of selected salient region from the original color image. More examples of the extracted salient-SIFT features are shown in Fig. 4.

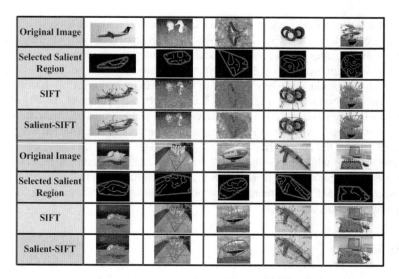

Fig. 4. Examples of salient-SIFT features

4 Experiments

We have implemented the proposed salient-SIFT algorithm using MATLAB R2009b on a platform of Intel(R) Core(TM)2 3.0GHZ Duo CPU with 4G memory. Two image datasets and three distance measurements are utilized to evaluate the performance of the salient-SIFT algorithm on image retrieval. We also compare our approach with the SIFT algorithm.

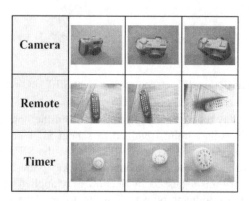

Fig. 5. Example images of the small dataset

4.1 Image Datasets

A small dataset used in [5] is used as one of the experimental dataset in this paper. There are in total 30 images from ten categories. In each category, there are three similar images photographed from different viewpoints. Some representative images with their categories are shown in Fig. 5. In addition, our proposed salient-SIFT is also compared with the SIFT algorithm in a larger dataset (100 images from 10 categories) which is selected from the Caltech-256 database [11]. The images in the same category of the large dataset have different objects in different types of background (see Fig. 6).

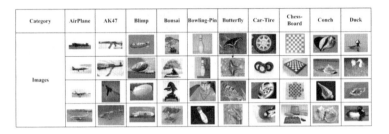

Fig. 6. Example images of the large dataset

4.2 Similarity Measures

In this paper, three matching strategies are applied to measure image similarity between the query and all candidate images in the dataset [7].

Nearest neighbor distance ratio (NNDR) (Eq. 1) proposed in [Lowe, 2004] is used to evaluate the correct matches of key points in the two images. The concept is based on comparing the distance of the closest neighbor to that of the second-closest neighbor. As shown in Eq. 1, after selecting the nearest neighbor key point D_B and second nearest neighbor key point D_c from candidate image I_B for a key point D_A in the query image I_A, a threshold T will determine whether D_A and D_B are matched. Three distance ratios (T), 0.6, 0.7, and 0.8, are adopted in the paper.

$$R = \frac{\|D_A - D_B\|}{\|D_A - D_C\|} . \tag{1}$$

We treat the number of correct matched key points as a similarity measure (S1) between the two images under consideration. The more matched key points, the more similar the two images.

Nearest neighbor rule (NNR) is also utilized to measure the image similarity in terms of local descriptors. A smaller distance indicates higher similarity. For example, Image A (I_A) has a set of key points K_A (k_i, i = 1, ..., M), and Image B (I_B) has a set of key points K_B (k_j, j = 1, ..., N), then the distance between I_A and I_B is defined as

$$S_2 = \frac{\sum_{i=1}^{M} min(d_{i,j}, j=1,2,...,N)}{M} , \tag{2}$$

where $d_{i,j}$ is the Euclidean Distance of (k_i, k_j).

Based on the idea of NNR, a similarity measure for image retrieval is proposed by using the saliency value to weigh nearest neighbor rule. The measure is termed as NNRWSV defined by

$$S_3 = \frac{\sum_{i=1}^{M} w_{i,j^*} min(d_{i,j}, j=1,2,...,N)}{\sum_{i=1}^{M} w_{i,j^*}} \tag{3}$$

where $j^* = arg \min_j(d_{i,j}, j = 1,2, ..., N)$ and $w_{i,j^*} = s_i \times s_{j^*}$. s_i is the saliency value of the key point k_i and s_{j^*} is the saliency value of the key point k_{j^*}. $\sum_{i=1}^{M} w_{i,j^*}$ is used to normalize the similarity measure.

4.3 Image Retrieval Performance

Recall rate is used to evaluate the image matching performance. It is defined in Eq. 4. Since there are in total two similar images in the small dataset and nine similar images in the large dataset for each query, we only consider the top 2 and top 9 retuned images, respectively. In other words, the number of images that should be returned for the small dataset is 2 while 9 for the large dataset.

$$Recall\ rate = \frac{The\ Number\ of\ Images\ Corretly\ Returned}{The\ Number\ of\ images\ that\ should\ be\ Returned}. \tag{4}$$

4.4 Experimental Results

The number of key points in salient-SIFT has been significantly reduced. The average number of key points of the small dataset is reduced from 1241 to 733 and the average number of key points of the large dataset is decreased from 725 to 441. Thus, the computational efficiency can be significant improved. Note that the number of extracted key points also depends on the image resolution. Since the images in the small dataset are of size 640 ×480 while the average image size is 311×401 in the large dataset, the average key point number for each image of the large dataset is only 725 while that of small dataset 1241. Table 1 shows a comparison of the SIFT and the Salient-SIFT in terms of the average number of key points (ANKP) and the total number of key points (TNKP).

Table 1. A comparison of the number of key points of the salient-SIFT and the original SIFT features in the two image datasets

	SIFT (ANKP / TNKP)	Salient-SIFT (ANKP / TNKP)
The Small Dataset	1241 / 37241	773 / 23196
The Large Dataset	725 / 72453	441 / 44097

Performance evaluation of image retrieval using the salient-SIFT and the original SIFT are conducted as follows. Firstly, for each image in the datasets, its corresponding SIFT key points and salient-SIFT key points are extracted using the corresponding algorithms. Secondly, the extracted SIFT and salient-SIFT key points are represented as 128-dimensional feature vectors. Thirdly, each image is used as a query for searching the dataset images, and similar images will be returned. The recall rates on the two datasets are shown in Fig. 7.

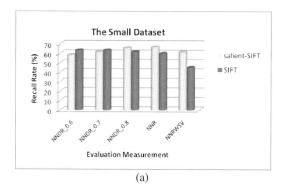

(a)

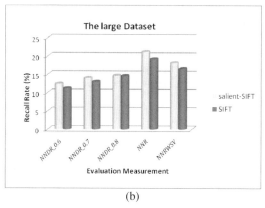

(b)

Fig. 7. Recall rates on the two datasets tested. (a) the small dataset; (b) the large dataset.

We can see that the proposed salient-SIFT clearly outperforms SIFT in these experiments when different similarity measures are adopted, in particular, the NNR and NNRWSV measures are used. On the other hand, the proposed NNRWSV measure performs well compared with NNDR in the large dataset which cannot beat NNR in both image datasets. Furthermore, the computational complexity of image retrieval can be greatly reduced because of more effective Salient-SIFT feature representation with a small number of key points utilized.

5   Discussion

A few points are discussed here. Firstly, the salient region selection plays a quite important role in the salient-SIFT algorithm. How to exactly extract hROIs is still an open problem. In this paper, an edge detection algorithm and the convex hull method are utilized to detect the contour of an object from the blurred saliency map as an attempt to obtain an approximate object boundary. Secondly, the SIFT and salient-SIFT features are quite similar when the background of an image is homogeneous. That is to say, the salient-SIFT cannot improve too much simple images with a pure background. It is noted that gradient features only are not powerful enough for an good image retrieval application. Experimental results show that the recall rate can be quite low for complex query images.

6 Conclusion

In this paper, a salient-SIFT descriptor is proposed for image retrieval, which considers the SIFT key points in the salient region only. The salient regions (human's region of interests) are obtained using the Canny edge algorithm and the convex hull method together with Itti's saliency model. In contrast with the original SIFT, the number of key points in the proposed salient-SIFT is significantly reduced, and the performance of image retrieval has been improved in terms of recall rate. In the paper, we also propose a similarity mesaure based on a Nearest neighbor Rule Weighted by Salient Value (NNRWSV). The proposed measure works well in a relative large dataset. In the future, some dimensional reduction algorithms will be incorporated into the system in order to reduce the feature dimension of a key point, and additional features such as color, shape, and size will be added to improve the image retrieval performance.

Acknowledgement

This work reported in this paper is substantially supported by the Research Grants Council of the Hong Kong Special Administrative Region, China (Project No.: PolyU 5141/07E) and the PolyU Grant (Project No.: 1-BBZ9).

References

1. Zou, W., Chi, Z., Chuen Lo, K.: Improvement of Image Classification Using Wavelet Coefficients with Structured-Based Neural Network. International Journal of Neural Systems 18(3), 195–205 (2008)
2. Chi, Z., Yan, H.: Feature Evaluation and Selection Based on An Entropy Measurement with Data Clustering. Optical Engineering 34(12), 3514–3519 (1995)
3. Lazebnic, S., Schmid, C., Ponce, J.: Spare Texture Representation Using Affine-invariant Neighborhoods. In: Proceedings of Computer Vision and Pattern Recognition, pp. 319–324 (2003)
4. Lowe, D.: Distinctive Image Features from Scale-Invariant Keypoints. International Journal of Computer Vision 2(60), 91–110 (2004)
5. Ke, Y., Sukthankar, R.: PCA-SIFT: A More Distinctive Representation for Local Image Descriptors. In: Proceedings of Computer Vision and Pattern Recognition, pp. 511–517 (2004)
6. Fu, H., Chi, Z., Feng, D.: Attention-Driven Image Interpretation with Application to Image Retrieval. Pattern Recognition 39(9), 1604–1621 (2006)
7. Mikolajczyk, K., Schmid, C.: A Performance Evaluation of Local Descriptors. IEEE Transactions on Pattern Analysis and Machine Intelligence 27(10), 1615–1630 (2005)

8. Itti, L., Koch, C., Niebur, E.: A Model of Saliency-Based Visual Attention for Rapid Scene Analysis. IEEE Transactions on Pattern Analysis and Machine Intelligence 20(11), 1254–1259 (1998)
9. Gao, K., Lin, S.X., Zhang, Y.D., Tang, S., Ren, H.M.: Attention Model Based SIFT Keypoints Filtration for Image Retrieval. In: Seventh IEEE/ACIS International Conference on Computer and Information Science, pp. 191–196 (2007)
10. Koch, C., Ullman, S.: Shifts in Selective Visual Attention: Towards The Underlying Neural Circuitry. Human Neurobiology 4(4), 319–327 (1985)
11. Griffin, G., Holub, A.D., Perona, P.: The Caltech-256. Caltech Technical Report, 1–20 (2007)

Combined Retrieval Strategies for Images with and without Distinct Objects

Hong Fu[1,2], Zheru Chi[1], and Dagan Feng[1,3]

[1] Department of Electronic and Information Engineering,
The Hong Kong Polytechnic University, Hong Kong
{enhongfu,enzheru}@inet.polyu.edu.hk
[2] Department of Computer Science, Chu Hai College of Higher Education, Hong Kong
hongfu@chuhai.edu.hk
[3] School of Information Technologies, The University of Sydney, NSW 2006, Australia
enfeng@polyu.edu.hk

Abstract. This paper presents the design of an all-season image retrieval system. The system handles the images with and without distinct object(s) using different retrieval strategies. Firstly, based on the visual contrasts and spatial information of an image, a neural network is trained to pre-classify an image as distinct-object or no-distinct-object category by using the Back Propagation Through Structure (BPTS) algorithm. In the second step, an image with distinct object(s) is processed by an attention-driven retrieval strategy emphasizing distinct objects. On the other hand, an image without distinct object(s) (e.g., a scenery images) is processed by a fusing-all retrieval strategy. An improved performance can be obtained by using this combined approach.

1 Introduction

In our previous study [1][2], we proposed an attention-driven image interpretation method to pop out visually distinct objects from an image iteratively by maximizing a global attention function. In the method, an image is interpreted as containing several perceptually distinct objects as well as the background, where each object is measured by an attention value. The attention values of distinct objects are then mapped to importance measures so as to facilitate the subsequent image retrieval. An attention-driven matching algorithm is proposed based on a retrieval strategy emphasizing distinct objects. Experiments show that the retrieval results from our attention-driven approach compare favorably with conventional methods, especially when important objects are seriously concealed by the irrelevant background.

Besides those images with distinct objects, there are images which do not contain any distinct object. Examples of these two classes of images are shown in Figure 1. The first class is the so-called "distinct-object image", as shown in Figure 1(a). These images contain distinct objects, such as "flower", "human face", "butterfly", etc. If the user submits such an image, he/she usually wants to retrieve images with the similar objects, not concerning the background. Obviously, an attention strategy is suitable for handling these distinct images. The second class is the so-called "no-distinct-object image", as shown in Figure 1(b). Different from the first category,

J. Blanc-Talon et al. (Eds.): ACIVS 2010, Part I, LNCS 6474, pp. 72–79, 2010.

there is no leading actor in an image without any distinct object. For no-distinct-object images, although a set of objects/regions and the background can be obtained using the attention-driven image processing, it is difficult to determine important objects or meaningful regions. In other words, laying emphasis on any object may lead an undesirable retrieval result. Therefore, a retrieval strategy which fuses all the factors in the query is more suitable for no-distinct-object images.

(a)

(b)

Fig. 1. (a) Twenty images with distinct objects and (b) twenty images without distinct object. (The images labelled with "*" are misclassified by the pre-classification step.).

The rest of this paper is organized as follows. Section 2 reviews the related work on Region of Interest (ROI) detection and image retrieval. Section 3 introduces the design of an all-season image retrieval system as well as the pre-classification module. Section 4 presents combined retrieval strategies that handle both types of images. Section 5 reports some experimental results with discussions. Finally, concluding remarks are drawn in Section 6.

2 Related Works

ROI (Region-Of-Interest) based image retrieval is a common approach for improving content based image retrieval. The current retrieval systems using ROI fall into two categories: user defined ROI and automatically-extracted ROI. In the user defined ROI, the user needs to select an region, normally a rectangle, a polygon or a self-defined shape on the image [3][4]. Although one can directly define one's interest regions, it is more favorable and useful to find the ROI automatically. In automatically-extracted ROIs, there are two sub-classes. The first class of approaches is based on human vision model [1] or some pre-defined rules [5][6]. For example, assuming that higher salient regions are user's interests, Hare and Lewis [7] proposed a method to detect the salient regions by computing multi-scale contrasts. The second class of approaches makes use of user's relevance feedback results to find out a common object from a group of positive images [8]. After a manual or automatic ROI detection, the ROI rather than the whole image will be used as the clue to retrieve images. The detected ROI forces the retrieval to focus on the essential part while ignoring irrelevant part, so that the accuracy and effectiveness of the retrieval can be improved. However, all the above methods are based on the same assumption: the query image contains a distinct object. This assumption is not necessarily tenable due to the existence of no-distinct-object images (Figure 1(b)), from which it is difficult to draw the outline of an object even for a human being. Although an automatic ROI detection method can figure out an interested region in many cases, it is very difficult to determine an ROI on a no-distinct-object image, since the whole image is more likely what the user looks for. Therefore, differentiating distinct-object images from no-distinct-object images is an important step not only for ROI detection but also for image retrieval.

3 Design of an All-Season Image Retrieval System

3.1 System Overview

In order to tackle both types of images, an all-season system as illustrated in Fig. 2 was designed. First, a pre-classification step is carried out to classify an image into distinct-object or no-distinct-object category. Then a desirable retrieval strategy is employed to perform the retrieval task for each type of images. For distinct-object images, an algorithm emphasizing attention getting objects is adopted. For no-distinct-object images, an algorithm that fuses all factors in the query image is used. More favorable retrieval results are expected by using this combined retrieval strategies.

3.2 Pre-classification Module

In this pre-classification module, an image is represented by an adaptive tree structure with each node carrying a set of normalized features that characterizes the object/region with visual contrasts and spatial information. Then a neural network is trained to classify an image as a "distinct-object" or "non- distinct-object" category by using the Back Propagation Through Structure (BPTS) algorithm [9][10][11]. A correct classification rate of more than 80% was obtained in the experiments. More detailed descriptions on the neural network architecture and the training algorithm can be found in our previous publication [12].

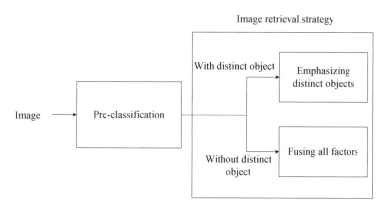

Fig. 2. Block diagram of an all-season image retrieval system

4   Combined Retrieval Strategies

In the all-season image retrieval system shown in Figure 1, an input image is firstly categorized into either distinct-object or no-distinct-object image class by a trained BTPS neural network and then a suitable strategy is adopted for image retrieval. For a distinct-object image, two attention-driven retrieval strategies (denoted as "attention" and "attention obj1", respectively) proposed in [1] are adopted so as to find images with similar objects to the query image. For a no-distinct-object image, a fusing-all retrieval strategy (denoted as "fusing-all") is used.

4.1   Attention-Driven Retrieval Strategy

Suppose that a query image $I_q = \{O_1,...,O_i,...,O_q\}$ and a candidate image $I'_c = \{O'_1,...,O'_j,...,O'_c\}$ have importance vectors $f_q = (f_1,...,f_i,...,f_q)$ and $f'_c = (f'_1,...,f'_j,...,f'_c)$, respectively. The importance factor measures the saliency of an object (the detailed definition was given in [1]. The similarity matrix among objects in two images is given by

$$S = \{s_{i,j} = sd(O_i,O'_j), i = 1,...,q; j = 1,...,c.\} \qquad (1)$$

where $sd(O_i,O'_j)$ is the Euclidean distance between the feature vectors of objects O_i and O'_j. An attention matrix, which measures the importance of each element in the similarity matrix, is defined as

$$W = \{w_{i,j} = f_i f'_j, i = 1,...,q; j = 1,...,c.\} \qquad (2)$$

Let each of the objects in the query image find its own most similar object in the candidate image, and we have a matching matrix defined by

$$M = \{m_{i,j}, i = 1,...,q; j = 1,...,c.\} \tag{3}$$

where

$$m_{i,j} = \begin{cases} 1, & \text{if } j = j^* \text{ and } j^* = \arg\min_{j}(s_{i,j}) \\ 0, & \text{otherwise.} \end{cases},$$

$$i = 1,...,q.$$

For each row of the M matrix, only one element is 1 and all the other elements are 0. The element 1 indicates that the corresponding $s_{i,j}$ achieves the minimum difference in the row. The distance between two images is defined as

$$(I_q, I'_c)_{attention} = \frac{\sum_{i=1}^{q}\sum_{j=1}^{c} m_{i,j} w_{i,j} s_{i,j}}{\sum_{i=1}^{q}\sum_{j=1}^{c} m_{i,j} w_{i,j}} \tag{4}$$

4.2 Fusing-All Retrieval Strategy

The distance between two images in a fusing-all retrieval strategy is defined as

$$(I_q, I'_c)_{fusing-all} = \frac{\sum_{i=1}^{q}\sum_{j=1}^{c} m_{i,j} s_{i,j}}{\sum_{i=1}^{q} m_{i,j}} \tag{5}$$

The only difference between the attention-driven retrieval strategy and the "fusing-all" retrieval strategy is that the former uses the attention matrix W which is generated from the importance factors f while the latter fuses the similarity matrix S using equal weights. Distinct objects are given higher weightings in the attention-driven retrieval process. On the other hand, all segments have the equal weighting in the fusing-all retrieval process.

5 Experimental Results and Discussion

The database for experiments includes 5314 images collected from the Internet, which are annotated manually. The retrieval criterion used is a semantic similarity measure. Suppose that images A and B have M and N keywords, respectively, the semantic similarity is defined as

$$s(A,B) = \frac{P}{(M+N)/2} \tag{6}$$

where P is the number of matched keywords between images A and B. Two experiments were conducted to evaluate the performance of our all-season retrieval system.

Experiment 1: We chose those images which are sure members of distinct-object or no-distinct-object class, as shown in Figure 1. We use the average semantic similarity versus the retrieval scope to evaluate the retrieval performance. A comparison of the combined method and individual methods on all the 40 images is shown in Fig(a). The combined method clearly shows a superior retrieval performance since it utilizes a suitable retrieval strategy for a query. Experimental results verify that it is beneficial to pre-classify images and to use different retrieval strategies accordingly.

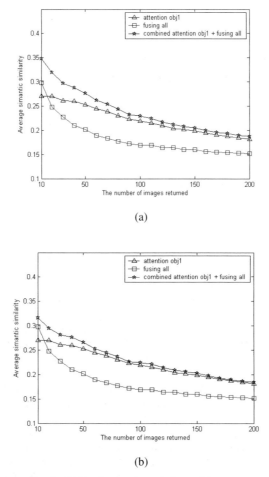

(a)

(b)

Fig. 3. Average semantic similarity versus the number of images returned for images pre-classified by human beings and the trained neural network. (a) The combined method versus individual methods based on human's classification; (b) The combined method versus individual methods based on the neural network classification.

78   H. Fu, Z. Chi, and D. Feng

Experiment 2: We also used the trained neural network to classify 40 images shown in Figure 1. Different from Experiment 1, the pre-classification is done by a neural network, not a human being. This experiment was designed to investigate the degree of degradation to the retrieval performance if the pre-classification is carried out by a neural network instead of a human being. The misclassified images are labeled as "*". Six no-distinct-object images have been mislabeled as distinct-object images. The same retrieval tests as in Experiment 1 were conducted and the results are shown in Fig(b), for the convenience of comparison. Although the improvement is reduced due to the misclassification in the pre-classification step, the effectiveness of the combined method is still noticeable. The trained neural network can produce an acceptable performance in distinguishing distinct-object images from distinct-object images for the image retrieval purpose.

6 Conclusion

In this paper, an all-season image retrieval system is proposed which handles both the images with and without distinct objects. First, based on the visual contrasts and spatial information of an image, a neural network is trained to pre-classify an image as a "distinct-object" or "no-distinct-object" image by using the Backpropagation Through Tree Structure (BPTS) algorithm. In the second step, a distinct-object image is processed by an attention-driven retrieval strategy emphasizing distinct objects. On the other hand, a "no-distinct-object" image is handled by a fusing-all retrieval strategy. Experimental results show an improved performance of our combined image retrieval strategies compared with individual retrieval strategies.

References

1. Fu, H., Chi, Z., Feng, D.: Attention-Driven Image Interpretation with Application to Image Retrieval. Pattern Recognition 39(9), 1604–1621 (2006)
2. Fu, H., Chi, Z., Feng, D.: An Efficient Algorithm for Attention-Driven Image Interpretation from Segments. Pattern Recognition 42(1), 126–140 (2009)
3. Vu, K., Hua, K.A., Tavanapong, W.: Image Retrieval Based on Regions of Interest. IEEE Transactions on Knowledge and Data Engineering 15(4), 1045–1049 (2003)
4. Tian, Q., Wu, Y., Huang, T.S.: Combine User Defined Region-Of-Interest and Spatial Layout for Image Retrieval. In: IEEE International Conference on Image Processing, vol. 3, pp. 746–749 (2000)
5. Zhang, J., Yoo, C.W., Ha, S.W.: ROI Based Natural Image Retrieval Using Color and Texture Feature. In: Proceedings - Fourth International Conference on Fuzzy Systems and Knowledge Discovery, FSKD 2007, vol. 4, art. no. 4406479, pp. 740–744 (2007)
6. Zhang, Q., Izquierdo, E.: Adaptive Salient Block-Based Image Retrieval in Multi-Feature Space. Signal Processing: Image Communication 22(6), 591–603 (2007)
7. Hare, J.S., Lewis, P.H.: Salient Regions for Query by Image Content. In: Enser, P.G.B., Kompatsiaris, Y., O'Connor, N.E., Smeaton, A., Smeulders, A.W.M. (eds.) CIVR 2004. LNCS, vol. 3115, pp. 317–325. Springer, Heidelberg (2004)

8. Guan, J., Qiu, G.: Modeling User Feedback Using a Hierarchical Graphical Model for Interactive Image Retrieval. In: Ip, H.H.-S., Au, O.C., Leung, H., Sun, M.-T., Ma, W.-Y., Hu, S.-M. (eds.) PCM 2007. LNCS (LNAI), vol. 4810, pp. 18–29. Springer, Heidelberg (2007)
9. Golloer, G., Kuchler, A.: Learning Task-Dependent Distributed Representations by Backpropagation through Structure. In: IEEE International Conferences on Neural Networks, pp. 347–352 (1996)
10. Cho, S.Y., Chi, Z.: Genetic Evolution Processing of Data Structures for Image Classification. IEEE Transactions on Knowledge and Data Engineering 17(2), 216–231 (2005)
11. Cho, S.Y., Chi, Z., Wang, Z., Siu, W.C.: An efficient learning algorithm for adaptive processing of data structure. Neural Processing letter 17(2), 175–190 (2003)
12. Fu, H., Chi, Z., Feng, D., Zou, W., Lo, K., Zhao, X.: Pre-classification module for an all-season image retrieval system. In: Proceedings of International Joint Conference on Neural Networks, Orlando, Florida, USA, paper 1688, 5 pages (August 12-17, 2007)

Spectral Matching Functions and Ellipse Mappings in Search for More Uniform Chromaticity and Color Spaces

Maryam Pahjehfouladgaran and Arto Kaarna

Lappeenranta University of Technology
Department of Information Technology
Machine Vision and Pattern Recognition Laboratory
P.O. Box 20, FI-53851 Lappeenranta, Finland
maryam.panjehfouladgaran@lut.fi,arto.kaarna@lut.fi

Abstract. In this study, modifying the CIE xyz color matching functions was considered to achieve a more uniform chromaticity space. New color matching functions resulting both from the non-negative tensor factorization and from the optimization were combined with two ellipse mapping approaches. In both approaches the original MacAdam ellipses were mapped to the new space. The first mapping approach depended on the dominant wavelengths and the second one on the spectral information for the five points on the locus of each ellipse. Equal semiaxis lengths (a constant radius) and equal areas for the mapped MacAdam ellipses were the characteristics for the uniformity of the new chromaticity space. The new color matching functions were modelled with the non-uniform rational B-splines and the optimization modified the independent parameters, namely the control points, for NURBS. The cost function was based on the size and shape of the mapped MacAdam ellipses. NURBS were also utilized as a smoothing operator when the color matching functions were directly output from the optimization task. The results indicate that modified color matching functions yield in more uniform chromaticity space. There still remains uncertainty about the ellipse mapping approaches and formulation on the cost function in the optimization tasks.

Keywords: Uniform Chromaticity Space, Color Matching Functions, MacAdam Ellipses, Non-uniform Rational B-splines, Non-negative Tensor Factorization, Smoothing.

1   Introduction

The original CIE color matching functions were developed in 1930's. Five resolutions were behind the development of these functions [1]:

1. Grassmann's Laws were assumed valid.
2. The wavelengths for R, G, and B were fixed and the luminance factors between them were fixed.

J. Blanc-Talon et al. (Eds.): ACIVS 2010, Part I, LNCS 6474, pp. 80–92, 2010.

3. All coordinates were non-negative.
4. The chromaticity coordinates for equal-energy spectrum would be equal.
5. The chromaticities should occupy the maximum area of a right triangle in the unit positive quadrant.
6. Setting the z-function to zeros at long wavelengths.

These settings were mostly practical at that time. The light sources for R, G, and B were available and the calculations were simplified for mechanical calculators. They also implied superposition of lights and their color matches [1]. There has been also some insufficient information in the original articles for implementation of the practical calculations [2]. The color matching functions are based on the perceptual experiments conducted by John Guild and W. David Wright. Thus, the color matching functions carry also features of human visual system along with the limitations from the computational point of view.

The problem of the non-uniformity can be compensated in three ways. Using CIE color matching functions, CIE Luv and CIE Lab color spaces were derived as more uniform spaces than CIE x, y chromaticity space or XYZ color space. This is achieved through compensating coefficients in defining the color space domains [3]. Then the Euclidean color difference formula is giving more correct results. In the second approach, the color difference formula is tuned for a specific color space. For CIE Lab space, the equations most often used are CIEDE94 (ΔE_{94}) and CIEDE2000 (ΔE_{00}) [4]. The third approach is based on the modification of the basis functions for deriving a new color space.

With this background our proposal is to release the original color matching functions such that also the uniformity of the chromaticity space is included in the definition of the functions. As the criteria for the uniformity we use MacAdam ellipse set even though its specific features and shortcomings are well known. Our approach is general in this sense and as such, also other ellipse sets can be used in defining and applying the criteria [5].

The structure of the report is following. In Chapter 2 the proposal is described. In Chapter 3, we give details on NTF are given. Then, in Chapter 4, the ellipse mapping methods are described. In Chapter 5, the optimal new basis functions are found. The conclusions are in Chapter 6.

2   Approaches to Uniform Color Spaces

The goal of this study is to modify CIE xyz color matching functions such that the resulting three-dimensional color space becomes more uniform than the ones obtained with original CIE xyz matching functions. Thus, it would be possible through a transform to map the MacAdam ellipse set to circular shapes with a constant radius.

A non-linear transformation of CIE xy chromaticity diagram has been developed by Farnsworth in 1958 in which the MacAdam ellipses were very close to circles with constant size [3]. The uniform chromaticity surface was divided into a number of planar sections such that each ellipse was surrounded by one section. The angle between x and y axis was determined in order the ellipse to become a circle of unit radius. The various planes' angles resulted in a new dimension. A similar result, higher dimensional color space, was also obtained in [6]. The spectral functions were defined such that their color coordinates matched to the given colors and at the same time, the color differences were uniform in the spectral space. The aspect ratios for all ellipses were equal to one which meant they became circles with a same size in all locations of the coordinate space. The drawback of the approach was the four-dimensional coordinate space. The first three coordinates came from the three-dimensional color matching functions and the uniformity was the fourth coordinate.

3   NTF Basis as Color Matching Functions

Non-negative tensor factorization (NTF) finds the optimal basis functions to describe the present data [7]. The factorization process minimizes the energy of the difference between the original data and the reconstructed data. Thus the goal is to find a solution for the problem

$$min||V_O - V_r|| \tag{1}$$

where V_O is the original data and V_r is the reconstructed data. In V_r all the components or substructures required in composition are non-negative. The reconstruction of V_r is obtained as a sum of tensor products

$$V_r = \sum_{j=1}^{k} u^j \otimes v^j \otimes w^j \tag{2}$$

where u^j are bases for the first domain, v^j are bases for the second domain and w^j are bases for the third domain for the three-dimensional dataset. k is the rank, a normal requirement is $k(r+s+t) \leq rst$, where r, s, and t are the number of samples in each domain. Every element in u^j, v^j, and w^j are non-negative. The solution for the three-dimensional data can be found iteratively as

$$u_i^j \leftarrow \frac{u_i^j \sum G_{i,s,t} v_s^j w_t^j}{\sum u_i^m \langle v^m, v^j \rangle \langle w^m, w^j \rangle} \tag{3}$$

where $\langle ., . \rangle$ refers to the inner product. The iterations for v^j and for w^j are analogous. Figure 1 shows the NTF color matching functions and Figure 2 shows the x_{NTF}, y_{NTF} chromaticity space. The spectral data applied was the spectra set from Munsell color chips.

NTF basis functions can be defined freely, they minimize the reconstruction error in the dataset. We maintained an extra requirement to keep up the NTF Y-component similar to CIE Y-component, see Figure 1 a). In a general case, one can release also this requirement. The chromaticities were calculated similarly to CIE modeling. In x_{NTF}, y_{NTF} chromaticity space the purple line becomes almost horizontal and the red area becomes larger that in CIE x, y space, see Figure 1 b).

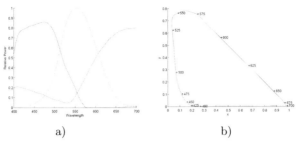

a)   b)

Fig. 1. a) NTF color matching functions from spectra set of Munsell chips. b) x_{NTF}, y_{NTF} chromaticity space derived from NTF basis functions.

When the NTF based chromaticity space is defined then one should find out how uniform the space is. The uniformity is not included in NTF basis functions, only the reconstruction quality controls the iteration.

4   Mapping Ellipses to New Chromaticity Spaces

4.1   Dominant Wavelength Projection

In this approach, the distance between the white point and points on ellipse geometry in CIE chromaticity space is calculated [8]. To define the ellipse shape, we were using totally 5 points for each ellipse: the center point and then two points at the ends of the major semiaxes and the two points at the ends of the minor semiaxes. The corresponding dominant wavelengths along the CIE xy locus related to each of these five points were defined. The line travelling through the white point and then the five ellipse points defined the dominant wavelengths. For the ellipses near the purple line, continuing the line from white point to ellipse's centre points crossed the purple line which does not correspond to any wavelengths. Therefore, for these ellipses we utilized the wavelengths defined by continuing the line in the opposite direction and using a negative ratio. In the mapping, the ratios and the dominant wavelengths of each ellipse should be the same in NTF x_{NTF}, y_{NTF} chromaticity space. As an experiment to test this mapping approach, we first calculated the ellipses' coordinates in LUV color space. Figure 2 a) shows the ellipses in LUV color space which are the same as the ellipses found from the literature [3]. Therefore, the same mapping approach found the ellipses in NTF x_{NTF}, y_{NTF} chromaticity space which is shown in Figure 2 b). The ellipses are shown 10 times larger to their original size. Ellipse 9 and part of ellipse 3 are outside of the locus. The negative ratio for these ellipses could initiate this problem.

4.2   Spectral Projection

Spectral projection utilizes the spectra of the five points for each ellipse. The corresponding spectrum for each point was found such that the color coordinates

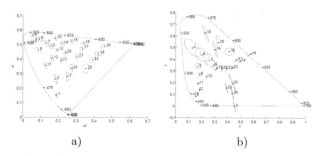

a)   b)

Fig. 2. a) MacAdam ellipses mapped into LUV chromaticity space utilizing the dominant wavelength projection. b) MacAdam ellipses mapped into NTF chromaticity space by utilizing the dominant wavelength projection. The ellipses are magnified ten times.

of the spectrum match to the given colors of ellipse points and at the same time the color differences were uniform in the spectral space [6]. The color coordinates of the MacAdam ellipse set were transformed to NURBS presentations. The NURBS were defined for the ellipse center point and for the four points at the ends of each ellipse semiaxis.

In Figure 3 a) top, left, the five NURBS for MacAdam ellipse 4 are shown. The vertical almost overlapping lines indicate the dominant wavelengths for the five ellipse points. Similar presentations are give for ellipses 1, 6, and 9. The spectral curves in Figure 3 a) are very close to each other, the five spectra can not be distinguished visually. This is natural, since the color differences for ellipses are also indistinguishable. The mapping is not unambiguous since in principle it is a mapping from a lower dimensional space to a higher dimensional space.

Figure 3 b) shows the ellipses in NTF x_{NTF}, y_{NTF} chromaticity space mapped with the spectral projection approach. The ellipses are shown two times larger

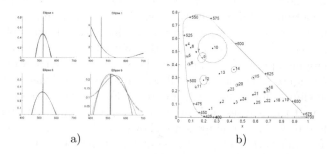

a)   b)

Fig. 3. a) The corresponding spectral presentations for MacAdam ellipses 4, 1, 6, and 9. Five points for each ellipse were mapped. The blue lines show the corresponding dominant wavelengths for the five points in each ellipse. b) MacAdam ellipses mapped into NTF x_{NTF}, y_{NTF} chromaticity space utilizing the spectral projection. The ellipses are magnified by two.

than their original size. The ellipse 10 includes a large area of the chromaticity space and some of the ellipses, like 16, 17, 18, 19 and 22, are placed in the red area between wavelengths 625-650, even though none of the MacAdam ellipses in CIE x, y chromaticity space are located in that area.

5   Optimizing Color Matching Functions

The goal of this study was to modify the color matching functions such that the resulting three-dimensional color space becomes more uniform. Thus, we start to optimize the NTF $x_{NTF}, y_{NTF}, z_{NTF}$ basis functions with the requirement that the mapped MacAdam ellipses become more like circles with a constant radius. Therefore, the uniformity of NTF x_{NTF}, y_{NTF} chromaticity space depends on the size and shape of ellipses after modification. In principle similar optimum can be achieved if CIE xyz color matching functions were used as the starting point.

Now we utilize Non-uniform rational B-splines (NURBS) to get more smooth shape for basis functions and at the end, also a smooth locus in a new x_{new}, y_{new} chromaticity space. NURBS are utilized in two separate approaches. First, the NURBS curves are representing the color matching functions directly. During the optimization, the control points of NURBS were modified. In the second approach NURBS were used to smooth the optimized x_{new}, y_{new} and z_{new} basis functions to result in a smoother chromaticity space.

5.1   Optimizing NURBS Presentations of Color Matching Functions

NURBS are widely used in defining geometric shapes, curves or surfaces, especially in computer aided design. A set of control points with associated weights are defining the geometry of NURBS curves. Finally, the internal knots can affect the geometry of curves. In this study, we use only the control points with weight one for shaping the curves. Eight control points are used for defining each of the three basis functions with their first coordinates fixed along the wavelength axes with a constant step, the wavelength range is from 400nm to 700 nm. The second coordinates are free to move along the value axes. Thus, there are eight variables in a two-dimensional space for each basis function. The NURBS curves exist in two-dimensional space with one parameter u as [9]

$$P(u) = \frac{\sum N_{i,k}(u) w_i P_i}{\sum N_{i,k}(u) w_i} \tag{4}$$

where $N_{i,k}$ are the basis functions defined as

$$N_{i,k} = \frac{u - u_i}{u_{i+k} - u_i} N_{i,k-1}(u) + \frac{u_{i+k+1} - u}{u_{i+k+1} - u_{i+1}} N_{i+1,k-1}(u) \tag{5}$$

and P_i are control points and w_i are the weights. The independent variable is u, $0 \le u \le 1$, and the knot sequence u_i is defined such that $u_i \le u_{i+1}$. A nonuniform knot sequence is now $u = \{0, 0, 0, 0, 0.25, 0.50, 0.75, 1, 1, 1, 1\}$ since the curve should visit the control points at the ends of the curve. The weights are constant for all control points, $w_i = 1.0 \; \forall \; i$. The initial values for each control point of three basis functions were defined the same as for the original color matching functions.

Various metrics can be selected by the user as a difference metric between the ellipses. In this study, we define the cost function in two parts. To achieve the uniformity in the chromaticity space, we focus on the area and radius of each ellipse. Thus the cost function c is defined as

$$c_1 = \frac{1}{n} \sum_{i=1}^{n} \left(\max \left(\frac{a_i}{b_i}, \frac{b_i}{a_i} \right) - 1 \right)^2 \quad c_2 = k * \left(\pi ab - \frac{1}{n} \sum_{i=1}^{n} \pi ab_i \right)^2$$

$$c = c_1 + c_2 \tag{6}$$

where a and b are the ellipse major axes and the minor axes respectively, n is the total number of MacAdam ellipses, $n = 25$. The constant k was experimentally set to $k = 5.0 * 10^8$.

The modified basis functions after the optimization are shown in Figure 4 a). As the mapping approach, the dominant wavelength projection was used. As it is clear, the basis function have now changed and approximately at the wavelength of 550nm they have their maximum values. Then, the new x_{new}, y_{new} chromaticity space is shown in Figure 4 b). The shape of the locus is not proper for color analysis, all ellipses are located outside the locus. Partly, the reason is in the mapping. It fixes the distances between the ellipses and the locus from the CIE x, y chromaticity space and these distances are not valid in the new space.

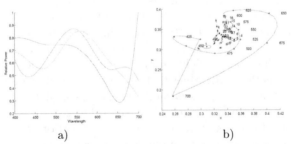

a)   b)

Fig. 4. a) Optimized color matching functions by utilizing the dominant wavelength projection in mapping ellipses. b) Optimized x_{new}, y_{new} chromaticity space and projected ellipses.

Figure 5 a) shows the ratios of two semiaxes after the optimization (circle bins) and of the MacAdam ellipses (star bins). The proportions for the last ellipses have increased which means that they have ellipse shapes. The ellipses numbered from 1 to 9 became more circular. Figure 5 b) shows the areas of the ellipses after the optimization and of the original MacAdam ellipses. Now the ellipses converge to a more constant area, the areas after the optimization are almost equal and less than the areas of original ellipses. Therefore, it seems that

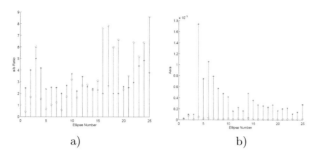

a)   b)

Fig. 5. a) Proportion of the semiaxis for optimized ellipses as circle and the original MacAdam ellipses as star. b) Areas for optimized ellipses as circles and areas of the original MacAdam ellipses as stars.

the optimization works well especially with respect to the area but not so well with respect to the shape. With a smaller value for k one can tune the weight between these two aspects.

Figure 6 a) shows the result of optimization when utilizing the spectral projection in ellipse mapping. The basis functions are smooth but heavily overlapping. This results in overlapping and mixtures for chromaticities. In Figure 6 b), showing the optimized x_{new}, y_{new} chromaticity space, there are sharp edges in the locus and the distribution of the wavelengths between 525 and 675 is not properly ordered.

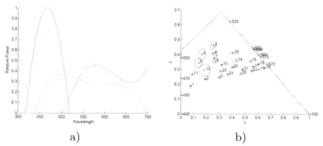

a)   b)

Fig. 6. a) Optimized color matching functions resulting from the spectral projection approach in ellipse mapping. b) Optimized x_{new}, y_{new} chromaticity space and projected ellipses.

Figure 7 shows the result of comparison between the MacAdam ellipses and the optimized ellipses with respect to shape a) and size b). The optimized ellipses are closer to a circle, their areas are larger than those for MacAdam ellipses and the areas are not equal. Especially ellipses 4, 5, 8, 12, and 14 have clearly larger areas than the average size.

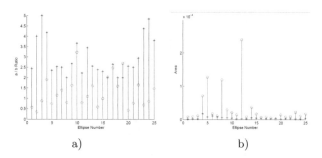

a)   b)

Fig. 7. a) Proportion of the semiaxis for optimized ellipses as circles and the original MacAdam ellipses as star. b) Areas for optimized ellipses as circles and areas for the original MacAdam ellipses as stars.

5.2   Smoothing with NURBS

In this approach, we first optimized the color matching functions and then NURBS were used to smooth the optimization results. The initial starting point for X, Y and Z was the CIE color matching functions and they were optimized such that the ellipses' two semiaxis become of equal size. Now the cost function c was calculated as a function of semiaxes sizes a and b as

$$c = \sum_{i=1}^{n}(a_i - b_i)^2 \qquad (7)$$

where n is the number of MacAdam ellipses, $n = 25$.

Figure 8 a) shows the modified color matching functions after optimization. They have many peaks and such functions do not result in a smooth locus for a x_{new}, y_{new} chromaticity space. Therefore, NURBS has been used to smooth them. The results are shown in Figure 8 b). The NURBS had 61 control points with weight one. Their horizontal coordinates were fixed and the vertical coordinates were free design parameters. The independent variable u was

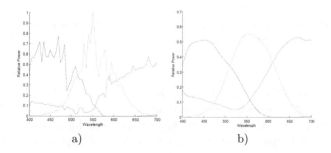

a)   b)

Fig. 8. a) The optimized color matching functions by utilizing the dominant wavelength projection. b) The optimized color matching functions after smoothing with NURBS.

$u = [0.0, \ldots, 1.0]$ with a knot sequence of 64 knots, the first 32 equal to zeros, and the last 32 equal to one. The smoothed, optimized basis functions ones are shown in Figure 8 b). Figure 11 a) shows the optimized chromaticity space.

Figure 9 a) shows the comparison between the ellipses resulting from the optimization and the original MacAdam ellipses. Some ellipses have more circle shape compared to the MacAdam ellipses but ellipses 3, and 23, 24, 25 have larger ratio for the semiaxis. At least by this modification all ellipses are located inside the locus. As Figure 9 b) shows, the area of the locus after the optimization does not change significantly related to the cost function.

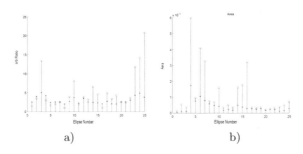

a)   b)

Fig. 9. a) Proportion of the semiaxis for optimized ellipses as circles and the original MacAdam ellipses as stars. b) Proportion of the area for optimized ellipses as circles and the original MacAdam ellipses as stars.

Figures 10 and 11 show the results of using same smoothing approach as previous one but the ellipse mapping was based on the spectral projection. The ellipses in Figure 11 b) are shown in real size. The semiaxis ratios are in Figure 12 a), all ellipses converge to circular shape because the ratios approach the value one.

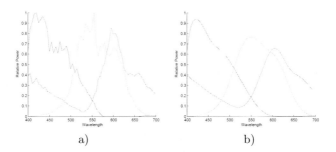

a)   b)

Fig. 10. a) The optimized color matching functions by utilizing the spectral projection. b) The optimized color matching functions after utilizing NURBS in smoothing.

The areas of the optimized ellipses are still far from unity. Especially ellipses 8, 9, and 10 are larger than others. The cost function contained now only the

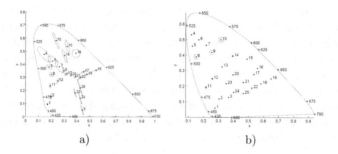

a)   b)

Fig. 11. a) The modified x_{new}, y_{new} chromaticity space and MacAdam ellipses mapped with dominant wavelength projection. b) The modified x, y chromaticity space, ellipses are projected by spectral information.

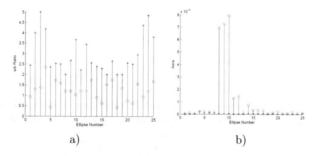

a)   b)

Fig. 12. a) Proportion of the semiaxis for optimized ellipses as circles and the original MacAdam ellipses as stars. b) Proportion of the area for optimized ellipses as circles and the original MacAdam ellipses as stars.

aspect ratio of the ellipses and this is the reason for the low quality results in unifying ellipse areas.

6   Conclusions

In this report, the goal was modifying the CIE xyz color matching functions to achieve higher uniformity in the chromaticity space. Also the NTF basis functions were utilized as originally proposed in [1]. The equations of the ellipse shape and size were selected to act as the parts of the cost function. The mapping of the MacAdam ellipses to the new chromaticity space happened with two projection approaches. In first approach, the dominant wavelengths were utilized and in the second approach, the spectral presentation was utilized. The ellipses were described with the center point and with the four endpoints of the two semiaxes.

The first step was projection of the ellipses to the NTF chromaticity space which was done with the two projection approaches. The dominant wavelength projection resulted in a better quality than the spectral projection in which some of the ellipses located in the red area.

The NURBS were utilized for optimization in the two approaches. When the NURBS were optimized directly then the mapping with spectral information produced more uniform chromaticity space. Still, the space was not uniform even though there was clear advance seen. The basis functions and finally the color space locus were not modified properly which could change the ellipses shape enough. At least all the ellipses located inside the locus. Finally, in the last optimization, the modified x_{new}, y_{new} chromaticity space seemed more uniform than from the previous results but still some of the ellipses were clearly larger than others. Unfortunately, the optimization process stuck to this local minima and uniformity could be found only partially.

At the end, we could not modify the color matching functions to get more uniform color space satisfying the preset requirements. Anyhow, some progress compared to CIE x, y, z chromaticity space was achieved. One important issue to consider is the projection of ellipses to the new chromaticity space which clearly needs more study. Also the formulation of the cost function needs more emphasis. The current modelling of the matching functions with NURBS allows enough design variables but at the same time the connection between the design variables and the cost function becomes more complex. The next steps would be to concentrate on the optimization task, both on the cost function and the constraints for design variables. Due to the shortcomings with the MacAdam ellipses, one should also use a larger set of ellipse data, which is available in *Lab* color space. The two mapping approaches should be also further studied. The first projection method used a constant distance between the ellipse, the white point, and the boundary of the locus. This constraint should be released but currently there is no proposal for that. In the second projection the one-to-many mapping allows also multiple spectra fulfilling the color constraint which was the only constraint in defining a suitable spectrum. Further constraints might mean more limited space in the mapping resulting in higher quality spectral presentations. When a more uniform chromaticity space is found then the general approach might be extended to a color space.

But one has to keep in mind that a uniform color space allows simple calculation of color differences. This general goal can be achieved also with more complex difference equation in a non-uniform color space. The current CIE xyz color matching functions are widely accepted in science and industry. A good viewpoint to fulfill the requirements set in this study would be to generate new color discrimination functions. Then the colors are still computed with CIE xyz color matching functions but the color differences are based on the color discrimination functions. This will be the guideline for our future studies.

References

1. Fairman, H.S., Brill, M.H., Hemmendinger, H.: How the CIE 1931 Color-Marthing Functions Were Derived from Wright-Guild Data. Color Research and Application 22(1), 11–23 (1997)

2. Broadbent, A.D.: Critical Review of the Development of the CIE1931 RGB Color-Matching Functions. Color Research and Application 29(4), 267–272 (2004)
3. Wyszecki, G., Stiles, W.S.: Color Science Concept and Methods, Quantitative Data and Formulae, 2nd edn. John Wiley & Sons Inc., Chichester (2000)
4. Luo, M.R., Cui, G., Rigg, B.: The development of the CIE2000 color-difference formula: CIEDE2000. Color Research and Application 26(5), 340–350 (2001)
5. Luo, M.R., Rigg, B.: Chromaticity-discrimination ellipses for surface colours. Color Research & Application 11(1), 25–42 (1985)
6. Kaarna, A.: Uniform Color Differences from NURBS Presentation of Color Coordinates. In: Proceedings of the Second International Workshop on Image Media Quality and its Applications, Chiba, Japan, March 9-10, pp. 37–46 (2007)
7. Hazan, T., Polak, S., Shashua, A.: Sparse Image Coding using a 3D Non-negative Tensor Factorization. In: 10th International Conference on Computer Vision (ICCV 2005), Beijing, China, vol. 1, pp. 50–57 (2005)
8. Kaarna, A.: NURBS Curves in Spectral Presentation of Colour Coordinates. In: Proceedings of The 10th Congress of the International Colour Association, AIC Color 05, Granada, Spain, May 8-13, pp. 1665–1668 (2005)
9. Piegl, L., Tiller, W.: The NURBS book. Monographs in Visual Communication. Springer, Berlin (1995)

Anatomy-Based Registration of Isometrically Transformed Surfaces Using Geodesic Area Functionals

Boaz Vigdor and Joseph M. Francos

Computer and Electrical Engineering Dpt., Ben-Gurion University, Israel

Abstract. A novel method for registration of isometrically transformed surfaces is introduced. The isometric transformation is locally decomposed into a sequence of low order transformations after manual analysis and partition of the template surface into its elementary parts. The proposed method employs geodesic moments, first, to find matching corresponding key points, and second, to generate matching regions for each of the object's parts. The local transformation is estimated using second order moments of the corresponding regions. The method operation is demonstrated on the TOSCA dog object.

Keywords: Isometric transformation, object registration.

1 Introduction

Registration of objects is an important task in a vast number of applications such as object recognition, gesture recognition, navigation, tracking, etc. In many of these applications, the transformations that an object undergoes can be roughly divided into geometric and radiometric. The geometric transformations occur as a result of the object movement in space, as it is mapped onto the imaging device's coordinate system. The radiometric transformations are the result of several factors. Among them are the changes in illumination sources and the reflectance properties of the object. In the current study we model and estimate the geometric deformations exclusively.

During the last several years there has been significant progress in the classification of isometrically transformed surfaces. This progress was enabled greatly due to the growing computational abilities and the development of methods to compute geodesic distances accurately and efficiently. Among the most prominent methods are the Fast Marching Method [1] and the Exact method [2], implemented by [3]. Over the last years there were many studies performing object recognition invariant to isometric transformations successfully, such as [4] [5][6].

However, there are almost no works tackling the registration of isometrically transformed surfaces, which requires the estimation of the transformation itself. Also, the studies mentioned are not suitable for surface registration, as they operate using intrinsic surface properties, while surface registration requires knowledge of how the surface is embedded in the ambient space.

J. Blanc-Talon et al. (Eds.): ACIVS 2010, Part I, LNCS 6474, pp. 93–104, 2010.
© Springer-Verlag Berlin Heidelberg 2010

In this work we introduce a scheme for the registration of isometrically transformed surfaces. First, the isometric transformation is explicitly modeled by manual decomposition of the template object into its parts and modeling each part's transformation by its anatomy. Second, we devise isometric invariant key-points matching scheme, based on geodesic area functionals. Incorporating geodesic distances measured from these key points with other cues, such as continuity of regions, is used to find matching regions for each part. Finally, each part's transformation is estimated using its matching regions. The proposed scheme decouples the global estimation of a highly complicated isometric transformation defined on all the surface into the estimation of many linear or low order polynomial transformations for each part. Section 2 presents the registration problem, the geodesic area functionals and the registration scheme, followed by experimentation and conclusions.

2   Registration of Isometrically Transformed Objects

2.1   Problem Definition

Let $\mathcal{S}, \mathcal{Q}$ be two differentiable surfaces with the parametrization $x(\xi), y(\xi) : \Omega \subset R^2 \rightarrow R^3$. Let $\phi : R^3 \rightarrow R^3$ be a differentiable transformation such that its restriction to $\mathcal{S}$ is an isometry where $y(\xi) = \phi(x(\xi))$. The registration task is to estimate the transformation ϕ given $x(\xi), y(\xi)$.

Let $y(\xi^1) = y^1 = \phi(x^1) = \phi(x(\xi^1))$ be two corresponding points on the surfaces. The isometric transformation ϕ preserves all the geodesic distances $G_\mathcal{S}\left(x(\xi), x(\xi^1)\right) = G_\mathcal{Q}\left(y(\xi), y(\xi^1)\right)$ between any two corresponding points on the surface.

In general, estimating the isometric transformation is a difficult task. First, to the best of our knowledge, there is no useful parametric form for the isometric transformations group. The isometric transformations group from the surface $\mathcal{S}$ is a subset of the transformations $\phi(x) = \sum \alpha_i \psi_i(x)$, where ψ forms a basis for the Euclidean space, such as the polynomial basis functions. The isometric transformation can be approximated by a finite order of the basis function $\phi(x) \approx \hat{\phi}(x) = \sum_{i=1}^{N} \alpha_i \psi_i(x)$. However, even in seemingly simple objects, the basis order required is high enough to proliferate the number of parameters to be estimated. For example, a fourth order polynomial basis results in $3 * 35 = 105$ parameters. Finding a low-order basis function set spanning the transformations typical for an object requires a large set of sampled surfaces, which is costly and rarely available.

Given enough correspondence points, the transformation can be approximated via points matching, but it is seldom the case. Using various local optimization methods in a high-dimensional space is prone to converge to a local minimum. In the case of object recognition converging to a local minimum might lead to acceptable results, but in the case of registration, it usually leads to meaningless solutions.

We propose to perform the registration after a scrutinized analysis of the template object's anatomy. In this approach, the user prior knowledge of the object is used to model the isometric transformation explicitly to ensure reliable and robust registration.

2.2   Anatomy-Based Registration

The majority of objects of interest can be partitioned into parts according to their position and relative movement. Each of these parts' movement in space is then modeled according to its anatomy. For example, a dog can be divided into a head, neck, tail, four articulated legs and a torso. The legs, each having three joints, are modeled each by four parts transformed by unitary transformations. The tail, neck and torso may undergo non-rigid transformations. The anatomic analysis is used to tailor the appropriate approximation to the isometric transformation. Denote the m-th partitioned object part and transformation model as $\mathcal{S}^{part,m}$ and ϕ^m, Respectively. The restriction of ϕ to $\mathcal{S}^{part,m}$ is ϕ^m

$$\phi|_{\mathcal{S}^{part,m}} = \phi^m \tag{1}$$

The transformation model for each part is modeled either by a linear unitary transformation, or a low order polynomial model. The local decomposition of ϕ into $\{\phi^m\}$, as well as the inclusion of prior knowledge on the object solves the problem of model order selection. The number of parameters to be estimated is derived directly from ϕ^m. For the dog example, the number of parameters to be estimated is $17 * 12 + 3 * 30 = 294$, where the non-rigid parts (tail, torso and neck) are estimated via a second order polynomial model.

Due to the high number of parameters, it is imperative to decouple the estimation task, such that each local transformation ϕ^m is estimated independently. We propose the following steps in order to perform the decoupling: (1) Find corresponding key-points invariant to isometric transformations using zero order geodesic area functionals, (2) Compute geodesic distances from correspondence key-points to find corresponding regions for each part on the object and (3) Use continuity constraints whenever phase 2 is not applicable.

2.3   Geodesic Area Functionals

The geodesic area functionals are the basic computational elements required for the registration process. Let ω be a bounded function and x^1 a point on the surface $\mathcal{S}$. The first and zero order geodesic moments $D_\omega^1(\mathcal{S}, x^1), D_\omega^0(\mathcal{S}, x^1)$ are defined as

$$D_\omega^1(\mathcal{S}, x^1) \triangleq \int_\Omega x(\xi)\omega \circ G_\mathcal{S}\left(x(\xi), x(\xi^1)\right)ds \in R^3$$

$$D_\omega^0(\mathcal{S}, x^1) \triangleq \int_\Omega \omega \circ G_\mathcal{S}\left(x(\xi), x(\xi^1)\right)ds \in R. \tag{2}$$

where the infinitesimal area is $ds = \left\|\frac{\partial x}{\partial \xi_1} \times \frac{\partial x}{\partial \xi_2}\right\| \partial \xi_1 \partial \xi_2$. Notice that the moment functionals $D_\omega^1(\mathcal{S}), D_\omega^0(\mathcal{S})$ are parametrization invariant, and as such, we have assumed the same parametrization ξ for both surfaces $\mathcal{S}, \mathcal{Q}$ for clarity. For further details see [7].

The geodesic distances and the infinitesimal area ds are invariant to isometric transformations. The zero order geodesic moment is an intrinsic property of the surface, i.e.

$$D_\omega^0(\mathcal{S}, x^1) = D_\omega^0(\phi(\mathcal{S}), \phi(x^1)) = D_\omega^0(\mathcal{Q}, y^1) \tag{3}$$

and will be exploited to find matching isometry invariant key points on the surfaces.

Multiplying the geodesic distances with $y(\xi)$

$$y(\xi)G_\mathcal{Q}(y(\xi), y(\xi^1)) = \phi(x(\xi))G_\mathcal{S}(x(\xi), x(\xi^1)). \tag{4}$$

and integrating over Ω yields

$$\int_\Omega y(\xi)\omega \circ G_\mathcal{Q}\left(y(\xi), y(\xi^1)\right) ds = \int_\Omega \phi(x(\xi))\omega \circ G_\mathcal{S}\left(x(\xi), x(\xi^1)\right) ds. \tag{5}$$

The first order geodesic moment is an extrinsic property of the surface that will be used to form linear equations for the estimation the isometric transformation ϕ.

2.4   Point Correspondence with Zeros Order GAD Functional

Assume two matching points $x^1, y^1 = \phi(x^1)$ and a composition function ω. The zero order functional $D_\omega^0(\mathcal{S})$ is invariant to isometric transformation (Equation 3). Let $\{d_j\}_{j=1}^{J+1}$ be a set of non-negative increasing values. Let us choose

$$\omega_j(x) = \begin{cases} 1 & d_j < x < d_{j+1} \\ 0 & otherwise \end{cases} \tag{6}$$

The compositions ω_j, that we shall refer to as indicator composition functions, partition the surface $\mathcal{S}$ into J disjoint sub-surfaces $\mathcal{S}^j$ where $D_{\omega_j}^1(\mathcal{S})$ are their first-order moments.

The Geodesic Area local Descriptor (GAD) $A_\mathcal{S}(x^1)$ of the surface $\mathcal{S}$ at the point x^1 is defined as the vector

$$A_\mathcal{S}(x^1) \triangleq \{D_{\omega_j}(\mathcal{S}, x(\xi^1))\}_{j=1}^J \in R^J. \tag{7}$$

Geometrically, the j-th GAD element is the surface area of the the sub-surface $\mathcal{S}^j$. The GAD vector can be used in order to find matching points in the following manner. Assume we have chosen a point x^1 on the template surface $\mathcal{S}$. The GAD vector $A_\mathcal{S}(x^1)$ is computed. Now we are presented with a new observation surface $\mathcal{Q}$, which is an isometric transformation of $\mathcal{S}$. We wish to find the corresponding point $y^1 = \phi(x^1)$. The GAD vector $A_\mathcal{Q}(y)$ is computed for all the points on $\mathcal{Q}$. We shall select the point $\hat{y} \in \mathcal{Q}$ as the one that minimize the norm

$$\hat{y} = \underset{y}{\operatorname{argmin}} \|A_\mathcal{Q}(y) - A_\mathcal{S}(x^1)\| \tag{8}$$

for some selected norm. The GAD signature is highly robust to noise due to the integration. Also, it is distinctive for geometrically unique regions, such as the dog's tail, legs, or nose.

2.5   Surface Partition Using Geodesic Distances

The geodesic distances from corresponding key-points x^1, y^1 are used to partition the template and observation surfaces into corresponding sub-surfaces. Let $\{d_j\}_{j=1}^{J+1}$ be a set of increasing distances. The sub-surface $\mathcal{S}^j$ is defined as

$$\mathcal{S}^j \triangleq \{x | d_j \leq G(x, x_1) < d_{j+1}\} \tag{9}$$

The decomposition of the observation $\mathcal{Q}$ into the sub-surface $\mathcal{Q}^j$ is performed identically. This decomposition is utilized for two purposes. First, in a larger scale, to find matching subsets for each of the object's parts. For example, the dog's tail can be segmented from the rest of the object using short geodesic distances measured from the tip of the tail. Matching subsets of the dog's torso can be found using set operations employed on sets obtained from geodesic distances from the tail and from the nose. In a smaller scale, a specific region $\mathcal{S}^j$ is partitioned into several sub-regions in order to obtain the required number of linear equations to estimate a non-linear transformation. The partitioning of the tail into 5 parts is illustrated in the different coloring in Figure 1.

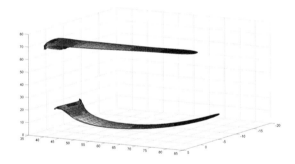

Fig. 1. Template (lower) and observation (upper) tails partitioned into 5 matching sub-regions using geodesic distances

2.6   Local Linearization of Non-rigid Isometric Transformation

The outputs of the previous stages are two matching regions for each of the object's parts. Denote the matching regions of the m-th object part as $\mathcal{S}^m \subseteq \mathcal{S}^{part,m}, \mathcal{Q}^m \subseteq \mathcal{Q}^{part,m}$. The task at hand is to estimate the local transformation ϕ^m operating on the m-th part. The non-rigid transformation $\phi^m = (\phi_1^m, \phi_2^m, \phi_3^m) : \mathcal{R}^3 \rightarrow \mathcal{R}^3$ is approximated using a linear subspace $\hat{\phi}_k^m(x) = \sum_{i=1}^{N} \alpha_{i,k} \psi_i(x), k = 1, 2, 3$ spanned by basis functions $\psi_i(x)$. Substituting the approximation in Equation 5 results in 3 linear constraints over the parameters $\alpha_{i,k}$

$$\int_{\Omega_m} y_k(\xi)\omega \circ G_{\mathcal{Q}}\left(y(\xi), y(\xi^1)\right) ds = \int_{\Omega_m} \phi(x(\xi))\omega \circ G_{\mathcal{S}}\left(x(\xi), x(\xi^1)\right) ds \approx$$
$$\approx \sum_{i=1}^{N} \alpha_{i,k} \int_{\Omega_m} \psi_i(x)\omega \circ G_{\mathcal{S}}\left(x(\xi), x(\xi^1)\right) ds, \tag{10}$$

where Ω_m is the domain of the m-th object part.

We approximate the isometric transformation as follows. First, the matching regions $\mathcal{S}^m, \mathcal{Q}^m$ are partitioned again, into smaller sub-regions $\mathcal{S}_j^m, \mathcal{Q}_j^m$ using geodesic distances. For each sub-region, $\mathcal{S}_j^m$, ϕ^m is locally approximated on $\mathcal{S}_j^m, \mathcal{Q}_j^m$ as linear unitary transformation

$$\phi^m(x) \approx U_j^m x + b_j^m, x \in \mathcal{S}_j^m. \tag{11}$$

The approximation of U_j^m is performed as follows. The principal axes of $\mathcal{S}_j^m, \mathcal{Q}_j^m$, denoted as U_x, U_y, are computed via centered second moments (computed from the eigenvectors of the vertices covariance matrix) and matched using their eigenvalues. The correct direction of the eigenvectors can be determined easily using the key-points and continuity cues. The unitary transformation U_j^m is estimated as the linear transformation from the template principal axes to the observation principal axes $U_j^m = U_y U_x^{-1}$.

Using the first order GAD functionals yields one linear equation for each sub-region

$$\int_{\Omega} y(\xi)\omega_j \circ G_{\mathcal{Q}}\left(y(\xi), y(\xi^1)\right) ds = \int_{\Omega} \phi(x(\xi))\omega_j \circ G_{\mathcal{S}}\left(x(\xi), x(\xi^1)\right) ds =$$
$$U_j^m \int_{\Omega} x\omega \circ G_{\mathcal{S}}\left(x(\xi), x(\xi^1)\right) ds + b_j^m \int_{\Omega} \omega \circ G_{\mathcal{S}}\left(x(\xi), x(\xi^1)\right) ds, \tag{12}$$

enabling the estimation of the matrices U_j^m and vectors b_j^m. Finally, the smooth parametric form $\phi^m(x)$ is estimated by the set of equations

$$\phi^m(x) \approx U_j^m x + b_j^m, x \in \mathcal{S}_j^m. \tag{13}$$

and the isometry conditions, now the linear equations

$$\left[\frac{\partial \hat{\phi}^m}{\partial x}\right]_{x_0} = U_j^m, x_0 \in \mathcal{S}_j^m. \tag{14}$$

2.7   Implementation of the GAD Functional

In reality, we do not have the differentiable surfaces $\mathcal{S}, \mathcal{Q}$, but only discrete parametrizations of the surfaces, or in a more general form, polygonal mesh structures (for details see [8]). In the following experiments we have assumed the form of triangular meshes. The structure is composed of N_v vertices, N_e edges and N_f triangular faces. Let us denote the coordinates of the i-th vertex by x_i, its corresponding vertex by i_0 and its weighted surface, defined below, by s_i.

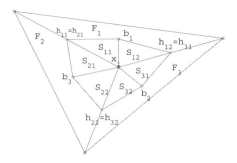

Fig. 2. The vertex i belongs to faces F_1, F_2, F_3 having barycenters b_1, b_2, b_3 and middle points $h_{11}, h_{12}, h_{21}, h_{22}, h_{31}, h_{32}$. The approximated weighted surface area s_i is the sum of $S_{11}, S_{12}, S_{21}, S_{22}, S_{31}, S_{32}$.

The weighted surface s_i is computed as follows: The vertex i with coordinates x_i belongs to J faces, each denoted as F_j. For each face F_j compute the coordinates of the face barycenter b_j, and the middle points of the two edges of face F_j intersecting at x_i. These middle points are denoted by h_{j_1}, h_{j_2}. For each face compute the area of the two triangles $x_i b_j h_{j_1}$ and $x_i b_j h_{j_2}$ and denote them by S_{j1} and S_{j2}, respectively. The weighted area s_i is the sum $\sum_{j=1}^{J}(S_{j1} + S_{j2})$ as illustrated in Figure 2. It is easy to verify that area of $\mathcal{S}$ is the sum $\sum_{i=1}^{N_v} s_i$.

The discrete geodesics $G_d(x_i, x_{i_0})$ computation was performed by the fast marching method[1][4] due to its low computational cost. The first and zero order geodesic moments functionals are approximated by

$$D_\omega^1(\mathcal{S}) = \int_\Omega x(\xi)\omega \circ G_{\mathcal{S}}\left(x(\xi), x(\xi^1)\right) ds \approx \sum_{i=1}^{N_v} x_i \omega \circ G_d(x_i, x_{i_0}) s_i$$

$$D_\omega^0(\mathcal{S}) = \int_\Omega \omega \circ G_{\mathcal{S}}\left(x(\xi), x(\xi^1)\right) ds \approx \sum_{i=1}^{N_v} \omega \circ G_d(x_i, x_{i_0}) s_i \tag{15}$$

3   Experimentation

The propose registration method is demonstrated and analyzed on the dog object from the TOSCA database [8] available at [9]. Each dog mesh has high (25290 vertices and 50528 faces) and low (3400 vertices and 6773 faces) resolution versions, and both were used during the registration. The 'dog4' mesh was omitted since the high and low resolution meshes did not correspond. We used 'dog1' as the template. All meshes were used as observations.

3.1   Pre-registration Analysis

The template mesh was first partitioned into its elementary parts (20 in total) manually. Second, robust scheme for key-points matching was devised. Third, proper geodesic distances were chosen, in order to find matching sub-regions for all the object's parts. After the manual analysis for the template object, the registration scheme was performed automatically for each observation mesh.

3.2   Step 1: Finding Initial Correspondence Points

In order to reduce the computational cost, we have embraced a crude-to-fine approach. First, we used the low resolution mesh with long geodesic distances. The matching points obtained in this manner were in the surrounding of the true matching points. Then we used the high resolution mesh with short geodesic distances in a small region to refine the search. We marked the initial correspondence points on the template mesh and calculated their GAD signatures. Figure 3 shows the GAD signature for all the vertices on the low resolution dog mesh with the using geodesic distances $[0, 20, 40]$. The vertices around the tail's edge (blue) are highly distinctive. The rear and front legs (red and green) are distinctive from the rest of the vertices (black), but can not be separated using the current geodesic distances exclusively.

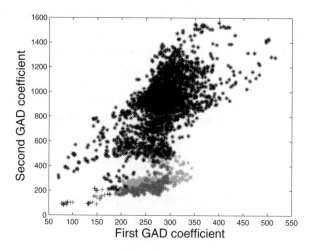

Fig. 3. GAD coefficients for the geodesic distances $[0,20,40]$ for the low resolution dog surface

Given the tail's edge estimated vertex, we can segment the object roughly using the geodesic distances measured from this vertex. The front and rear legs have different geodesic distance to the tail (80-100 and 140-160). Although their form and GAD signature are quite similar, the geodesic distance from the tail segments the rear from the front legs.

The first matching point chosen for the front legs was the one minimizing the L_2 norm for the template GAD signature of the front legs and having a geodesic distance of 120 or larger. This point can be on either one of the front legs. In order to find a point on the other front leg, we use the geodesic distances from the tail's edge and from the new front leg point. The points on the other leg have a minimal geodesic distance 80. The point minimizing the L_2 norm for the GAD signature on the other leg was the second matching point for the front leg. The rear legs and nose's edge points were found similarly to the front legs using different geodesic distances from the tail's edge. The remaining task is to find out which of the front (rear) legs belongs to the right and left legs. This is a non-trivial task, since both left and right legs are symmetrical, and thus, have the same (or very similar) GAD signatures. In the current study, we have used the true correspondence points in order to distinguish between the left and right front and rear legs.

3.3   Step 2: Legs Registration

Each leg is modeled as an object with four parts and three joints. Each part is rigid and its transformation is approximated by a unitary transformation $\phi^m(x) = U^m x + b^m, U^m \in SO(3)$. The three lower parts are segmented using geodesic distances from the appropriate corresponding point. The upper thigh can not be segmented in this manner due to large variations in the geodesic distances and area. These parts do not fit into the isometric transformation model, as will be demonstrated in the registration results.

3.4   Step 3: Tail Non-linear Registration

The tail registration was performed using a second order polynomial model. The tail sub-mesh was formed by the points whose geodesic distance from the tail's edge correspondence points was less than 45. This sub-mesh was refined, to increase the number of vertices from 444 to 3879, using spline interpolation of the face edges done by the Opposite Edge Method [10]. The tail was partitioned into 11 parts with the geodesic distances $[0:4:45]$.

3.5   Step 4: Head and Neck Registration

The head, neck and torso parts were modeled as rigid parts. The geodesic distances for the two parts taken from the nose were $[0:5:30], [35:7:50]$, respectively. Isolating a part in the torso required the intersection of the points whose geodesic distance from the tail were smaller than 105 and geodesic distances from the nose were smaller than 100. However, since the deformations in this region are not entirely isometric due to stretching and contractions, we use continuity cues. The bordering tail and neck parts are already registered. We chose several registered points bordering the neck and the torso as new correspondence points for the torso. The same was performed for points bordering the tail and the torso. Adding these points with the GAD first order functionals with the geodesic distances $[70:10:100]$ provided a robust registration of the torso.

3.6   Step 5: Legs Revisited

The remaining upper parts of the legs that were impossible to register using GAD functionals due to their variation in their geodesic distances and area can now be registered using continuity cues from the torso and the lower parts of the leg, similarly as was performed in the registration of the torso.

3.7   Registration Accuracy Analysis

In order to assess and analyze the registration process, we performed three different registration schemes. The 'Full' registration process using the estimated key-points and local isometric approximation. The 'Partial' scheme estimates the local isometric approximation given the true key-points. The 'Model' schemes estimate via Least square each part using all vertices.

The 'Model' registration is the lower bound for the registration accuracy given the transformation model, since it uses the correspondence between the template and observation at each vertex. The 'Partial' registration, compared to the 'Model' one, quantifies the error generated in the proposed estimation of the local isometries. The 'Full' registration enables us to assess the effect of key-points correspondence error to the registration error. The mean registration L_2 error between the registered templates and the observations for each part are presented in Table 1. For comparison, the dog's dimensions are roughly $150 \times 70 \times 30$.

Following the estimation of the isometric transformation ϕ using the 'Full' scheme, we synthesized each of the 8 observation meshes using the the template mesh. The observations (leftmost and second from right columns) and the registered templates (rightmost and second left columns) are shown in Figure 4.

Table 1. L_2 registration error

Name	Tail	Head	Neck	Left front	Right front	Left back	Right back	Torso	Thighs
Model	0.48	0.16	0.89	0.26	0.34	0.5	0.49	2.18	2.38
Partial	0.6	1.47	1.72	1.31	0.86	0.94	1.16	4.7	3.87
Full	0.69	2.75	1.82	2.45	2.78	1.35	1.6	4.9	3.9

The model assumptions are quite accurate for most of the parts, except for the thighs and torso. The error in the corresponding key-points and the unitary estimation produce additional error, as expected.

3.8   Computation Time

The computational bottleneck in the proposed registration scheme is the key-points matching due to the exhaustive search ,requiring the computation of the full geodesic distances matrix (3400×3400) for the low resolution mesh, and non-negligible sub-matrix of the geodesic distances matrix for the high resolution mesh. This stage took between 5 to 10 minutes, using the Fast Marching Method

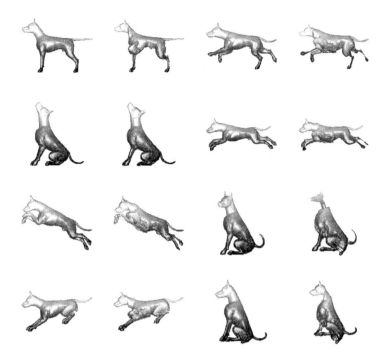

Fig. 4. Eight pairs of observations (leftmost and second from right columns) and registered templates (rightmost and second left columns)

implementation offered by the TOSCA project [9] on a T60 Lenovo laptop. The computation of moments and the estimation of the unitary transformations was negligible in comparison with the key-points correspondence.

4   Conclusions

We have introduced a scheme to register an isometrically transformed surface and provided a constructive demonstration on a complex surface. The scheme provided robust registration results due to a thorough analysis of the template surface. The proposed method can be incorporated with local optimization to enhance the registration results. Also,it is imperative to fully automate ,or reduce, the preparatory work required by the user in the template surface analysis.

References

1. Sethian, J.A.: Level set methods and fast marching methods, Cambridge (1999)
2. Mitchell, J.S.B., Mount, D.M., Papadimitriou, C.H.: The discrete geodesic problem. Found. Comput. SIAM Journal of Computing (1987)
3. Surazhsky, V., Surazhsky, T., Kirsanov, D., Gortler, S., Hoppe, H.: Fast Exact and Approximate Geodesics on Meshes. ACM Transactions on Graphics (2005)

4. Bronstein, A.M., Bronstein, M.M., Kimmel, R.: Numerical geometry of non-rigid shapes. Springer, Heidelberg (2008)
5. Elad, A., Kimmel, R.: On bending invariant signatures for surfaces. IEEE Transactions on Pattern Analysis and Machine Intelligence (2003)
6. Memoli, F., Sapiro, G.: A Theoretical and Computational Framework for Isometry Invariant Recognition of Point Cloud Data. Found. Comput. Math., 313–347 (2005)
7. do Carmo, M.P.: Differential Geometry of Curves and Surfaces. Prentice-Hall, Englewood Cliffs (1976)
8. De Berg, M., Van Kreveld, M., Overmars, M., Schwarzkopf, O.: Computational Geometry. Springer, Heidelberg (2000)
9. Tosca project, http://tosca.cs.technion.ac.il/
10. Shirman, L.A.: Construction of smooth curves and surfaces from polyhedral models. PhD dissertation, Berkeley University (1990)

Trabecular Bone Anisotropy Characterization Using 1D Local Binary Patterns

Lotfi Houam[1], Adel Hafiane[2], Rachid Jennane[1],
Abdelhani Boukrouche[3], and Eric Lespessailles[4]

[1] Institut PRISME, UPRES EA 4229, Université d'Orléans, 12 rue de Blois BP 6744,
45067 Orléans, France
[2] Institut PRISME, UPRES EA 4229, ENSI de Bourges, 88 boulvard Lahitolle,
18000 Bourges, France
[3] Laboratoire LAIG, Université 8 Mai 1945, 24000 Guelma Algérie
[4] Inserm U658, CHR Orléans, 1 rue Porte-Madeleine BP 2439, 45032 Orléans, France

Abstract. This paper presents a new method to characterize the texture of gray level bone radiographic images. The technique is inspired from the Local Binary Pattern descriptor which has been classically applied on two dimensional (2D) images. Our algorithm is a derived solution for the 1D projected fields of the 2D images. The method requires a series of preprocessing of images. A clinical study is led on two populations of osteoporotic and control patients. The results show the ability of our technique to better discriminate the two populations than the classical LBP method. Moreover, they show that the structural organization of bone is more anisotropic for the osteoporotic cases than that of the control cases in accordance with the natural evolution of bone tissue linked to osteoporosis.

Keywords: texture, classification, anisotropy, bone, osteoporosis.

1 Introduction

Osteoporosis is considered as a public health issue [1]. The numbers of hip fractures worldwide are projected to increase almost 4-fold from 1990-2050 [2,3]. Prevention of fracture normally determines which populations are at risk for fracture. At the present time, osteoporosis has been defined as a disease characterized by low bone mass and microarchitectural alterations of bone tissue, leading to enhance bone fragility and consequent increase in fracture risk [4]. One of these two elements, bone mass is well evaluated in clinical practice by bone mineral density (BMD) determination, whereas the other one, microarchitectural alterations, is not[5]. The development of a useful microarchitecture indicator providing an appropriate risk factor of osteoporotic fractures would lead to a better diagnosis of osteoporosis [6]. This indicator should be independent from BMD and thus yield complementary information versus BMD to osteoporotic bone changes. It also must be reproducible, convenient, noninvasive, and inexpensive. For a long time, trabecular bone microarchitecture has been

J. Blanc-Talon et al. (Eds.): ACIVS 2010, Part I, LNCS 6474, pp. 105–113, 2010.

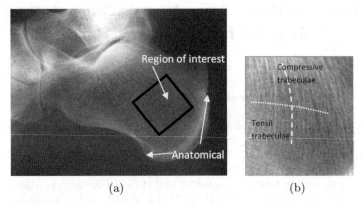

(a)   (b)

Fig. 1. Calcaneus radiograph and its region of interest (dark square) (a) Region of interest measuring 256 x 256 pixels (2.7 x 2.7 cm^2) used for processing and testing (b)

characterized by histomorphometry [7,8] but this method is invasive and cannot be applied to large populations. Our goal is to distinguish between two populations including patients with osteoporotic fractures (OP) and control cases (CT).

The calcaneus (heel bone) is well suited to measure the anisotropy (figure 1(a)). This bone is submitted to compression and tension forces produced by the walking and by the gravity. As a result, it is a very anisotropic structure as shown in figure 1(b). The evolution of the orientations of the trabeculae enables quantifying the degree of deterioration of the bone. For a normal subject both types of trabeculae are uniformly distributed. For an osteoporotic subject the number of tensile trabeculae decreases gradually until a complete disappearance for a patient with severe osteoporosis. On the other hand, compression trabeculae become thinner and their number decreases much less quickly during the disease. As a result, a radiograph of an osteoporotic subject will be more anisotropic than the normal subject.

Texture analysis applied to trabecular bone images offers the ability of exploiting the information present on conventional radiographs [9,10]. There exists a wide variety of image texture analysis techniques, the main approaches use: Gauss Markov Random Fields (GMRF) [11], Gabor filters [12], histogram of local characteristics, [13,14]. However, the performance of each approach depends on the application and the type of the texture. Nevertheless, The Local Binary Pattern (LBP) method [13] have shown nice performance for different applications including texture phenomena. It is interesting to use such kind of approach for bone texture classification, for its simplicity and high discriminative properties for textures. However, the bone texture of osteoporotic and control patients is not much distinctive and needs deep expert analysis with prior acknowledge to separate the two classes of patients.

The calcaneus texture is characterized by both the direction of the global and the local patterns figure 1(b). The LBP is useful to capture the local patterns, but it is less suitable for the global patterns. In order to handle this issue, we propose in this paper, a new approach that adapt the classical LBP for 1D projected fields of the images (1DLBP which stands for One Dimensional LBP). The technique consists in three stages procedure. First, a high pass spatial frequency filter is applied to keep the essential information of the texture. The second step is the quantization of the gray level texture from 256 to 8 gray levels. Next, the image is projected into two orthogonal directions. Finally, the local binary method is applied on the 1D obtained signal. Compared to the original LBP, the K-nearest neighbors classifier yields better classification rate of the two populations (OP and CT) with the proposed method.

The paper is organized as follows: first, we present the preprocessing performed to enhance the data. Then, we recall the previous work on the original LBP. Next, the 1DLBP is described. Finally, the results from the statistical analysis are reported and discussed.

2   Features Enhancement

Trabeculae in bone are organized so as to supply a mechanical resistance adapted to various constraints. Trabeculae in the directions undergoing weak constraints are less numerous and less thick. The non uniform changes due to osteoporosis induce variations of the degree of anisotropy. A precise analysis of the mean periodogram performed on the lines of trabecular images presents two distinct frequency regimes as shown on figure 2. These two regimes are separated by a frequency cut ω. The low frequencies $|f| < \omega$, or, equivalently, the large scales correspond to the intertrabecular area. While the high frequencies $|f| > \omega$, or, equivalently, the small scales correspond to the trabecular area.

To highlight the significance of this frequency cut, we have filtered two images from an osteoporotic patient and a control one. A circular filter in the frequency domain is used for this purpose. The high frequency part of these images is presented on figure 3. The low frequency part corresponds to the area which is not concerned by osteoporosis and belongs to the intertrabecular spacing.

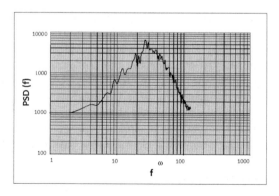

Fig. 2. A representative mean periodogram (power spectral density or PSD) of the lines of an X-ray image

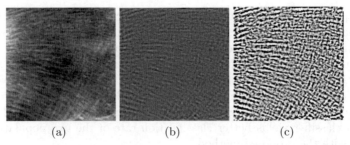

Fig. 3. Original image of the calcaneus of an osteoporotic patient(a), high pass filtered image (b), and high pass filtered and quantized image for 8 gray levels (c)

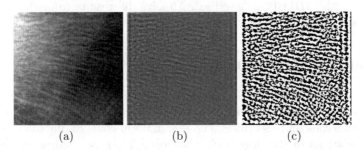

Fig. 4. Original image of the calcaneus of a control case (a), high pass filtered image (b), and high pass filtered and quantized image for 8 gray levels (c)

While the high frequency part corresponds to the area concerned by osteoporosis namely the trabeculae area.

To sum up, the architecture of bone is mainly described by the arrangement of trabeculae and thickness. The evolution of architecture in osteoporosis results in variations at scales that match our images at high frequencies. To analyze the phenomena in this band, it would be necessary to perform preprocessing of the trabecular bone images to support this range of analysis. For this purpose we choose to make a high-pass filtering of the images. This filter is sometimes called "flattening of the image". According to figure 2, the first 20 spatial frequencies of the spectrum are removed before performing the next processing.

Further, in our case, 256 values of gray levels are not useful for proper characterization of the image. To enhance the trabecular bone patterns we reduce the number of gray levels. A reduction to 8 gray levels provides better and easier exploitable images more convenient for bone texture analysis. Figures 3 and 4 show the effect of quantization and the filtering processes. We can notice also, from these figures, the high visual similarity between the control cases and osteoporotic patients which make the classification task more difficult.

3   Local Binary Pattern

The LBP and its variants [13,15] become one of the best texture descriptors, in terms of performance and their highly discriminative abilities. LBP based

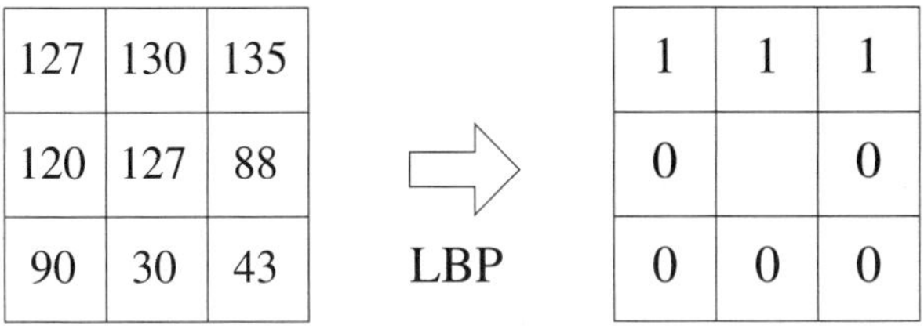

127	130	135
120	127	88
90	30	43

⇨ LBP

1	1	1
0		0
0	0	0

Fig. 5. LBP operator performed over a 3 × 3 neighborhood

methods are in general comprised of two steps: first, extracting texels or elementary structures in the local region; and, second, analyzing the spatial distribution of the same. The method is designed to enhance the local properties by using spatial operators and transform the image into a new representation. Then, it seeks to code, characterize and quantify the spatial arrangement of basic structures observed in the newly transformed image. The basic LBP technique uses a local thresholding over a 3 × 3 neighborhood associated to each pixel. The central pixel intensity is chosen as the threshold value. A value of 1 is assigned to each neighboring pixels whose intensity is of above or equal to the threshold, and 0 for others. The resulting pattern is captured as an 8-bit binary number representing one of 256 distinct known patterns. Then, the histogram is computed for the transformed image and considered as a texture-descriptor. For instance, in figure 5 the threshold value is 127; and, the central pixel does not belong to the pattern. The LBP may fail in many cases for anisotropy phenomena since it is more complex than the natural textures. This phenomenon is characterized by the global direction of the structures. The 2D local patterns are less sensitive to such characteristics, because they encode only the frequency of local structures regardless their global orientations. In the next section we present a method that uses local patterns to capture more information about global directions.

4   One Dimensional Local Binary Pattern

The 1D projection of row and columns of an image provides a mean to describe better the global and local patterns. Figure 6 presents an example of vertical and horizontal projections. Our aim is to derive from the classical LBP descriptor used to characterize 2D images a new descriptor more convenient for 1D fields. The concept of the One Dimensional Local Binary Pattern (1DLBP) consists in a binary code describing the local agitation of a segment in a 1D signal. It is calculated by thresholding the neighborhood values of the central element. All the neighbors will get the value 1 if they are greater or equal to the current element and 0 otherwise. Then, each element of the resulting vector is multiplied by a weight according to its position (see figure 7). Finally, the current element is replaced by the sum of the resulting vector. This can be summarized as follows:

$$\text{1DLBP} = \sum_{n=0}^{N-1} S(g_n - g_o)2^n \qquad S(x) = \begin{cases} 1 & \text{if} \quad x \geq 0 \\ 0 & \text{otherwise} \end{cases} \tag{1}$$

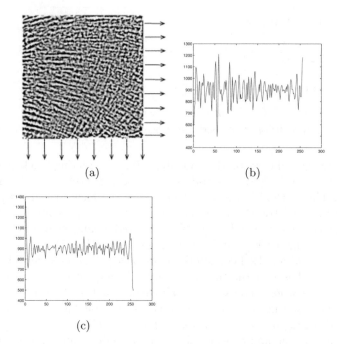

(a)   (b)

(c)

Fig. 6. A Quantized radiographic trabecular bone image (a), resulting 1D projected signals in the horizontal direction (b) and in the vertical direction (c)

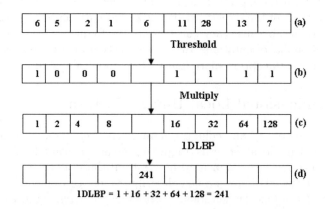

Fig. 7. Performing the 1DLBP on the central element of a vector with 8 elements (a), threshold (b), coding (c), resulting 1DLBP (d)

g_o and g_n are respectively the values of the central element and its 1D neighbors. The index n increases from the left to the right in the 1D string as shown in figure 7 (c). The 1DLBP descriptor is defined by the histogram of the 1D patterns. As result, the size of this descriptor depends on the size of the neighborhood, N. For instance, 8 neighbors yield 256 bins in the histogram.

5   Experiments and Results

Calcaneus radiographs were performed after a standardized protocol. We used X-ray clinical apparatus with a tungsten tube and an aluminum filter of 1-mm thickness. The tube voltage was fixed to 36 kV and the exposure condition was 18 mA, with an exposure time of 0.08 s. The source-calcaneus distance was settled at 1 m, and the calcaneus was placed in contact with the sensor.

An image of a region of interest (256 x 256 pixels) from a calcaneus radiography is extracted thanks to two anatomical marks (figure 1(a)). This region was scanned with 256 gray levels to obtain a trabecular bone texture image as presented in figure 1(b). Our technique was tested on a population composed of 109 women provided by the medical stuff at the hospital. Among these subjects, there were 39 patients with osteoporotic fractures (OP) (vertebral fracture) and 70 control cases (CT). Because age has an influence on bone density and on trabecular bone texture analysis, the fracture cases were age-matched with the control cases. The classical LBP and the 1DLBP methods are compared on

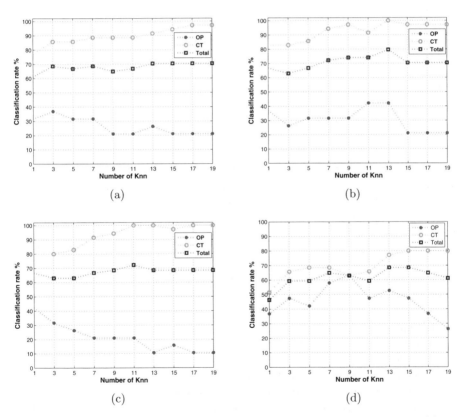

Fig. 8. Classification rates of: the original LBP performed on the raw data (a) the original LBP performed on the enhanced data (b) the 1DLBP performed on the vertical projected fields (c) with the 1DLBP performed on the horizontal projected fields (d)

these data to characterize the anisotropy of the structure, and check if it yields evaluating bone changes.

The K-nearest neighbors (K-nn) classifier is used to measure the performance of the proposed method. This classifier presents the advantage of parameter free algorithm, only the number of neighbors in feature space need to be set. We vary this parameter to test the influence of the number of nearest neighbors size over the classification correctness. The Euclidean distance is used to compare the feature vectors. The original LBP is applied to the raw and to the enhanced data. Depending on the number of K-nn, figure 8 shows that our enhancement of the texture features improves the classification rate with no spectacular effect. The 1DLBP applied to the 1D fields from the projected images shows better and complementary performances. While the texture features from 1DLBP over the vertical projection better classifies the CT samples (figure 8(c)), the texture features from the horizontal projection better classifies the OP samples (figure 8(d)). These results are in accordance with our expectations in that the non uniform changes due to osteoporosis induce variations of the degree of anisotropy. The measurement of the trabecular bone texture anisotropy could reveal this disease.

6   Discussion

The aim of this study was to investigate the efficiency differences between two texture classification techniques for discrete 2D gray level images. The first, issued from the literature, LBP [13] and the second, an original method based on LBP and the use of the information contained in the projected field of the 2D images in two directions. These two techniques have been compared in terms of classification efficiency of two different populations composed of OP (osteoporotic) and CT (control patients). In a first part, plotting the periodogram of the increments of the lines of the images (figure 2) helped us acknowledge that the texture of our data is composed of two areas. The first area related to the intertrabecular spacing and the second one related to the trabecular spacing. This finding led us to use a high pass filter to keep only the information linked to the trabecular bone microarchitecture modifications due to osteoporosis. Next, a quantization process is applied to reduce the number of gray levels required to represent the image gray levels. Finally, to enhance and condense the information contained in the resulting images, two projections in the two orthogonal directions are performed. This leads to two 1D signals for each image. An original 1DLBP method is implemented to compute the resulting signals. The statistical results from a clinical study of two populations composed of osteoporotic and control patients lead to informative remarks. As we can notice on figure 8, the proposed method shows better performance to recognize the osteoporotic patients and realize good trade off between OP and CT classification.

In a long-term work, this technique could be used by physicians to efficiently complete their osteoporosis diagnosis using 2D X ray radiographic images.

Further work is to be led on the anisotropy of the trabecular bone texture. This requires performing our method on different projections from more orientations.

Acknowledgements. This work is part of the project FRACTOS supported by the Region Centre (France) and part of the project ANR-09-BLAN-0029-01. We would like to thank gratefully the two institutions for their support.

References

1. Johnell, O.: The socioeconomic burden of fractures: today and in the 21st century. Am. J. Med. 103(2A), 20S–25S (1997) (discussion 25S–26S)
2. Cooper, C., Campion, G., Melton, L.J.: Hip fractures in the elderly: a world-wide projection. Osteoporos Int. 2(6), 285–289 (1992)
3. Gullberg, B., Johnell, O., Kanis, J.A.: World-wide projections for hip fracture. Osteoporos Int. 7(5), 407–413 (1997)
4. NIH: Consensus development conference: diagnosis, prophylaxis, and treatment of osteoporosis. Am. J. Med. 94(6), 646–650 (1993)
5. Genant, H.K., Engelke, K., Fuerst, T., Gler, C.C., Grampp, S., Harris, S.T., Jergas, M., Lang, T., Lu, Y., Majumdar, S., Mathur, A., Takada, M.: Noninvasive assessment of bone mineral and structure: state of the art. J. Bone Miner. Res. 11(6), 707–730 (1996)
6. Dempster, D.W.: The contribution of trabecular architecture to cancellous bone quality. J. Bone Miner. Res. 15(1), 20–23 (2000)
7. Compston, J.E., Mellish, R.W., Garrahan, N.J.: Age-related changes in iliac crest trabecular microanatomic bone structure in man. Bone 8(5), 289–292 (1987)
8. Parfitt, A.M., Drezner, M.K., Glorieux, F.H., Kanis, J.A., Malluche, H., Meunier, P.J., Ott, S.M., Recker, R.R.: Bone histomorphometry: standardization of nomenclature, symbols, and units. report of the asbmr histomorphometry nomenclature committee. J. Bone Miner. Res. 2(6), 595–610 (1987)
9. Geraets, W.G., Van der Stelt, P.F., Netelenbos, C.J., Elders, P.J.: A new method for automatic recognition of the radiographic trabecular pattern. J. Bone Miner. Res. 5(3), 227–233 (1990)
10. Link, T.M., Majumdar, S., Lin, J.C., Augat, P., Gould, R.G., Newitt, D., Ouyang, X., Lang, T.F., Mathur, A., Genant, H.K.: Assessment of trabecular structure using high resolution ct images and texture analysis. J. Comput. Assist. Tomogr. 22(1), 15–24 (1998)
11. Cohen, F.S., Fan, Z., Patel, M.A.: Classification of rotated and scaled textured images using gaussian markov random field models. IEEE Transactions on Pattern Analysis and Machine Intelligence 13(2), 192–202 (1991)
12. Grigorescu, S.E., Petkov, N., Kruizinga, P.: Comparison of texture features based on gabor filters. IEEE Trans. Image Process 11(10), 1160–1167 (2002)
13. Ojala, T., Pietikäinen, M., Mäenpää, T.: Multiresolution gray-scale and rotation invariant texture classification with local binary patterns. IEEE Transactions on Pattern Analysis and Machine Intelligence 24(7), 971–987 (2002)
14. Varma, M., Zisserman, A.: A statistical approach to material classification using image patch exemplars. IEEE Trans. Pattern Anal. Mach. Intell. 31(11), 2032–2047 (2009)
15. Ahonen, T., Pietikäinen, M.: Image description using joint distribution of filter bank responses. Pattern Recognition Letters 30(4), 368–376 (2009)

Watershed Based Document Image Analysis

Pasha Shadkami and Nicolas Bonnier

Oce Print Logic Technologies,
1 rue Jean Lemoine, Creteil 94015 cedex, France
{pasha.shadkami,nicolas.bonnier}@oce.com
http://www.oce.com

Abstract. Document image analysis is used to segment and classify regions of a document image into categories such as text, graphic and background. In this paper we first review existing document image analysis approaches and discuss their limits. Then we adapt the well-known watershed segmentation in order to obtain a very fast and efficient classification. Finally, we compare our algorithm with three others, by running all the algorithms on a set of document images and comparing their results with a ground-truth segmentation designed by hand.

Results show that the proposed algorithm is the fastest and obtains the best quality scores.

Keywords: Page Layout Analysis, Document Image Processing, Watershed Segmentation.

1   Introduction

Digital documents or pages are usually composed of different regions: text, images, tables, diagrams, and background. Automatic classification of the various regions within a document can be challenging, especially when the document is pixel-based (as opposed to vector-based). Various methods of Document Image Analysis (DIA) and classification have been proposed in the literature [1,2,3,4,5,6,7]. DIA can be extremely useful to retrieve information from the document database and allow efficient indexing and archiving. DIA can also help detect text regions in a preliminary stage of an Optical Character Recognition (OCR) system. In this study, the long term goal is to use the results of the DIA to apply different image and color processes to the different categories of regions. Such an adaptive approach could be embedded in the image processing workflow of a printing system in order to improve the image quality. To achieve this long term goal, we need a fast and efficient classification method.

In this paper we first discuss existing approaches and their limits. In the second section we propose a new algorithm. Finally we proceed to an experimental evaluation on a set of images, in which we compare our algorithm with three others from the literature. The results of this experiment are presented and commented.

2   Existing Methods

Several existing algorithms have been investigated, each composed of a series of sub-components. To simplify the discussion, we group the algorithms into three approaches,

J. Blanc-Talon et al. (Eds.): ACIVS 2010, Part I, LNCS 6474, pp. 114–124, 2010.

according to their main component: *pixel based*, *frequency decomposition* and *statistical* approaches.

The *pixel based* approach groups methods based on pixel information such as the intensity or the transition between pixels. Wang et al. [7] have presented a X-Y Cut segmentation, using the projections of the intensities of the pixels in the vertical and horizontal directions. Chuai-aree et al. [1] and Cai et a. [8] have used Fuzzy C-Mean (FCM) clustering to achieve the segmentation of document images and Journet et al. [3] have exploited the properties of the image texture such as the orientation and the frequency.

In the *frequency decomposition* approach, the image is first decomposed into several frequency bands. This decomposition is used to separate text from non-text regions. Li et al. [4] have proposed to use wavelet coefficients to classify the regions by discriminating between the distribution of wavelet coefficients in text and image zones. Gupta et al. [2] introduced another wavelet based method which examines the energy differences of wavelets using a multi-resolution analysis. Pati et al. [6] have used the banks of Gabor filters and a threshold stage to separate text from graphics. In the *statistical* approach, the use of tools such as Artificial Neural Networks (ANN) is proposed by K. Nakamura et al. in [5] to solve the document page segmentation problem.

Despite all the work already performed, there are still some limits in existing methods. Most require a long processing time and their resulting classifications are often not optimal. Some of the methods use *a priori information* or make assumptions that are not compatible with the kinds of document images that can be processed.

In the *pixel based* approach, we observed that methods based on pixel intensity like x-y cut are not adapted to complex layout document images having colored or textured background areas. Methods that exploit the mean or the standard deviation (e.g. FCM) or methods based on wavelet properties, have difficulty selecting a suitable pixel block size. The setting of the pixel block size has a strong impact: increasing the pixel block size decreases the execution time but also the precision of the resulting classification. Hence, it is difficult to find a fixed and optimal block size for all document images.

Furthermore, some methods in the *pixel based* and *frequency decomposition* approaches reach their limits when strong similarities exist between the pixels or the frequency content of two adjacent regions of different categories. For example, if the contrast between an image and its background is very low, the segmentation will not be perfect. One alternative is to find the bounding boxes of image regions instead of processing and classifying each block of pixels in the document independently. This is why we propose to use a contour-based approach. In this research, our goal is to find a fast and versatile algorithm to identify text, image and background regions in a pixel-based document.

3   Proposed Watershed-Based Method

We propose a new contour-based method using a watershed segmentation algorithm to discriminate the text, image and background regions of documents. This method is fast, robust and does not use blocks of pixels, therefore avoiding the difficult selection of a suitable pixel block size. Watershed is a well-known segmentation and edge detection algorithm proposed by Digabel et al. [9] as a final step of a segmentation process in 1978. It was used as an edge detection by Beucher et al. [10] in 1979. Beucher later worked on drawbacks of the watershed algorithm and proposed a hierarchical use of markers for watershed segmentation in 1994 [11]. Watershed is based on the topology of the image. The length of the gradient is interpreted as a topographical image. Topographical reliefs of the image, which have adjacent catchment basins, construct watersheds. Usually this process is not completely adequate for segmentation purposes, because of the risk of over-segmentation, especially for noisy images. Therefore, a pre-processing step is required to prevent over-segmentation.

In the following we present our categorization approach based on watershed segmentation and expose its advantages for classification of document images. The proposed method can be summarized by its four main steps:

1. pre-processing,
2. watershed segmentation,
3. classification by size-filtering,
4. text merging.

3.1   Pre-processing

The first step consists of computing gradient G of the image I_k, the 8-bit linear combination of the red I_r, green I_g and blue I_b color layers of the original 3x8-bit document image I:

$$I_k = 0.2989 \times I_r + 0.5870 \times I_g + 0.1140 \times I_b. \tag{1}$$

Several filters exist to compute gradients of the image such as *Roberts, Sobel & Prewitt*, or *Canny*. We use a 3-by-3 *Sobel* filter because it is more accurate than *Roberts* and simpler to calculate than *Canny*. Figure 2(b) shows the gradient transform G of the document image reproduced in Figure 2(a).

As mentioned in the previous section, some pre-processing is needed in watershed-based methods to avoid over-segmentation. This pre-processing step consists of modifying the gradient transform of the document image by removing irrelevant minima with mathematical morphology operations. This is achieved by geodesic dilatation and reconstruction. The original image is first inverted to its complement G_c:

$$G_c = 1 - G, \tag{2}$$

and subtracted by the height threshold $T1$:

$$G_s = G_c - T1. \tag{3}$$

In this study we set $T1 = 65$ to remove shallow minima in gradients of the image, approximately 10 % of the maximum value of the gradient. This value was set experimentally, by varying $T1$ to obtain the best correlation with ground truth segmentations. A larger $T1$ will produce over-segmentation, whereas a smaller $T1$ will cause merging of independent regions.

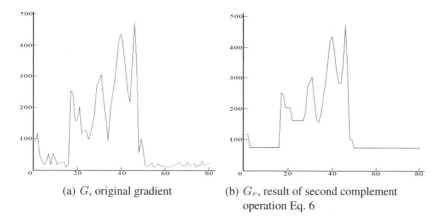

(a) G, original gradient

(b) G_r, result of second complement operation Eq. 6

Fig. 1. Removing irrelevant minima using geodesic dilatation

Then G_s is dilated:

$$\delta^G(G_s) = \delta(G_s) \wedge G, \tag{4}$$

and a reconstruction of G_s is computed in the initial complement G_c of the image:

$$E_s^G = sup\{n \geq 0\{(\delta^G)^n(G_s)\}, \tag{5}$$

Its complement is computed to obtain the processed gradient image G_r:

$$G_r = 1 - E_s^G. \tag{6}$$

When comparing Figures 1(a) and 1(b), we can see that some minima have been re-moved by the pre-processing stage in Figure 1(b). Topologically, some of the non-important basins have been merged together to conserve only the significant regions of the document image and avoid over-segmentation. The limit between significant and not significant is set by T1.

3.2   Watershed Segmentation

After this pre-processing stage, watershed algorithm can be applied. There are sev-eral watershed algorithms in the literature, among them four well-knowns are: *Vincent-Soille*, *Meyer*, *Cost-based* and *Topological* [12]. In the following we use the *Meyer* watershed [13] as it is simple and efficient. The Meyer algorithm takes the pre-processed gradient G_r as input, considers its minima as markers and expands them while preserv-ing the number of connected components (equal to the number of markers). L. Najman et. al. [12] describe the Meyer algorithm in 3 steps as in Algorithm 1:

The result of watershed segmentation is a segmented image I_w with watershed regions (labeled connected components). Each watershed region contains an initial minimum (marker). Watershed pixels p_{wb} constitute the boundaries of the watershed regions. In the final step of this watershed segmentation, all the watershed pixels are turned on, $p_wb = 1$, and all the other pixels turned off, $p_w = 0$, as shown in Figure 2(c).

Algorithm 1. Meyer Watershed

1. Mark gradient areas using the minima of G_r. Insert every neighbors x of every marked area in a hierarchical queue, with a priority level corresponding to the gradient G_r level.

2. Extract a point x from the hierarchical queue, at the highest priority level, that is, the lowest gradient level. If the neighborhood of x contains only points with the same label, then x is marked with this label, and its neighbors that are not yet marked are put into the hierarchical queue.

3. If the hierarchical queue is not empty go to the step 2.

In the result of the watershed segmentation, contours of characters are extracted separately and even a low contrast between image zones and background zones is sufficient to build a boundary between image zones. Hence, a classification based on a distinction criterion shall suffice to classify the document image.

3.3 Classification by Size-Filtering

In this third step, image and character zones are segmented from background zones by turning on all pixels situated in any closed contour of I_w, as in Figure 2(d). This is achieved by labeling all connected components of the complement of I_w, then attributing "1" to all zero pixels both situated in connected components and not on the document boundaries.

As described above, boundaries of image zones are extracted by watershed segmentation using the contrast between image and background zones. In cases where there is no contrast between image zones and background zones, as several components or segmented objects will likely be segmented in image zones, images zones will still be correctly classified. Furthermore, boundaries of characters are extracted and characters are segmented by filling their boundaries.

As characters are usually smaller and separated from each other, we propose to separate character from images based on the size of the components. We understand that this a priori assumption is limiting, since some document might have large fonts. Yet in our processing pipeline, such a large font is likely to be handled more as a image would than as small size fonts. We use the size-filtering algorithm described here:

Algorithm 2. Size-filtering

1: Label all connected components from $I_w f$.
2: Compute the surface of each connected component (number of the pixels).
3: If $SC_n \geq T2$
    label C_n as an image zone,
  Else
    label C_n as a text zone.

Where C_n denotes the n_{th} connected component and SC_n presents its surface.

In our study, we propose to set the threshold $T2$ to approximately 0.25% of the total pixel number of the image, i.e. around $T2 = 1200$ pixels. This value was set experimentally, by varying $T2$ to obtain the best correlation with ground truth segmentations.

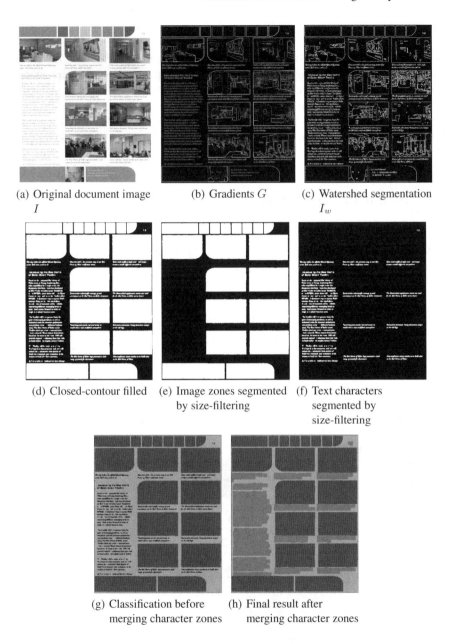

(a) Original document image
    I

(b) Gradients G

(c) Watershed segmentation
    I_w

(d) Closed-contour filled

(e) Image zones segmented
    by size-filtering

(f) Text characters
    segmented by
    size-filtering

(g) Classification before
    merging character zones

(h) Final result after
    merging character zones

Fig. 2. Different steps of proposed watershed segmentation

A larger $T2$ might cause images to be considered as text, whereas a smaller $T2$ will cause text to be considered as images. Figures 2(e) and 2(f) show successively the image zones and the text characters after labeling and size-filtering. At last, Figure 2(g) presents the final classification result.

3.4   Text Merging

Finally in this last step, text characters segmented are merged onto text regions, by scanning the document image with a 8×8 template and computing the percentage of text characters in the template for each pixel x. The pixel x is considered as a text pixel if the percentage of text pixels around the central pixel within the template is bigger than a threshold $T3$. In this study and for our experimental setup, we have set $T3 = 0.01$. Varying $T3$ will cause the text areas to vary accordingly. Figure 2(h) illustrates the result of this final step.

4   Experimental Evaluation

The goal of this experiment was to evaluate the gain of the proposed algorithm compared to a selection of existing algorithms. This experiment consisted of running all the algorithms on a set of document images and comparing their results with a ground-truth segmentation designed by hand.

(a) Simple layout   (b) Textual

(c) Complex layout

Fig. 3. Types of document images within our evaluation set

4.1 Experimental Setup

Document Image Set. The first step of the setup consisted of building an evaluation set. The selected images composed a realistic and various set, which included photographs, engineering plans, maps, posters, advertisements, book and journal pages, in different languages, with different orientations, and different amount of noise. Our set includes 40 document images: 15 *simple layout*, 21 *complex layout* and 4 *textual* document images. As shown in Figure 3(a), *simple layout* document images are composed of separate and simple blocks of text or image, on a white background. *Complex layout* document images are composed of text, image and background zones, either superposed or of complex forms, on a colored or textured background, as illustrated in Figure 3(c). Lastly, *textual* document images are composed of text and background regions, as in Figure 3(b).

Ground-Truth. The goal of this evaluation was to test the ability of the algorithms to distinguish text zones, image zones and background zones. For each of the 40 document images, we manually drew the ground-truth using the image drawing software *PhotoFiltre* and defined each pixel as being part of the image, text or background classes.

Compared Algorithms. We selected the following algorithms:

1. *DWT*, the *frequency decomposition* based on wavelet proposed by Li et al. [4]
2. *FCM*, the *pixel based* fuzzy c-mean proposed by Chuai-aree et al. [1],
3. *GAB*, the *frequency decomposition* based on Gabor filters proposed by Pati et al. [6]
4. *WAT*, our watershed-based method.

These algorithms were applied successively to each image of our evaluation set.

Quality Criteria. Results of the different algorithms were then compared with the ground-truth data. Based on the expert work of Antonacopoulos and Bridson [14], we used two quality criteria to measure the quality of the results provided by the different algorithms:

1. **Correctly classified** is, for each class and each algorithm, the relative percentage of correctly classified pixels obtained as follows:

$$CC_{class,algo} = \frac{N^{CC}_{class,algo}}{N_{class,ground}} \times 100, \tag{7}$$

where $N^{CC}_{class,algo}$ is the number of pixels correctly classified as the same class as the ground-truth, for a class and an algorithm, and $N_{class,ground}$ is the number of pixels for a class in the ground-truth data.

2. **Wrongly classified** is, for each class and each algorithm, the relative percentage of wrongly classified pixels obtained as follows:

$$WC_{class,algo} = \frac{N^{WC}_{class,algo}}{N_{class,algo}} \times 100, \tag{8}$$

where $N^{WC}_{class,algo}$ is the number of pixels classified as another class than the ground-truth for a class and an algorithm, $N_{class,algo}$ is the total number of pixels classified as one class for a class and by an algorithm.

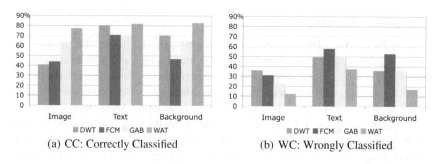

(a) CC: Correctly Classified   (b) WC: Wrongly Classified

Fig. 4. Comparison of the scores CC and WC obtained by the four algorithms

4.2 Results

Figure 4 shows that our watershed-based method obtains the best correctly classified percentage $CC_{class,algo}$ score and the less wrongly classified percentage $WC_{class,algo}$ score.

In the following, in order to simplify the comparison between methods, we propose to combine correct percentage $CC_{class,algo}$ and wrong $WC_{class,algo}$ percentage as one quality metric QM_{algo}:

$$CC_{algo} = \frac{1}{3} \sum_{class} CC_{class,algo}, \tag{9}$$

$$WC_{algo} = \frac{1}{3} \sum_{class} WC_{class,algo}, \tag{10}$$

$$QM_{algo} = CC_{algo} - \frac{1}{3} WC_{algo}, \tag{11}$$

The wrongly classified percentages $WC_{class,algo}$ were computed separately on the three classes (text, image and background). Hence, to give more importance to correctly classified percentage, we decided to weight the $WC_{class,algo}$ by a coefficient of 1/3.

Results reported in Figure 5(a) show that WAT obtains the best QM score.

Furthermore, to extend the comparison to other criteria, the average execution time of each method is also compared in Figure 5(b). According to these results, our

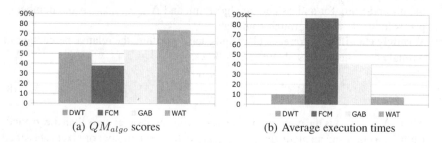

(a) QM_{algo} scores   (b) Average execution times

Fig. 5. (a) QM_{algo} scores and (b) Average execution times

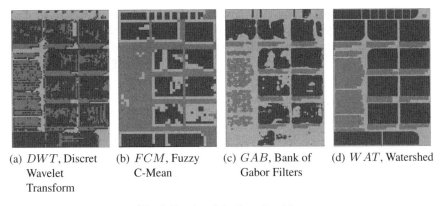

(a) *DWT*, Discret Wavelet Transform   (b) *FCM*, Fuzzy C-Mean   (c) *GAB*, Bank of Gabor Filters   (d) *WAT*, Watershed

Fig. 6. Results of the four algorithms

watershed-based method is the fastest with a processing time of 6-7 seconds on average compared to the DWT, Gabor filter and FCM methods with successively 10, 41 and 86 seconds on Matlab 2008a with a processor *Intel Pentium 4 CPU 2.80GHz*, for 40 images of 800x600 pixels.

4.3 Discussion

An example of the results of the four algorithms applied to image I (Figure 2(a)) is illustrated in Figure 6. Notice that the results of DWT and FCM Figures 6(b) and 6(a) lack precision. This is due to the image processing of blocks of pixels instead of individual pixels. For example, this lack of precision is noticeable at the round corners of image regions. The use of blocks of pixels has two drawbacks: the first is aliasing, the second is the difficulty of defining an adequate block size, adapted to all kinds of document images.

Another clear issue with the results of the DWT, FCM and GAB methods is the lack of precision in image zones, especially when the contrast between an image and its background is low. Furthermore in detection of the text regions, we observe a consequent noise in the result of DWT, Figure 6(a), some false detection in result of FCM Figure 6(b) and some non-detection in the result of GAB Figure 6(c). These problems are not observed in the result of watershed segmentation WAT, Figure 6(d) . Unfortunately, on some other document types, such as a subway map, with a significant amount of crossing lines encapsulating uniform areas, our algorithm performs poorly. Moreover, large text or text embedded in images will be considered as image areas. We will focus on these problems in the future.

5 Conclusions

In this paper, we presented a new approach of document page segmentation and classification, that is simple, fast and has a limited number of parameters. Then we carried out an experimental evaluation in which our watershed-based method obtained the overall best quality scores in the shortest execution time. In the future, we will focus on automatic setting of the thresholds, and on separating different structures overlaid in the same region, such as lines crossing text or image zones. More test experiments will also be conducted.

Acknowledgments

We would like to thank Christophe Leynadier and Isabelle Bloch for the enlightening discussions.

References

1. Chuai-aree, S., Lursinsap, C., Sophatsathit, P., Siripant, S.: Fuzzy c-mean: A statistical feature classification of text and image segmentation method. International Journal of Uncertainty, Fuzziness and Knowledge-Based Systems 9(6), 661–671 (2001)
2. Gupta, P., Vohra, N., Chaudhury, S., Joshi, S.D.: Wavelet based page segmentation. In: Proc. Indian Conf. on Computer Vision, Graphics and Image Processing, pp. 51–56 (2000)
3. Journet, N., Ramel, J.Y., Mullot, R., Eglin, V.: Document image characterization using a multiresolution analysis of the texture: application to old documents. International Journal on Document Analysis and Recognition 11(1), 9–18 (2008)
4. Li, J., Gray, R.M.: Text and picture segmentation by the distribution analysis of wavelet coefficients. In: Proceedings of International Conference on Image Processing, vol. 3, pp. 790–794 (October 1998)
5. Nakamura, K., Jiang, H., Yamamoto, S., Itoh, T.: Document image segmentation into text, continuous-tone and screened-halftone region by the neural networks. In: IAPR Workshop on Machine Vision Application (12-14), pp. 450–453 (November 1996)
6. Pati, P.B., Raju, S.S., Pati, N., Ramakrishnan, A.G.: Gabor filter for document analysis in indian bilingual documents. In: Proc. Internat. Conf. on Intelligent Sensing and Info. Process., pp. 123–126 (2004)
7. Wang, H., Li, S.Z., Ragupathi, S.: A fast and robust approach for document segmentation and classification. In: MVA 1996 IAPR Workshop on Machine Vision Applications, pp. 333–336 (November 1996)
8. Cai, W., Chen, S., Zhang, D.: Fast and robust fuzzy c-means clustering algorithms incorporating local information for image segmentation. Pattern Recognition 40, 825–838 (2007)
9. Digabel, H., Lantuéjoul, C.: Iterative algorithms. In: 2nd European Symp. Quantitative Analysis of Microstructures in Material Science, pp. 85–99 (1978)
10. Beucher, S., Lantuéjoul, C.: Use of watersheds in contour detection. In: International Workshop on Image Processing, Real-Time Edge and Motion Detection (1979)
11. Beucher, S.: Watershed, hierarchical segmentation and waterfall algorithm. In: Mathematical Morphology and its Applications to Image Processing, pp. 69–76 (1994)
12. Najman, L., Couprie, M.: Watershed algorithms and contrast preservation. In: International Conference on Discrete Geometry for Computer Imagery (11), pp. 62–71 (2003)
13. Meyer, F.: Topographic distance and watershed lines. Signal Processing 38, 113–125 (1994)
14. Antonacopoulos, A., Bridson, D.: Performance analysis framework for layout analysis methods. In: 9th International Conference on Document Analysis and Recognition, pp. 1258–1262 (September 2007)

A Fast External Force Field for Parametric Active Contour Segmentation

Jonas De Vylder, Koen Douterloigne, and Wilfried Philips

Department of Telecommunications and Information Processing,
IBBT - Image Processing and Interpretation Group,
Ghent University, St-Pietersnieuwstraat 41, B-9000 Ghent, Belgium
jonas.devylder@telin.ugent.be
http://telin.ugent.be/ipi/

Abstract. Active contours or snakes are widely used for segmentation and tracking. We propose a new active contour model, which converges reliably even when the initialization is far from the object of interest. The proposed segmentation technique uses an external energy function where the energy slowly decreases in the vicinity of an edge. Based on this energy a new external force field is defined. Both energy function and force field are calculated using an efficient dual scan line algorithm. The proposed force field is tested on computational speed, its effect on the convergence speed of the active contour and the segmentation result. The proposed method gets similar segmentation results as the *gradient vector flow* and *vector field convolution* active contours, but the force field needs significantly less time to calculate.

Keywords: Active contours, segmentation, edge and force propagation.

1 Introduction

The reliable estimation of object features in images is a time consuming task. In many application areas the analysis requires human intervention. This is e.g. the case in cell analysis, where a microscopist first has to identify cells of interest, then delineate them in order to measure the cell growth. Although interactive software tools can ease this work, the approach becomes impractical in monitoring when huge amounts of images need to be processed. In order to decrease the time used by human operators, the aid of automatic or semi-automatic image analysis algorithms is desired.

The active contour framework is widely used for automatic and supervised segmentation. This method translates and deforms an initial contour in order to minimize an energy function, which results in a contour delineating the object of interest. Depending on the application, different energy functions have been proposed. The adjustability of the energy function has resulted in numerous energy functions which can incorporate prior knowledge of motion [1,2,3], region statistics [4,5], expected shapes [1,6,7], etc.

Two main classes of active contours are found in literature: the first class represents the contour explicitly as a parametric curve; the second class represents the contour implicitly using level sets. In this paper we will define a new external force field which can be calculated in a fast and efficient way, which results in good segmentation and

J. Blanc-Talon et al. (Eds.): ACIVS 2010, Part I, LNCS 6474, pp. 125–134, 2010.

which has straightforward parameters. The proposed force is defined to be used with parametric active contours. In [8,9] the use of similar external forces and energies are used for geometric active contours, which suggest that the proposed technique can be adjusted to work with geometric active contours as well. However, in the scope of this paper we will limit ourselves to parametric active contours.

This paper is arranged as follows. The next section provides a detailed description of active contours. In section 3 our proposed algorithm is presented. Section 4 shows the results of our technique and is compared to the results from other active contour formulations. Section 5 recapitulates and concludes.

2   Active Contours

2.1   Parametric Active Contours

The original parametric active contour model proposed by Kass et al. [4], defines the active contour as a parametric curve, $\mathbf{r}(s) = (x(s), y(s))$, which moves in the spatial domain until the energy functional in Eq. (1) reaches its minimum value.

$$E_{snake}[\mathbf{r}(.)] = E_{int}[\mathbf{r}(.)] + E_{ext}[\mathbf{r}(.)] \tag{1}$$

$E_{int}[\mathbf{r}(.)]$ and $E_{ext}[\mathbf{r}(.)]$ represent respectively the internal and external energy of the contour. The internal energy enforces smoothness along the contour. A common internal energy function is defined as follows:

$$E_{int}[\mathbf{r}(.)] = \frac{1}{2} \int \left(\alpha \left| \frac{d\mathbf{r}(s)}{ds} \right|^2 + \beta \left| \frac{d^2\mathbf{r}(s)}{ds^2} \right|^2 \right) ds. \tag{2}$$

where α and β are weighting parameters. The first term, also known as the tension energy, prevents the contour from sticking to isolated points by penalizing *stretching* of the contour. The second term, known as the bending energy, measures the smoothness, e.g. by penalizing sharp corners. More complex energy terms, for example based on Fourier descriptors, have also been reported in literature [6,10,7].

The external energy is derived from the image, such that the contour will be attracted to features of interest. Given a gray level image $I(x, y)$, a common external energy is defined as:

$$E_{ext}[\mathbf{r}(.)] = - \int F(\mathbf{r}(s))ds. \tag{3}$$

where $F(x, y)$ is a feature map. Common features of interest are edges, e.g.

$$F(x, y) = |\nabla I(x, y)|^2 \tag{4a}$$

or

$$F(x, y) = \left| \nabla \left(G_\sigma(x, y) * I(x, y) \right) \right|^2 \tag{4b}$$

where ∇ is the gradient operator, $G_\sigma(x, y)$ a 2D Gaussian kernel with standard deviation σ and where $*$ is the convolution operator.

Eq. (1) can be minimized by treating $\mathbf{r}(s)$ as a function of time, i.e. $\mathbf{r}(s,t)$. This requires finding $\mathbf{x}(s,t)$ and $\mathbf{y}(s,t)$ such that

$$\frac{\partial \mathbf{x}(s,t)}{\partial t} = \alpha \frac{\partial^2 \mathbf{x}(s,t)}{\partial s^2} - \beta \frac{\partial^4 \mathbf{x}(s,t)}{\partial s^4} + \frac{\partial F(\mathbf{r}(s,t))}{\partial x} \tag{5a}$$

and

$$\frac{\partial \mathbf{y}(s,t)}{\partial t} = \alpha \frac{\partial^2 \mathbf{y}(s,t)}{\partial s^2} - \beta \frac{\partial^4 \mathbf{y}(s,t)}{\partial s^4} + \frac{\partial F(\mathbf{r}(s,t))}{\partial y} \tag{5b}$$

vanish for all s. This can be achieved by iteratively solving a discretization of s using a finite difference approach [11,12].

2.2   Force Based Active Contours

The external energy term defined in the previous section usually requires a good initialization, close to the object boundary, in order to achieve correct convergence. This limitation is caused by the nature of the external energy term, which is typically non-flat only in the proximity of the object's boundary. To overcome this problem, Xu and Prince [13] proposed the use of an external force field, $\mathbf{v}(x,y) = (P(x,y), Q(x,y))$, where $P(\mathbf{r}(s,t))$ and $Q(\mathbf{r}(s,t))$ replace the partial derivatives of $F(\mathbf{r}(s,t))$ in Eq. (5),i.e.

$$\frac{\partial \mathbf{r}(s,t)}{\partial t} = \alpha \frac{\partial^2 \mathbf{r}(s,t)}{\partial s^2} - \beta \frac{\partial^4 \mathbf{r}(s,t)}{\partial s^4} + \mathbf{v}(\mathbf{r}(s,t)) \tag{6}$$

The vector field $\mathbf{v}(.,.)$ is calculated by minimizing the following energy functional:

$$E_{GVF}[\mathbf{v}(.,.)] =$$
$$\iint \mu \left(\frac{\partial P(x,y)}{\partial x}^2 + \frac{\partial P(x,y)}{\partial y}^2 + \frac{\partial Q(x,y)}{\partial x}^2 + \frac{\partial Q(x,y)}{\partial y}^2 \right)$$
$$+ \mid \nabla F(x,y) \mid^2 \mid \mathbf{v}(x,y) - \nabla F(x,y) \mid^2 dxdy \tag{7}$$

where μ is a nonnegative parameter expressing the degree of smoothness imposed on the field $\mathbf{v}$ and where F is a feature map such as in Eq. (4). The first term of Eq. (7) keeps the field $\mathbf{v}$ smooth, whereas the second term forces the field $\mathbf{v}$ to resemble the original edge force in the neighbourhood of edges. This external force is called *Gradient Vector Flow* (GVF) field. The force field with minimal energy can be found using gradient descent [13].

A different approach is proposed by Li et al. [14] and by Wang et al. [15], who define an external force by using *Vector Field Convolution* (VFC), i.e.

$$\mathbf{v}(x,y) = \left(K * \frac{\partial F(x,y)}{\partial x}, K * \frac{\partial F(x,y)}{\partial y} \right) \tag{8}$$

where K can be any kernel function.

3 Force Propagation

The GVF force field extends the capturing range of the active contours by iteratively updating the external force field. Although this force field has been proven useful, it comes at a great cost: iteratively updating of the force field in order to minimize an energy function is both memory and time consuming. The VFC force field does not suffer from this problem, but it is difficult to find an optimal kernel function for a specific application. In the following section we propose a new external energy based on edge and force propagation (*ep* and *fp* respectively), which does not need the iterative optimization of a force field, but which has straightforward parameters.

We start from a force field $\mathbf{v}_{fp}(x, y)$ which is zero everywhere and a feature map $F_{ep}(x, y)$, such as in Eq. (4) where the feature map expresses how much *evidence* there is that there is an edge at pixel (x, y). The goal is to create a new feature map, where there is high edge evidence at the edge itself and where the edge evidence gradually decreases if you get further away from the edge. The main idea is to propagate strong edge evidence at a certain pixel to its neighbouring pixels with lower edge evidence. This step only propagates edge evidence to the direct neighbours, which would require an iterative process as well. This can however be avoided by the following dual scan line algorithm:

1. Scan the edge map row by row from top to bottom
2. In each row, the pixels are scanned from left to right
3. Define the already processed neighbourhood of a pixel (x,y), i.e.

$$\mathbf{n}(x, y, i) = \begin{cases} (x, y - 1) & \text{if } i = 1 \\ (x - 1, y - 1) & \text{if } i = 2 \\ (x - 1, y) & \text{if } i = 3 \\ (x - 1, y + 1) & \text{if } i = 4 \end{cases} \tag{9}$$

In Fig. 1(a) the already processed neighbour pixels for P are shown in pink.
4. Update the pixel in the feature map by:

$$F_{ep}(x, y) = \max \begin{cases} \gamma \max_i F_{ep}\big(\mathbf{n}(x, y, i)\big) & \text{(a)} \\ F_{ep}(x, y) & \text{(b)} \end{cases} \tag{10}$$

where $\gamma \in [0, 1]$ is a weighting coefficient, which determines the speed at which edge evidence decreases. This propagates edge evidence of a pixel beyond its direct neighbours in the scanning direction. Note that all pixels of $F_{ep}(\mathbf{n}(x, y, .))$ are already processed in previous steps, due to the scanning order.
5. The feature map resulting from this scanning algorithm defines a new external energy. Instead of using the gradient of this external energy we propose to propagate the force corresponding to the external energy, i.e.

$$\mathbf{v}_{fp}(x, y) =$$
$$\max \begin{cases} \mathbf{v}_{fp}(\mathbf{n}(x, y, i)) + \mathbf{n}(x, y, i) - (x, y) & \text{if (a) was used in eq. (10)} \\ \mathbf{v}_{fp}(x, y) & \text{if (b) was used in eq. (10)} \end{cases} \tag{11}$$

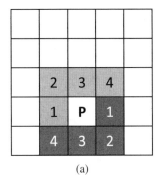
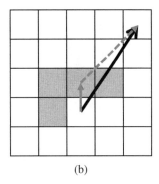

(a)   (b)

Fig. 1. Example of edge and force propagation. In (a) the feature map is show, together with the two processed neighbourhoods. The red one is used in the first run, the green neighbourhood is used for the second run. (b) The force at the pixel is the sum of the force of its neighbouring pixel and the vector to that pixel.

where $i = \arg \max F_{ep}(\mathbf{n}(x, y, i))$. In Fig. 1 an example is shown. Assume that the feature map is maximal in its top neighbour, i.e. $i = 3$. The force vector is equal to the sum the force vector in $\mathbf{n}(x, y, 3)$, shown as a dashed blue arrow, and the vector pointing from the current pixel to $\mathbf{n}(x, y, 3)$, shown as the small blue arrow. This results in a vector pointing from the current pixel to the same point as to which the vector in $\mathbf{n}(x, y, 3)$ points, shown as a black arrow.

This algorithm propagates edge evidence from top to bottom and from left to right of the image. Repeat the algorithm in order to propagate edge evidence in the remaining directions, but in opposite scanning direction, i.e. from bottom to top and from right to left. Then the already processed neighbourhood of a pixel (x,y) is:

$$
\mathbf{n}'(x, y, i) = \begin{cases}
(x, y + 1) & \text{if } i = 1 \\
(x + 1, y + 1) & \text{if } i = 2 \\
(x + 1, y) & \text{if } i = 3 \\
(x + 1, y - 1) & \text{if } i = 4
\end{cases}
\tag{12}
$$

Fig. 1(a) this new neighbourhood is shown in dark green. After the second run, the vector field should be adjusted in order to have a proper norm. There are two common approaches:

– Set the norm of a force vector equal to its value in the feature map, i.e.

$$
\mathbf{v}_{fp}(x, y) = F_{ep}(x, y) \frac{\mathbf{v}_{fp}(x, y)}{\|\mathbf{v}_{fp}(x, y)\|}
\tag{13}
$$

This results in a vector field where there is a strong force in the vicinity of edges and a weak force far away of edges, i.e. far away of edges the active contour is mainly regulated by the internal energy, whereas in the vicinity of edges it is mainly deformed by the external force.

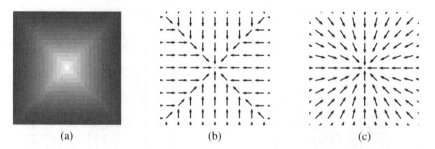

(a)   (b)   (c)

Fig. 2. (a) An example of the feature map of an isolated point in the centre of the image. (b) The force field defined by the gradient of the feature map. (c) The force field resulting from force propagation.

– Normalize the force, i.e.

$$\mathbf{v}_{fp}(x, y) = \frac{\mathbf{v}_{fp}(x, y)}{\|\mathbf{v}_{fp}(x, y)\|} \tag{14}$$

This results in an active contour which evolves at nearly constant speed, such as proposed in [12].

Force propagation active contours can be optimized by replacing the external force in Eq.(6) by $\mathbf{v}_{fp}(\mathbf{r}(s, t))$. In Fig. 3 an example is shown. In (a) the feature map of an image with an isolated point in the centre of the image is shown. In (b) the gradient of the feature map is shown, whereas in (c) the proposed force field can be seen. Note that a free particle placed in both force fields will move to the same point, i.e. the maximum of the feature map. The particle moving according to the proposed force field will move the shortest distance possible to arrive at the steady state, which is clearly not the case for the particle moving according to the gradient of the feature map.

4   Results

4.1   Error Metric

For the validation of the segmentation, the Dice coefficient is used. If S is the resulting segment from the active contour, i.e. the region enclosed by $\mathbf{r}(s)$, and GT the ground truth segment, then the Dice coefficient between S and GT is defined as:

$$d(S, GT) = \frac{2 \operatorname{Area}(S \wedge GT)}{\operatorname{Area}(S) + \operatorname{Area}(GT)} \tag{15}$$

where $S \wedge GT$ consist of all pixels which both belong to the detected segment as well as to the ground truth segment. If S and GT are equal, the Dice coefficient is equal to one. The Dice coefficient will approach zero if the regions hardly overlap.

4.2   Convergence

To test the convergence of the active contours using the proposed external energy, a database with pictures of leaves was used. This tests how the proposed technique converges to realistic shapes with concavitys. The database contains 355 pictures of isolated leaves from five different plant species. These are colour pictures of 512×512 pixels. The leaves were extracted by thresholding the RGB values. An example of such a leaf is shown in the left part of Fig. 3. The active contour was initialised by a square delineating the full image. Then the Dice coefficient between the active contour and the leaf was measured every 10 iterations. The average results can be seen in Fig. 4.a. The proposed active contours (FP) are compared with the GVF and VFC active contours [13,14]. The VFC force field was calculated using a kernel based on a quadratic function as defined in [14], the gvf force fields was calculated with $\mu = 0.2$. As can be seen, the proposed method converges approximately to the same result as the GVF active contours, but converges significantly faster: it reaches a Dice coefficient of 0.88 in 40 iterations, compared to GVF which needs approximately 48 iterations to achieve the same Dice coefficient. The VFC active contours converge slower than the force propagation active contours and never reach the same accurate result as GVF or the proposed method.

Fig. 3. Examples of images used to test the active contours: left a binary image of the leaf database, right an example of an isolated cell in a fluorescent micrograph

In a second experiment, the proposed technique is tested on real data. The goal is to segment isolated cells in fluorescent micrographs. On the right of Fig. 3 an example of such a micrograph is shown. Twenty cells were manually segmented and compared with the resulting segments from both the proposed and the GVF active contours. For both methods tests were done with several parameter combinations, i.e. μ in Eq. (7) and γ in Eq. (10). For GVF, $\mu = 0.22$ resulted in the best average dice coefficient, $\gamma = 0.97$ gave the best result for the proposed method. The resulting Dice coefficients for GVF with $\mu = 0.22$, and the result for our method with $\gamma = 0.97$ are compared in the bottom part of Fig. 4. Both methods perform well with almost all Dice coefficients between 0.8 and 1, except for cell 18, where the GVF active contour converged to a false optimum due to clutter in the micrograph.

4.3   Computational Cost

The proposed scanning algorithm recalculates the value of each pixel twice, resulting in a $O(N^2)$ algorithm for a square image with dimension $N \times N$. The VFC force computation has a complexity of $O(N^2 \log N^2)$ which is determined by the complexity of the 2D FFT and IFFT algorithms used. Since the GVF field needs $O(N^2)$ operations

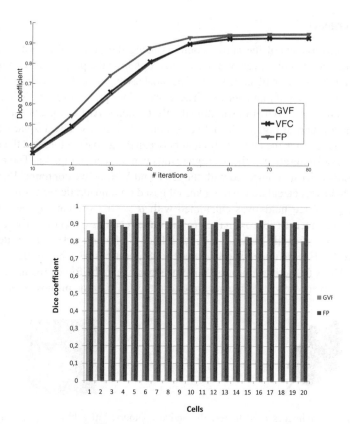

Fig. 4. Top, convergence of different active contours. Bottom, the resulting Dice coefficients of GVF and force propagation active contours.

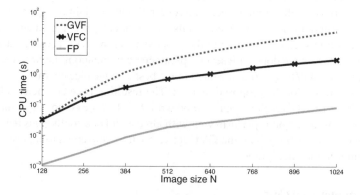

Fig. 5. Computational cost of GVF, VFC and force propagation for a NxN image

for each iteration and N iterations are generally needed to calculate the force field [14], the GVF field has an $O(N^3)$ complexity. In Fig. 5 the computation time of GVF, VFC and the proposed force field are compared in function of the image size. Note that the time axis is log scaled. These experimental results were calculated on a computer with an Intel core I7 1.60 GHz CPU and 4 GB RAM. All algorithms were programmed in C. The GVF code was provided by Xu and Prince [13]. The code for VFC was provided by the Virginia Image & Video Analysis group [14]. In agreement with the theoretical complexity analysis, the GVF field is the slowest to calculate. The VFC field is much faster than GVF, but is significantly slower than the proposed method, while the proposed method outperforms VFC on segmentation quality as well.

5   Conclusion

In this paper a new variant on the active contour framework is defined. This method propagates both edge evidence and the corresponding force vector in order to extend the capturing range of active contours. Experiments show that the proposed method is much faster than GVF and VFC, while resulting in similar segmentation results as GVF. It produces better segmentation results than VFC. The method has been tested both on binary and real fluorescent micrographs and shows good convergence properties. The proposed method only has one parameter which allows easy tuning.

Acknowledgment

The authors would like to thank T.G. Dietterich and the Plant and Botany Department, Oregon State University, for providing the digital herbarium. This research has been made possible by the Institute for the Promotion of Innovation by Science and Technology in Flanders (IWT).

References

1. Isard, M., Blake, A.: Active contours. Springer, Heidelberg (1998)
2. Ray, N., Acton, S.: Motion gradient vector flow: An external force for tracking rolling leukocytes with shape and size constrained active contours. IEEE Transaction on Medical Imaging 23, 1466–1478 (2004)
3. Tang, J.: A multi-direction gvf snake for the segmentation of skin cancer images. Pattern Recognition (2008)
4. Chan, T., Vese, L.: An active contour model without edges. In: Nielsen, M., Johansen, P., Fogh Olsen, O., Weickert, J. (eds.) Scale-Space 1999. LNCS, vol. 1682, pp. 141–151. Springer, Heidelberg (1999)
5. Mille, J.: Narrow band region-based active contours and surfaces for 2d and 3d segmentation. Computer Vision and Image Understanding 113(9), 946–965 (2009)
6. Charmi, M.A., Derrode, S., Ghorbel, S.: Fourier-based geometric shape prior for snakes. Pattern Recognition Letters 29, 897–904 (2008)
7. Rochery, M., Jermyn, I.H., Zerubia, J.: Higher order active contours. International Journal of Computer Vision 69(1), 27–42 (2006)

8. Paragios, N., Mellina-Gottardo, O., Ramesh, V.: Gradient vector flow fast geometric active contours. IEEE Transactions on Pattern Analysis and Machine Intelligence 26(3), 402–407 (2004)
9. Xu, C.Y., Yezzi, A., Prince, J.L.: On the relationship between parametric and geometric active contours. In: Conference Record of the Thirty-Fourth Asilomar Conference on Signals, Systems & Computers, pp. 483–489 (2000)
10. Goobic, A., Welser, M., Acton, S., Ley, K.: Biomedical application of target tracking in clutter. In: Proc. 35th Asilomar Conference on Signals, Systems and Computers, vol. 1, pp. 88–92 (2001)
11. Kass, M., Witkin, A., Terzopoulos, D.: Snakes: active contour models. International Journal of Computer Vision, 321–331 (1988)
12. Cohen, L.D., Cohen, I.: Finite-element methods for active contour models and balloons for 2-d and 3-d images. IEEE Transactions on Pattern Analysis and Machine Intelligence 15(11), 1131–1147 (1993)
13. Xu, C., Prince, J.: Snakes, shapes and gradient vector flow. IEEE Transactions on Image Processing 7, 359–369 (1998), http://iacl.ece.jhu.edu/projects/gvf/
14. Li, B., Acton, S.: Active contour external force using vector field convolution for image segmentation. IEEE Transactions on Image Processing 16, 2096–2106 (2007), http://viva.ee.virginia.edu/research_vfc.html
15. Wang, Y.Q., Jia, Y.D.: External force for active contours: Gradient vector convolution. In: Ho, T.-B., Zhou, Z.-H. (eds.) PRICAI 2008. LNCS (LNAI), vol. 5351, pp. 466–472. Springer, Heidelberg (2008)

The Extraction of Venation from Leaf Images by Evolved Vein Classifiers and Ant Colony Algorithms

James S. Cope[1], Paolo Remagnino[1], Sarah Barman[1], and Paul Wilkin[2]

[1] Digital Imaging Research Centre, Kingston University, London, UK
{j.cope,p.remagnino,s.barman}@kingston.ac.uk
[2] Royal Botanic Gardens, Kew, London, UK
p.wilkin@kew.org

Abstract. Leaf venation is an important source of data for research in comparative plant biology. This paper presents a method for evolving classifiers capable of extracting the venation from leaf images. Quantitative and qualitative analysis of the classifier produced is carried out. The results show that the method is capable of the extraction of near complete primary and secondary venations with relatively little noise. For comparison, a method using ant colony algorithms is also discussed.

1 Introduction

In the field of comparative biology, novel sources of data are continuously being sought to enable or enhance research varying from studies of evolution to generating tools for taxon identification. Leaves are especially important in this regard, because in many applied fields, such as studies of ecology or palaeontology, reproductive organs, which may often provide an easier form of identification, are unavailable or present for only a limited season. Leaves are present during all seasons when plants are in growth. There are also millions of dried specimens available in herbaria around the world, many of which have already been imaged. While these specimens may possess reproductive organs, the main character features are often concealed in images through being internal or poor preparation. However, almost all specimens possess well-preserved and relatively easily imaged leaf material.

Traditional methods employed by botanists for describing leaves rely on terminology and are wholly qualitative and open to some level of interpretation [3]. In recent decades plant science has begun to use a range of quantitative morphometric methods in comparative studies [12,5]. However, such data currently exist for a small minority of plant taxa, largely due to the limitations imposed by manual data capture. Research such as that cited above has shown that the most useful features of leaves for use in comparative biology are usually the two-dimensional outline shape, characters of the margin and structure of the vein network (Figure 1). Thus a fully automated method of extracting consistent,

J. Blanc-Talon et al. (Eds.): ACIVS 2010, Part I, LNCS 6474, pp. 135–144, 2010.

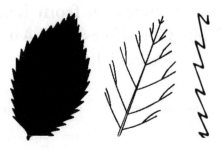

Fig. 1. Leaf Shape, Venation & Margin

mathematically sound information from images of leaves would be a great aid in plant comparative biology.

This paper presents a first step towards extracting the primary and secondary venation from leaf images, using a classifier that has been evolved to recognise those pixels which belong to veins. For comparison we also explore the use of ant colony algorithms for vein extraction.

2   Previous Work

In recent years, a number of techniques have been employed for extracting leaf venation. Clarke [1] compares the results from two simple methods, smoothing and edge detection, and a scale space algorithm, with the best results that they could achieve manually using Photoshop. Fu & Chi [4] used a two stage approach on leaves which had been photographed using a fluorescent light bank to enhance the venation. First, edge detection methods were used to determine a suitable greyscale threshold for removing most of the non-vein pixels. An artificial neural network classifier was then used to refine the results. Li & Chi [7] successfully extracted the venation from leaf sub-images using Independent Component Analysis (ICA) [2], though when used on whole leaves, the results were only comparable to the Prewitt edge detection operator. Artificial ant swarms were also used by Mullen [9] to trace venation and outlines in leaves via an edge detection method. Kirchgeßner [6] describes a method of tracking vein structures on leaves, and representing them using b-splines which contain the hierarchical venation information. This method, however, required some manual interaction to initialise a search.

The method presented in this paper produces robust vein extractions from whole leaf images without backlighting the leaves. Section 3.1 outlines how the pixels are classified. The features used are specified in section 3.2, whilst section 3.3 describes how the classifiers are evolved. Results for this method are given in section 3.5. Section 4.1 describes how ant colony algorithms can be used for vein extraction, with section 4.2 containing the results for this and a comparison of the two methods, with discussion of how they might be combined to further improve the results.

3   Extraction by Evolved Vein Classifiers

3.1   Classifying the Vein Pixels

A genetic algorithm is used to evolve a set of classifiers for detecting veins. Each classifier consists of a pair of bounds for each of the features used. If the values of all the features for a pixel fall within all the bounds for a classifier, then it is classified as vein. The vein pixels found by all the classifiers in the set are combined, and all other pixels are classified as non-vein. These classifiers are similar those used by Liu & Tang [8]. More specifically, the set of vein pixels, V, is determined as follows:

$$V = \{(x,y)|0 \leq x < w, 0 \leq y < h,$$
$$\exists c \in C s.t. \forall f_i \in F_{xy}(c_{i0} \leq f_i \leq c_{i1})\}$$

where

- w,h are the image width and height respectively
- C is the set of all classifiers
- c_{i0} is the lower bound for the ith feature for the classifier c
- c_{i1} is the upper bound for the ith feature for the classifier c
- F_{xy} is the set of feature values for the pixel at (x, y)
- f_i is the value for the ith feature

3.2   Feature Extraction

A set of 9 features are extracted for each pixel for use in classification. The features used are as follows:

1. Pixel greyscale value $f_1 = I(x, y)$
2. Edge gradient magnitude (from Sobel)
3. Average of greyscale values in a 7×7 neighbourhood

$$f_3 = \frac{1}{49} \sum_{\substack{x-3 \leq i \leq x+3 \\ y-3 \leq j \leq y+3}} I(i, j)$$

4. Greyscale value minus neighbourhood average

$$f_4 = I(x, y) - \frac{1}{49} \sum_{\substack{x-3 \leq i \leq x+3 \\ y-3 \leq j \leq y+3}} I(i, j)$$

5. Greyscale value minus leaf lamina average

$$f_5 = I(x, y) - \frac{1}{|lamina|} \sum_{\substack{0 \leq i < width \\ 0 \leq j < height \\ (i,j) \in lamina}} I(i, j)$$

Where *lamina* is the set of all pixels which are part of the leaf's lamina (surface), found by using Otsu's thresholding [10] to remove the leaf from the background.

The average local gradient direction of pixels in a 11×11 neighbourhood around the current pixel is calculated. This size neighbourhood was chosen because for most vein pixels this will include both sides of the vein. The greyscale values of the points 5 pixels from the current one in both directions along the gradient and perpendicular to the gradient are calculated. If the current pixel is part of a vein, the pixels perpendicular to the gradient direction are likely to also be vein pixels, and so similar to the current pixel, whilst the pixels along the gradient direction are likely to be non-vein, and therefore quite different.

$$i_1 = I(x + 5 * Sin(\alpha), y + 5 * Cos(\alpha))$$

$$i_2 = I(x - 5 * Sin(\alpha), y - 5 * Cos(\alpha))$$

$$j_1 = I(x + 5 * Sin(\alpha + \frac{\pi}{2}), y + 5 * Cos(\alpha + \frac{\pi}{2}))$$

$$j_2 = I(x - 5 * Sin(\alpha + \frac{\pi}{2}), y - 5 * Cos(\alpha + \frac{\pi}{2}))$$

where α is the gradient direction.
The remaining features are then:

6. The difference between pixels either side of potential vein $f_6 = |i_1 - i_2|$
7. The difference between pixels along potential vein

$$f_7 = |j_1 - j_2|$$

8. Greyscale value minus average value of the two pixels either side of the potential vein

$$f_8 = I(x, y) - \frac{i_1 + i_2}{2}$$

9. Greyscale value minus average value of the two pixels along the potential vein

$$f_9 = I(x, y) - \frac{j_1 + j_2}{2}$$

To allow the same genetic operators to be used on features with very varied distributions, the feature values for the training data are mapped to a uniform distribution. This mapping is recorded and applied to any data being subsequently classified.

3.3   Evolving the Classifiers

Classifiers are evolved one after another using a genetic algorithm, and added to the classifier set until no more classifiers with a fitness above a certain threshold can be generated. The only genetic operators used are mutations, as crossover operations are likely to combine classifiers that work on different types of vein pixels, thereby having a negative effect. For example, a classifier that finds thin sections of vein may require higher edge gradient values and lower greyscale values than a classifier finding the pixels in the middle of thicker veins. Crossing over these two classifiers would result in ones which classified neither of these vein pixel types. Bounds are mutated with probability 0.3 by adding or subtracting an amount randomly drawn from the range [0,0.01]. The population is re-initialised after each classifier is added to the set. Each individual is initialised by centring the bounds around the feature values for a vein pixel randomly selected from the training data, with the width of the bounds drawn from a Gaussian distribution. This increases the likelihood of the classifier being effective, as one vein pixel will always be correctly classified by it, along with any similar vein pixels.

The fitness function used is as follows:

$$fitness_i = \frac{|T_i \setminus \bigcup_{j \in C} T_j|}{|F_i \setminus \bigcup_{j \in C} F_j| + k}$$

where:

- T_i is the set vein pixels correctly classified by classifier i (true positives).
- F_i is the set non-vein pixels incorrectly classified by classifier i (false positives).
- C is the current set of classifiers selected in previous iterations and k is a constant.

This function grants high fitnesses to individuals which, if added to the classifier set, would significantly increase the number of true positives, but not the number of false positives. The constant k is used to adjust the balance between a high true positive/false positive ratio, and a high total number of true positives. If k is set too low the ratio will be very high, but the final classifier set may over-fit the training data. If k is set too high it will result in a high number of false positives. A value of $k = 5$ was found to be appropriate.

3.4   Redundancy

Classifiers can potentially be made redundant by other classifiers added to set later. In other words, a classifier may no longer uniquely classify many vein pixels whilst still incorrectly classifying some non-vein pixels. It is beneficial to remove such classifiers as this may greatly reduce the number of false positives whilst only slightly reducing the number of true positives.

Redundant classifiers are identified by removing candidates from the set and measuring any improvement in overall classification quality. The classifier whose removal produces the largest increase in quality is permanently removed from the set. This process is repeated until no more classifiers are found to be redundant.

3.5   Results

The classifier was trained using 8000 pixels randomly selected from 14 leaf images, 2 from each of 7 species. These pixels were then manually labelled as either

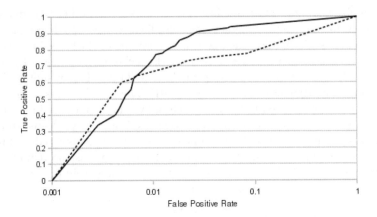

Fig. 2. ROC Curve. Solid line - evolved classifiers. Dashed line - ant algorithm.

vein or non-vein. The resulting classifier was then tested on 7 new leaf images, one from each of the species used for training. The ROC curve in figure 2 shows the results (solid line). With a false positive rate of 0.0166, a true positive rate of 0.853 was achieved. The curve was produced by varying the value of k, and the size of the initial classifier bounds.

The classifier was also used on the full leaf images from the test set, in order to extract the full venation pattern. Examples of these results are shown in figure 3.

4   Extraction by Ant Colonies

4.1   The Algorithm

Our second approach to vein extraction is to use an ant colony algorithm. A population of ant-like agents are placed at random across the image. These "ants" then move across the image, moving from pixel to pixel based upon some heuristic evaluation of that pixel, known as the pixel's visibility, and also based on the level of "pheromone" at that pixel. The pheromones are an indicator deposited by ants to signal to other ants the value of a particular pixel. As time progresses, the pheromone levels build up to create a pheromone map for the image, with high levels in desirable regions, and low levels in undesirable regions. In our case we use the edge magnitude as the measure of visibility, to encourage the ants to traverse along the veins, thereby extracting continuous sections of venation. The probability, P_{ij}, of an ant at pixel i moving to pixel j is calculated as follows:

$$P_{ij} = \begin{cases} \dfrac{\tau_j^{\alpha} \eta_j^{\beta}}{\displaystyle\sum_{k \in K_i} \tau_k^{\alpha} \eta_k^{\beta}} & \text{if } j \in K_i \\ 0 & \text{otherwise} \end{cases}$$

(a) Quercus Shumardii

(b) Quercus Rubra

(c) Quercus Ellipsoidalis

Fig. 3. Results for extraction by evolved classifers

where τ_j and η_j are the pheromone level and visibility respectively at pixel j, α and β are the weightings for these two components, and K_i is the set of pixels neighbouring pixel i. To prevent the ants converging on the strong edges outlining the leaf instead of the venation, the visibility for all background pixels (again calculated using Otsu's method) and all pixels within a short distance of the background (in this case, a distance of 10 pixels) is set to 0. After all the ants have performed one move, the pheromone levels are updated:

$$\tau_i = (1 - \rho)\tau_i + \delta a_i \eta_i$$

where ρ is the rate at which pheromones evaporate, δ is the update rate, and a_i is the number of ants at pixel i. There is a risk that ants will simply move between the same small set of pixels, building up pheromone levels until it is highly unlikely for them to escape. This is prevented by keeping a list of the last 10 pixels visited by each ant, and forbidding the ant from re-visiting any of these pixels. After a set number of moves have taken place, the pheromone map is thresholded to produce a binary vein classification. This method is based on the method described in [9].

4.2   Results and Comparison of Methods

Figure 4 contains examples of typical results obtained using this method. For each leaf the algorithm was run for 500 steps, using 2000 ants. The pheromone map was then thresholded at 2% of the maximum pheromone level. These values were chosen as they appeared to give the best qualitative results. The results differ from those obtained using the evolved classifiers in a number of ways. Firstly, due to the use of only the edge gradients to guide the ants across the image, the results contained only the hollow outline of the venation, whereas the other method extracts the full vein. One advantage of using ants is that it helps in extracting continous venation, whilst the evolved classifiers extract veins with many small gaps in them. On the downside, when a vein contains a section with only a low edge magnitude, the ants are unable to continue to extract the rest of that vein as the pixel-by-pixel evolved classifiers are able to do. The effects of

Fig. 4. Results using the ant colony algorithm

Fig. 5. Results after morphological closing

this can be seen near the top of the first image in figure 4, where a large section of venation is completely absent. Furthermore, whereas much of the false positive results from the first method are isolated pixels that can be easily removed, the ants produce larger, connected areas of noise, that may be harder to distinguish from the actual venation.

By applying morphological closing, the hollow vein centres can be filled in (figure 5). From these, quantitative results can be calculated, as shown in figure 2 (dashed line). It can be see that the ant algorithm still performs worse than the evolved classifiers, except when the true positive rate falls below approximately 0.63.

5   Conclusion

In this paper, a method of evolving classifiers capable of extracting the venation pattern from leaf images was presented. Qualitative results show that near complete primary and secondary venation patterns can extracted with relatively little noise. Extraction of tertiary venations is less reliable. This was compared to a vein extraction method using an ant colony algorithm. Whilst the ants were able to extract more continuous venation, the gaps which were present tended to be larger, as did the regions of noise. With this in mind, it may be possible to combine the two methods to achieve even better results. The evolved classifier could be adapted to provide a probabilistic, rather than binary, classification, with a different ant colony using each classifier as its visibility measure to extract complete, continuous venation. This is one possible area for future work. Other future work will first involve finding a method of refining the extracted venation so that only the complete primary and secondary venation remains. A system for automatically generating a venation description, preserving the hierarchical vein structure, will then be developed. This will allow the venation from different leaves to be accurately compared.

References

1. Clarke, J., Barman, S., Remagnino, P., Bailey, K., Kirkup, D., Mayo, S., Wilkin, P.: Venation pattern analysis of leaf images. In: Bebis, G., Boyle, R., Parvin, B., Koracin, D., Remagnino, P., Nefian, A., Meenakshisundaram, G., Pascucci, V., Zara, J., Molineros, J., Theisel, H., Malzbender, T. (eds.) ISVC 2006. LNCS, vol. 4292, pp. 427–436. Springer, Heidelberg (2006)
2. Comon, P.: Independent component analysis, a new concept? Signal Processing 36(3), 287–314 (1994)
3. Ellis, B., Daly, D.C., Hickey, L.J., Johnson, K.R., Mitchell, J.D., Wilf, P., Wing, S.L.: Manual Of Leaf Architecture. Cornell University Press, Ithica (2009)
4. Fu, H., Chi, Z.: Combined thresholding and neural network approach for vein pattern extraction from leaf images. In: IEE Proceedings. Vision Image And Signal Processing, vol. 153, pp. 881–892. Institution of Electrical Engineers (2006)
5. Jensen, R.J., Ciofani, K.M., Miramontes, L.C.: Lines, outlines, and landmarks: Morphometric analyses of leaves of acer rubrum, acer saccharinum (aceraceae) and their hybrid. Taxon 51(3), 475–492 (2002)
6. Kirchgessner, N., Scharr, H., Schurr, U.: Robust vein extraction on plant leaf images. In: 2nd IASTED International Conference Visualisation, Imaging And Image Processing (2002)
7. Li, Y., Chi, Z., Feng, D.D.: Leaf vein extraction using independent component analysis. In: IEEE International Conference On Systems, Man, And Cybernetics, pp. 3890–3984. IEEE, Los Alamitos (2006)
8. Liu, J., Tang, Y.Y.: Adaptive image segmentation with distributed behavior-based agents. IEEE Trans. Pattern Anal. Mach. Intell. 21(6), 544–551 (1999)
9. Mullen, R., Monekosso, D., Barman, S., Remagnino, P., Wilkin, P.: Artificial ants to extract leaf outlines and primary venation patterns. In: Dorigo, M., Birattari, M., Blum, C., Clerc, M., Stützle, T., Winfield, A.F.T. (eds.) ANTS 2008. LNCS, vol. 5217, pp. 251–258. Springer, Heidelberg (2008)
10. Otsu, N.: A threshold selection method from gray level histograms. IEEE Trans. Systems, Man and Cybernetics 9, 62–66 (1979)
11. Park, J., Hwang, E., Nam, Y.: Utilizing venation features for efficient leaf image retrieval. Journal of Systems and Software 81(1), 71–82 (2008)
12. Plotze, R.d.O., Falvo, M., Padua, J.G., Bernacci, L.C., Vieira, M.L.C., Oliveira, G.C.X., Martinez, O.: Leaf shape analysis using the multiscale minkowski fractal dimension, a new morphometric method: A study with passiflora (passifloraceae). Canadian Journal Of Botany 83(3), 287–301 (2005)

Segmentation of Inter-neurons in Three Dimensional Brain Imagery

Gervase Tuxworth[1,2], Adrian Meedeniya[2], and Michael Blumenstein[1]

[1] School of Information Communication and Technology,
Griffith University, Queensland, Australia
[2] National Centre for Adult Stem Cell Research,
Griffith University, Queensland, Australia

Abstract. Segmentation of neural cells in three dimensional fluorescence microscopy images is a challenging image processing problem. In addition to being important to neurobiologists, accurate segmentation is a vital component of an automated image processing system. Due to the complexity of the data, particularly the extreme irregularity in neural cell shape, generic segmentation techniques do not perform well. This paper presents a novel segmentation technique for segmenting neural cells in three dimensional images. Accuracy rates of over 90% are reported on a data set of 100 images containing over 130 neural cells and subsequently validated using a novel data set of 64 neurons.

1 Introduction

Microscopy and image acquisition technology has undergone a recent revolution, generating multidimensional data sets that require significant automation to analyse efficiently. Studies have shown that many neurodegenerative disorders (including Parkinson's disease and Alzheimer's disease) have a significant impact on neuronal structure. The ability to recognize changes in the morphology of neurons together with more subtle changes that occur within the cells with respect to the distribution of cytoplasmic proteins and cell organelles, will allow cell function to be determined. The capacity to analyse the morphology of these cells using unbiased, automated techniques would greatly facilitate advances in the field. In order to analyse the morphology of individual neural cells, we must first segment them from the rest of the image.

Our previous work in cell morphology analysis [1] used manually guided segmentation techniques to conduct experiments on our initial data set, but with increasing data becoming available, there is a need for accurate automated image analysis systems. In addition, manual techniques are subject to human bias, making automated quantitative techniques desirable. However, the automated segmentation of neural cells of the central nervous system presents a major challenge due to inherent features such as irregularity of cell shape and size, and arborising interconnecting cell processes.

Many existing segmentation techniques in fluorescent microscopy concentrate on the segmentation of morphological structures such as the cell nuclei [2, 3], or the complete cell (nucleus and cytoplasm) [4]. Fernandez et al. [2] and Jarkrans [3] both

J. Blanc-Talon et al. (Eds.): ACIVS 2010, Part I, LNCS 6474, pp. 145–152, 2010.
© Springer-Verlag Berlin Heidelberg 2010

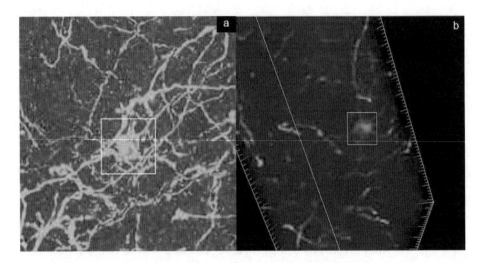

Fig. 1. An olfactory bulb neuron in a) 2D MIP Image; b) 3D Volume image

try to detect and separate directly neighbouring cell nuclei. Fernandez et al. propose the detection of dominant or concave points on the binary contour of the region as points where a splitting of the nuclei might be possible. In contrast, Jarkrans uses a contour analysis based on a smoothed chain code, which reflects the curvature of the nucleus contour.

We have developed a method for generating optically resolvable, thick tissue specimens [5]. The cellular and sub-cellular compartments of these specimens are probed using multiple fluorescent probes. These structures may be resolved in three dimensional space using structured illumination and wide-field microscopy ([6], [7]). Thus, we are able to produce large data sets of high resolution three dimensional (3D) images probed with multiple markers [5]. These images contain more informa-tion than their two dimensional (2D) counterparts, and present new possibilities for automated analysis. Figure 1 shows a cell that would normally be difficult or impos-sible to segment in a two dimensional image become a more manageable image proc-essing task when analysed in three dimensions. When considering a three dimensional image, new segmentation techniques are needed to facilitate further processing.

Current three dimensional segmentation techniques can be broken down into edge based techniques and region based techniques. In edge-based approaches such as [8] , the points located on the edges are first identified, followed by edge linking, contour analysis and surface definition. In region-based approaches a number of seed regions are first chosen. These seed regions grow by adding neighbouring points based on a compatibility threshold [9]. In the context of fluorescence microscopy, goal seed regions are the cell nuclei or centres where the signal intensity is highest. As the re-gion growing reaches the edges of the cell, the intensity values drop off and therefore don't meet the compatibility threshold.

In [10], Yu et al. propose a seed region finding approach to segmenting tightly packed cell nuclei within 3D confocal images of neurospheres. They focused on a method to find seed regions in the centre of objects of different sizes and then use an

"Evolving" Generalized Voronoi Diagram to separate touching nuclei. Another nuclei segmentation algorithm proposed by Long *et al* [11] uses the 3D watershed method to segment cell nuclei. They combine a foreground contour mask with intensity-based watershed segmentation and post-process the segmentation results to correct over and under segmentation errors.

Our project goals required the entire cell body to be segmented, so these nuclei segmentation techniques may not be suitable. In this paper, we propose a method that involves a 2D slice by slice analysis as per Cai *et al* in [12], as well as intensity based analysis as used in [11], and then use contour tracking to merge 2D slices into 3D neuron masks. We tested this algorithm on 100 images of the olfactory bulb of mice and found we were able to segment cells with high accuracy.

2   Research Methodology

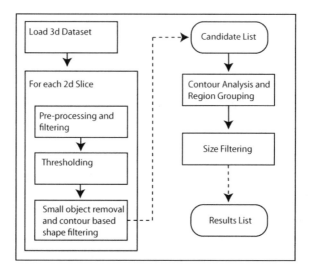

Fig. 2. Overview of segmentation process

2.1   Pre-processing

The 3D image data is loaded as a 'stack' of 2D images. All the individual 2D images ('slices') share the same x and y dimensions. The number of images is variable depending on the thickness of the tissue sample, but a typical stack has between 80 and 120 slices, each slice representing $0.25 - 0.5$ µm of cell thickness along the z axis.

2.2   Slice Analysis

Each slice has a 3x3x3 Gaussian filter applied to it to remove noise and is then thresholded to separate the foreground from the background. Similar works ([13], [11]) use Otsu's method [14] for automatically detecting a threshold that separates foreground background. Whilst using an automated thresholding technique does provide more tolerance for intensity variations in the data set, it also has the drawback of looking to discriminate foreground and background data regardless of the image contents. In some images with little 'real' foreground data (an image with no neurons in it), an automatic thresholding technique is more likely to produce false positive objects. Both methods will be used in experimentation.

Once thresholded, each slice then has a series of morphological operations performed on it to remove irrelevant or insignificant objects. Firstly, the slices are filtered again to remove any noise or stray pixels created in the thresholding process. After the slices have been filtered, morphological opening (erosion followed by dilation) is performed to remove small objects followed by morphological closing (dilation followed by erosion) to fill in holes inside foreground objects.

Once the objects have been separated, we identify potential neuron cross sections by eliminating small objects and computing a contour roundness metric. After estimating the perimeter and area of each object in the scene, an isoperimetric value is calculated using the formula:

$$\frac{4\,\pi\,area}{perimeter^2}$$

If the objects isoperimetric value is below a preset threshold, the object is discarded as a candidate; else it is added to the candidate list. With an appropriate threshold, this filtering allows our technique to remove foreground objects like thick axon trunks, whose cross sections are typically more rectangular shaped than neural cell bodies.

2.3 Neuron Segmentation

Once each slice has been individually analysed and objects placed on the candidate list, the objects on the list need to be grouped to create 3D masks. Assuming a conservative minimum cell thickness of 3 microns, an object must be present in at least 12 slices (at 0.25 µm slice thickness) to be considered. We discard any neurons touching image boundaries as they may not contain complete neurons. Objects that overlap in the x and y planes on adjacent images are examined for contour similarity. A high rate of change of the contour of the object over a series of slices can be used to identify overlapping or touching objects, or identify slices with noisy data around the cell. By creating a rate of change threshold, objects that have irregularities in their contours between Z-slices can be discarded.

Once the neurons have been identified, they can be segmented in one of two ways. A bounding box can be created using the maximum detected radius of any slice to identify where a neuron is located. This is useful for cell counting applications, but does not suit applications where the morphology of the cell is important. Instead, a three dimensional matrix can be constructed as a mask over the original image, with the detected cell cross-section in each slice used to create a series of two dimensional masks. This extracts the morphology of the cell for further analysis.

2.4 Algorithm Pseudo-code

Psuedo-code for the segmentation technique can be seen below.

Segmentation Algorithm

```
mThresh = metricThreshold
cThresh = contourThreshold

for each Slice S ∈ Image
{
  Filter and threshold S;
  Perform opening and closing on S;
  Fill holes and detect objects in S;

  for each object K ∈ S;
  {
    Calculate roundness metric for K;
    if (isoperimetric > mThresh && K does not touch
        image edges)
      Add K to candidate list C
  }
}

for each candidate X ∈ C
{
  Remove X from candidate list C
  Add X to Neuron N

  for each candidate Y ∈ C
  {
    if (contourChange(Y,N) < cThresh && X and Y
        are adjacent)
      Add Y to Neuron N
      X is assigned Y
      Remove Y from candidate list C
  }

  if(N.sizeZ > minZSize)
    Add N to results list R
}
```

3 Experimental Results, Analysis and Discussion

To develop our proposed segmentation technique, 100 images of olfactory bulb neurons were obtained. Tissue specimens were harvested from laboratory mice, embedded in PEG using the protocol detailed in [5] and sectioned coronally at a thickness of 40 μm. Fifty images were taken of olfactory neurons from wild type laboratory mice and another 50 were taken from mice with a focal deletion of the gene sequence coding for the neurotrophic factor neurturin.

Images were taken at 630x magnification using a Zeiss AxioImager Z1 equipped with an Apotome system to create Z-stacks. These images were manually analysed by neurobiologists and found to contain 134 cells. We tested our algorithm using several different parameters for threshold, minimum object size and isoperimetric threshold.

Table 1. Results using manual threshold values

Minimum Object Size	Isoperimetric Threshold	Threshold	Accuracy
2500	0.7	0.2	74%
2500	**0.7**	**0.3**	**88%**
2500	0.7	0.4	80%
4000	0.7	0.2	77%
4000	0.7	0.3	83%
4000	0.7	0.4	72%

The highest accuracy was obtained using a fairly low threshold (0.3), with 123 detected cells and 5 miss-classifications, resulting in an accuracy of 118/134 (88%). Lowering the threshold to 0.2 increased the number of false positives, while any higher resulted in an increased number of missed cells. We then used Otsu's method to automatically calculate the threshold for the dataset.

Table 2. Otsu's thresholding vs. manual thresholding

Threshold	False Positives	Missed Cells	Accuracy
0.3	5	11	88.1%
Otsu	**7**	**8**	**88.8%**

The use of Otsu's thresholding technique yielded 126 detected cells, but 7 miss-classifications giving an overall accuracy of 88.8%. As expected, Otsu's technique created more foreground data than a preset manual value and resulted in an increase in false positives. To attempt to reduce the number of false positives, we tested Otsu's technique with higher post processing thresholds for object size and isoperimetric values.

Table 3. Adjusting algorithm parameters with Otsu's thresholding technique

Minimum Object Size	Isoperimetric Threshold	False Positives	Missed Cells	Accuracy
2500	0.7	7	8	88.8%
2500	0.75	6	17	82.8%
4000	**0.7**	**2**	**10**	**91.1%**
4000	0.75	2	19	84.3%

By increasing the post-processing thresholds we are able to eliminate nearly all of the false positives without significantly compromising the correctly labelled cells. This is particularly useful in our application where we can generate large data sets, so missed cells will have little impact, but a large number of false positives could cause inaccuracies in the analysis of cell morphologies.

To test our results, a separate validation data set of 30 images was obtained and segmented using the parameters that produced the best results on our original "development" dataset.

Table 4. Accuracy of algorithm on validation dataset. Minimum object size 4000, Isoperimetric threshold 0.7.

Dataset	False Positives	Missed Cells	Accuracy
Original (100 images, 134 cells)	2	10	91.1%
Validation (30 images, 64 cells)	2	5	89.1%

The validation images contained a high density of neurons per image in comparison to the development data set. Despite the increased density of cells in the validation set, our segmentation technique was able to segment cells with an accuracy of 89.1%. The number of false positives was relatively low, and only 5 out of the 64 cells were not recognized.

Our overall accuracy of 91.1% and 89.1% is comparable to other segmentation techniques ([11], [12]) developed for related 3D microscopic image analysis tasks. A closer inspection of the results also showed that 7/10 (70%) of the missed cells in the original data set occurred in just 4 (4%) of the images where there is a low signal to noise ratio either due to a weak fluorescent signal or a high non-specific background signal. As our aim is to completely automate the image analysis process, the weak images are not manually removed from the dataset, however an extension to our work will involve the automated identification of poor images and their removal from the dataset to prevent biasing of the study outcomes.

4   Conclusions and Future Research

In this paper we have presented a technique for segmenting neurons in 3-Dimensional images that combines both edge based and region growing techniques. This algorithm requires very little manual input and is able to automatically detect seed points in complex scenes. Using contour analysis we can accurately detect objects over a series of slices and determine whether or not they are a neuron. The technique was validated using a novel data set of greater complexity and demonstrated to work accurately. This work provides a critical component for future automated image analysis. Using the segmented neuron data, we can develop techniques to automatically analyse neuron morphology and population numbers to aid neurobiological and other cell biological research.

Acknowledgements

The authors would like to acknowledge the invaluable assistance of the members of the Transplant Therapy and Neuro Anatomy group at the National Centre for Adult Stem Cell Research, Griffith University. In particular, we would like to thank Brenton Cavanagh and Maria Nguyen for tissue preparation and imaging.

References

[1] Alavi, A., Cavanagh, B., Tuxworth, G., Meedeniya, A., Mackay-Sim, A., Blumenstein, M.: Automated classification of dopaminergic neurons in the rodent brain. Presented at the International Joint Conference on Neural Networks, Atlanta (2009)

[2] Fernandez, G., Zyrd, J.P., Kunt, M.: A New Plant Cell Image Segmentation Algorithm. Presented at the ICIAP (1995)

[3] Jarkrans, T.: Algorithms for Cell Image Analysis in Cytology and Pathology. Faculty of Science and Technology, Uppsala University, Sweden (1996)

[4] Byriel, J.: Neuro-Fuzzy Classification of Cells in Cervical Smears. Technical University of Denmark, Lyngby (1999)

[5] Nguyen, M.N., Cavanagh, B., Davenport, T., Norazit, A., Meedeniya, A.: Tissue processing for epifluoresence microscopy. In: Méndez-Vilas, A., Diaz, J. (eds.) Microscopy: Science, Technology, Applications and Education, vol. 4. Formatex, Badajoz (2010)

[6] Schaefer, L.H., Schuster, D., Herz, H.: Generalized approach for accelerated maximum likelihood based image restoration applied to three-dimensional fluorescence microscopy. Journal of Microscopy 204, 99–107 (2001)

[7] Murray, J.M., Appleton, P.L., Swedlow, J.R., Waters, J.C.: Evaluating performance in three-dimensional fluorescence Microscopy. Journal of Microscopy 228, 390–405 (2007)

[8] Benlamri, R.: Range image segmentation of scenes with occluded curved objects. Pattern Recognition Letters 21, 1051–1060 (2000)

[9] Jiang, X., Bunke, H., Meier, U.: High level feature based range image segmentation. Image and Vision Computation 18, 817–822 (2000)

[10] Yu, W., et al.: Segmentation of Neural Stem/Progenitor Cells Nuclei within 3-D Neurospheres. In: Bebis, G., et al. (eds.) Advances in Visual Computing, vol. 5875, pp. 531–543. Springer, Heidelberg (2009)

[11] Long, F., et al.: Automatic Segmentation of Nuclei in 3D Microscopy Images of C.Elegans. In: 4th IEEE International Symposium on Biomedical Imaging: From Nano to Macro, ISBI 2007, pp. 536–539 (2007)

[12] Cai, H., et al.: Using nonlinear diffusion and mean shift to detect and connect cross-sections of axons in 3D optical microscopy images. Medical Image Analysis 12 (2008)

[13] Yu, W., et al.: Segmentation of Neural Stem/Progenitor Cells Nuclei within 3-D Neurospheres. In: Advances in Visual Computing, pp. 531–543 (2009)

[14] Otsu, N.: A Threshold Selection Method from Gray-Level Histograms. IEEE Transactions on Systems, Man and Cybernetics 9, 62–66 (1979)

Noise-Robust Method for Image Segmentation

Ivana Despotović, Vedran Jelača, Ewout Vansteenkiste, and Wilfried Philips

Ghent Univesity, Department of Telecommunications and Information Processing,
TELIN-IPI-IBBT,
Sint-Pietersnieuwstraat 41, 9000 Ghent, Belgium
{ivek,vjelaca,ervsteen,philips}@telin.ugent.be
http://telin.ugent.be/ipi/drupal

Abstract. Segmentation of noisy images is one of the most challenging problems in image analysis and any improvement of segmentation methods can highly influence the performance of many image processing applications. In automated image segmentation, the fuzzy c-means (FCM) clustering has been widely used because of its ability to model uncertainty within the data, applicability to multi-modal data and fairly robust behaviour. However, the standard FCM algorithm does not consider any information about the spatial image context and is highly sensitive to noise and other imaging artefacts. Considering above mentioned problems, we developed a new FCM-based approach for the noise-robust fuzzy clustering and we present it in this paper. In this new iterative algorithm we incorporated both spatial and feature space information into the similarity measure and the membership function. We considered that spatial information depends on the relative location and features of the neighbouring pixels. The performance of the proposed algorithm is tested on synthetic image with different noise levels and real images. Experimental quantitative and qualitative segmentation results show that our method efficiently preserves the homogeneity of the regions and is more robust to noise than other FCM-based methods.

Keywords: Image segmentation, Noise, Fuzzy clustering, Fuzzy C-Means, Spatial information.

1 Introduction

Image segmentation is often a critical component in many image applications and is typically used to partition images into a set of non-overlapping, homogeneous regions with similar attributes such as intensity, texture, depth, color, etc. The diversity of image applications have led to the development of various segmentation techniques that vary in both algorithmic approach and the quality and nature of the segmentation produced. Some applications require the image to be segmented in details, while others require coarse homogeneous regions. Since unsupervised fuzzy clustering is one of the most commonly used methods for automatic image segmentation [1, 2] and has been successfully applied in fields such as astronomy, geology, medical and molecular imaging, it will be considered in this paper.

J. Blanc-Talon et al. (Eds.): ACIVS 2010, Part I, LNCS 6474, pp. 153–162, 2010.
© Springer-Verlag Berlin Heidelberg 2010

Fuzzy clustering methods involve the idea of partial membership and allow pixels to belong to multiple classes with certain degree. This idea is very important in applications where uncertainty, poor contrast, limited spatial resolution and noise are present (e.g. satellite and medical images). Among fuzzy clustering methods, the fuzzy c-means (FCM) algorithm [3] is the most popular one. However, the conventional FCM algorithm has a drawback, it classifies pixels in the feature space without considering their spatial distribution in the image and thus it is highly sensitive to noise.

To overcome above mentioned problem and reduce segmentation errors, many extensions of the FCM algorithm have been proposed [4, 5, 6, 7, 8, 9]. The most common approach is to include spatial neighbourhood information by modifying the FCM objective function [4,5] or a similarity measure between cluster centres and elements [6]. Ahmed et al. [4] modified the objective function of the standard FCM algorithm to allow the immediate neighbours of the pixel to influence its labelling. On the other hand, to keep the continuity from the FCM algorithm, Shen et al. [6] introduced a new similarity measure that depends on spatial neighbourhood information, where the degree of the neighbourhood attraction is optimized by a neural network. Beside these modifications, there are also other methods that can be used to enhance the FCM performance. For example, one can combine the pixel-wise classification with preprocessing (noise cleaning in the original image) [10, 7] and post-processing (noise cleaning on the classified data). Xue et al. [10] proposed an algorithm where they firstly denoise images, then classify the pixels using the standard FCM method and finally refine the segmentation with post-processing filtering. All of these methods can reduce the noise to a certain extent, but still have some drawbacks such as increased complexity [4,6,9] and image smoothing [10,7] that can result in loss of important image details.

In this paper, we present a new noise-robust FCM-based algorithm for image segmentation. Our algorithm iteratively integrates spatial neighbourhood information of the image elements (pixels) into both the similarity measure and the membership function. The spatial information depends on the relative location, intensities and membership degree values of the neighbouring pixels. The efficiency of our method is tested on synthetic and real images with different noise levels. Experimental results indicate that our method successfully reduces the effect of noise and biases the algorithm toward homogeneous clustering.

The paper is organized as follows. In Section 2, we explain the standard FCM method and our modified FCM algorithm. Experimental results together with comparison with other methods are presented and discussed in Section 3. Finally, we conclude this paper in Section 4.

2   Method

2.1   FCM Algorithm

The FCM algorithm, initially developed by Dunn and later generalized by Bezdek [3], is an iterative, unsupervised, soft classification method that can obtain much more information from the original image than hard segmentation methods (e.g. k-means). While hard segmentation methods classify pixels to belong exclusively to one class, FCM allows pixels to belong to multiple classes with different membership degrees.

Let $X = \{\mathbf{x}_j, j = 1, 2, ..., N \mid \mathbf{x}_j \in \mathbb{R}^q\}$ represent feature vectors of the image with N pixels that needs to be partitioned into C classes, where every component of the vector $\mathbf{x}_j$ represents a feature of the image at position j and q is the dimension of the feature vector. The FCM clustering algorithm is based on minimizing the following objective function:

$$J_m = \sum_{i=1}^{C} \sum_{j=1}^{N} u_{ij}^m D_{ij} \ , \tag{1}$$

where u_{ij} is the membership function of the feature $\mathbf{x}_j$ belonging to the i-th cluster, m is the weighting exponent that controls the fuzziness of the resulting partition (most often is set to $m = 2$) and $D_{ij} = d^2(\mathbf{x}_j, \mathbf{v}_i)$ is the similarity measure between $\mathbf{x}_j$ and the i-th cluster center $\mathbf{v}_i$. The most commonly used similarity measure is the squared Euclidean distance:

$$D_{ij} = d^2(\mathbf{x}_j, \mathbf{v}_i) = \|\mathbf{x}_j - \mathbf{v}_i\|^2 \ . \tag{2}$$

The objective function J_m (Eq. (1)) is minimized under the following constraints:

$$u_{ij} \in [0,1], \ \sum_{i=1}^{C} u_{ij} = 1 \ , \forall j \ \text{ and } \ 0 < \sum_{j=1}^{N} u_{ij} < N \ , \forall i \ , \tag{3}$$

where low membership values are assigned to pixels far from the cluster centroid, and high membership values to pixels close to the cluster centroid. Considering the constraints u_{ij} from Eq. (3) and calculating the first derivatives of J_m with respect to u_{ij} and $\mathbf{v}_i$ and setting them to zero, results in two following conditions for minimizing J_m:

$$u_{ij} = \left[\sum_{k=1}^{C} \left(\frac{D_{ij}}{D_{kj}} \right)^{\frac{1}{m-1}} \right]^{-1} \tag{4}$$

and

$$\mathbf{v}_i = \frac{\sum_{j=1}^{N} u_{ij}^m \ \mathbf{x}_j}{\sum_{j=1}^{N} u_{ij}^m} \ , (i = 1, 2, ..., C) \ . \tag{5}$$

The FCM algorithm iteratively optimizes J_m, by evaluating Eq. (4) and Eq. (5), until the following stop criterion is satisfied:

$$\max_{i \in [1,C]} \left\| \mathbf{v}_i^{(l)} - \mathbf{v}_i^{(l+1)} \right\|_\infty < \epsilon \ , \tag{6}$$

where l is the iteration index and $\| \cdot \|_\infty$ is the L_∞ norm. Once a membership value u_{ij} for each class i is assigned to each pixel j, a defuzzification of the fuzzy clusters $\{F_k\}_{k=1}^C$ into its crisp version $\{H_k\}_{k=1}^C$ is done by assigning the pixel to the class with the highest membership value as follows:

$$\max_{i \in [1,C]} (u_{ij}) = u_{kj} \implies \mathbf{x}_j \in H_k \ . \tag{7}$$

The main drawback of the standard FCM for image segmentation is that the objective function does not take into account any spatial information and deals with the pixels as separate points. Therefore, the standard FCM algorithm is sensitive to outliers and very often those pixels are wrongly classified. To illustrate this, we consider an example shown in Fig. 1, where we have a simple synthetic image with two classes (grey background and white foreground) Fig. 1a. The white foreground and the black background are corrupted by the noise pixels, which have the same intensity value as the opposite class, the background and the foreground respectively. The segmentation result using the FCM Fig. 1b is affected by the noise pixels, while the desired segmentation result is shown in Fig. 1c.

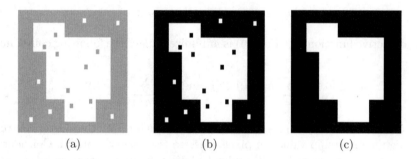

(a)	(b)	(c)

Fig. 1. Example: (a) a synthetic image with a noise, (b) the FCM segmentation result and (c) the expected segmentation result

2.2   Proposed Method

One of the important characteristics of the image is that majority of its neighbouring pixels have similar feature values and the probability that they belong to the same cluster is great. Therefore, to improve the performance and overcome the limitation of the standard FCM algorithm, we considered the spatial neighbourhood information in our method.

If we look at the objective function of the FCM algorithm (Eq. (1)) and its two necessary conditions for the convergence (Eq. (4) and Eq. (5)), we can conclude that the segmentation result is significantly influenced by membership values u_{ij} and the choice of the similarity measure D_{ij}. The novelty of our method is that in each iteration of the algorithm we modify both the similarity measure and the membership values, in two separate steps, using the spatial information of the neighbouring pixels. The new similarity measure includes the intensity and distance of the neighbouring pixels, while the new membership function is calculated using the membership degree values of the neighbouring pixels weighted by their spatial position in the image. In the following lines we explain these two steps in more details.

Firstly, we define the spatially dependent similarity measure as follows:

$$D_{ij} = \|\mathbf{x}_j - \mathbf{v}_i\|^2 (1 - \alpha S_{ij}), \tag{8}$$

where S_{ij} represents the spatial neighbourhood information and $\alpha \in [0, 1]$ is the parameter that controls the relative importance of the neighbourhood attraction. If $\alpha = 0$, D_{ij} is the squared Euclidean distance and we have the standard FCM. The spatial information S_{ij} depends on the feature attraction a_{jr} (pixel intensities) and the distance attraction d_{jr} (relative location of neighbouring pixels), and is defined as:

$$S_{ij} = \frac{\sum_{r=1}^{N_r} u_{ir} a_{jr} d_{jr}^{-1}}{\sum_{r=1}^{N_r} a_{jr} d_{jr}^{-1}} \;, \tag{9}$$

where N_r is the number of neighbours surrounding the element $\mathbf{x}_j$ in a square window Ω_j, and u_{ir} is the membership degree of the neighbouring element $\mathbf{x}_r$ to the cluster i. If we define the neighbourhood configuration Ω_j as an $n \times n$ square window with the central element $\mathbf{x}_j$, then $r = n^2 - 1$ and $\Omega_j = \{\mathbf{x}_r | r = 1, 2, ..., n^2 - 1\}$. Feature attraction a_{jr} is defined as the absolute intensity difference between $\mathbf{x}_j$ and its neighbour $\mathbf{x}_r$

$$a_{jr} = |\mathbf{x}_j - \mathbf{x}_r| \;. \tag{10}$$

The distance attraction d_{jr} is the squared Euclidean distance between the coordinates of elements $\mathbf{x}(p_j, q_j)$ and $\mathbf{x}(p_r, q_r)$

$$d_{jr} = (p_j - p_r)^2 + (q_j - q_r)^2 \;. \tag{11}$$

Secondly, after modifying the similarity measure, we calculate the membership values using Eq.(4). Then, we use the spatial neighbourhood information again to calculate the new spatially dependent membership values in the following way:

$$u_{ij}^* = \frac{u_{ij} M_{ij}^2}{\sum_{k=1}^{C} u_{kj} M_{kj}^2} \tag{12}$$

and

$$M_{ij} = \sum_{r=1}^{N_r} u_{ir} d_{jr}^{-1}, \tag{13}$$

where u_{ij}^* is the new spatially dependent membership value, C is the number of classes, N_r is the number of neighbours surrounding the element $\mathbf{x}_j$ and M_{ij} is the spatial membership function that represents the probability that element $\mathbf{x}_j$ belongs to the cluster i.

In both equations, Eq. (9) and Eq. (13), the reciprocal of the distance d_{jr}^{-1} is used because the neighbours $\mathbf{x}_r$ close to the central element $\mathbf{x}_j$ should more influence the result, while further neighbours should be less important.

The idea behind this new integration of spatial information in the FCM algorithm is as follows. Consider the local $n \times n$ neighbourhood where the central element $\mathbf{x}_j$ has large intensity differences with the closest neighbouring elements $\mathbf{x}_r$, which have similar intensities as the cluster center $\mathbf{v}_i$. After running the standard FCM algorithm, the neighbouring elements will be classified in a cluster i, while the central element will be in a different cluster. However, if we consider spatial information and calculate the neighbourhood attraction S_{ij}, which will be large in this case and the expression $(1 - \alpha S_{ij})$ will be small for $\alpha \neq 0$, the new spatially dependent similarity measure will be smaller than before. That means that after one iteration of the algorithm the central element $\mathbf{x}_j$ will be attracted to the neighbouring cluster i. Next, if we calculate the new spatial membership function M_{ij} and update the membership values, we will get that in a homogeneous regions the new membership values stay unchanged, while for a noisy pixel the new membership value is influenced by the labels of its neighbouring pixels. In our case, the central element $\mathbf{x}_j$ is then even stronger attracted to the cluster i. If the neighbourhood attraction S_{ij} and M_{ij} are continuously large till the end of the algorithm, the central element $\mathbf{x}_j$ will be forced to belong to the cluster i despite being dissimilar to it. Precisely, this property biases the algorithm towards homogeneous clustering.

The outline of the proposed algorithm is:

Step 1. Set the number of clusters C, degree of fuzziness m, stop criterion ϵ and neighbourhood size.

Step 2. Initialize the centres of the clusters $\mathbf{v}_i | i = 1, 2, ..., C$ and using FCM calculate u_{ij}.

Step 3. Calculate the spatially dependent similarity measure Eq. (8).

Step 4. Update u_{ij} using the new similarity measure Eq. (4).

Step 5. Calculate the new membership values u_{ij}^* using the spatial membership function Eq. (12).

Step 6. Update $\mathbf{v}_i$ using new membership values u_{ij}^* Eq. (5).

Repeat steps 3-6 until the stop criterion Eq.(6) is satisfied.

As with all clustering algorithms, the segmentation result may highly depend on the choice of parameter values used for initialization. Therefore, we use intensity-based thresholding [11] to reliably initialize the cluster centres.

3   Results

In this section, the experimental results of our algorithm to synthetic and real images are presented. For all experiments we set the weighting exponent $m = 2$, the stop criterion $\epsilon = 0.01$, the neighbourhood size 3×3 and the parameter that controls the effect of the neighbours $\alpha = 1$.

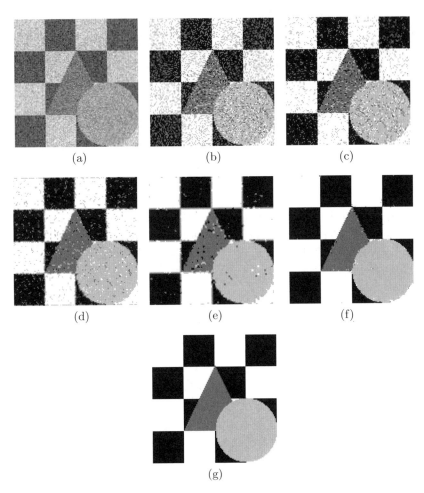

Fig. 2. Results comparison of the five segmentation methods on a synthetic image with four grey levels and three different shapes: (a) the image corrupted by zero mean Gaussian noise (SNR=12dB); (b) the FCM method [3]; (c) Shen *et al.* method [6]; (d) Ahmed *et al.* method [4]; (e) Xue *et al.* method [10]; (f) the segmentation result of our algorithm; (g) the "ground truth" - original synthetic image

To investigate the sensitivity of the proposed method to noise and to show the quantitative comparative results with other FCM-based methods [3, 4, 6, 10], we use the synthetic image (size 128×128) shown in Fig. 2g. It contains four-class pattern with three different shapes and is corrupted by zero mean Gaussian noise (Fig. 2a), where Signal-to-Noise Ratio (SNR) between the original and noisy image is 12dB.

As can be seen in Fig. 2b, the FCM algorithm [3] can not correctly classify four classes and is highly sensitive to outliers. The methods of Shen *et al.* [6] and Ahmed *et al.* [4], with results given in Fig. 2c and Fig. 2d respectively, although incorporating spatial information, are not sufficient enough to segment the image with very low SNR. The method from Xue *et al.* [10], which uses image filtering before and after the segmentation, also does not give satisfactory result and still contains artefacts and additional edge blurring (Fig. 2e). However, the result of our method Fig. 2f shows good performance and achieves the best segmentation result comparing with the "ground truth" image Fig. 2g.

In order to obtain a quantitative comparison, we plot the validation results of five methods for different noise levels in Fig. 3. The similarity index ρ, used for the comparison and quantitative evaluation, is the Dice coefficient:

$$\rho = \frac{2|A_i \cap B_i|}{|A_i| + |B_i|}, \tag{14}$$

where A_i and B_i denote the set of pixels labelled into i by the "ground truth" and our method respectively, and $|A_i|$ denotes the number of elements in A_i. In our experiment, the results for ρ are averaged over all four classes.

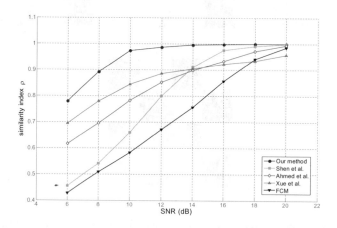

Fig. 3. Validation result for different noise levels. Comparison of FCM [3], Ahmed *et al.* [4], Xue *et al.* [10], Shen *et al.* [6] and our algorithm. From the graph, we can clearly see that our algorithm outperforms the standard FCM and popular spatial clustering variants, especially for the lower SNR.

From the Fig. 3 we can clearly see that our algorithm outperforms other FCM-based methods and acquires the best segmentation performance for all noise levels.

The performance of our algorithm is also demonstrated on four real images corrupted with noise: the cameraman, a house, a CT (Computer Tomography) image of the liver and an MRI (Magnetic Resonance Imege) of the brain. Segmentation results of the FCM and our algorithm are shown in the figure Fig. 4.

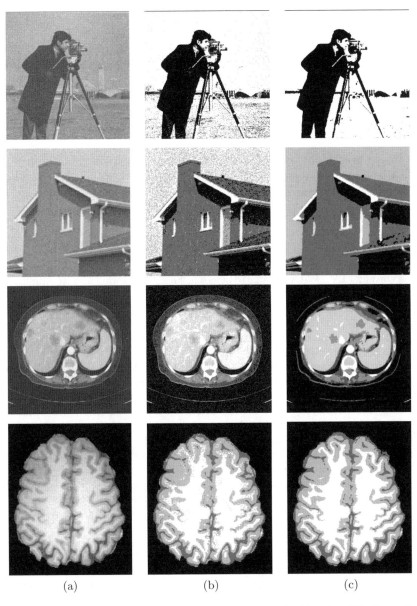

(a)   (b)   (c)

Fig. 4. Segmentation results on four real images corrupted with noise. The first column (a) shows noisy images, the second column (b) shows the results using FCM algorithm and the third column (c) shows the segmentation performance of our algorithm. The first two images, the cameraman and a house, are segmented in two and four labels respectively. Next, the CT image of the liver is segmented in five labels. Finally, the MRI of the brain, with a lesion on the upper-left side, is segmented in three labels. Comparing the second and third columns, it is clear that our method is effective and gives noise-free segmentation.

4   Conclusion

We have presented a new algorithm for unsupervised and automatic segmentation of images corrupted with noise. Our method is based on the FCM clustering approach, feature space and spatial contextual information of the neighbouring pixels in the image. The quantitative and qualitative experimental results for simulated and real images show that our method is very efficient and can effectively reduce the sensitivity of fuzzy segmentation algorithms to noise, without blurring the image. Also, it is good at resolving classification ambiguity for data in the overlapping region of two clusters. Our method could be useful in applications such as image texture segmentation, medical image segmentation and multispectral image segmentation, where spatial contextual information is important.

References

1. de Oliveira, J.V., Pedrycz, W.: Advances in Fuzzy Clustering and its Applications. John Wiley & Sons, Inc., New York (2007)
2. Pal, N., Pal, S.: A review on image segmentation techniques. Pattern Recognition 26, 1277–1294 (1993)
3. Bezdek, J.C.: Pattern Recognition with Fuzzy Objective Function Algorithms. Plenum Press, New York (1981)
4. Ahmed, M.N., Yamany, S.M., Mohamed, N., Farag, A.A., Moriaty, T.: A modified fuzzy c-means algorithm for bias field estimation and segmentation of MRI data. IEEE Trans. Med. Imag. 21, 193–199 (2002)
5. Zhang, D., Chen, C.: A novel kernelized fuzzy c-means algorithm with application in medical image segmentation. Artificial Inteligence in Medicine 32, 37–50 (2004)
6. Shen, S., Sandham, W., Granat, M., Sterr, A.: MRI fuzzy segmentation of brain tissue using neighborhood attraction with neural-network optimization. IEEE Trans. Inf. Technology in Biomedicine 9, 459–467 (2005)
7. Cai, W., Chen, S., Zang, D.: Fast and robust fuzzy c-means clustering algorithms incorporating local information for image segmentation. Pattern Recognition 40, 825–838 (2007)
8. Cao, A.Z., Song, Q.: Robust information clustering for automatic breast mass detection in digitized mammograms. Comput. Vision Image Understanding 109, 87–96 (2008)
9. Wang, Z.M., Soh, Y.C., Song, Q., Sim, K.: Adaptive spatial information-theoretic clustering for image segmentation. Pattern Recognition Letters 42, 2029–2044 (2009)
10. Xue, J.-H., Pižurica, A., Philips, W., Kerre, E., Van de Walle, R., Lemahieu, I.: An integrated method of adaptive enhancement for unsupervised segmentation of MRI brain images. Pattern Recognition Letters 24, 2549–2560 (2003)
11. Reddi, S.S., Rudin, S.F., Keshavan, H.R.: An optical multiple threshold scheme for image segmentation. IEEE Trans. System Man Cybernet. 14, 661–665 (1984)
12. Unnikrishnan, R., Pantofaru, C.E., Hebert, M.: Toward objective evaluation of image segmentation algorithms. IEEE Trans. Pattern Anal. Machine Intell. 29, 929–943 (2007)

High Definition Feature Map for GVF Snake by Using Harris Function

Andrea Kovacs[1] and Tamas Sziranyi[2]

[1] Pazmany Peter Catholic University
Prater 50/A, 1083, Budapest, Hungary
[2] Hungarian Academy of Sciences, Computer and Automation Research Institute
Distributed Events Analysis Research Group
Kende 13-17, 1111, Budapest, Hungary
{kovacs.andrea,sziranyi}@sztaki.hu

Abstract. In image segmentation the gradient vector flow snake model is widely used. For concave curvatures snake model has good convergence capabilities, but poor contrast or saddle corner points may result in a loss of contour. We have introduced a new external force component and an optimal initial border, approaching the final boundary as close as possible. We apply keypoints defined by corner functions and their corresponding scale to outline the envelope around the object. The Gradient Vector Flow (GVF) field is generated by the eigenvalues of Harris matrix and/or the scale of the feature point. The GVF field is featured by new functions characterizing the edginess and cornerness in one function. We have shown that the $max(0, log[max(\lambda_1, \lambda_2)])$ function fulfills the requirements for any active contour definitions in case of difficult shapes and background conditions. This new GVF field has several advantages: smooth transitions are robustly taken into account, while sharp corners and contour scragginess can be perfectly detected.

Keywords: Shape Analysis, Active-contour, Corner detection, Harris function.

1 Introduction

Snake models were introduced by [1] in 1988. Since then deformable models proved to be efficient tools in fitting contours nestling to objects' boundaries. This motion is controlled by internal and external forces; internal forces are responsible for the smooth and reasonable curves, while external forces represent the constraints of the original image data.

Another separate formula is the region based active contour model [2], which works efficiently even if there are only weak edges and can be solved in a level set framework. To avoid the drawbacks of the level set approach and to improve computational complexity, Fast Active Contour (FAC) was introduced in [3] as a new method similar to the geodesic active contour model.

The newest approach [4] uses Hidden Markov Model and Viterbi opitimization, results more robustness to noise, captures regions of very high curvature, and exhibits limited dependence on contour initialization or parameter settings.

J. Blanc-Talon et al. (Eds.): ACIVS 2010, Part I, LNCS 6474, pp. 163–172, 2010.

External forces are responsible for moving the model curve towards an optimum in the feature field. The external force is usually a type of edge information over the intensity distribution. However, the edge information itself is a poor description of local contours: in many cases noises and low contrast cause the loss of valid outline, resulting in muddled contour. Several methods try to exploit some new calculus of external forces to improve the efficiency of GVF snakes, like [5] with extended gradient vector flow, [6] by using dynamic directional gradient vector flow and [7] with vector field convolution, they are not sufficient enough in the featuring of very sharp corners along with smooth edges.

The weak definition of edges is coming from the next issues:

- weak contrast with unsettled edge-transition, perturbed by heavy noises;
- lack of coherent neighborhood: no local structure is found;
- scale of local features is not obvious: noises in small neighborhood cause similar responses as a well defined edge or corner from a distance;
- strong blobs, as e.g. faces, can be found better than their outlines;
- strong attraction centers, like noisy corner points inside the shape, are to be avoided by compressing dynamics in GVF.

To overcome these shortcomings, we have introduced the following feature definitions for generating the vector flow in the external force:

- Both edges and corners are to be detected by the same function;
- The starting contour is to be as close as possible to the object;
- Edges should fit the outline of the shape while sharp corners can be reached by the contour line without rounding off.

We propose the next solution for the above constraints:

- Edges and corners are detected by a meaningful function of Harris corner detector instead of edge detection: its response is quite good for edges, moreover it is very successful in detecting corner points as well. By this we can avoid the poor definition of smooth transition or saddle effects (multi-direction) of edges around corners;
- The starting contour is spanned from the most attractive corner points. The scale around the corner ensures that the initial contour is situated outside the object. The appropriate scale radius around the feature point can be detected by [8];
- We generate a balanced map of feature points emphasizing the corners while avoiding too strong attraction centrals. For this reason the dynamics of the Harris function must be compressed into a balanced distribution by keeping the necessary strength of the main attractors.

2   Main Steps of the Method

Our process first generates the main keypoints with scales, then they are enveloped to get the initialization. Harris function is used instead of edge functions as feature map for generating GVF snake.

2.1   Harris Corner Detector

The detector was introduced by Chris Harris and Mike Stephens in 1988 [9]. The algorithm is based on the principle that at corner points intensity values change largely in multiple directions. By considering a local window in the image and determining the average changes of image intensity result from shifting the window by a small amount in various directions, all the shifts will result in large change in case of a corner point. Thus corner can be detected by finding when the minimum change produced by any of shifts is large.

The method first computes the Harris matrix (M) for each pixel in the image. M is related to the convolution of first order derivatives' products and Gaussian window. Originally R corner response is defined based on the determinant and trace of the M matrix. This R charasteristic function is used to detect corners. R is large and positive in corner regions, and negative in edge regions.

$$R = Det(M) - k * Tr^2(M) \tag{1}$$

where Det and Tr denote the determinant and trace and k is a coefficient (usually arround 0.04).

In our case, when searching for both corners and edges, the eigenvalues can perform better. Denoting the eigenvalues of M by λ_1 and λ_2, the R_{eig}, R_{max}, R_{logmax}, R_{logmin}, $R_{sc*logmax}$ characteristic functions are as follows (log: natural logarithm):

$$R_{eig} = (\lambda_1 + 1)(\lambda_2 + 1) - 1 \tag{2}$$

$$R_{max} = max(\lambda_1, \lambda_2)$$

$$R_{logmax} = max(0, log[max(\lambda_1, \lambda_2)])$$

$$R_{logmin} = max(0, log[min(\lambda_1, \lambda_2)])$$

$$R_{sc*logmax} = (R_{scale} * max(0, log[max(\lambda_1, \lambda_2)])$$

Here R_{scale} is the scale parameter as defined in the next section. As we will see in the experimental part, nonzero eigenvalues together are good estimations for the cornerness, but we must keep the edge points as well. One of the λ_1 and λ_2 functions has high value in edge regions and both of them are high in corner regions. Therefore, a high eigenvalue can emphasize contours better and in a way is more suitable for detection of contours and corners together. By searching for local maxima of normalized $R_{...}$ functions, the keypoints can be found. These corner points serve as basis to calculate the starting contour. The number of found keypoints can be controlled by thresholding (like in the original Harris detector [9]).

Although $R_{min} = min(\lambda_1, \lambda_2)$ [10] was a good choice for corner detection, when our purpose is to detect both corners and edges, the $R_{max} = max(\lambda_1, \lambda_2)$ function may result in better contour detection function. However, both R_{min} and R_{max} have great dynamic ranges, so they need to be compressed to a balanced distribution. The natural logarithm (log) function proved to be appropriate to solve the interval compression by keeping the necessary strength of the main attractors.

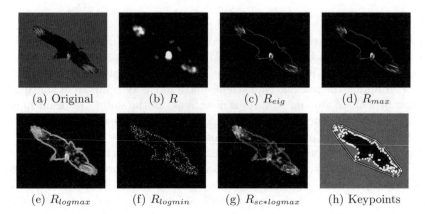

(a) Original   (b) R (c) R_{eig} (d) R_{max}

(e) R_{logmax} (f) R_{logmin} (g) $R_{sc*logmax}$ (h) Keypoints

Fig. 1. (a): the original image, (b)–(g): different characteristic functions illustrating Eq. 1 and Eq. 2, (h): result of the keypoint detection based on R_{logmax} function and the generated initial contour

Figure 1 shows the different characteristic functions generated for 1(a). Figure 1(b) is the generally used R (Eq. 1), the other pictures are the above-mentioned eigenvalue-related functions (Eq. 2). In each image, light regions shows the larger values, so keypoints can be detected in these areas. In Figure 1(c),...,1(g) the edge regions are also emphasized, so keypoints from these regions can also be found. Figure 1(h) shows the detection result based on the R_{logmax} characteristic function. Detected keypoints are in white, the boundary is the convex hull of the detected white keypoints, the calculation will be explained in Section 2.2.

$R_{sc*logmax}$ overemphasizes some keypoints in the inner part of the object (see Figure 1(g)) and results an unbalanced feature map. Our goal is to generate balanced map of feature points of both edges and thin corners, together with the suppression of too strong attraction centrals. Therefore we compared the two most promising candidates: $R_{logmin} = max(0, log(min(\lambda_1, \lambda_2)))$ and $R_{logmax} = max(0, log(max(\lambda_1, \lambda_2)))$. On Figure 2 the comparison of R_{logmin} and R_{logmax} values can be seen. The horizontal axis shows the values occurring in R_{logmin} function, the vertical axis shows the values occuring in R_{logmax} function. The brighter pixel, the more number of occurence of a value-pair. On this occurence map, pixels in the bottom-left corner has small eigenvalues (flat points). Therefore, edge points can be found on the left, narrow stripe of the picture. Heading along the main diagonal towards the upper right corner, corner points are situated. When counting R_{logmin}, both flat and edge points get small values. This causes the loss of edges in contour detection. When calculating R_{logmax}, edge and corner points also assign high values and by the smoothing effect of log the feature map becomes balanced. Figure 1(e) and 1(f) confirms the statistical demonstration, in the latter image many edge points are missing, which makes the further detection more difficult. While in case of R_{logmax} the edge of the eagle is emphasized equally.

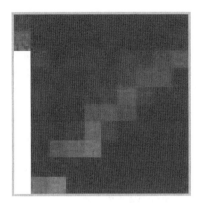

Fig. 2. Comparing R_{logmin} and R_{logmax} on Figure 1(a) ; horizontal axis: R_{logmin}, vertical axis: R_{logmax} values. While R_{logmin} gives equally approximately zero values for both flat points and edge points (left, narrow stripe), R_{logmax} function is able to emphasize both edge and corner points as well

According to this consideration we expect R_{logmax} to outperform R_{logmin}.

2.2 Scale Selection

Scale selection has become a main attribute of recent feature detection algorithms: for example when finding SIFT (Scale Invariant Feature Transform) keypoints [11] or extracting ridge curves are supported by finding the optimal scale over the local structure.

[12] introduces a heuristical principle stating that local extrema over scales of different combinations of normalized scale invariant derivatives are likely candidates to correspond to interesting structures. Therefore we can avoid the poor definition of smooth transition or saddle effects (multi-direction) of edges around corners by selecting optimal scale. This appropriate scale is proportional to the radius around the keypoint where relevant local structures should be detected.

In our case these scales are used in two, different ways.

First, they serve as basis to construct the R_{scale} map used in the last expression of Eq. 2. This R_{scale} component contributes to generation of $R_{sc*logmax}$ characteristic function.

Second, the scales are used to define the initial contour for the snake algorithm. The local area around the generated keypoints, with radius defined by the optimal scale should be considered as part of the region of interest. Points, representing the outline of the supported area, should be added to the Harris keypoint set. After this, the initial contour is defined as the convex hull of the extended set of keypoints. (See Figure 1(h), generated Harris keypoints are in white, initial scale based contour in black and white.)

2.3 Active Contour

Active contour (AC) [1] is used in computer vision especially for locating object boundaries. It is an energy minimizing algorithm, where the curve (also known as snake) is guided and influenced by different forces. These forces include external constraint forces (like the initial contour given by the user) and image forces (like the edges and ridges in the image, which moves the snake). The basic version had limited utility as the initialization should have been near the real contour of the object. Problems also occurred while detecting concave boundaries.

GVF (Gradient Vector Flow) was a new external force used for snakes [13]. It is computed as a diffusion of the gradient vectors of a gray-level or binary edge map derived from the image. The resultant field has a large capture range and forces active contours into concave regions.

In our work we used the active contour with GVF (called as GVF snake). The f edge map and E_{ext} external force of the original GVF snake ($\mathbf{v}(x,y) = (u(x,y), v(x,y))$ is the vector field that minimizes E_{ext}) [13]:

$$f(x,y) = |\nabla(G_\sigma(x,y) * I(x,y))| \tag{3}$$

$$E_{ext} = \int\int \mu(u_x^2 + u_y^2 + v_x^2 + v_y^2) + |\nabla f|^2 \, |\mathbf{v} - \nabla f|^2 \, dxdy \tag{4}$$

where μ is a regularization parameter (for further discussion see [13]), G_σ is Gaussian function with σ standard deviation and ∇ is the gradient operator.

Instead of calculating the original intensity-based edge map, we used the normalized, eigenvalue-based, scale-dependent Harris field as a feature map.

$$f_{R_{...}}(x,y) = |\nabla(G_\sigma(x,y) * R_{...}(x,y))| \tag{5}$$

where $R_{...}$ denotes any function from eq.1.

3 Experiments

Figure 3 shows the results of the contour detection. The GVF snake was tested with different feature maps, introduced in Section 2.1. Definition of the initial contour is explained in Section 2.2. (See Figure 1(h) for example.)

Figure 3(a) and Figure 3(b) uses the R_{eig} and R_{max} characteristic function respectively. The problem with these functions is that the points from corner regions have higher values, than points from edge regions. Thus, the snake sticks to high-valued cornerpoints on the wings and skips the real contour.

R_{logmin} on Figure 3(c) performs much better than the previous ones. As the log function balances the values, more parts of the wings are detected. In spite of the smoothness, this function also prefers corners to edges (see Sec. 2.1), so some regions of the peak of the wings are still missing.

R_{logmax} function, used in Figure 3(d), expected to be better (Sec. 2.1). It emphasizes edge and corner regions equally and the real contour can be found almost precisely.

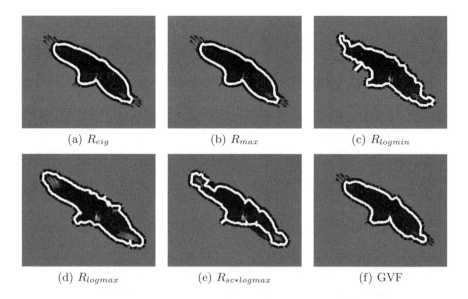

(a) R_{eig} (b) R_{max} (c) R_{logmin}

(d) R_{logmax} (e) $R_{sc*logmax}$ (f) GVF

Fig. 3. Contour detection with different feature maps

Figure 3(e) uses the $R_{sc*logmax}$ function. This is expected to emphasize some points, where important local structures can be found. The results shows that the accentuated points distorted the contour instead of specifying it in sharp regions (like the beak of the eagle).

Finally in Figure 3(f), the result of the original, intensity-based GVF detection can be seen. This also skips the end of the wings and performs similar to R_{eig} and R_{max}.

Spline weighting parameters are set to the optimal in every case, therefore the presented images reflect the most accurate result which could be achieved by each method.

On the whole, results of the experiments confirmed our expectation (Sec. 2.1), R_{logmax} performed the best. Therefore, we kept on testing this function on various images.

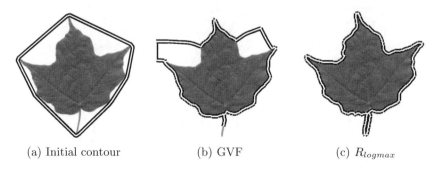

(a) Initial contour   (b) GVF   (c) R_{logmax}

Fig. 4. Leaf

Figure 4 shows that our method was able to detect the sharp peaks and stem of the leaf. (Initial contour on the left.) While the original, intensity-based GVF missed these peaks, the R_{logmax}-based method detected them accurately.

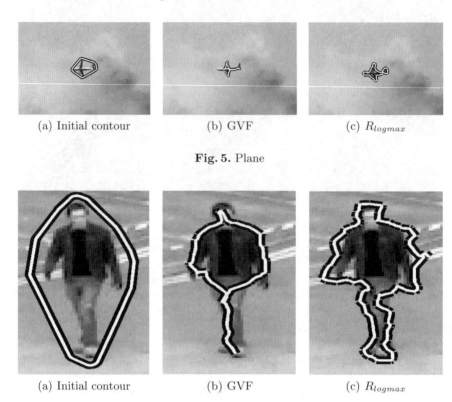

(a) Initial contour   (b) GVF   (c) R_{logmax}

Fig. 5. Plane

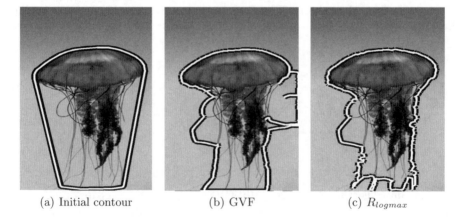

(a) Initial contour   (b) GVF   (c) R_{logmax}

Fig. 6. Pedestrian

(a) Initial contour   (b) GVF   (c) R_{logmax}

Fig. 7. Medusa

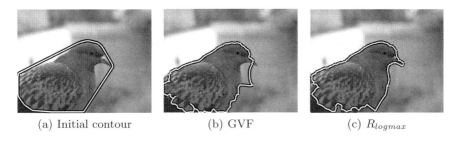

(a) Initial contour   (b) GVF   (c) R_{logmax}

Fig. 8. Image 'DSCF3583' from the Weizmann segmentation evaluation dataset

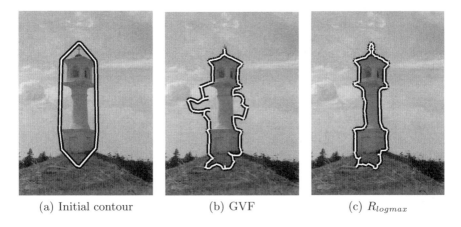

(a) Initial contour   (b) GVF   (c) R_{logmax}

Fig. 9. Image '112255696146' from the Weizmann segmentation evaluation dataset

Figure 5, 6 and 7 show the performance of active contour with original (GVF) and R_{logmax}-based feature map. (Initial contour on the left.)

Images from the Weizmann segmentation dataset [14] was also used for evaluation. Some of these results are represented in Figure 8 and 9. Our R_{logmax} based algorithm was able to converge to the real boundaries, including such small parts like the cross on the top of the pillar (Figure 9(c)) and the beak of the bird (Figure 8(c)), while the original GVF method missed them.

4   Conclusion

We have introduced a new external component for active contours instead of edge function. The main advantage of our method is the joint function of edginess and cornerness. We have found that the $max(0, log(max(L1, L2)))$ function fulfills the requirements: edges should fit the outline of the shape while sharp corners can be reached by the contour line without rounding off. We have also introduced the corner detection for generating a convex hull as starting contour around the shape by assigning scale estimation to the corners spanning the envelope.

Acknowledgements

This work was supported by the Hungarian Scientific Research Fund under grant number 80352.

References

1. Kass, M., Witkin, A.P., Terzopoulos, D.: Snakes: Active contour models. International Journal of Computer Vision 1(4), 321–331 (1988)
2. Chan, T.F., Vese, L.A.: Active contours without edges. IEEE Transactions on Image Processing 10(2), 266–277 (2001)
3. Bresson, X., Esedoglu, S., Vandergheynst, P., Thiran, J.P., Osher, S.: Fast global minimization of the active contour/snake model. Journal of Mathematical Imaging and Vision 28(2), 151–167 (2007)
4. Mishra, A.K., Fieguth, P.W., Clausi, D.A.: Decoupled active contour (dac) for boundary detection. IEEE Transactions on Pattern Analysis and Machine Intelligence 99 (preprints) (2010)
5. Chuang, C., Lie, W.: A downstream algorithm based on extended gradient vector flow field for object segmentation. IEEE Transactions on Image Processing 13, 1379–1392 (2004)
6. Cheng, J., Foo, S.: Dynamic directional gradient vector flow for snakes. IEEE Transactions on Image Processing 15, 1563–1571 (2006)
7. Li, B., Acton, T.: Active contour external force using vector field convolution for image segmentation. IEEE Transactions on Image Processing 16(8), 2096–2106 (2007)
8. Lindeberg, T.: Edge detection and ridge detection with automatic scale selection. International Journal of Computer Vision 30, 465–470 (1996)
9. Harris, C., Stephens, M.: A combined corner and edge detector. In: Proceedings of the 4th Alvey Vision Conference, pp. 147–151 (1988)
10. Shi, J., Tomasi, C.: Good features to track. In: Proceedings of the IEEE Conference on Computer Vision and Pattern Recognition, pp. 593–600 (1994)
11. Lowe, D.G.: Distinctive image features from scale-invariant keypoints. International Journal of Computer Vision 60, 91–110 (2004)
12. Lindeberg, T.: On scale selection for differential operators. In: Proceedings of the 8th Scandinavian Conference on Image Analysis, pp. 857–866 (1993)
13. Xu, C., Prince, J.L.: Gradient vector flow: A new external force for snakes. In: Proceedings of the IEEE Conference on Computer Vision and Pattern Recognition, pp. 66–71 (1997)
14. Alpert, S., Galun, M., Basri, R., Brandt, A.: Image segmentation by probabilistic bottom-up aggregation and cue integration. In: Proceedings of the IEEE Conference on Computer Vision and Pattern Recognition (June 2007)

Adaptive Constructive Polynomial Fitting

Francis Deboeverie, Kristof Teelen, Peter Veelaert, and Wilfried Philips

Ghent University - Image Processing and Interpretation/IBBT,
St-Pietersnieuwstraat 41, B9000 Ghent, Belgium
University College Ghent - Engineering Sciences,
Schoonmeersstraat 52, B9000 Ghent, Belgium
Francis.Deboeverie@telin.ugent.be, Kristof.Teelen@hogent.be,
Peter.Veelaert@hogent.be, Wilfried.Philips@telin.ugent.be

Abstract. To extract geometric primitives from edges, we use an incremental linear-time fitting algorithm, which is based on constructive polynomial fitting. In this work, we propose to determine the polynomial order by observing the regularity and the increase of the fitting cost. When using a fixed polynomial order under- or even overfitting could occur. Second, due to a fixed treshold on the fitting cost, arbitrary endpoints are detected for the segments, which are unsuitable as feature points. We propose to allow a variable segment thickness by detecting discontinuities and irregularities in the fitting cost. Our method is evaluated on the MPEG-7 core experiment CE-Shape-1 database part B [1]. In the experimental results, the edges are approximated closely by the polynomials of variable order. Furthermore, the polynomial segments have robust endpoints, which are suitable as feature points. When comparing adaptive constructive polynomial fitting (ACPF) to non-adaptive constructive polynomial fitting (NACPF), the average Hausdorff distance per segment decreases by 8.85% and the object recognition rate increases by 10.24%, while preserving simplicity and computational efficiency.

1 Introduction

Extraction of geometric primitives plays an important role in computer vision applications, such as object recognition and reconstruction, position estimation, image or curve segmentation. In this work we consider the segmentation of digitized curves into polynomial segments. Curve segmentation has been used for curve coding and representation, length and tangent estimation, and the location of feature points for shape matching.

In discrete geometry, a popular approach is to segment a curve into digital straight segments (DSS). A rather complicated linear time-algorithm for DSS segmentation was presented by Smeulders and Dorst [2]. Debled-Renesson and Réveillès [3] gave a simple, easy to implement algorithm. Buzer [4] developed an algorithm for the recognition of straight lines of arbitrary thickness, based on convex hulls. Other function-based representations are B-spline, nonuniform rational B-splines (NURBS) [5], rational Gaussian [6], radial basis function (RBF) [7] and implicit polynomials (IPs). Over time, several algorithms for fitting IPs were developed. A recent fitting algorithm is 3L [9,10],

J. Blanc-Talon et al. (Eds.): ACIVS 2010, Part I, LNCS 6474, pp. 173–184, 2010.

which solves a Least Squares problem. Another advanced algorithm [11,12] uses a topo-logical approach to obtain IPs. State-of-the-art fitting algorithms are Gradient-One [13], Min-Max [14], Min-Var [14], and Ridge-Regression [13].

Non-adaptive constructive polynomial fitting (NACPF) is a primitive extraction al-gorithm, which looks for subsets of points in an edge map that lie close to a polynomial function [15]. A geometric primitive is a curve or surface that can be characterized by an algebraic equation with a number of parameters. How well a subset corresponds to a primitive is measured by a uniform fitting cost, computed by a simple formula. We use a simple, linear-time algorithm for polynomial segmentation [15]. The method is based on the estimation of the fitting error, not the exact computation, and therefore also the segmentation will not always be exact. The amount of errors can be reduced, however, by increasing the number of computations, and for most applications the er-rors are acceptable. The problem statement in [15] was to find a subset of points in an edge map such that a polynomial function of fixed order can be fitted to the points of the subset with a fitting cost below an a-priori given threshold. This threshold defines a fixed polygonal segment thickness and segment endpoints with arbitrary location, un-suitable as feature points. Feature points are points of interest, which are used e.g. for correspondence problems and object recognition.

In this paper, we propose a technique for adaptive constructive polynomial fitting (ACPF), which allows variable polynomial order and variable segment thickness, pro-viding segment endpoints suitable as feature points. Variable orders for polynomial functions avoid under- and overfitting: straight edges are expected to be approximated by lines, while higher order polynomials are used for curved edges. In this work, the orders of polynomial functions are determined by observing the increase and the regu-larity of the fitting cost. A drawback of thresholding the fitting cost is a fixed segment thickness, which is often chosen too large. We propose to do edge segmentation based on the regularity of the fitting cost, providing a variable segment thickness. The end-points of the segments are stable and robust, giving rotational invariance.

The segmentation techniques are evaluated on the MPEG-7 core experiment CE-Shape-1 database part B [1] containing images of shapes with single closed contours. Part B of the MPEG-7 CE-Shape-1 database contains a total number of 1400 binary images with 70 different classes, each of which contains 20 images. A few examples

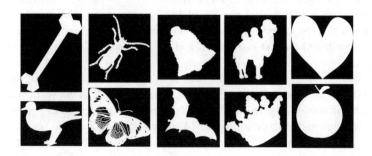

Fig. 1. Examples of the MPEG-7 core experiment CE-Shape-1 database part B [1]

are shown in Figure 1. The segmentation results presented for ACPF are promising. Edges with different smoothness are approximated by polynomials of expected order. Moreover, the endpoints of the segments correspond to corners in the edges, which are suitable as feature points.

When the parameters from ACPF are used as a lower bound for the parameters from NACPF, the segments with variable order and variable segment thickness from ACPF are on average 1.5 times longer than the segments with fixed order and fixed segment thickness from NACPF, while giving a better approximation. As a general measure, the average Hausdorff distance per segment decreases by 8.85%. When evaluating the MPEG-7 database, the endpoints for the segments from NACPF have an average Euclidean distance of 9.21 pixels, while the endpoints for the segments from ACPF have an average Euclidean distance of 0.45 pixels. ACPF is rotational invariant and delivers stable and robust endpoints, suitable as feature points.

The method is quantitatively assessed through the bull's-eye test applied to the MPEG7 CE-shape-1 database part B [1]. When using our shape matching technique for polynomial segments [16,17], the object recognition rate for ACPF increases by 10.24% compared to NACPF.

This paper is organized as follows. Section 2 describes NACPF. In section 2.1 we review the mathematical basis of the segmentation algorithm. In section 2.2, we discuss the problems that appear in NACPF, with fixed polynomial order and fixed segment thickness. In section 3, we propose ACPF, allowing variable polynomial order and variable segment thickness. Section 4 presents the segmentation results. Finally, we conclude our paper in section 5.

2   Non-adaptive Constructive Polynomial Fitting

2.1   Mathematical Formulation

We briefly review the basics of our fitting method [15], on which the region growing processes in this paper are based. The method is called constructive fitting because it allows us to construct global fits to an entire data set from so-called elemental fits to small parts of the data. The purpose of region growing and segmentation is to partition a curve or edge map into segments that satisfy a certain criterion, such as being straight or smooth. To find such segments, a typical region growing algorithm starts from a small seed segment, and then repeatedly tries to add new points to this segment, while verifying whether the segmentation criterion is still satisfied for the enlarged segment. If not, a new segment is started, or another point is chosen. In general, the verification of the segmentation criterion requires increasingly more computation time when the segment gets longer. This computation time can be reduced considerably by comparing the extension point with a small, but well-chosen set of reference points within the segment. Since the number of reference points is constant during the entire region growing process, the resulting algorithms have linear time complexity.

The edge map is derived from the Canny edge detector [18]. The Canny edge detector is suitable in this application, because it results in thin edges of one pixel thickness and it is less sensitive to noise. Connected curves are obtained from the edge map by a simple boundary scan algorithm.

Let $p_i = (x_i, y_i) \subset \mathbb{Z}^2$ be the points of a finite curve $C_k = \{p_0, \ldots, p_k\}$. Let G be a vector space of fitting functions, for instance, the vector space of polynomial functions of the form

$$g(x) = \alpha_0 + \alpha_1 x + \ldots + \alpha_n x^n. \tag{1}$$

To simplify the properties that follow, we impose the mild constraint that the current segment $C_m = \{p_0, \ldots, p_m\}$, which is part of C_k, contains at least $n + 1$ distinct points, $n + 1 \leq m \leq k$, where $n + 1$ denotes the dimension of the vector space of the fitting functions G or n denotes the polynomial order of the fitting functions. The uniform fitting cost of fitting $g(x)$ to the curve C_m is defined as

$$r_n(C_m) = \max_{(x_i, y_i) \in C_m} |g(x_i) - y_i|. \tag{2}$$

Note that this is also called the Chebyshev, minimax, or L_∞ fitting cost. The best fit is the function $g(x)$ in G for which $r_n(C_m)$ is minimal. We denote this minimal cost as $\hat{r}_n(C_m)$, and we call it the fitting cost over C_m. To be precise,

$$\hat{r}_n(C_m) = \min_{g \in G} r_n(C_m). \tag{3}$$

The first property of constructive fitting that we need is that the best fit and its fitting cost can be computed from fits to the so-called elemental subsets of C_m. These are subsets of the curve C_m that contain precisely $n + 2$ points and have a nontrivial fitting cost. The fitting cost over an elemental subset itself can be computed in a straightforward manner. To be precise, let $D = \{(x_1, y_1), \ldots, (x_{n+2}, y_{n+2})\}$ be an elemental subset of C_m. Let E_j denote the cofactor of the element at the intersection of the last column and the jth row of the augmented matrix:

$$(A_D | B_D) = \begin{pmatrix} 1 & x_1 & \ldots & x_1^n & y_1 \\ & \ldots & & & \\ 1 & x_{n+2} & \ldots & x_{n+2}^n & y_{n+2} \end{pmatrix} \tag{4}$$

Then one can show that the fitting cost of an elemental subset D can be computed by

$$\begin{aligned} \hat{r}_n(D) &= \frac{\det(A_D | B_D)}{(|E_1| + \ldots + |E_{n+2}|)} \\ &= \frac{(|E_1 y_1 + \ldots + E_{n+2} y_{n+2}|)}{(|E_1| + \ldots + |E_{n+2}|)}, \end{aligned} \tag{5}$$

provided the denominator is non-vanishing. Furthermore, one can prove that the fitting cost over C_m is the maximal value of the elemental fitting costs over all elemental subsets of the curve C_m.

$$\hat{r}_n(C_m) = \max_{D \in M} \hat{r}_n(D), \tag{6}$$

where M is the collection of all elemental subsets D of C_m for which $|E_1| + \ldots + |E_{n+2}| > 0$. We can obtain a reliable estimate of the fitting cost with far less computations than required for computing the fitting cost itself. The fitting cost of a data set can be estimated from the fitting costs of a few of its elemental subsets. Instead of calculating $\hat{r}_n(C_m)$, we compute

$$\tilde{r}_n(C_m) = \max_{D \in \tilde{M}} \hat{r}_n(D), \tag{7}$$

where $\tilde{M}$ forms a so-called rigid subcollection of elemental subsets of M. One can prove that $\tilde{r}_n(C_m) \leq \hat{r}_n(C_m) \leq \gamma \tilde{r}_n(C_m)$, for some value γ that only depends on the way in which the elemental subsets are chosen, not on the data points themselves [15].

The fitting parameters are only computed when needed explicity, after we have found a subset that satisfies our objectives with regard to the fitting cost. The fitting parameters of the best fit are equal to the fitting parameters of the elemental subset that has the largest fitting cost.

2.2   Shortcomings

We give an overview of the shortcomings in NACPF, with fixed polynomial order and fixed segment thickness.

First, the most important drawback of thresholding the fitting cost is the a-priori fixed segment thickness.

The edges are segmented in arbitrary locations. Instead, we prefer to find endpoints for segmentation at locations where the direction or the regularity of the edges changes. These changes in direction and regularity correspond to discontinuities in the fitting cost. Figure 2 (a) gives an example for a car image from the MPEG7 database. Figure $2(c)$ shows the first order polynomial fitting cost $\tilde{r}_1(C_m)$, when running through the edge from the red cross p_1 to the blue plus p_3, via the green circle p_2, as shown in Figure $2(b)$. A threshold on the fitting cost $T_r = 1$, incorrectly segments the edge in p_3, which corresponds to the blue dotted lines. Instead, we prefer a segmentation of the edge in p_2, which corresponds to the green dotted lines.

The second drawback of fitting polynomials with fixed order are under- and overfitting of edges.

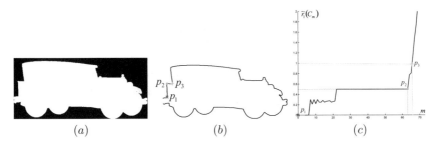

(a)   (b)   (c)

Fig. 2. (a) Image of a car from the MPEG-7 core experiment CE-Shape-1 database part B. (b) The edge obtained from the canny edge detector. Indication of run trough the edge from the red cross p_1 to the blue plus p_3, via the green circle p_2. (c) The first order polynomial fitting cost. The blue plus p_3 indicates the location of segementation after thresholding. The green circle p_2 indicates the prefered location of segmentation.

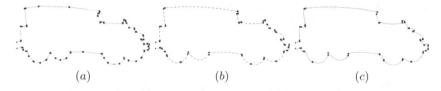

Fig. 3. Figure (a),(b) and (c) show the segmentation results for a threshold on the fitting cost $T_r = 1$, polynomial functions of orders $n = 1, 2, 3$ and represented with red dotted lines, green dashed lines and blue solid lines, respectively

First order polynomials underfit curved edges, while higher order polynomials overfit straight edges. Figure 3 (a),(b) and (c) show the segmentation results for a car image from the MPEG7 database for a threshold on the fitting cost $T_r = 1$, polynomial functions of orders $n = 1, 2, 3$ and represented with red dotted lines, green dashed lines and blue solid lines, respectively. The polynomial functions of order $n = 1$ underestimate the wheels of the car, while the polynomial functions of order $n = 3$ overestimate the straight edges from the back of the car.

In this work, we propose a solution for these problems by making the segmentation of the edges and the decision of polynomial order adaptive. We extend NACPF by allowing a variable polynomial order and segment thickness.

3   Adaptive Constructive Polynomial Fitting

We propose a constructive polynomial fitting algorithm extended with techniques to allow variable polynomial order and variable segment thickness.

The segmentation algorithm starts its run through the edge map in three consecutive points of the digitized curve, where the starting point is randomly chosen. We start looking for first order polynomial functions, so the initial parameter values are $n = 1$ and $C_2 = \{p_0, p_1, p_2\}$. When extending the curve C_m with a new point, $m = m + 1$, we evaluate the size and the regularity of the fitting cost, in order to make decisions about segmentation and polynomial order.

The segmentation is made dependent on the regularity of the fitting cost. More precisely, we segment edges in locations where the direction or the regularity of edges changes, which correspond to discontinuities in the fitting cost. To avoid detection of discontinuities in the fitting cost due to noise, we observe the running average of the fitting cost. The current running average $A_n^c(C_m)$ of the fitting cost is

$$A_n^c(C_m) = \sum_{i=1}^{u} \tilde{r}_n(C_{m-u+i})/u, \qquad (8)$$

where u is the window size of the running average, e.g. $u = 5$. To detect dicontinuities in the fitting cost, we also observe the future running average

$$A_n^f(C_m) = \sum_{i=1}^{v} \tilde{r}_n(C_{m+i})/v, \qquad (9)$$

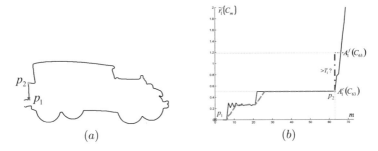

Fig. 4. Figure (a) indicates a run trough the edge from the red cross p_1 to the green circle p_2. Figure (b) shows the corresponding first order fitting cost $\tilde{r}_1(C_m)$. The magenta dashed line, the orange dotted line and the blue dashed-dottted line correspond to the current running average $A_1^c(C_m)$, the future running average $A_1^f(C_m)$ and the value I_1, respectively.

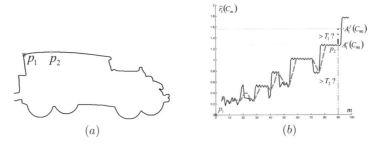

Fig. 5. Figure (a) indicates a run trough the edge from p_1 to p_2. Figure (b) shows the corresponding first order fitting cost $\tilde{r}_1(C_m)$. The same notations, markers and colors are used as in Figure 4. The value I_2 corresponds to the green dashed-double dotted line.

where v is the window size of the future running average, e.g. $v = 5$. Discontinuities in the fitting cost are detected in the evaluation of the value I_1, which we define as the difference in future running average $A_n^f(C_m)$ and current running average $A_n^c(C_m)$

$$I_1 = A_n^f(C_m) - A_n^c(C_m). \tag{10}$$

A new segment is found, if the value I_1 exceeds the threshold T_1, e.g. $T_1 = 0.6$. The process starts a new segment with the remaining points of the digitized curve for polynomial functions with order $n = 1$. Figure 4 (a) indicates a run trough the edge from the red cross to the green circle, for which the fitting cost $\tilde{r}_1(C_m)$ is plot in Figure 4 (b). The magenta dashed line, the orange dotted line and the blue dashed-dottted line correspond to the current running average $A_1^c(C_m)$, the future running average $A_1^f(C_m)$ and the value I_1, respectively.

The order of the polynomial function is determined by observing the value I_2, which is defined as the current running average $A_n^c(C_m)$,

$$I_2 = A_n^c(C_m). \tag{11}$$

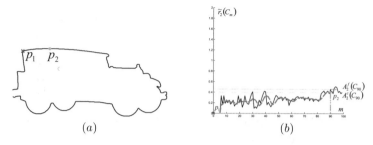

Fig. 6. Figure (a) indicates a run trough the edge from the red cross p_1 to the green circle p_2. Figure (b) shows the corresponding second order fitting cost $\tilde{r}_2(C_m)$. The same markers and colors are used as in Figure 5. The notations for the current running average and future running average are $A_2^c(C_m)$ and $A_2^f(C_m)$, respectively. The value I_2 is again within the limit of T_2.

If the value I_2 exceeds the threshold T_2, e.g. $T_2 = 1.3$, the order of the polynomial function is increased by one, $n = n + 1$. The order is increased until the value I_2 is again within the limit of the threshold T_2. The segmentation process continues with the remaining points of the digitized curve. Figure 5 (a) indicates a run trough the edge from the red cross p_1 to the green circle p_2, for which the fitting cost $\tilde{r}_1(C_m)$ is plot in Figure 5 (b). The green dashed-double dotted line corresponds to the value I_2. When the order is increased, as shown in Figure 6, the value I_2 is again within the limit of T_2.

For each extension of the segment C_m with a new point, we evaluate if I_1 and I_2 exceed T_1 and T_2, respectively. The first value is responsible for a segmentation of the edge, while the second value is responsible for an increase of the polynomial order.

4   Results

The segmentation techniques are evaluated on the MPEG-7 core experiment CE-Shape-1 database part B [1] containing images of shapes with single closed contours. Part B of the MPEG-7 CE-Shape-1 database contains a total number of 1400 binary images in 70 different classes, each of which contains 20 images. The recognition rate of an algorithm in the MPEG-7 database is commonly measured by the so called bull's eye test. Every shape in the database is compared to all other shapes, and the number of shapes from the same class among the 40 most similar shapes is reported. The bulls eye retrieval rate is the ratio of the total number of shapes from the same class to the highest possible number (which is 20 x 1400).

In ACPF, there are four parameters to optimize, namely the window sizes u and v for the current and future running average and the thresholds T_1 and T_2. The optimal parameters are found for the maximal object recognition rate R when evaluating the MPEG-7 database, using our shape matching technique for polynomial segments as in [16,17]. Our technique considers an integrated shape distance function for polynomial segments from two different objects under different viewing angles.

To find the optimal parameter subset, a sweep over all parameters values is conducted to locate the maximal R, as shown in Figure 7. The maximum object recognition rate

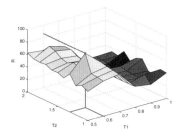

Fig. 7. Optimalization of the window sizes u and v of the current running average and the thresholds T_1 and T_2. The optimum for the maximum object recognition rate R is found, when evaluating the MPEG7 database.

$R = 86.80\%$. The optimal values for the parameters are $u = 5$, $v = 5$, $T_1 = 0.6$ and $T_2 = 1.3$.

We look at a few segmentation results for the MPEG-7 database. Figure 8 (a) shows the segmentation result for a car using ACPF. The red dotted lines and the green dashed lines correspond to first and second order polynomials, respectively. It is satisfying to see that the wheels are separately approximated by parabolas, while the edges at the back of the car are approximated by lines. The endpoints of the segments correspond to the corners in the edge and are suitable as feature points.

Values for the average fitting cost per edge point, the average order per edge point, the average length of the segments and the average Hausdorff distance per segment can be found in table 1. In order to compare, the parameter values for the average order

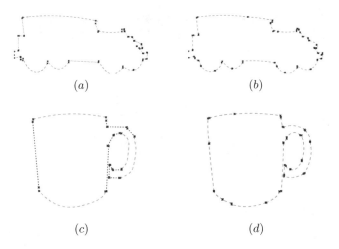

Fig. 8. Figure (a) shows the segmentation result for a car using ACPF. The red dotted lines and the green dashed lines correspond to first and second order polynomials, respectively. Figure (b) shows the segmention result for NACPF, when the ACPF serves as a lower bound. Figure (c) and (d) show the segmentation result for a cup using ACPF and NACPF, respectively.

Table 1. Values for the average fitting cost per edge point, the average order per edge point, the average length of the segments and the average Hausdorff distance per segment, when comparing ACPF to NACPF, for the car and the cup in Figure 8

	Car		Cup	
	ACPF	NACPF	ACPF	NACPF
Average fitting cost per edge point	1.25	1.25	1.16	1.16
Average order per edge point	1.84	2	1.76	2
Average length of the segments	53.54	39.42	90.44	52.23
Average Hausdorff distance per segment	2.36	2.92	3.58	3.83

per edge point and the average fitting cost per edge point from ACPF serve as a lower bound for the parameter values for NACPF, e.g. we take the fixed order equal to 2 and the threshold for the fitting cost equal to 1.25. The segmention result for NACPF is shown in Figure 8 (b). When evaluating the values from Table 1, we can conclude that ACPF gives longer segments, which are more accurate approximations to the edge map, when compared to NACPF. Similar results for a cup are shown in Figure 8 (c) and (d), when using ACPF and NACPF, respectively.

We prove rotational invariance by experiments in which we chose different random starting points for segmentation. For two different random starting points, we consider the distance between the corresponding endpoints of the segments. When evaluating the MPEG-7 database, the endpoints from the segments for NACPF have an average Euclidean distance of 9.21 pixels, while the endpoints from the segments for ACPF have an average Euclidean distance of 0.45 pixels. ACPF gives significantly more rotational

Fig. 9. The segmentation result for a realistic image when using ACPF. Red dotted lines, green dashed lines, blue solid lines and yellow dashed-dotted lines correspond to first, second, third and fourth order polynomials, respectively.

invariance than NACPF, which results in stable and robust endpoints, suitable as feature points.

As mentioned earlier, the maximum object recognition rate using ACPF for the MPEG-7 database is 86.80%. If ACPF serves as a lower bound for NACPF, experiments show that the recognition rate for ACPF is 10.24% higher than the recognition rate for NACPF. Moreover, the average Hausdorff distance for segments from ACPF is 8.85% lower than the average Hausdorff distance for segments from NACPF. Although it was not the main goal, our method performs comparable with or better than reported results in literature on the MPEG-7 database [19]. The highest score reported in literature is 93.32% [20].

The segmentation result for ACPF applied to a realistic image is shown in Figure 9. Red dotted lines, green dashed lines, blue solid lines and yellow dashed-dotted lines correspond to first, second, third and fourth order polynomials, respectively. We notice that the expected order is applied by our system for each type of curve in the image.

5   Conclusion

In this work, incremental linear-time fitting based on constructive polynomial fitting is extended with methods which provide a variable polynomial order and a variable segment thickness. The extensions give a solution for shortcomings such as under- and overfitting and arbitrary endpoints. We propose to determine polynomial orders by observing the regularity and the size of the fitting cost and to a achieve a variable segment thickness by detecting discontinuities and irregularities in the fitting cost. The methods are evaluated on the MPEG-7 core experiment CE-Shape-1 database part B. In the results, the expected polynomial order is applied by our system for each type of curve. Furthermore, the polynomial segments have endpoints suitable as feature points, due to rotational invariance. When comparing ACPF to NACPF, the average Hausdorff distance per segment decreases by 8.85% and the object recognition rate increases by 10.24%, while preserving simplicity and computational efficiency.

References

1. Jeannin, S., Bober, M.: Description of core experiments for mpeg-7 motion/shape, Technical Report ISO/IEC JTC 1/SC 29/WG 11 MPEG99/N2690 (1999)
2. Dorst, L., Smeulders, A.W.M.: Length estimators for digitized contours. Computer Vision, Graphics, and Image Processing 40(3), 311–333 (1987)
3. Debled-Rennesson, I., Reveills, J.-P.: A Linear Algorithm for Segmentation of Digital Curves. Int. J. of Pattern Recognition and Artificial Intelligence 9(4), 635–662 (1995)
4. Buzer, L.: An Incremental Linear Time Algorithm for Digital Line and Plane Recognition Using a Linear Incremental Feasibility Problem. In: Braquelaire, A., Lachaud, J.-O., Vialard, A. (eds.) DGCI 2002. LNCS, vol. 2301, pp. 372–381. Springer, Heidelberg (2002)
5. Piegl, L.: On NURBS: A Survey. IEEE Computer Graphics and Applications 11(1), 55–71 (1991)
6. Goshtasby, A.: Design and Recovery of 2D and 3D Shapes Using Rational Gaussian Curves and Surfaces. International Journal of Computer Vision 10(3), 233–256 (1993)

7. Turk, G., O'Brien, J.F.: Variational Implicit Surfaces. Technical Report GIT-GVU-99-15, Graphics, Visualization, and Usability Center, Georgia Technical Univ. (1999)
8. Taubin, G.: Estimation of Planar Curves, Surfaces and Nonplanar Space Curves Defined by Implicit Equations, with Applications to Edge and Range Image Segmentation. IEEE Trans. PAMI 13(11), 1115–1138 (1991)
9. Blane, M.M., Lei, Z., Civi, H., Cooper, D.B.: The 3L Algorithm for Fitting Implicit Polynomial Curves and Surfaces to Data. IEEE Trans. PAMI 22(3), 298–313 (2000)
10. Sahin, T., Unel, M.: Stable Algebraic Surfaces for 3D Object Representation. Journal of Mathematical Imaging and Vision 32(2), 127–137 (2008)
11. Keren, D., Gotsman, C.: Fitting Curves and Surfaces with Constrained Implicit Polynomials. IEEE Trans. PAMI 21(1), 31–41 (1999)
12. Keren, D.: Topologically Faithful Fitting of Simple Closed Curves. IEEE Trans. PAMI 26(1), 118–123 (2004)
13. Tasdizen, T., Tarel, J., Cooper, D.: Improving the Stability of Algebraic Curves for Applications. IEEE Trans. Image Processing 9(3), 405–416 (2000)
14. Helzer, A., Barzohar, M., Malah, D.: Stable Fitting of 2D Curves and 3d Surfaces by Implicit Polynomials. IEEE Trans. PAMI 26(10), 1283–1294 (2004)
15. Veelaert, P., Teelen, K.: Fast polynomial segmentation of digitized curves. In: Kuba, A., Nyúl, L.G., Palágyi, K. (eds.) DGCI 2006. LNCS, vol. 4245, pp. 482–493. Springer, Heidelberg (2006)
16. Deboeverie, F., Veelaert, P., Teelen, K., Philips, W.: Face Recognition Using Parabola Edge Map. In: Blanc-Talon, J., Bourennane, S., Philips, W., Popescu, D., Scheunders, P. (eds.) ACIVS 2008. LNCS, vol. 5259, pp. 994–1005. Springer, Heidelberg (2008)
17. Deboeverie, F., Teelen, K., Veelaert, P., Philips, W.: Vehicle tracking using geometric features. In: Blanc-Talon, J., Philips, W., Popescu, D., Scheunders, P. (eds.) ACIVS 2009. LNCS, vol. 5807, pp. 506–515. Springer, Heidelberg (2009)
18. Canny, J.F.: A computational approach to edge detection. IEEE Trans. PAMI, 679–698 (1986)
19. http://knight.cis.temple.edu/shape/MPEG7/results.html
20. Yang, X., Koknar-Tezel, S., Latecki, L.J.: Locally Constrained Diffusion Process on Locally Densified Distance Spaces with Applications to Shape Retrieval. In: CVPR, pp. 357–364 (2009)

Long-Range Inhibition in Reaction-Diffusion Algorithms Designed for Edge Detection and Stereo Disparity Detection

Atsushi Nomura[1], Makoto Ichikawa[2], Koichi Okada[3], and Hidetoshi Miike[4]

[1] Faculty of Education, Yamaguchi University, Japan
[2] Faculty of Letters, Chiba University, Japan
[3] Center for the Promotion of Higher Education, Yamaguchi University, Japan
[4] Graduate School of Science and Engineering, Yamaguchi University, Japan

Abstract. The present paper demonstrates the significance of long-range inhibition in reaction-diffusion algorithms designed for edge detection and stereo disparity detection. In early visual systems, the long-range inhibition plays an important role in brightness perception. The most famous illusory perception due to the long-range inhibition is the Mach bands effect, which is observed in a visual system of an animal and also in the human visual system. The long-range inhibition also appears in the computer vision algorithm utilising the difference of two Gaussian filters for edge detection. Upon evidence implying analogy between brightness perception and stereo depth perception, several psychologists have suggested that such the long-range inhibition works not only in the brightness perception, but also in the depth perception. We previously proposed biologically motivated reaction-diffusion algorithms designed for edge detection and stereo disparity detection. Thus, we show that the long-range inhibition also plays an important role in both of the reaction-diffusion algorithms through experimental study. Results of the study provide a new idea of improving performance of the reaction-diffusion stereo algorithm.

1 Introduction

Long-range inhibition plays an important role in pattern recognition processes of visual systems. Mach had firstly found an interesting effect for a step-wise brightness change in brightness perception [1]. The human visual system perceives brighter or darker bands than physical brightness at the step-wise change of brightness. The effect is now called Mach bands and the effect is caused by the lateral inhibition. Lateral eyes of *Limulus*, which is a kind of crab, also perceive the Mach bands for a step-wise brightness change. The effect for the animal is found in physiological experiments by Hartline et al., who also presented a mathematical model [2]. Then, their mathematical model modified by Barlow and Quarles is found to be completely consistent with physiological experimental results [3]. The important point of the modified model is the long-range inhibition. When signals propagating from discretely spaced ommatidium

J. Blanc-Talon et al. (Eds.): ACIVS 2010, Part I, LNCS 6474, pp. 185–196, 2010.

(individual elements organising lateral eyes) are summed, it is found that inhibitory interactions among widely distributing ommatidium are important.

The human visual system perceives interesting illusory effects for specific image stimuli, in addition to the Mach bands effect. Typical examples of illusory effects are the Hermann grid illusion, the Chevreul illusion and the Craik-O'Brien-Cornsweet illusion. All of these illusions, which are categorised into the contrast effect in brightness perception, are explained with the lateral inhibition.

Several illusory effects for brightness perception appear also in stereo depth perception. Anstis and Howard found the Craik-O'Brien-Cornsweet illusion also in stereo depth perception; the illusion was originally found in brightness perception [4]. Brookes and Stevens presented several examples of random-dot stereogram, of which some cause illusory depth perception [5], and discussed the analogy between brightness perception and stereo depth perception on the human visual system. As well as they showed evidence of the analogy, they suggested that the lateral inhibition exists in the stereo depth perception of the human visual system.

Reaction-diffusion systems describe pattern formation processes in several biological systems. Turing proposed a scenario in order to understand biological pattern formation processes [6]. He showed that stationary patterns self-organised in biological systems are due to the rapid inhibitory diffusion in comparison to the excitatory diffusion. After that, Gierer and Meinhardt, who were approaching the biological pattern formation problem from a realistic point of view, proposed more realistic models of equations in the framework of reaction-diffusion systems [7]. They also imposed the rapid inhibitory diffusion on the models, as proposed by Turing. More recently, much evidence supporting the Turing scenario has been found in biological systems [8,9].

A light-sensitive chemical reaction system, which is known as one of reaction-diffusion systems, detects edges from an image intensity distribution [10]. An excitatory diffusion in the reaction-diffusion system causes a chemical wave, which initially indicates an edge position for the distribution. Thus, the position of the chemical wave indicates an edge position. However, the diffusion also drives propagation of the chemical wave. Thus, although the system can indeed detect edges, those detected edges propagate spatially and finally disappear after certain duration of time. Since the excitatory diffusion constant is almost same as the inhibitory one in the chemical reaction system, we can not expect stationary patterns of edge detection results.

If we turn our attention to the computer vision research, we can find initial work done by Marr and his co-workers for modelling the human visual system. Marr and Hildreth proposed an edge detection algorithm with two versions [11]. One of the versions utilises the difference of two Gaussian filters: excitatory and inhibitory Gaussian filters. The inhibitory Gaussian filter spatially spreads more than the excitatory one. A Gaussian filter is a solution of a diffusion equation and the spatial spread of the Gaussian filter depends on its diffusion coefficient [12]. Thus, a pair of the two Gaussian filters is equivalent to a pair of two diffusion equations having slow excitatory diffusion and rapid inhibitory diffusion, or long-range inhibition in comparison to short-range excitation.

For the stereo depth perception, Marr and Poggio presented an algorithm that detects a stereo disparity map from random-dot stereogram [13]. Their algorithm consists of multi-layered networks; each network governs areas of its corresponding disparity level and each grid point simulates a cell response. When a grid point at a disparity level is in an excited state, the algorithm judges the point to have the corresponding disparity level. They imposed two constraints: continuity and uniqueness on a disparity map; mutual exclusive connections among the multi-layered networks realises the uniqueness constraint and a spatial summation of signals from neighbouring cells realises the smoothness constraint. The uniqueness constraint states that a particular grid point has only one disparity level. Thus, at each grid point an excitation process must be inhibited mutually among the networks. On the one hand, the continuity constraint propagates the excited state into neighbouring areas and works as a filling-in process into undefined areas of a disparity level; on the other hand, the uniqueness constraint guarantees the uniqueness of a disparity level at each grid point against the filling-in process.

Algorithms of edge detection and stereo disparity detection have been extensively developed. Many researchers have proposed edge detection algorithms with anisotropic diffusion [14] and for detecting multi-scale edges [15]. The co-operative stereo algorithm has been also developed to incorporate edge information [16] and to detect occlusion areas [17]. However, there is little study on discussing both edge detection and stereo disparity detection in a unified framework employing a biologically motivated model of equations.

We have previously proposed reaction-diffusion algorithms for edge detection [18] and stereo disparity detection [19]. Those algorithms utilise the FitzHugh-Nagumo reaction-diffusion equations [20,21], on which we imposed the long-range inhibition. In contrast to the experimental results reported by Kuhnert et al., the reaction-diffusion algorithm for edge detection provides stationary results of detected edges. The reaction-diffusion algorithm for stereo disparity detection utilises multi-layered reaction-diffusion networks being similar to the cooperative algorithm proposed by Marr and Poggio. However, each network has the long-range range inhibition, which improves performance of the stereo disparity detection, in contrast to the algorithm not having the long-range inhibition.

Although previous studies done by other researchers have focused on the long-range inhibition in brightness perception, little study in particular in the computer vision research does not pay attention to the long-range inhibition in stereo depth perception. We believe that the long-range inhibition plays an important role in most of visual functions. Thus, our final objective is to propose models of visual functions by taking account of the long-range inhibition and to show how much the long-range inhibition improves the performance of each visual function in comparison to the short-range inhibition.

This paper demonstrates the significance of the long-range inhibition in reaction-diffusion algorithms through experimental study. In particular, we confirm the effect of the long-range inhibition in stereo disparity detection, by varying the inhibitory diffusion coefficient and also by comparing the reaction-diffusion stereo algorithm with the cooperative stereo algorithm revised with a reaction-diffusion equation. Main results obtained in the experimental study is that the long-range inhibition is necessary to obtain static results of edge detection and is necessary to obtain precise structure in a stereo disparity map.

The FitzHugh-Nagumo reaction-diffusion equations simulate a non-linear reaction of excitation and inhibition for an external stimuli and propagating pulses of excitation. On the one hand, the reaction-diffusion equations describe microscopic phenomena for external stimuli; on the other hand, psychological experimental results show macroscopic phenomena for visual stimuli. We would like to contribute towards describing and building macroscopic models of visual functions with reaction-diffusion equations describing microscopic biological behaviour of excitation and inhibition. It would be interesting, if we can predict unknown illusory effects of the human visual system and suggest mechanisms inducing the effects upon the reaction-diffusion algorithms.

2   Reaction-Diffusion Algorithms

2.1   Reaction-Diffusion System

A pair of reaction-diffusion equations with two variables $u(x, y, t)$ and $v(x, y, t)$ defined in a two-dimensional space (x, y) and time t consists of

$$\partial_t u = D_u \nabla^2 u + f(u, v), \quad \partial_t v = D_v \nabla^2 v + g(u, v), \tag{1}$$

where D_u and D_v are diffusion coefficients, $\partial_t = \partial/\partial t$, $\nabla^2 = \partial^2/\partial x^2 + \partial^2/\partial y^2$ is the Laplacian operator and $f(u, v)$ and $g(u, v)$ are reaction terms. For modelling a pulse propagation process observed along a nerve axon, FitzHugh [20] and Nagumo et al. [21] proposed a pair of reaction-diffusion equations with the following reaction terms:

$$f(u, v) = [u(u - a)(1 - u) - v]/\varepsilon, \quad g(u, v) = u - bv, \tag{2}$$

where a and b are positive constants and ε is a positive small constant ($0 < \varepsilon \ll 1$). The pair of the FitzHugh-Nagumo reaction-diffusion equations refers to Eq. (1) with Eq. (2).

Let us consider the ordinary differential equations derived from Eqs. (1) and (2) under no-spatial coupling $D_u = D_v = 0$, as follows:

$$du/dt = f(u, v) = [u(u - a)(1 - u) - v]/\varepsilon, \quad dv/dt = g(u, v) = u - bv. \tag{3}$$

The pair of Eq. (3) has steady states satisfying $du/dt = 0$ and $dv/dt = 0$, depending on the parameter values a and b. Figure 1 shows two different types of phase plots, one of which has a steady state denoted by A and the other of

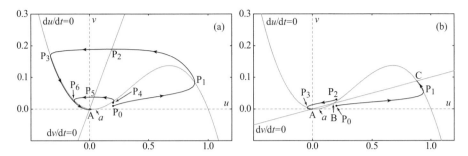

Fig. 1. Phase plots of the FitzHugh-Nagumo equations $du/dt = f(u,v)$ and $dv/dt = g(u,v)$ [see Eq. (3)]. The horizontal axis denotes u and the vertical axis denotes v. The solid grey lines denote $du/dt = 0$ and $dv/dt = 0$. Parameter settings are $a = 0.05$, $\varepsilon = 10^{-2}$ and $b = 1.0$ in (a) and $b = 10.0$ in (b). The steady states denoted by A and C are stable and that denoted by B is unstable. In the uni-stable system (a), a solution starting from the point P_0 traces the trajectory $P_0 \to P_1 \to P_2 \to P_3 \to A$ and a solution starting from the point P_4 traces the trajectory $P_4 \to P_5 \to P_6 \to A$. In the bi-stable system (b), a solution starting from the point P_0 traces the trajectory $P_0 \to P_1 \to C$ and that from the point P_2 traces the trajectory $P_2 \to P_3 \to A$.

which has three steady states denoted by A, B and C. By utilising the linear stability analysis, we can understand that the points A and C are stable and the point B is unstable. Thus, any solution (u,v) converges at the point A or C. The uni-stable system refers to the pair with one stable steady state, as shown in Fig. 1(a); the bi-stable system refers to the pair with two stable steady states, as shown in Fig. 1(b). In the uni-stable system of Fig. 1(a), on the one hand, a solution starting from a point P_0 traces the global trajectory denoted by $P_0 \to P_1 \to P_2 \to P_3 \to A$, according to signs of temporal derivatives $du/dt > 0, dv/dt > 0$ in $P_0 \to P_1$, $du/dt < 0, dv/dt > 0$ in $P_1 \to P_2$, $du/dt < 0, dv/dt < 0$ in $P_2 \to P_3$ and $du/dt > 0, dv/dt < 0$ in $P_3 \to A$. On the other hand, in the same uni-stable system, a solution starting from a point P_4 traces the local trajectory denoted by $P_4 \to P_5 \to P_6 \to A$. We can understand that a small difference in v causes quite different trajectories and the increasing variable v inhibits the variable u from tracing the global trajectory. Thus, the variable v is an inhibitor variable and the variable u is an activator variable. The state located at around the point P_1 is an excited state and the state located at around the point A is a resting state. In the bi-stable system of Fig. 1(b), we can also understand that the variable v inhibits the variable u from increasing.

In order to understand how the parameter a of Eq. (3) works in a trajectory of a solution (u,v), we focus on the stable steady state A and its surroundings in the phase plots shown in Fig. 1. When we externally stimulate a solution located at the state A $(u = 0, v = 0)$ by adding $\delta u > a$ to $u = 0$, we can observe that the solution traces the global trajectory. In comparison, when we utilise $\delta u < a$ in the stimulation, the solution directory returns to the state A. Thus, the parameter a works as a threshold level for an external stimulus to the system.

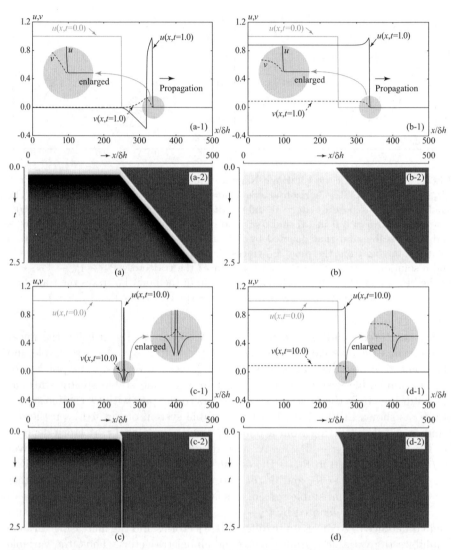

Fig. 2. One-dimensional numerical results obtained for the FitzHugh-Nagumo reaction-diffusion Eqs. (1) and (2) with (a) $D_v/D_u = 0.0$ and $b = 1.0$, (b) $D_v/D_u = 0.0$ and $b = 10.0$, (c) $D_v/D_u = 3.0$ and $b = 1.0$ and (d) $D_v/D_u = 3.0$ and $b = 10.0$. The system is uni-stable in (a) and (c) and bi-stable in (b) and (d). Figures (a-1), (b-1), (c-1) and (d-1) show one-dimensional distributions of $u(x, t = 0.0)$ denoted by grey solid lines, $u(x, t = 1.0)$ denoted by solid black lines and $v(x, t = 1.0)$ denoted by broken lines. Figures (a-2), (b-2), (c-2) and (d-2) show spatiotemporal distributions of $u(x, t)$. The initial condition $u(x, t = 0.0)$ provided for the equations is a step function having 1.0 in the left half of the space and 0.0 in the right half, and the initial condition $v(x, t = 0.0)$ is zero for any position in the space. Other parameter settings are as follows: $D_u = 1.0, a = 0.05, \varepsilon = 1.0 \times 10^{-3}, \delta h = 0.2, \delta t = 1.0 \times 10^{-4}$. Grey circular areas in (a-1), (b-1), (c-1) and (d-1) are enlarged.

The reaction-diffusion equations describe diffusely coupled reaction systems, as described in Eq. (1). The FitzHugh-Nagumo reaction-diffusion equations have two variables: the activator variable u and the inhibitor variable v. Thus, in the pair of Eqs. (1) and (2) the activator and the inhibitor diffuse with their diffusion coefficients D_u and D_v. If D_v is larger than D_u, the inhibitor v diffuses rapidly more than the activator u. Thus, when the ratio D_v/D_u is larger than 1.0, the system exhibits the long-range inhibition due to large D_v, in comparison to the short-range excitation due to small D_u.

When numerically solving the FitzHugh-Nagumo reaction-diffusion equations in a one-dimensional space x, we can observe that the equations self-organise a pulse or an interface, as shown in Fig. 2. Figures 2(a) and 2(b) show a pulse or an interface propagating in the space. These two cases of a propagating pulse and a propagating interface are due to the ratio $D_v/D_u = 0.0$. If we consider the long-range inhibition of $D_v/D_u = 3.0$ for a discretely spaced system of the FitzHugh-Nagumo equations with a finite difference δh in space, we can observe a static pulse or a static interface remaining at around the edge of the step function provided as the initial condition of u [18]. Figures 2(c) and 2(d) show numerical results in the case of the long-range inhibition. Let us focus on the areas denoted by grey circles in the one-dimensional distributions of $u(x, t = 1.0)$ and $v(x, t = 1.0)$ shown in Figs. 2(a-1), 2(b-1), 2(c-1) and 2(d-1). In the case of $D_v/D_u = 0.0$ of Figs. 2(a-1) and 2(b-1), since the inhibitor variable v is almost zero in front of the pulse or the interface, the pulse or the interface can propagate. In comparison with the situations observed in $D_v/D_u = 0.0$, in the case of the long-range inhibition $D_v/D_u = 3.0$ of Figs. 2(c-1) and 2(d-1), since the inhibitor variable v has some positive values in front of the pulse or the interface, it prevents the system from entering the excited state and prevents the pulse and the interface from propagating. Therefore, when the inhibitor variable v diffuses rapidly more than the activator variable u, the pulse or the interface remains at around its initial position.

2.2   Edge Detection

As shown in Fig. 2(c), a discretely spaced uni-stable system of the FitzHugh-Nagumo reaction-diffusion Eqs. (1) and (2) detects edges from an initially provided distribution of $u(x, y, t = 0.0)$. The parameter value a works as a threshold level for the initial distribution. Areas larger than the threshold level a firstly enter the excited state and then the inside of the areas returns to the resting state along the global trajectory; areas smaller than a directly return to the resting state along the local trajectory [see Fig. 1(a)]. In the processes tracing the global trajectory and the local one, a pulse located at the edge position survives. Thus, by providing an image intensity distribution $I(x, y)$ for the initial distribution $u(x, y, t = 0.0)$, that is, by setting the initial condition as $u(x, y, t = 0.0) = I(x, y)$, we obtain pulses at edge positions dividing the distribution into brighter or darker areas with the threshold level a [18]. By searching $u(x, y, t)$ for the pulses, we can perform edge detection for the image intensity distribution $I(x, y)$. In the reaction-diffusion algorithm designed for edge detection, the long-range inhibition plays an important role to obtain static pulses indicating edge positions. If we have short-range inhibition $D_v/D_u < 1.0$, the reaction-diffusion system does not organise static pulses, but organise propagating pulses or does not organise any pulse.

2.3   Stereo Disparity Detection

A stereo vision system projects a point in a three-dimensional space onto image planes of left and right eyes or cameras. A difference between the corresponding positions on the image planes refers to a stereo disparity, which provides the depth of the point. Thus, stereo disparity detection requires finding one-to-one correspondence. A simple way for obtaining the correspondence is to compute cross-correlation or similarity measure between the stereo images. Several approaches for the stereo disparity detection compute an initial estimate of a stereo disparity map, according to a similarity measure, and then update the disparity map recursively or iteratively so that the disparity map satisfies conditions such as continuity and uniqueness. The cooperative algorithm [13] consists of multiple networks, each of which represents existence or non-existence of its corresponding disparity level at a particular grid point. Let N be the number of possible disparity levels, let d_n be a disparity level ($n \in \{0, 1, \cdots, N-1\}$) and let $C_n(x, y)$ be a similarity measure computed at the position (x, y) and at the disparity level d_n. Then, the original cooperative algorithm can be revised with multiple reaction-diffusion systems, as follows [22]:

$$\partial_t u_n = D_u \nabla^2 u_n + u_n \{u_n - a(u_0, u_1, \cdots, u_{N-1})\}(1 - u_n)/\varepsilon + \mu C_n(x, y). \quad (4)$$

The function $a(u_0, u_1, \cdots, u_{N-1})$ realises the uniqueness constraint with

$$a(u_0, u_1, \cdots, u_{N-1}) = a_0 + \frac{\max_{n'} u_{n'}}{2} \left[1 + \tanh \left(\left| d_n - \arg\max_{n'} u_{n'} \right| - a_1 \right) \right], \quad (5)$$

where a_0 and a_1 are constants and the operators: max and argmax are performed in an inhibition area [17] for (x, y) and d_n. Equation (4) realises a filling-in process into undefined areas of disparity with the diffusion term $D_u \nabla^2 u_n$, where D_u controls the speed of the filling-in process. After sufficient duration of time, the following equation provides a stereo disparity map $M(x, y, t)$.

$$M(x, y, t) = d_n, \quad n = \arg\max_{n \in \{0, 1, \cdots, N-1\}} u_n(x, y, t). \quad (6)$$

We previously proposed a stereo algorithm by utilising multiple systems of the FitzHugh-Nagumo reaction-diffusion equations [19], as follows:

$$\partial_t u_n = D_u \nabla^2 u_n + [u_n \{u_n - a(u_0, u_1, \cdots, u_{N-1})\}(1 - u_n) - v_n]/\varepsilon + \mu C_n(x, y),$$
$$\partial_t v_n = D_v \nabla^2 v_n + u_n - b v_n, \quad (7)$$

where the function $a(u_0, u_1, \cdots, u_{N-1})$ is the same as Eq. (5) and Eq. (6) provides a stereo disparity map. The algorithm with Eq. (7) is an extended version of the cooperative algorithm; it has the inhibitor variable v_n and its inhibitory diffusion $D_v \nabla^2 v_n$, which prevents the area of the disparity level d_n from extending.

3   Experimental Results

In order to confirm the significance of the long-range inhibition, we performed edge detection and stereo disparity detection with different values of the inhibitory diffusion coefficient D_v. Table 1 shows parameter settings utilised in the present experiments. We have constraints on some of the parameters, as follows. The finite difference δt in time t must be quite smaller than the finite difference δh in space (x, y) for stable numerical computation of reaction-diffusion equations; a and a_0 must be in the range of $(0, 0.5)$; b is fixed at 1.0 for edge detection and at 10 for stereo disparity detection; and ε must be quite small $(0 < \varepsilon \ll 1.0)$ to trace trajectories shown in Fig. 1. Upon the constraints, we roughly adjusted the parameter values for presentation of Figs. 3 and 4.

First, we report results on the edge detection algorithm consisting of the reaction-diffusion Eqs. (1) and (2), as shown in Fig. 3. Figure 3(b) shows $u(x, y, t)$ obtained by the algorithm with $D_v/D_u = 0.0$ from an initial condition of the image shown in Fig. 3(a). As shown in Fig. 3(b-2), the algorithm extracted edges from the initial image; however, the edges propagated like waves and spiral waves were organised [Fig. 3(b-3)]. Thus, the edges extracted with the short-range inhibition were transient. Figure 3(c) shows $u(x, y, t)$ obtained by the same algorithm with the long-range inhibition $(D_v/D_u = 5.0)$. Edges extracted with the long-range inhibition remained at their initial positions; the edges did not propagate. These two results show that the long-range inhibition plays an important role in the edge detection with the reaction-diffusion equations.

Next, we report results of stereo disparity detection with the cooperative algorithm and the reaction-diffusion stereo algorithm. The cooperative algorithm revised with a reaction-diffusion equation consists of Eqs. (4), (5) and (6) and the reaction-diffusion stereo algorithm consists of Eqs. (5), (6) and (7). We applied these two stereo algorithms to a stereo image pair [24]. Figure 4 shows the results of stereo disparity maps and error dependence on the inhibitory diffusion coefficient D_v. Focusing on the stereo disparity maps, we can confirm that the reaction-diffusion stereo algorithm can detect small parts of stereo disparity maps. For example, by comparing small parts indicated by circles in Figs. 4(b) and 4(c), we can confirm that the small parts survived in the result of the reaction-diffusion algorithm with the long-range inhibition. However, the small

Table 1. Parameter settings utilised in the experiments of edge detection and stereo disparity detection. Reaction-diffusion equations of Eqs. (1), (4) and (7) were discretely expressed with finite differences δh in space (x, y) and δt in time t. We fixed the diffusion coefficient of the activator at $D_u = 1.0$.

Figure	Finite differences	Parameter settings
Fig. 3(b)	$\delta h = 0.2, \delta t = 1.0 \times 10^{-4}$	$D_v = 0.0, a = 0.05, b = 1.0, \varepsilon = 1.0 \times 10^{-2}$
Fig. 3(c)	$\delta h = 0.5, \delta t = 1.0 \times 10^{-4}$	$D_v = 5.0, a = 0.20, b = 1.0, \varepsilon = 1.0 \times 10^{-2}$
Fig. 4	$\delta h = 0.2, \delta t = 1.0 \times 10^{-2}$	$D_v = 3.0, a_0 = 0.13, a_1 = 1.5, b = 10$
		$\varepsilon = 1.0 \times 10^{-2}, \mu = 3.0$

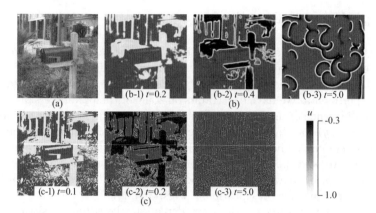

Fig. 3. Two dimensional results obtained with Eqs. (1) and (2). (a) The test image provided on the website http://marathon.csee.usf.edu/edge/edge_detection.html for performance evaluation of edge detection algorithms [23]. The image size is 512×512 (pixels). Spatial distributions of $u(x, y, t)$ obtained with (b) $D_v/D_u = 0.0$ at $t = 0.2, 0.4, 5.0$ and (c) $D_v/D_u = 5.0$ at $t = 0.1, 0.2, 5.0$. See Table 1 for the other parameter settings.

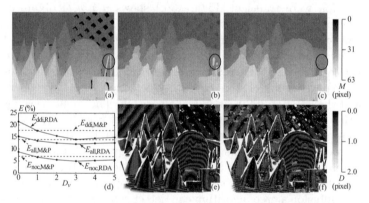

Fig. 4. Results of stereo disparity detection with the reaction-diffusion stereo algorithm (RDA) and the cooperative algorithm revised with a reaction-diffusion equation (M&P). A stereo image pair tested here has stereo disparity levels of $d_n \in \{0, 1, \cdots, 59\}$ (pixels) ($N = 60$) and an image size of 450×375 (pixels). (a) The ground-truth data of the stereo disparity map. Stereo disparity maps $M(x, y, t = 10)$ (pixel) were obtained by (b) the reaction-diffusion stereo algorithm and (c) the cooperative algorithm. (d) The dependence of bad-match-percentage error (solid lines) on the inhibitory diffusion coefficient D_v utilised in the reaction-diffusion stereo algorithm and the bad-match-parentage error (broken lines) evaluated for (c). Evaluated areas are the depth-discontinuity area (ddi), non-occlusion area (noc) and all area (all). Figures (e) and (f) show distributions of absolute error D (pixel) evaluated for the disparity maps (b) and (c). Circles depicted in (a), (b) and (c) show areas focused in Section 3. The website http://vision.middlebury.edu/stereo provides the stereo image pair and its ground-truth data. Table 1 shows the other parameter settings utilised in the algorithms.

parts did not survive in the result of the cooperative algorithm not having the inhibitor variable. In addition, by changing D_v in the reaction-diffusion algorithm, we confirmed the effectiveness of the long-range inhibition. Figure 4(d) shows the results, where we evaluated stereo disparity maps with the bad-match-percentage error measure in depth discontinuity area (ddi), non-occlusion area (noc) and all area (all). These numerical results show that the algorithm achieved the minimum error at $D_v = 3.0$. The long-range inhibition is effective, in particular, in depth discontinuity areas. This is also the evidence showing that the long-range inhibition works for small parts of a stereo disparity distribution.

The results of the present experimental study suggest a new idea to improve performance of the reaction-diffusion stereo algorithm. As shown in Fig. 4(d), the long-range inhibition is quite effective in areas having small parts and depth discontinuity. Thus, if we can preliminarily know those areas according to other information sources, such as, intensity edge, texture, defocusing and motion, we can apply anisotropic inhibitory diffusion coefficient modulated with the sources to the stereo algorithm. Then, we can expect the performance improvement of the algorithm in those areas. Previous edge detection algorithms utilising anisotropic diffusion [14] weakened the diffusion coefficient in discontinuity areas. In comparison to the previous algorithms, the reaction-diffusion stereo algorithm must strengthen the anisotropic diffusion coefficient on the inhibitor variable in such the discontinuity areas.

4   Conclusions

The present paper presented the significance of the long-range inhibition in reaction-diffusion algorithms designed for edge detection and stereo disparity detection. It has been known that several pattern formation and pattern recognition processes in natural and biological systems are due to the long-range inhibition. As being similar to the systems, the long-range inhibition is the necessary condition for the reaction-diffusion algorithm designed for edge detection, and is effective, in particular, in small parts and depth discontinuity areas for that designed for stereo disparity detection. These findings suggested a new idea of improving performance of the reaction-diffusion stereo algorithm.

Acknowledgement. The present study was supported in part by a Grant-in-Aid for Scientific Research (C) (No. 20500206) from the Japan Society for the Promotion of Science.

References

1. Mach, E.: Über die Wirkung der raumlichen Vertheilung des Lichterizes auf die Netzhaut, I. Sitzungsberichte der Mathematisch-Naturwissenschaftlichen Classe der kaiserlichen Akademie der Wissenschaften 52, 303–322 (1865)
2. Hartline, H.K., Wagner, H.G., Ratliff, F.: Inhibition in the eye of *Limulus*. Journal of General Physiology 39, 651–673 (1956)
3. Barlow, R.B., Quarles, D.A.: Mach bands in the lateral eye of *Limulus*. Journal of General Physiology 65, 709–730 (1975)

4. Anstis, S.M., Howard, I.P., Rogers, B.: A Craik-O'Brien-Cornsweet illusion for visual depth. Vision Research 18, 213–217 (1978)
5. Brookes, A., Stevens, K.A.: The analogy between stereo depth and brightness. Perception 18, 601–614 (1989)
6. Turing, A.M.: The chemical basis of morphogenesis. Philosophical Transactions of the Royal Society of London. Series B, Biological Sciences 237, 37–72 (1952)
7. Gierer, A., Meinhardt, H.: A theory of biological pattern formation. Kybernetik 12, 30–39 (1972)
8. Kondo, S., Asai, R.: A reaction-diffusion wave on the skin of the marine angelfish *Pomacanthus*. Nature 376, 765–768 (1995)
9. Sick, S., Reinker, S., Timmer, J., Schlake, T.: WNT and DKK determine hair follicle spacing through a reaction-diffusion mechanism. Science 314, 1447–1450 (2006)
10. Kuhnert, L., Agladze, K.I., Krinsky, V.I.: Image processing using light-sensitive chemical waves. Nature 337, 244–247 (1989)
11. Marr, D., Hildreth, E.: Theory of edge detection. Proceedings of the Royal Society of London. Series B, Biological Sciences 207, 187–217 (1980)
12. Koenderink, J.J.: The structure of images. Biological Cybernetics 50, 363–370 (1984)
13. Marr, D., Poggio, T.: Cooperative computation of stereo disparity. Science 194, 283–287 (1976)
14. Black, M.J., Sapiro, G., Marimont, D.H., Heeger, D.: Robust anisotropic diffusion. IEEE Transactions on Image Processing 7, 421–432 (1998)
15. Elder, J.H., Zucker, S.W.: Local scale control for edge detection and blur estimation. IEEE Transactions on Pattern Analysis and Machine Intelligence 20, 699–716 (1998)
16. Luo, A., Burkhardt, H.: An intensity-based cooperative bidirectional stereo matching with simultaneous detection of discontinuities and occlusions. International Journal of Computer Vision 15, 171–188 (1995)
17. Zitnick, C.L., Kanade, T.: A cooperative algorithm for stereo matching and occlusion detection. IEEE Transactions on Pattern Analysis and Machine Intelligence 22, 675–684 (2000)
18. Kurata, N., Kitahata, H., Mahara, H., Nomura, A., Miike, H., Sakurai, T.: Stationary pattern formation in a discrete excitable system with strong inhibitory coupling. Physical Review E 79, 56203 (2009)
19. Nomura, A., Ichikawa, M., Miike, H.: Reaction-diffusion algorithm for stereo disparity detection. Machine Vision and Applications 20, 175–187 (2009)
20. FitzHugh, R.: Impulses and physiological states in theoretical models of nerve membrane. Biophysical Journal 1, 445–466 (1961)
21. Nagumo, J., Arimoto, S., Yoshizawa, S.: An active pulse transmission line simulating nerve axon. Proceedings of the IRE 50, 2061–2070 (1962)
22. Nomura, A., Ichikawa, M., Miike, H.: Disparity estimation from stereo images with multilayered reaction-diffusion models of activation-inhibition mechanism. In: Proceedings of 2006 IEEE International Conference on Acoustics, Speech and Signal Processing. Part II, pp. 509–512 (May 2006)
23. Heath, M.D., Sarkar, S., Sanocki, T., Bowyer, K.W.: A robust visual method for assessing the relative performance of edge-detection algorithms. IEEE Transactions on Pattern Analysis and Machine Intelligence, PAMI 19, 1338–1359 (1997)
24. Scharstein, D., Szeliski, R.: A taxonomy and evaluation of dense two-frame stereo correspondence algorithms. International Journal of Computer Vision 47, 7–42 (2002)

An Edge-Sensing Universal Demosaicing Algorithm

Alain Horé and Djemel Ziou

MOIVRE, Département d'Informatique, Université de Sherbrooke, 2500 Boulevard de l'Université, Sherbrooke (Québec), Canada, J1K 2R1
{alain.hore,djemel.ziou}@usherbrooke.ca

Abstract. In this paper, we introduce an edge detection algorithm for mosaiced images which can be used to enhance generic demosaicing algorithms. The algorithm is based on pixels color differences in the horizontal, vertical and diagonal directions. By using our edge-detection technique to enhance the universal demosaicing algorithm of Lukac *et al.*, experimental results show that the presence of color shifts and artefacts in demosaiced images is reduced. This is confirmed in regard to both subjective and objective evaluation.

1 Introduction

A full-color image is usually composed of three color planes and, accordingly, three separate sensors are required for a camera to measure an image. To reduce the cost, many cameras use a single sensor covered with a color filter array (CFA). The CFA consists of a set of spectrally selective filters that are arranged in an interleaved pattern so that each pixel samples one of three primary color components. These sparsely sampled color values are termed *mosaiced* images. To render a full-color image from a mosaiced image, an image reconstruction process, commonly known as CFA interpolation or demosaicing [1], is required to estimate for each multispectral pixel its two missing color values. Many demosaicing algorithms have been proposed over the last decade [2]. They play a major role in the demosaicing process, as summarized in Fig. 1, in order to obtain a final image close to the original image.

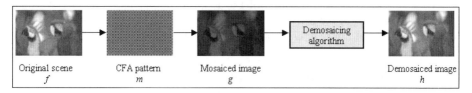

Fig. 1. Demosaicing process

The demosaicing algorithms are broadly divided into two categories: those that are non edge-directed and those that are edge-directed. In the first category, simple non-adaptive algorithms such as nearest neighbour, bilinear, cubic interpolation [3], or algorithms exploiting the cross-correlation between the color channels [4-7] are found. They perform interpolation in a fixed pattern for every pixel. Even though they

J. Blanc-Talon et al. (Eds.): ACIVS 2010, Part I, LNCS 6474, pp. 197–208, 2010.
© Springer-Verlag Berlin Heidelberg 2010

may be computationally efficient, they introduce large errors in edge regions that degrade the resulting image. In the second category of demosaicing algorithms which are edge-directed [1, 8-11], local spatial features present in the pixel neighbourhood are detected. In the presence of edges, the interpolation is made along the edge, which enhances the quality of images on edges regions. However, we note that finding edges is not an easy task, since we need to compute derivatives/gradients although two primary colors are missing at each pixel. All the algorithms described previously were designed especially for the Bayer pattern [12] shown in Fig. 2(a). Even if the Bayer pattern is the most widely used in digital cameras, other CFA models exist [13-17] and some are shown in Fig. 2. The existing CFA patterns vary significantly in the distribution of red, green and blue pixels, and thus, have different anti-aliasing capabilities and complexities in the reconstruction of images. In [18], Lukac et al. have introduced a universal demosaicing algorithm which can be used for any CFA. However, the algorithm does not direct the interpolation along any edge. The edge-sensing model proposed by the authors simply reduces the color difference between neighbouring pixels, but does not include any edge detection, and resulting images are subject to artefacts such as color aliasing (see Fig. 7 further for experimental results).

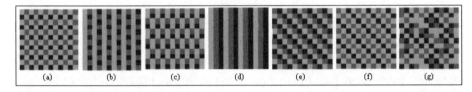

Fig. 2. RGB CFAs: (a) Bayer CFA [12]. (b) Yamanaka CFA [13]. (c) Lukac et al. CFA [14]. (d) Vertical stripe CFA [15]. (e) Diagonal stripe CFA [15]. (f) Modified Bayer CFA [15]. (g) HVS-based CFA [16].

In this paper, we propose an edge-detection algorithm which can be used to detect edges in mosaiced images obtained using any RGB-CFA. Thus, at edge points, the interpolation of pixels can be made along the edges and not across, which reduces the presence of artefacts such as color aliasing. The rest of the paper is organized as follows: in Section 2, we describe our edge-detection algorithm, and in Section 3 we introduce the demosaicing algorithm of Lukac et al. In Section 4, we present some experimental results of the use of our edge-detection algorithm to enhance the demosaicing algorithm of Lukac et al. Final comments are given in Section 5.

2   The Universal Algorithm of Lukac *et al.*

Due to the monochromatic nature of the sensor, the captured values from a CFA pattern create an $M \times N$ image $F: Z^2 \rightarrow Z$. This CFA image represents a two-dimensional matrix of integer samples $F(p,q)$ with $p = 1, 2, \ldots, M$ and $q = 1, 2, \ldots, N$ denoting the image rows and columns, respectively. The demosaicing step re-arranges the acquired sensor data to an RGB-like vectorial field, and completes missing color components using adjacent sensor data through spectral interpolation. The process produces a color (RGB) image $I : Z^2 \rightarrow Z^3$ with color pixels $I(p,q) = [I(p,q)_1, I(p,q)_2, I(p,q)_3]$

represented as vectors in the RGB vectorial space. In the color vector $I(p,q)$, the $I(p,q)_k$ value, for $k = 1, 2, 3$, denotes the kth vector's spectral component. Namely, $I(p,q)_1$ represents the red (R) component, $I(p,q)_2$ the green (G) component, and $I(p,q)_3$ the blue (B) component. Since information about the arrangement of color filters in the actual CFA is readily available either from the camera manufacturer (when demosaicing is implemented in the camera), or obtained from the raw CFA image, a $M \times N$ vectorial field $d : Z^2 \rightarrow \{1,2,3\}$ of the corresponding location flags $d(p,q)$ is initialized using the default value $d(p,q) = k$ to indicate that the primary color indexed by k is the color found in the CFA at position (p,q).

After initialization, Lukac *et al.*'s algorithm follows some conventional practices [19-20] and starts the demosaicing process by estimating the missing green components through a weighted sum-based interpolation. Then, the red (respectively blue) components are estimated from the neighbouring red (respectively blue) components as well as the green components by using a constant color-difference model. Finally, a post-processing step is applied on the green components and then on the red and blue components to improve the image quality [21].

3   The Universal Edge-Detection Algorithm

Human visual systems are sensitive to high frequencies (e.g., edges) present in images, and non-adaptive color interpolation algorithms often fail around edges since they are not able to detect them. The universal demosaicing algorithm of Lukac *et al.* also suffers this issue since it does not embed an edge-detection model. Heuristic models such as the color-difference model imply the use of linear interpolation to compute missing color pixels, which is generally done within a neighbourhood for each pixel [22]. However, linear interpolation, which is computed as weighted sums in the case of Lukac *et al.*'s demosaicing algorithm, fails around edges since neighbouring pixels that are not in the direction of an edge are used to compute the color of pixels of that edge. To enhance the universal algorithm designed by Lukac *et al.*, we propose to include an edge-detection step. The idea is to detect, at a missed pixel, if there is a potential horizontal, vertical or diagonal edge. If we detect a horizontal (respectively vertical or diagonal) edge, then we interpolate the missed pixel by using only the known pixels along the horizontal (respectively vertical or diagonal) direction. To detect the edge points in RGB mosaiced images, we draw our inspiration from the methods used in some demosaicing algorithms based on Bayer CFA [2, 6, 23, 24], and we generalize our approach to any CFA pattern. The idea is to approximate, at a missed pixel, the horizontal gradient as the sum of two-by-two differences between successive known pixels of the same color in the horizontal line containing the missed pixel. The vertical gradient is computed similarly. The diagonal gradient is computed in two directions: the North-West South-East direction (indexed *WE*) and the North-East South-West (indexed *EW*) direction (see Figure 3). The idea of summing the differences between pixels of the same color allows to detect changes in any of the red, green and blue channels along a direction. Thus, by considering edge points as sharp changes in the red, green and blue channels along a given direction, we are able to detect them. This can be seen as a simplified approximation of the multispectral gradient proposed in [25]. In fact, instead of looking for the direction of the greatest contrast among all possible directions, we reduce the possible directions to the horizontal, vertical and diagonal directions. This is done to simplify the complexity of the model and reduce the computing time. Also, we use the 1-norm instead of the 2-norm as the measure for computing the multispectral/color gradient between neighbouring pixels in the horizontal, vertical and diagonal directions. Knowing the horizontal, vertical and diagonal gradients, we are able to interpolate pixels using neighbouring pixels that are located in the direction of the smallest contrast in order to preserve edges as much as possible without altering smooth regions. Thus, let us suppose that we want to compute the horizontal, vertical and diagonal gradients at a position (p,q) surrounded by a window (neighbourhood) $\Psi(p,q)$ centered on (p,q). Let us define by ζ the set of all positions of pixels forming $\Psi(p,q)$. Let us also define by ζ_h (respectively ζ_v) the set of horizontal (respectively vertical) positions of the pixels in the same horizontal (respectively vertical) line than the pixel $I(p,q)$ in $\Psi(p,q)$. In the same way, let us define by ζ_{WE} (respectively ζ_{EW}) the set of positions of the pixels in the North-West South-East direction (respectively North-East South-West direction) of $I(p,q)$ in $\Psi(p,q)$. If $g_h(p,q)$ denotes the horizontal gradient, $g_v(p,q)$ the vertical gradient, and $g_{WE}(p,q)$ and $g_{EW}(p,q)$ the diagonal gradients at location (p,q), then we have:

$$g_h(p,q) = \sum_{k \in \{1,2,3\}} \sum_{\substack{(p,j_1),(p,j_2) \in \xi_h(p,q) \\ j_1 < j_2 \\ d(p,j_1)=d(p,j_2)=k \\ \forall(p,j_3) \in \xi_h(p,q),\, j_1 < j_3 < j_2 \Rightarrow d(p,j_3) \neq k}} \left| I(p,j_1)_k - I(p,j_2)_k \right| \tag{1}$$

The condition $(p,j_1),(p,j_2) \in \xi_h(p,q)$ means that the gradient is computed for pixels in the same horizontal line than the pixel (p,q). The condition $j_1 < j_2$ simply creates a direction for computing the differences (in this case, from the pixels at the left in the horizontal neighbourhood to the pixels at the right). The condition $d(p,j_1)=d(p,j_2)=k$ means that the differences are computed only for known pixels from the CFA patterns. Finally, the last condition $\forall(p,j_3) \in \xi_h(p,q),\, j_1 < j_3 < j_2 \Rightarrow d(p,j_3) \neq k$ simply indicates that the differences are computed between consecutive known pixels in the direction imposed by the condition $j_1 < j_2$. The other color gradients are computed similarly to $g_h(p,q)$ as:

$$g_v(p,q) = \sum_{k \in \{1,2,3\}} \sum_{\substack{(j_1,q),(j_2,q) \in \xi_v(p,q) \\ j_1 < j_2 \\ d(j_1,q)=d(j_2,q)=k \\ \forall(j_3,q) \in \xi_v(p,q),\, j_1 < j_3 < j_2 \Rightarrow d(j_3,q) \neq k}} \left| I(j_1,q)_k - I(j_2,q)_k \right| \tag{2}$$

$$g_{WE}(p,q) = \sum_{k \in \{1,2,3\}} \sum_{\substack{(i_1,j_1),(i_2,j_2) \in \xi_{WE}(p,q) \\ i_1 < i_2,\, j_1 < j_2 \\ d(i_1,j_1)=d(i_2,j_2)=k \\ \forall(i_3,j_3) \in \xi_{WE}(p,q),\, i_1 < i_3 < i_2 \text{ and } j_1 < j_3 < j_2 \Rightarrow d(i_3,j_3) \neq k}} \left| I(i_1,j_1)_k - I(i_2,j_2)_k \right| \tag{3}$$

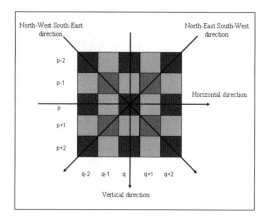

Fig. 3. Example of CFA configuration with the directions of gradient computation

$$g_{EW}(p,q) = \sum_{k \in \{1,2,3\}} \sum_{\substack{(i_1,j_1),(i_2,j_2) \in \xi_{EW}(p,q) \\ i_1 < i_2, j_1 > j_2 \\ d(i_1,j_1)=d(i_2,j_2)=k \\ \forall (i_3,j_3) \in \xi_{EW}(p,q), i_1 < i_3 < i_2 \text{ and } j_1 > j_3 > j_2 \Rightarrow d(i_3,j_3) \neq k}} \left| I(i_1,j_1)_k - I(i_2,j_2)_k \right| \tag{4}$$

To determine if the missed pixel belongs to an edge, we compare the horizontal, vertical and diagonal gradients to a threshold T. The idea is to interpolate using pixels in the direction of smallest contrast. The following test guides the interpolation process for the green pixels ($k=2$). Let us define *gmin* by:

$$g_d = \underset{i \in \{h,v,WE,EW\}}{\arg\min} \ g_i(p,q) \tag{5}$$

i. if $g_d \leq T$ (we may be along an edge), then we interpolate along the direction given by d (horizontal if $d=h$, vertical if $d=v$, diagonal North-West South-East if $d=WE$, diagonal North-East South-West if $d=EW$).
ii. if $g_d > T$, we are not on an edge, and we interpolate using the complete neighbourhood ζ containing the missing pixel.

In the case of Lukac *et al.*'s demosaicing algorithm for example, interpolating in the horizontal direction (h) can be described using the following equation:

$$I(p,q)_k = \sum_{\substack{(i,j) \in \xi_h \\ d(i,j)=k}} w_{pq}(i,j)_k \ I(i,j)_k \tag{6}$$

where w_{pq} are interpolation weights. We will not address the computation of these weights in this paper.

The interpolation in the other directions is computed similarly by replacing in (6) ζ_h with ζ_v, ζ_{WE} or ζ_{EW}. The interpolation using the complete neighbourhood is computed by replacing ζ_h with ζ. The effect of T on the performance of the demosaicing will be discussed in the experimental results section.

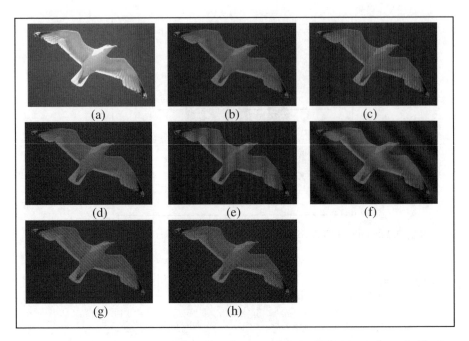

Fig. 4. (a) Original image; (b)-(h) Mosaiced images using the CFA (a)-(g) shown in Fig. 2

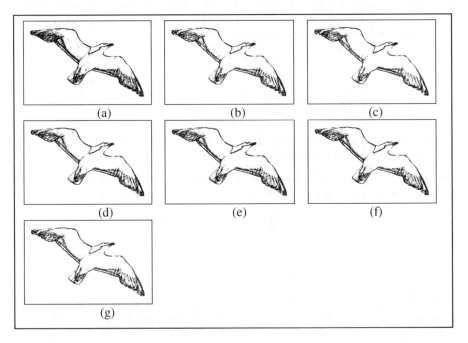

Fig. 5. (a)-(g) Edges extracted from the mosaiced images (b)-(h) shown in Fig. 4

In Fig. 4, we show a set of mosaiced images corresponding to the CFA patterns presented in Fig. 2, and we show in Fig. 5 the edges extracted from these images by using the equations defined in (1)-(4) and a threshold value T=15. We have used a fixed 5×5 window size for computing the gradients corresponding to the mosaiced images. As can be observed, the edges are well defined even if the mosaiced images miss two primary colors at each pixel location. Thus, our general model of extracting edges from mosaiced images coming from various CFA patterns appears to be efficient and reliable. Of course, this model can still be improved by computing not only the gradient in four directions, but in all possible directions depending on the size of the window used. However, as we already mentioned, this approach adds more complexity to our model and is time consuming. As a final remark, we should note that the edges points found are not the same for all the CFA patterns. This is the consequence of the different arrangements of primary color pixels on the CFA. Thus, the CFA patterns perform differently in detecting edges, which may also impact the global demosaicing of images.

4 Experimental Results

In this section, we make a series of tests on 24 images which are shown in Fig. 6. The images are extracted from the Kodak database. We also use 7 CFA patterns, shown in Fig. 2, for comparing the original demosaicing algorithm of Lukac *et al.*, and a new version of this algorithm which is based on improvements among which is the edge-detection model proposed in this paper. The experimentation protocol is as follows: an original image is sampled using a CFA pattern and the output is a mosaiced image. A demosaicing algorithm is then applied to the mosaiced image and we obtain a final image. The final image is further compared to the original image in order to assess the quality of reconstruction. An initial subjective comparison is made by inspecting some visual artefacts like color aliasing on the images obtained through the demosaicing algorithms. For objective comparison, we use the mean squared error (MSE) quality measure. The MSE for a color image is computed as the mean value of all the pixel-by-pixel squared differences for all color bands. A small value of the MSE indicates small reconstruction errors, while a high value of the MSE indicates non-negligible reconstruction errors. In Fig. 7, we present a part of an original image and the results of the images obtained through Lukac *et al.*'s demosaicing algorithm and the improved version for the Bayer CFA shown in Fig. 2(a) and for the CFA pattern shown in Fig. 2(g). As we can notice, Lukac *et al.*'s algorithm produces a lot of color aliasing artefacts which is not the case for the improved algorithm. Thus, the improved algorithm reduces the presence of color aliasing artefacts, which is desirable for the human visual system.

The improved algorithm is also able to reduce zipper effects as can be observed in Fig. 8 where we show an original image, a part of that image, and the resulting images obtained through the two demosaicing algorithms applied to the CFA pattern shown in Fig. 2(b). The zipper effect refers to artificial "on-off" patterns created in smooth regions around edges and mainly caused by improper fusion of neighbouring color values across edges [7]. As can be observed in Fig. 8, Lukac *et al.*'s algorithm has

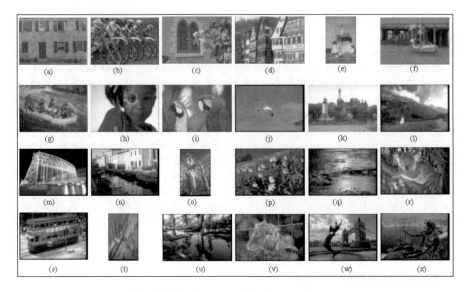

Fig. 6. Color images used in the experiments

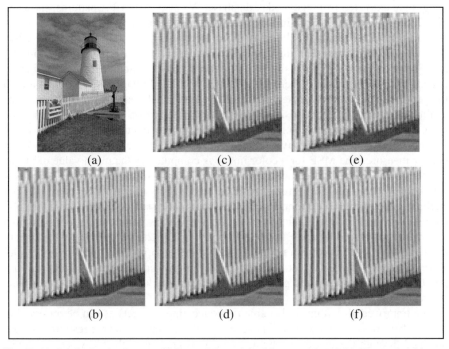

Fig. 7. (a) Original color image. (b) Part of the original image. (c) and (e) Demosaiced image using Lukac *et al.*'s algorithm for the CFA pattern in Fig. 2(a) and Fig. 2(g) respectively. (d) and (f) Corresponding demosaiced images for the improved algorithm.

Fig. 8. (a) Original color image. (b) Part of the original image. (c) Demosaiced image using Lukac *et al.*'s algorithm. (d) Demosaiced image using the improved algorithm.

produced a lot of zipper effects on the window compared to our algorithm, which degrades the visual quality of the global image. Thus, it appears that the introduction of an edge-detection model contributes to increase the performance of the universal demosaicing algorithm in reducing zipper effects.

The increase in visual quality of the improved demosaicing algorithm compared to Lukac *et al.*'s original algorithm is confirmed numerically by using the MSE. In Fig. 9, we plot the mean values of the MSE (i.e., the MSE is computed for each of the test images, and we take the mean value) for edge regions for the different patterns in order to observe how the pixels values of the demosaiced images are close to the values of the original image for edge regions. We have used a threshold $T=25\%$, meaning that 25% of all the pixels are considered to be potential edge pixels. For detecting the edge points, the method proposed in [25] is applied to the original images. Thus, the same edge points are used for the two algorithms being compared. As can been noticed in Fig. 9, the mean values of the MSE for the different images and CFA patterns is smaller for the improved algorithm compared to Lukac's algorithm, meaning smaller reconstruction errors and less color distortions for the improved algorithm.

The study of the effect of the threshold T on the performance of the demosaicing algorithm is represented in Fig. 10 where we plot the difference between the mean values of the MSE at edge regions for the Lukac *et al.*'s algorithm and the improved

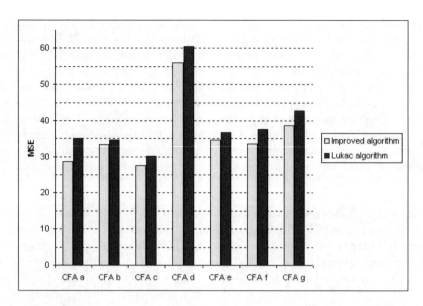

Fig. 9. MSE mean values for edge regions for the various CFA patterns: T=25%

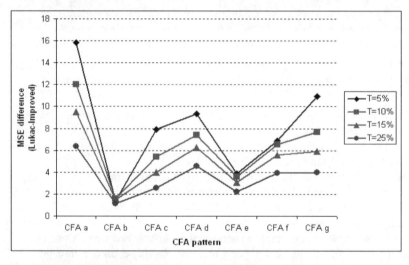

Fig. 10. MSE difference for edge regions between Lukac *et al.*'s demosaing algorithm and the improved demosaicing algorithm for the various CFA patterns and for various threshold representing the percentage of potential edges points

algorithm for the various CFA patterns. As we can notice, for each CFA pattern, the difference between the MSE values increases when the threshold T decreases (the exception is the CFA b for which the improvement is relatively constant for all values of T). In fact, smaller values of T represent the most realistic and sharp edge regions. In the other hand, higher values of T include the most realistic edge regions and also edge regions that may not be so sharp. Consequently, the performance for smaller values of T indicates how the improved algorithm really performs on sharp edge regions. Thus, we can conclude from Fig. 10 that the universal edge-detection algorithm enhances the quality of images for the demosaicing algorithm of Lukac et *al.*, and the improvement is more perceptible on sharp edge regions.

In general, all the results presented in Fig. 9-10 indicate that the choice of the CFA has a great impact on the overall quality of images since different performances are obtained for the various CFA patterns. This is not surprising since the various CFA have different arrangements of red, green and blue pixels which may influence their anti-aliasing capability and the reconstruction of images.

5 Conclusion

An efficient edge-detecting method was proposed for detecting edges present in mosaiced images extracted using any RGB-CFA pattern. It enables, at edge points, to direct the interpolation along the edge and not across the edge. Experimental results have shown that better images, in terms of both visual quality and objective quality measures, are obtained when this edge-detecting algorithm is embedded in the demosaicing algorithm of Lukac *et al.* We have also noticed that the performance of the demosaicing algorithms depends on the CFA pattern used as well as the image captured. Thus, a CFA pattern may give the best results for one image and be less effective for another image. An interesting future work may be the study of the automatic generation of the optimal CFA pattern given an image.

References

1. Tsai, C.Y., Song, K.Y.: A new edge-adaptive demosaicing algorithm for color filter arrays. Image and Vision Computing 25, 1495–1508 (2007)
2. Lee, W., Lee, S., Kim, J.: Cost-effective color filter array demosaicing using spatial correlation. IEEE Transactions on Consumer Electronics 52(2), 547–554 (2006)
3. Keys, R.G.: Cubic convolution interpolation for digital image processing. IEEE Transactions on Acoustic, Speech and Signal Processing ASSP-29, 1153–1160 (1981)
4. Cok, D.R.: Signal processing method and apparatus for producing interpolated chrominance values in a sampled color image. U.S. patent 4642768 (1987)
5. Adams, J.E.: Interactions between color plane interpolation and other image processing functions in electronic photography. In: Proceedings of SPIE, vol. 2416, pp. 144–151 (1995)
6. Chung, K.H., Chan, Y.H.: Color demosaicing using variance of color differences. IEEE Transactions on Image Processing 15(10), 2944–2955 (2006)
7. Chang, L., Tan, Y.P.: Effective use of spatial and spectral correlations for color filter array demosaicking. IEEE Transactions on Consumer Electronics 50(1), 355–365 (2004)
8. Kakarala, R., Baharav, Z.: Adaptive demosaicing with the principle vector method. IEEE Transactions on Consumer Electronics 48, 932–937 (2002)
9. Li, X., Orchard, M.T.: New edge directed interpolation. IEEE Transactions on Image Processing 10(10) (2001)

10. Pei, S.C., Tam, I.K.: Effective color interpolation in CCD color filter arrays using signal correlation. IEEE Transactions on Circuits and Systems for video technology 13(6), 503–513 (2003)

11. Lukac, R., Plataniotis, K.N., Hatzinakos, D.: A new CFA interpolation framework. Signal Processing 86, 1559–1579 (2006)

12. Bayer, B.E.: Color imaging array. U.S. Patent 3971065 (1976)

13. Yamanaka, S.: Solid state camera. U.S. Patent 4054906 (1977)

14. Lukac, R., Plataniotis, K.N.: Color filter arrays: design and performance analysis. IEEE Transactions on Consumer Electronics 51(4), 1260–1267 (2004)

15. FillFactory: Technology image sensor: the color filter array,
    http://web.archive.org/web/20051219223659/www.fillfactory.com/htm/technology/htm/rgbfaq.htm

16. Parmar, M., Reeves, S.J.: A perceptually based design methodology for color filter arrays. In: Proceedings of the IEEE International Conference on Acoustics, Speech, and Signal Processing (ICASSP), vol. 3, pp. 473–476 (2004)

17. Hirakawa, H., Wolfe, P.J.: Spatio-spectral color filter array design for optimal image recovery. IEEE Transactions on Image Processing 17(2), 1876–1890 (2008)

18. Lukac, R., Plataniotis, K.N.: Universal demosaicking for imaging pipelines with an RGB color filter array. Pattern Recognition 38, 2208–2212 (2005)

19. Gunturk, B.K., Glotzbach, J., Altunbasak, Y., Schaffer, R.W., Murserau, R.M.: Demosaicking: color filter array interpolation. IEEE Signal Processing Magazine 22(1), 44–54 (2005)

20. Lukac, R., Plataniotis, K.N.: Data adaptive filters for demosaicking: a framework. IEEE Transactions on Consumer Electronics 51(2), 560–570 (2005)

21. Lukac, R., Plataniotis, K.N.: A robust, cost-effective postprocessor for enhancing demosaicked camera images. Real-Time Imaging 11(2), 139–150 (2005)

22. Li, X.: Demosaicing by successive approximations. IEEE Transactions on Image Processing 14(3), 370–379 (2005)

23. Ramanath, R., Snyder, W.E., Bilbro, G.L., Sander III, W.A.: Demosaicking methods for Bayer color arrays. Journal of Electronic Imaging 11(3), 306–315 (2002)

24. Su, C.Y.: Highly effective iterative demosaicing using weighted-edge and color-difference interpolations. IEEE Transactions on Consumer Electronics 52(2), 639–645 (2006)

25. Drewniok, C.: Multi-spectral edge detection: some experiments on data from Landsat-TM. International Journal of Remote Sensing 15(18), 3743–3765 (1994)

A New Perceptual Edge Detector in Color Images

Philippe Montesinos and Baptiste Magnier

Ecole des Mines d'ALES,
LGI2P,
Site EERIE, Parc Scientifique G.Besse
30035 Nimes Cedex 1
{Philippe.Montesinos,Baptiste.Magnier}@mines-ales.fr

Abstract. In this paper we propose a new perceptual edge detector based on anisotropic linear filtering and local maximization. The novelty of this approach resides in the mixing of ideas coming both from perceptual grouping and directional recursive linear filtering. We obtain new edge operators enabling very precise detection of edge points which are involved in large structures. This detector has been tested successfully on various image types presenting difficult problems for classical edge detection methods.

Keywords: Edge detections, perceptual organization, anisotropic filters.

1 Introduction and Background

This work is motivated by applications needing strongly for a "good" edge detector, providing precise and really informative edge points with the fewest false detection rate as possible. For example, in the domain of object finding or object recognition, in natural scenes or in Internet images, objects may present various shapes and color aspects. For such cases, many local methods involving for example points of interest and color invariants fail.

In such applications, edge detection remains a central key point as it can provide geometrical information. However, commonly used edge detectors does not lead directly to object contours which must be searched among numerous edge points. Then to avoid or simplify a difficult geometrical search, many works on perceptual organisation in computer vision have been carried out [8], [12], [11], with the aim of selecting edge points involved in large "perceptual" structures. Independently of these works, new edge detection techniques using anisotropic filtering have been defined [7], [9]. These methods are able to correctly detect large linear structures.

In Practice, the generalization of perceptual organization methods for the automatic segmentation of various image types remains a difficult task in regard to the necessity of adjusting multiple thresholds and parameters. For the second class of methods (anisotropic filtering), the robustness against noise depends strongly on the filter's smoothing parameter. If this parameter increases, the

J. Blanc-Talon et al. (Eds.): ACIVS 2010, Part I, LNCS 6474, pp. 209–220, 2010.

detection is less sensitive to noise (and small structures considered as noise). Consequently, the precision of detected edge points decreases strongly at corners points and for non straight object contour parts.

We describe in this paper a new method for the precise detection of edge points belonging to large structures. Contrary to recent works involving edges, junctions and texture detection [1] [3] this work does not at this time address texture. Consequently the method described here is computationally much simpler and faster. The aim of this method is to obtain the most reliable geometrical information for object contour extraction as possible by just image differentiation. The method described, involves directional linear filtering by means of recursive filters followed by the computation of an edge operator built with a local directional maximization of the response of the filters. This method is inspired from perceptual organisation works [11], and anisotropic filtering [9].

Paper Organization :
In the section 2, we remember first the basics of perceptual organization with saliency networks, and then the basics of anisotropic edge detection with the anisotropic tensor. In the section 3, we present our method implementing a robust edge detector on gray-scale and color images having some features pointed out at section 2. Finally, at section 4, we present the results obtained with our method and we compare our results with other methods.

2 Perceptual Organization and Anisotropic Edge Detection

2.1 Perceptual Organization with Saliency Networks

Based on the works described in [12] and [11], let us consider a path crossing a pixel P of an edge segmented image. We can divide this path into three parts: the path coming from the left of P, the pixel P under consideration and the path leaving on the right (see Fig. 1). A quality function of a path can be defined as the sum of left and right lateral quality terms multiplied by a coupling factor based on the local curvature of the path at P.

$$F\left(P\right) = \left[F_l\left(P - 1\right) + F_r\left(P - 1\right)\right] C_{\left(P-1, P+1\right)} . \tag{1}$$

For these terms, it has been shown in [12] that some classes of quality functions involving grey levels and curvature could be optimized with locally connected saliency networks, by a local to global way. In [11] we have differently written these quality functions to establish a link with active contour function used in snakes. These functions are also composed of grey levels and curvature well separated into two different terms.

2.2 Anisotropic Edge Detection

Anisotropic edge detection can be seen as a generalization of color edge detection [6]. Suppose that the image is smoothed with a bank of rotated anisotropic Gaussian kernels:

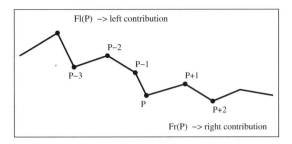

Fig. 1. A path crossing a considered pixel P

$$G_\theta(x,y) = C\, e^{-(x\ y)\, P_\theta^{-1} \begin{pmatrix} \frac{1}{2\sigma_1^2} & 0 \\ 0 & \frac{1}{2\sigma_2^2} \end{pmatrix} P_\theta \begin{pmatrix} x \\ y \end{pmatrix}}$$

where C is a normalization coefficient, P_θ a rotation matrix of angle θ and σ_1 and σ_2 are the standard-deviations of the Gaussian filter.

By convolution with these rotated kernels, we obtain a collection of smoothed images $I_\theta = I * G_\theta$ which can be derived along X and Y axis to obtain anisotropic directional derivatives:

$$I_{\theta X} = \frac{\partial I_\theta}{\partial X} \quad \text{and} \quad I_{\theta Y} = \frac{\partial I_\theta}{\partial Y}.$$

These derivatives can now be combined in an orientation tensor [9]. From this tensor, an anisotropic gradient and its orientation can be computed respectively with the square root of the largest eigenvalue and its associated eigenvector. Extension to color is straightforward [6].

3   A Perceptual Edge Detector

As pointed out in section 1, the anisotropic edge detector described in section 2.2 performs well at linear portions of contours, but near corners, the gradient magnitude decreases as the edge information under the scope of the filter decreases (see Fig. 2.a). Consequently, the robustness to the noise decreases.

The simplest solution to bypass this effect is to consider paths crossing each pixel in several directions. We simply "cut" the smoothing kernel in two parts: a first part along the path coming from the left and a second part along the path leaving on the right as seen in Fig. 2.b). In the direction of the contour, "half smoothing" is performed, in the perpendicular direction a derivation filter is applied to obtain a derivative information. In order to obtain edge information, we have to combine entering and leaving paths. Now, the edge detection problem becomes an optimization problem similar to path optimization in saliency networks.

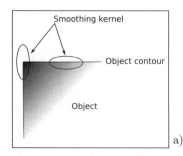 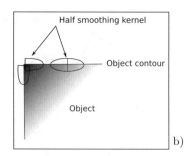

Fig. 2. Anisotropic Gaussian kernels at linear portions of contours and at corners, a) Full anisotropic Gaussian kernels. b) Half anisotropic Gaussian kernels (smoothing along the contour, derivation in the orthogonal direction of the edge).

3.1   Filters and Their Implementation

Considering edge detection, it is now well established that the Gaussian and its derivatives form optimal filter in the sense of the SNR, localization and uniqueness of detection [2]. Due to their euclidean invariance and also to the emergence of scale-space theory, these filters have received a great attention in edge detection. But several other filters based on the exponential filter presenting also optimality features have been pointed out by [4], [13]. These filters do not present isotropic invariance but are interesting for their lower computational complexity in regard to Gaussians [5]. The Shen filter can be implemented recursively at order 1 and Deriche filter at order 2, as the Gaussian filter can be recursively implemented at order 4 with a good approximation.

In our case, firstly, we aren't concerned with isotropic property of filters. Secondly, the better SNR of the Gaussian filter in regard to the exponential filters is not fundamental as we are going to use a large standard-deviation in the smoothing direction (in any way this important smoothing will remove the noise). According to these considerations, we can use any of the three filters for smoothing. If we need small computational complexity, we will prefer Shen filter to the Gaussian filter. At the contrary, for derivation, we will preferably use the first derivative of the Gaussian according again to SNR considerations.

In order to obtain all the rotated filtering (see Fig. 3 b)), we just proceed in an inverse rotation of the image at discredited orientations from 0 to 360 degrees (of 1, 2, 5, or 10 degrees, depending on the precision needed and the smoothing parameter) before applying non rotated filters. We always use the "half smoothing" filter along the Y direction, and the derivation filter along the X direction (as illustrated in Fig. 3 a)). As the image is rotated instead of the filters, the filtering implementation is quite straightforward. The "half smoothing" uses slightly different implementations that those described in [13], [4] or [5].

It is well known that for implementing a recursive filter, we need to decompose the filter function into causal and anti-causal parts. In this case, we need

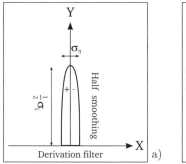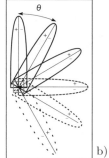

Fig. 3. a) Edge operator (*derivation filter on X and half smoothing filter on Y*). b) Rotated filters with an angle of θ.

exactly "half filtering", for normalization considerations. We then decompose the smoothing filter as:

$$F(x) = F^+(x) + F^-(x)$$

where:

$$F^+(x) = \begin{cases} F(x) & \text{if } x > 0 \\ \frac{1}{2}F(x) & \text{if } x = 0 \\ 0 & \text{if } x < 0 \end{cases} \qquad (2)$$

and

$$F^-(x) = \begin{cases} 0 & \text{if } x > 0 \\ \frac{1}{2}F(x) & \text{if } x = 0 \\ F(x) & \text{if } x < 0 . \end{cases}$$

Only the filter of equation 2, representing the "half smoothing" will be implemented. If the chosen filter is the Gaussian, we will speak of σ_ξ for the standard-deviation of the smoothing filter and of σ_η for the standard-deviation of the derivation filter. But for a Shen smoothing filter (equation 3), we will continue speaking of σ_ξ, in this case we just define it as: $\sigma_\xi = 1/\sqrt{2\alpha}$ since the Shen filter is defined as:

$$F(x) = C\, e^{-\alpha|x|} . \qquad (3)$$

3.2 Edge Extraction

After the filtering stage, for each pixel, we obtain a quality measure $\mathcal{Q}(x, y, \theta)$ of a path entering this pixel at the orientation θ. This measure is an integration of the slope of the image function in this direction. For obtaining an edge operator $E(x, y)$ and a gradient direction $\eta(x, y)$, we have now to combine two entering paths (inspired by [11]). For a fast practical computation of $E(x, y)$, we first compute local extrema of the function $\mathcal{Q}(x, y, \theta)$, θ_1 and θ_2 (illustrated in Fig. 4 b)). Then two of these local extrema are combined to maximize $E(x, y)$.

$$E(x, y) = \mathcal{Q}(x, y, \theta_1) - \mathcal{Q}(x, y, \theta_2)$$

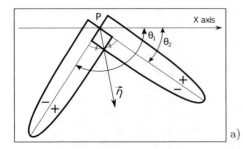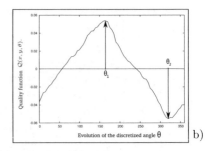

a)   b)

Fig. 4. a) Computation of $\eta(x,y)$ from θ_1 and θ_2. b) Example of a function $\mathcal{Q}(x,y,\theta)$ (*the x-axis corresponds to the value of* $\mathcal{Q}(x,y,\theta)$ *and the y-axis to* θ).

Then we simply estimate $\eta(x,y)$ by a linear combination of θ_1 and θ_2 with the coefficients $\mathcal{Q}(x,y,\theta_1)$ and $\mathcal{Q}(x,y,\theta_2)$ (see Fig. 4 a)).

Once we have obtained $E(x,y)$ and $\eta(x,y)$, edges can easily be extracted by computing local maxima of $E(x,y)$ in the $\eta(x,y)$ direction followed by an hysteresis threshold.

3.3   Adaptation to Color Images

A color image is composed of three image planes : red, blue and green. Our perceptual detector above can be applied on gray-scale images, but it can also be adapted separately to the three planes of a color image as three gray-scale images. We can combine them into the following formula:

$$\|\nabla I\|_{color} = \max(\|\nabla R\|, \|\nabla G\|, \|\nabla B\|),$$
$$\eta_{color} = \arg\max\nolimits_{\|\nabla R\|,\|\nabla G\|,\|\nabla B\|}(\eta_R, \eta_G, \eta_B).$$

After this step, edges can easily be extracted by computing local maxima of $\|\nabla I\|_{color}$ in the $\eta_{color}(x,y)$ direction followed by an hysteresis threshold.

4   Results and Computational Time

We present results obtained both on synthetic and real images using our perceptual edge detector with derivative and half-smoothing Gaussian filters.

4.1   Synthetic Images

The first group of images (Fig. 5) is composed of two synthetic images. The first binary image (Fig. 5 a)) contains geometrical shapes without noise, dotted lines and a perceptual triangle. The image is filtered with $\sigma_\xi = 15$, $\sigma_\eta = 1$ and a discretization angle of 10 degrees. Note that all contours are detected, moreover the triangle on the down right of the image is completely visible with our perceptual edge detector and dotted lines are detected as straight lines. The second synthetic gray-scale image containing small geometrical objects, (Fig. 5 c)) is

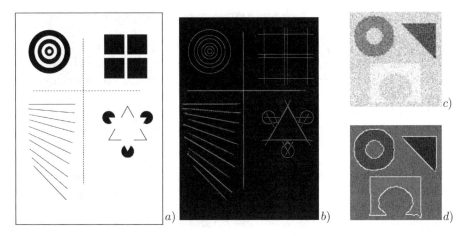

Fig. 5. a) Synthetic input image with lines, dotted lines, nearby squares and circles. b) Result of the perceptual edge operator. c) Noisy synthetic input image. d) Result of the perceptual edge operator.

small (128× 128) and noisy. The amplitude of the noise is greater than the amplitude of the edges (the white figure is very difficult to segment correctly both with classical edge detection and with the method described at section 2.2). The three objects and their corners are easily extracted using our perceptual edge detector with $\sigma_\xi = 10$, $\sigma_\eta = 1$, the hysteresis lower threshold is equal to 0.01, the higher threshold is equal to 0.15 and the discretization angle is equal to 2 degrees. As stated in section 3.1, if objects to segment are small, the parameter σ_ξ should not be too "high" ($\sigma_\xi = 10$ is a good compromise).

4.2   Real Gray-Scale Images

The second group of images (Fig. 6) consists of an omnidirectional image and a real textured image. The first image (Fig. 6 a)) (omnidirectional) contains a lot of warped objects. Within this experiment, we compare the anisotropic method described at section 2.2 and our perceptual edge detector. The first result (Fig. 6 b) is obtained with the anisotropic Gaussian filter with $\sigma_\xi = 10$, $\sigma_\eta = 1$, the hysteresis lower threshold is equal to 0.01, the higher threshold is equal to 0.1 and the discretization angle is equal to 10 degrees. The second result (Fig. 6 c)) is obtained with our perceptual edge detector using the same parameters (except the higher threshold which is equal to 0.5) and gives better results on many small details. Contours of small objects are more accurate, corners also are better defined, even in blurred regions of the image. Also, the second circle at the center of the image is detected almost complete with our perceptual edge operator. All these details (corners, circle in the center) are important for the calibration of this kind of sensor as well as various applications in robotics [10]. At Fig.6 d) we plot the obtained $\mathcal{Q}(x, y, \theta)$ function of θ at the pixel indicated by the yellow cross on the Fig. 6 c). In the second image of this

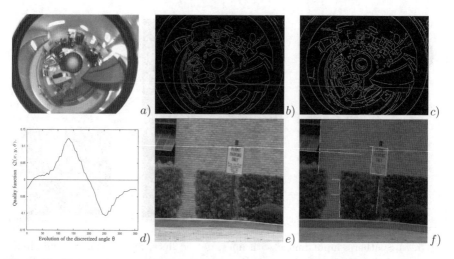

Fig. 6. a) Omnidirectional image. b) Edges obtained with the Gaussian anisotropic edge detector. c) Result of the perceptual edge operator. d) $\mathcal{Q}(x,y,\theta)$ function in one pixel (*indicated by the yellow cross in the Fig. c)*) of the perceptual edge operator. (*the x-axis corresponds to the value of* $\mathcal{Q}(x,y,\theta)$ *and the y-axis to* θ). e) Difficult real image. f) Edges obtained containing a vertical component.

group (Fig.6 e)), we have been interested here in the extraction of the panel and its post. The image is filtered using our perceptual edge operator, with $\sigma_\xi = 50$, $\sigma_\eta = 1$, the hysteresis lower threshold is equal to 0.01, the higher threshold is equal to 0.15 and the discretization angle is equal to 2 degrees. We then have thresholded connex components presenting vertical angles. The panel and its post are correctly extracted (Fig. 6 f)).

4.3   Real Color Images

We have tested our method on color images. The result of the first image is compared with the Gaussian anisotropic edge detector [9], the color Gaussian detector [5], the color Deriche detector [4] and the gPb [1].

The first result (Fig. 7 b)) is obtained with the anisotropic Gaussian filter with $\sigma_\xi = 10$, $\sigma_\eta = 1$, the discretization angle is equal to 5 degrees with hysteresis lower threshold equal to 0.001 and higher threshold equal to 0.15. The second result (Fig. 7 c)) is the result of our perceptual edge detector with $\sigma_\xi = 10$, $\sigma_\eta = 1$, the discretization angle is equal to 5 degrees with hysteresis lower threshold equal to 0.05 and higher threshold equal to 0.15. The Fig. 7 d) is obtained using the color Gaussian edge detector with $\sigma = 1$, hysteresis lower threshold is equal to 0.01 and higher threshold is equal to 0.1. The Fig. 7 e) is obtained using the color Deriche edge detector with $\alpha = 1$, hysteresis lower threshold is equal to 0.001 and higher threshold is equal to 0.04. As compared to the anisotropic Gaussian filter, our perceptual edge detector gives better results on many small details, this can be seen at the arm of the man in the picture, moreover, our perceptual detector

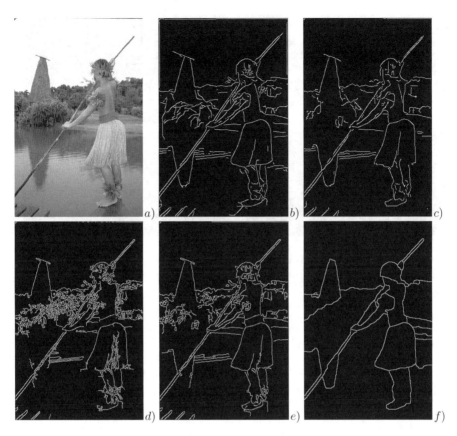

Fig. 7. a) Real color image. b) Edges obtained with the Gaussian anisotropic edge detector. c) Result of the perceptual edge operator. d) Contours obtained with the isotropic Gaussian operator. e) Results of the color Deriche operator. f) Results with the gPb operator.

is more robust to noise on complex textures. Results obtained by Gaussian and Deriche filtering are more noisy. If we increase the threshold, many important edge points disappear. We have also compared our result with gPb (Fig. 7 f)) and we obtain more details.

The second image (Fig. 8 a)) contain difficult textures, the aim is to segment the car. The first result (Fig. 8 b)) is obtained with the anisotropic Gaussian filter with $\sigma_\xi = 10$, $\sigma_\eta = 1$, the discretization angle is equal to 5 degrees with hysteresis lower threshold equal to 0.001 and higher threshold equal to 0.3. If the higher threshold decreases, the noise caused by leaves increases, on the contrary, if the higher threshold becomes greater than 0.3, contours of the car disappear. The second result (Fig. 8 c)) is the result of our perceptual edge detector with $\sigma_\xi = 10$, $\sigma_\eta = 1$, the discretization angle is equal to 5 degrees with hysteresis lower threshold equal to 0.01 and higher threshold equal to 0.5. We are able to extract the edge of the car from "leaves" texture. The third result (Fig. 8 d)) is

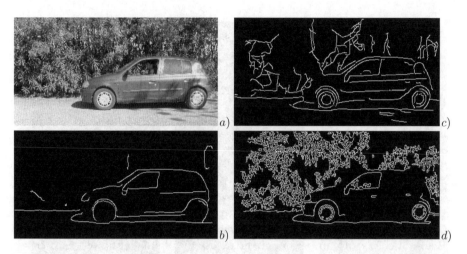

Fig. 8. a) Real color image. b) Edges obtained with the Gaussian anisotropic edge detector. c) Result of the perceptual edge operator. d) Results with the isotropic Gaussian edge operator.

obtained with the Gaussian isotropic edge detector, with $\sigma = 1$, hysteresis higher threshold is equal to 0.2 and lower threshold is equal to 0.01. If the hysteresis higher threshold becomes greater than 0.2, we lost totally edges of the car and the noise remains so this result can not be exploited. We present other results with our perceptual detector in Fig. 9 and an images data base with results is available on-line [14].

4.4   Computational Time

The code of our detector is written in C++ on a Linux Operating System. For testing the detector with derivative and half-smoothing Gaussian filter, we have used a 8-core processor running at 2.6 GHz. For processing a 256x256 grey level image (with a discretization angle of 5 degrees), the whole process takes 1.3 seconds. Note that this process is divided in two stages: derivation stage and gradient stage. At the derivation stage, derivation images are computed and written to the disk. At the gradient stage, derivation images are loaded again, to optimize input and output directions, then the gradient and its angle are written to the disk. Within this experiment 72 derivation images are computed and written and loaded again. Only the derivation stage is parallelized on the 8 processors. Many time could be saved firstly by the parallelization of the gradient stage and secondly by avoiding the saving of derivation images. The memory occupation for the whole process is small and the detector is not limited by image size. For example, images of size 1000x1000 can be easily computed with 2 GB of RAM.

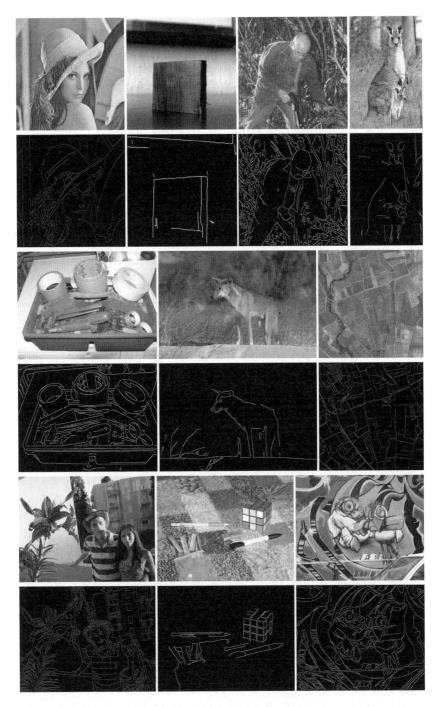

Fig. 9. Image contours selection using our perceptual edge detector with $\sigma_\xi = 10$, $\sigma_\eta = 1$ and the discretization angle is equal to 5 degrees

5 Conclusion

We have presented a new precise, robust and fast perceptual edge detector based on anisotropic linear filtering and local maximization. Our method is designed for the detection of edge points which are involved in large structures. It enables a really precise detection for edges even in very noisy cases. This detector has been tested successfully on various image types presenting difficult problems for classical edge and detection methods. At this time, threshold parameters are almost stable, in the future we plan to bring automatic threshold.

References

1. Arbelaez, P., Maire, M., Fowlkes, C., Malik, J.: From Contours to Regions: An Empirical Evaluation. In: IEEE Computer Vision and Pattern Recognition, Miami, pp. 2294–2301 (2009)
2. Canny, J.F.: A Variational Approach to Edge Detection. In: Proceedings 3rd National Conference on Artificial Intelligence, Washington, D.C., pp. 54–58 (1983)
3. Catanzaro, B., Su, B., Sundaram, N., Lee, Y., Murphy, M., Keutzer, K.: Efficient, High-quality Image Contour Detection. In: IEEE International Conference on Computer Vision, Kyoto (2009)
4. Deriche, R.: Using Canny's Criteria to Derive a Recursively Implemented Optimal Edge Detector. International J. of Computer Vision 1(2), 167–187 (1987)
5. Deriche, R.: Recursively Implementing the Gaussian and its Derivatives. In: IEEE International Conference on Image Processing, Singapore, pp. 263–267 (1992)
6. Di Zenzo, S.: A Note on the Gradient of a Multi image. J. Computer Vision, Graphics, and Image Processing. 33, 116–125 (1986)
7. Geusebroek, J., Smeulders, A., Van De Weijer, J.: Fast Anisotropic Gauss Filtering. In: Heyden, A., Sparr, G., Nielsen, M., Johansen, P. (eds.) ECCV 2002. LNCS, vol. 2350, pp. 99–112. Springer, Heidelberg (2002)
8. Guy, G., Medioni, G.: Inferring Global Perceptual Contours from Local Features. In: IEEE DARPA Image Understanding Workshop, Washington, D.C., pp. 881–892 (1993)
9. Knossow, D., van de Weijer, J., Horaud, R., Ronfard, R.: Articulated-body Tracking Through Anisotropic Edge Detection. In: Vidal, R., Heyden, A., Ma, Y. (eds.) WDV 2005/2006. LNCS, vol. 4358, pp. 86–99. Springer, Heidelberg (2007)
10. Magnier, B., Comby, F., Strauss, O., Triboulet, J., Demonceaux, C.: Highly Specific Pose Estimation with a Catadioptric Omnidirectional Camera. In: IEEE Int. Conference on Imaging Systems and Techniques, Thessaloniki (2010)
11. Montesinos, P., Alquier, L.: Perceptual Organization of thin Networks with Active Contour Functions Applied to Medical and Aerial Images. In: Proceedings 13th IEEE International Conference on Pattern Recognition, Vienna, pp. 647–651 (1996)
12. Sha'ashua, A., Ullman, S.: Grouping Contours Elements Using a Locally Connected Network. Neural Information Processing Systems. Morgan Kaufmann, San Francisco (1990)
13. Shen, J., Castan, S.: An Optimal Linear Operator for Step Edge Detection. Computer Vision, Graphical Models and Image Processing 54(2), 112–133 (1992)
14. Magnier, B., Montesinos, P.: Perceptual Edge Detector Results,
   http://www.lgi2p.ema.fr/~montesin/Demos/perceptualedgedetection.html

Combining Geometric Edge Detectors for Feature Detection

Michaël Heyvaert, David Van Hamme, Jonas Coppens, and Peter Veelaert

University College Ghent, Engineering Sciences - Ghent University Association,
Schoonmeersstraat 52, B9000 Ghent, Belgium
michael.heyvaert@hogent.be, david.vanhamme@hogent.be,
jonas.coppens@hogent.be, peter.veelaert@hogent.be

Abstract. We propose a novel framework for the analysis and modeling of discrete edge filters, based on the notion of signed rays. This framework will allow us to easily deduce the geometric and localization properties of a family of first-order filters, and use this information to design custom filter banks for specific applications. As an example, a set of angle-selective corner detectors is constructed for the detection of buildings in video sequences. This clearly illustrates the merit of the theory for solving practical recognition problems.

1 Introduction

The traditional approach in feature detection is to start with filter kernels that yield accurate localization in space and frequency [12]. General corner detectors, e.g. Harris, FAST and SUSAN are rotationally insensitive, as this is a desirable property in many feature matching applications. Steerable filters, e.g. Gabor filters and Derivative of Gaussian (DoG) filters, incorporate orientation to increase the selectivity. Since one cannot convolve an image with kernels for all possible orientations, scales and positions, only a small set of filters is used to sample the space for a finite set of orientations and scales. The response for arbitrary orientations or scales is obtained by interpolation.

The detection of more specific patterns, such as wedges or junctions, requires specially tuned filters. Perona demonstrates the use of 2-sided, endstopped and 1-sided endstopped filters for the detection of junctions, where each of these tuned filters is a suitable combination of a limited set of basic kernels [12]. Simoncelli et al use steerable wedge filters to avoid 180 degree periodic response [11]. Jacob et al use the degrees of freedom of steerable functions to design shape-adaptable filters, in particular for ridges and wedges [4]. The drawback of using steerable filters, however, is that basic kernels of high order are needed, requiring relatively large templates (typically with radius 10 or larger).

In this work we construct filters in a design space which differs from the classical approach. The major novelty is that we will exploit the relation between position selectivity and orientation selectivity. We will make explicit use of the property that the orientation selectivity actually depends on the position of the edge relative to the filter kernel. To highlight the advantages of the proposed scheme we will use filter response models that are relatively simple, without referring to scale or frequency.

J. Blanc-Talon et al. (Eds.): ACIVS 2010, Part I, LNCS 6474, pp. 221–232, 2010.

Modeling the dependency between position uncertainty and orientation uncertainty makes it easier to design detectors for specific features. To detect features that consist of two or more edge segments, e.g., corners or junctions, we have to combine the response of multiple edge detectors for edges at different orientations and positions. The proposed scheme indicates which edge detectors have to be combined. Furthermore, there is still the freedom to choose the selectivity of the edge filters that will be used. The inclusion of a large number of highly selective filters will yield high accuracy. A small set of filters with limited selectivity requires less computation. The edge filters used in this work all have a small radius (≤ 2.5) with very few non-zero coefficients. The filters are much smaller and simpler than the high-order steerable filters, since we combine filter responses at different positions in the image.

Section 2 introduces the mathematical model used to characterize edge filters. Section 3 shows how to evaluate the performance of combined edge filters. The technique is illustrated in Section 4 for the detection of corners in buildings.

2 Discrete Geometry Approach to Edge Detection

To model the dependency between orientation and position selectivity we need to define some concepts related to the digitization of straight edges and lines.

Let $U = \{u_1, \ldots, u_n\}$ and $V = \{v_1, \ldots, v_m\}$ be two finite and non-empty subsets of Z^2 such that U can be linearly separated from V. Then the lines separating these regions satisfy the following conditions:

$$y_i - ax_i - b > 0, \; (x_i, y_i) \in U \tag{1}$$

$$y_j - ax_j - b < 0, \; (x_j, y_j) \in V \tag{2}$$

Thus the parameters of the separating lines lie in an open convex region or domain in the ab-parameter plane, which will be denoted as $D(U, V)$. This domain is related to the preimage of a discrete straight line segment [5], but it is not exactly the same concept, since the preimage of a discrete subset considers all the lines that stab a set of pixel squares, while here we consider the lines that separate two sets of points.

Fig. 1(a) shows two disjoint point sets. The straight lines that separate these two sets cover a butterfly shaped region. We note that the range of possible orientations of lines that pass through p_1 is different from the range of orientations at the point p_2. Likewise, given an arbitrary straight line which separates U and V, the distance by which this line can be displaced while keeping the separation intact depends on the orientation of the line. For example, the line L_1 can be displaced much further vertically than the line L_2. Also in Fig. 1(b) it is clear that there is a relation between position and slope uncertainty. Fig. 1(b) shows the domain that contains the parameters of the separating lines. When the domain is sliced into vertical segments, the height of each vertical segment depends on the position of the segment in the domain, that is, on the slope parameter a.

The digital edge filters used in this work are first order filters that are directly related to two disjoint sets of grid points. Let $f(x, y) : R^2 \rightarrow R$ be an image function of two continuous variables. We use a simple sampling model: a digital image $f[x, y]$ is formed from the function $f(x, y)$ by the relationship $f[x, y] = f(x, y)$, for integer values of x and y, $0 \leq x \leq M, 0 \leq y \leq N$.

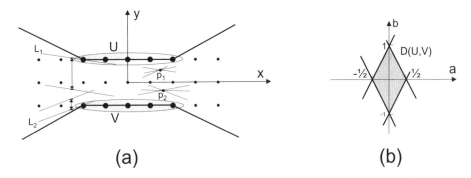

(a)   (b)

Fig. 1. (a) Straight lines that separate two discrete sets U and V, and (b) the parameter domain of all the separating lines

Let $U = \{u_1, \ldots, u_n\}$ and $V = \{v_1, \ldots, v_m\}$ be two disjoint subsets of Z^2. We define a digital 2D filter $h[x, y]$ as follows:

$$h[x, y] = \begin{cases} \frac{1}{2n} & |(x, y) \in U \\ \frac{-1}{2m} & |(x, y) \in V \\ 0 & otherwise \end{cases} \tag{3}$$

When we apply the filter $h[x, y]$ to the digital image of an edge, i.e. $g = h * u$, and consider its response at $g[0, 0]$, we find that there is direct relation between the filter response and the domain $D(U, V)$. Let $u(x, y)$ denote an edge function of the form $u(x, y) = 1$ if $0 \leq y - ax - b$, and $u(x, y) = -1$ if $0 > y - ax - b$, for some real numbers a, b. Let $u[x, y]$ denote the discrete sampling of $u(x, y)$. Let $g[] = h[] * u[]$ denote the response of the filter for the edge function $u[x, y]$. Clearly, the response $|g[0, 0]|$ will be maximal, i.e, $|g[0, 0]| = 1$ provided $u[x, y] = 1$ for all $(x, y) \in U$ and $u[x, y] = -1$ for all $(x, y) \in V$. The values of a and b for which this holds true define the edges that separate the two sets U and V. Their line parameters a, b lie in the domain shown in Fig. 1. For any other edge outside the domain the response $|g[0, 0]|$ will be less than 1. To summarize, the filter response is maximal for the edges whose parameters lie in the domain $D(U, V)$.

Fig. 2. Response of four filters with different orientations

2.1 Signed Rays

To be able to combine filters for the detection of features we will decompose domains into elementary domain cells. To this end we introduce the simple but convenient notion of a signed ray of points. A signed set X is a set together with a partition $\{X_p, X_n\}$ where the elements in X_p have positive signs, and the elements in X_n have negative signs.

Definition 1. *Let S be a finite set of points in the plane, and let R be an ordered signed subset of S. Then R is a signed ray if:*

- *R is the intersection of a straight line with S;*
- *the ordering of R preserves the betweenness-relation of Euclidean geometry;*
- *the sign changes only once along the ray.*

A signed ray can be denoted as $R = \ldots p_1 p_2 \overline{p_3 p_4} \ldots$, where p_1 and p_2 have positive signs, and p_3 and p_4 have negative signs. Because of the last condition in the definition, we cannot have rays of the form $p_1 p_2 \overline{p_3 p_4} p_5 \ldots$, where the sign alternates more than once. But it is possible to start with negative signs, e.g., $R = \overline{p_1 p_2} p_3 p_4$. All points may also have the same sign.

A signed ray $R = p_1 \ldots \overline{p_n}$ divides the points of S into two parts. The points in $R \cap S$ already have a sign. Let L be the straight line passing through the points of R. Since R is an ordered sequence, the points induce an orientation on the line L, from p_1 to p_n. With this orientation we can attribute signs to the points in S not in R. Points that lie at the right side of L receive a positive sign, points at the left side receive a negative sign. The two signed parts of S will be denoted as R^+ and R^-, respectively. Thus the signs of the points of the ray serve to add these points to either R^+ or R^-.

There is a direct relation between rays and linear separations of sets.

Proposition 1. *Let $S = S^+ \cup S^-$ be a partition of a finite set S induced by a straight line L that does not pass through any of the points of S. Then there exists a signed ray R such that $S^+ = R^+$ and $S^- = R^-$. Conversely, if R is a signed ray in S, then the subsets R^+ and R^- can be linearly separated by a straight line not passing through any of the points of S.*

As a result each signed ray corresponds to a domain. Suppose R separates the points of S into two non-empty parts, S^+ and S^-. The straight lines separating S^+ and S^- satisfy the following conditions:

$$y_i - a x_i - b > 0, \ (x_i, y_i) \in S^+ \tag{4}$$

$$y_j - a x_j - b < 0, \ (x_j, y_j) \in S^- \tag{5}$$

The parameters a and b that satisfy these conditions occupy an open convex region in parameter space, the domain of the signed ray, which is denoted as $D_S(R^+, R^-)$.

Distinct rays may represent the same domain. Fig. 3 shows four distinct rays that separate the four points such that p_1, p_2 receive positive signs and p_3, p_4 negative signs, namely, $p_1 p_2$, $\overline{p_3} p_2$, $p_1 \overline{p_4}$, and $\overline{p_3 p_4}$. Likewise, $\overline{p_2 p_1}$, $\overline{p_2} p_3$, $p_4 \overline{p_1}$, and $p_4 p_3$ separate the points such that p_1, p_2 receive negative signs and p_3, p_4 positive signs, which yields the

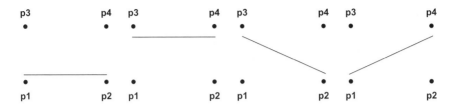

Fig. 3. Four signed rays that separate the points into $\{p_1, p_2\}$ and $\{p_3, p_4\}$: (a) $p_1 p_2$, (b) $\overline{p_3 p_4}$, (c) $\overline{p_3} p_2$, and (d) $p_1 \overline{p_4}$

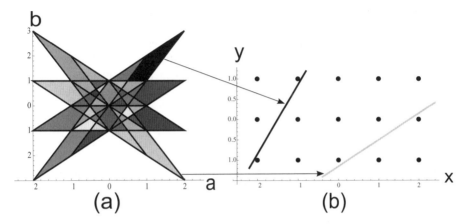

Fig. 4. (a) Finite domains of the signed rays for a 3×5 set of points. (b) Examples of member lines for two of the domains.

same partition but with interchanged signs. Among these 8 rays of the same partition, we can select a unique ray by imposing an ordering relation on the points of S (not to be confused with the ordering of R). For example, with $p_1 < p_2 < \ldots < p_n$, and using lexicographic ordering, the smallest representant is $p_1 p_2$. From now on, we will use the term 'signed ray' to denote the smallest representant corresponding to a certain partition of S.

Fig. 4(a) shows the bounded domains for the set S of 3×5 grid points shown in Fig. 4(b). Only domains that are bounded are shown, i.e, domains that do not include parameters of vertical lines.

With rays we decompose domains into elementary domains. Let U and V be subsets of a set S, such that U and V can be linearly separated. The union $U \cup V$ does not necessarily constitute the entire set S. Clearly the domain of lines that separate U and V can be decomposed into elementary domains that correspond to rays. Let $R(U, V)$ denote the set of all signed rays R that divide the set S into parts R^+ and R^- so that either $V \subseteq R^+ \wedge U \subseteq R^-$ or $U \subseteq R^+ \wedge V \subseteq R^-$. The topological closure of the domain of the disjoint subsets is the union of the closure of the elementary domains of the rays in $R(U, V)$:

$$\mathrm{cl}\left(D(U, V)\right) = \cup_{R \in R(U,V)} \mathrm{cl}\left(D_S(R^+, R^-)\right)$$

In fact, $R(U, V)$ corresponds to all the possible ways in which the subsets U and V can be maximally extended until their extensions coincide with a complete linear separation of S. Furthermore, no pair of subsets in S can have a domain $D(U, V)$ smaller than that of any ray in S. and the domains of two distinct rays are always disjoint.

The size of the set S defines the resolution of the decomposition into elementary domains. When S is enlarged, the ray domains become smaller, that is, if $S_1 \subseteq S_2$ then cl $D_{S_1}(R^+, R^-) \supseteq$ cl $D_{S_2}(R^+, R^-)$.

Ray domains are very similar to the cells in a Farey fan for digitized straight lines as defined in [5, 2]. The definition of a ray domain is more general, however, as the decomposition can be defined for an arbitrary set S. Furthermore, as mentioned earlier, ray domains correspond to sets of separating lines, while Farey cells correspond to common line stabbings.

The importance of decomposing domains of disjoint subsets is that a first order edge filter can be considered as the detector of a given collection of partitions of S. The decomposition into elementary domains, where each elementary domain corresponds to a filter with maximal selectivity, therefore allows us to identify all the possible overlaps and gaps in a bank of edge filters.

2.2 Localization Constraints

A second reason for introducing rays is that they are well suited to formulate constraints concerning localization, e.g. all straight lines passing through a polygon. Let us assume that the vertices of the polygon are points of S. In practical applications, this is a reasonable assumption, since it only requires that the vertices coincide with image sample points. Then it is sufficient to list all rays that do not attribute the same sign to all vertices. To be explicit, let P be a set of vertices of a convex polygon, with $P \subset S$, then the closed set

$$\cup_{R | R^+ \cap P \neq \emptyset \wedge R^- \cap P \neq \emptyset} \text{cl } D_S(R^+, R^-)$$

contains the parameters of the straight lines that pass through the polygon P.

If the vertices of the polygon are not points of S, the use of rays can still hold merit. Consider the extension of this polygon to its smallest bounding polygon made up by points in S. Any ray that does not cross this bounding polygon, cannot contain a line which crosses the original polygon. Thus rays can still be used to form boundaries delimiting the parameter space to be searched.

2.3 Angular Relations

Rays were introduced to discretize the parameter space of straight lines. As a result, angles between rays are determined in terms of intervals. For each pair of rays we can determine the minimum and maximum angle between any two of their lines by looking at the extrema of their domains in the a-axis (see Fig. 1). Rays are considered parallel when the angle intervals overlap, that is, when their domains contain at least one pair of parallel lines. Similarly, two rays are considered perpendicular if their domains contain at least one perpendicular pair of lines.

3   Combining Edge Detectors

The well-defined geometric properties and localization constraints of rays and the domain based approach allow us to easily design custom detectors for compound structures such as perpendicular corners, T-junctions or Y-junctions. Each detector will consist of one or more simple filters, and in general, multiple detectors will be needed to detect all occurrences of a feature. Furthermore, the size and the shape of the filters will determine their selectivity. The performance of each detector can be evaluated by computing ray domains. The general approach is as follows:

- First we select a set S of grid points for which all the ray domains will be computed. The set S determines the resolution of the domains. It makes no sense to choose S too large, however. It suffices that S encompasses all the sample points of the digital filters that will be used, and the vertices of the polygons that are used to define localization constraints.
- Next, we list all the rays or combinations of rays that define the features that we are interested in. The result is a list of ray tuples, for example pairs of rays that form corners, or triples of rays that form Y-junctions.
- Feature detectors are constructed by combining edge detectors. For each feature detector we can verify which ray tuples are detected, i.e, for which the detector will yield a maximal response. This will show whether all tuples are covered. The selectivity of the detectors is examined by looking at ray tuples for which more than one detector responds or by verifying whether the detector responds to tuples that do not correspond to the features that we are interested in.

Fig. 5 illustrates a simple example. The features that we are interested consist of perpendicular corners, for which one edge has a slope in $[0.85; 1.15]$ and the second edge has a slope in $[-1.15; -0.85]$. To make sure that we can detect this feature at any position in the image, we will examine the detection performance in the gray square shown in Fig. 5. The vertices of the square are four neighboring pixels. The detector that will be analyzed consist of the two simple filters F and G shown in Fig. 5, with filter coefficients equal to $-1/2$ at the dark dots, and equal to $1/3$ at the light dots.

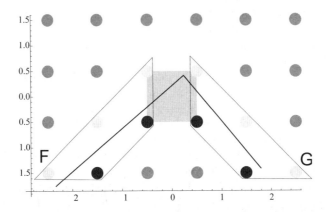

Fig. 5. Detection of perpendicular corners in a square. Two filters F and G are shown.

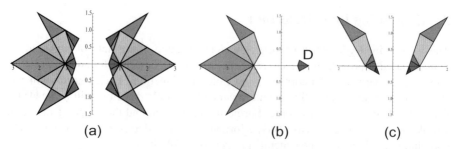

Fig. 6. Domains of the signed rays for a 4×6 set of points. (a) Shows all the domains of rays that cover slopes of either 1 or -1 and that enter the gray square. (b) Orthogonal pairs of domains. (c) Domain pairs for which both F and G yield a maximal response.

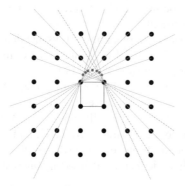

Fig. 7. Illustration of outer bound for intersection of perpendicular lines crossing a square

Fig. 6(a) shows the domains of all rays that contain lines passing through the square and have one of the required slopes. In this case a domain is included as soon as its closure contains a line with a slope in the specified intervals. Since there are 14 domains at the left side and 14 domains at the right side we can form 196 ray pairs. To select perpendicular corners, in this collection of 196 pairs all the ray pairs are listed that contain at least one perpendicular pair of lines. Fig. 6(b) shows a domain D that contains lines with slope in $[0.85; 1.15]$. The domains at the left side of Fig. 6(b) each contain at least one line that is perpendicular to one of the lines in D. In total there are 122 ray pairs that contain perpendicular corners.

Fig. 6(c) shows to which ray pairs the filters F and G will both give a maximal response. At the left side of Fig. 6(c) the ray domains are shown for which G responds, at the right side those for which F responds. Note that F (and G) also responds to a domain with lines that do not have the required slope. Since each filter gives a maximal response for 5 domains, the detector formed by F and G is triggered by 25 distinct ray pairs. Only 13 of them, however, contain orthogonal corners. Hence, the detector is not very selective since about half of the pairs by which it is triggered do not contain perpendicular corners. Clearly, the selectivity of the detector can be improved by using filters with a larger extent defined in a larger set S. Furthermore, the filter pair F,G only covers 13 of the 122 perpendicular pairs. More corner pairs can be covered by including more filter pairs, as will be illustrated in the next section.

Also note that although Fig. 6(a) only considers rays that cross the square, the detector may respond to pairs of perpendicular lines that intersect outside the square. This localization inaccuracy is bounded, however, by four half-circles with a side of the square as diameter, and is therefore also independent of the size of the grid S in which the rays are considered. This is illustrated in Fig. 7.

4   Application: Corner Detection in Buildings

One of the most defining features of buildings and man-made structures in general is that they tend to be constructed almost exclusively out of horizontal and vertical surfaces. The presence of a multitude of perpendicular corners is therefore a useful feature for detecting buildings in video. However, as they are viewed through a perspective transformation, these corners can be significantly skewed. In common cinematography, two of the camera axes are more or less perpendicular to the ground plane. This means that the vertical edge of a perpendicular corner can be assumed to remain vertical through the perspective transformation, while the horizontal edge will generally be rotated. We therefore need a set of detectors which respond maximally to any combination of a vertical with a non-vertical edge.

We will construct a filter bank following the reasoning of the previous section. This means combining a first order filter which responds maximally to vertical rays crossing a square, with a complete set of first order filters which respond maximally to all other orientations of rays crossing the square. Note that the minimum angle of the corner is defined by the orientation selectivity of the vertical first order filter, which itself is bounded by the grid size in which it is defined.

As a proof of concept we design a bank of filters as shown in Fig. 8. Only the filters for rays between 0 and 45 degrees are pictured. The remainder can be obtained by mirroring over the horizontal and vertical axes, resulting in a bank of 52 unique filters. For implementation purposes, further reduction is possible, as many of the filters have an identical point configuration, but a different point of origin.

By enumerating for each filter the rays to which responds, we can prove that this set of filters is both complete and non-overlapping for a 2 by 2 square, meaning that for each line which crosses a 2 by 2 square there is exactly one filter which yields maximal response. The proof is illustrated in Fig. 9. The leftmost graph shows the parameter domains of all rays in the 7 by 7 array containing a line angled between 0 and 45 degrees which crosses the 2 by 2 square. The remaining graphs show the parameter domains of

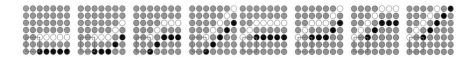

Fig. 8. 8 first order filters from a bank of 52. The remainder is obtained through horizontal and vertical mirroring.

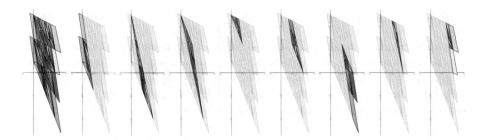

Fig. 9. Domains in the ab parameter space of all rays containing lines crossing the 2 by 2 square with a slope between 0 and 1 (left), and of rays with maximal response for each of the filters (remainder)

maximal response for each filter shown in Fig. 8. In Fig. 9 it can be seen that the union of the domains of the individual filters makes up the whole set of domains as shown on the left, while the intersection between the filters is empty. Due to the symmetries, these properties apply to the entire filter set.

To translate the theoretical results to a practical application, we need to swap the notion of maximal response with a threshold on the response, as real edges in an image do not correspond to the theoretical concept of the infinitely sharp edge. In this case, a locally adaptive threshold was chosen based on the average intensity of the image patch with a Gaussian filter mask of size 11×11. Next each non-vertical response is thresholded and combined with the vertical responses. The resulting masks contain all the detected corners. Due to the non-ideal edges, a non-maximal suppression step is needed to remove multiple detections of the same corner. This step is implemented by only retaining the corner with the strongest response in a 3×3 neighborhood. The measure for determining the strongest response is the sum of the squared response magnitudes for both edges.

Fig. 10. Corner detection, the color gives a coarse indication of the corner angle

Fig. 11. Comparison of our corner detector and the Harris corner detector, red corners are matches, green corners are only detected by our method and blue corners are only detected by the Harris corner detector

Fig. 10 shows corners angle indicated with the different color labels. The angular selectivity of the filters divides the building into zones of similar perspective skew. This is a good illustration of the orientation selectivity of the filter pairs. We also compared the detected corners with the Harris corner detector [3]. Fig. 11 shows the 400 strongest Harris corners, and the 400 strongest corners according to our method. The results of the theoretical domain analysis are confirmed in several ways. First, when both methods detect the same corner, the positions coincide, proving the accuracy of localization. Second, our corners cover 48% of the Harris corner set, which is not surprising, as the detectors were designed for a limited set of corner shapes, while Harris is a general corner detector. On the other hand, our method provides a classification of the corners into corner types.

5   Conclusion

We have proposed a theoretical framework to model the properties of first-order filters in a discrete geometric approach. The definition of rays allows us to simply deduce localization and geometric properties of families of filters, and offers an interesting insight into the consequences of a discrete sampling of edges in a continuous image function. The usefulness of the theory is illustrated by an example application, where the angular properties of real-world structures are evaluated by a custom filter set. Some aspects remain to be explored in more depth, such as the relation between angular selectivity and choice of grid size and density, and the best way to construct first order filters from the chosen grid. Even so, we can conclude that the ray-based framework is already a useful tool to model the properties of discrete filters.

References

1. Chinneck, J.: Feasibility and Infeasibility in Optimization. International Series in Operations Research and Management Science. Springer, Heidelberg (2008)
2. Coeurjolly, D., Sivignon, I.: Measure of straight lines and its applications in digital geometry. In: Progress in Combinatorial Image Analysis, pp. 37–48. Research Publishing (2010)
3. Harris, C., Stephens, M.: A combined corner and edge detector. In: Alvey Vision Conference, pp. 147–151 (1988)
4. Jacob, M., Unser, M.: Design of Steerable Filters for Feature Detection Using Canny-Like Criteria. IEEE Transactions on Pattern Analysis and Machine Intelligence 26, 1007–1019 (2004)
5. Lindenbaum, M., Bruckstein, A.: On recursive $O(N)$ partitioning of a digitized curve into digital straight line segments. IEEE Transactions on Pattern Analysis and Machine Intelligence 15, 949–953 (1993)
6. Lowe, D.G.: Distinctive image features from scale-invariant keypoints. International Journal of Computer Vision 60, 91–110 (2004)
7. Rosten, E., Drummond, T.: Machine learning for high-speed corner detector. In: Computer Conference on Computer Vision, pp. 430–443 (2006)
8. Smith, S.M., Brady, J.M.: SUSAN – a new approach to low level image processing. International Journal of Computer Vision 23, 45–78 (1997)
9. Trajkovic, M., Hedley, M.: Fast corner detection. Image and Vision Computing 16, 75–87 (1998)
10. Veelaert, P.: Constructive fitting and extraction of geometric primitives. CVGIP: Graphical Models and Image Processing 59, 233–251 (1997)
11. Simoncelli, E.P., Farid, H.: Steerable Wedge Filters for Local Orientation Analysis. IEEE Transactions on Image Processing 5, 1377–1382 (1996)
12. Perona, P.: Steerable-scalable kernels for edge detection and junction analysis. In: Sandini, G. (ed.) ECCV 1992. LNCS, vol. 588, pp. 3–18. Springer, Heidelberg (1992)

Canny Edge Detection Using Bilateral Filter on Real Hexagonal Structure

Xiangjian He[1,5], Daming Wei[2], Kin-Man Lam[3], Jianmin Li[4], Lin Wang[5],
Wenjing Jia[1], and Qiang Wu[1]

[1] Centre for Innovation in IT Services and Applications (iNEXT)
University of Technology, Sydney, Australia
{xiangjian.he,wenjing.jia-1,qiang.wu}@uts.edu.au
[2] Biomedical Information Technology Laboratory
University of Aizu, Japan
dm-wei@u-aizu.ac.jp
[3] Department of Electronic & Information Engineering
Hong Kong Polytechnic University, Hong Kong
enkmlam@inet.polyu.edu.hk
[4] College of Mathematics and Computer Science
Fuzhou University, China
animation@fzu.edu.cn
[5] Video Surveillance Laboratory
Guizhou University for Nationalities, China
wanglin@gznc.edu.cn

Abstract. Edge detection plays an important role in image processing area. This paper presents a Canny edge detection method based on bilateral filtering which achieves better performance than single Gaussian filtering. In this form of filtering, both spatial closeness and intensity similarity of pixels are considered in order to preserve important visual cues provided by edges and reduce the sharpness of transitions in intensity values as well. In addition, the edge detection method proposed in this paper is achieved on sampled images represented on a real hexagonal structure. Due to the compact and circular nature of the hexagonal lattice, a better quality edge map is obtained on the hexagonal structure than common edge detection on square structure. Experimental results using proposed methods exhibit also the faster speed of detection on hexagonal structure.

Keywords: Canny edge detection, image processing, image analysis, Gaussian filtering, bilateral filtering, hexagonal image structure.

1 Introduction

As described in [1], computer vision involves compositions of picture elements (pixels) into edges, edges into object contours and object contours into scenes. The determination of edges depends on detection of edge points (pixels) of a 3-D physical object in a 2-D image. This first step in the process is critical to the functioning of

J. Blanc-Talon et al. (Eds.): ACIVS 2010, Part I, LNCS 6474, pp. 233–244, 2010.
© Springer-Verlag Berlin Heidelberg 2010

machine vision. As the success of subsequent steps are sensitive to the quality of results at this step, the performance of higher level processes such as extraction of object contours and object recognition relies heavily on the complete and correct determination of edges. Edges contain major image information and need only a small amount of memory storage space compared to the original image. Hence, edge detection simplifies images and thus facilitates image analysis and interpretation.

Edge detection is based on the relationship a pixel has with its neighbours. It extracts and localizes points (pixels) around which a large change in image brightness has occurred. A pixel is unsuitable to be recorded as an edge if the brightness around a pixel is similar (or close). Otherwise, the pixel may represent an edge.

During the last three decades, many algorithms have been developed for edge detection e.g. Roberts edge detector, Sobel edge detector, Marr-Hildreth edge detector, etc. All these edge detectors resolve some problems but still have their disadvantages. In 1986, Canny [2] developed an optimal edge detection scheme using linear filtering with a Gaussian kernel to suppress noise and reduce the sharpness of transition in intensity values. In order to recover missing weak edge points and eliminate false edge points, two edge strength thresholds are set to examine all the candidate edge points. Those below the lower threshold are marked as non-edge. Those which are above the lower threshold and can be connected to points whose edge strengths are above the higher threshold through a chain of edge points are marked as edge points [3].

However, the performance of Canny edge detection relies on Gaussian filtering. Gaussian filtering not only removes image noise and suppresses image details but also weakens the edge information [3].

In [1], an additional filter called range filter [4] is combined with the conventional Gaussian filter to get a bilateral filter in order to reduce the blur effect using the Gaussian filter only. The approach was based on a virtual hexagonal structure. In the hexagonal image structure, image is represented by a collection of hexagonal pixels of the same size (in contrast with the traditional representation using square pixels). The importance of the hexagonal representation is that it possesses special computational features that are pertinent to the vision process [3]. Although the results shown in [1] have improved the performance on traditional square structure, it has following two limitations. In [1], the original image for edge detection was converted to hexagonal structure based on a sub-pixel based massive computation algorithm, and the edge strengths obtained on hexagonal structure were converted to the square structure again using another sub-pixel based massive algorithm. Hence the time costs for the overall edge detection on the sub-pixel approach hexagonal structure were much higher than the same approach on the square structure. Moreover, the thresholding step for Canny detection was implemented on the square structure rather than the hexagonal structure and this downgraded detection accuracy.

In this paper, a new edge detection algorithm is implemented on a real hexagonal structure. The complete steps of Canny edge detection is performed on the hexagonal structure. Because a simpler conversion algorithm is used for image conversion between the image structures, the computation costs are efficient while improving the detection accuracy.

The organization of this paper is as follows. A new and real hexagonal structure is constructed in Section 2. Canny edge detection using a bilateral filter is performed in Section 3. Section 4 presents the experimental results. Conclusions are given in Section 5.

2 Hexagonal Structure

The possibility of using a hexagonal grid to represent digital images has been studied for more than thirty years. Hexagonal grids have higher degrees of symmetry than the square grids. This symmetry results in a considerable saving of both storage and computation time [5, 6]. In order to properly address and store hexagonal images data, Sheridan [7] proposed a one-dimensional addressing scheme for a hexagonal structure, called Spiral Architecture, as shown in Fig. 1.

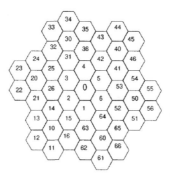

Fig. 1. Spiral Architecture with spiral addressing [3]

Because there has been no hardware available for image display and capture on hexagonal structure, in [1], a software approach was introduced to the construction of a hexagonal structure. To simulate hexagonal pixels, each square pixel was first separated into 7×7 small pixels, called *sub-pixels*. The light intensity for each of these sub-pixels was set to be the same as that of the pixel from which the sub-pixels are separated. Each virtual hexagonal pixel is formed by 56 sub-pixels that were unevenly spread into 8 sub-pixel rows and 9 sub-pixel columns [1]. The light intensity of each constructed hexagonal pixel is computed as the average of the intensities of the 56 sub-pixels forming the hexagonal pixel. Because of much larger amount of sub-pixels involved in the image conversion computation and in the Canny detection algorithm, the computation cost was a lot higher than bilateral based Canny edge algorithm on the traditional square structure.

Unlike all previous approaches for Canny edge detection on hexagonal structure, in this paper, we no longer use the sub-pixels for the simulation of hexagonal pixels. On the new hexagonal structure in this paper, the hexagonal pixel shape is a real hexagon. Furthermore, in this new structure, each row has only half as many pixel samples as those on the square structure (Fig. 2). The row and column arrangement of this new hexagonal structure is displayed in Fig. 2.

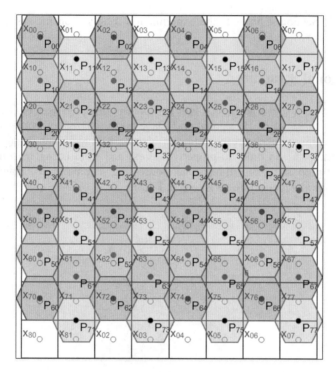

Fig. 2. This figure shows a 9x8 square structure and a constructed 14x8 hexagonal structure

As shown in Fig.2, the hexagonal pixels appear only on the columns where the square pixels are located. Let us assume that the distance between two neighbouring square pixels on the same row or column is 1. Then, the distance between two neighbouring hexagonal pixels is set to be $2/\sqrt{3}$. This indicates that the size of each hexagonal pixel is slightly larger than a square pixel, and hence the number of hexagonal pixels required to represent an image is smaller than that on square structure. This, however, does not reduce the image resolution in theory because image displayed on hexagonal structure allows us to use about 13% less pixels to achieve the same resolution level as the one displayed on square structure [5].

As illustrated in Fig. 2, for a given hexagonal pixel (denoted by X), there exist two square pixels denoted by A and B, lying on two consecutive rows and the same column of X, such that point X falls between A and B. Therefore, we can use the linear interpolation algorithm to obtain the light intensity value of X from the intensities of A and B.

Fig. 3 shows an original Lena image represented on square structure (left) and its representation on the hexagonal structure (right) using the linear interpolation approach mentioned above. In the right figure of Fig. 3, we see the black part on the bottom of the image. This black part actually illustrates the number of pixels saved when representing an image on hexagonal structure. The remaining figure is divided into two parts above the black part. The left half is formed by all hexagonal pixels on the odd rows (and hence the odd columns) of pixels on hexagonal structure, and the right half is formed by all hexagonal pixels on the even rows and even columns.

Fig. 3. Original Lena image. Left: on square structure; right: on hexagonal structure

3   Edge Detection

In this section, the performance of edge detection will go through three steps: noise filtering using a bilateral filter, edge detection using an edge operator defined on hexagonal structure and edge refining using thresholds.

3.1   Noise Filtering

Before the edge map of an image is found, it is common that image noise is removed (or suppressed) by applying a filter that blurs or smoothes the image.

One commonly used filter is implemented by convolution of the original image function with a Gaussian kernel as defined in Equation (2) below. In order to achieve a more desirable level of smoothing in applications, a bilateral filter has recently been introduced as shown in [3]. Bilateral filtering replaces the intensity value of a pixel with a weighted average intensity value of those pixels that either have similar intensity values as that of the given pixel or are close to the given pixel. In this form of filtering, a *range filter* is combined with a *domain filter*. A domain filter enforces spatial closeness by weighing pixel intensity values with coefficients that fall off as distance of the neighbouring pixel increases [3]. A range filter, on the other hand, assigns greater coefficients to those neighbouring pixel values that are more similar to the given reference pixel value. Hence, the original intensity value at a given pixel would be better preserved after the value replacement. Range filtering by itself is of little use because values of the pixels that are far away from a given pixel should not contribute to the new value. In one word, the kernel coefficients of a bilateral filter are determined by the combined closeness and similarity function. We explain how a bilateral filter works using mathematical terms as follows [3].

Let $f : \Re^2 \to \Re$ be the original brightness function of an image which maps the coordinates of a pixel, (x, y) to a value in light intensity. Let a_0 be the reference pixel.

Then, for any given pixel a at location (x, y), the coefficient assigned to intensity value $f(a)$ at a for the range filter is $r(a)$ computed by the similarity function s as:

$$r(a) = s(f(a), f(a_0)) = e^{-\frac{(f(a)-f(a_0))^2}{2\sigma_1^2}} \qquad (1)$$

Similarly, the coefficient assigned for the domain filter is $g(a)$ computed by the closeness function c as:

$$g(a) = c(a, a_0) = e^{-\frac{(a-a_0)^2}{2\sigma_2^2}} \qquad (2)$$

Therefore, for the reference pixel a_0, its new intensity value, denoted by $h(a_0)$, is

$$h(a_0) = k^{-1} \sum_{i=0}^{n-1} f(a_i) \times g(a_i) \times r(a_i) \qquad (3)$$

where k is the normalization constant and is defined as

$$k = \sum_{i=0}^{n-1} g(a_i) \times r(a_i). \qquad (4)$$

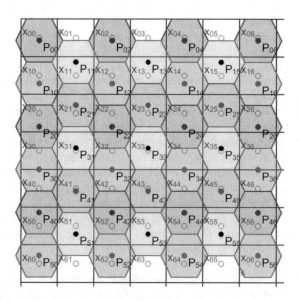

Fig. 4. An 11x7 hex kernel window applying to hexagonal pixel at P_{33}

Equation (3) above is called a convolution of the image brightness function f with domain filter g and range filter r. It will take a long time to carry on the convolution processing as shown in (3) if n is large. Considering about 99.5% of energy is found in the central area of "Mexico cap" (the curve of Gaussian function with parameter σ)

within the radius of 3σ, in order to increase the computation speed, Equation (3) in this paper is computed only over a small area (called *convolution window*) surround-ding each reference pixel and covering the rectangle with centre at the reference pixel and length and width of $3\sigma_2$. In this paper, σ_2 is set to be 1. By computation, the con-volution window is found to be square containing 49 hexagonal pixels (assuming the distance between two adjacent square pixels is 1) on square structure. Similarly, when an image represented on the hexagonal structure is filtered using either a Gaussian filter or bilateral filter, its window is found to be a rectangle shown in Fig. 4 for weighted average computation using Equations (3) and (4), and the convolution win-dow consists of the 39 hexagonal pixels (10 pixels less than those in the window on square structure) centred at the reference pixel. Furthermore, σ_1, the parameter for the range filtering, is computed as the standard deviation of grey values in input image.

3.2 Edge Detection

Conventional Sobel edge detector [8] is an edge detector using a 3×3 mask as an edge operator on square structure. It is used widely in image processing area, and is used in this paper for Canny edge detection on square structure for comparison pur-pose. In order to implement edge detection on the hexagonal structure, a modified Sobel operator, as presented in [3] and shown in Fig. 5, is applied in this paper. It is worth to know that the use of operators is not critical on hexagonal structure and we have proved this property in a paper submitted to a journal for publication. Using the modified Sobel operator, edge strength and direction at each sub-pixel can be calcu-lated in the similar way as on the square structure. Each pixel with maximum gradient magnitude in the gradient direction is recorded as possible edge point. Otherwise, the pixel is recorded as a non-edge point.

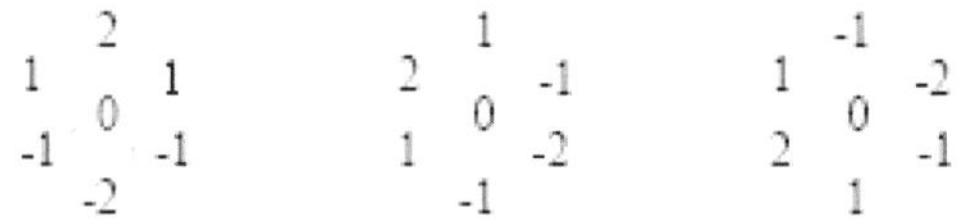

$$
\begin{array}{ccc}
2 & 1 & -1 \\
1 \quad 1 & 2 \quad -1 & 1 \quad -2 \\
0 & 0 & 0 \\
-1 \quad -1 & 1 \quad -2 & 2 \quad -1 \\
-2 & -1 & 1
\end{array}
$$

Fig. 5. Modified Sobel operator [3]

3.3 Edge Refining

After the edge detection step shown in the previous subsection, all pixels have been marked as either possible edge points or non-edge points. We can then follow the remaining steps of Canny's method to obtain the final edge map by computing and using one lower threshold and one higher threshold. The higher threshold is computed based on the percentage of possible edge points that is manually set as the strong edge points by the user. The lower threshold is computed based on the ratio of the high to low threshold that is manually set by the user.

The same as the original Canny's detection algorithm, we first mark the pixels that have gradient magnitudes bigger than the higher threshold as the edge pixels. Then, an iterative process is performed on every neighbouring pixel of the marked edge pixels such that the neighbouring pixel is marked as an edge pixel if its gradient magnitude is larger than the lower threshold, or non-edge pixel otherwise.

The advantage of implementation on the hexagonal structure for this edge refining process instead of performing this step in square structure as shown in all previous approaches is that we need only consider and perform on 6 neighbouring pixels during each iteration compared to 8 neighbouring pixels on square structure, and hence reduce the computation time.

3.4 Display Edge on Square Structure

After the edge pixels are identified on the hexagonal structure, we need to convert the results to square structure to display. On the square structure, we first set all pixels as non-edge pixels. Instead of performing on all square pixels, we then perform only on the square pixels that are only away from the hexagonal edge pixels with at most half of the distance (i.e., $1/\sqrt{3}$) between two connected hexagonal pixels. In another word, a square pixel is marked as an edge pixel only if on the same column, there is a hexagonal pixel such that the distance between the square pixel and the hexagonal pixel is less than or equal to $1/\sqrt{3}$. This approach again greatly improves the conversion speed for display of edge results.

4 Experimental Results

To study the effect of new edge detection method on the real hexagonal structure and compare with the results obtained on square structure, 8-bit grey level Lena image of size 256×256 is chosen as our sample image to be processed, because it is one of most widely accepted testing images to evaluate the performance of edge detection algorithm (see Fig. 3). We also use other images including the Mary image as shown in [9] for testing our algorithm.

Four different edge maps are produced in order to demonstrate the performance improved by new edge detection method. The first edge map is produced by common Canny edge detection through Gaussian filtering on square structure. The second and the fourth edge maps are obtained based on the hexagonal structure. The second edge map is created using the Gaussian filtering and the fourth edge map is produced after using the bilateral filtering as shown in Section 3. The third edge map is obtained after the bilateral filtering but based on square structure.

All the above edge maps are generated based on the consistent environment parameters such as $\sigma_2=1$ for Gaussian filtering and bilateral filtering. Recall that the size of window for carrying out the Gaussian convolution and bilateral processes is 49 on square structure and 39 on hexagonal structure. In addition, the same lower and higher thresholds are used to locate the exact edge points for all edge maps. The percentage to set the higher threshold is 0.125 and the ratio used to set the lower threshold is 0.05 [3] (Refer to Subsection 3.3 above).

Fig. 6 shows the various image smoothing results based on Gaussian and bilateral filtering on square structure and on hexagonal structure respectively. The top row shows the Gaussian filtering and the bottom row shows the bi-lateral filtering. The left column shows the filtering on square structure and the right column shows the

(a) Gaussian filtering on square structure   (b) Gaussian filtering on hexagonal structure

(c) Bilateral filtering on square structure   (d) Bilateral filtering on hexagonal structure

Fig. 6. Images processed by different filtering operations on different image structures

filtering on hexagonal structure. As can be seen in Fig. 6, the filtered images on using the bilateral kernel shows clearer pictures than those using Gaussian kernel. This proves that bilateral filtering not only suppresses the image noise but also maintains (actually enhance) the edge significance as can be seen in Fig. 7 below.

Fig. 7 shows four edge images obtained from the original image shown in Fig. 3 using different filtering operations on different image structures. It is shown that changing image structure from square to hexagonal structure reduces the edge details a little while still keeping the important edge information no matter if we use Gaussian or bilateral filtering. In Figs. 7(b) and 7(d), we see less edge points on the nose contour but better nose shape. It is also shown that the hexagonal structure maintains the curvature features better. This can be seen from the contour of the lower lip. A better looking round shape of the lower lip is displayed on the hexagonal structure (Fig. 7(b) and Fig. 7(d)) than on square structure (Fig. 7(a) and Fig. 7(c)).

(a) Edge map after Gaussian on square structure   (b) Edge map after Gaussian on hexagonal structure

(c) Edge map after bilateral on square structure   (d) Edge map after bilateral on hexagonal structure

Fig. 7. Edge maps of the filtered images shown in Fig. 6

Fig. 7(c) and Fig. 7(d) show that bilateral filtering further improves the quality of edge map because it enhances edge area information while suppressing image noise and trivial edge pixels. It can be clearly seen in Figs. 7(c) and 7(d) that the finer details of eye balls (in particular on the right eye) have been extracted.

We have also tested our algorithm on other images including the Mary image [9]. Similar findings showing the advantages of bilateral filtering on hexagonal structure are obtained.

In order to show the computation efficiency, a comparison of time costs using the above mentioned various approaches for Lena and Mary images are listed in Table 1. We run the various algorithms for comparison on a laptop PC featured with an Intel(R) Core(TM) i3 CPU of speed 2.13GHz. The RAM size is 4GB. It shows that the time costs on hexagonal structure on the new hexagonal structure are always less than on square structure no matter if we use Gaussian or bilateral filtering even though

Table 1. Time costs (in seconds) for Canny edge detection using Gaussian filtering and bilateral filtering on square structure and hexagonal structure respectively

Image	Gaussian filtering on square structure	Bilateral filtering on square structure	Bilateral filtering on old hexagonal structure ([1])	Gaussian filtering on hex	Bilateral filtering on new hexagonal structure (Proposed)
Lena	0.125	0.203	0.687	0.109	0.125
Mary	0.110	0.172	0.702	0.109	0.125

we have taken into account the image conversion times. Furthermore, the speed for bilateral Canny edge detection on the new hexagonal structure is more than 5 times faster than the approach on the old hexagonal shown in [1].

5 Conclusions

In this paper, a new Canny edge detection method is presented. The use of bilateral filtering combined with the advantages of hexagonal image architecture has achieved efficient edge detection performance under the same experimental conditions.

Unlike the work done in [1], the new edge detection algorithm is based on a newly constructed and real hexagonal structure and avoids the complicated and time-consuming conversion between the square and hexagonal structure. We take the advantages of higher degree of symmetry and equality of distances to neighbouring pixels that are special to the real hexagonal structure for better performance of image filtering and more accurate computation of gradients including edges and their strength. All steps for Canny algorithm are completely implemented on the hexagonal structure to achieve the accurate detection approach.

Note that in this paper, unlike the approach in [1], the value of parameter σ_1 used for image range filtering is computed as the standard deviation of the intensity function on the whole image either on the square structure or hexagonal structure. This approach avoids the uncertainty of the parameter selection.

Acknowledgement

This work was supported by the Houniao program through Guizhou University for Nationalities (China).

References

1. He, X., Jia, W., Hur, N., Wu, Q., Kim, J., Hintz, T.: Bilateral Edge Detection on a Virtual Hexagonal Structure. In: Bebis, G., Boyle, R., Parvin, B., Koracin, D., Remagnino, P., Nefian, A., Meenakshisundaram, G., Pascucci, V., Zara, J., Molineros, J., Theisel, H., Malzbender, T. (eds.) ISVC 2006. LNCS, vol. 4292, pp. 176–185. Springer, Heidelberg (2006)

2. Canny, J.F.: A Computational Approach to Edge Detection. IEEE Trans. On Pattern Analysis and Machine Intelligence PAMI-8, 679–698 (1986)
3. Wu, Q., He, X., Hintz, T.: Bilateral Filtering Based Edge Detection on Hexagonal Architecture. In: Proc. 2005 IEEE International Conference on Acoustics, Speech, and Signal Processing, Philadelphia, PA, USA, vol. II, pp. 713–716 (2005)
4. Barash, D.: Fundamental relationship between bilateral filtering, adaptive smoothing, and the nonlinear diffusion equation. IEEE Transactions on Pattern Analysis and Machine Intelligence 24, 844–847 (2002)
5. Mersereau, R.M.: The Processing of Hexagonally Sampled Two-Dimensional Signals. Proc. the IEEE 67, 930–949 (1979)
6. Her, I.: Geometric Transformations on the Hexagonal Grid. IEEE Trans. on Image Processing 4 (1995)
7. Sheridan, P., Hintz, T., Alexander, D.: Pseudo-invariant Image Transformations on a Hexagonal Lattice. Image and Vision Computing 18, 907–917 (2000)
8. Davis, L.S.: A Survey of Edge Detection Techniques. Computer Graphics and Image processing 4, 248–270 (1975)
9. He, X., Jia, W., Wu, Q.: An Approach of Canny Edge Detection with Virtual Hexagonal Image Structure. In: Proceedings of 10th International Conference on Control, Automation, Robotics and Vision (ICARCV 2008), pp. 879–882 (2008)

Automated Segmentation of Endoscopic Images Based on Local Shape-Adaptive Filtering and Color Descriptors

Artur Klepaczko and Piotr Szczypiński

Technical University of Lodz, Institute of Electronics
90-924 Lodz, ul. Wolczanska 211/215
{aklepaczko,pms}@p.lodz.pl

Abstract. This paper presents a novel technique for automatic segmentation of wireless capsule endoscopic images. The main contribution resides in the integration of three computational blocks: 1) local polynomial approximation algorithm which finds locally-adapted neighborhood of each pixel; 2) color texture analysis which describes each pixel by a vector of numerical attributes that reflect this pixel local neighborhood characteristcs; and 3) cluster analysis (k-means) for grouping pixels into homgeneous regions based on their color information. The proposed approach leads to a robust segmentation procedure which produces fine segments well matched to the image contents.

1 Introduction

Diagnosis of the human gastrointestinal tract often involves its visualization using endoscopy imaging techniques. Wireless Capsule Endoscopy (WCE) is one such method, that has been relatively recently developed and introduced to the clinical practice [1,2]. Its supremacy over the other techniques lies in the capability of WCE to visualize the small intestine non-invasivly. A patient must only swallow a pill-shaped capsule equipped with a video camera which communicates wirelessly with a video recorder attached to the patient body. Transmitted at a rate of 5 frames per second, WCE images eventually compose a 8-hour video sequence, later analyzed by a diagnostician. For a trained gastroenterologist, this may take even 2 hours or more. The procedure is a monotonous and time-consuming task, requiring high level of concentration, so that none of clinically important details, especially pathological alterations appearing on the intestine walls, are not missed. This breeds the need for automation of WCE video interpretation process.

Apparently, in the literature the problem of automatic segmentation of WCE images has attracted little attentionIn the majority of studies related to the general problem of WCE image processing (e.g. [3,4,5,6]) the aim is to identify different sections of the gastrointestinal system. Thus, instead of concentrating on single WCE frames, a whole video sequence is devided into appropraite parts allowing a clinician to examine only relevant portions. It is worth noticing

J. Blanc-Talon et al. (Eds.): ACIVS 2010, Part I, LNCS 6474, pp. 245–254, 2010.
© Springer-Verlag Berlin Heidelberg 2010

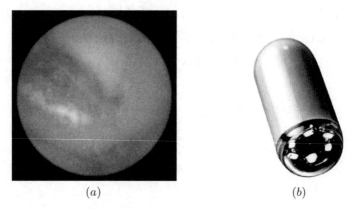

(a)   (b)

Fig. 1. Example of a WCE image (a) and a WCE camera (b)

that combined color and texture information is widely exploited in these works showing its potential in application to endoscopic image analysis.

Another category of approaches utilize color and texture features to detect certain structures (like polyps, bleeding, ulcers and lesions) with or without performing image segmentation. In [7] WCE frames are first submitted to the smoothing procedure and then segmented by the region growing algorithm. Identified regions and their mean RGB color values are used to train a neural network classifier so that it recognizes a range of abnormal patterns in new images. Similar studies — although they involve different classifiers, color and texture models — are described in [8,9] and [10,11]. However, in these approaches images are divided uniformly into a predefined number of square or circular ROIs, disregarding particular shapes visible in a given frame. The focus is put on determination of characteristics of chosen patterns in endoscopic images. These characteristics can be used to build classifiers capable of distinguishing classes of ideally shaped image snippets. Although such classifiers may to some extent help indicate diagnostically valuable WCE frames, precise delineation, visualization and quantification of interesting regions remains an unsolved task.

This paper undertakes the problem of automatic segmentation of 2D WCE images. The primary goal of this study is to faciliate unsupervised recognition of various ulcerations, bleedings and lesions visible in the internal lumen of the small intenstine and their precise delineation from normal or irrelevant regions. The proposed approach integrates local polynomial approximation (LPA) [12] algorithm with the well-founded color texture analysis and unsupervised classification (k-means) methods. As a first step, LPA performs pixel-wise analysis of the circular view given by a WCE camera (cf. Fig. 1) and for each pixel it defines a corresponding region of interest (ROI) whose size and shape is adapted to this pixel local neighborhood. Then, using histogram information calculated separately for 8 different color channels, each ROI (and thus also its associated pixel) is described by a vector of color texture features. Eventually, these vectors are grouped in the unsupervised manner by the k-means algorithm with the number of clusters set a priori. This combination of methods leads to a robust, three-phase fully automated segmentation procedure which produces fine-grained segments well matched to the image contents.

In the following we present details of our approach to WCE image segmentation. Section 2 provides concise review of the materials and methods used in this research. In Sect. 3 we present preliminary results of segmentation obtained for sample WCE images taken from several different examinations. We compare these results with segmentation performed manually by two independent experts in WCE-based diagnosis. High level of correspondence between both types of segmentation techniques (manual and the automatic one) makes us believe that the proposed method can be successfully introduced to the clinical practice. Conclusions and possible improvements are outlined in Sect. 4.

2   Materials and Methods

2.1   Wireless Capsule Endoscopy

In this study we examined ten WCE video sequences among which we selected 60 sample images comprising of various forms of ulcerations, bleedings and petechiae. Within these images, pathology regions were manually delineated by the cooperating gastroenterologists. This segmentation revealed that there are 6 alterations to consider:

1. focal ulcerations – yellowish, relatively small regions;
2. focal fibrotic ulcerations – light, almost white regions;
3. extensive fibrotic ulcerations – large areas of white and light pink color;
4. focal bleedings – small areas of blood;
5. extensive bleedings – large areas of blood;
6. petechiae - reddish, rather small spots.

Example images of each of the pathology classes included in our experiments with their corresponding regions of interest are depicted in Fig. 2.

2.2   Local Polynomial Approximation

The task of the LPA algorithm invoked in the first step of the segmentation procedure is to define for each pixel a region that is adapted to the shape of this pixel local neighborhood. It is presumed that such a neighborhood exhibits homogenous color and texture characteristics. Consequently, it can be expected that in the subsequent texture analysis step pixels gain credible description, representative for a wider range of points. This in turn allows making the resulting texture description independent from local fluctuations in pixel values caused by noise and other imaging artifacts.

The LPA algorithm itself is a technique of non-parametric regression recently adopted in various image processing applications. Using low order polynomial function, LPA models a non-linear relationship between an independent variable X and a dependent variable Y. Data are fitted to a modeled polynomial function

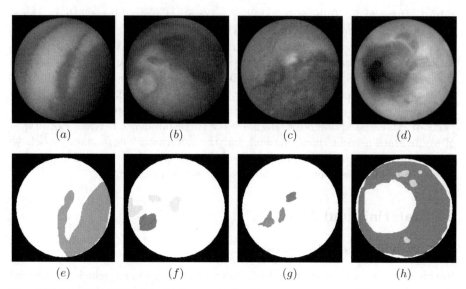

Fig. 2. Example WCE video frames containing extensive bleeding (a), focal bleedings (a,b), focal ulceration (c), focal fibrotic ulcer (b), extensive fibrotic ulceration (d), petechiae (d) and their corresponding manually delineated regions of interest (e-h)

within a sliding window positioned at subsequent observations (X, Y) — e.g. measured values of a sampled signal. In a window, a signal is convolved with a kernel function of a known form. This enables estimating values of the Y signal in the neighborhood of a given data point X. Window size h is a key parameter of the method. It is defined as a number of data samples beyond which it becomes impossible to estimate signal Y basing on values measured in the proximal neighborhood of X.

In our study we apply the LPA algorithm following the approach presented in [13]. Firstly, a color WCE video frame is converted into a gray-scaled image. Next, we filter each pixel neighborhood in 8 distinct directions θ_i deviated from the horizontal East-oriented axis at angles $0°, 45°, 90°, 135°, 180°, 225°, 270°$ and $315°$ (cf. Fig. 3a). For a given pixel X we calculate

$$\mu^{(h)} = \sum_{j=1}^{h} g_j^{(h)} I(X + (j-1)\theta_i), \tag{1}$$

where $g^{(h)}$ is a discrete convolution kernel of scale h (window size), $g_j^{(h)}$ with $j = 1, \ldots, h$ denote kernel weights which sum to unity and decrease with the increasing distance from a center pixel X. The exact procedure of weights generation is described in [12]. Eventually, I is a matrix of image intensity values.

Adjusting the window size to local image contents is performed using the *intersection of confidence intervals* (ICI) rule. The idea is to test several values of scale h, i.e. $h \in \{h_1 \ldots, h_k\}$ and $h_1 < h_2 < \ldots < h_k$ and for each of them evelute (1) as well as local standard deviation value

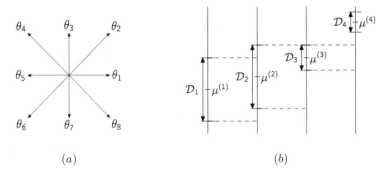

Fig. 3. Directions in the LPA algorithm (a) and the concept of the ICI rule (b)

$$\sigma_{\mu^{(h)}} = \sigma \|g^{(h)}\|, \tag{2}$$

where σ is the global standard deviation determined for the whole image. Then for each direction θ_i and scale h one calculates confidence intervals

$$\mathcal{D}_h = [\mu^{(h)} - \Gamma\sigma_{\mu^{(h)}}, \mu^{(h)} + \Gamma\sigma_{\mu^{(h)}}], \tag{3}$$

in which $\Gamma > 0$ denotes a global parameter that allows controlling noise tollerance. The lower Γ, the stronger requirement for local homogeneity is, and thus fewer pixels are included in the resulting neighborhood regions. The ICI rule states that for each direction one should choose a maximum value of h that ensures nonempty intersection of all previous confidence intervals, i.e. (cf. Fig. 3b)

$$h_{\mathrm{max},i} = \max_{h \in \{h_1, \ldots, h_k\}} \{h : (\mathcal{D}_1 \cap \mathcal{D}_2 \cap \cdots \cap \mathcal{D}_h) \neq \emptyset\}. \tag{4}$$

In our experiments, we arbitrarily set $h \in \{1, 2, 3, 5, 7, 9, 12, 15, 18, 21\}$, hence the upper bound for the window size in any direction amounts to 21 pixels. On completion, pixels determined by relations $X + h_{\mathrm{max},i}\theta_i$ constitute a set of polygon vertices whose interior determines a locally adapted ROI of a pixel X. Although we invoke LPA for a gray-scaled image, at the current stage of the research, for performance reasons, the resulting ROIs are used for each color channel in the texture analysis step.

2.3   Color Texture Analysis

Visual examination of a typical WCE image that its inherent color information is decisive for further diagnostic procedure. However, as in the case of other color medical images (including endoscopy and dermatoscopy), an original RGB bitmap has to be decomposed and transformed into several color channels which together convey complete color characteristics. In this study, we analze a WCE frame in the following color spaces:

- brightness (according to the CCIR Recommendation 601-1),
- RGB,

- HSV, and
- U channel ($(886R - 587G - 299B)/1772$),

which gives 8 color channels in total. For each channel and every pixel we calculate its associated ROI first-order histogram (256 bins). The histogram is computed from the intensity of pixels, without taking into consideration any spatial relations between the pixels within the image. Features are simply statistical parameters of the histogram distribution such as: mean brightness, variance, skewness, kurtosis and percentiles [14]. However, distinct regions of WCE images differ mainly by color and second-order regularities appear less important. Moreover, determination of histogram features is time-efficient and thus reduces the computational load.

2.4   K-Means Clustering

As a last step in our segmentation technique we perform cluster analysis for unsupervised grouping of image pixels described by their corresponding ROI texture features. For that purpose we employ k-means algorithm [15] due to its low complexity and ease of implementation. An important drawback of k-means is its intrinsic tendency to get stuck in a local minimum of the optimization criterion (sum of squared distances between feature vectors and their corresponding cluster centers). Thus, we call a clustering procedure 5 times, each time with different initialization. Then, the result with the best score is chosen to represent final segmentation.

2.5   Morphological Post-processing

After clustering, a segmented image can be still difficult to interpret. First of all, segments borders are to much extent distracted and penetrating each other (cf. Fig. 4a). Thus, we submit the result of clustering to a morphological closing operation. In order to preserve circular and elliptical contours of image objects, we used a disk-shaped structuring element with a 5-pixel-long diameter. Closing still leaves isolated small groups fo pixels surrounded by larger areas (holes

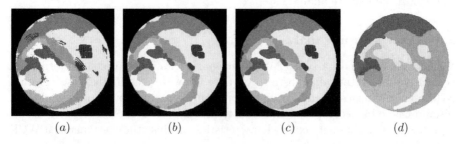

Fig. 4. Subsequent results of segmentation and morphological operations: a) segments obtained directly clustering, b) closing result, c) opening result, and d) identified connected components

and islands). To deal with this problem, we apply binary opening operation to each segment separately. We imposed a minimum threshold of 200 pixels for a region not to be removed during opening. If any pixel remains unclassified after opening, it is assigned to its closest neighbor. Eventually, detection of connected components must be performed so that none of the segments posses a colony spatially detached from it. Figure 4a-d presents subsequent results of the morphological transformations applied to the image from Fig. 2b.

3   Results

As stated before, we have tested the propsed algorithm on the series of 60 sample WCE images. We have invoked our segmentation procedure presuming arbitrarily that number of segments is equal to 8 in each case. By dividing an image into at least 8 segments (a higher number may eventually result from detection of connected components) we expect to encapsulate six pathology patterns (see Sect. 2.1) and also normal tissue and gastrointestinal lumen. This may of course lead to unnecessary subdivisions of some patterns if there are fewer distinguishable regions in a given frame.

   In Fig. 5 we present yet another example of an analyzed WCE image, as well as 4 ROIs produced by the LPA algorithm. Note, how regions A,C and D are well fitted to the surrounding tissue. On the other hand, region B placed in the interior of the intestinal canal covers larger area even though underlaying pixels do not exhibit homogeneouse texture. This observation shows that the algorithm — remaining local in nature — posses capability of reflecting general characteristics of a given pixel neighborhood.

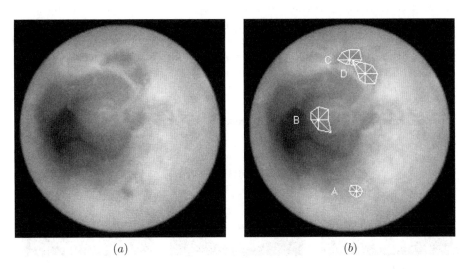

(a)   (b)

Fig. 5. Subsequent results of segmentation and morphological operations: a) segments obtained directly clustering, b) closing result, c) opening result, and d) identified connected components

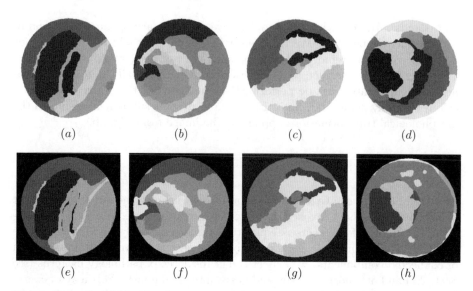

(a)   (b)   (c)   (d)

(e)   (f)   (g)   (h)

Fig. 6. Example WCE video frames containing extensive bleeding (a), focal bleedings (a,b), focal ulceration (c), focal fibrotic ulcer (b), extensive fibrotic ulceration (d), petechiae (d) and their corresponding manually delineated regions of interest (e-h)

Segmentation results obtained for four images viewed in Fig. 2a-d are depicted in Fig. 6a-d. When overlayed by the manually delineated regions, it appears that human expertise agrees with autmatically found segments. The level of this agreement largely depends on an image, pathology type, its area and tissue color charateristics. In order to qunatify it, we have calculated the Jaccard coefficient between corresponding regions. It turned out, that pathologies covering larger areas (such as extensive bleedings and ulceration) gain the highest score, i.e. 89% (with 5% standard deviation). On the other extreme, for focal ulcers and petechiae the algorihtm exhibits poorer performance, receiving the value 65% of the Jaccard criterion. However, even in then, location of the produced segments is correct, although they occupy larger tissue are than clinically important. In

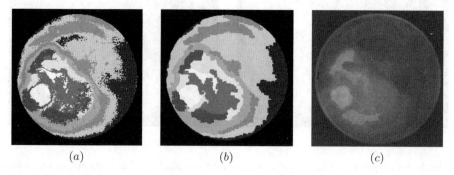

(a)   (b)   (c)

Fig. 7. Segmentation results (a-b) for the image from Fig. 2b; c — identified segments overlaid on the manually delineated regions of interest

that case, quantification of a given pathology would be corrupted, but qualitative information about a potentially dangerous pattern can be properly signalled to a diagnostician.

In order to evaluate effectiveness of processing locally adapted pixel neighborhoods instead of single points, we compare our segmentation procedure with the results obtained by imposing clustering on isolated pixels described only by their intensities in the 8 considered color channels. As shown in the example depicted in Fig. 7, image obtained directly after clustering (Fig. 7a) exhibits to a much extent chaotic set of small pixel groupings. This makes morphological operations (cf. Fig. 7b) much more responsible for final result than it is in the case of LPA filtered images. However, even after this post-processing the segmented image may cause misinterpretation of the original. There is a number of small regions which do not correspond to any clinically significant objects and one of the bleeding regions (the left-most one) is not recognized at all.

4   Summary

In this paper we presented a novel method for automatic segementation of the WCE video frames. We demonstrated robustness of the proposed technique in application to several WCE images taken from real examinations. The obtained results are exhibit high rate of agreement between automatically identified segments and regions manually delineated by gastroenterologists. Naturally, these results must be further validated with the use of larger set of sample images.

It must be noted that our study is still in the development phase. Further research is required to reduce time complexity associated with determination of pixels local neighborhoods. Number of LPA executions while processing a single WCE frame ranges the order of 10^5. Fortunatelly, the LPA algorithm can be relatively easily parallelized and implemented efficiently eg. on a multicore GPU. Moreover, postprocessing should be added after clustering step in order to cope with segmentation holes and islands, and also to identify clusters which include distal regions and thus should be subdivided.

Acknowledgments. This work was supported by the Polish Ministry of Science and Higher Education grant no. 3263/B/T02/2008/35.

References

1. Iddan, G., Meron, G., Glukhowsky, A., Swain, P.: Wireless capsule endoscopy. Nature 405(6785), 417–418 (2000)
2. Swain, P., Fritscher-Ravens, A.: Role of video endoscopy in managing small bowel disease. GUT 53, 1866–1875 (2004)
3. Coimbra, M., Cunha, J.: MPEG-7 visual descriptors–contributions for automated feature extraction in capsule endoscopy. IEEE Transactions on Circuits and Systems for Video Technology 16(5), 628–637 (2006)

4. Mackiewicz, M., Berens, J., Fisher, M., Bell, G.: Colour and texture based gastrointestinal tissue discrimination. In: Proceedings of the IEEE International Conference on Acoustics, Speech and Signal Processing, ICASSP, vol. 2, pp. 597–600 (2006)
5. Mackiewicz, M., Berens, J., Fisher, M.: Wireless capsule endoscopy video segmentation using support vector classifiers and hidden markov models. In: Proc. International Conference Medical Image Understanding and Analyses (June 2006)
6. Mackiewicz, M., Berens, J., Fisher, M.: Wireless capsule endoscopy color video segmentation. IEEE Transactions on Medical Imaging 27(12), 1769–1781 (2008)
7. Bourbakis, N.: Detecting abnormal patterns in WCE images. In: 5th IEEE Symposium on Bioinformatics and Bioengineering (BIBE 2005), pp. 232–238 (2005)
8. Lau, P.Y., Correia, P.: Detection of bleeding patterns in WCE video using multiple features. In: 29th Annual International Conference of the IEEE Engineering in Medicine and Biology Society, EMBS 2007, pp. 5601–5604 (2007)
9. Li, B., Meng, M.Q.H.: Computer-based detection of bleeding and ulcer in wireless capsule endoscopy images by chromaticity moments. Computers in Biology and Medicine 39(2), 141–147 (2009)
10. Szczypinski, P., Klepaczko, A.: Selecting texture discriminative descriptors of capsule endpscopy images. In: Proceedings of 6th International Symposium on Image and Signal Processing and Analysis, ISPA 2009, pp. 701–706 (2009)
11. Szczypinski, P., Klepaczko, A.: Convex hull-based feature selection in application to classification of wireless capsule endoscopic images. In: Blanc-Talon, J., Philips, W., Popescu, D., Scheunders, P. (eds.) ACIVS 2009. LNCS, vol. 5807, pp. 664–675. Springer, Heidelberg (2009)
12. Katkovnik, V., Egiazarian, K., Astola, J.: Local Approximation Techniques in Signal and Image Processing. SPIE Press, San Jose (2006)
13. Bergmann, Ø., Christiansen, O., Lie, J., Lundervold, A.: Shape-adaptive DCT for denoising of 3d scalar and tensor valued images. Journal of Digital Imaging 22(3), 297–308 (2009)
14. Szczypinski, P., Strzelecki, M., Materka, A., Klepaczko, A.: MaZda - a software package for image texture analysis. Computer Methods and Programs in Biomedicine 94, 66–76 (2009)
15. Duda, R., Hart, P., Stork, D.: Pattern Classification. John Wiley & Sons, Chichester (2001)

Dense Stereo Matching from Separated Views of Wide-Baseline Images

Qian Zhang and King Ngi Ngan

Department of Electronic Engineering, The Chinese University of Hong Kong,
Shatin, N.T., Hong Kong
{qzhang,knngan}@ee.cuhk.edu.hk

Abstract. In this paper, we present a dense stereo matching algorithm from multiple wide-baseline images with separated views. The algorithm utilizes the coarse-to-fine strategy to propagate the sparse feature matching to dense stereo for image pixels. First, the images are segmented into non-overlapping homogeneous partitions. Then, in the coarse step, the initial disparity map is estimated by assigning the sparse feature correspondences, where the spatial location of these features is incorporated with the over-segmentation. The initial occlusion status is obtained by cross-checking test. Finally, the stereo maps are refined by the proposed discontinuity-preserving regularization algorithm, which directly coupling the disparity and occlusion labeling. The experimental results implemented on the real date sets of challenging samples, including the wide-baseline image pairs with both identical scale and different scale, demonstrated the good subjective performance of the proposed method.

Keywords: color segmentation, sparse matching, stereo estimation, wide-baseline images.

1 Introduction

Multi-view stereo matching is a classic vision problem and has attracted increasing attentions in the recent decades. Even though extensive breakthroughs and developments have been taken place, it is still a challenging task because of inherent difficulties such as the lack of texture, occlusion and repetitive patterns in the scene. Many related topics (three-dimensional (3D) reconstruction and modeling ([1,2]), image-based rendering and virtual view synthesis ([3,4])) in computer vision and graphics can be generalized into the stereo matching problem. The outcomes of stereo matching (disparity/depth) facilitate various multi-ocular applications, for example, layer separation [5], object tracking [6], multi-view video coding [7] and free-view video generation [8]. Since we expect the vision system that is capable of understanding and reasoning the real 3D environment from two-dimensional (2D) images, one of solutions is to utilize the known multiple points from stereo matching to reconstruct the 3D structures. Stereo matching aims to find the corresponding pairs in 2D images referring to the same points in the 3D space and determine their disparities. Additionally, occlusion reasoning is an important task in stereo matching. A good stereo

J. Blanc-Talon et al. (Eds.): ACIVS 2010, Part I, LNCS 6474, pp. 255–266, 2010.

matching algorithm should not only estimate accurate disparity for the visible point, but also provide reasonable hypothesis of correspondence for the occluded one.

Short-baseline stereo matching is to seek the disparity from recorded images with slightly different viewpoint and small baseline distance. A good survey on the stereo estimation algorithm of short-baseline can be found in [9]. In generally, the methodologies of dense stereo matching with short-baseline can be categorized into local and global approaches. The local algorithms compute the disparity for a given points within a finite local window only relying on the intensity values. On the other hand, the global algorithms explicitly enforce the smoothness assumptions of disparity field and solve the matching problem as global cost minimization, using various optimization techniques such as simulated annealing [10], probabilistic diffusion [11], scanline optimization [12], belief propagation [13,14], dynamic programming [15,16] and graph cut [1,17,18].

Stereo matching algorithms that take the advantages of color segmentation have always drawn great interests due to its excellent performance in disparity estimation, especially in the texture-less regions. In the end of 1980's, Gagalowicz in [19] had incorporated segmented regions in stereo matching using global region features and epipolar constraint. In the recent segment-based approaches [20,21,22,23], they first divide the images into non-overlapping over-segmented regions, then implement disparity plane fitting from local pixel matching by approximating scene structure as a collection of planar surface, and finally assign labels in segment or pixel domain by minimizing the cost function. The assumption of planar scene structure in disparity space is supported in the short-baseline images, whereas invalid for wide-baseline case because of more general scene resulting from large disparity range and camera angle.

Comparing with the extensive works dedicated to the short-baseline stereo matching, disparity estimation and occlusion reasoning from image pairs of wide-baseline is largely unexplored, due to the difficulties such as large disparity range, severe self-occlusion, significant appearance change and geometric transformation as shown in Fig. 1(a) and 1(b). One class of wide-baseline stereo matching algorithms is feature-based approaches [24,25] that recover the matching of sparse features and obtain the depth for a small fraction of image pixels. Dense stereo algorithms [26,27] as its counterpart aim to seek a dense disparity map as output, which is requisite in further applications such as image-based rendering and virtual view synthesis.

This paper presents a novel dense stereo matching algorithm for wide-baseline image pairs with largely separated views. We utilize coarse-to-fine strategy that first propagate the sparse feature matching to image pixels, and then refine the initialization by minimizing the proposed energy function. There are two major contributions in this paper. Firstly, unlike the other segment-based stereo algorithms [20,21,22,23] that incorporate the segmentation in the disparity plane fitting and labeling stage, we confine the over-segmentation effect in the coarse initialization which implicitly makes use of the spatial information of sparse matching. Secondly, different from other disparity estimation frameworks using regularization scheme [28,29] without occlusion reasoning, a discontinuity-preserving regularization algorithm is proposed by directly coupling the disparity and occlusion labeling under geometry constraint to refine the initial stereo maps in the pixel domain.

The rest of the paper is organized as follow. Section 2 describes the stereo initialization by sparse matching propagation. In Section 3, we discuss the refinement using regularization algorithm. Experimental results implemented on the self-recorded real images demonstrate the algorithm's efficiency in Section 4. Conclusions are finally drawn in Section 5.

2   Stereo Initialization

Given the calibrated multi-view images, the first component of algorithm is to initialize the stereo estimation from sparse matching using color over-segmentation. We separately discuss the sparse matching, color segmentation and initial assignment in the following sections.

2.1   Sparse Feature Matching

Dense matching of wide-baseline stereo pair is much challenging due to the large perspective distortion and increasing occlusions. One alternative is to establish the sparse correspondence and propagate the matching of sampled pixels to a dense stereo map. In the matching scheme, we detect and match a bag of affine features (Harris and Hessian) [30], which are invariant to the scale change,

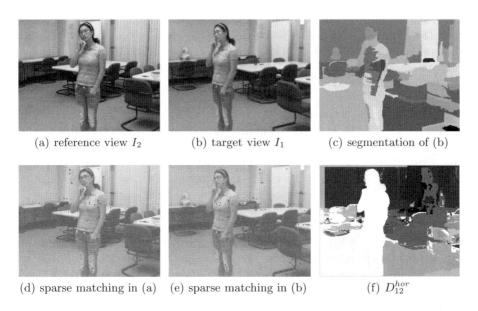

(a) reference view I_2 (b) target view I_1 (c) segmentation of (b)

(d) sparse matching in (a)   (e) sparse matching in (b)   (f) D_{12}^{hor}

Fig. 1. Disparity initialization

affine deformation and illumination variation. RANSAC fitting based on epipolar geometry is performed to filter out the mismatch, and epipolar geometry is then estimated using the correct correspondences. Finally, we combine these features and apply non-maximum suppression to remove the redundant feature points that are very close to each other, and re-estimate the scene by a bag of features. The matched sparse features marked as red points are shown in Fig. 1(d) and Fig. 1(e), which provides intuitions for the rest of unmatched points.

2.2 Color Segmentation

By assuming the disparity values vary smoothly in the homogenous color segments while occur discontinuities along the segments boundaries, the stereo matching algorithms that incorporate color segmentation achieve superior performance. Mean-shift [31] as a sophisticated clustering technique has been widely adopted in many segment-based approaches [20,21,22,23,32] to decompose the images into over-segmented regions. Similar to these works, we over-segment the images into homogenous color and consistent spatial partitions by mean-shift color segmentation. The over-segmentation of the target view in a stereo pair is illustrated in Fig. 1(c).

2.3 Disparity Initialization

Given the sparse matching results, the disparity between point p in the image I_1 and its counterpart q in image I_2 is defined as the offset of this correspondence. Only assuming the horizontal disparity is impractical when a large number of cameras are involved and placed randomly. In the wide-baseline case, we consider the disparity in both horizontal and vertical directions and $D_{12}^{hor}(p) = q_x - p_x$ and $D_{12}^{ver}(p) = q_y - p_y$. The disparity set $D = \{d_i\}$ is composed of N two-dimensional vectors, where N is the number of sparse matching point. The goal of disparity initialization is to assign a reasonable labeling from D for each pixel in the images. Instead of labeling each segment as the same disparity plane, we allow each segment sharing the same matching hypothesis from either self segment or neighboring segments.

As discussed in [33], directly combining the spatial and color proximities would mislead the correct support. Due to the sparsity and non-uniform distribution of the sparse matching as in Fig. 1(d) and Fig. 1(e), some segments have no less than one matching point $NS(s) \geq 1$ while no matching point can be found in the other segments $NS(s) = 0$. In the proposed algorithm, we build a neighboring pyramid for each segment to incorporate the spatial location of sparse correspondences with color segmentation. The construction of neighboring pyramid for a specified segment is shown in Fig. 2, where for each segment s, its neighboring segments are divided into K different layers. The sparse matching candidates (SMC) are selected from the segment itself or belonging to the neighboring pyramid $NP_k(s)$. The creation of neighboring pyramid lies in three aspects. Firstly, the number of matching candidates is limited and the matching points that are far away from the segment can not be selected. Secondly, the segments without matching

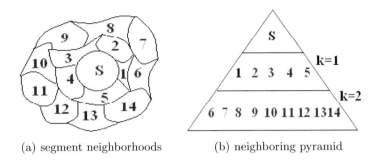

(a) segment neighborhoods   (b) neighboring pyramid

Fig. 2. Neighborhoods and neighboring pyramid of segment S

points can extract some candidates from neighboring segments. Finally, the cost function for the matching candidates varies according to the located layers.

To assign a reasonable labeling from SMC for not only the visible pixels but also the occluded ones, we divide the SMC into two groups for a certain point: within-range match is defined as that the counterpart in the other images is within the height and width limit of image plane by selecting this sparse matching and beyond-range match otherwise.

For the within-range match, we use the local matching to define a matching score within the supported pattern. To enforce the photo-consistency, some dissimilarity measurements such as mean absolute difference (MAD) and mean square error (MSE) are commonly used in the matching score. In our approach, by selecting the disparity d of SMC sm_d, we use MSE as matching score for p in the segment s of image I_1 and its matching candidate q $(q = p + d)$ in image I_2, which is defined as follow:

$$Score_{mse}(p, d) = \begin{cases} \dfrac{1}{n} \sum\limits_{p_i \in N_p, q_i \in N_q} dist(I_1(p_i), I_2(q_i)) : NS(s) \geq 1 \land sm_d \in s & \text{(1a)} \\ \dfrac{(1+k)}{n} \sum\limits_{p_i \in N_p, q_i \in N_q} dist(I_1(p_i), I_2(q_i)) : NS(s) = 0 \land sm_d \in NP_k(s) & \text{(1b)} \end{cases}$$

where N_p and N_q are the 3×3 surrounding window of p and q respectively, and n is the window size. $dist(I_1(p), I_2(q)) = \frac{1}{3} \sum\limits_{c \in R, G, B} \| I_1^c(p) - I_2^c(q) \|^2$ is the average color difference in RGB channels. In this photo-consistency matching score of (1b), the weight for the SMC in the different layer of neighboring pyramid varies, and higher layer (bigger k) means further away from the points with larger penalty.

For some pixel p that generally locates at the image boundaries and is occluded, its SMC may include beyond-range match thus the dissimilarity of photo-consistency can not be derived. We assign a matching score for beyond-range match using spatial distance:

$$Score_{space}(p,d){=}\begin{cases} \| p - sm_d \| + \| d - \mu \|: NS(s) \geq 1 \wedge sm_d \in s & \text{(2a)} \\ \| p - sm_d \| + \| d - \mu_k \|: NS(s) = 0 \wedge sm_d \in NP_k(s) & \text{(2b)} \end{cases}$$

where μ and μ_k are the average disparity in the segment and in the kth layer of neighboring pyramid, respectively. (2) expects that not only the suitable matching is close to the target point but also its disparity complies with the mean disparity of SMC. Among all the SMC, the one that give the minimal matching score is selected as the initial disparity. For the point that contains both within-range and beyond-range matches, we prefer to choose the beyond-range match unless small photo-consistency error is satisfied. The initial horizontal disparity D_{12}^{hor} of Fig. 1(b) is shown in Fig. 1(f), which dominates the disparity field. The disparity initialization is performed simultaneously for the target and reference image, and the initial occlusions are filtered out by the cross-checking test which applies the consistency of the estimated disparity. We assign binary label that OC_o if occlusion and OC_n otherwise.

3   Stereo Refinement

By providing tentative disparity estimation from initialization, we develop a discontinuity-preserving regularization algorithm to refine the coarse field, which directly coupling the disparity labeling and occlusion reasoning under epipolar constraint.

3.1   Epipolar Constraint

The epipolar geometry is the intrinsic projective geometry between two views, and the fundamental matrix F computed using the sparse features encapsulates this intrinsic geometry. Let F_{12} denote the fundamental matrix of view V_1 and V_2 for pixel p in image I_1 and pixel q in image I_2.

$$q^T F_{12} p = 0 \tag{3}$$

Equivalently, q lies on the epipolar line

$$l_{12} = F_{12} p \tag{4}$$

The advantage of using the epipolar constraint is twofold. Firstly, the epipolar constraint converts the matching from a two dimensional problem to a one dimensional problem, which greatly reduce the solution space and computational complexity. Secondly, the epipolar constraint removes possible outliers which may occur because of repetitive pattern or lack of texture. In the algorithm, we set starting point q by projecting p on l_{12} using initial disparity, and search within a range centered q along epipolar line. The optimal q is determined as the one which can minimize the proposed energy function in the following refinement step.

3.2   Disparity Refinement

In the proposed algorithm, the disparity refinement is formulated as energy minimization problem. The occlusion reasoning is derived directly from its definition that if a pixel cannot find a correspondence in the reference image. The energy function simultaneously models the disparity labeling and occlusion reasoning. Let I_1 is the target image and I_2 is the reference image which are the input pair. D_{12} and O_{12} denote the disparity map and occlusion map of I_1 with respect to (w.r.t) I_2 respectively, and D_{21} and O_{21} vice verse. The proposed algorithm is asymmetric in the sense that it simultaneously outputs the disparity of the target view D_{12} and occlusion of reference view O_{21}, and the energy function is defined as:

$$E = E_{dd}(D_{12}) + \lambda_d E_{ds}(D_{12}) + E_{vd}(D_{12}) + E_{od}(O_{21}) + \lambda_o E_{os}(O_{21}) \quad (5)$$

where E_{dd} is the disparity data term which measures photo-consistency covering a small neighborhood of the target pixel p and its matching candidate q. E_{ds} is the disparity smoothness term. E_{vd} is the view consistency term to propagate the disparity of the one view to the other view. E_{od} and E_{os} are the occlusion data term and occlusion smoothness term respectively. λ_d and λ_o are the parameters for disparity and occlusion regularization. The definition of five terms in the energy function (5) are defined as follow:

$$E_{dd}(p, q) = \frac{1}{n} \sum_{p_i \in N_p, q_i \in N_q} dist(I_1(p_i), I_2(q_i)) \quad (6)$$

$$E_{ds}(p) = \frac{1}{n} \sum_{p_i \in N_p, O_{12}(p_i) \neq OC_o} \frac{\| D_{12}(p_i) - D_{12}(p) \|}{f(dist(I_1(p_i), I_1(p)), T) + 1} \quad (7)$$

$$E_{vd}(p, q) = \begin{cases} \| D_{12}(p) + D_{21}(q) \| : D_{12}(p) = OC_o \vee D_{12}(p) + D_{21}(q) \neq 0 \\ 0 : otherwise \end{cases} \quad (8)$$

$$E_{od}(q) = -|O_{21}(q) - OC_n| \quad (9)$$

$$E_{os}(q) = \frac{1}{n} \sum_{q_i \in N_q, O_{21}(q_i) \neq OC_o} \frac{\| O_{21}(q_i) - OC_n \|}{f(dist(I_2(q_i), I_2(q)), T) + 1} \quad (10)$$

$$f(x, T) = \begin{cases} x : x > T \\ 0 : x < T \end{cases} \quad (11)$$

In the above energy functions, view consistency term E_{vd} motivates the consistent assignment across views, which means that the sum of disparity vector of p in I_1 and its correspondence q in I_2 should be zero. A non-negative penalty will be charged if this constraint violates. As the smoothness term E_{ds} and E_{os} incorporate the image gradient information in the denominator, the disparity and occlusion maps can be well smoothed in the texture-less regions while discontinuities are preserved at the edges. f is a truncation function used to suppress noise in the gradient images.

The novelty of the proposed algorithm lies in the terms of E_{od} and E_{os}. The purpose of adding the occlusion data term is twofold. The first is to avoid labeling all the pixels as occluded. In addition, it enables the uniqueness characteristic as a soft constraint. The advantage of adding the occlusion smoothness term is to ensure piecewise smoothness within the occlusion map, avoiding holes and isolated occluded points.

4   Experimental Results

To evaluate the performance of our approach, we implement the experiments on the data sets containing wide-baseline images with identical scale and different scale. The tested images are captured in the real environment with normal indoors fluorescent lighting of resolution 320×240, including challenging difficulties for stereo estimation such as large texture-less regions, severe occlusions, repetitive patterns, dramatic appearance change and geometric transformation. There are several parameters in the proposed algorithm and we fix them in all the experimental settings to validate the insensitivity of the algorithm to the parameters. The number of layers K in the neighboring pyramid is set to be 2. λ_d and λ_o control the smoothness of disparity map and occlusion map respectively, both are 0.5 in (5). T is the threshold of truncation function for the gradient map and equals to 10 in (11).

4.1   Identical Scale

An example of stereo pair with identical scale is shown in Fig. 1(a) and 1(b). The maximal disparity (horizontal) of Fig. 1(b) by taking Fig. 1(a) as reference is -140 pixels, which is nearly half of the image width. The number of sparse matching pairs in Fig. 1(d) and Fig. 1(e) is 107. The D_{12}^{hor} from the perspective of target view after refinement in Fig. 3(a) and the detected occlusion map O_{12}

(a) D_{12}^{hor} (b) O_{12}

Fig. 3. The disparity map and occlusion map of target view for identical scale images

in Fig. 3(b) present the subjective quality of the resulting stereo maps. The black points in Fig. 3(b) are labeled as OC_n and gray points are OC_o. The estimated disparity map in Fig. 3(a) shows consistency and smoothness within the same depth and discontinuity between different depths in the scene. Apart from the accurate disparity value in the visible part, the structure of objects in the background such as the chairs and the yellow duck is well preserved even though they are occluded in Fig. 3(b).

4.2 Changed Scale

Supporting from the scale-invariant feature matching, the stereo estimation algorithm can be applied to the image pair with different scale shown in Fig. 4(a) and 4(b). The maximal disparity (horizontal) of target view w.r.t the reference view is +115 pixels. The refined disparity map and the occlusion map of the target view are presented in Fig. 4(c) and 4(d) respectively. Obvious disparity transition in different depth and smooth disparity assignment within the same depth in the real and complex scene can be observed from Fig. 4(c). Fig. 4(d) highlights the effectiveness of occlusion reasoning. Even though assisted by quite sparse features which are only 49 matching, the algorithm can obtain accurate estimation of disparity and occlusion maps with good subjective quality.

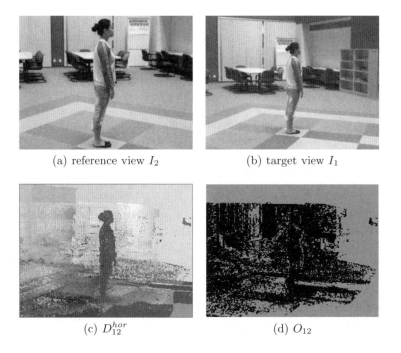

(a) reference view I_2 (b) target view I_1

(c) D_{12}^{hor} (d) O_{12}

Fig. 4. The disparity map and occlusion map of target view for different scale images

5   Conclusions

In this paper, we propose an effective algorithm of dense stereo matching from wide-baseline images with separated views. The algorithm utilize the coarse-to-fine strategy that the outputs from the coarse level are used to constraint a local search in the finer level. In the disparity initialization, a coarse disparity map is obtained by selecting sparse matching toward appropriate assignment for the visible point and reasonable hypothesis for the occlusions, where the color over-segmentation is incorporated with the spatial location of feature matching. To refine the initial stereo maps, a global energy function is formulated in the minimization framework. Discontinuity-preserving regularization algorithm is developed by simultaneously modeling the disparity labeling and occlusion reasoning under epipolar constraint. The experimental results on the challenging wide-baseline image pairs captured in the real and complicated 3D scene with both identical scale and different scale, demonstrates the performance of the proposed algorithm with accuracy of stereo estimation and robustness to different scenarios.

Acknowledgments. The work described in this paper was partially supported by a grant from the Research Grants Council of the Hong Kong SAR, China (Project CUHK415707).

References

1. Kolmogorov, V., Zabih, R.: Multi-camera Scene Reconstruction via Graph Cuts. In: European Conference on Computer Vision, pp. 82–96 (2002)
2. Quan, L., Wang, J.D., Tan, P., Yuan, L.: Image-Based Modeling by Joint Segmentation. International Journal of Computer Vision 75(1), 135–150 (2007)
3. Shum, H.Y., Sun, J., Yamazaki, S., Li, Y., Tang, C.K.: Pop-up light field: An inter-active image-based modeling and rendering system. ACM Transactions on Graphics (TOG) 23(2), 143–162 (2004)
4. Zitnick, C.L., Kang, S.B.: Stereo for Image-Based Rendering using Image Over-Segmentation. International Journal of Computer Vision 75(1), 49–65 (2007)
5. Kolmogorov, V., Criminisi, A., Blake, A., Cross, G., Rother, C.: Probabilistic fusion of stereo with color and contrast for bi-layer segmentation. IEEE Transactions on Pattern Analysis and Machine Intelligence 28(9), 1480–1492 (2006)
6. Zhao, T., Aggarwal, M., Kumar, R., Sawhney, H.: Real-Time Wide Area Multi-Camera Stereo Tracking. In: IEEE Conference on Computer Vision and Pattern Recognition, pp. 976–983 (2005)
7. Grammalidis, N., Strintzis, M.G.: Disparity and occlusion estimation in multiocular systems and their coding for the communication of multiview image sequences. IEEE Transactions on Circuits and Systems for Video Technology 8(3), 328–344 (1998)
8. Dongbo, M., Donghyun, K., SangUn, Y., Kwanghoon, S.: 2D/3D freeview video generation for 3DTV system. Signal Processing: Image Communication 24(1-2), 31–48 (2009)

9. Scharstein, D., Szeliski, R.: A Taxonomy and Evaluation of Dense Two-Frame Stereo Correspondence Algorithms. International Journal of Computer Vision 47(1-2), 7–42 (2002)

10. Barnard, S.T.: Stochastic Stereo Matching over Scale. International Journal of Computer Vision 3(1), 17–32 (1989)

11. Scharstein, D., Szeliski, R.: Stereo Matching with Nonlinear Diffusion. International Journal of Computer Vision 328(2), 155–174 (1998)

12. Mattoccia, S., Tombari, F., Stefano, D.L.: Stereo Vision Enabling Precise Border Localization Within a Scanline Optimization Framework. In: Asian Conference on Computer Vision, pp. 517–527 (2007)

13. Sun, J., Zheng, N.N., Shum, H.Y.: Stereo Matching Using Belief Propagation. IEEE Transactions on Pattern Analysis and Machine Intelligence 25(7) (2003)

14. Yang, Q.X., Wang, L., Yang, R.Q., Stewnius, H., Nistr, D.: Stereo Matching with Color-Weighted Correlation, Hierarchical Belief Propagation and Occlusion Handling. IEEE Transactions on Pattern Analysis and Machine Intelligence 31(3), 492–504 (2009)

15. Veksler, O.: Stereo correspondence by dynamic programming on a tree. In: IEEE Conference on Computer Vision and Pattern Recognition, pp. 384–390 (2005)

16. Lei, C., Selzer, J., Yang, Y.: Region-tree based stereo using dynamic programming optimization. In: IEEE Conference on Computer Vision and Pattern Recognition, pp. 2378–2385 (2006)

17. Kolmogorov, V., Zabih, R.: Computing visual correspondence with occlusions using graph cuts. In: International Conference on Computer Vision, pp. 508–515 (2001)

18. Miyazaki, D., Matsushita, Y., Ikeuchi, K.: Interactive shadow removal from a single image using hierarchical graph cut. In: Asian Conference on Computer Vision (2009)

19. Gagalowicz, A., Vinet, L.: Region matching for stereo pairs. In: Proceedings of the Sixth Scandinavian Conference on Image Analysis, Oslo (1989)

20. Klaus, A., Sormann, M., Karner, K.: Segment-based stereo matching using belief propagation and a self-adapting dissimilarity measure. In: International Conference on Pattern Recognition, pp. 15–18 (2006)

21. Bleyer, M., Gelautz, M.: Graph-based surface reconstruction from stereo pairs using image segmentation. In: SPIE Symposium on Electronic Imaging, vol. 5665, pp. 288–299 (2005)

22. Hong, L., Chen, G.: Segment-based Stereo Matching Using Graph Cuts. In: IEEE Conference on Computer Vision and Pattern Recognition, pp. 74–81 (2004)

23. Tao, H., Sawhney, H., Kumar, R.: A Global Matching Framework for Stereo Computation. In: International Conference on Computer Vision, pp. 532–539 (2001)

24. Torr, P.H.S., Zisserman, A.: Feature Based Methods for Structure and Motion Estimation. In: Triggs, B., Zisserman, A., Szeliski, R. (eds.) ICCV-WS 1999. LNCS, vol. 1883, pp. 278–294. Springer, Heidelberg (2000)

25. Lowe, D.G.: Distinctive Image Features from Scale-Invariant Keypoints. International Journal of Computer Vision 60(2), 91–110 (2004)

26. Strecha, C., Tuytelaars, T., Gool, L.V.: Dense Matching of Multiple Wide-baseline Views. In: IEEE International Conference on Computer Vision, pp. 1194–1200 (2003)

27. Tola, E., Lepetit, V., Fua, P.: DAISY: An Efficient Dense Descriptor Applied to Wide-Baseline Stereo. IEEE Transactions on Pattern Analysis and Machine Intelligence 32(5), 815–820 (2010)

28. Kim, H., Sohn, K.: Hierarchical disparity estimation with energy-based regularization. In: International Conference on Image Processing, pp. 373–376 (2003)

29. Yang, W., Ngan, K.N., Lim, J., Sohn, K.: Joint motion and disparity fields esti-
    mation for stereoscopic video sequences. Signal Processing: Image Communication,
    265–276 (2005)
30. Mikolajczyk, K., Tuytelaars, T., Schmid, C., Zisserman, A., Matas, J., Schaffal-
    itzky, F., Kadir, T., Gool, L.V.: A Comparison of Affine Region Detectors. Inter-
    national Journal of Computer Vision 65(1), 43–72 (2005)
31. Dorin, C., Meer, P.: Mean Shift: A Robust Approach Toward Feature Space Anal-
    ysis. IEEE Transactions on Pattern Analysis and Machine Intelligence 24(5), 603–
    619 (2002)
32. Zhang, G.F., Jia, J.Y., Wong, T.T., Bao, H.J.: Consistent Depth Maps Recov-
    ery from a Video Sequence. IEEE Transactions on Pattern Analysis and Machine
    Intelligence 31(6), 974–988 (2009)
33. Tombari, F., Mattoccia, S., Stefano, L.D.: Segmentation-based adaptive support
    for accurate stereo correspondence. In: IEEE Pacific-Rim Symposium on Image
    and Video Technology, pp. 427–438 (2007)

Modeling Wavelet Coefficients for Wavelet Subdivision Transforms of 3D Meshes

Shahid M. Satti, Leon Denis, Adrian Munteanu, Jan Cornelis, and Peter Schelkens

Department of Electronics and Informatics – Interdisciplinary Institute for Broadband Technology, Vrije Universiteit Brussel, Pleinlaan 2, B-1050 Brussels, Belgium
smsatti@etro.vub.ac.be

Abstract. In this paper, a Laplacian Mixture (LM) model is proposed to accurately approximate the observed histogram of the wavelet coefficients produced by lifting-based subdivision wavelet transforms. On average, the proposed mixture model gives better histogram fitting for both normal and non-normal meshes compared to the traditionally used Generalized Gaussian (GG) distributions. Exact closed-form expressions for the rate and the distortion of the LM probability density function quantized using generic embedded deadzone scalar quantizer (EDSQ) are derived, without making high-rate assumptions. Experimental evaluations carried out on a set of 3D meshes reveals that, on average, the D-R function for the LM model closely follows and gives a better indication of the experimental D-R compared to the D-R curve of the competing GG model. Optimal embedded quantization for the proposed LM model is experimentally determined. In this sense, it is concluded that the classical Successive Approximation Quantization (SAQ) is an acceptable, but in general, not an optimal embedded quantization solution in wavelet-based scalable coding of 3D meshes.

1 Introduction

The increasing computational power of personal computers and the accurate acquisition of complex shapes made recently available have enabled the use of highly-detailed 3D meshes in graphics applications both in industry and entertainment. These meshes are difficult to handle in their raw form due to their large size and irregular structure. In the past, efforts have been made for their compact representation to accommodate a wide variety of end-user terminals, transmission environments and computational capabilities. Resulting compression algorithms include both single-rate [1-3] and progressive [4-6] mesh coding techniques. Due to the highly irregular topology of the input mesh, a large source rate is usually reserved by these techniques for the lossless encoding of the connectivity information.

As an alternative to this problem, a number of remeshing techniques were proposed to convert the original irregular mesh into a mesh consisting of regular elements, such as B-spline [7] or subdivision connectivity patches [8, 9]. The regular mesh behaves more nicely in what it concerns compression, and when compared to

J. Blanc-Talon et al. (Eds.): ACIVS 2010, Part I, LNCS 6474, pp. 267–278, 2010.
© Springer-Verlag Berlin Heidelberg 2010

irregular meshes, a much lower rate is need to code the connectivity information. This was confirmed in the state-of-the-art compression system of [10] where almost all of the connectivity was recovered at the decoder side using subdivision. The scheme of [10], combines a subdivision wavelet transform with the zero-tree coding paradigm [11], successfully used in the past in scalable wavelet-based coding of images.

In our previous work [12], we have experimentally demonstrated that for 3D meshes, the wavelet coefficients exhibit significantly different statistical dependencies when compared to images. Based on these observations, we proposed octtree-based intraband [13] and composite [14] mesh coding designs, giving higher compression performance and better scalability of the compressed bitstream in comparison to the state-of-the-art zero-tree based interband coder of [10].

The wavelet coefficients in subdivision transforms are generally modeled as an i.i.d Generalized Gaussian (GG) random variable [15]. In the past, GG distributions have been used to model the subband histograms in wavelet transforms for images [16, 17]. However, no theoretical or experimental justification is available for their use in 3D mesh coding. This paper experimentally justifies the use of a Laplacian Mixture (LM) model in wavelet-based coding of 3D meshes. It is experimentally confirmed that, on average, the LM model provides better histogram fitting than the GG model. Additionally, due to the simplicity of the expression of the probability density function (pdf), the model D-R function can be exactly computed in closed-form. For GG pdfs, however, only approximate closed-form rate and distortion expressions [18], [19] or numerical solutions are known. It is shown that the LM model also allows for modeling the experimental D-R very accurately and better than the GG model. Additionally, using the LM model one can address a critical aspect in any scalable codec design, which is making an appropriate choice of the employed embedded quantizer. With this respect, 3D mesh codecs use Successive Approximation Quantization (SAQ) [11], [20] to achieve quality scalability. However, no theoretical study investigated the optimality of SAQ in such application scenarios, the only reason justifying this choice being SAQ's ease in implementation. Using the LM model, we determined the optimal embedded deadzone scalar quantizer (EDSQ) [20] to be used in scalable mesh coding. In this sense, SAQ is shown to be not an optimal choice. However, its near-optimal behavior and its ease in implementation using simple binary arithmetics make it an acceptable choice for scalable wavelet-based coding of 3D meshes.

The remainder of this paper is organized as follows. Section 2 briefly explains the wavelet decomposition of a 3D mesh. The histogram and D-R modeling using the proposed and the commonly-used models are presented in sections 3 and 4, respectively. The proposed LM model is experimentally validated in section 5. Optimal embedded quantization for the LM model is analyzed in section 6. Finally, section 7 draws the conclusion of this work.

2 Lifting-Based Wavelet Transform

In a lifting-based mesh wavelet transform [21], the highest resolution semi-regular mesh $M^J(\mathbf{v}^J, \mathbf{p}^J)$ at level J is obtained by remeshing the irregular input mesh M_{irr}, with $\mathbf{v}^J$ and $\mathbf{p}^J$ denoting the positions of vertices in the 3D space and the list of polygons of M^J respectively. M^J is first decimated to $\tilde{M}^{J-1}$ using inverse triangulation. Prediction of the high-resolution vertices, i.e. vertices that are present in M^J but not in $\tilde{M}^{J-1}$, is done by employing the commonly used Butterfly [22] or Loop [23] subdivision schemes. The prediction errors i.e. the wavelet coefficients are stored in a vector $\mathbf{d}^{J-1}$. Based on the values of its neighboring wavelet coefficients, each vertex of $\tilde{M}^{J-1}$ is then displaced using the update step [21], to create an accurate low-resolution approximation $M^{J-1}(\mathbf{v}^{J-1}, \mathbf{p}^{J-1})$ of the input M^J. A further application of the same lifting-based transform on M^{J-1} produces the pair { $M^{J-2}(\mathbf{v}^{J-2}, \mathbf{p}^{J-2})$, $\mathbf{d}^{J-2}$ }. Similarly, J successive applications of such a transform result in J subbands of wavelet coefficients $\mathbf{d}^{J-1}, \mathbf{d}^{J-2} ... \mathbf{d}^0$ and a coarser level geometry $M^0(\mathbf{v}^0, \mathbf{p}^0)$, also known as the base mesh. Note that $\left|\mathbf{v}^{j+1}\right| = \left|\mathbf{v}^j\right| + \left|\mathbf{d}^j\right|$ for $0 \leq j < J$.

3   Histogram Modeling

For both normal and non-normal meshes, wavelet coefficients are represented using local frame coordinate components as in [10]. The observed histogram h_i^j of the ith coordinate component of the wavelet subband $\mathbf{d}^j$ is symmetric around zero. A large mass of the histogram is situated near the center and the frequency of occurrence decays with the magnitude of the wavelet coefficient. An example is given in Figure 1, which depicts the observed *normal* component histograms of the $\mathbf{d}^{J-3}$ subband of Rabbit (non-normal) and Dino (normal) meshes obtained using the Butterly transform. The histograms are plotted using 255 bins. One points out that the two *tangential* components have similar histogram shapes but have smaller variance σ^2. It is observed experimentally that, in general, $\sigma^2(h_i^{j+1}) < \sigma^2(h_i^j)$ for any i and j. For Dino, almost all the coefficients fall in the central bin (or the zero-bin, as the histogram mean is zero) and the histogram decays abruptly towards higher magnitudes. For Rabbit, however, fewer coefficients fall in the central bin and the decay is more gradual. In the literature, the observed histogram of any component of a wavelet subband is generally modeled using a zero mean GG distribution [15], expressed by:

$$\forall x \in \mathbb{R} \quad f_{GG}(x, \sigma, \alpha) = \frac{\alpha \upsilon^{\frac{1}{\alpha}}}{2\Gamma(1/\alpha)} e^{-\upsilon|x|^\alpha} , \tag{1}$$

where $0 < \alpha \leq 2$ is the shape (or decay) control parameter, $\upsilon > 0$ is the scaling factor and $\upsilon^{1/\alpha} = \sqrt{\Gamma(3/\alpha)/\sigma^2 \Gamma(1/\alpha)}$, where Γ is the Gamma function. Note that, for $\alpha = 1$, equation (1) is a zero-mean Laplacian pdf given by:

$$\forall x \in \mathbb{R} \quad f_L(x, \sigma) = \frac{1}{\sigma\sqrt{2}} e^{-\frac{\sqrt{2}}{\sigma}|x|} = \frac{\lambda}{2} e^{-\lambda|x|} \quad \text{for } \lambda = \frac{\sqrt{2}}{\sigma} , \tag{2}$$

from here onward referred to as the single Laplacian (SL) pdf; we note also that for $\alpha = 2$ equation (1) corresponds to a zero-mean Gaussian pdf.

3.1 Proposed Model

The pdf of the proposed LM model is given by:

$$\forall x \in \mathbb{R} \quad f_{LM}(x) = a_1 . f_{L_1}(x, \sigma_1) + a_2 . f_{L_2}(x, \sigma_2),\tag{3}$$

where $0 < a_i < 1$ for $i = 1, 2$ such that $a_1 + a_2 = 1$. Note that $f_{LM}(x)$ indeed defines a probability function, as $\int_{-\infty}^{\infty} f_{LM}(x)\,dx = 1$.

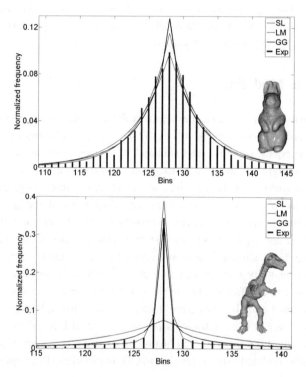

Fig. 1. Probability function fitting over the observed histogram (Exp) for $\mathbf{d}^{J-3}$-normal component for Rabbit (above) and Dino (below)

In our approach, the EM algorithm [24] is used to estimate the fitting parameters. The E- and M- steps are executed in tandem till the algorithm converges. A better convergence rate is achieved by initially taking $\sigma_1^2 = 0.5\sigma_E^2$, $\sigma_2^2 = 2\sigma_E^2$, $a_1 = 0.9$ and $a_2 = 0.1$, where σ_E^2 is the estimated data variance. Histogram fitting for the SL and GG models is done using the brute-force method.

Figure 1 shows also the histogram plots for the LM model. For comparison, the fitted SL pdf is also shown. For Rabbit, all three models give comparable fitting results in terms of *KL* (Kullback-Leibler) divergence [25]. The LM in this case gives slightly better fitting, especially in the middle range values, than the other two models. However, for Dino, the LM can clearly model the fast decay of the observed histogram more accurately than the GG. The SL model in this case only gives a very coarse approximation of the actual distribution.

4 D-R Modeling

The wavelet subbands are quantized using a generic family of EDSQ [20] in which every wavelet coefficient component X is quantized to an index $q_{\xi,n}$ as:

$$
q_{\xi,n} = \begin{cases} sign(X). \left\lfloor \dfrac{|X|}{\Delta_n} + \xi_n \right\rfloor & if \quad \dfrac{|X|}{\Delta_n} + \xi_n > 0 \\ 0 & otherwise \end{cases},
$$

where $n \in \mathbb{Z}_+$ denotes the quantization level. ξ_n and Δ_n denote the deadzone control parameter and the quantization cell size for any $n \geq 0$, respectively, with $\xi_n = \xi_0/2^n$ and $\Delta_n = 2^n \Delta_0$, where ξ_0 and Δ_0 are the parameters for the highest-rate quantizer $(n = 0)$. Note that $\xi_0 = 0$ corresponds to the well-known SAQ in which the deadzone size is twice the step size Δ_n for any n.

Closed-form expressions for the output distortion D_L and the output rate R_L of the SL source, quantized using an n level EDQS are derived in the Appendix. Note that both quantities are computed exactly and no high-rate approximations are made.

Since the distortion is a linear function of the pdf, the output distortion D_{LM} of the LM pdf for any quantization level n can be written as:

$$
D_{LM}\left(Q_{\delta_n,\Delta_n}\right) = a_1.D_{L1}\left(Q_{\delta_n,\Delta_n}\right) + a_2.D_{L2}\left(Q_{\delta_n,\Delta_n}\right), \text{ with } \delta_n = 1 - \xi_n . \tag{4}
$$

This does not hold, however, for the output rate R_{LM} as the entropy involves the non-linear $\log(.)$ function. Instead, R_{LM} can be computed as an infinite sum:

$$
P_0 = 2\int_0^{\delta_n \Delta_n} f_{LM}(x)\,dx , \quad P_k = \int_{(k-1+\delta_n)\Delta_n}^{(k+\delta_n)\Delta_n} f_{LM}(x)\,dx , \quad k = 1,2,3... ,
$$

and

$$
R_{LM}(Q_{\delta_n,\Delta_n}) = -\sum_{k=-\infty}^{\infty} P_k \log_2 P_k , \tag{5}
$$

where P_k denotes the probability mass of the *k*th quantization cell ($k = 0$ corresponds to the deadzone). Since the LM model is symmetric around its mean, $P_k = P_{-k}$.

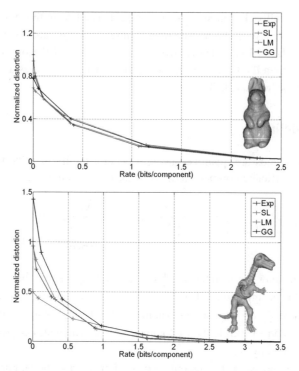

Fig. 2. Modeled and observed D-R functions for the histograms of Figure 1

Note that the probability mass function (pmf) can be computed exactly due to the analytical integration of $f_{LM}(x)$. For GG however, only numerical integration is possible.

To our knowledge, only approximate rate and distortion expressions for uniformly quantized GG distributions are known [18], [19]. Extensions of these expressions to a general EDSQ are not evident due to the fact that the rate and distortion functions for such distributions are not easily tractable. For comparison purposes, we implemented a numerical solution by approximating the continuous GG pdf with a discrete pmf $\mathbf{p}_m = \{p_1, p_2 \dots p_m\}$ having m bins. First, the GG pdf is discretized to m samples $\mathbf{f}_m = \{f_1, f_2 \dots f_m\}$, such that $f_i = f_{GG}(x_i) \cdot \tilde{\Delta}$, where $x_0 = x_{\min} + (\tilde{\Delta}/2)$ and $x_0 = x_{\max} - (\tilde{\Delta}/2)$. $x_{\min}$ and $x_{\max}$ denote the smallest and largest value of the coordinate component in the subband. The pmf $\mathbf{p}_m$ is then calculated by the normalization $p_i = f_i / F$, where F is the sum of all f_i's. $\tilde{\Delta}$ is chosen small enough (i.e. m is chosen to be large enough), such that high-rate assumptions do not come into play. Distortion and rate of the quantized GG random variable can then be approximately written as:

$$D_{GG}(Q_{\delta_n, \Delta_n}) \approx \underbrace{\sum_{\forall i, x_i \in S_0} x_i^2 p_0}_{D_{DZ}} + 2 \underbrace{\sum_{k=1}^{\infty} \sum_{\forall i, x_i \in S_k} (x_i - \hat{x}_k)^2 p_i}_{D_{REST}}, \qquad (6)$$

and

$$R_{GG}(Q_{\delta_n,\Delta_n}) \approx \underbrace{-P_0 \log_2 P_0}_{R_{DZ}} \underbrace{-2\sum_{k=1}^{\infty} P_k \log_2 P_k}_{R_{REST}}, \quad P_k = \sum_{\forall i, x_i \in S_k} p_i, \tag{7}$$

where S_k denotes the cell-range of the kth quantization cell. $k = 0$ corresponds to the deadzone.

Figure 2 shows the observed and model D-R curves for the same histograms shown in Figure 1. For Rabbit, the LM D-R almost completely overlaps the observed D-R curve. In both cases, the D-R function for the proposed LM model follows the experimental D-R curve more closely than the D-R curves of the other two models.

5 Model Validation

5.1 Histogram Fitting

In Table 1 and Table 2, the average KL divergence results for the SL, GG and LM models for both normal (Dino, Skull) and non-normal (Venus, Rabbit) meshes are shown.

Table 1. KL divergence for three coordinate components averaged over five subbands. Filters: *U-BF*(unlifted Butterfly), *L-BF*(lifted Butterfly) and Loop.

MESH	SL			LM			GG		
(FILTER)	*NOR*	*TAN 1*	*TAN 2*	*NOR*	*TAN 1*	*TAN 2*	*NOR*	*TAN 1*	*TAN 2*
Venus(U-BF)	0.097	0.114	0.103	0.075	0.100	0.091	0.086	0.102	0.089
Venus(L-BF)	0.137	0.137	0.104	0.090	0.108	0.080	0.112	0.121	0.092
Venus(Loop)	0.113	0.102	0.091	0.085	0.090	0.069	0.098	0.092	0.081
Rabbit(U-BF)	0.170	0.171	0.172	0.134	0.136	0.132	0.150	0.143	0.147
Rabbit(L-BF)	0.208	0.188	0.177	0.143	0.140	0.138	0.160	0.152	0.153
Rabbit(Loop)	0.167	0.207	0.173	0.115	0.156	0.135	0.136	0.177	0.152
Dino(U-BF)	0.527	0.656	0.971	0.145	0.147	0.154	0.165	0.132	0.141
Skull(U-BF)	1.108	1.473	1.877	0.120	0.138	0.157	0.145	0.141	0.141

Table 2. KL divergence for three subbands averaged over three coordinate components

MESH (FILTER)	SL			LM			GG		
	$\mathbf{d}^{J-1}$	$\mathbf{d}^{J-2}$	$\mathbf{d}^{J-3}$	$\mathbf{d}^{J-1}$	$\mathbf{d}^{J-2}$	$\mathbf{d}^{J-3}$	$\mathbf{d}^{J-1}$	$\mathbf{d}^{J-2}$	$\mathbf{d}^{J-3}$
Venus(U-BF)	0.044	0.038	0.039	0.014	0.008	0.025	0.027	0.024	0.033
Venus(L-BF)	0.050	0.070	0.076	0.010	0.010	0.027	0.029	0.041	0.049
Venus(Loop)	0.051	0.054	0.038	0.016	0.009	0.023	0.036	0.031	0.032
Rabbit(U-BF)	0.064	0.062	0.082	0.008	0.011	0.035	0.029	0.032	0.054
Rabbit(L-BF)	0.069	0.093	0.111	0.007	0.011	0.035	0.029	0.040	0.058
Rabbit(Loop)	0.082	0.088	0.085	0.011	0.013	0.034	0.042	0.038	0.058
Dino(U-BF)	1.208	0.873	0.623	0.029	0.074	0.049	0.031	0.042	0.058
Skull(U-BF)	2.039	1.981	1.832	0.054	0.040	0.076	0.036	0.068	0.066

For the large majority of cases, the LM model gives better fitting over the observed histogram than the competing GG model. Note that, SL gives always the worst fitting results. Also, the LM model gives equally good fitting for both *normal* (*NOR*) and *tangential* (*TAN 1* and *TAN 2*) components.

It is also observed that the GG model performs slightly better for the low-resolution subbands of some meshes. The observed histograms in such cases are more Gaussian-alike, i.e. they have a round top. In general, the LM model faces difficulty in approximating such a round-top histogram due to the peaky nature of each of its Laplacian component; the GG fits well such histograms, as it corresponds to a Gaussian distribution for $\alpha = 2$. Nevertheless, the results show that, on average, the LM model outperforms the SL and the GG models in *KL* sense.

5.2 D-R Fitting

The model accuracy in D-R sense is measured using the percentage modeling error *ME*(%) defined as:

$$ME(\%) = \int_{R \in \Re} \left| D_M(R) - D_E(R) \right| * 100 \Big/ \int_{R \in \Re} \max_R \{ D_M(R), D_E(R) \}, \qquad (8)$$

Table 3. *ME*(%) for three coordinate components averaged over five resolution subbands

MESH (FILTER)	SL			LM			GG		
	NOR	TAN 1	TAN 2	NOR	TAN 1	TAN 2	NOR	TAN 1	TAN 2
Venus(U-BF)	6.3	10.3	8.9	1.3	3.3	2.8	4.7	5.0	4.7
Venus(L-BF)	11.4	10.1	6.0	2.0	2.9	1.9	8.1	5.4	4.1
Venus(Loop)	9.4	7.3	6.7	3.3	1.8	1.7	7.1	3.9	5.0
Rabbit(U-BF)	8.6	10.4	10.2	1.4	2.0	1.8	5.7	5.2	6.2
Rabbit(L-BF)	12.0	10.7	8.4	2.5	1.5	1.8	6.7	5.1	5.3
Rabbit(Loop)	11.2	11.2	8.3	2.4	1.8	2.3	7.9	7.6	5.2
Dino(U-BF)	16.2	34.3	42.7	5.6	7.8	9.4	7.5	23.4	30.3
Skull(U-BF)	37.2	44.9	50.4	3.9	7.9	20.5	12.8	15.4	19.9

Table 4. *ME*(%) for three subbands averaged over three coordinate components

MESH (FILTER)	SL			LM			GG		
	d^{J-1}	d^{J-2}	d^{J-3}	d^{J-1}	d^{J-2}	d^{J-3}	d^{J-1}	d^{J-2}	d^{J-3}
Venus(U-BF)	13.6	8.4	3.5	2.9	0.85	1.5	9.5	5.6	2.8
Venus(L-BF)	13.8	13.9	7.6	2.1	1.5	1.7	9.9	10.1	4.1
Venus(Loop)	13.8	11.0	4.0	2.4	1.6	0.80	11.0	6.8	2.7
Rabbit(U-BF)	14.0	11.4	8.1	1.5	1.0	1.3	8.6	6.8	4.9
Rabbit(L-BF)	14.2	13.9	11.2	1.5	1.1	1.8	8.6	8.6	5.9
Rabbit(Loop)	16.4	14.7	9.0	2.0	1.9	2.0	11.5	8.7	5.4
Dino(U-BF)	56.7	46.7	34.7	13.7	12.8	4.6	41.3	32.9	20.4
Skull(U-BF)	65.7	49.9	32.4	34.2	7.6	5.1	40.2	15.1	8.3

where $D_M(R)$ and $D_E(R)$ are the model and the experimental D-R functions, respectively. Table 3 and Table 4 show percentage ME results for the same meshes and transforms as shown in Table 1 and Table 2. A clear advantage of using the LM model over the other two models is evident from these results. On average, it is found that the proposed LM model performs better than the GG and SL models in ME sense. It is worth mentioning here that a best histogram fitting in KL sense may not always yield the lowest ME. However, one concludes that, on average, the LM model outperforms the SL and GG models in D-R sense.

6 Optimal Embedded Quantizer

In this section, the optimal EDSQ to be used in scalable wavelet-based coding of meshes is experimentally determined. Let z denote the ratio between the deadzone size and the step size of a general EDSQ. One defines the total average Signal-to-Noise Ratio (SNR) difference, given by:

$$\frac{1}{N}\sum_{\Re}\left(\underset{z=1}{SNR(R)} - \underset{z>1}{SNR(R)} \right),$$

which is computed over the a rate range $\Re$ for N rate points, where $SNR(R)$ denotes the discrete SNR-rate function. The $SNR = 10\log_{10}(\sigma^2/D)$ is taken in dBs, where D is the total distortion in the transform domain. The difference in SNR is computed relative to the uniform embedded quantizer (UEQ), for which $z=1$. The SNR difference for five embedded deadzone quantizers is plotted in Figure 3 over a wide range of standard deviation ratios σ_2/σ_1. Commonly observed proportion $a_1 = 0.9$ and $a_2 = 0.1$ are considered here.

We found experimentally that at lower standard deviation ratios, the total SNR difference is positive and the UEQ is optimal for $\sigma_2/\sigma_1 < 120$. For $120 < \sigma_2/\sigma_1 < 290$, the quantizer with $z = 1.5$ performs better compared to all the others. Similarly, $z = 2$ (i.e. the SAQ) performs the best in the range $290 < \sigma_2/\sigma_1 < 600$, while $z = 2.5$ performs the best for $600 < \sigma_2/\sigma_1$. In general, small standard deviation ratios correspond to α close to 1, observed in non-normal meshes, while higher ratios correspond to $\alpha \ll 1$, observed in normal meshes. These results show that one cannot determine a single embedded quantizer that provides the best performance for *all* 3D meshes. However, an optimal quantizer per wavelet coordinate can be determined based on the corresponding σ_2/σ_1 extracted from the model. Overall, for $\sigma_2/\sigma_1 < 120$, the difference between SAQ and the UEQ is significant, and hence UEQ is the optimal choice. For $\sigma_2/\sigma_1 \geq 120$, SAQ is not always the optimum, but lies not far from the optimum. Given the fact that SAQ is closely linked to bit-plane coding and that it can be implemented using simple binary arithmetic, one concludes that SAQ is not an optimal, but an acceptable solution in scalable coding of meshes.

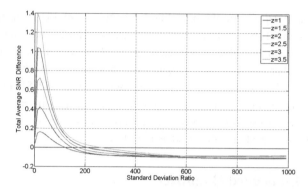

Fig. 3. *SNR* difference for five EDSQs with respect to UEQ

7 Conclusion

Based on the experimental results of section 5, we can conclude that the LM probability function allows for modeling the observed histogram and D-R curves better than the GG and SL models for both normal and non-normal meshes. On average, the LM model performs equally well for different subdivision transforms. The results show also that the SL model can only provide a rough approximation in cases where $\alpha \ll 1$ (i.e. for normal meshes). It is also concluded that optimal quantization depends on the standard deviation ratio σ_2/σ_1 in a subband. In this sense, one concludes that the classical SAQ is an acceptable near-optimal and easy to implement solution for embedded quantization of wavelet subbands in 3D mesh coding based on wavelet subdivision surfaces.

Acknowledgments

This work was supported by the Fund for Scientific Research (FWO) Flanders (postdoctoral fellowships of A. Munteanu and P. Schelkens), and the Flemish Institute for the Promotion of Innovation by Science and Technology (IWT) (OptiMMA project). Models are courtesy of Cyberware, Headus, The Scripps Research Institute, Washington University. The authors are particularly grateful to Igor Guskov for providing them with the normal meshes.

References

[1] Rossignac, J.: Edgebreaker: Connectivity compression for triangle meshes. IEEE Transaction on Visualization and Computer Graphics 5(1), 47–61
[2] Touma, C., Gotsman, C.: Triangular mesh compression. In: Proceedings of Graphics Interface, pp. 26–34 (1998)
[3] Taubin, G., Rossignac, J.: Geometric compression through topological surgery. ACM Transactions on Graphics 17(2), 84–115 (1998)

[4] Pajarola, R., Rossignac, J.: Compressed progressive meshes. IEEE Transactions on Visualization and Computer Graphics 6(1-3), 79–93 (2000)

[5] Taubin, G., Guéziec, A., Horn, W., Lazarus, F.: Progressive forest-split compression. In: Proceedings of SIGGRAPH, pp. 123–132 (1998)

[6] Li, J., Kuo, C.-C.J.: Progressive coding of 3-D graphic models. Proceedings of the IEEE 86(6), 1052–1063 (1998)

[7] Eck, M., Hoppe, H.: Automatic reconstruction of B-spline surfaces of arbitrary topological type. In: Proceedings of SIGGRAPH, pp. 325–334 (1996)

[8] Eck, M., DeRose, T., Duchamp, T., Hoppe, H., Lounsbery, M., Stuetzle, W.: Multiresolution analysis of arbitrary meshes. In: Proceedings of SIGGRAPH, pp. 173–182 (1995)

[9] Lee, A.W.F., Sweldens, W., Schröder, P., Cowsar, L., Dobkin, D.: Multiresolution adaptive parameterization of surfaces. In: Proceedings of SIGGRAPH, pp. 95–104 (1998)

[10] Khodakovsky, A., Schroder, P., Sweldens, W.: Progressive geometry compression. In: Proceedings of SIGGRAPH, pp. 271–278 (2000)

[11] Shapiro, J.M.: Embedded image coding using zerotrees of wavelet coefficients. IEEE Transactions on Signal Processing 41(12), 3445–3462 (1993)

[12] Satti, S.M., Denis, L., Munteanu, A., Schelkens, P., Cornelis, J.: Estimation of interband and intraband statistical dependencies in wavelet-based decomposition of meshes. In: Proceedings of IS&T/SPIE, San Jose, California, pp. 72480A–10A (2009)

[13] Denis, L., Satti, S.M., Munteanu, A., Schelkens, P., Cornelis, J.: Fully scalable intraband coding of wavelet-decomposed 3D meshes. In: Proceedings of Digital Signal Processing (DSP), Santorini (2009)

[14] Denis, L., Satti, S.M., Munteanu, A., Schelkens, P., Cornelis, J.: Context-conditioned composite coding of 3D meshes based on wavelets on surfaces. In: Proceedings of IEEE International Conference on Image Processing (ICIP), Cairo, pp. 3509–3512 (2009)

[15] Payan, F., Antonini, M.: An efficient bit allocation for compressing normal meshes with an error-driven quantization. Computer Aided Geometric Design 22(5), 466–486 (2005)

[16] Mallat, S.: A theory for multiresolution signal decomposition: the wavelet representation. IEEE Transactions on Pattern Analysis and Machine Intelligence 11(7), 674–693 (1989)

[17] Antonini, M., Barlaud, M., Mathieu, P., Daubechies, I.: Image coding using wavelet transform. IEEE Transactions on Image Processing 1, 205–220 (1992)

[18] Fraysse, A., Pesquet-Popescu, B., Pesquet, J.-C.: Rate-distortion results for generalized Gaussian distributions. In: Proceedings of IEEE International Conference on Acoustics, Speech and Signal Processing (ICASSP), Las Vegas, pp. 3753–3756

[19] Fraysse, A., Pesquet-Popescu, B., Pesquet, J.-C.: On the uniform quantization of a class of sparse sources. IEEE Transactions on Information Theory 55(7), 3243–3263 (2009)

[20] Taubman, D., Marcelin, M.W.: JPEG2000: Image Compression Fundamentals, Standards, and Practice. Kluwer Academic Publishers, Norwell (2002)

[21] Schröder, P., Sweldens, W.: Spherical wavelets: efficiently representing functions on the sphere. In: Proceedings of SIGGRAPH, pp. 161–172 (1995)

[22] Dyn, N., Levin, D., Gregory, J.: A butterfly subdivision scheme for surface interpolation with tension control. Transaction on Graphics 9(2), 160–169 (1990)

[23] Loop, C.: Smooth subdivision surfaces based on triangles. Department of Mathematics, Master's Thesis, University of Utah (1987)

[24] Dempster, A.P., Laird, N.M., Rubin, D.B.: Maximum likelihood from incomplete data via the EM algorithm. The Royal Statistical Society, Series B 39(1), 1–38 (1977)

[25] Cover, T.M., Thomas, J.A.: Elements of Information Theory. Wiley Series in Telecommunications. Wiley, New York (1991)

Appendix

The output distortion D_L of a Laplacian pdf, quantized using an n level EDSQ and reconstructed using midpoint reconstruction, can be written as:

$$D_L(Q_{\xi_n,\Delta_n}) = \lambda \underbrace{\int_0^{(1-\xi_n)\Delta_n} x^2 e^{-\lambda x}\, dx}_{D_{DZ}} + \lambda \underbrace{\sum_{k=1}^{\infty} \int_{(k-\xi_n)\Delta_n}^{(k+1-\xi_n)\Delta_n} \left(x - (k+0.5-\xi_n)\Delta_n\right)^2 e^{-\lambda x}\, dx}_{D_{REST}},$$

where D_{DZ} and D_{REST} denote the distortion contributions of the deadzone and the other quantization cells, respectively. By proper substitution and letting

$$\sum_{k=1}^{\infty} e^{-\lambda \Delta_n k} = \frac{e^{-\lambda \Delta_n}}{1 - e^{-\lambda \Delta_n}}, \text{ as } e^{-\lambda \Delta_n} \leq 1, \tag{9}$$

the following closed-form expression for the distortion is obtained:

$$D_L(Q_{\delta_n,\Delta_n}) = \frac{2}{\lambda^2} + e^{-\lambda \Delta_n \delta_n}\left\{\left(\frac{1}{4} - \delta_n^2\right)\Delta_n^2 - \left(2\delta_n + \coth\left(\frac{\lambda \Delta_n}{2}\right)\right)\frac{\Delta_n}{\lambda}\right\}, \tag{10}$$

where $\delta_n = 1 - \xi_n$.

Similarly, the output rate R_L of a Laplacian pdf, quantized using an n level EDSQ can be written as:

$$R_L(Q_{\xi_n,\Delta_n}) = -2\underbrace{\left(\frac{\lambda}{2}\int_0^{(1-\xi_n)\Delta_n} e^{-\lambda x}\, dx\right)\log_2 2\left(\frac{\lambda}{2}\int_0^{(1-\xi_n)\Delta_n} e^{-\lambda x}\, dx\right)}_{R_{DZ}}\dots$$

$$\dots -2\underbrace{\sum_{k=1}^{\infty}\left(\frac{\lambda}{2}\int_{(k-\xi_n)\Delta_n}^{(k+1-\xi_n)\Delta_n} e^{-\lambda x}\, dx\right)\log_2\left(\frac{\lambda}{2}\int_{(k-\xi_n)\Delta_n}^{(k+1-\xi_n)\Delta_n} e^{-\lambda x}\, dx\right)}_{R_{REST}}.$$

Again making use of the summation reduction identity of (9) along with the identity

$$\sum_{k=1}^{\infty} e^{-\lambda \Delta_n k}\log_2\left(e^{-\lambda \Delta_n k}\right) = \log_2\left(e^{-\lambda \Delta_n}\right)\sum_{k=1}^{\infty} k\left(e^{-\lambda \Delta_n}\right)^k = \frac{\log_2\left(e^{-\lambda \Delta_n}\right)e^{-\lambda \Delta_n}}{\left(1 - e^{-\lambda \Delta_n}\right)^2},$$

the expression for the rate can be reduced to the following closed-form:

$$R_L(Q_{\delta_n,\Delta_n}) = c_\delta \log_2\left(\frac{2d_{\delta_n}}{d_1 c_1^{1/d_1} e^{\lambda \Delta_n (1-\delta_n)} d_{\delta_n}^{1/c_{\delta_n}}}\right), \tag{11}$$

where $c_{\delta_n} = e^{-\lambda \Delta_n \delta_n}$ (hence $c_1 = e^{-\lambda \Delta_n}$) and $d_{\delta_n} = 1 - c_{\delta_n}$ (hence $d_1 = 1 - c_1$).

3D Surface Reconstruction Using Structured Circular Light Patterns

Deokwoo Lee and Hamid Krim

Department of Electrical and Computer Engineering
North Carolina State University
Raleigh NC 27606, USA
{dlee4,ahk}@ncsu.edu
http://www.vissta.ncsu.edu/

Abstract. Reconstructing a 3D surface in $\mathbb{R}^3$ from a 2D image in $\mathbb{R}^2$ has been a widely studied issue as well as one of the most important problems in image processing. In this paper, we propose a novel approach to reconstructing 3D coordinates of a surface from a 2D image taken by a camera using projected circular light patterns. Known information (i.e. intrinsic and extrinsic parameters of the camera, the structure of the circular patterns, a fixed optical center of the camera and the location of the reference plane of the surface) provides a mathematical model for surface reconstruction. The reconstruction is based on a geometrical relationship between a given pattern projected onto a 3D surface and a pattern captured in a 2D image plane from a viewpoint. This paper chiefly deals with a mathematical proof of concept for the reconstruction problem.

Keywords: 3D reconstruction, Structured light system, Circular light pattern, Geometrical relationship.

1 Introduction

3D image reconstruction from a 2D projected image on the basis of structured light patterns has been of much interest and an important topic in image processing. Applications are in the areas of object recognition, medical technologies, robotic visions and inspections of properties of target images, etc ([1], [2]). 3D surface reconstruction from a 2D projected image can be solved using a geometric relationship between the target image(3D) and the projected image(2D). There are two main approaches to the reconstruction problem : active and passive. The general principle involved in the passive method is triangulation using 2 or more cameras(usually 2 cameras) [3]. The relative positions of two cameras and an object in each image plane provides the necessary information to reconstruct 3D coordinate information ([3], [4]). This is also called a stereo correspondence problem, for which many techniques have been proposed ([3], [7]). In the passive

J. Blanc-Talon et al. (Eds.): ACIVS 2010, Part I, LNCS 6474, pp. 279–289, 2010.

method, prior knowledge (i.e. projection of object points in the image plane) necessitates high computational complexity for the solution. The 3D measurement also depends on the distance between two cameras and the result is sometimes distorted [10]. The alternative approach to the reconstruction problem is an active stereo vision, or an active method, using a structured light system which is used widely [5]. Generally one camera is replaced by a light source such as an LED or a laser beam that projects a known pattern. Only one camera is used to capture the projected pattern on a 3D object to be measured. Structured light patterns with high resolution can achieve a large number of sampling points over the surface and result in high accuracy [6]. In this paper, we assume that the position of a camera and a light source are known, a camera is modeled as an ideal camera (often called a pinhole model) and the light projection is parallel [7](Fig. 6). In practice, however, a camera is not usually calibrated to a pinhole model and structured patterns do not exactly preserve their shape by a set of lenses (lens distortion), but it is very difficult to model the system [4]. The observed deformation of the projected pattern on a 3D object provides information of its real world 3D coordinates (x_w, y_w, z_w). In order to improve the accuracy of the reconstruction, stripe patterns ([1], [8], [9]), pyramidal laser rays resulting in a matrix of dots (genetic algorithm) [10], occluding contours [11] and coded structured light [4] techniques were developed. Known information about the patterns(i.e. structure of patterns or the location of the points belonging to each pattern) are required prior to the projection in the previous works. Circular patterns have very good characteristics such as a closed and continuous form, and a symmetric shape leading to a lower computational complexity. Moreover, only a single point(i.e. the center of a circle) and the radii of the circles are needed. This advantage can improve the algorithm efficiency. Our approach is based on analyzing a deformed circular pattern acquired by the camera providing the 3D coordinate information of an object. (Fig. 1). This paper gives an account of proof of concept for a reconstruction and some simple simulated results. The outline of this paper is as follows. The overview of our system is described and some initial assumptions are explained in Section 2. Section 3, containing the major contribution of this paper, presents notations for image representation(Section 3.1) and details the proposed mathematical model to achieve the reconstruction procedure (Section 3.2). Some preliminary experimental results are shown in Section 4 to

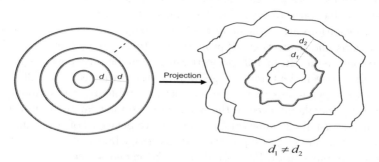

Fig. 1. Ideal and deformed circles

substantiate the mathematical model proved in Section 3.2. Finally, Section 5 presents the conclusion and future works.

2 System Architecture

2.1 Overall System Description

Basically, the structured light system (Fig. 3) ([12], [13]) is composed of a high-power and a noninvasive LED light source, a spatial light modulator(LC2002) generating a structured light pattern and a series of lenses to collimate a light beam. This is low-cost and effective system to generate a structured light patterns, to try using different kind of light sources and to establish a mathematical

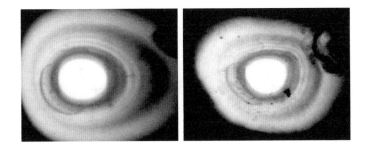

Fig. 2. Ideal and projected(observed) circular patterns

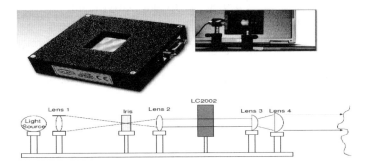

Fig. 3. Setup of structured light projection system using LC2002

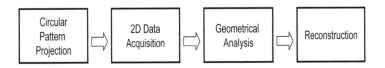

Fig. 4. Block diagram of an overall system

modeling for a 3D coordinates reconstruction. Overall system (Fig. 4) consists of a pattern projection, acquisition of 2D data points, geometrical analysis of 2D data and real world 3D coordinates, and a reconstruction. As discussed previously, our structured light pattern is circular and a reconstruction is based on the relationship between ideal circular patterns and deformed ones. In this paper, we assume that the patterns are projected in parallel, a camera is calibrated(i.e. known intrinsic and extrinsic parameters) to a pinhole model, and all the components(a camera, a 3D surface and a light source) are in fixed positions.

3   3D Surface Reconstruction

3.1   Notations and Geometrical Representation

Let $S \in \mathbb{R}^3$ be a domain of a 3D object of interest, then a point $P_w \in S$ is represented as

$$P_w = \{(x_w, y_w, z_w) \in \mathbb{R}^3\}, \tag{1}$$

where an index w is used to denote real world coordinates. Let $L \in \mathbb{R}^3$ be a domain of a circular structured light source and the origin defined as a center of a pattern(or a curve), then a point $P_L \in L$ is represented as

$$P_L = \{(x_{Lij}, y_{Lij}, z_{Lij}) \in \mathbb{R}^3 \mid x_{Lij}^2 + y_{Lij}^2 = R_j^2, \ z_{Lij} = 0\},$$
$$i = 1, 2, \ldots, M, j = 1, 2, \ldots, N. \tag{2}$$

Let $S_3 \in \mathbb{R}^3$ be a domain of projected circular patterns on a 3D object, then $P_3 \in S_3$ is represented as

$$P_3 = \{(x_{wij}, y_{wij}, z_{wij}) \in \mathbb{R}^3\}, \ i = 1, 2, \ldots, M, j = 1, 2, \ldots, N. \tag{3}$$

After the patterns projected, P_3 and P_w defined in the intersection of S and S_3 are identical,

$$P_3 = \{P_w \mid P_w \in S \cap S_3\} \ or \ P_w = \{P_3 \mid P_3 \in S \cap S_3\}. \tag{4}$$

Let $S_2 \in \mathbb{R}^2$ be a domain of 2D image plane of a camera, then $P_2 \in S_2$ is represented as

$$P_2 = \{(u_{ij}, v_{ij}) \in \mathbb{R}^2\}, \ i = 1, 2, \ldots, M, j = 1, 2, \ldots, N, \tag{5}$$

where M is a number of patterns and N is a number of sampled points in each pattern. The 3D reconstruction problem is analyzing a relationship between $P_3 \in S_3$, $P_L \in L$ and $P_2 \in S_2$ (Fig. 5). Let $f : L \rightarrow S_3$ be a map of a light projection and $g : S_3 \rightarrow S_2$ be a map of reflection respectively, then a reconstruction problem can be described as functions

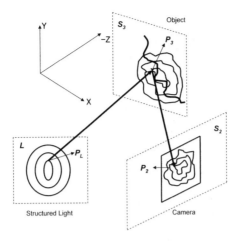

Fig. 5. Geometrical representation of the experimental setup

$$f(P_L) = P_3, \tag{6}$$
$$g(P_3) = P_2. \tag{7}$$

Recall that we assume parallel light projection which preserves (x_{Lij}, y_{Lij}) after projection onto a 3D object such as

$$I : (x_{Lij}, y_{Lij}) \rightarrow (x_{wij}, y_{wij}), \forall i, j,$$
$$i = 1, 2, \ldots, M, j = 1, 2, \ldots, N, \tag{8}$$

where I is an identity function. As discussed previously, under the assumption of parallel projection, (x_{Lij}, y_{Lij}) and (x_{wij}, y_{wij}) obey same constraints as follows:

$$x_{Lij}^2 + y_{Lij}^2 = R_i^2, \tag{9}$$
$$x_{wij}^2 + y_{wij}^2 = R_i^2, \tag{10}$$

where i denotes the ith positioned pattern. While preserving (x_{Lij}, y_{Lij}) coordinates, parallel projection makes the depth(z_{wij}) varies after projection onto an object. We call these variation of depth, z_{wij}, a *deformation factor*. 3D reconstruction problem is composed of analyzing a deformed circular patterns and depth recovery.

3.2 Mathematical Model

This section details the reconstruction technique of real world 3D coordinates of an object from a planar image of its patterned lighted surface. The geometrical structure, describing the physical measurement setup, is defined in 3D space and the reference plane is chosen prior to the reconstruction (Fig. 6). We assume that a camera is calibrated to a pinhole model[7]. To solve a reconstruction problem,

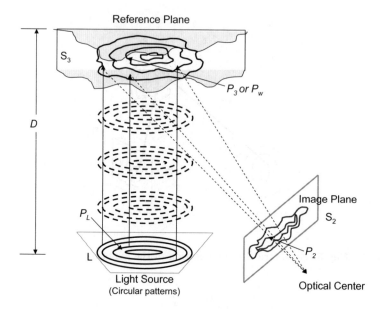

Fig. 6. Reconstruction experimental setup based on parallel projection

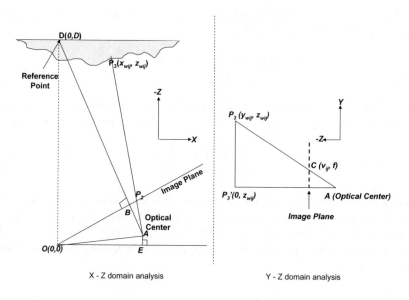

Fig. 7. $(X - Z)$ and $(Y - Z)$ domain analysis

we opt for two distinct coordinate systems. One lies on (X, Z) domain and the other lies in (Y, Z)domain(see Fig. 7). From Fig. 7 along with associated attributes, we can solve the 3D reconstruction problem. Assuming again that the structured light patterns remain parallel, camera is calibrated to a pinhole model, we know the locations of a camera, reference plane of an object and light source, we can write as follows:

$$\overline{AO} = d, \quad \overline{AB} = f,$$
$$\overline{BO} = \sqrt{d^2 - f^2} = d_1,$$
$$d\cos(\angle AOB) = d\cos\theta_2 = \sqrt{d^2 - f^2},$$
$$\overline{OP_2} = |\overrightarrow{BO} + \overrightarrow{BP_2}|, \tag{11}$$

where the point $P_2(u_{ij}, v_{ij})$ defined in the 2D image plane, is the result of reflection from the point P_3, A is the optical center and B is the origin point in the 2D image plane. Since the coordinate system of a 3D object and that of a 2D image plane are different, denoting the $\angle(AOE)$ by θ_1, we transform the domain S_2 to S_3 associated with $(X - Z)$ domain as follows:

$$\theta_1 + \theta_2 = \theta,$$
$$A : (-d\cos\theta_1, d\sin\theta_1),$$
$$B : (-d_1\cos\theta, d_1\sin\theta),$$
$$P_2 : (-d_2\cos\theta, d_2\sin\theta), \tag{12}$$

where $\theta_1, \theta_2, \theta, d, d_1$ and d_2 are known information. Using a property that the lines $\overline{P_2P_3}$ and $\overline{DB}$ meet at the point A(see Fig. 3), we can write the relationship between x_w and z_w as

$$d\sin\theta_1 = \frac{-d\cos\theta_1}{x_{wij} + d_2\cos\theta}\left(z_{wij} + \frac{d_2^2}{2}\sin 2\theta\right) + \frac{d_2 x_{wij}\sin\theta - z_{wij}}{x_{wij} + d_2\cos\theta},$$
$$\Rightarrow z_{wij} = F(x_{wij}). \tag{13}$$

To completely reconstruct 3D coordinates (x_w, y_w, z_w), we can show the $(Y - Z)$ domain analysis(Fig. 3) as

$$\frac{v_{ij}}{f} = \frac{y_{wij}}{z_{wij} - d\sin\theta_1},$$
$$z_{wij} = \frac{f}{v_{ij}} y_{wij} + d\sin\theta_1$$
$$= \frac{f}{v_{ij}}\sqrt{R^2 - x_{wij}^2} + d\sin\theta_1, \tag{14}$$
$$\Rightarrow z_{wij} = H(x_{wij}). \tag{15}$$

Concerning all above steps, we can determine 3D coordinates of the deformed curves on a 3D object,

$$F(x_{wij}) = z_{wij}, \tag{16}$$
$$H(x_{wij}) = z_{wij}, \tag{17}$$
$$x_{wij}^2 + y_{wij}^2 = R_j^2. \tag{18}$$

4   Examples of Reconstruction

To substantiate these reconstruction steps, some examples are shown in Fig.s 8, 9, 10 and 11. In experiments, 9 circular patterns are projected using a LC2002 light modulator which is a device for displaying images(e.g. structured light patterns) with a resolution up to SVGA format(800×600 pixels)[12]. A regular camera is used to take a picture of patterns projected on the target object. 2D data points (u_{ij}, v_{ij}) are manually selected, usually in pixel unit, (Fig. 8) and used to reconstruct $(x_{wij}, y_{wij}, z_{wij})$.

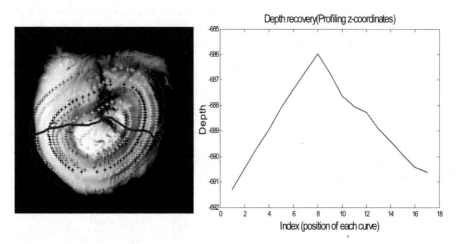

Fig. 8. Simulation of a profiling z_{wij} coordinates(relative depths) of a red line

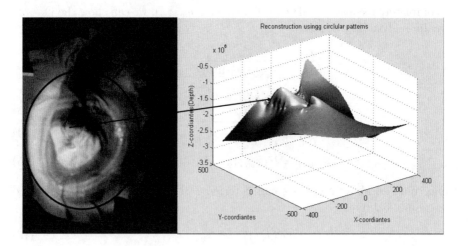

Fig. 9. Reconstructed 3D face from a measurement of 3D coordinates (x_w, y_w, z_w)

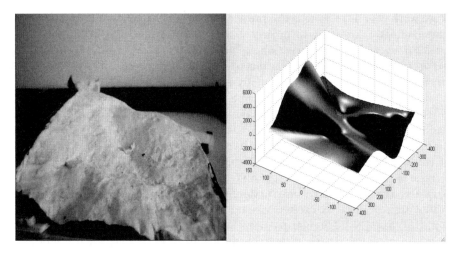

Fig. 10. Reconstruction example of a terrain model

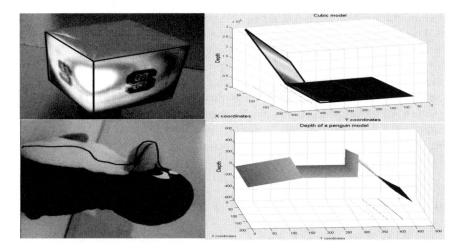

Fig. 11. Reconstruction examples of a cubic and a penguin model(depth recovery)

5   Conclusion and Further Works

In this paper we have presented an algorithm for 3D image reconstruction using circular structured light patterns. However our purpose in this paper is to
emphasize the theoretical proof of the reconstruction procedure. 3D image reconstruction is of great importance to many fields of image processing : surveillance
and inspection, and the proposed algorithm can be used for reconstructions of
an unknown object. 3D coordinates (x_w, y_w, z_w) were computed using a relationship between ideal and deformed circular patterns. The example reconstructions
are preliminary results and there are some technical issues to be resolved in

future work. The first issue is the projection : an LED light source and a spatial light modulator are used to project a light pattern onto the 3D surface, and the accuracy of the reconstruction results have not been examined and this is also an important aspect for continued work. In this paper, low resolution of a structured light pattern and manually extracted 2D data points result in low quality of reconstruction results. From a practical perspective, we need a better projection system to increase resolution leading to high quality of reconstruction results. The better projection system also plays a very important role in acquisition of 2D data points in imaged patterns. The second one is the calibration of the camera : in this paper, we assume that the camera is calibrated(i.e. constant intrinsic parameters) to make a possible mathematical model for a measurement setup and a geometrical reconstruction. Calibration is also one of the most important task in an active stereo vision and a lot of works have been presented ([14], [15], [16], [17]). Circular patterns provide important information and algorithm efficiency for 3D reconstruction problems, in particular when the objects are generic surfaces. Especially the characteristics of circular patterns(Section. 1) contributes an improvement in the mathematical model for the reconstruction process and computation efficiency. Quantifying the algorithm efficiency (i.e. computation times) compared to other method is also required in the future. Furthermore, with high sampling density (i.e. a great number of circular patterns), the reconstruction result is extremely accurate. Provided this accurate result, we can calculate the minimum sampling rate(minimum number of circular patterns) to successfully reconstruct the 3D surface. In the future, we are planning to determine the minimum sampling rate for a generic 3D signal, and the algorithm proposed in this paper is promising as an initial step toward the sampling rate. In the future, our goal is determining a sampling criterion specifying the necessary number of circular patterns required for 3D reconstruction and this work is in progress.

References

1. Wei, Z., Zhou, F., Zhang, G.: 3D coordinates measurement based on structured light sensor. Sensors and Actuators A: Physical 120(2), 527–535 (2005)
2. Zhang, G., He, J., Li, X.: 3D vision inspection for internal surface based on circle structured light. Sensors and Actuators A: Physical 122(1), 68–75 (2005)
3. Dhond, U.R., Aggarwal, J.K.: Structure from Stereo - A Review. IEEE Transaction on systems, man, and cybernetics 19(6) (November/December 1989)
4. Batlle, J., Mouaddib, E., Salvi, J.: Recent Progress in Coded Structured Light as a Technique to solve the Correspondence Problem: A Survey. Pattern Recognition 31(7), 963–982 (1998)
5. Will, P.M., Pennington, K.S.: Grid coding: a preprocessing technique for robot and machine vision. In: Proc. Int. Joint Conf. on Artificial Intelligence, pp. 66–70 (1971)
6. Pagés, J., Salvi, J., Matabosch, C.: Implementation of a Robust Coded Structured Light Technique for Dynamic 3D Measurements. In: IEEE International Conference on Image Processing, Barcelona, Spain, pp. 1073–1076 (September 2003)

7. Gaugeras, O., Luong, Q.-T.: The Geometry of Multiple Images. The MIT Press Cambridge, Massachusetts, London, England
8. Asada, M., Ichikawa, H., Tsuji, S.: Determining of surface properties by projecting a stripe pattern. In: Proc. Int. Conf. on Pattern Recognition, pp. 1162–1164 (1986)
9. Frueh, C., Zakhor, A.: Capturing 2 1/2D Depth and Texture of Time-Varying Scenes Using Structured Infrared Light. In: Proceedings of the Fifth International Conference on 3-D Digital Imaging and modeling (3DIM 2005) (2005)
10. Dipanda, A., Woo, S.: Towards a real-time 3D shape reconstruction using a structured light system. Pattern Recognition 38(10), 1632–1650 (2005)
11. Boyer, E., Cerger, M.-O.: 3D Surface Reconstruction Using Occluding contours. International Journal of Computer Vision 22(3), 219–233 (1997)
12. LC2002 Spatial Light Modulator Operating Instruction, HOLOEYE Photonics AG (2004)
13. HOLOEYE, Pioneers in Photonic Technology, http://www.holoeye.com/spatial_light_modulator_lc_2002.htm
14. Pollefeys, M., Koch, R., Van Gool, L.: Self-Calibration and Metric Reconstruction Inspite of Varying and Known Intrinsic Camera Parameters. International Journal of Computer Vision 32(1), 7–25 (1999)
15. Heyden, A., Åström, K.: Euclidean Reconstruction from Constant Intrinsic Parameters. In: Proc. 13th ICPR, Vienna, Austria, pp. 339–343 (1996)
16. Salvi, J., Armangué, X.: A comparative review of camera calibrating methods with accuracy evaluation. The Journal of Pattern Recognition 35, 1617–1635 (2002)
17. Strum, P.: On Focal Length Calibration from Two Views. In: Conf. on Computer Vision and Pattern Recognition, Kauai, USA, vol. II, pp. 145–150 (December 2001)

Computing Saliency Map from Spatial Information in Point Cloud Data

Oytun Akman and Pieter Jonker

Delft Biorobotics Laboratory, Department of BioMechanical Engineering,
Delft University of Technology, 2628 CD, Delft, The Netherlands
{o.akman,p.p.jonker}@tudelft.nl
http://www.3me.tudelft.nl

Abstract. Saliency detection in 2D and 3D images has been extensively used in many computer vision applications such as obstacle detection, object recognition and segmentation. In this paper we present a new saliency detection method which exploits the spatial irregularities in an environment. A Time-of-Flight (TOF) camera is used to obtain 3D points that represent the available spatial information in an environment. Two separate saliency maps are calculated by employing local surface properties (LSP) in different scales and the distance between the points and the camera. Initially, residuals representing the irregularities are obtained by fitting planar patches to the 3D points in different scales. Then, residuals within the spatial scales are combined and a saliency map in which the points with high residual values represent non-trivial regions of the surfaces is generated. Also, another saliency map is generated by using the proximity of each point in the point cloud data. Finally, two saliency maps are integrated by averaging and a master saliency map is generated.

Keywords: saliency detection, point cloud, local surface properties, time-of-flight camera.

1 Introduction

Selective visual attention is the mechanism by which we can direct our gaze towards interesting objects/regions in the scene and it allows us to break down the problem of scene understanding into rapid series of computationally less demanding, localized visual analysis problems [1]. Selective visual attention emerges from the joint impact of the visual saliency via goals (top-down influences) that people have and the stimuli (bottom-up influences) that have influence on them [2]. A general definition of visual saliency would be the subjective perceptual quality that makes some objects or regions in an environment stand out from their neighbors and grab the attention of the subject. These salient regions may represent non-trivial locations that can possess the information necessary to accomplish further tasks like recognition, manipulation, grasping or mapping. Most of the saliency detection methods in 2D images employ the color, texture and orientation contrast between the salient regions and their surroundings in order to

J. Blanc-Talon et al. (Eds.): ACIVS 2010, Part I, LNCS 6474, pp. 290–299, 2010.

detect regions standing out. However, these methods are still severely affected by many shortcomings, such as illumination differences, complex colored objects, objects without color or texture etc. In this respect, 3D saliency detection is becoming more popular due to the exploitation of 3D information that can cope with these drawbacks of 2D image based saliency detection methods.

In this research effort, we propose a novel saliency detection method based on the combination of spatial and geometric information available in 3D point cloud data (obtained via a TOF camera). The novelty of the proposed method is the utilization of local surface properties (LSP) to detect non-trivial regions in a scene and the combination of LSP with depth information to detect saliency. Initially, a scale space is generated by using a Gaussian kernel and subsampling the (registered) input point cloud. Then, in each scale, a small planar patch is fitted to each point in the point cloud to estimate the spatial irregularity at that point. Afterwards, calculated residual values in different scales are combined to create the first saliency map. The second saliency map is calculated by using the depth information and points that are closer to the camera are given high saliency values. Finally, these maps are combined to generate a master saliency map. In the master map, regions (3D points) with relatively high values with respect to their neighbors represent the salient regions. Also, saliency detection results of some other algorithms are presented and compared with the results of the proposed method.

The paper is organized as follows: in the next section related work is explained. The proposed method is introduced in the third section. Finally experimental work and results are presented.

2   Related Work

Saliency detection in 2D and 3D images has been attempted in many research efforts. Most of the 2D methods employ a low-level approach (bottom-up) to compute the saliency by determining the difference between image regions and their surroundings by means of color, intensity and orientation. Itti et al. [3] proposed a saliency-based visual attention model for rapid scene analysis which builds on a second biologically plausible system introduced by Koch and Ullman [1]. They combined bottom-up cues coming from feature detectors tuned to color, orientation and intensity contrast. Also there are other computational methods that are not based on biological vision principles [4,5]. In [5] Hou and Zhang exploited the frequency domain to calculate the saliency map. They used the spectral residual of an image in spectral domain to extract the nontrivial part (unexpected portion) of an image. Achanta et al. [4] presented a frequency-tuned approach of computing saliency in images using luminance and color. However, these saliency detection methods via 2D image features are inefficient when the color/texture of an object is similar to the background or other objects in the scene. Also they are very sensitive to the lighting condition in an environment. Moreover, some of these methods [3,5] can only generate very low resolution maps.

Detecting salient regions in 3D images has also been studied in the past. Almost all of the methods rely on depth information or combination of depth with 2D features [6,7,8,9,10,11,12]. In [6,7,8,9,10] depth information is combined with different 2D features such as color and motion to generate a saliency map for different applications like selective rendering, scene segmentation or guiding blind people. In [11], Frintrop et al. present a bimodal attention system based on laser scanner data. Depth mode image and reflectance mode image are fed into the Koch and Ullman's [1] saliency detection algorithm. All these methods use depth as a measure for saliency and they are unable to detect irregularities on continuous surfaces. Moreover, they assign approximately the same saliency values to the regions with similar color and depth values, which is not valid in some situations. In [12] Ouerhani and Hugli tested depth, mean curvature and depth gradients to calculate the saliency. However, in the final algorithm they have sticked to the depth information due to the noise in curvature and gradient calculations. This method also has similar drawbacks with the previous methods. In [13,14,15] saliency detection is used to extract informative geometric features for shape matching, scene segmentation and feature extraction. Primarily, the curvature and the size of the part/patch relative to the whole object are used to calculate saliency. However, the depth information is not involved in feature detection process and the proposed methods are not suitable for a generic saliency detection in an unknown environment since the relative size can vary between different scenarios.

3   Proposed Saliency Map Generation

Point cloud data encapsulate the available 3D information in an environment. This information can be exploited to extract the geometric structure and irregularities in a scene. Irregularities represent the non-trivial components and can be used as a measure of saliency. This approach has similarities with the 2D image-based saliency detection methods in which different features such as color and texture are employed to detect irregularities in different domains. For instance, color-based saliency detection methods usually scan an image for regions with different color values with respect to their neighborhood. However, utilization of local surface properties in point cloud data instead of 2D features can be used to overcome previously mentioned shortcomings. In the proposed method irregularities are extracted by calculating LSP for each point and the regions with different LSP than their neighbors are labeled as salient. Moreover, the depth information is considered in the saliency detection process. Points that are closer to the camera are labeled as more salient than the other points. The architecture of the method described in this paper is summarized in Fig.1.

First, sparse (noisy) points (outliers) are eliminated from the point cloud. Then, a scale space is created and the local surface properties (surface normal, curvature and residual) of remaining points are calculated in each scale. Residual values in different scales are combined and used as a saliency measure since they represent the irregularity on the surface of an object. Then the distance of each

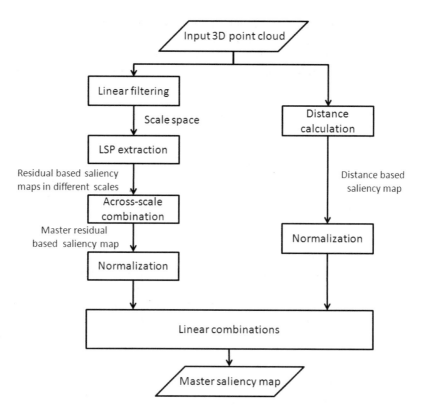

Fig. 1. Overall system architecture

point to the camera is utilized to calculate a separate saliency map. Finally, these maps are combined together to generate a master saliency map.

3.1 Outlier Rejection

Noisy measurements, especially at the object boundaries and on the relatively less visible surfaces, result in outliers in the point cloud. However, these outliers can be eliminated since they generally situated far from their neighboring points.

A small sphere with radius r is fitted to each point and the number of neighboring points inside the sphere is counted. If the number of points is greater than some certain threshold then the point is labeled as inlier. Otherwise it is labeled as outlier and eliminated from the point cloud. In our setup, we used radius $r = 5$ cm.

3.2 Saliency via Local Surface Properties

Point clouds can be used to find geometric information in a scene since they explicitly represent the surfaces. However, surface properties, surface normals and curvatures, of the points in the point cloud are defined by their local neighbors rather than a single point. Therefore, local surface properties must be estimated from the local neighborhood of a query point. Eigenanalysis of the covariance matrix of a local neighborhood can be used to estimate local surface properties [16].

Scale Space Construction. Initially, the input (registered) point cloud data is expanded by a factor of 2, using bilinear interpolation, prior to building the pyramid. This initial expansion enables the system to detect small regions that are hardly visible due to the low resolution of the camera. Then, five spatial scales are generated by using a dyadic Gaussian pyramids [17], which progressively filter by Gaussian kernel and subsample the (registered) input point cloud, using bilinear interpolation. Afterwards, LSP are calculated in each scale space in order to extract the features from different spatial scales.

Residual Estimation. In their comparison paper [18] Dey et al. compared different normal estimation methods for point clouds. Weighted plane fitting (WPF), adaptive plane fitting (APF) and big Delaunay balls (BDB) methods are considered and tested to decide on their performances. Their conclusions about these three methods are observed performances are almost equal (though WPF gives the best results) to each other when the noise level is low and the point cloud samples the surface more or less evenly. Also, BDB works the best when the noise level is relatively high and the sampling is skewed along some curves or is not dense enough for thin parts. Finally, they conclude that if the size of the point cloud is no more than a few million points ($\approx$ 5 million points), BDB is safer to use if one does not have specific knowledge about the quality of the input. Otherwise, WPF or APF should be preferred. By considering their conclusion, their experimental results and the resolution of MESA range camera (176×144) we decided to focus on the WPF method to estimate the surface normals.

The estimated normal n of the point p in the point cloud data can be approximated with the normal of the local neighborhood of p. The normal of the local neighborhood of p can be found by estimating the best plane fitting to the local patch. A plane can be parameterized with its unit normal $\mathbf{n} = (n_x \ n_y \ n_z)$, and its distance from the origin ρ. The distance of any given point $\mathbf{p} = (p_x \ p_y \ p_z)$ from the plane is given by $\mathbf{n} \cdot \mathbf{p} - \rho$. Given a set of m points in 3D belonging to the plane, direct solution for ρ in terms of $\mathbf{n}$ is

$$\rho = -\mathbf{n} \cdot \bar{\mathbf{p}} \tag{1}$$

where

$$\bar{\mathbf{p}} = \frac{1}{m} \sum_m (p_x \ p_y \ p_z) \tag{2}$$

Then,

$$\sum_{i=0}^{k} (\mathbf{p}_i - \bar{\mathbf{p}})^T (\mathbf{p}_i - \bar{\mathbf{p}}) \begin{pmatrix} n_x \\ n_y \\ n_z \end{pmatrix} = \lambda \begin{pmatrix} n_x \\ n_y \\ n_z \end{pmatrix} \tag{3}$$

$$A\mathbf{n} = \lambda\mathbf{n} \tag{4}$$

The minimum solution is given by the eigenvector of A corresponding to its minimum eigenvalue. The eigenvalue gives the *residual* of the plane fitting. Given a solution for $\mathbf{n}$ of the plane ρ can be calculated using $\rho = -\mathbf{n} \cdot \bar{\mathbf{p}}$.

The weighted covariance matrix from the points $\mathbf{p}_i$ of the local neighborhood where $i = 1...m$ is:

$$C = \sum_{i=1}^{m} \omega_i (\mathbf{p}_i - \bar{\mathbf{p}})^T (\mathbf{p}_i - \bar{\mathbf{p}}) \tag{5}$$

The weight ω_i for point $\mathbf{p}_i$ is defined as:

$$\omega_i = \left\{ \begin{array}{cc} exp(-\frac{d_i^2}{\mu^2}) \; if \; \mathbf{p}_i \; is \; outlier \\ 1 \quad\quad if \; \mathbf{p}_i \; is \; inlier \end{array} \right\} \tag{6}$$

where μ is the mean distance from the query point $\mathbf{p}$ to all its neighbors $\mathbf{p}_i$, and d_i is the distance from point $\mathbf{p}$ to a neighbor $\mathbf{p}_i$. This weighting method reduces the effect of the outliers in the surface normal calculation process.

3.3 Saliency via Depth and Map Integration

It is assumed that the objects which are close to the subject (camera) become more salient due to proximity since it is important for many applications to be aware of immediate surrounds. This is achieved by using a (distance) saliency measure, exponential decay function, given as

$$S_{d_i} = \frac{1}{\alpha\sqrt{2\pi}} exp(-\frac{d_i^2}{\mu^2}) \tag{7}$$

where d_i is the distance between point i and the camera, α and μ are the constants used to adjust the amount of decay. Such a decay function eliminates the unstable saliency detection response for very close 3D points.

The generated depth-based saliency map is combined with a LSP-based saliency map. First, saliency maps in different scales are resized back to the coarsest scale and combined by averaging the saliency values of each point in different scales. Then, the final LSP-based saliency map is normalized and combined with the normalized depth-based saliency map by averaging.

4 Experimental Results

Various test scenarios and scenes are generated and tested by using the explained saliency detection algorithm. We have tested our algorithm on both real point cloud data captured via a TOF camera and on artificially generated data. A typical input sequence is given in Fig.2. To test the 2D saliency methods, grayscale

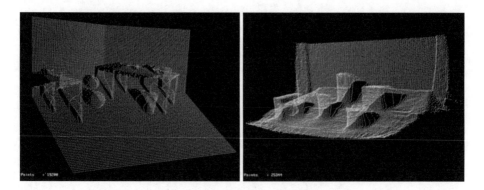

Fig. 2. Input point cloud data left to right, artificially generated and obtained via Time-of-Flight camera

output of the TOF camera is used. Also, created artificial scenes are rendered in grayscale mode to obtain the image of the scene. Captured images are used for visualization in which the 2D pixels corresponding to the 3D points are given values related with the saliency of their counterparts.

We have compared our method with the 2D algorithms presented in [5] and [4], and the 3D algorithm based on the distance between the 3D points and the camera. The first method takes grayscale images as input while the second one is designed for color images. However, the TOF camera is not able to output color images. Therefore, we used grayscale images while testing the second algorithm to see its performance since it is one of the best 2D algorithms in the literature. Typical results are given in Fig.3.

First two 2D segmentation methods fail in detecting saliency in grayscale images since the contrast level between the objects and the background is very small in the input images. Also different lighting conditions and shadows in the scene result in false salient regions. The main drawback of the third method is the lack of a saliency measure except distance. Although the method is good at detecting spatial discontinuities in point cloud data, it is ineffective in continuous surfaces. Such a measure does not distinguish between the close points and the salient points. Therefore, close regions without any non-trivial part are also labeled as salient.

The proposed algorithm achieved better detection results on tested data compared to the other three methods. Considering the overall performance, the advantages of this algorithm are twofold. Detection results are more accurate and the algorithm is independent of environmental conditions such as lighting because of the 3D sensor. Scale space exploration enables the system to detect the irregularities in different scales and also fills the gaps between the irregular regions on objects.

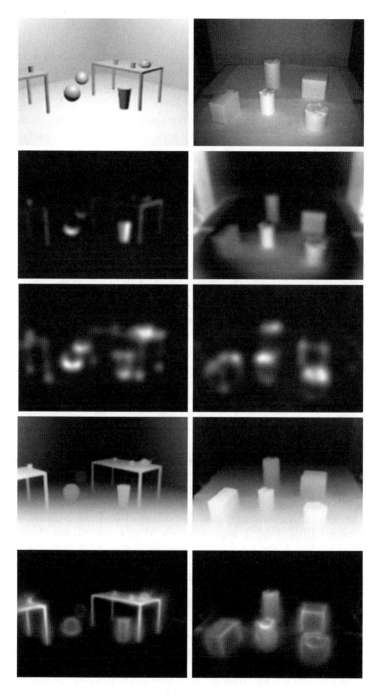

Fig. 3. Saliency detection results of two input images (columns)top to bottom, input images, results of 2D saliency detection methods [5] and [4], 3D saliency detection by using only depth information and the proposed method

5   Conclusion

In this work we present the algorithm to detect salient regions in a range data captured by a TOF camera. Proposed algorithm exploits the fact that irregularities on objects/surfaces represent the non-trivial regions in the scene. Local surface properties are extracted from 3D point cloud data in different scales by fitting planar surfaces to the points. Then, extracted features are utilized to construct a saliency map. Afterwards, the second saliency map based on the distance of the points is constructed. Finally, two maps are combined to generate a master saliency map.

Experimental results showed that the locations of the salient regions/objects are determined accurately. Compared to the tested methods proposed algorithm is less sensitive to the noise, less environment dependent and leads more accurate segmentation results. Moreover, proposed 3D saliency detection method can be combined with 2D methods by integrating a TOF camera and a standard color camera. Such a configuration would lead to saliency detection in different domains and compensate for the failures in individual systems.

Acknowledgments. This work has been carried out as part of the FALCON project under the responsibility of the Embedded Systems Institute with Vanderlande Industries as the carrying industrial partner. This project is partially supported by the Netherlands Ministry of Economic Affairs under the Embedded Systems Institute (BSIK03021) program.

References

1. Koch, C., Ullman, S.: Shifts in selective visual attention: towards the underlying neural circuitry. Human Neurobiology 4, 219–227 (1985)
2. Pashler, H., Johnston, J., Ruthruff, E.: Attention and performance. In: Annual Review of Psychology (2001)
3. Itti, L., Koch, C., Niebur, E.: A model of saliency-based visual attention for rapid scene analysis. IEEE Transactions on Pattern Analysis and Machine Intelligence 20, 1254–1259 (1998)
4. Achanta, R., Hemami, S., Estrada, F., Ssstrunk, S.: Frequency-tuned Salient Region Detection. In: IEEE International Conference on Computer Vision and Pattern Recognition, CVPR (2009)
5. Hou, X., Zhang, L.: Saliency detection: A spectral residual approach. In: IEEE Conference on Computer Vision and Pattern Recognition, CVPR (2007)
6. Sundstedt, V., Debattista, K., Longhurst, P., Chalmers, A., Troscianko, T.: Visual attention for efficient high-fidelity graphics. In: Spring Conference on Computer Graphics (SCCG), pp. 162–168 (2005)
7. Courty, N., Marchand, E., Arnaldi, B.: A new application for saliency maps: Synthetic vision of autonomous actors. In: IEEE International Conference on Image Processing, ICIP (2003)
8. Maki, A., Nordlund, P., Eklundh, J.O.: Attentional scene segmentation: integrating depth and motion. Computer Vision and Image Understanding 78, 351–373 (2000)

9. Maki, A., Nordlund, P., Eklundh, J.O.: A computational model of depth-based attention. In: International Conference on Pattern Recognition (ICPR), vol. 4, p. 734. IEEE Computer Society, Los Alamitos (1996)
10. Deville, B., Bologna, G., Vinckenbosch, M., Pun, T.: Guiding the focus of attention of blind people with visual saliency. In: Workshop on Computer Vision Applications for the Visually Impaired, Marseille, France (2008)
11. Frintrop, S., Rome, E., Nchter, A., Surmann, H.: A bimodal laser-based attention system. Computer Vision and Image Understanding, Special Issue on Attention and Performance in Computer Vision 100, 124–151 (2005)
12. Ouerhani, N., Hugli, H.: Computing visual attention from scene depth. In: International Conference on Pattern Recognition (ICPR), vol. 1, pp. 1375–1378. IEEE Computer Society, Los Alamitos (2000)
13. Sukumar, S., Page, D., Gribok, A., Koschan, A., Abidi, M.: Shape measure for identifying perceptually informative parts of 3d objects. In: International Symposium on 3D Data Processing Visualization and Transmission, pp. 679–686. IEEE Computer Society, Los Alamitos (2006)
14. Hoffman, D.: Salience of visual parts. Cognition 63, 29–78 (1997)
15. Gal, R., Cohen-Or, D.: Salient geometric features for partial shape matching and similarity. ACM Transactions on Graphics (TOG) 25, 130–150 (2006)
16. Pauly, M., Gross, M., Kobbelt, L.P.: Efficient simplification of point-sampled surfaces. In: IEEE Conference on Visualization (VIS), pp. 163–170 (2002)
17. Greenspan, H., Belongie, S., Perona, P., Goodman, R., Rakshit, S., Anderson, C.: Overcomplete steerable pyramid filters and rotation invariance. In: IEEE Conference on Computer Vision and Pattern Recognition (CVPR), pp. 222–228 (1994)
18. Dey, T., Li, G., Sun, J.: Normal estimation for point clouds: a comparison study for a voronoi based method. In: Proceedings Eurographics/IEEE VGTC Symposium Point-Based Graphics, pp. 39–46 (2005)

A Practical Approach for Calibration of Omnidirectional Stereo Cameras

Kang-San Lee[1], Hyun-Soo Kang[1,*], and Hamid Gholamhosseini[2]

[1] College of ECE, ChungBuk National University, Cheongju, Korea
masieno@nate.com, hskang@cbnu.ac.kr
[2] School of Eng., Auckland University of Technology, Auckland, New Zealand
hgholamh@aut.ac.nz

Abstract. This paper presents a calibration method of an omnidirectional stereo camera (ODSC) for the purpose of long distance measurement. Existing calibration methods can be used for calibration of an ODSC, but they may be applicable either to calibration of the ODSC with a small baseline or to individual calibration of its two cameras independently. In practice, it is difficult to calibrate the ODSC with a large baseline. A calibration test pattern, which is simultaneously captured by the two cameras of an ODSC system, appears very small in at least one of the cameras. Nevertheless, the baseline should be large enough for long distance measurement to ensure consistency of the estimated distance. In this paper, therefore, we propose a calibration method of the ODSC with a large baseline and verify its feasibility by presenting the experimental results of its distance estimation.

Keywords: camera calibration, omnidirectional camera, baseline.

1 Introduction

Omnidirectional cameras with a wide field of view are useful for many computer vision applications such as monitoring systems and robot navigation systems in need of an omnidirectional view. However, they require more precise calibration and more detailed camera models to ensure that the performance is coherent over the entire field of view. Many methods for calibration of omnidirectional cameras have been studied, taking into account the characteristics of catadioptric mirrors and dioptric lenses [1-6]. In central catadioptric cameras, lines in a scene project to conic curves in the image [2]. It has been showed that the unified model for the catadioptric cameras via a spherical projection is equivalent to a pin hole-based model with radial distortions and thus it can be directly employed to model the fish eye cameras [7-9].

While most of the conventional works have focused on calibration methods and camera models, in this paper, we aim at simultaneous calibration of an ODSC with a large baseline for the purpose of extracting metric information.

---

* Corresponding author.

J. Blanc-Talon et al. (Eds.): ACIVS 2010, Part I, LNCS 6474, pp. 300–308, 2010.
© Springer-Verlag Berlin Heidelberg 2010

Fig. 1. A pair of images from an ODSC

With a large baseline, we suffer from the practical problem in calibration. A calibration test pattern, which is simultaneously captured by the two cameras of an ODSC, appears very small in at least one of the cameras. This problem causes inaccurate calibration as well as incoherent calibration over the entire field of view. Because the test pattern may be mapped to a small region in the image plane of either left or/and right camera. One solution to this problem is to use a very large test pattern, which is not practical from its manufacturing and installation point of view. Thus, we propose a practical method to solve the problem by analytic derivations of camera parameters for a large baseline using calibration results of an ODSC with a small baseline.

Fig. 1 shows an example where a test pattern, the check board of $1.2m \times 1.2m$, is captured by a stereo camera with the baseline of 1m. The left image may provide infidelity in calibrating of the left camera since the test pattern was mapped to a small region in the right-center part of the image. As the baseline increases, the test pattern reduces to a point on the image plane and therefore, it becomes more difficult to be used for calibration purpose.

2 Proposed Method

In this section, we introduce a practical solution to calibrating the stereo camera with a large baseline to overcome the problem addressed in the previous section. A large baseline causes very small images of a test pattern in the left camera or/and the right camera. Thus, based on camera parameters resulted by calibration for a stereo camera with an appropriate baseline for which a calibration process is practically feasible, we have theoretically derived new camera parameters for the stereo camera with different baselines obtained by shifting one of two cameras along the baseline as much as required. In our derivation, the right camera is assumed to be shifted along the baseline because it is not easy to practically measure the change of the coordinate frames after arbitrarily shifting it in the real 3D space. Shifting along the baseline is measurable by employing an equipment where two cameras are installed on a guide rail and their shifting away from each other is allowed along the rail. Since the intrinsic parameters of the camera represent its features, they are shift invariant. Thus, the intrinsic parameters can be used without alternation regardless of shifting. Accordingly, the stereo camera with a different configuration where its baseline was changed by shifting has only different external parameters from the ones before changed. Thus, we mainly describe derivation of the external parameters after shifting as follows.

The omnidirectional camera mapping is generally represented by

$$\alpha \cdot \mathbf{p} = \mathbf{P} \cdot \mathbf{X}_w \tag{1}$$

where $\mathbf{P} \in R^{3 \times 4}$ is a projection matrix, $\mathbf{X}_w \in P^4$ is a scene point in 4-D projective space represented by a homogeneous 4-D vector, and $\mathbf{p} \in P^3$ is an image point expressed by a homogeneous 3-D vector. The general form of $\mathbf{p}$ is,

$$\alpha \cdot \mathbf{p} = (u, v, f(u, v))^t \tag{2}$$

where (u, v) denotes coordinates of the image plane and $f(u, v)$ represents radial distortions by a lens.

In the omnidirectional cameras, $f(u, v)$ in Eq. (2) corresponds to the intrinsic parameters, and $\mathbf{P}$ in Eq. (1) consists of only external parameters, that is,

$$\mathbf{P} = [\mathbf{R} \mid -\mathbf{R}\mathbf{C}] = [\mathbf{R} \mid \mathbf{t}] \tag{3}$$

where $\mathbf{C}$ is the camera center and $\mathbf{R} \in R^{3 \times 3}$ and $\mathbf{t} \in R^3$ are the rotation matrix and the translation vector, respectively.

It should be emphasized that the intrinsic parameters are fixed with no manipulation of the camera, regardless of a change of the baseline. Thus, once the parameters were found for a feasible baseline we can focus on finding the external parameters for a different baseline.

Let's consider the relationship in mapping between the camera coordinates, $\mathbf{X}_{cam}$, and the world coordinates, $\mathbf{X}_w$, as follows.

$$\mathbf{X}_{cam} = \begin{pmatrix} \mathbf{R} & \mathbf{t} \\ \mathbf{0} & 1 \end{pmatrix} \mathbf{X}_w = \mathbf{P}_{4 \times 4} \mathbf{X}_w \tag{4}$$

where $\mathbf{X}_{cam} \in P^4$ is a homogeneous vector in camera coordinates and $\mathbf{P}_{4 \times 4}$ is the 4×4 projective matrix where the first three rows come from the 3×4 projective matrix $\mathbf{P}$ in Eq. (3) and the last row is the row vector $(0\ 0\ 0\ 1)$. For simplicity, we removed the last row of the matrix in Eq. (4), and obtained a concise form as

$$\mathbf{x}_{cam} = [\mathbf{R} \mid \mathbf{t}]\mathbf{X}_w = \mathbf{P}\mathbf{X}_w \tag{5}$$

where $\mathbf{x}_{cam} \in R^3$ is the vector in Euclidean 3-D space. Applying Eq. (5) to each of the left and the right cameras, $\mathbf{P}_L$ and $\mathbf{P}_R$, it results to

$$\mathbf{x}_L = \mathbf{P}_L \mathbf{X}_W = \mathbf{R}_L \mathbf{x}_w + \mathbf{t}_L, \quad \mathbf{x}_R = \mathbf{P}_R \mathbf{X}_W = \mathbf{R}_R \mathbf{x}_w + \mathbf{t}_R \tag{6}$$

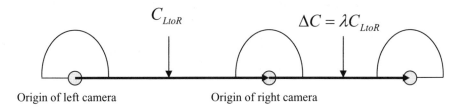

$$C_{LtoR} \qquad\qquad \Delta C = \lambda C_{LtoR}$$

Origin of left camera   Origin of right camera

Fig. 2. Camera shifting along the baseline

where $\mathbf{x}_w \in R^3$ is the scene point represented in Euclidean 3-D space. These equations lead to the following formula

$$\mathbf{x}_R = \mathbf{R}_R \mathbf{R}_L^{-1}(\mathbf{x}_L - (\mathbf{t}_L - (\mathbf{R}_R \mathbf{R}_L^{-1})^{-1}\mathbf{t}_R))$$
$$\equiv \mathbf{R}_{LtoR}(\mathbf{x}_L - \mathbf{C}_{LtoR}) \qquad (7)$$
$$where \quad \mathbf{R}_{LtoR} = \mathbf{R}_R \mathbf{R}_L^{-1}, \quad \mathbf{C}_{LtoR} = \mathbf{t}_L - (\mathbf{R}_R \mathbf{R}_L^{-1})^{-1}\mathbf{t}_R$$

which shows the mapping from the left camera coordinates to the right camera coordinates. It reveals that two coordinate systems of the left and the right cameras are related via a rotation and a translation.

Having the mapping relationship between the coordinates of the two cameras, we consider the case for a large baseline. As in Fig. 2, suppose that the right camera was shifted along the baseline by $\Delta\mathbf{C}$, which was rewritten as $\lambda\mathbf{C}_{LtoR}$ for a general notation where λ is a constant to control the amount of the displacement and $\mathbf{C}_{LtoR}$ is the vector from one principal point to the other principal point. Then let's compute the rotation matrix and the translation vector of the right camera shifted by $\Delta\mathbf{C}$.

Replacing the translational term $\mathbf{C}_{LtoR}$ in Eq. (7) with $\mathbf{C}_{LtoR} + \Delta\mathbf{C}$, it results to

$$\mathbf{x}'_R = \mathbf{R}_{LtoR}(\mathbf{x}_L - (\mathbf{C}_{LtoR} + \Delta\mathbf{C}))$$
$$= \mathbf{R}_R \mathbf{x}_w + \mathbf{t}_R - \lambda\mathbf{R}_{LtoR}\mathbf{C}_{LtoR} \equiv \mathbf{R}_R \mathbf{x}_w - \mathbf{t}'_R \qquad (8)$$
$$where \quad \mathbf{t}'_R = \mathbf{t}_R - \lambda\mathbf{R}_{LtoR}\mathbf{C}_{LtoR}$$

In Eq. (8), we observe that the rotation matrix is not changed but the translation vector is varying as λ, which makes sense since the right camera was only shifted along the baseline. With Eq. (7), $\mathbf{t}'_R$ is rewritten as

$$\mathbf{t}'_R = \lambda\mathbf{R}_R \mathbf{R}_L^{-1}\mathbf{t}_L - (\lambda+1)\mathbf{t}_R \qquad (9)$$

Finally, we have the projection matrix of the shifted right camera as

$$\mathbf{P}'_R = [\mathbf{R}_R \mid \lambda\mathbf{R}_R \mathbf{R}_L^{-1}\mathbf{t}_L - (\lambda+1)\mathbf{t}_R] \qquad (10)$$

The following describes the proposed algorithm for long distance measurement.

- Perform calibration for two cameras with a baseline $|\mathbf{C}_{LtoR}|$ where the baseline should be appropriately selected so that a test pattern may appear large enough on both of the left image and the right image. Then obtain the intrinsic and the external parameters. Let's denote the intrinsic and the external parameters, $f_L(u, v)$ and $\mathbf{P}_L$ for the left camera, $f_R(u, v)$ and $\mathbf{P}_R$ for the right camera, respectively.
- The right camera is shifted by $\Delta\mathbf{C}$ along the baseline to provide a large baseline. Then compute $\mathbf{P}'_R$ using Eq. (10). After shifting, new calibration should be performed but it is not realistic because the large baseline causes very small images of the test pattern. However, it is noticed that only $\mathbf{P}_R$ of the four parameters obtained in the previous step is changed and can be obtained by Eq. (10). Finally, the stereo camera with the large baseline takes $f_L(u, v)$ and $\mathbf{P}_L$ for the left camera, and $f_R(u, v)$ and $\mathbf{P}'_R$ for the right camera.
- Find disparities between the left camera and the shifted right camera and then compute the distances associated with the disparities using $f_L(u, v)$, $\mathbf{P}_L$, $f_R(u, v)$ and $\mathbf{P}'_R$.

3   Experimental Results

To evaluate the performance of calibration methods, in general, one uses the root of mean squared distance (RMS) in pixels between image points on a test pattern image and image points reprojected by the camera parameters. In case of large baselines, however, a test pattern image is too small to distinguish each of the image points. As a result, extracting the camera parameters would be complicated. Thus, we first evaluated our method for the case of small baselines where we could practically extract the camera parameters. After that, for evaluation of large baselines we considered long distant objects. The estimated distance of the proposed method was compared with the distance by a distance measurement equipment such as a laser telescope.

The proposed method was tested for small baselines, 20cm, 40cm, and 60cm, which are practical for extracting camera parameters. It was found that as far as a test pattern is not large enough it is practically impossible to perform calibration for a stereo camera with baselines of more than 60cm. Though a very large test pattern is available, it is not easy to establish it in the air for image acquisition.

To gather the reference camera parameters for evaluating our method, the camera parameters for each baseline of 20cm, 40cm, and 60cm, were taken by the conventional method [4]. Meanwhile, we computed the camera parameters for two baselines of 40cm and 60cm, applying the camera parameters for the baseline of 20cm to the proposed method. Table 1 shows the RMS values of the conventional method and the proposed method, where three test pattern images for each baseline and 30 image points for each test pattern image were selected. The size of each image was 640x480 pixels. Since the proposed method

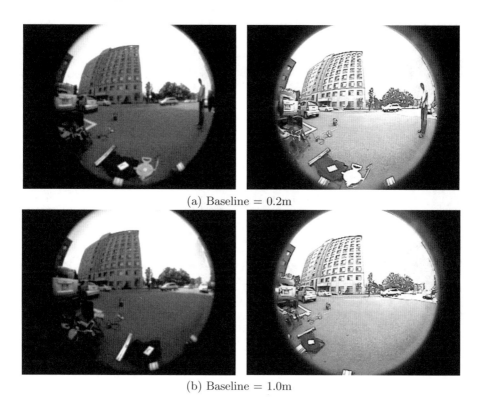

(a) Baseline = 0.2m

(b) Baseline = 1.0m

Fig. 3. A pair of images where the distance to the building = 15m

supplies the camera parameters without calibration, it is slightly inferior to the conventional method. However, it resulted in similar performance in RMS. Unlike the conventional methods, the proposed method can be easily applied to the large baselines for which the calibration process is infeasible. In addition, it does not require physical calibration any more after performing the first calibration for a small baseline.

For evaluation of large baselines, the test images in Fig. 3 and Fig. 4 were acquired with a small baseline of 0.2m and a large baseline of 1.0m. Using the proposed method, we estimated the distance to two buildings which were 15m and 30m far from the camera. Based on the camera parameters for the baseline of 0.2m obtained by physical calibration, the camera parameters for the large baseline of 1.0m were computed by the proposed method. Then the average of the estimated distances to the specific points on the buildings in the images was found using disparity information and the computed camera parameters.

Table 2 shows the distances estimated by the conventional method and the proposed method. The rows in the table where the baseline is equal to 0.2m show the distance estimation results by conventional method since calibration for the small baseline was feasible. On the other hand, the other rows where the baseline is equal to 1.0m present the distance estimation results by the proposed

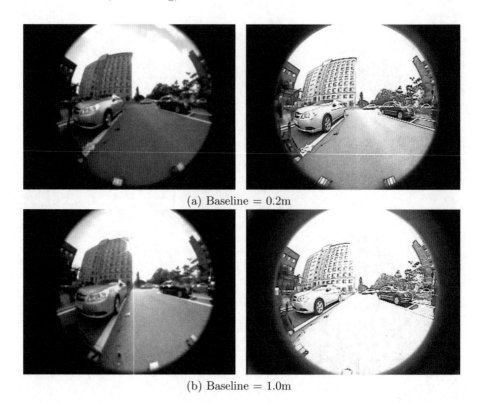

(a) Baseline = 0.2m

(b) Baseline = 1.0m

Fig. 4. A pair of images where the distance to the building = 30m

method. As mentioned previously, the distance for the baseline of 1.0m is not available by the conventional method as calibration is infeasible due to such a large baseline. Thus, we compared our results to the true distances instead of conventional ones. As shown in Table 2, the baseline of 0.2m is so small in recognizing the distance of 30m that it might cause a large error over 100%. In contrast, with the baseline of 1.0m, we achieved good results close to the true distance values. It explains that the camera parameters by the proposed method are very useful for large baselines. In the meantime, the fact that the result for 15m is more accurate than that for 30m is coincident with the analysis made in the previous section.

Table 1. Reprojection errors (RMS)

Baseline	Conventional method	Proposed method	Difference
40cm	1.694527 pixels	1.982364 pixels	0.287837 pixels
60cm	1.833266 pixels	2.049611 pixels	0.216345 pixels

Table 2. Results of distance estimation

Baseline (meter)	True distance (meter)	Average disparity (pixels)	Estimated distance (meters)	Estimation error (%)
0.2*	15	3.5	15.97	6.47
	30	0.8	60.87	102.9
1.0**	15	16.4	14.86	0.93
	30	7.8	31.20	4.00

* Calibration by the conventional method, ** Calibration by the proposed method and calibration unavailable by conventional method.

4   Conclusion

The camera calibration process is essential to extract the distance to a scene point using stereo camera systems. In ODSC systems, however, we may suffer from physical limitation in space for the calibration because the baselines should be large enough to ensure the accuracy of the distance. Moreover, the large baselines of the ODSC system make the test pattern images to be mapped to very small shapes in the images. In this paper, we proposed a practical solution to overcome the problem of calibration for large baselines by extending the calibration results for a small baseline. As a result, the proposed method can be employed for the purpose of long distance measurement using ODSC systems. Currently, we have a study on the cloud height estimation using our method. We expect that it will be realized after resolving a camera installation problem caused by huge shifting in the order of several decade meters for the application.

Acknowledgement

This work was conducted as a part of the research projects of "The Development of Security and Safety Systems based on Ubiquitous Technology for Shipping and Logistics" financially supported by the Ministry of Land, Transport and Maritime Affairs (MLTM) of Korea.

References

1. Kang, S.B.: Catadioptric self-calibration. In: Proceedings of International Conference on Computer Vision and Pattern Recognition, vol. 1, pp. 201–207 (2000)
2. Barreto, J.P., Araujo, H.: Geometric properties of central catadioptric line images and their application in calibration. IEEE Trans. on Pattern Analysis and Machine Intelligence 27(8), 1327–1333 (2005)
3. Ying, X., Hu, Z.: Catadioptric camera calibration using geometric invariants. IEEE Trans. on Pattern Analysis and Machine Intelligence 26(10), 1260–1271 (2004)
4. Scaramuzza, D., Martinelli, A.: A flexible technique for accurate omnidirectional camera calibration and structure from motion. In: Proceedings of IEEE International Conference on Computer Vision Systems, pp. 45–52 (2006)

5. Kannala, J., Brandt, S.S.: A generic camera calibration method for fish-eye lenses. In: Proceedings of International Conference on the Pattern Recognition, vol. 1, pp. 10–13 (2004)
6. Kannala, J., Brandt, S.S.: A generic camera model and calibration method for conventional, wide-angle and fish-eye lenses. IEEE Trans. on Pattern Analysis and Machine Intelligence 28(8) (August 2006)
7. Geyer, C., Daniilidis, K.: A unifying theory for central panoramic systems and practical implications. In: Vernon, D. (ed.) ECCV 2000. LNCS, vol. 1843, pp. 159–179. Springer, Heidelberg (2000)
8. Toepfer, C., Ehlgen, T.: A unifying omnidirectional camera model and its applications. In: IEEE International Conference on Computer Vision, pp. 1–5 (2007)
9. Courbon, J., Mezouar, Y., Eck, L., Martinet, P.: A generic fisheye camera model for robotic applications. In: Proc. Of 2007 IEEE/RSJ International Conference on Intelligent Robots and Systems, pp. 1683–1688 (October 2007)

Surface Reconstruction of Wear in Carpets by Using a Wavelet Edge Detector

Sergio Alejandro Orjuela Vargas[1,3,*], Benhur Ortiz Jaramillo[4],
Simon De Meulemeester[2], Julio Cesar Garcia Alvarez[4], Filip Rooms[1],
Aleksandra Pižurica[1], and Wilfried Philips[1]

[1] Department of Telecommunications and Information Processing,
(TELIN-IPI-IBBT), Ghent University, Belgium
[2] Department of Textiles, Ghent University, Belgium
{SergioAlejandro.OrjuelaVargas,Simon.DeMeulemeester,Filip.Rooms,
Aleksandra.Pizurica,Wilfried.Philips}@UGent.be
[3] Perception and Robotics Group, Antonio Nariño University, Colombia
[4] Control and Digital Signal Processing Group, National University, Colombia
{bortizj,jcgarciaa}@unal.edu.co

Abstract. Carpet manufacturers have wear labels assigned to their products by human experts who evaluate carpet samples subjected to accelerated wear in a test device. There is considerable industrial and academic interest in going from human to automated evaluation, which should be less cumbersome and more objective. In this paper, we present image analysis research on videos of carpet surfaces scanned with a 3D laser. The purpose is obtaining good depth images for an automated system that should have a high percentage of correct assessments for a wide variety of carpets. The innovation is the use of a wavelet edge detector to obtain a more continuously defined surface shape. The evaluation is based on how well the algorithms allow a good linear ranking and a good discriminance of consecutive wear labels. The results show an improved linear ranking for most carpet types, for two carpet types the results are quite significant.

Keywords: Carpet wear, LBP technique, Kullback-Leibler, Image analysis, Automated labeling assessment.

1 Introduction

One of the most important parameters for the classification of the quality of floor coverings is the conservation of appearance after an accelerated wear process. To assess their aspect preservation, textile floor coverings were initially compared with previously rated reference samples. As the physical features of these reference samples may change over time, a normalization committee decided to propose certified photographs by international committees instead. In

* Sergio Orjuela is supported by a grant of the LASPAU Academic and Professional Programs for the Americas in agreement with the COLCIENCIAS Science & Technology Program, Colombia.

J. Blanc-Talon et al. (Eds.): ACIVS 2010, Part I, LNCS 6474, pp. 309–320, 2010.
© Springer-Verlag Berlin Heidelberg 2010

the assessment process, the carpets are first subjected to accelerated mechanical wear to simulate traffic exposure. Consequently, a group of trained experts compare the original carpet with the carpet subjected to an accelerated mechanical wear. Experts evaluate the wear level from color appearance and 3D structure, attributing values between 1 and 5 to each carpet. Value 1 corresponds to a total loss of structure and value 5 is attributed to a carpet that did not undergo a structure change. This visual evaluation method lacks in reproducibility and the method requires at least three experts, which is not always possible, especially within a small company. The human evaluation assessment is also somewhat subjective and industry is very interested in converting these traditional standards to automated objective standards. However, no automated system exists yet to enable the labeling process.

Research in automated rating has progressed, specifically on image analysis for extracting texture features from digital color images. Approximations to the human evaluation have been achieved using Fourier transform [1], second order statistics [2], random markov fields [3] and neural networks [4]. However, practical applications were limited at that time by factors such as the amount of incorrect assessments exceeding 5% and algorithms being considered not generic enough for a broad variety of carpets.

Recently, some researchers have been exploring the use of depth information capturing the three dimensional structures of the carpets also evaluated by the experts. Initially, a scanner for 3D objects was used to capture the 3D shape of the carpet surfaces [5]. However, with that scanner the depth data were captured into nonstructured grids, with the number of acquired points highly dependent on the colors of the object. To extract texture features from these data using image analysis, the information of depth had to be structured first into 2D images. This has two disadvantages, an additional computational cost and the possibility of distortion of the surface shape due to interpolation methods involved in this process [6]. Although a classification over 95% was achieved, the extracted features did not change accordingly with the wear labels as should be expected. Nevertheless, research in automating the labeling process now attempts to find a universal classification system for carpets using depth and/or intensity data.

To optimize the feature extraction process a methodology based on experimental design has been proposed [7]. The methodology assumes that for a correct description the features must not only change monotonically according to the wear labels but also must be highly discriminate between consecutive wear labels.

This methodology has been tested extracting Local Binary Pattern statistics on references from different standards [8,9], obtaining rank correlations over 0.9, linear correlations over 0.88 and a 89% of statistical distinction between consecutive wear labels. Additionally, a novel 3D scanner based on structured light for specifically scanning carpets has been developed [10]. 3D data, termed range data, are obtained by video capturing with a camera the reflection of a uniform laser line on the surface of the carpet. Then, the depth information is calculated from the highest position of the brightest reflection on the columns of each frame. This system offers better linear and linear-rank correlations between wear labels and texture features computed from depth data. Experiments suggest that depth and color information are complementary to generalize the description on several carpets [11]. However, discrimination is still better using data from intensity images.

In this paper we present our proposed method to improve the surface representation on depth images. The method increases the discriminance of texture by extracting the depth from the 3D range data using edge detection based on multiresolution analysis. Thus, the relevant edges can be detected and separated from noise. This type of analysis offers excellent results for texture analysis and classification [12,13,14,15,16] and will be shown that the proposed method achieves a better linear ranking of wear labels than the previous method for all carpet types. We compare the results of our proposed method to the method applied in [10] as well as the optimal results from both methods to results using images of intensity.

The paper is organized as follows. In Section 2 we describe the materials used in this apporach. In Section 3 we describe the method that we propose to improve the construction of depth images as well as the methodology employed to compare the methods. In Section 4 we report the results of the comparison. Finally, in Sections 5 findings are discussed and conclusions are drawn.

2   Materials

In this approach we use eight types of reference sets provided from the EN1471 standard. Each reference contains a collection of samples of a particular textile floor covering priorly subjected to different revolutions on the Vettermann tester. The samples have been collected from carpet types loop, cut/loop, woven cut pile, fris and shaggy. Each reference includes eight labelled samples of transitional degrees of wear. These sets do not include label 5 and the labels vary from 4.5 to 1, with steps of half point. Label 4.5 represents a minor change in appearance and label 1 a several change.

We composed a database of videos using the scanner based on structured light. For this, the samples were scanned one sample at a time. The sample was first vacuum cleaned and held with elastic bands upon an inox-drum with a diameter of 25 cm. On the surface of the sample a uniform line was projected. The line was produced with a line laser generator model LDM-4-650-1-PF200-UL60. This type of lasers produce a bright, crisp laser line of uniform intensity with a fan angle of 60°. It was fixed at 20 cm above the drum projecting on the surface of the sample a high quality uniform line with a length of 20 cm and with a thickness of 0.5 mm.

The reflection of the line was seen with a progressive 3CCD Sony camera model DXC-9100P using a Sony macro lens model VCL-707BXM. The camera was fixed at a distance of 30 cm from the line to the objective lens. Figure 1 shows the reflection of the uniform laser line on the surface of samples from the same reference with different degrees of change in appearance. To cover the surface of the sample with the line, the drum was moved using a motor model

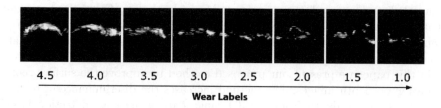

Fig. 1. Surface appearance change captured by the camera on carpet type loop

Parvalux 400-753 with gear box. This allowed us to control the distance between captured lines. The speed of the motor was controlled using an AC Inverter Drive Speed Controller with model Parker SSD Drives 650. Thus, 50 seconds of video have been recorded for each sample with 25 fps. The frames are spaced 0.24 mm on the surface, each frame with a resolution of 720×576 pixels.

As a result we have composed a database of 64 videos, capturing the 3D structure of eight types of reference fatigued specimens. Each reference with samples of eight wear labels. Figure 1 displays sections of frames showing the change of appearance on the surface of reference samples.

3 Methods

To be able to use classic image analysis, the depth information given by the reflection of the light must be stored into an image. For this, Orjuela *et al.* have proposed in [10] and [11] to search in each column of the frame for the highest position of the highest intensity value corresponding to the reflected light on the surface. That position represents the depth and an array is constructed using one depth value per column from the frame. Then, the image is built adding the arrays when the drum is rotating. In the following, we will refer to this method as the *RefLight* method.

From Figure 1 it can be observed that the reflected light forms discontinuous segments with a high variation in width. We are however particularly interested in obtaining fine lines representing small details that describe changes in surface between wear labels. Using the RefLight method on this kind of images has two disadvantages. The first one is that it is highly dependent on the intensity of the reflected light; the second one is that the detected points are unconnected between columns since they are independently calculated. Since this method does not assure a good reconstruction with a continuous surface shape, we propose to use an edge detection procedure instead.

For a better reconstruction of the surface shape, we propose to detect the edge of the laser line frame by frame using a wavelet representation [17]. The need for a multiresolution evaluation relies on the fact that edges such as those describing the reflection of the light are optimally detected by using different scales and classical edge detectors (like Canny) only use a single scale parameter for the whole image [18]. Thus, the basic single scale edge detection has been

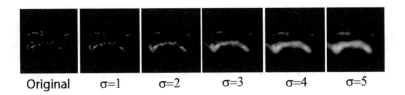

Fig. 2. Visual selection of the number of scale to evaluate

extended to an approach that combines information about the behaviour of the edges across a set of different scales [19]. The number of scales is determined by applying a Gaussian lowpass filter with increasing standard deviation, termed σ, from 1 to 5 until separate fibers can no longer be distinguished in the image [20]. In our case the separated fibers are no longer perceptible beyond $\sigma = 3$. This is illustrated in Figure 2.

The edges are detected in each sub–band by using a Canny second–order filter. Additionally, lower resolution sub-bands are merged by using a Sobel filter in order to preserve the position of the edge in the image. This filter is used because the edge is selected when the amplitude of the filter response increases from the finer to the lower scale sub-bands and eliminated when the amplitude decreases from finer to coarser scales [17]. In a more formal way, we compute the Lipschitz exponents for all positions in the image. This Lipschitz exponent expresses the local regularity of an image at a certain location. The Lipschitz exponent is small where only fine texture or noise are present and large where smoother features or continued edges are present. Recent works that use the Lipschitz exponent in multiresolution edge detection can be found in [21] and [22]. Using the Lipschitz exponent implicitly separates the noise from the edges. In the following, we will refer to this method for detecting edges as the *EdgeWav* method. Comparative methods can be found in [20,23], where merging is stated with an additional training phase in order to select the edges. For this application, only the moduli of edge pixel coefficients are required.

For the methods considered in this paper, depth images are again constructed by adding arrays when the drum is rotating, as it is defined in [10] and [11]. Thus, in the EdgeWav method, the highest position of the edges instead of the highest intensity value is searched in each column of the frame. This improves the representation of the depth of the surface by using connected points between adjacent columns. Figure 3 shows cut out examples of the change in appearance of the surface captured with both methods.

We want to compare the performance of both methods EdgeWav and RefLight in discriminating between consecutive wear labels and in correctly ranking them. For this, the texture transitions due to wear are first numerically represented by extracting texture features from the images. Then, we use two measures that quantify characteristics from the description of both methods. Finally, we evaluate which method offers the closest description of the wear label to the visual analysis by comparing both the measures.

Fig. 3. Comparison of the reconstruction of the surface on wear labels of carpet type shaggy

To extract texture features, we compute a symmetrized adaptation of the Kullback-Leibler (SKL) [24] divergence on the distribution of Local Binary Patterns (LBP) [7] from the images. We use the Rotational, Mirrored and Complemented invariance extension of the LBP technique (LBPRMC) [7]. This technique has been tested on both intensity and depth images, revealing good performance for multiple types of carpets [7,11]. To characterize the texture, relationships between points on a circle around a central pixel are evaluated. Equally spaced points are considered on the circle and a corresponding pixel value in each point is interpolated from the four pixels closest to the point. Each point gets a code bit 0 or 1 assigned depending on whether it has a higher or lower gray value than the central pixel. These bits are read out clock wise and placed in a diadic code word named pattern. Mirror and complement versions of patterns are grouped using a look up table. This is because a carpet reflected in a mirror or with the colors inverted would be assigned the same rating by human assessors. The distribution of the patterns corresponding to wear labels are represented with histograms. In human visual inspection samples with changes in appearance are compared to samples of original appearance. However, there are not samples from original appearance in the database. We estimate the LBPRMC histograms corresponding to original appearance by using the pattern distributions of the respective changes in appearance, with wear labels from 1.0 to 4.5. Thus, the bin values for the histogram corresponding to label 5.0 are estimated using a linear regression model since the frequency of a pattern is expected to change monotonically from labels 1.0 to 5.0 [7]. We quantify the difference in texture between the original appearance and the changes by comparing the corresponding LBPRMC histograms. We compute the symmetric Kullback-Leibler difference, termed κ, between two histograms as follows:

$$\kappa = \sum_{i=1}^{N} h_1(i) \log h_1(i) + \sum_{i=1}^{N} h_2(i) \log h_2(i) - \sum_{i=1}^{N} h_p(i) \log h_p(i) \qquad (1)$$

where $h_1(i)$ and $h_2(i)$ are the two histograms, which must be normalized first, i is the bin index, $h_p(i) = h_1(i) + h_2(i)$ and N is the total number of bins.

For each image in the database, we composed a set of 32 image variations, consisting in combinations of complements, rotations of 0, 90, 180, 270 degrees and mirrored up-down and left-right. Some of these κ values from the same worn sample can be significantly larger or smaller than the others because of the presence of factors such as flecks or speckles that could not be removed by the vacuum cleaning. These outliers are detected using the Mahalanobis distance and then replaced with the associated median to allow statistical comparisons with an equal number of κ values per worn sample.

To be consistent with the visual analysis, the κ values are expected to change monotonically with the wear labels as well as to be clearly distinguished between consecutive wear labels [7]. To compare the WavEdge to the Reflight Method, we quantify both characteristics from the description of both methods.

The first characteristic is satisfied if the relation between κ values and the wear labels is at least linear-ranked. To check this, we compute the Spearman linear-rank correlation between the wear labels and the mean values of the associated κ values. The Spearman rank correlation assign a significance of correspondence between -1 to 1, with 1 indicating a perfect rank correlation.

The second characteristic can be evaluated by checking the number of Consecutive Wear labels that can be Statistically Discriminated, termed CWSD [7]. This number can be quantified by counting how many times the difference between consecutive means is larger than the threshold for a statistic significance. The statistic significance is computed based on the Tukey test which allows pairwise comparisons. For this, an equal number of κ values per wear label is required.

Most of the changes due to wear appear in the tips of the pile yarns tufts. As their size depends of the type of carpet, a multiresolution analysis is required [7]. This can be achieved by changing the number of circular neighbors and their distance from the center pixel [25]. However, we prefer then to keep these parameters fixed and to resize the images instead. To resize, we use bilinear interpolation, analysing pictures on scale factors from 0.6 to 1 with intervals of 0.1. We present results only in this range because experiments show that the optimal resolution is found to always lie in it.

The linear rank correlation and CWSD are called the response variables and are computed for each one of the combinations of the elements shown in Table 1.

We are interested in evaluate whether the EdgeWav method offers a more monotonic and higher discriminant representation of the κ values related to wear labels than the RefLight method. For this, we independently evaluate the response variables using ANalysis Of VAriance tests (ANOVA) [26]. We test for each response variable the null hypothesis 'κ *values related to wear labels offer*

Table 1. Elements evaluated in this experiment

Method Type	Scale Factor	Reference Type
RefLight	0.6	Shaggy1
EdgeWav	0.7	Cut/loop
	0.8	Shaggy2
	0.9	High/Low loop
	1.0	Frisé
		Cut
		Loop
		Cut Design

the same representation for both methods'. ANOVA results are probabilities, termed *p*-values, where a *p*-value less than a given α rejects the null hypothesis, meaning that there is a significant difference in the response variables of both methods with $100(1 - \alpha)\%$ of confidence.

For valid *p*-values, the methods must be independent of scale factors and carpet types. These dependences are identified also by ANOVA evaluating the null hypothesis *'there are no dependences between combinations of methods in Table 1'*, with *p*-values, where a *p*-value less than a given α rejects the null hypothesis, meaning that there are dependences between the associated elements. In case of dependences, the group is subdivided performing analysis in each subgroup that does not reveal dependences among methods and scale factors and/or carpet types. This assures the validity of the *p*-values.

4   Results

The ANOVA results show that using the EdgeWav method to construct depth images improves significantly the discriminance between consecutive wear labels as well as the linear rank between κ values and wear labels. The results also show that the method works well for seven of the eight carpet types evaluated.

To obtain these results, we tested for significant differences in the response variables computed from images constructed with both the RefLight and the EdgeWav method. Therefore, we first checked for dependencies between the type of construction method and the type of carpets. During this analysis, the scale factors were not evaluated since there was no evidence that scale factors are dependent on either type of carpet or type of method. Afterwards, we searched in each type of carpet for the best scale factor using only images constructed with the EdgeWav method. In the following, we will describe the ANOVA results in detail.

- **Evaluation of Linear Rank Correlation (LRC).** The ANOVA test shows dependences between the type of methods and the type of carpets (*p*-value < 0.01). However, there is no evidence of dependences between scale factors and the other two elements (*p*-value $= 0.894$ for dependences with methods and *p*-value $= 0.252$ for dependences with type of carpets). There is also no evidence at this point of significant differences between scale factors (*p*-value $= 0.617$). From this, we separated the type of carpets in the following three groups:
  1. Carpets with high significant differences in LRC. This group is composed of carpets in which the EdgeWav method improves over 0.1 the linear rank correlation. Carpet type shaggy1 and cut/loop are in this group. There is no evidence in this group of dependences between carpet types and methods (*p*-value $= 0.24 > 0.5$) and the LRC values are identified to be significantly different (*p*-value > 0.01).
  2. Carpets with low significant differences in LRC. This group is composed of carpets in which the EdgeWav method improves less than 0.1 the

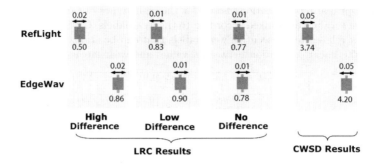

Fig. 4. Comparison of linear rank correlations between the RefLight and the EdgeWav methods

linear rank correlation. There is no evidence in this group of dependences between carpet types and methods (p-value $= 0.067 > 0.5$) and the LRC values are identified to be significantly different (p-value > 0.01). This group contains carpet types shaggy2, high/low loop and frisé.

3. Carpets with no significant differences. This group is composed of carpets in which the EdgeWav method does not improve the linear rank correlation. There is no evidence in this group of dependences between carpet types and methods (p-value $= 0.89 > 0.5$). There is neither evidence in this group of significant differences in LRC values (p-value $= 0.89 > 0.5$). This group is composed of carpet types loop and cut design

– **Evaluation of the number of Consecutive Wear labels that can be Statistically Discriminated (CWSD).** The ANOVA results shows no evidence of dependences between carpet types and methods (p-value $= 0.091 > 0.5$). CWSD values are identified to be significantly different (p-value > 0.01) for all the eight types of carpets.

Figure 4 summarize the ANOVA results. Mean values, at the bottom of the boxes, and standard deviations, represented with $\leftrightarrow$ at the top of the boxes, are shown.

– **Selecting for each type of carpet the optimal scale factor.** As a final step we choose the scale factor with the best combination of response variables. Thus, the wear labels of the eight types of carpets are optimally represented with the combination presented in Table 2. The table lists the quantified characteristics, including linear correlations values for comparison purposes with other approaches. Results obtained in [11] are also displayed to state the advantages of the EdgeWav method over the RefLight method as well as to compare the wear label description from depth images constructed using the EdgeWav method to the wear label description obtained using intensity images. The values corresponding to the EdgeWav method proposed in this approach are highlighted in italics. Additionally, for cases where EdgeWav performs better than intensity images, the values have been highlighted in bold.

Table 2. Optimal representation chosen for the eight types of carpets. LRC specifies how well the κ values are ranked according to the wear labels, CWSD determinates the number of κ related to consecutive wear labels that can be statistically discriminated and LC is the linear correlation between κ values and wear labels.

Carpet Type	Image Type	Scale Factor	LRC	CWSD	LC
	EdgeWav	*0.7*	*0.97*	*5.00*	*0.93*
Shaggy1	RefLight	0.7	0.93	4.00	0.92
	Intensity	0.7	0.93	4.60	0.75
	EdgeWav	*0.6*	*0.96*	*5.00*	*0.96*
Cut/loop	RefLight	0.7	0.53	4.00	0.48
	Intensity	0.9	0.49	5.20	0.49
	EdgeWav	*0.9*	*0.87*	*4.40*	*0.89*
Shaggy2	RefLight	0.9	0.77	4.00	0.80
	Intensity	1.0	0.92	5.60	0.87
	EdgeWav	*0.6*	*0.95*	*4.20*	*0.96*
High/Low loop	RefLight	0.6	0.88	4.00	0.93
	Intensity	0.9	0.99	6.40	0.97
	EdgeWav	*0.9*	*0.99*	*6.2*	*0.99*
Frisé	RefLight	0.9	0.97	5.40	0.97
	Intensity	1.0	0.89	5.20	0.82
	EdgeWav	*0.8*	*0.99*	*5.00*	*0.91*
Cut	RefLight	0.9	0.95	3.60	0.93
	Intensity	1.0	0.99	6.00	0.96
	EdgeWav	*1.0*	*1.00*	*6.60*	*0.91*
Loop	RefLight	0.8	1.00	6.60	0.94
	Intensity	0.9	0.98	6.20	0.97
	EdgeWav	*0.9*	*0.70*	*4.00*	*0.68*
Cut Design	RefLight	1.0	0.65	3.80	0.73
	Intensity	0.9	0.87	4.20	0.81

5   Discussions and Conclusions

In this paper a comparison between two methods for reconstructing the surface of carpets from depth images has been presented. The novel use of a wavelet edge detection algorithm has been compared to a previously used algorithm that only looked at the highest position of the brightest reflection in the images. The images were taken from samples of 8 types of carpets provided from the EN1471 standard. The texture features were extracted comparing the distribution of LBP patterns between images of original and change in appearance of carpets. Then two characteristics were used to evaluate the algorithms against each other, these characteristics are first how well the relation of the κ values (obtained from the Symmetric Kullback-Leibler difference) and the wear labels is linear ranked and second how well consecutive wear labels can be statistically discriminated using their κ values. The results of this evaluation show that the wavelet edge detector significantly improves the linear ranking compared to the original algorithm for six of the eight carpet types. For two carpet the method tend to perform better but without statistical evidence of significant improvement. The statistical discriminance between consecutive wear labels improves for all types of carpets. As a last step, the optimum (giving best response variables) scale factor of the images was researched and both characteristics and linear correlation coefficient were given. These measures permit comparison of results from images obtained with our method to results using depth images obtained with the original method as well as intensity intensity images, both evaluated in [11]. Wear labels in four carpet types are best represented with depth images and the other four with intensity images. This confirms that the texture features from both types of images are complementary for representing the wear label. Particularly, wear labels in carpet type cut/lop could be now represented, which was not possible in the previous approach. We have shown that using the wavelet edge detector, texture features with a more monotonical description with wear labels can be obtained for depth images. These types of features combined with features from intensity images can be used for developing an automated carpet assessment system dealing with multiples carpets.

References

1. Wang, J., Wood, E.J.: A new method for measuring carpet texture change. Textile Research Journal 65, 196–202 (1994)
2. Sobus, J., Pourdeyhimi, B., Gerde, J., Ulcay, Y.: Assessing changes in texture periodicity due to appearance loss in carpets: Gray level co-occurrence analysis. Textile Research Journal 61, 557–567 (1991)
3. Wang, J., Campbell, R.A., Harwood, R.J.: Automated inspection of carpets. In: Proc. SPIE, Optics in Agriculture, Forestry, and Biological Processing, vol. 2345, pp. 180–191. SPIE, San Jose (1995)
4. Sette, S., Boullart, L., Kiekens, P.: Self-organizing neural nets: A new approach to quality in textiles. Textile Research Journal 65, 196–202 (1995)
5. Waegeman, W., Cottyn, J., Wyns, B., Boullart, L., De Baets, B., Van Langenhove, L., Detand, J.: Classifying carpets based on laser scanner data. Engineering Applications of Artificial Intelligence 21(6), 907–918 (2008)
6. Copot, C., Syafiie, S., Orjuela, S.A., De Keyser, R., Van Langenhove, L., Lazar, C.: Carpet wear classification based on support vector machine pattern recognition approach. In: Proceedings of the 5th IEEE Int. Conference on Intelligent Computer Communication and Processing, pp. 161–164 (2009)
7. Orjuela, S.A., Vansteenkiste, E., Rooms, F., De Meulemeester, S., De Keyser, R., Philips, W.: Evaluation of the wear label description in carpets by using local binary pattern techniques. Textile Research Journal (2010) (published online)
8. The Carpet and Rug Institute: Assessment of carpet surface appearance change using the cri reference scales. Technical Bulletin (2003)
9. European Committee for standardization. Constructional details of types of textile floor covering available as reference fatigued specimens (1996)
10. Orjuela, S.A., Vansteenkiste, E., Rooms, F., De Meulemeester, S., De Keyser, R., Philips, W.: Feature extraction of the wear label of carpets by using a novel 3d scanner. In: Proc. of the Optics, Photonics and Digital Technologies for Multimedia Applications Conference (2010)
11. Orjuela, S.A., Vansteenkiste, E., Rooms, F., De Meulemeester, S., De Keyser, R., Philips, W.: A comparison between intensity and depth images for extracting features related to wear labels in carpets. In: Proc. of SPIE Applications of Digital Image Processing XXXIII, vol. 7798 (2010)
12. Luo, J., Savakis, A.: Texture-based segmentation of natural images using multiresolution autoregressive models. In: IEEE Western New York Image Processing Workshop (September 1998)

13. Daoudi, K., Frakt, A.B., Willsky, A.S.: An efficient method for texture defect detection: sub-band domain co-occurrence matrices. Image and Vision Computing 18(6-7), 543–553 (2000)
14. Han, Y., Shi, P.: An adaptive level-selecting wavelet transform for texture defect detection. Image and Vision Computing 25(8), 1239–1248 (2007)
15. Wang, Z.-Z., Yong, J.-H.: Texture analysis and classification with linear regression model based on wavelet transform. IEEE Trans. Image Processing 17(8), 1421–1430 (2008)
16. He, Z., You, X., Yuan, Y.: Texture image retrieval based on non-tensor product wavelet filter banks. Signal Processing 89(8), 1501–1510 (2009)
17. Mallat, S., Hwang, W.L.: Singularity detection and processing with wavelets. IEEE Trans. Information Theory 38(2), 617–643 (1992)
18. Elder, J.H., Zucker, S.W.: Local scale control for edge detection and blur estimation. IEEE Trans. Pattern Analysis and Machine Intelligence 20(7), 699–716 (1998)
19. Li, J.: A wavelet approach to edge detection. Master's thesis, Sam Houston State University (August 2003)
20. Ducottet, C., Fournel, T., Barat, B.: Scale-adaptive detection and local characterization of edges based on wavelet transform. Signal Processing 84(11), 2115–2137 (2004)
21. Bao, P., Zhang, L., Wu, X.: Canny edge detection enhancement by scale multiplication. IEEE Trans. on Pattern Analysis and Machine Intelligence 27(9), 1485–1490 (2005)
22. Xue, L., Pan, J.: Edge detection combining wavelet transform and canny operator based on fusion rules. In: Proc. of Wavelet Analysis and Pattern Recognition (2009)
23. Laligant, O., Truchetet, F., Miteran, J., Gorria, P.: Merging system for multiscale edge detection. Optical Engineering 44(3), 035602-1–035602-11 (2005)
24. Petrou, M., Sevilla, P.G.: Image Processing Dealing with Texture. Wiley, Chichester (January 2006)
25. Ojala, T., Pietikäinen, M., Mäenpää, T.: Multiresolution gray scale and rotation invariant texture classification with local binary patterns. IEEE Trans. on Pattern Analysis and Machine Intelligence 24(7), 971–987 (2002)
26. Kutner, M., Nachtsheim, C.J., Neter, J., Li, W.: Applied Linear Statistical Models, 5th edn. McGraw-Hill, New York (2004)

Augmented Reality with Human Body Interaction Based on Monocular 3D Pose Estimation

Huei-Yung Lin and Ting-Wen Chen

Department of Electrical Engineering
National Chung Cheng University
168 University Rd., Min-Hsiung, Chiayi 621, Taiwan

Abstract. We present an augmented reality interface with markerless human body interaction. It consists of 3D motion capture of the human body and the processing of 3D human poses for augmented reality applications. A monocular camera is used to acquire the images of the user's motion for 3D pose estimation. In the proposed technique, a graphical 3D human model is first constructed. Its projection on a virtual image plane is then used to match the silhouettes obtained from the image sequence. By iteratively adjusting the 3D pose of the graphical 3D model with the physical and anatomic constraints of the human motion, the human pose and the associated 3D motion parameters can be uniquely identified. The obtained 3D pose information is then transferred to the reality processing subsystem and used to achieve the marker-free interaction in the augmented environment. Experimental results are presented using a head mounted display.

1   Introduction

One important issue of augmented reality (AR) is to design an interface for seamless interaction between the virtual objects and the real world. Since the first AR interface was built in the 1960's, researchers have proposed various types of techniques to increase the interactivity in the augmented space [1]. In its early development, 3D AR interfaces focus on providing spatially seamless interaction with special-purpose input devices. Recent advances on tangible AR interfaces, on the other hand, emphasize the use of physical objects as tools for projecting the virtual objects onto the surfaces [2]. Nevertheless, both approaches are not capable of "tool-free" interaction only with the bare hands. In the past few years, some techniques with gesture or finger tracking were proposed for augmented desk applications. Although there is no need for specific tools, the interaction is still restricted to 2-dimensional or requires markers for vision-based tracking [3,4]. Marker-free interaction for AR interfaces is only adopted for the pose estimation between the objects and the camera [5,6].

The objective of this work is to develop an AR interface with markerless human body interaction. It consists of 3D motion capture of the human body

J. Blanc-Talon et al. (Eds.): ACIVS 2010, Part I, LNCS 6474, pp. 321–331, 2010.
© Springer-Verlag Berlin Heidelberg 2010

and the processing of 3D human poses for augmented reality applications. Although there exist some approaches for human computer interaction (HCI) using commercially available motion capture system, the underlying technologies are usually expensive, obtrusive, and require the users to wear special markers for joint or body parts identification [7,8]. The proposed AR system uses only a video camera and a head mounted display (HMD) as the input and output devices, respectively. Since the application domain is less restrictive with only a single camera, especially for low-cost AR systems, the human pose estimation from monocular image capture has become an emerging issue to be properly addressed.

The major difficulties of monocular human pose estimation include the high dimensionality of the pose configuration space, lacking of depth information, self-occlusion, and perspective effect of the camera model [9]. These problems are caused by the inherent ambiguity in 3D to 2D mapping, and have to be resolved with additional constraints [10]. In the previous work, Loy et al. adopted a keyframe based approach to estimate the 3D pose of human motion in sports sequences [11]. The 3D reconstruction is derived using a video footage, which is not capable of on-site processing. Chen et al. presented a method to reconstruct 3D human motion parameters using image silhouettes [12]. A weighted-XOR cost metric was used for object alignment, shape fitting and motion tracking.

In this work, we present a model and appearance based method for markerless 3D pose estimation from a single camera view. It is the first step toward the monocular human motion capture for a complete tool-free AR interface. The input to our system includes an initialization image for the adjustment of the human body model and an on-site captured image for 3D pose estimation. First, an articulated 3D human model is created and the dimension of each body part is adjusted using the initialization image silhouette. To estimate the pose of a subsequent image, the modified 3D model is adjusted such that its projection is aligned with the image silhouette. We have proposed a cost function to facilitate the shape fitting and fast movement of the body part. Furthermore, the high dimensionality of search space for alignment and the ambiguities in 3D pose reconstruction are reduced by anatomic and physical constraints of human motion, as well as the appearance information from the intensity image. The resulting pose parameters and an articulated graphical 3D model are then used for full body interaction in the augmented environment. Experimental results have demonstrated the feasibility of the proposed camera/HMD AR interface.

2   3D Pose Estimation Technique

The proposed 3D pose estimation algorithm is based on the comparison of the perspectively projected graphical 3D human model and the captured image. An articulated graphical human model is created and adjusted iteratively to align with the input image based on the silhouette and color information of the object region.

2.1   Modeling a Human Body

Due to the lack of 3D information from the input images, a graphical 3D model of the human body has to be generated for 3D pose estimation. It should be capable of performing a large variety of human motion and easy to identify from the silhouettes. Most articulated 3D human model is generated with a number of rigid body parts and joints. The number of degrees of freedom is thus a key factor to the construction of the graphical 3D human model.

In this work, the 3D human model is created using OpenGL library. It consists of 10 body parts, 9 joints and 22 degrees of freedom. The body parts are represented by spheres, ellipsoids and cylinders. Different colors are assigned to different body parts to facilitate the pose recognition process. Since the graphical 3D model is projected to a virtual image plane for template matching and alignment with the real scene image, the object regions in both images should have a similar size and orientation. Thus, a canonical 3D human model is created first, and an on-site model initialization process is carried out for the user in the scene.

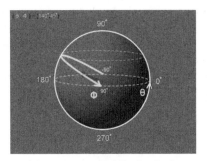
(a) 2 rotation DOF of a limb.

(b) Changes due to foreshortening.

Fig. 1. Silhouette matching between images

2.2   Silhouette Based Pose Estimation

Given the foreground silhouette image of a human body, the associated pose is estimated by minimizing the difference between the silhouette in the real scene image and the projection of the 3D model on the virtual image. To find the best pose of the graphical model which matches the human pose, a suitable metric and cost functions should be provided. In the early work, Chen et al. presented a Euclidean distance transform approach to calculate the pixel-wise distances between the real and virtual image silhouettes [12]. A cost function defined by the summation of pixel-wise distances was then used to adjust the 3D model. Since both of the entire images were used for comparison, the computational cost was relatively high and the results tended to converge to a local minimum.

Different from their whole silhouette matching approach, we propose a multi-part alignment technique. The body parts in the real and 3D model projected silhouette images are compared and adjusted one by one using a core-weighted XOR operation. The pixel difference is processed locally for each body part so that better alignment results with less computation can be achieved. Furthermore, it is well suited for articulated 3D models with a number of joints and rigid body parts.

To perform the multi-part pose estimation, the most significant body part, i.e. the trunk, is identified first. It is the central part of the foreground silhouette, connecting the rest of the body parts. Once the trunk is extracted, the regions of the head, upper and lower limbs can be easily acquired. To identify the trunk, an erosion operation is first carried out recursively to remove the limbs in the foreground silhouette. The projected 3D model is then overlaid on the center of the silhouette, followed by a 3 DOF rotation to minimize the difference between the trunk of the foreground silhouette and the 2D projection of the 3D model.

After the 3D pose of the trunk is derived, the upper and lower limbs are processed in the order of arms, wrists, thighs and legs. The identification of the limbs is carried out by comparing the foreground-background ratio of the graphical model. For these body parts, we define 2 DOF for rotation (without the rotation along their main axes). As shown in Figure 1(a), a limb is capable of rotating 360° on the image plane (represented by the angle θ) and 180° off the image plane (represented by the angle ϕ). When searching the pose of a limb, the angle θ is identified first by rotating the corresponding body part in the 3D model. Several initial orientations separated by 45° are used to avoid the full range search and speedup the alignment process. The angle ϕ is then calculated by detecting the size change of the projected body part due to the foreshortening as shown in Figure 1(b).

2.3   Appearance Constraints

It is well known that the foreground silhouette does not provide the self-occlusion information of the object. To make the pose estimation algorithm more robust, one commonly used approach is to take the color and edge information of the object into account [13]. By extracting the individual parts of the object, the associated poses can then be identified.

In this work, the physical and kinematic constraints are enforced on the motion of an initial 3D human model [14]. Thus, self-occlusions of the body parts need not be properly extracted prior to the pose estimation process. One can identify the end of each limb, combine with the above constraints to estimate the 3D human pose up to a projective ambiguity. In this case, each body part is considered as a link of the human skeleton model, and the positions of the hands and feet will be identified within the foreground silhouette.

3   Augmented Reality System Architecture

The proposed markerless augmented reality interface consists of two subsystems: one is for 3D motion capture of the human body as described in Section 2, and the

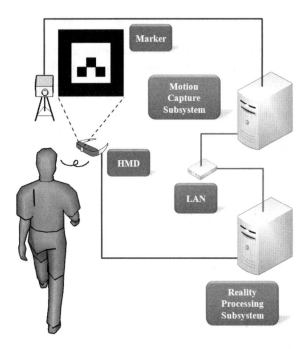

Fig. 2. The augmented reality system architecture

other is for the processing of augmented reality applications. Figure 2 illustrates the overall system architecture. The 3D pose estimation and the augmented image synthesis are accomplished by two separate computers communicated via a local area network. The input for the markerless human body interaction is the image sequence captured by a video camera, and the output for the augmented reality system is through the head mounted display.

The data transmission between the motion capture and the reality processing subsystems is developed on the TCP/IP protocol using WinSock interface. It includes the information requests, the transmission of the 3D pose parameters and the captured image sequence. In general situations, the reality processing subsystem requests the immediate 3D pose information from the motion capture subsystem. Thus, the former and the latter computer systems are defined as the client and the server, respectively. For the large amount of data transmission, especially the images, the data stream is partitioned and transmitted with smaller and fixed packet sizes. To prevent the data lost during transmission, several registers are adopted on both the client and server computers. The transmission quality is improved by holding the data packets temporally in the registers for sending and receiving.

As described previously, the motion capture and reality processing subsystems are in charge of heavy image processing tasks with the high frame rate constraint. To reduce the data streaming overhead, multi-threading using POSIX thread libraries is adopted on both computers. A single thread is used exclusively for the data transmission task.

Similar to most augmented reality systems, marker identification and tracking are used for manipulating the virtual objects in this work. We adopt the AR-ToolKit for marker tracking and HMD calibration in our implementation [15]. However, the marker in the application scenario is mainly used for generating a virtual interface at the program initialization stage. The interaction between the human and the virtual objects can be completely marker-free. The motion capture information is used to register the 3D human pose to the virtual environment. Through the HMD, the real scene and virtual objects are simultaneously accessible for manipulation.

4 Implementation and Results

This section describes the hardware and environment setup for our application scenario. Some implementation details of the motion capture subsystem and the related issues on augmented reality are also addressed.

4.1 Hardware and Environment

Figure 3 shows the experimental environment. The client (motion capture) and server (reality processing) systems are illustrated in the left and right images, respectively. The motion capture subsystem consists of a PC with Intel Core 2 Quad processor, a Logitech QuickCam Sphere AF camera with image resolution of 1600×1200, and a green background for facilitating the foreground human segmentation. The camera is connected to the PC via USB 2.0 interface with the frame rate of 30 fps.

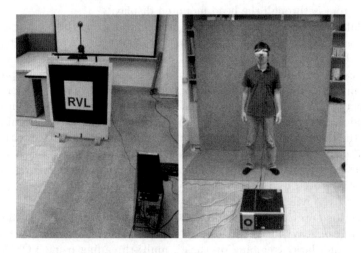

Fig. 3. The experimental environment

Fig. 4. On-site model initialization

The reality processing subsystem consists of a PC with Intel Pentium D processor, a Cyberman HMD (GVD-310A) attached with a Logitech QuickCam Pro 5000 camera, and a marker for creating the program initialization interface. The input and output image resolutions of the camera and HMD are 640 × 480 and 800 × 255, respectively. The distance between the user and the camera for motion capture is about 3.8 meters, and the dimension of the marker is 70 × 70 cm^2. A local area network is used to connect the motion capture and reality processing subsystems.

4.2 Motion Capture Interface

The first step of model based pose estimation is to extract the image silhouette of the foreground region. For a given background image sequence, the intensity distributions of each image pixel are calculated for the red, blue, green, and hue channels. Two times of the standard deviations for each pixel are used to model the channel intensity ranges for segmentation. Since the RGB model is more sensitive to the illumination change and the HSV model is better for color discrimination, we use the hybrid approach to derive the robust background model for foreground segmentation.

To make the resulting silhouette image more suitable for model based template matching, morphological operations and median filtering are carried out to remove the holes inside the foreground region. Although the foreground region is not perfectly extracted in most cases, the noise presented in the image is not significant enough to affect the subsequent pose estimation stage. This result also suggests that the sophisticated segmentation algorithm is not always required for our pose estimation technique.

As shown in the previous section, the location of a body part within the foreground silhouette is identified by the color information. The most significant feature in the foreground region is the skin color of the hands. To extract the associated color model, a simple and robust method is to detect the face color in the initialization stage. The head in the foreground silhouette is first identified using model-based template matching. Histogram analysis on the head region is carried out to separate the skin and hair colors. The threshold for the face color segmentation is then used to extract the hand regions in the foreground.

(a) The GUI for system initialization.

(b) The augmented environment.

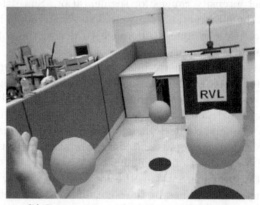

(c) Interaction with the virtual objects.

Fig. 5. The results of augmented reality with markerless human body interaction

4.3   Reality Processing Interface

In the reality processing subsystem, the real world scene is captured by the camera attached on the HMD. The images are transferred to the client PC for virtual objects overlay, and then transferred back to the HMD for display. At the system initialization stage, a user friendly interface is displayed at the marker position. As shown in Figure 5(a), the GUI provides the program control by real-time full body interaction for selecting the available options.

For more accurate comparison between the foreground silhouette and the projection of the 3D model, it is clear that there should exist a similarity transformation between the graphical 3D model and the real human body. That is, the dimension of each body part should be identical up to a unique scale factor for both the graphical model and real object. Since only one canonical 3D model is created for all situations, it has to be modified for different users according to their shapes. We refer to this step as an "on-site model initialization".

To perform the on-site model initialization, an image of the user with a pre-defined pose is captured. After extracting the foreground object region, the run-length encoding is used to scan the silhouette image and derive the features of the body parts. Since the initial human pose is pre-defined, the dimension and orientation of each body part in the 3D model can be easily identified by the image features such as head, shoulder, elbow, etc. Figure 4 shows the 3D models prior to and after the on-site model initialization step.

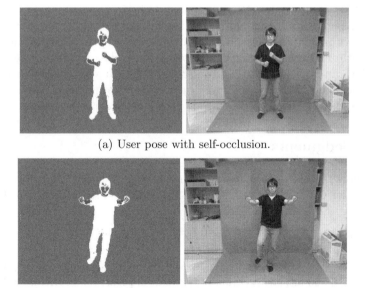

(a) User pose with self-occlusion.

(b) User pose with foreshortening.

Fig. 6. 3D pose estimation results. The left figures show the foreground silhouettes and skin color detection. The original images with estimated 3D graphical model overlay are shown in the right figures.

4.4 Results

In our application scenario, the pose estimation results and the augmented reality with full body interaction can be illustrated separately. Since the 3D motion parameters are essential to the proposed augmented reality system, we have tested several image sequences with various types of human postures. Two results of non-trivial tasks with the arms occluding the body silhouette and severe foreshortening of the arms are shown in Figures 6(a) and 6(b), respectively. In both cases, the 3D poses are correctly identified with the assistance of skin color.

For the augmented reality application, we initiate several balls at the marker position and make them bounce in the environment with different velocities and directions as shown in Figure 5(b). The balls will be bounced back if they are hit by the user according to the vision-based 3D pose estimation results. Otherwise, the balls will disappear when they pass beyond the user location. Figure 5(c) shows an image capture of markerless interaction with the virtual objects seen through the HMD.

5   Conclusions and Future Work

In this work, we present a monocular vision based human pose estimation technique and its application to augmented reality. An articulated graphical human model is created for 3D pose estimation of each body part. The foreground silhouette and color information are used to evaluate the 3D parameters of the graphical 3D model under the anatomic and physical constraints of the human motion. Experimental results of markerless human body interaction in the augmented environment are presented. In future work, we plan to extend the current system with multiple image capture devices. Since the omnidirectional 3D pose estimation can be achieved using the surrounding cameras in the environment, total immersion with free mobility of the user becomes possible. The augmented reality system will thus be able to work in a large scale environment.

Acknowledgments

The support of this work in part by the National Science Council of Taiwan, R.O.C. under Grant NSC-96-2221-E-194-016-MY2 is gratefully acknowledged.

References

1. Zhou, F., Duh, H.B.L., Billinghurst, M.: Trends in augmented reality tracking, interaction and display: A review of ten years of ismar. In: ISMAR 2008: Proceedings of the 7th IEEE/ACM International Symposium on Mixed and Augmented Reality, pp. 193–202. IEEE Computer Society, Washington (2008)
2. Azuma, R., Baillot, Y., Behringer, R., Feiner, S., Julier, S., MacIntyre, B.: Recent advances in augmented reality. Computer Graphics and Applications 21, 34–47 (2001)

3. Starner, T., Leibe, B., Minnen, D., Westyn, T., Hurst, A., Weeks, J.: The percep-
   tive workbench: Computer-vision-based gesture tracking, object tracking, and 3d
   reconstruction for augmented desks. Machine Vision and Applications 14, 59–71
   (2003)
4. Finger tracking for interaction in augmented environments. In: ISAR 2001: Proceedings of the IEEE and ACM International Symposium on Augmented Reality
   (ISAR 2001), Washington, DC, USA, p. 55. IEEE Computer Society, Los Alamitos
   (2001)
5. Comport, A.I., Marchand, E., Pressigout, M., Chaumette, F.: Real-time markerless tracking for augmented reality: The virtual visual servoing framework. IEEE
   Transactions on Visualization and Computer Graphics 12, 615–628 (2006)
6. Lee, T., Höllerer, T.: Multithreaded hybrid feature tracking for markerless augmented reality. IEEE Transactions on Visualization and Computer Graphics 15,
   355–368 (2009)
7. Chua, P.T., Crivella, R., Daly, B., Hu, N., Schaaf, R., Ventura, D., Camill, T.,
   Hodgins, J., Pausch, R.: Training for physical tasks in virtual environments: Tai
   chi. In: VR 2003: Proceedings of the IEEE Virtual Reality 2003, Washington, DC,
   USA, p. 87. IEEE Computer Society, Los Alamitos (2003)
8. Chan, J., Leung, H., Tang, K.T., Komura, T.: Immersive performance training
   tools using motion capture technology. In: ImmersCom 2007: Proceedings of the
   First International Conference on Immersive Telecommunications, pp. 1–6 (2007)
9. Howe, N.R.: Silhouette lookup for monocular 3d pose tracking. Image Vision Comput. 25, 331–341 (2007)
10. Bregler, C., Malik, J., Pullen, K.: Twist based acquisition and tracking of animal
    and human kinematics. Int. J. Comput. Vision 56, 179–194 (2004)
11. Loy, G., Eriksson, M., Sullivan, J., Carlsson, S.: Monocular 3d reconstruction of
    human motion in long action sequences. In: Pajdla, T., Matas, J(G.) (eds.) ECCV
    2004. LNCS, vol. 3024, pp. 442–455. Springer, Heidelberg (2004)
12. Chen, Y., Lee, J., Parent, R., Machiraju, R.: Markerless monocular motion cap-
    ture using image features and physical constraints. Computer Graphics Interna-
    tional 2005, 36–43 (2005)
13. Poppe, R.: Vision-based human motion analysis: An overview. Comput. Vis. Image
    Underst. 108, 4–18 (2007)
14. Ning, H., Tan, T., Wang, L., Hu, W.: Kinematics-based tracking of human walking
    in monocular video sequences. Image Vision Comput. 22, 429–441 (2004)
15. Kato, H., Billinghurst, M.: Marker tracking and hmd calibration for a video-based
    augmented reality conferencing system. In: Proceedings of 2nd IEEE and ACM
    International Workshop on Augmented Reality (IWAR 1999), pp. 85–94 (1999)

Fusing Large Volumes of Range and Image Data for Accurate Description of Realistic 3D Scenes

Yuk Hin Chan[1], Patrice Delmas[1], Georgy Gimel'farb[1], and Robert Valkenburg[2]

[1] The University of Auckland, Auckland, New Zealand
ycha171@aucklanduni.ac.nz,{p.delmas,g.gimelfarb}@auckland.ac.nz
[2] Industrial Research Ltd., Auckland, New Zealand
r.valkenburg@irl.cri.nz

Abstract. Hand-held time-of-flight laser scene scanners provide very large volumes of 3D range (coordinate) and optical (colour) measurements for modelling visible surfaces of real 3D scenes. To obtain an accurate model, the measurement errors resulting e.g. in gaps, uncertain edges and small details have to be detected and corrected. This paper discusses possibilities of using multiple calibrated scene images collected simultaneously with the range data for getting a more complete and accurate scene model. Experiments show that the proposed approach eliminates a number of range errors while still may fail on intricate disjoint surfaces that can be met in practice.

Keywords: time-of-flight range scanner, data fusion, scene description.

1 Introduction

3D scene imaging and modelling helps in solving various practical problems of reverse engineering, mobile robotics, surveying and mapping, computer-assisted civil and military training, video gaming, archeological site and artefacts mapping, police examination of accident and crime scenes to cite just a few applications [1,2,3,4,5,6]. A digital 3D scene model has to realistically describe both geometry and visual appearance, i.e. texture of optical (visible) surfaces, of the scene.

Accurate modelling of large real indoor and outdoor scenes is a challenging task. Each application poses specific requirements on spatial resolution and accuracy of 3D measurements as well as constraints on data collection and processing time. Today's active and passive imaging and range measurement devices have different and often complementary pros and cons. Time-of-flight (TOF) laser range scanners are popular for static or dynamic depth measurements on short (up to 1 m) to medium (1 - 10 m) distances from a surface. However, the acquisition might suffer from poor refection, high noise on mirroring or highly uneven surfaces, and data losses at object edges. Field-of-view of an individual scan in some scanners, especially, mobile hand-held ones is relatively narrow, so that large surfaces have to be scanned by parts. Passive binocular or multi-view stereo vision systems typically have larger fields-of-view but fail on featureless

J. Blanc-Talon et al. (Eds.): ACIVS 2010, Part I, LNCS 6474, pp. 332–343, 2010.

(uniform) areas and areas with repetitive visual patterns. Their spatial resolution is decreasing with the distance from the imaging devices (cameras). Both 3D acquisition techniques have difficulties in the presence of multiple disjoint surfaces and mutual occlusions.

Fusing complementary range and image data to build a more complete and accurate 3D scene model has been widely explored for autonomous navigation of robotic vehicles [7,8,9], separation of road obstacles and evaluation of their spatial positions [10,11,12], and general 3D scene modelling [11,13,14]. These approaches exploit simple local stereo matching techniques and apply sequential heuristic rules to eliminate mutually contradicting range and stereo measurements. In particular, the range data in [14,15] constrain correlation based search for stereo correspondences in a passive binocular stereo system. Then both the data sets are combined into a unique depth map where points with inconsistent range and stereo measurements are labelled as outliers.

A more advanced strategy in [16] uses a joint Markov random field model to fuse range and stereo data in a specific stationary sensor system containing a TOF range scanner (200K points per field-of-view) and two cameras with the same field-of-view for capturing stereo pairs of images. The range measurements are combined with depth maps produced by belief propagation based binocular stereo matching. 3D ground truth for a test scene to verify complex photometric and geometric calibration of the system was obtained with a separate structured light device. Comparing to the ground truth, the overall depth error was reduced from 1.8% down to 0.6%. But the basic assumption in [16] that every field-of-view point is characterised with a single pair of image signals and a single range measurement rarely holds in practice for a vast majority of real outdoor and indoor scenes. The required modelling accuracy and physical limitations of the available range and stereo sensors dictate sequential scanning of a middle- or large-scale 3D scene from different positions and in multiple directions. Thus the amounts of range, stereo, and image data available for each 3D point may vary considerably. Moreover, model-based fusion permits not only to use stereo data to fill in gaps and detect other range data inaccuracies but also guide 3D stereo reconstruction with reliable range data in order to improve the accuracy and completeness of the scene model.

This paper explores capabilities of the range and image data fusion for a multi-purpose hand-held 3D laser TOF scene scanner outlined in [17]. A set of pre-placed beacons enables real-time scanner calibration and registration to a world coordinate system. The operator sweeps the scanner over a static 3D scene covering more densely surfaces of interest and glossing over other parts of the scene. The scanner produces a large "cloud" of 3D points indicating surfaces of interest. During the scan sweeps, a colour camera mounted on the scanner produces a video stream that captures the scene texture. Both the scanner and camera are continuously calibrated in order to link every video frame and range data to the world coordinates. We focus below on accurate scene modelling by fusing the collected image and range data. Previous works on fusion such as [16] assumed a stationary range scanner and stationary stereo cameras viewing a small-size scene from a single fixed direction only. Such a setup drastically reduces range errors from occlusions and on sharp edges. In contrast, a hand-held mobile scanner views the same scene from multiple directions, and thus edge errors, occlusions of camera views, homogeneously coloured surfaces with poor reflection, and multiple disjoint surfaces play a much larger role.

This paper elaborates further the data fusion process proposed in [18,19]. A more accurate dense scene model is built by filling in gaps and correcting errors of range measurements using 3D stereo reconstruction guided with reliable range data. The reliability is associated with colour consistency of 3D points observed in multiple scene images. Experiments revealed that such a guidance may be misled by reliable surfaces occluded on stereo pairs. Simple ad hoc heuristics reduce the number of such errors and suggest that measurements of scanning directions and scanner positions should be used, in addition to the currently acquired range and image data, to eliminate the incorrect guidance.

2   Data Characteristics

TOF range scanners compute surface hits with respect to the scanner position. For a mobile scanner, the measurements are converted to a world coordinate system and form a cloud of 3D points located potentially on a goal optical surface. Depending on the scanner, auxiliary information such as the returning laser signal strength and the scanning direction for each individual 3D point may also be recorded. Additionally, one or more calibrated imaging cameras capture images of the scene during the scan. Due to camera calibration, each image can be associated with the range data and the whole scene.

The camera unit of our hand-held mobile scanner is mounted rigidly with respect to the laser unit, views approximately in the same direction as the laser scan-line, and captures the images at a fixed frame rate during the scan. Although the scanner used capture the images simultaneously with the range data, the calibrated scene images can be obtained separately as long as the scene is not changing.

Generally, range measuring with a TOF laser unit may produce uncertain (unreliable) 3D point coordinates. The uncertainty of 3D point coordinates is typically small for a stationary scanner and can be neglected. But it is quite sizable for a mobile scanner in adverse conditions such as poor surface reflection. Because such uncertainties depend of external factors they are not shown in the scanner specifications to a full extent and mostly have to be estimated experimentally. The mobile scanner has multiple sources of errors including, for example, inaccuracies of computing its position and orientation at any instant from inertial measurements or a system of calibration beacons. These inaccuracies affect the calculated position of every surface hit.

Our scene scanner uses six positioning video cameras on the laser unit to track fixed beacons while traversing the scene. Under normal operating conditions, it is experimentally found that the error in the pose of the scanner is sufficiently small to be neglected. The laser scanning unit utilises a rotating mirror to direct the

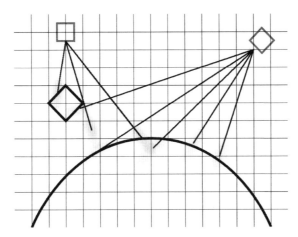

Fig. 1. Surface hits from two scanning positions (red boxes) to exemplify large distance (central yellow hit) and edge errors (central blue hit) and uncertainty volumes associated with each hit (yellow and blue ellipses) overlaid with a grid

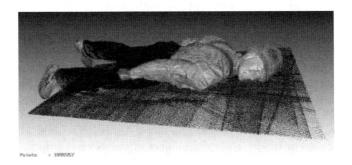

Fig. 2. Measured by our scene scanner 3D surface points ($\approx 10^6$) of a mannequin

laser beam at different angles in a horizontal line. The angular uncertainty of the mirror position at the moment of measurement causes a small deviation (known as jitter) in the angle of the beam and subsequently in the spatial coordinates of a 3D point that had produced the returned signal. The distance to the latter point is determined by sending and receiving a coded laser signal, their mutual time shift being determined by correlation. In terms of the magnitude, the distance error is much greater than the jitter. Combining all these uncertainties permits us to model locations of a measured 3D point with a point-centred ellipsoidal probability distribution stretched along the scanning direction, the long axis (or distance) uncertainty being one–two orders of magnitude larger than the short axes (jitter) uncertainties.

Mobile scanners collect range measurements from multiple directions. For example, Fig. 1 depicts two scanning positions, multiple hits from each of them (some containing incorrect measurements caused by sharp edges), and probability distributions (uncertainty ellipsoids) of 3D point locations associated with each hit. In real applications, the measured 3D points form a dense and very large "cloud" shown e.g. in Fig. 2.

3   Probabilistic Modelling of Data Fusion

Points from the range scanner are measured in a fixed Cartesian XYZ coordinate system specified by an on-line calibration. The Spatial resolution of a goal scene model depends on application and is limited by spatial resolution of the scanner. Let the whole 3D space be partitioned into a coordinate-wise oriented grid of cubic voxels of a size corresponding to the desired resolution. Each voxel is given by its spatial location (x, y, z) in the scene coordinates. Each voxel that potentially belongs to a surface having been scanned and/or captured on a scene image is characterised with one or more volumes of the range measurement uncertainty associated with this location along with directional vectors of range measurements, and optical properties. Due to multiple views acquired during scanning, each potential surface voxel can be generally described with a bidirectional texture function (BTF) [20] simplified in this case due to the fixed scene illumination to represent (at least approximately) the outgoing colours in different directions depending on the voxel location and outgoing azimuth and zenith angles.

The goal of probabilistic data fusion is to combine the collected range and image data with a prior knowledge about geometric and optical properties of a goal surface such as smoothness, continuity, and admissible BTF changes at neighbouring locations in order to reconstruct more accurate and realistic 3D scene models. Typical real outdoor or indoor scenes acquired by a mobile scanner have sizes from 1 metre to 10 metres and more. Assuming a millimetre or higher resolution of a scene model, the total number of voxels can be up to $10^9 \dots 10^{12}$. Therefore, a conventional probability model of a single optical surface in the XYZ space represented by one range and one stereo Z-measurement for each (X, Y) location to infer an optimal surface from the collected range and image data (like e.g. in [16]) becomes computationally unfeasible. Moreover, it does not account for multiple disjoint surfaces, their mutual occlusions, and multiple positions and directions of data collection by the mobile scanner. At the same time, optical and geometric properties of surfaces of natural 3D objects are local in that each potential surface voxel depends mostly on its neighbourhood specified by the uncertainty volumes rather than from more distant voxels.

As indicated in Section 2, each individual calibrated range measurement produces an elongated and narrow uncertainty volume of probable surface locations along the scanning direction. Multiple intersecting volumes for different scanning directions result in a practically reliable surface location. Assuming that ambiguous cases where the locations should be refined are relatively rare, the mesh model of a scene surface such as in Fig. 2 is built through only the reliable locations using a few heuristics to exclude outliers. Such a straightforward modelling may fail in more intricate practical cases, e.g. when multiple small foreground details with poor surface reflection occlude the background objects.

Depending on the actual measurements, the set of voxels to be considered as a probabilistic search space for the goal surfaces can be partitioned into: (*i*) measured potential candidates along each scanning direction; (*ii*) gaps, or voxels that belong to no measurement uncertainty volume but are adjacent to and form a continuous surface patch with the candidates, and (*iii*) edges, or adjacent voxels such that locations of their uncertainty volumes differ too much along the same scanning directions. The fusion based inference may be constrained to only ambiguous parts of the goal surface by considering each time a limited part of the search space that depends on the uncertainty volumes and directions of the relevant range measurements and on spatial probability distribution of the measured candidates. Because only neighbouring relationships in the surfaces are taken into account, the influence of distant locations on the globally optimum solution for any position within the search space becomes negligibly small quickly with increasing distance. Therefore, reducing the search space by separate probabilistic modelling of an uncertain patch should not significantly impact the optimality of its refinement on the basis of fusing the range and image data available for this patch.

Let V denote a set of voxels forming a search space for the goal surface patch. For simplicity, let us consider a dense "moving-window" 3D search space xyz such that the goal patch is represented by the voxels $v_{xyz} \in V$ supported by the xy-plane P. The position and orientation of this partial (sub)model with respect to the scene coordinate system XYZ is assumed to be known. Each voxel either lies on the goal surface, or is transparent, or is inside a solid object. Each scanning ray r_m; $m = 1, \ldots, M$, associated with this model passes through a voxel sequence $\boldsymbol{\rho}_m$ specified by the scanner position (x_m, y_m, z_m) and angular scanning direction (θ_m, ϕ_m) with respect to the xyz-space. Providing a valid range measurement is returned, each voxel within the ellipsoidal uncertainty volume representing the known probabilistic error model gets a probabilistic (soft) indicator $\gamma_{xyz}(m) \in [0, 1]$ of being on the goal surface: $\sum_{(x,y,z) \in \boldsymbol{\rho}_m} \gamma_{xyz}(m) = 1$, reflecting the conditional voxel uncertainty with respect to this range measurement.

Capturing images of the scene from many directions associates each voxel v_{xyz} with a set C_{xyz} of colour texture measurements. Instead of using a complex BTF, one may assume for simplicity that a non-occluded voxel of an optical surface has the same or at least very similar colouring (i.e. voxel-wise hue H and saturation S in HSV colour space) for different reflection angles. However, the colours in the set C_{xyz} may not relate all to the voxel v_{xyz} under consideration due to possible multiple disjoint surfaces and occlusions. Under the above simplifying assumption, the "template" (H, S)-pair for a candidate voxel is provided by the image captured during the range measurement of this voxel. The nuisance colours due to occlusions can be separated by matching all the pairs in C_{xyz} for other images to the template. Similar clustering of the (H, S)-pairs might help also in adding to the candidate voxels their neighbours in order to fill in gaps between the measured voxels. In the case that gaps in the range data result from limited resolution of the scanner, deviations of the colourings over a gap from the candidates on the gap boundary are expected to be small. Edge voxels viewed under different angles may manifest larger colouring changes but still considerably smaller than the voxels that are not associated with a surface. The latter have notably larger HS-deviations from all scanning directions except in rare cases when all the scene surfaces are of the same colour.

To infer an optimal surface by range and image data fusion, one needs a posterior surface model $(v_{xyz} : (x,y) \in P)$ that combines characteristics $(\gamma_{xyz}(m),$ $C_{xyz})$ of the measured and associated voxels with additional results of image analysis (e.g. stereo matching) and takes account of prior geometric and optical relationships between the neighbouring voxels. Generally, such a probabilistic random field model is too complicated in practice due to different numbers of signals measured for or associated with each voxel and their spatially variant properties. To simplify the case, our consideration is restricted to building dense (gap-less) scene models using only reliable surface voxels obtained by the range measurements and associated surface voxels obtained by passive stereo matching with the symmetric dynamic programming stereo (SDPS) algorithm [21]. The matching is based on a joint Markov random field model of continuous surface profiles, i.e. chains of voxels with the same y-coordinates, and voxels colours on a stereo pair of images. The reliable voxels (with $\gamma_{xyz} \approx 1$) guide the stereo matching within a moving window showing a particular part of the scene [18,19]. These guiding 3D points are selected first by intersecting the individual uncertainty volumes for several different scanning directions (the current scene scanner system returns just such measured voxels) and then are refined checking their colour HS-consistency in multiple images captured during the scanner's movements around the scene. As in [19] the voxels are considered as unreliable to guide the stereo matching if their colours in different images of the scene are inconsistent, or if after guided reconstruction the reconstructed colour consistency decreases.

4   Experiments in Data Fusion and Conclusions

As shown in [18,19], measuring the colour consistency of a potentially visible voxel from the multiple views alone is insufficient to ensure the accurate guidance of stereo matching. Potentially, this kind of detection of range data unreliability is based on two assumptions: (i) the voxels placed due to measurement errors either ahead of or behind the true surface are visible both in a stereo pair and other views of the same scene and (ii) colours of these erroneous voxels differ in the different images. However, this simple consistency criterion fails when multiple scene surfaces occlude each other on different views and contain large homogeneous colour areas. For example, a majority of the voxels in a stereo pair in Fig. 3 are considered as reliable due to their consistent colours in a large number of images. The unreliable points in Fig. 3(c) follow from the above two assumptions. Note the "halo" around the edges of the chair, particularly the legs, from the range data points that are incorrect due to the aforementioned edge effects and dark surfaces. The guided stereo reconstruction improves the accuracy for and fills gaps between the visible voxels provided by the range measurements. At the same time, as Fig. 3(e) shows, the distant reliable floor

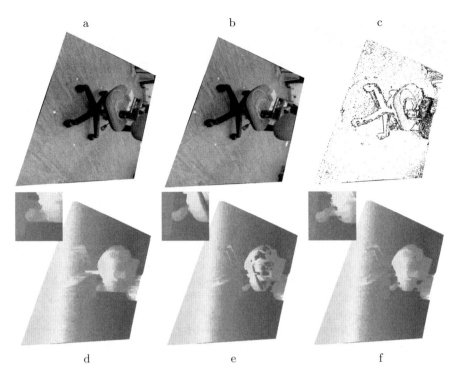

Fig. 3. Rectified stereo pair (a,b) from images of a chair with various objects on top captured during scanning; the mask (c) of unreliable range guidance points; stereo reconstruction using SDPS [21] with no guidance (d), guidance (e), and occlusion culling of guidance (f). The inset details the area around the lever of the chair to show its correct reconstruction with the guidance.

points are also used for guiding the stereo reconstruction despite these points are actually occluded in both the images of this stereo pair. Such sources of errors that results from large featureless foreground objects are undetectable by simple colour consistency criteria.

A simple heuristic approach based on the viewing direction of a laser scan allows us to remove the occluded but colour consistent background points and partly resolve the problem of large homogeneous colour areas. Let a 3D point be considered occluded if it lies within a certain culling distance r away from another 3D point with a higher disparity (i.e. closer to the cameras) in the disparity space. In practice, a occlusion mask is constructed from the 3D points in the disparity space. The closest points (with the largest disparity values) are processed first. Each point casts a shadow of radius r onto the mask. Any subsequent points further away (with a lower disparity) that lies within the occlusion mask are excluded as being potentially occluded. Combining the colour consistency checks and occlusion culling (Fig. 3(f)) makes it possible to improve the accuracy of the scene further in comparison to the stereo alone, or with only the colour consistency guidance. While the incorrect guiding points from the floor render

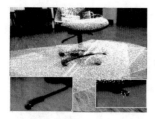

Fig. 4. Another view on the same scene (range points in white). Sparsity and errors of the range data on the lever (see the left insets) and stereo reconstruction constrained to a single optical surface result in the inaccurate surface model shown by its depth map (centre) and cyclopean view (right).

part of the chair's surface incorrect, this is corrected using the simple heuristic occlusion culling ($r = 4$ pixels in this experiment). Note that now the difficult areas such as the chair's lever are modelled correctly while the chair seat is unaffected by the colour-consistent background floor points. Nonetheless, the errors near the edges of the chair seat remain due to the imprecise nature of the culling heuristic used.

We expect to eliminate in future the need for such a heuristic to improve the data accuracy by measuring both the directions and positions of the scene scanning and viewing, and using this additional information to determine the possible occlusions. One more problem to be addressed is due to sparse range measurements for disjoint parts of a scene with poor reflection: in such a case a guided stereo reconstruction assuming only a single continuous visible surface remains inaccurate as illustrated in Fig. 4. Because a few range data points on the lever are inaccurate and lie outside the surface of the lever, the range data are deemed as unreliable and offers no extra information in that area, and the fusion of range and stereo data cannot improve the accuracy of the lever model in this case.

Table 1 shows the accuracy of modelling the same scene from three selected views. Ground-truth that is complete and reliable on large natural scenes are often difficult to obtain, and in this case access to special measuring devices such as a structured light scanner is impossible in the experimental setup. Thus in these results, the accuracy is compared to a manually generated sparse ground truth illustrated in Fig. 5. It was generated by careful visual inspection of stereo

Table 1. Overall accuracy of combining the active range and passive stereo data for 3 views on the test scene

Fusion type	View 1	View 2	View 3
No guidance	90.6%	84.6%	91.4%
All guidance	74.0%	75.2%	72.1%
Colour consistency	90.2%	84.7%	91.4%
Occlusion culling and colour consistency	90.2%	84.6%	91.5%

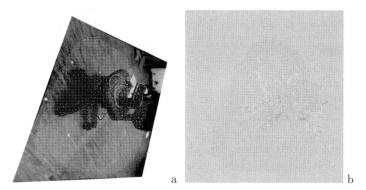

Fig. 5. Distribution (a) of the manually generated ground truth and the accuracy (b) of the surface modelling with occlusion culling with respect to the ground truth

pairs with the aid of an image enhancement visualisation program and contains ≈ 6000 points out of ≈ 500000 visible pixels in the common field of view of the stereo pairs, giving the overall coverage of about 1.2%. This method of ground truth generation is expected to be accurate to ± 1 disparity level but requires substantial time and labour. We intend to generate the ground truth by more convenient automated means in the future. The location of ground truth points are independent of the guiding range data, and are evenly distributed across the images, with extra density (up to 5%) at various places of interest. The ground truth is provided even at problematic areas where with no range data (e.g. dark chair legs). Stereo reconstruction was considered correct if its absolute disparity difference from the ground truth is not greater than one.

Although the total accuracy seemingly is not improved, the errors in the specific areas of interest notably decrease after the data fusion. The chosen scenes have relatively large areas comparing to the areas of interest, so the parts where the modelling meets with the greatest difficulties were examined further, e.g. the surfaces of poor reflection or missing range data such as the dark legs and lever of the chair, homogeneous areas such as the seat and back of the chair, and occluded areas with reliable range data. Table 2 highlights the accuracy improvements due to different fusion techniques for these parts of the scenes. Each part contains approximately 800 ground truth points. The introduced simple colour consistency based selection of the guiding range data with occlusion culling to exclude the occluded points gives statistically significant increase in accuracy for the two out of three test cases. The overall errors are now associated with edges of reconstructed parts rather than completely incorrect as in Fig. 4.

These and our other experiments show that the range and image data fusion based on guiding stereo reconstruction with reliable (colour-consistent) range data improves the accuracy of modelling some parts of a 3D scene but adds new inaccuracies due to errors on edges and due to occluded colour-consistent areas. While the overall accuracy is not increased, the local accuracy for some parts

Table 2. Accuracy for the scene parts with sparse guiding data or of homogeneous colour (case A: view 1, part 1; case B: view 1, part 2; case C: view 2, part 1)

Fusion type	Case A	Case B	Case C
No guidance	71.9%	73.5%	80.2%
All guidance	49.6%	53.7%	43.9%
Colour consistency	72.0%	75.6%	78.2%
Occlusion culling and colour consistency	77.3%	76.2%	81.0%

difficult for the range scanning is significantly better if colour consistency is combined with occlusion culling whereas the colour consistency alone is insufficient.

References

1. Ip, W.L.R., Loftus, M.: Shaded image machining: a reverse engineering approach using computer vision techniques and analytical methods to reproduce sculptured surfaces. International Journal of Production Research 34, 1895–1916 (1996)
2. Iocchi, L., Konolige, K., Bajracharya, M.: Visually realistic mapping of a planar environment with stereo. In: Proc. 7th Int. Symp. on Experimental Robotics (ISER), pp. 521–532 (2001)
3. Tosovic, S., Sablatnig, R.: 3d modeling of archaeological vessels using shape from silhouette. International Conference on, 3D Digital Imaging and Modeling 0, 51–58 (2001)
4. Moslah, O., Klee, M., Grolleau, A., Guitteny, V., Couvet, S., Foliguet, P.S.: Urban models texturing from un-calibrated photographs. In: Proc. 23rd Int. Conf. Image & Vision Computing New Zealand, November 26–28, pp. 1–6 (2008)
5. Thales: 3d chrono: A 3d modelling tool for mission rehearsal (2010) Retrieved online on the (January 12 , 2010)
6. van Iersel, M., Veerman, H., van der Mark, W.: Modelling a crime scene in 3d and adding thermal information. In: Huckridge, D.A., Ebert, R.R. (eds.) Electro-Optical and Infrared Systems: Technology and Applications VI, vol. 7481, p. 74810M. SPIE, San Jose (2009)
7. Knoll, A., Schröder, R., Wolfram, A.: Generation of dense range maps by data fusion from active and passive colour stereo vision. In: Proc. 1996 IEEE/SICE/RSJ Int. Conf. Multisensor Fusion and Integration for Intelligent Systems (MFI), Washington, USA, pp. 410–415 (1996)
8. Scherba, D., Bajscy, P.: Depth estimation by fusing stereo and wireless sensor locations. Technical Report alg04–005, Automated Learning Group, National Center for Supercomputing Applications, Champaign, IL 61820 (2004)
9. Kim, M.Y., Lee, H., Cho, H.: Dense range map reconstruction from a versatile robotic sensor system with an active trinocular vision and a passive binocular vision. Applied Optics 47, 1927–1939 (2008)
10. Morgenthaler, D., Hennessy, S., DeMenthon, D.: Range-video fusion and comparison of inverse perspective algorithms in static images. IEEE Transactions on Systems, Man, and Cybernetics 20(6), 1301–1312 (1990)
11. Biber, P., Fleck, S., Duckett, T.: 3d modeling of indoor environments for a robotic security guard. In: Proc. IEEE Computer Society Conf. Computer Vision and Pattern Recognition - Workshops, Advanced 3D Imaging for Safety and Security (SafeSecur05), vol. 3, pp. 124–124 (2005)

12. Frintrop, S.: VOCUS: A Visual Attention System for Object Detection and Goal-Directed Search. Lecture Notes in Computer Science / Lecture Notes in Artificial Intelligence. Springer, Heidelberg (2006)
13. Curtis, P., Yang, C.S., Payeur, P.: An integrated robotic multi-modal range sensing system. In: Instrumentation and Measurement Technology Conference, Proceedings of the IEEE, Ottawa, Canada, vol. 3, pp. 1991–1996 (2005)
14. Kuhnert, K., Stommel, M.: Fusion of stereo-camera and pmd-camera data for real-time suited precise 3d environment reconstruction. In: IEEE/RSJ International Conference on Intelligent Robots and Systems, Beijing, China, pp. 4780–4785 (2006)
15. Perrollaz, M., Labayrade, R., Royere, C., Hautiere, N., Aubert, D.: Long range obstacle detection using laser scanner and stereovision. In: Proceedings of the IEEE Intelligent Vehicles Symposium, Tokyo, Japan, pp. 182–187 (2006)
16. Zhu, J., Wang, L., Yang, R., Davis, J.: Fusion of time-of-flight depth and stereo for high accuracy depth maps. In: IEEE Conference on, Computer Vision and Pattern Recognition, pp. 1–8. IEEE Computer Society, Los Alamitos (2008)
17. Valkenburg, R.J., Penman, D.W., Schoonees, J.A., Alwesh, N.S., Palmer, G.T.: Interactive hand-held 3d scanning. In: Proc. Int. Conf. Image and Vision Computing New Zealand, Great Barrier Island, Auckland, pp. 245–250 (2006)
18. Chan, Y.H., Delmas, P., Gimel'farb, G., Valkenburg, R.: On fusion of active range data and passive stereo data for 3d scene modeling. In: Proc. 23rd Int. Conf. Image & Vision Computing New Zealand, November 26–28, pp. 234–239 (2008)
19. Chan, Y.H., Delmas, P., Gimel'farb, G., Valkenburg, R.: Accurate 3d modelling by fusion of potentially reliable active range and passive stereo data. In: Jiang, X., Petkov, N. (eds.) CAIP 2009. LNCS, vol. 5702, pp. 848–855. Springer, Heidelberg (2009)
20. Liu, X., Hu, Y., Zhang, J., Tong, X., Guo, B., Shum, H.Y.: Synthesis and rendering of biderectional texture functions on arbitrary surfaces. IEEE Transactions on Visualization and Computer Graphics 10, 278–289 (2004)
21. Gimel'farb, G.: Probabilistic regularisation and symmetry in binocular dynamic programming stereo. Pattern Recognitioin Letters 23, 431–442 (2002)

Design of a Real-Time Embedded Stereo Smart Camera

Frantz Pelissier and François Berry

LASMEA CNRS,
24 avenue des Landais 63177 AUBIERE Cedex - France
frantz.pelissier@gmail.com,
berry@univ-bpclermont.fr

Abstract. This paper describes the architecture of a new smart vision system called BiSeeMos. This smart camera is designed for stereo vision purposes and the implementation of a simple dense stereo vision algorithm. The architecture has been designed for dedicated parallel algorithms in using a high performance FPGA. This chip provides the user with useful features for vision processing as integrated RAM blocks, embedded multipliers, phase locked loops and plenty of logic elements. In this paper, a description of our architecture and a comparison versus others works is done. A dense stereo vision algorithm has been implemented on the platform using the Census method.

1 Introduction

Goals of computer vision are to extract information from images. It can then be used for 3D recognition, speed detection, pose detection or object recognition. In robotics, the 3D information of a scene is useful because it can lead to obstacle avoidance, path computation or object recognition. Therefore several ways to get this type of information have been developed in the last decades.

One of these methods is the stereo vision; it uses two or more images of a scene taken from different angles. Then with some stereo algorithms the images are fused and the elevation map of the scene can be computed. This very elevation map contains the depth information of the scene. A famous instance of such a system is the human vision system, the two eyes are watching the environment from different angles, and the brain fuses the two sights to compute the 3D human perception that we know.

We have tried to artificially reproduce this very system for decades, the problem resides in the huge amount of data to process when real time is the goal. Moreover the stereo algorithms need plenty of resources and performances to achieve the real time rate. For these reasons a standard computer cannot even reach the derisory computation rate of 1 frame per second.

For the last three decades a considerable effort has been made in developing dedicated hardware architectures to overcome this unfortunate problem. One solution consists in designing a dedicated embedded vision system classically called "smart camera".

J. Blanc-Talon et al. (Eds.): ACIVS 2010, Part I, LNCS 6474, pp. 344–356, 2010.

1.1   Smart Camera

A smart camera can be globally defined as a vision system that not only integrates an image sensing device but also signal processing elements and communication peripherals. One of the major advantages of this kind of embedded system is that it is able to handle a wide range of problems, presenting several advantages which can be categorized as:

- Communication bottlenecks: embedded processing allows to reduce the data communication between sensors and the host system, avoiding the bottlenecks that frequently occur in real-time image processing.
- Autonomous or Mobile devices: avoiding the use of a mainframe computer system, compact sizes (for unmanned aerial vehicles for example) and low power consumption can be obtained.
- Active perception: for these systems, a high-speed feedback link is essential between sensing and processing units. To accomplish an intensive real-time exchange, where higher level processes drive the perception tasks. This feedback is performed at different levels, ranging from analog threshold setting and dynamic configuration of the image sensor at the low level, up to region of interest (ROI) selection at the high level. This implies a direct 'private link' between sensors and processing units, which is impossible with classical field buses such as firewire, USB, ethernet, etc...
- Camera networks: distributed processing using smart cameras has major advantages over centralized processing systems, as it avoids the transmission of large amounts of information. This has a two-fold result, in that both transmission of sensed data as well as transmission of camera control information is reduced or even avoided.

When designing a smart camera for a given application, several processing structures can be considered. This includes embedded general purpose processors, dedicated signal processing devices like GPU's, DSP's and media processors, or reconfigurable devices like FPGA or CPLD. Furthermore, heterogeneous approaches containing two or more of the previously cited components can also be considered. Each of these options presents its advantages and disadvantage. Design choices must not only be made by considering the image processing tasks to be performed, but also considering the desired flexibility (will this camera be used for another application?) and the implementation/programming techniques (high-level programming, hardware description language (HDL), etc.).

Although it is impossible to generalize image processing flow, but it is realistic to consider SIMD (Single Instruction, Multiple Data) and MIMD (Multiple Instructions, Multiple Data) machines, because these machines allow the manipulation of multiple data items and give relatively fast response. Without losing generality, mostly the image processing task can be divided into three main levels.

"Low level" processes will often involve operations performed on a group of adjacent pixels, like mask convolution for filtering, or sample correlation for feature matching. These "neighborhood" operations require lots of memory transactions,

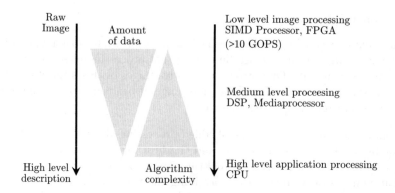

Fig. 1. Amount of data vs. algorithm complexity. (GOPS = Giga (10^9) Operations per Second).

and can quickly become a constraining bottleneck if the systemï¿s hardware and architecture are not tailored for such kind of processing. Furthermore, "medium level" (e.g. segmentation) and "high level" processes (e.g. recognition) can require complex iterative or recursive mathematical routines, like matrix inversion or minimization methods. These processes are quite challenging, specially under embedded context where clock frequencies must be kept low to reduce power consumption. The figure 1 illustrates the inverse relationship between data amounts and algorithm complexity. Low level image processing performs a few simple repetitive operations over huge amounts of raw data. These processes are highly parallel, and suitable for processing structures such as FPGA or SIMD processors (Single Instruction Multiple Data). Meanwhile, higher level processes often involve complex sequential routines with a big number of instructions and operations, applied over a reduced set of feature descriptors. Dedicated signal processing structures and high-level programming are desired features, making these processes suitable for CPU-based devices like DSP and mediaprocessors.

1.2   Previous Works

As standard processor architectures are not matched for stereo vision computation, works have been done with DSP chips. In 1997, K. Konolige, et al. [2] designed miniature stereovision smart cameras called SVM and SVM II, the last one use a DSP TMS320C60x from Texas Instruments. The depth processing can reaches more than 30 Fps with a resolution of 160x120 pixels. In 2007, Hengstler et al presented the MeshEye [3], a microcontroller based architecture. The system is a multiple camera system that can host up to 9 cameras modules. It is completely embedded and has a wireless communication port.

Unfortunately, we cannot have satisfactory processing with only DSP chips. Because vision processing includes often parallel tasks, using parallel architectures seems to be more efficient. That is why several designs have been developed with ASIC based architectures. In 2003, M. Kuhn et al. [4] have designed an ASIC-based system which can run a depth computation at 50 Fps with a resolution of 256x192 and a disparity of 25 pixels. The DeepSea system has been developed by J. I. Woodfill et al. [5] in 2004, it is based on the DeepSea ASIC. It computes the depth at 200 Fps with a resolution of 512x480 pixels and with 52 disparities.

ASIC architectures are dedicated to one task, therefore the use of FPGAs is more flexible because we can change its configuration, it enables faster prototyping and is more suitable for research and development. In 1997, J. I. Woodfill et al. [6] used the PARTS engine computer to compute a real time depth system at 42 Fps with a resolution of 320x240 pixels and with 24 disparities. The PARTS engine is a PCI card based on 16 Xilinx 4025 FPGAs. In 2003, A. Darabiha et al. [7] designed a four FPGA-based board with four Virtex FPGA, it was called the TM-3A Board. This system reaches 30 Fps at a resolution of 256x360 pixels with 20 disparities.

As the FPGA technologies improved, the number of FPGA onto the design decreased in the same time, then several single FPGA-based designed have been developed. Y. Jia et al. [8,9] developed trinocular stereo vision systems called the MSVMs in 2003-2004. The last one of them, the MSVM-III, computes depth frames at a rate of 30 Fps in a resolution of 640x480 with 64 disparities on an architecture based on a single FPGA Virtex 2 chip. In 2006, A. Naoulou et al. [10] used a FPGA based board with the Stratix I FPGA to compute a 130 Fps depth map at a resolution of 640x480 pixels and with 64 disparities. And lately in 2010, S. Jin et al. [11] developed a stereo vision system based on a Virtex 4 FPGA which computes depth frames at 230 Fps in a 640x480 resolution with 64 disparities.

Finally, some hybrids systems have been presented with the use of both DSPs and FPGAs. The stereo TriMedia smart camera has been conceived by J. van der Horst et al. [12] in 2006, it consists of two cameras TriMedia from Phillips Corporation and a processing board. The processing board is provided with a Virtex II FPGA and a TriMedia DSP, the whole system runs at a 19 Fps rate in a 256x256 resolution and with 18 disparities.

Later, in 2008, another hybrid system has been used by Kleihorst et al. [13] [14]. It is a wireless smart camera system based on a SIMD, a CPLD and a 8051 microprocessor architecture. The system computes 37 disparity pixels at 30 Fps on a resolution of 320x240 pixels.

In 2009, P. Liu et al. [15] have realized a stereo vision system with motorized lens which enable 10x zoom features. The system is based on a Spartan 3 FPGA and a Blackfin BF537 DSP architecture.

This paper is organized as follows. The next section depicts the architecture of our smart camera and its features. In section 3 an implementation of dense stereo vision algorithm and the results is given. Finally, the last section concludes the paper.

2   BiSeeMos Architecture

Tremendous work has been realized in the development of stereovision smart cameras. It seems realistic to consider that the most interesting results are those from FPGA-based and ASIC-based systems. This is due to the parallel nature of these chips which particularly suits the needs of stereo algorithms. Nevertheless some of these systems suffer the communication interface due to the classical bottleneck between sensing and processing part. Moreover the monitoring of the sensors is more limited when the sensors and the processing system are separated by a serial communication layer such I2C.

The architecture presented in this paper consists of a FPGA based stereo smart camera based on Cyclone III EP3C120F780 FPGA chip. The sensors used are two MV-A1024 Photon Focus matrixes that can attain a rate of 160 Fps with a resolution of 1024 by 1024 pixels. The sensor chips are directly connected to the FPGA inputs/outputs through an analog interface. Finally the FPGA is connected to a SXGA interface in order to perform easy visualization of results. Furthermore, the FPGA is also connected to a Camera Link interface to provide the data to a computer and then to achieve post computing figure 2.

Fig. 2. BiSeeMos board with one of its 2 cameras plugged in

2.1   Hardware Feature

The hardware architecture of the system is summarized in Figure 3.

The key components of the BiSeeMos smart camera are:

- The FPGA is the core of the system. It is a Cyclone III EP3C120F780 FPGA from ALTERA's corporation. It provides the user with 119,088 logic elements, 3.888 Kbits of embedded memory, 288 multipliers and 4 Phase Locked Loops.
- A couple of sensors MV-A1024 from Photon Focus corporation are soldered in two daughter card modules. These modules have been designed to be

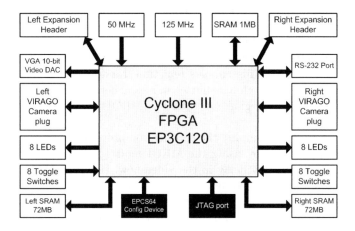

Fig. 3. BiSeeMos hardware architecture

plugged into the main board. The sensors have a resolution of 1024x1024
pixels at a possible rate of 160 Fps. The access of data can be full random
and the capture mode can be either global shutter or rolling shutter.
- SXGA Interface has been designed to provide easy display of the video flow
  before or after processing into the FPGA without any additional computer
  required. It can handle a SXGA flow of 1280x1024 pixels at 60Hz.
- The Camera Link Interface has been incorporated in the design and provides
  a fast video data flow interface which can attain 2.04 Gbit/s that is a rate
  of 255 Fps in full resolution.
- In addition to the FPGA memory blocks, memory chips have been included
  into the design. Two Cypress CY7C1470BV33 Synchronous pipelined burst
  SRAMs of 72 MB organized in 2Mx36 Bytes with No Bus Latency and one
  Cypress CY7C1059DV33 SRAM of 1MB have been integrated in the design.
- The configuration of the FPGA device is possible through a JTAG port in
  Active Serial mode and it can be stored in the flash memory device onto the
  board.

2.2   Design Strategies

One of the most striking problem in real time vision processing is the bottleneck
of the communication layers. We have avoided this potential problem in this
design by using communication interfaces that provide bigger data flow capabilities than the maximum data flow of the sensors. Indeed, by connecting directly
the sensor's inputs and outputs to the FPGA, we avoid to use an other interface
that could have slowed down the video flow. After processing, the video flow can
be send to an other system, like a computer, with the Camera Link Interface
which provides higher data rate than required.

Connecting the sensors directly to the FPGA inputs and outputs has other
advantages, it enables full control of the sensors by the FPGA and therefore

by the user. Indeed, in others smart cameras systems, the sensors used to be handled by external chips as microcontrolers via I2C which is much more slower than a direct control by FPGA.

In our architecture the configuration of the sensors can be changed between each frame at 160 Fps. This enables real time random access of the sensor's matrix in either rolling or global shutter modes. Therefore the system is highly versatile and Multiple Region Of Interest (MROI) is possible without any limitation.

The use of MROI can simplify the rectification process when using the system in stereo vision. Indeed, by using the MROI modes it is possible to align the matrix frames without any delay in the video flow. However, this has for effect to reduce the number of exploitable lines in each frames.

Another key point of this architecture concerns the total exposure control and exposure updating between frames capture. The sensors provide as well the possibility to be programmed for either linear or logarithmic or hybrids response for exposure. And finally the Rolling shutter mode and the Global shutter mode are fully handled.

All these features were required for the simultaneous object pose and velocity computation algorithm[1] when using a single view from the rolling shutter capture.

3   Stereo Vision Algorithm Example

In this part, implementation of a well known census transform on BiSeeMos is proposed in order to demonstrate its efficiency in real time processing.

3.1   The Census Algorithm

Census algorithm is a good candidate for matching algorithm in programmable logic because it can be described by a fully combinational design. Therefore real time speeds are easily attained in accordance to the amount of logic elements available in the programmable chip. The Census algorithm can be decomposed in three steps: the Census transform, the Hamming scores computation, and the score selection.

Census transform. Census Transform is a form of non-parametric local transform (i.e. relies on the relative ordering of local intensity values, and not on the intensity values themselves) used in image processing to map the intensity values of the pixels within a square window to a bit string, thereby capturing the image structure. The centre pixeli¿s intensity value is replaced by the bit string composed of set of boolean comparisons such that in a square window, moving left to right.

Figure 4 depicts an example of Census transform for a 5×5 pixels correlation window, then the processed binary string has $5 \times 5 - 1$ bits because the center pixel of the window is not used.

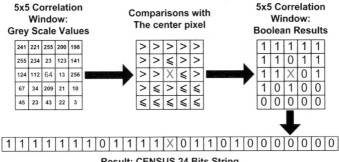

Result: CENSUS 24 Bits String

Fig. 4. Example of Census transform for a 5x5 Correlation window

Hamming scores computation. It consists in comparing each pixel of the left frame with each candidate pixels of the right frame. The candidates pixels are usually selected on the same line coordinate as the left selected pixel if the bench has been rectified. Then the number of candidate is determined by the maximum disparity handled by the system.

If this maximum disparity is 64 pixels, then we have 64 Hamming comparisons to compute. Hamming comparison of two Census strings consists in counting the number of similarities in the two strings. This score is called *Hamming score*. When Hamming score is high implies that strings are similar.

Therefore in this example we compute 64 Hamming scores for each pixel of the left frame. Each Hamming score is associated to one of the candidate pixel of the right frame.

Score selection. Final step consists in selecting the winner among all the candidates. Simple selection (WTA: Winner Takes All) consists in selecting the best Hamming score and get the coordinate of the corresponding pixel in the right image. Therefore this very pixel is the winner and the difference between its column coordinate and the column coordinate of the left pixel is the disparity. This very disparity is proportionally equal to the distance between the camera and the solid point of the space.

Fig. 5. Example of a depth result with a Census window of 15×15 pixels

Example of figure 5 has shown that the quality of the depth frame is indeed improving when the correlation window grows. Anyway, when the correlation window continues to grow bigger than 15×15 pixels, the quality of the depth frame seems to stabilize. The left and right frames used are from the middleburry university's website [18] to evaluate the algorithm performance.

4   Hardware Implementation

This part presents the hardware implementation of the Census algorithm which summarized on the Figure 6.

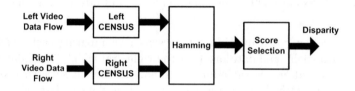

Fig. 6. Overview of the whole Census stereo vision algorithm

The system is a pipeline with the processing directly connected to the video flow. There is no latency where a complete frame is stored in memory before the end of the algorithm.

4.1   Census Transformation

The first stage is the Census transform and has the organization depicted in figure 7:

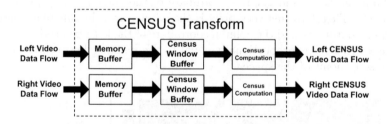

Fig. 7. Census transform stage

First both video left and right synchronized flow are entering into the FPGA. As theses flows are transmitted pixel by pixel, the firsts two blocks of the algorithm are RAM-based memories for buffering the frames data. The transformation needs windows with a size of 15×15 pixels, therefore the two memory blocks are to store 16 lines of the incoming left and right frames before to start any

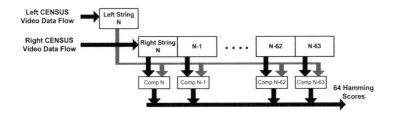

Fig. 8. Hamming computation stage

processing. After this stage, the both windows buffer are shift registers which has at each clock period a whole Census window, then at the next clock cycle it read a new column from the memory buffer and shift the window on the right.

Finally 224 comparisons are combinatory done between each pixel of the window with its center pixel. The results of these 224 comparisons are saved into 224 bits register for the next stage of the algorithm. This is done simultaneously for the left and the right frame. At each clock cycle, we have therefore two new 224 bits strings coming out of this stage.

4.2 Hamming Scores Computation

This stage consist in comparing the left 224 bits strings with the 64 previous right 224 bits strings(Fig 8).

64 cells shift register for the right flow and a single cell register for the left flow are instantiated. The right register stores the last 64 Census strings while

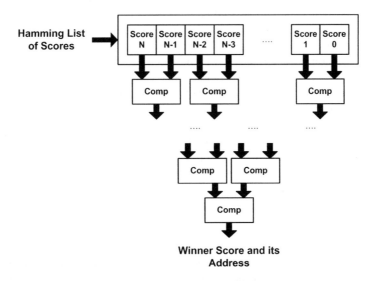

Fig. 9. Hamming score selection stage

Table 1. Synthesis report

Block	Number of LEs	Memory bits	Clock Frequency
Census Transform	1124 (< 1%)	131072 bits (3%)	160 MHz
Hamming Scores Computation	57760 (48%)	0	160 MHz
Hamming Scores Selection	1789 (2%)	0	160 MHz
Whole Algorithm	60673 (51%)	131072 bits (3%)	160 MHz

the left register store the current left Census string. The 64 comparisons are combinatory computed at each cycle.

4.3   Score Selection

This final step consists in selecting the best hamming score in each collection of 64 scores.

This stage has a pyramidal structure of comparators. Each comparator selects the greater score between two scores and a multiplexer selects the address (the disparity) of the winner. When the top of the pyramid is reached, the last score is the greater and its address in the 64 cells string is the disparity (fig. 9). As final results, the synthesis report is given below.

5   Conclusion

This work has presented the design of the BiSeeMos platform. It has shown its real-time capabilities with the implementation of a simple Census stereo algorithm. Even though a wide Census window has been used, there are plenty of logic Elements and Memory blocks available. Indeed, the architecture uses only (51%) of the Logic Elements available and (3%) of the Memory blocks. There is then enough place to implement both a rectifier system and a stronger algorithm. Furthermore, we could divide the Logic Elements used by serialize the hamming score computation stage. As the clock of the system is 160 MHz and that the logics in the FPGA can reach more than the double, then we could multiply the system clock by two and this will lend us to significatively reduce the logic elements needed.

With the rectification stage, we can use the MROI system of the sensors to save more Memory Blocks inside the FPGA. Concerning the algorithm, we can use a double census transform to compute left-right and right-left correlations in the same time, then fuse them to get a better disparity map. We can as well implement an other algorithm in parallel as the SAD to combine the advantages of both. This will be the continuing of this work.

References

1. Ait-Aider, O., Andreff, N., Lavest, J.M., Martinet, P.: Simultaneous object pose and velocity computation using a single view from a rolling shutter camera. In: Leonardis, A., Bischof, H., Pinz, A. (eds.) ECCV 2006. LNCS, vol. 3952, pp. 56–68. Springer, Heidelberg (2006)

2. Konolige, K.: Small vision systems: Hardware and implementation. In: Eighth International Symposium on Robotics Research, Hayama, Japan, pp. 203–212. Springer, London (1997)
3. Hengstler, S., Prashanth, D., Fong, S., Aghajan, H.: MeshEye: A Hybrid-Resolution Smart Camera Mote for Applications in Distributed Intelligent Surveillance. In: Proc. of the 6th Int. Symposium on Information Processing in Sensor Networks IPSN 2007, April 25-27, pp. 360–369 (2007)
4. Kuhn, M., Moser, S., Isler, O., Gurkaynak, F.K., Burg, A., Felber, N., Kaeslin, H., Fichtner, W.: Efficient ASIC implementation of a real-time depth mapping stereo vision system. In: Proc. IEEE Int. Circuits Syst. (MWSCAS 2003), Cairo, Egypt, December 2003, vol. 3, pp. 1478–1481 (2003)
5. Woodfill, J.I., Gordon, G., Buck, R.: Tyzx DeepSea high speed stereo vision system. In: Proc. IEEE Comput. Soc. Workshop Real-Time 3-D Sensors Use Conf. Comput. Vision Pattern Recog., Washington D.C., pp. 41–46 (June 2004)
6. Woodfill, J., Von Herzen, B.: Real-time stereo vision on the PARTS reconfigurable computer. In: IEEE Workshop on FPGAs for Custom Computing Machines (1997)
7. Darabiha, A., Rose, J.R., MacLean, W.J.: Video rate stereo depth measurement on programmable hardware. In: IEEE Conference on Computer Vision & Pattern Recognition, pp. 203–210 (June 2003)
8. Jia, Y., Xu, Y., Liu, W., Yang, C., Zhu, Y., Zhang, X., et al.: An: A Miniature Stereo Vision Machine for Real-Time Dense Depth Mapping. In: 3rd International Conference Computer Vision Systems, Graz, Austria, pp. 268–277 (2003)
9. Jia, Y., Xu, Y., Liu, W., Yang, C., Zhu, Y., Zhang, X., et al.: An: A Miniature Stereo Vision Machine (MSVM-III) for Dense Disparity Mapping. In: 17th International conference on Pattern Recognition, Cambridge, UK, August 23-26, vol. 1, pp. 728–731 (2004)
10. Naoulou, A., Boizard, J.-L., Fourniols, J.Y., Devy, M.: A 3D real-time vision system based on passive stereo vision algorithms: application to laparoscopic surgical manipulations. In: Proceedings of the 2nd International Conference on Information and Communication Technologies (ICTTA 2006), Damascus, Syria, vol. 1, pp. 1068–1073 (April 2006)
11. Jin, S., Cho, J., Pham, X.D., Lee, K.M., Park, S.-K., Kim, M., Jeon, J.W.: FPGA Design and Implementation of a Real-Time Stereo Vision System. IEEE transactions on circuits and systems for video technology 20(1), 15–26 (2010)
12. van der Horst, J., van Leeuwen, R., Broers, H., Kleihorst, R., Jonker, P.: A Real-Time Stereo SmartCam, using FPGA, SIMD and VLIW. In: Proc. 2nd Workshop on Applications of Computer Vision, pp. 1–8 (2006)
13. Kleihorst, R., Abbo, A., Schueler, B., Danilin, A.: Camera mote with a high-performance parallel processor for realtime frame-based video processing. In: ICDSC, pp. 109–116 (Semptember 2007)
14. Gao, X., Kleihorst, R., Schueler, B.: Stereo vision in a smart camera system. In: Proc. ECV/CVPR 2008, Anchorage, USA (June 2008)
15. Liu, P., Willis, A., Sui, Y.: Stereoscopic 3D Reconstruction using Motorized Zoom Lenses within an Embedded System. In: Niel, K.S., Fofi, D. (eds.) Proceedings of Image Processing: Machine Vision Applications II, 72510W (February 2, 2009)
16. Volpe, R., Balaram, J., Ohm, T., Ivlev, R.: The rocky 7 mars rover prototype. In: International Conference on Intelligent Robots and Systems, Osaka, Japan, vol. 3, pp. 1558–1564 (1996)

17. Point Grey Research (1997), http://www.ptgrey.com
18. Scharstein, D., Szeliski, R.: A taxonomy and evaluation of dense two-frame stereo correspondence algorithms. International Journal of Computer Vision 47(1/2/3), 7–42 (2002), Microsoft Research Technical Report MSR-TR-2001-81 (November 2001)

Optimal Trajectory Space Finding for Nonrigid Structure from Motion

Yuanqi Su, Yuehu Liu, and Yang Yang

Institute of Artificial Intelligence and Robotics,
Xi'an Jiaotong University. 710049, Xi'an Shaanxi, China
yuanqisu@hotmail.com, liuyuehu@mail.xjtu.edu.cn, yyang@aiar.xjtu.edu.cn

Abstract. The deformation in nonrigid structure from motion can be modeled either in shape domain or in time domain. Here, we view the deformation in time domain, model the trajectory of each 3D point as a linear combination of trajectory bases, and present a novel method to automatically find the trajectory bases based on orthographic camera assumption. In this paper, a linear relation is explicitly derived between 2D projected trajectory and 3D trajectory bases. With this formulation, an approximation is formulated for finding 3D trajectory bases which cast the trajectory bases finding into a problem of finding eigenvectors. Using the approximated trajectory bases as a start point, an EM-like algorithm is proposed which refine the trajectory bases and the corresponding coefficients. The proposed method demonstrates satisfactory results on both the synthetic and real data.

Keywords: Nonrigid Structure form Motion, Image Sequences Processing, Video Signal Processing, Structure from Motion, Singular Value Decomposition, EM algorithm.

1 Introduction

Structure from motion is a fundamental problem in video signal processing which seeks to infer the 3D geometry of the object and the camera motion from a group of tracked 2D points. It is used in a wide range of applications such as 3D face reconstruction, robot navigation etc. Due to the fact that the image forming process is invertible, the problem is ill-posed; however, it can be solved with additional information. To solve the structure from motion problem, assumptions about the camera and the object should be made. On the camera side, both affine camera model[1,8,16,5,3,7,2,11] and projective camera model [4,9,12,13,6,15]are widely used. On the object side, both the rigid [1,8,16,5] and nonrigid [11,3,2,4,9,12,13,6,15] assumptions were used depending on the problem to be solved. We concentrate on affine camera model and nonrigid case, and developed a novel factorization method in this paper to deal with the problem. The deformation in nonrigid structure from motion can be modeled in both the shape domain and the trajectory domain [1]. In shape domain, the instantaneous shape in each frame is typically a linear combination of a group of shape bases.

J. Blanc-Talon et al. (Eds.): ACIVS 2010, Part I, LNCS 6474, pp. 357–366, 2010.
© Springer-Verlag Berlin Heidelberg 2010

For time domain, the 3D trajectory of each point is modeled as the linear combination of trajectory bases. No matter which domain is used, determining the proper bases is crucial and yet hard for nonrigid structure from motion. In the paper, we view the deformation from time domain, and propose a novel method for nonrigid structure from motion, which automatically determines the trajectory space based on the linear relation between 2D trajectory and 3D trajectory bases. The proposed method contains three steps: camera motion calculation, trajectory bases finding and coefficients optimizing which are further explained in section 3. And our method falls into the domain of factorization methods for structure from motion.

2   Related Work

Factorization method starting from Tomasi-Kanade's work [10] is a main branch in the research of structure from motion. The algorithm is easy to implement; for some occasions, results generated by factorization are sufficient for its precision. The results can be used as an initialization for other methods such as [8]. Tomasi and Kanade [10] proved that under the orthographic assumption, the centered measurement matrix of tracked points can be decomposed into two rank-3 matrices: one for the camera motion, and the other for the 3D geometry. SVD is used for factorizing the centered measurement matrix. The factorization method is extended for the paraperspective camera model in [7]. Moreover, Kanatani et al. pointed out in [4] that for affine camera model, the factorization method for structure from motion can be viewed as subspace fitting. They used the conclusion that 2D trajectory of each point lies in the subspace spanned by four vectors determined by the rotation and translation of camera. The structure from motion problem is then recasted as subspace fitting through optimization. They gave the conclusion that singular value decomposition (SVD) used by Tomasi and Kanade fits subspaces in the least square manner. Besides affine camera assumption, Triggs [13] extended the Tomasi-Kanade factorization to perspective cameras, where projection depth for each point is first estimated by using fundamental matrix and epipoles with image data. A corresponding measurement matrix is formed, followed by a factorization similar to SVD. All previous methods are designed for rigid object, where the shape of object is fixed across frames. And the conclusions drawn by these methods are all relied on the point. For the nonrigid case, factorization can also be used where shape in each frame is represented as a linear combination of a group of shape bases, first proposed by Bregler et.al in [3]. In their method, two SVD followed by a metric updating are used to compute the camera motion, shape bases and coefficients. Based on the same assumption, several other methods are proposed for nonrigid structure from motion which could be found in [11,3,2] . Because the shape bases are not unique, there may be multiple solutions which lead to the ambiguities in the factorization. To eliminate the ambiguities, Xiao et al. [17] combined a group of basis constraints with the rotation constraints, resulting in a closed-form solution to the problem. Besides the basis constraints, other constraints are proposed for eliminating the ambiguities. Wang et al. [15] used the convex combination instead of linear combination for interpolating instantaneous shape, which requires that the coefficients for shape in each frame to be nonnegative and summed up to one. As pointed out in [1], there is an alternative for viewing the deformation of nonrigid objects, from the time domain. Instead of approximating shape in each frame with a linear combination of shape bases, the assumption that the trajectory of each 3D point across all frames is a linear combination of trajectory bases can be adopted. Akhter et al. [1] proved the equivalence between the two representations for nonrigid deformation. If instantaneous shape is a linear combination of K shape bases, then the trajectory of each 3D point is the combination of at most K trajectory bases. They reported that bases with K lowest frequencies for discrete cosine transform (DCT) produce a good approximation to the trajectory shape bases. In this paper, taking the time domain into consideration, we derive a linear relation between the 2D trajectory and 3D trajectory bases for orthographic cameras and propose a method to automatically determine the trajectory bases depending on the given data.

3   Trajectory Subspace Optimizing and 3D Trajectory Approximation

The projected coordinates of point p in frame f is a 2×1 vector denoted by $\mathbf{x}_p^f$, with $p = 1, \cdots, P$ and $f = 1, \cdots F$ with P, F the number for points and frames respectively. Under the orthographic camera model, projection from 3D point to 2D is shown as bellow:

$$\mathbf{x}_p^f = \mathbf{R}^f \mathbf{X}_p^f + \mathbf{b}^f \tag{1}$$

$\mathbf{X}_p^f$ is the corresponding 3D coordinate of point p in frame f, recorded as 3×1 vector; $\mathbf{R}^f$ is a matrix which contains the first two rows of rotation matrix with elements denoted as $\mathbf{R}_{ij}^f$, $i = 1, 2; j = 1, 2, 3$. Through the paper, i is used for indexing 2D point, and j for 3D. $\mathbf{b}^f$ is the displacement, which is usually assigned the average value of $\mathbf{x}_p^f$ across all points. For convenience, all points $\mathbf{x}_p^f$ are centered by subtracting $\mathbf{b}^f$ in the following sections. With centered $\mathbf{x}_p^f$, $\mathbf{R}^f$ can be solved by SVD decomposition and a subsequent corrective step by metric updating as shown in [1,16,3]. Here we take method proposed by Akhter et al. [1] for calculating . For deformation in nonrigid structure from motion, it is usually modeled in shape domain. For a 3D nonrigid object, its instantaneous shape $\mathbf{S}_f$ in frame f is usually expressed as a linear combination of a group of shape bases shown in bellow.

$$\mathbf{S}^f = \begin{bmatrix} \mathbf{X}_1^f & \cdots & \mathbf{X}_P^f \end{bmatrix} = \sum_{i=1}^{K} \alpha_k^f \mathbf{B}_k \tag{2}$$

where $\mathbf{B}_k$, a $3 \times P$ matrix, is the shape basis fixed across all frames, with α_k^f the coefficient; K the number of shape bases. Coefficients $\{\alpha_k^f\}$ change with frames.

As pointed out in [1], non-rigidity can also be modeled in time domain; correspondingly, a similar linear relationship exists with the same number of bases called trajectory bases. Let $\mathbf{T}_p = [\mathbf{T}_{p1}, \mathbf{T}_{p2}, \mathbf{T}_{p3}]$ denote the 3D trajectory, $\mathbf{T}_{pj}$ a column vector by packing the jth coordinates of all frames. Borrowing the linear relation in shape domain, it can be written as follow:

$$\mathbf{T}_{pj} = \left[\sum_{k=1}^{K} \alpha_k^1 \mathbf{B}_{k,jp}, \cdots, \sum_{k=1}^{K} \alpha_k^F \mathbf{B}_{k,jp} \right]^T \tag{3}$$

where $\mathbf{B}_{k,jp}$ is the element of jth row and pth column in shape basis matrix $\mathbf{B}_k$. Let $\mathbf{\Lambda}$ a $F \times K$ matrix with $\mathbf{\Lambda}_{fk} \overset{\Delta}{=} \alpha_k^f$, (3) can then be written as follows.

$$\mathbf{T}_{pj} = \mathbf{\Lambda} \left[\mathbf{B}_{1,jp}, \cdots, \mathbf{B}_{K,jp} \right]^T \tag{4}$$

where $\mathbf{T}_{p1}, \mathbf{T}_{p2}, \mathbf{T}_{p3}$ give point p's trajectory in first, second, and third coordinate respectively. $\mathbf{\Lambda}$ records all the shape coefficients corresponding to the shape bases $\{\mathbf{B}_k | k = 1, \ldots, K\}$. When trajectory space used, each column in matrix $\mathbf{\Lambda}$ can be viewed as a trajectory basis in 3D space while $[\mathbf{B}_{1,jp}, \cdots, \mathbf{B}_{K,jp}]^T$ are the corresponding coefficients. The dual relation is first reported in [1].

Since for any matrix, rank of row vectors is equal to that of the column vectors. The rank of $\mathbf{\Lambda}$ is at most K; reflected in the trajectory space, it means there are at most K bases. For simplicity, we denote K bases as column vectors $\mathbf{\Lambda}_1, \cdots, \mathbf{\Lambda}_K$; then the trajectory is the linear combination of the bases in non-degenerated case as follow.

$$\mathbf{T}_{pj} = \sum_{k=1}^{K} \beta_{pj,k} \mathbf{\Lambda}_k, \tag{5}$$

$\beta_{pj,k}$ give the weight of trajectory basis k for point p's jth coordinate.

In [1], Akhter et al. used discrete cosine transform (DCT) for interpolating trajectories; and achieved significant improvements in the factorization of nonrigid structure from motion. As pointed in their paper, they tried several other groups of bases; among these bases, DCT bases outperformed others. However, using DCT bases is independent of the given data, optimizing for the best trajectory bases is still an unsolved problem.

To find proper trajectory bases from data, we proposed a EM-like algorithm that recasts the task of finding the proper trajectory bases as a subspace fitting problem. For convenience, the trajectory in 2D space is recorded as $\mathbf{u}_{pi}$ obeying the same rule as $\mathbf{T}_{pj}$ except that i can only takes value from $\{1, 2\}$. In the rigid case, only the camera motion is involved which makes $\mathbf{u}_{pi}$ in a space spanned by the camera motion vectors. However, for the nonrigid case, the situation is complicated by the fact that the camera motion and the motion led by deformation are entangled together. By expanding (1), we have:

$$\mathbf{x}_{pi}^f = \mathbf{R}_{i1}^f \mathbf{X}_{p1}^f + \mathbf{R}_{i2}^f \mathbf{X}_{p2}^f + \mathbf{R}_{i3}^f \mathbf{X}_{p3}^f. \tag{6}$$

Given $\mathbf{M}_{ij} = \mathrm{diag}\left(\left[\mathbf{R}_{ij}^1, \cdots, \mathbf{R}_{ij}^F\right]\right)$, (6) can be expressed as:

$$\mathbf{u}_{pi} = \sum_{j=1}^{3} \mathbf{M}_{ij}\mathbf{T}_{pj} = \sum_{j=1}^{3} \mathbf{M}_{ij}\left(\sum_{k=1}^{K} \beta_{pj,k}\mathbf{\Lambda}_k\right). \tag{7}$$

Exchange the summation order, (7) changes to:

$$\mathbf{u}_{pi} = \sum_{k=1}^{K}\sum_{j=1}^{3} \beta_{pj,k}\left(\mathbf{M}_{ij}\mathbf{\Lambda}_k\right). \tag{8}$$

The upper equation helps us reach a similar conclusion as in [4]; $\left\{\mathbf{u}_j^p\right\}$ are constrained to the subspace spanned by $\{\mathbf{M}_{ij}\mathbf{\Lambda}_k\}$. Since that $\beta_{pj,k}$ is invariant for both $i=1$ and $i=2$, here we pack $\mathbf{u}_{p1}$ and $\mathbf{u}_{p2}$ together into a $2F \times 1$ vector $\mathbf{u}_p$. At the same time, $\mathbf{M}_{ij}$ is packed as:

$$\mathbf{M}_j = \begin{bmatrix} \mathbf{M}_{1j} \\ \mathbf{M}_{2j} \end{bmatrix}, \tag{9}$$

then equation for trajectory is re-casted as follows

$$\mathbf{u}_p = \sum_{k=1}^{K}\sum_{j=1}^{3} \beta_{pj,k}\left(\mathbf{M}_j\mathbf{\Lambda}_k\right) \tag{10}$$

With the above formula, finding proper trajectory bases is converted into finding a group of linearly independent bases $\mathbf{\Lambda}_k$ such that $\mathbf{M}_j\mathbf{\Lambda}_k$ can properly form the bases for $\mathbf{u}_p$. Here, we propose an approximation method for finding the proper trajectory bases. Given vector $\mathbf{v} \in \mathcal{R}^{F\times1}$, the projected component of $\mathbf{u}_p$ in the direction of $\mathbf{M}_j\mathbf{v}$ is $\mathbf{u}_p^T\mathbf{M}_j\mathbf{v}$, the corresponding energy is given in (11).

$$\left(\mathbf{u}_p^T\mathbf{M}_j\mathbf{v}\right)^2 = \mathbf{v}^T\left(\mathbf{M}_j^T\mathbf{u}_p\mathbf{u}_p^T\mathbf{M}_j\right)\mathbf{v} \tag{11}$$

If $\mathbf{v}$ belongs to space spanned by $\{\mathbf{\Lambda}_k\}$, then it is reasonable to assume that energy along the direction is large. With the assumption, finding trajectory bases is re-casted as finding direction such that energy of the trajectory along this direction is maximized.

$$\operatorname*{arg\,max}_{\|\mathbf{v}\|=1}\sum_{j,p}\mathbf{v}^T\left(\mathbf{M}_j^T\mathbf{u}_p\mathbf{u}_p^T\mathbf{M}_j\right)\mathbf{v} \tag{12}$$

Maximum value of (12) corresponds to the maximum eigenvalue whose corresponding eigenvector is $\mathbf{v}$.

Eigenvectors with maximum eigenvalues give us a good start point for finding optimal trajectory bases. In practice, an iterative way is then implemented for refining the bases which consists refining trajectory bases with fixed coefficients and optimizing coefficients with trajectory bases.

First, given the trajectory bases, coefficients $\{\beta_{pj,k}\}$ are optimized in a least square manner by minimizing the (13) where $\|\cdot\|$ measures the Euclidean distance.

$$\arg\min_{\beta_{pj,k}} \sum_p \left\| \mathbf{u}_p - \sum_{k=1}^{K}\sum_{j=1}^{3} \beta_{pj,k}\left(\mathbf{M}_j\boldsymbol{\Lambda}_k\right) \right\|^2 \tag{13}$$

With coefficients $\beta_{pj,k}$ calculated, the corresponding trajectory bases can be refined through optimizing $\{\boldsymbol{\Lambda_k}\}$ with orthonormal constraints posed.

$$\arg\min_{\boldsymbol{\Lambda}_k} \sum_p \left\| \mathbf{u}_p - \sum_{k=1}^{K}\sum_{j=1}^{3} \beta_{pj,k}\left(\mathbf{M}_j\boldsymbol{\Lambda}_k\right) \right\|^2$$
$$\text{s.t. } \forall k_1 \neq k_2 \quad \boldsymbol{\Lambda_{k_1}^T}\boldsymbol{\Lambda_{k_2}} = \mathbf{0} \tag{14}$$
$$\forall k \quad \|\boldsymbol{\Lambda_k}\| = \mathbf{1}$$

The iterative process gives a EM-like algorithm which can refine the trajectory bases and corresponding coefficients. With optimized coefficients and bases, $\hat{\mathbf{X}}_p^f$ for 3D object across all frames can be computed by linear combination. The whole process for the proposed algorithm is summarized in Fig.1.

1: given $\mathbf{x}_p^f$, and K
2: construct the matrix Γ with

$$\Gamma = \begin{bmatrix} \mathbf{x}_1^1 & \cdots & \mathbf{x}_P^1 \\ \vdots & \ddots & \vdots \\ \mathbf{x}_1^1 & \cdots & \mathbf{x}_P^F \end{bmatrix} \tag{15}$$

3: using SVD to get $\Gamma = \mathbf{UV}$
4: Given $\mathbf{U}$ matrix of $2F \times n$ with n the rank of Γ, the first three columns $\mathbf{Q}_{n\times 3}$ of an orthonormal matrix is optimized for finding $\mathbf{R}^f$, with the following relations:

$$\begin{cases} \mathbf{R}_{2i-1}^f = \mathbf{U}_{2i-1,\cdot} \cdot \mathbf{Q} \\ \mathbf{R}_{2i}^f = \mathbf{U}_{2i,\cdot} \cdot \mathbf{Q} \\ \|\mathbf{R_{2i}^f}\| = 1 \quad \|\mathbf{R_{2i-1}^f}\| = 1 \\ \mathbf{R_{2i}^f}\mathbf{R_{2i-1}^{fT}} = \mathbf{0} \\ \mathbf{Q^T Q} = \mathbf{I_{3\times 3}} \end{cases}$$

5: pack $\mathbf{M}_j$ and $\mathbf{u}_p$
6: initialize $\left\{\boldsymbol{\Lambda_k^{(0)}}\right\}$ with (12)
7: **repeat**
8:     optimize (13) for $\beta_{pj,k}$
9:     optimize (14) for $\{\boldsymbol{\Lambda_k}\}$
10: **until** conditions are satisfied
11: output $\mathbf{R}^f$ and 3D trajectory $\mathbf{T}_{pj}$ computed from 5

Fig. 1. Algorithm for candidates voting and iterative refinement

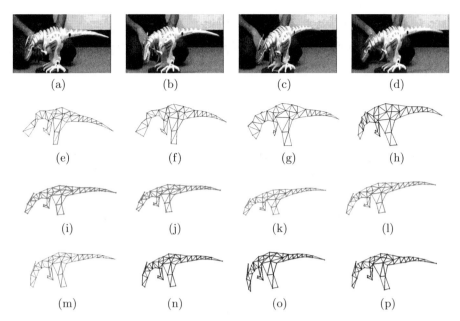

Fig. 2. Comparison results of methods for randomly selected four frames of dinosaur data. 2(a),2(b),2(c),2(d) are images from dinosaur data with frame number 49,84,143,191, 2(e),2(f),2(g),2(h) are the results generated by using method proposed by Akhter et al., 2(i),2(j),2(k),2(l)Torresani et al.s method and 2(m),2(n),2(o),2(p) our method, respectively.

4   Experiments and Evaluation

To demonstrate the effectiveness of the proposed method, experimental comparisons with [1] and [11] are performed on both the synthetic and real data. For Akhter et al.s method, the number of shape bases is set to be the same with ours which is listed in Table 1. For Torresani et al.s method [11], code supplied by the authors is used, and is tuned for the best performance. Our experiments show that for large number of shape bases, Torresani et al.s method is easy to run into error, thus the parameters are manually tuned as to give the best performance. For comparison, the mean camera motion error and the mean 3D geometry error [1] are adopted where is the average Frobenius difference between original rotations and estimated rotations matrix, and is the average distance between original 3D points and aligned reconstructed points across frames.

For the synthetic data, a sequence with $F = 200$ frames and $P = 50$ points is generated. The points are generated from randomly linear combining $K = 10$ randomly generated shape bases. For the real data, the nonrigid shape data from [1] is used for experiments where the rotation matrix is randomly generated.

Comparing results are reported in Table I, where for each data, the first column gives the mean rotation error E_R, and second the mean shape error E_S. Besides the quantitative comparisons, Fig.2 also gives reconstructed geometry of

Fig. 3. 3(a),3(b),3(c),3(d),3(e),3(f),3(g),3(h),3(i) are the frames from dancer sequence with frame number $30, 43, 88, 130, 148, 194, 225, 230, 234$. The red dot circles give the original location of the tracked points, while the green squares give the reprojected locations from the reconstructed camera parameters and 3D shape.

randomly selected four frames from the dinosaur data. Some reprojected results on dancer sequences can also be find in fig3.

According to the reported evaluations, compared to the other two methods, ours achieves a stable result for the nonrigid structure from motion. For method

Table 1. Comparison Results of Different Methods on Synthetic and Real Data

	Shark $(K=2)$		Dinosaur $(K=12)$		pickup $(K=12)$		Cubes $(K=2)$		Synthetic $(K=10)$	
	E_R	E_S	E_R	E_S	E_R	E_S	E_R	E_S	E_R	E_S
Akhter et al.'s	**1.029**	1.816	0.897	0.782	**0.027**	0.099	**0.009**	0.138	**1.493**	3.056
Torresani et al.'s	1.064	2.255	**0.800**	0.887	0.443	0.706	0.348	1.212	N/A	N/A
Our Method	**1.029**	**1.645**	0.896	**0.736**	**0.027**	**0.032**	**0.009**	**0.012**	**1.493**	**0.759**

[1], the trajectory bases are selected in a random way which cannot always capture the deforming structure of nonrigid objects, thus for some dataset, it cannot perform very well which can be seen from the synthetic data. The DCT basis used by Akhter et al. can only capture the smooth and slowly changed deformation led by nonrigid deformation, thus it fails in the cases where the nonrigid deformation changes rapidly. In the paper, trajectory bases are selected data-dependently, compared to DCT bases, which are pre-computed without looking at the data.

5   Conclusion

In nonrigid structure from motion, the nonrigid deformation of a point is entangled with the camera motion. Here we propose a method to disentangle these two motions, and automatically search for the proper trajectory bases for the nonrigid deformation. For the purpose, a linear relation between 2D trajectory and 3D trajectory is explicitly derived, then used for guiding the search of the trajectory bases in a data-dependent way. With trajectory bases, trajectory coefficients for each point are calculated with least square fitting. Results show that our method achieves a better reconstruction performance than former methods, and successfully capture the deformation of nonrigid objects.

References

1. Akhter, I., Sheikh, Y.A., Khan, S., Kanade, T.: Nonrigid structure from motion in trajectory space. In: Neural Information Processing Systems 2008 (December 2008)
2. Brand, W.: Morphable 3d models from video. In: Proceedings of the 2001 IEEE Computer Society Conference on Computer Vision and Pattern Recognition, CVPR 2001, pp. II–456–II–463, vol. 2 (2001)
3. Bregler, C., Hertzmann, A., Biermann, H.: Recovering non-rigid 3d shape from image streams, pp. 690–696 (2000)
4. Bue, A.D., Smeraldi, F., de Agapito, L.: Non-rigid structure from motion using ranklet-based tracking and non-linear optimization. Image Vision Comput. 25(3), 297–310 (2007)
5. Kanatani, K., Sugaya, Y.: Factorization without factorization: a complete recipe. Mem. Fac. Eng. Okayama Univ. 38, 61–72 (2004)

6. Olsen, S.I., Bartoli, A.: Implicit non-rigid structure-from-motion with priors. Journal of Mathematical Imaging and Vision 31(2), 233–244 (2008)
7. Poelman, C.J., Kanade, T.: A paraperspective factorization method for shape and motion recovery. IEEE Trans. Pattern Anal. Mach. Intell. 19(3), 206–218 (1997)
8. Rabaud, V., Belongie, S.: Re-thinking non-rigid structure from motion. In: IEEE Conference on Computer Vision and Pattern Recognition, CVPR 2008, pp. 1–8 (23-28, 2008)
9. Rosin, P.L., Marshall, A.D. (eds.): PNon-rigid 3D factorization for projective reconstruction. British Machine Vision Association (2005)
10. Tomasi, C., Kanade, T.: Shape and motion from image streams under orthography: a factorization method. International Journal of Computer Vision 9(2), 137–154 (1992)
11. Torresani, L., Hertzmann, A., Bregler, C.: Learning non-rigid 3d shape from 2d motion. In: Thrun, S., Saul, L., Schölkopf, B. (eds.) Advances in Neural Information Processing Systems, vol. 16. MIT Press, Cambridge (2004)
12. Torresani, L., Hertzmann, A., Bregler, C.: Nonrigid structure-from-motion: Estimating shape and motion with hierarchical priors. IEEE Trans. Pattern Anal. Mach. Intell. 30(5), 878–892 (2008)
13. Triggs, B.: Factorization methods for projective structure and motion. In: Proceedings of IEEE Computer Society Conference on Computer Vision and Pattern Recognition, CVPR 1996, pp. 845–851 (18-20, 1996)
14. Vogler, C., Li, Z., Kanaujia, A., Goldenstein, S., Metaxas, D.: The best of both worlds: Combining 3d deformable models with active shape models. In: IEEE 11th International Conference on Computer Vision, ICCV 2007, pp. 1–7 (14-21, 2007)
15. Wang, G., Wu, Q.M.J.: Stratification approach for 3-d euclidean reconstruction of nonrigid objects from uncalibrated image sequences. IEEE Transactions on Systems, Man, and Cybernetics, Part B 38(1), 90–101 (2008)
16. Xiao, J., Chai, J., Kanade, T.: A closed-form solution to non-rigid shape and motion recovery. International Journal of Computer Vision 67(2), 233–246 (2006)
17. Xiao, J., Kanade, T.: Uncalibrated perspective reconstruction of deformable structures. In: Tenth IEEE International Conference on Computer Vision, ICCV 2005, vol. 2, pp. 1075–1082 (17-21, 2005)

Fast Depth Saliency from Stereo for Region-Based Artificial Visual Attention

Muhammad Zaheer Aziz and Bärbel Mertsching

GET LAB, Universität Paderborn, 33098 Paderborn, Germany
{last name}@upb.de
http://getwww.uni-paderborn.de

Abstract. Depth is an important feature channel for natural vision organisms that helps in focusing attention on important locations of the viewed scene. Artificial visual attention systems require a fast estimation of depth to construct a saliency map based upon distance from the vision system. Recent studies on depth perception in biological vision indicate that disparity is computed using object detection in the brain. The proposed method exploits these studies and determines the shift that objects go through in the stereo frames using data regarding their borders. This enables efficient creation of depth saliency map for artificial visual attention. Results of the proposed model have shown success in selecting those locations from stereo scenes that are salient for human perception in terms of depth.

1 Introduction

Depth cue from stereo vision plays an important role in visual attention mechanism of primates [1]. There have been several efforts to include the depth channel into computational attention models for making artificial visual attention biologically plausible. For example [2] uses disparity from video image sequence, [3] extracts disparity from stereo, and [4] creates depth map from laser range scanner for finding depth saliency. Although depth saliency is important for obstacle avoidance and self survival of artificial vision systems, a major problem in using depth as a feature channel is the computation time needed to process it. This paper presents a fast depth estimation method inspired from natural stereo processing in human/animal brain able to quickly generate a saliency map sufficient for pre-attention stage. The main objective of this work is to identify depth-wise salient locations in a given scene for focusing covert or overt attention. Detailed, computationally heavy, depth analysis could be restricted to these selected locations. Such strategy is commonly applied by biological vision systems for optimized utilization of resources.

Studies of human brain done through functional magnetic resonance imaging (fMRI), e.g. those presented in [5] and [6], show that the neurons in V3A area of visual cortex are involved in depth amplitude perception using stereo input. On the other hand, it has been established in [7] that V2 part of the visual cortex has relation to object recognition. Experiments with fMRI reported in [8]

J. Blanc-Talon et al. (Eds.): ACIVS 2010, Part I, LNCS 6474, pp. 367–378, 2010.

conclude that the border ownership selectivity is performed in V2 area whereas this selection results into figure-ground segregation. Since V3A receives input from V2, there is a clear indication of the role of object detection in stereo-based depth perception.

Evidence of object-based depth perception in human vision can also be found in literature on psychology. The work in [9] suggests that intrinsic borders of viewed objects help in processing depth. These contours are distinguished in a relatively early stage of visual processing and are useful for object segmentation. The experiments presented in [10] lead to the inference that depth segregation is accomplished after accessing memories of objects.

Based upon the above mentioned role of object detection in finding disparity in stereo input, the depth estimation in the proposed methodology is done by approximating the magnitude of object shifts in the pair of stereo frames. Since a reliable (multicolored) object segregation is a long standing problem for computer vision, homogeneously colored regions are taken as simulation of objects in the current status of the model.

The next section gathers some references regarding saliency with respect to depth and efforts on computation of region-based disparity. Section 3 describes the proposed methodology, section 4 demonstrates some samples from output of the proposed system, section 5 evaluates the results, and section 6 concludes the paper.

2   Related Literature

Saliency of objects at a nearer distance from the vision system is usually high. On the other hand, a sudden change of depth may also attract visual attention. Report on psychophysical experiments showing coding of greater depth at early stages of human vision processing can be seen in [11]. The conclusion that the depth contrast effect decreases with distance in [12] also indicates that near objects offer high visual saliency. The study presented in [13] establishes a clear relation between depth contrast and visual attention showing that high disparity contrast attract human attention first. The depth saliency map from stereo camera input computed by [3] gives high conspicuity to near objects.

The proposed method of depth estimation uses segmented regions in its procedure; hence a brief overview of other region-based stereo processing algorithms is provided here for comparison with the state-of-the-art. The method proposed in [14] uses an over-segmentation approach with an assumption that all pixels on a segment possess the same depth. The technique consists of heavy computational steps with iterative processing leading to reasonably good disparity output with a minimum processing time of 90 seconds for the 0.11 mega pixel (Tsukuba) image on a 3.2 GHz PC. The algorithm in [15] finds the initial disparity using adaptive correlation window matching, estimates the disparity parameters based upon plane fitting, and optimizes these parameters using cooperative optimization. The processing time reported for this method is 20 seconds for the Tsukuba image on a 1.6 GHz machine. The method in [16] uses segments from the reference image in a local window-based matching with the target image. A set of disparity planes is extracted and then an optimization process computes the final disparity of each plane. They have recorded a minimum computation time of 14 seconds on a 64 bit 2.21 GHz computer.

The work presented in [17] segments the input and computes the initial matching cost using contrast context histogram descriptors. Then it uses a two-pass weighted cost aggregation with segmentation-based adaptive support weight. The study presented in [18] establishes that, in region-based stereo correspondence, dependence upon proximity of only color is prone to errors. Although counting on region shape can improve the accuracy but it still remains non-robust. The basic reason is that the corresponding regions in both frames always suffer from some differences because of overlapping borders, varying view perspective, and segmentation errors.

Work on depth from stereo by members of our research group includes the method involving cost relaxation with occlusion detection [19][20], correspondence using features of segmented regions [21], and scan-line segment based algorithm for motion analysis [22].

3   Region-Based Depth Saliency

The efforts presented in this paper aim to estimate object shifts that occur from the right frame into the left one. Difference of the two overlapped frames recorded into an image clearly shows traces of these shifts in form of line strips. Depth activity at object borders can be quickly estimated by allocating these strips to relevant objects and finding lengths of these strips along epipolar lines. The depth cue obtained in such a way is sufficient for pre-attention saliency with respect to depth. Detailed perception of depth for selected objects can be done in post-attention stage.

Three preprocessing steps are performed before computation of depth saliency from the given stereo pair. Firstly, the left frame is clipped at its left side and the right one is clipped at its right side proportional to the inter-axial separation of cameras. This helps to avoid processing of the areas consisting of totally non-matching objects. Secondly, both clipped images, $I^l(x,y)$ and $I^r(x,y)$, are smoothed by convolution with a 3×3 averaging mask. Thirdly, the reference image (the right image $I^r(x,y)$) is segmented using a simple color segmentation routine based upon seed-to-neighbor distances measured in hue, saturation, and intensity (HSI) color space. Output of this process is a list $\Re$ consisting of regions R_i^r, $1 \leq i \leq n$ and a label image $L(x,y)$ such that

$$L(x,y) = i \; \forall \; (x,y) \; \in \; R_i^r \tag{1}$$

The first step in depth saliency processing is production of a difference image $\Delta(x,y)$. Since minor differences of color need to be noticed, e.g. difference between shades on the same object appearing because of curvature or faces in different directions, $\Delta(x,y)$ is computed using the red, green, and blue (r,g,b) color channels of $I^l(x,y)$ and $I^r(x,y)$ as follows

$$\Delta(x,y) = \begin{cases} L(x,y) & \text{for } max\left(|I^l_c(x,y) - I^r_c(x,y)| \;\forall\; c \in \{r,g,b\}\right) > \tau \\ 0 & \text{otherwise} \end{cases} \tag{2}$$

Where $I^l_c(x,y)$ and $I^r_c(x,y)$ represent the color components (red, green, and blue) of the concerned pixel from left and right input respectively. τ is the threshold for color-component similarity. The advantage of storing the region labels $L(x,y)$ in $\Delta(x,y)$ is border preservation of regions/objects involved in disparity. The pixels showing no depth activity get filtered out in this process.

The length of horizontal strips containing the same label in each row of $\Delta(x,y)$ provide clue about the magnitudes of shifts that the objects have gone through at that vertical position. One problem with these strips is that the thin regions produce their imprint two times in $\Delta(x,y)$ as they cause difference below them at both of their distinct occurrences in $I^l(x,y)$ and $I^r(x,y)$. In order to solve this problem the proposed method selects only those strips that belong to the objects of the reference frame $I^r(x,y)$ and go through a rightward shift in $I^l(x,y)$. Such strips can be identified by checking whether they are aligned to border of some R^r_i. Testing alignment of the difference strips with the left border of the considered R^r_i is sufficient to identify strips that remain inside R^r_i. Having $B^r_i(x_l, y_l)$ as the left-side border points of region R^r_i and $E(x,y)$ as the map of edge points of difference strips in $\Delta(x,y)$ the ratio of strips aligned to $B^r_i(x_l, y_l)$ is computed as

$$\rho^b_i = \frac{\sum \left(B^r_i(x_l, y_l) E(x_l, y_l)\right) \;\forall(x_l, y_l) \in B^r_i(x_l, y_l)}{H(R^r_i)} \tag{3}$$

where $H(R^r_i)$ is the height of R^r_i. Only vertical edges are stored into $E(x,y)$ keeping in view the condition of epipolarity. Hence

$$E(x,y) = \begin{cases} 0 & \text{for } \Delta(x-1,y) = \Delta(x,y) \\ 1 & \text{otherwise} \end{cases} \tag{4}$$

Now the difference strips aligned to each region R^r_i are gathered into a map $S(x,y)$ as follows:

$$S(x,y) = \begin{cases} \Delta(x,y) & \forall(x,y) \in R^r_i \text{ s.t. } \rho^b_i > \epsilon \text{ and } \Delta(x,y) = i \\ 0 & \text{otherwise} \end{cases} \tag{5}$$

There are two ways in which $S(x,y)$ could be used to provide an estimate of object shifts. Length of these strips could either be measured in its current status, i.e. lengths of similarly labeled strips, or these strips could be joined together and the merged strips could be considered as the amount of shift. The first option is prone to errors because there can be consecutive thin regions involved in an area where a large shift took place, for example regions occluded in one frame that appear in the other. Hence, lower depth activity could be falsely recorded if length measurement is stopped at borders of these regions. The second option can lead to falsely elongated shift estimation when strips of two adjacent regions touch each other. The proposed method uses the second option but splits the strips at potential depth borders to minimize error. For this purpose those $B_i^r(x_l, y_l)$ are chosen whose R_i^r are overlapped by a moderate amount of difference strips from $S(x, y)$ because regions highly or fully overlapped by difference strips have a high probability of being occluded regions. The magnitude of overlap for a region R_i^r with difference strips is computed as

$$\rho_i^o = \frac{\sum \Delta'(x, y) \ \forall (x, y) \in R_i^r}{A(R_i^r)} \tag{6}$$

where $\Delta'(x, y)$ is the occupancy map of $\Delta(x, y)$, i.e $\Delta'(x, y) = 1$ when $\Delta(x, y) > 0$, and $A(R_i^r)$ extracts the area under the given region. The difference strips are broken at borders of those R_i^r that have $\delta_1 \le \rho_i^o \le \delta_2$, where δ_1 and δ_2 are lower and upper thresholds for ρ_i^o. Hence

$$S(x, y) = 0 \ \forall (x, y) \in B_i^r(x_l, y_l) \ \text{s.t.} \ \delta_1 \le \rho_i^o \le \delta_2 \tag{7}$$

The contiguous strips in each row of $S(x, y)$ are now merged together and each point on the strip is replaced by the length of the merged strip. In its final status $S(x, y)$ serves as a raster depth saliency map in which high intensity reflects greater depth contrast at the respective location. This map is segmented using gray-scale region growing to cluster together two-dimensional contiguous regions with similar depth saliency. Focus of attention is diverted to these regions in order of high saliency. Promising results were obtained from implementation of the proposed method. The next section presents the intermediate as well as the final output.

4   Results

Figure 1 demonstrates the intermediate output of the proposed method applied on the Tsukuba image pair (http: //bj .middlebury .edu/ ˜schar /stereo /data /tsukuba/) at different stages. Subfigure (a) presents the right frame from the stereo pair and subfigure (b) shows results of the process summarized in equations 1 and 2. Contiguous strips along epipolar lines were merged together and their pixels were replaced with the magnitude of the strip lengths to generate the output shown here. Subfigure (c) shows the output after processing with equation 5. It may be noted that double imprints of the lamp arms (right middle of image) are eliminated here. Up to this step some difference strips that belong to neighboring objects remain joined together, e.g. the strip in the middle of the subfigure (c) where the left corner of the lamp overlaps the statue. Such strips are broken at depth borders determined by the process described in equation 7. The considered border pixels are shown in subfigure (d). The result after breaking the difference strips by equation 7, merging the contiguous epipolar strips, and replacing the strip pixels with the length of strips is shown in subfigure (e). The output of segmenting together the contiguous strips with similar lengths

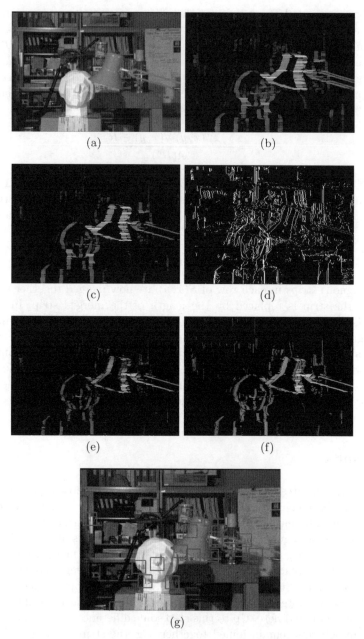

Fig. 1. (a) Right frame of a sample stereo pair. (b) Raw difference image after replacing horizontal strips with their lengths. (c) Difference strips aligned to objects in right input frame. (d) Borders of regions offering depth contrast (e) Difference strips splitted at depth contrast borders. (f) Contiguous difference strips with similar depth activity segmented together. (g) Fixations of the attention system based upon the depth saliency.

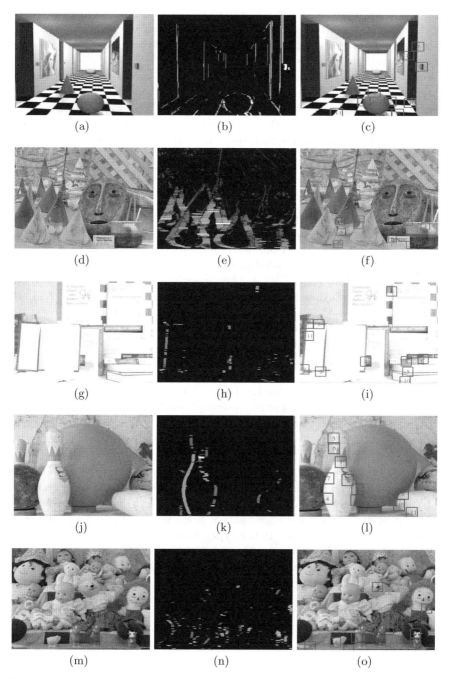

Fig. 2. Output of depth saliency detection and attention fixations on some samples of stereo images. Right frames of the stereo pairs are shown in the first column, depth saliency maps in the second column, and attended locations in the third.

is shown in subfigure (f) where brightness of the region reflects the amount of depth saliency. The attention system fixates on the salient locations in order of high to low saliency magnitude. Subfigure (g) shows results of these attention fixations using the obtained depth map.

Figure 2 demonstrates depth saliency maps and locations attended by the system for some other samples of stereo data used in experimentation. It is observable that the fixations of the proposed attention mechanism fall mostly on those locations that are either near to the viewer (camera) or offer a high depth contrast. A quantitative evaluation of the system performance is presented in the next section.

5   Evaluation

Figure 3 presents the processing time taken by the proposed method recorded against image resolution and number of segmented regions present in the right frame using a large selection from different datasets available at Middlebury resource [23]. The images were scaled to same resolution for evaluating time against the number of regions (figure 3(b)). The algorithm was executed on a 3.33 GHz CPU to see its performance on current hardware facilities. An older 1.14 GHz machine was also used in the experiments in order to allow a comparison with previously available fast stereo algorithms. It may be noted that the proposed method computes depth saliency in less than 300 ms for the 0.11 mega pixel image even on the 1.14 GHz CPU. The minimum reported time for the same image by contemporary methods is 14 seconds on a 2.21 GHz machine (details in section 2). Hence a clear edge has been achieved in computational speed.

In order to evaluate success of the proposed system in determining depth-wise salient locations its foci of attention were compared with depth saliency marked by human subjects. Since it is difficult to train human subjects to concentrate only on depth feature in eye-tracking experiments; the gray-level contrast in the ground truth disparity maps was used to collect data on depth saliency in perspective of human vision. The subjects was asked to mark areas that seem to be important in terms of depth after training them to use intensity as an indication of depth. Figure 4 shows salient areas marked by human subjects on one of the sample images used in the experiments.

Having the manually marked salient locations as benchmark; we evaluate the results of our model in terms of detection efficiency ε^d and detection capability σ^d. ε^d measures the ability of a system to fixate on all salient locations in minimum number of attempts. If there are N_s salient locations/objects in a given scene then a highly efficient system should be able to detect all of them in N_s fixations. Hence, a system will be allowed to make only N_s attempts of attention and the number of correctly detected salient objects within this limit will be counted as N_d. Now

$$\varepsilon^d = \frac{N_d}{N_s} \tag{8}$$

Obviously, $0 \le \varepsilon^d \le 1$. It is quite common that the attention models are not able to detect all N_s salient objects within N_s attempts. For such situations we

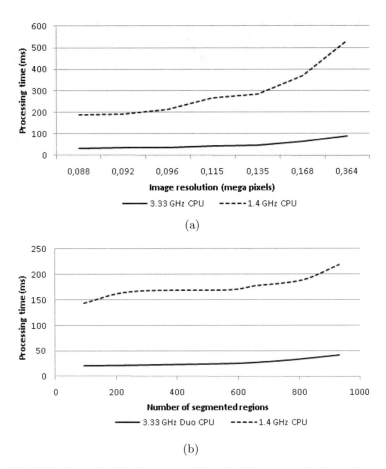

Fig. 3. (a) CPU time taken by the proposed method for processing input images with different resolutions. (b) Performance of the system against number of segmented regions in input images scaled to same resolution.

use the measure σ^d that allows the system to run for N_t attempts in order to provide an opportunity to fixate on all N_s salient objects in the given scene. N_t is the maximum number of fixations permissible in the application for which the attention model is being evaluated. The number of correctly found salient objects in these attempts is counted as N_f and the number of fixations attempts used are counted as N_a. The system is not allowed to go beyond N_t even if it could not mark some of the salient locations. It is obvious that $N_f \leq N_s \leq N_a \leq N_t$. Using readings for these values, the bottom-up detection capability σ^d is defined as

$$\sigma^d = \frac{N_f \left(N_t - (N_a - N_s) \right)}{N_s N_t} \tag{9}$$

The first factor (N_f/N_s) quantifies the capability of finding salient objects; a system able to find all salient objects of a given scene scores a 1 in this factor.

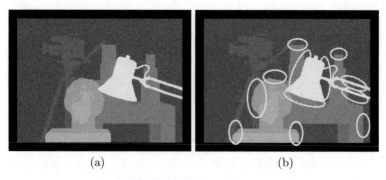

(a)   (b)

Fig. 4. (a) Ground-truth disparity map of a stereo sample shown in figure 1. (b) Depth-wise salient areas marked by human subjects.

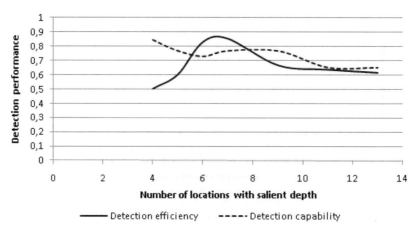

Fig. 5. (a) Evaluation of attention by the proposed model in terms detection efficiency ε^d and detection capability σ^d against number of salient locations marked by human subjects (N_s) in various stereo pairs

The second factor $((N_t - (N_a - N_s))/N_t)$ imposes a penalty on extra fixations taken by the model to cover the N_s salient objects. A system capable of fixating on all N_s locations within $N_a = N_s$ will score a 1 in this factor. Figure 5 summarizes results of evaluation experiments to determine the detection efficiency and capability of the proposed model against the manually marked (N_s) salient locations for various stereo pairs.

6   Conclusion

The method introduced in this paper is meant for quick detection of those locations in stereo scenes that contain high amount of depth saliency. A non-traditional approach was experimented as a milestone towards object-based stereo analysis similar to processing in the human/animal brain. In its current status, it obviously does not deliver a dense and perfect disparity map but the quality of results is sufficient to identify depth-wise salient locations. Evaluation of output has shown success of the proposed method in selecting locations important for human perception. Its significantly low computational complexity allows its use in visual attention systems that require coarse clues of feature contrasts to select foci of attention. Computationally heavy feature analysis can be confined to salient locations or objects selected by this pre-attention stage.

Contributions of this paper is two-fold. Firstly, a step has been taken towards the direction of biologically plausible stereo processing leading to object-based disparity computation. Object borders were used to estimate depth contrast as suggested in literature on natural vision, such as [8] and [9]. Secondly, output of this pre-attention step was utilized in an attention mechanism to determine locations salient with respect to depth . Avoiding the conventional correspondence searches has significantly reduced the computational complexity of the proposed model.

Future work in this direction may include creation of cyclopean view for each attended object for obtaining refined object disparity. Further depth information with fine details could be included by applying monocular depth cues, e.g. shape from shading, on the selected objects. Another advancement in making the artificial stereo vision according to the recent findings in biological vision would be to learn the structure of objects as 3D models. After a coarse analysis of depth and other visual features for an attended object the whole object model could be fitted there to make the depth perception fast and precise.

Acknowledgment

We gratefully acknowledge the funding of this work by the German Research Foundation (DFG) under grant Me 1289/12-1(AVRAM).

References

1. Wolfe, J.M., Horowitz, T.S.: What attributes guide the deployment of visual attention and how do they do it? Nature Reviews. Neuroscience 5, 495–501 (2004)
2. Zhang, Y., Jiang, G., Yu, M., Chen, K.: Stereoscopic visual attention model for 3d video. In: Boll, S., Tian, Q., Zhang, L., Zhang, Z., Chen, Y.-P.P. (eds.) MMM 2010. LNCS, vol. 5916, pp. 314–324. Springer, Heidelberg (2010)
3. Jang, Y.M., Ban, S.W., Lee, M.: Stereo saliency map considering affective factors in a dynamic environment. In: Ishikawa, M., Doya, K., Miyamoto, H., Yamakawa, T. (eds.) ICONIP 2007, Part II. LNCS, vol. 4985, pp. 1055–1064. Springer, Heidelberg (2008)
4. Frintrop, S., Rome, E., Nüchter, A., Surmann, H.: A bimodal laser-based attention system. Computer Vision and Image Understanding 100(1-2), 124–151 (2005)
5. Backus, B.T., Fleet, D.J., Parker, A.J., Heeger, D.J.: Human cortical activity correlates with stereoscopic depth perception. Journal of Neurophysiology 86, 2054–2068 (2001)

6. Georgieva, S., Peeters, R., Kolster, H., Todd, J.T., Orban, G.A.: The processing of three-dimensional shape from disparity in the human brain. Journal of Neuroscience 29(3), 727–742 (2009)

7. López-Aranda, M.F., López-Téllez, J.F., Navarro-Lobato, I., Masmudi-Martín, M., Gutiérrez, A., Khan, Z.U.: Role of layer 6 of v2 visual cortex in object-recognition memory. Science 325(5936), 87–89 (2009)

8. Fang, F., Boyaci, H., Kersten, D.: Border ownership selectivity in human early visual cortex and its modulation by attention. Journal of Neuroscience 29(2), 460–465 (2009)

9. Nakayama, K., Shimojo, S., Silverman, G.: Stereoscopic depth: its relation to image segmentation, grouping, and the recognition of occluded objects. Perception 18(1), 55–68 (1989)

10. Peterson, M.A.: Organization, segregation and object recognition. Intellectica 28(1), 37–53 (1999)

11. Mitsudo, H., Nakamizo, S., Ono, H.: Greater depth seen with phantom stereopsis is coded at the early stages of visual processing. Vision Research 45, 1365–1374 (2005)

12. van Ee, R., Erkelens, C.: Anisotropy in werner's binocular depth-contrast effect. Vision research 36, 2253–2262 (1996)

13. Jost, T., Ouerhani, N., Wartburg, R.v., Müri, R., Hügli, H.: Contribution of depth to visual attention: comparison of a computer model and human. In: Early Cognitive Vision Workshop, Isle of Skye, Scotland (2004)

14. Tagichi, Y., Wilburn, B., Zitnick, C.L.: Stereo reconstruction with mixed pixels using adaptive over-segmentation. In: CVPR 2008, Alaska, USA, pp. 1–8. IEEE, Los Alamitos (2008)

15. Wanng, Z.F., Zheng, Z.G.: A region based matching algorithm using cooperative optimization. In: CVPR 2008, Alaska, USA, pp. 1–8. IEEE, Los Alamitos (2008)

16. Klaus, A., Sormann, M., Karner, K.: Segment-based stereo matching using belief propagation and a self-adapting dissimilarity measure. In: ICPR 2006, pp. 15–18 (2006)

17. Liu, T., Zhang, P., Luo, L.: Dense stereo correspondence with contrast context histogram, segmentation-based two-pass aggregation and occlusion handling. In: Wada, T., Huang, F., Lin, S. (eds.) PSIVT 2009. LNCS, vol. 5414, pp. 449–461. Springer, Heidelberg (2009)

18. Tombari, F., Mattocia, S., Stefano, L.D.: Segmentation-based adaptive support for accurate stereo correspondence. In: Mery, D., Rueda, L. (eds.) PSIVT 2007. LNCS, vol. 4872, pp. 427–438. Springer, Heidelberg (2007)

19. Brockers, R., Hund, M., Mertsching, B.: A fast cost relaxation stereo algorithm with occlusion detection for mobile robot applications. In: VMV, pp. 47–53 (2004)

20. Brockers, R., Hund, M., Mertsching, B.: Stereo matching with occlusion detection using cost relaxation. In: ICIP, vol. (3), pp. 389–392 (2005)

21. Aziz, M.Z., Stemmer, R., Mertsching, B.: Region-based depth feature map for visual attention in autonomous mobile systems. In: AMS 2005, Stuttgart - Germany, Informatic Actuell, pp. 89–95. Springer, Heidelberg (2005)

22. Shafik, M.S.E.N., Mertsching, B.: Real-time scan-line segment based stereo vision for the estimation of biologically motivated classifier cells. In: Mertsching, B., Hund, M., Aziz, Z. (eds.) KI 2009. LNCS, vol. 5803, pp. 89–96. Springer, Heidelberg (2009)

23. Scharstein, D., Szeliski, R.: A taxonomy and evaluation of dense two-frame stereo correspondence algorithms. International Journal of Computer Vision 47, 7–42 (2001)

A Caustic Approach of Panoramic Image Analysis

Siyuan Zhang and Emmanuel Zenou

Université de Toulouse
Institut Supérieur de l'Aéronautique et de l'Espace
10 Avenue Edouard Belin, BP54032, 31055 Toulouse, France
{siyuan.zhang,emmanuel.zenou}@isae.fr
http://www.isae.fr

Abstract. In this article, the problem of blur in a panoramic image from a catadioptric camera is analyzed through the determination of the virtual image. This determination is done first with an approximative method, and second through the caustic approach. This leads us to a general caustic approach of panoramic image analysis, where equations of virtual images are given. Finally, we give some direct applications of our analysis, such as depth of field (blur) or image resolution.

Keywords: Catadioptric camera, Caustics, Panoramic image, Virtual image, Blur, Depth of Field.

1 Introduction

Catadioptric systems [1] offer many advantages in the field of computer vision. A catadioptric system is an optical system which is composed of a reflector element (mirror) and a refractive element (lens) [6]. The field of view is of 360° around the central axis of the mirror, which can be of many types [1] [2], as spherical, conical, parabolic, hyperbolic...

However, in some systems where the mirror and the camera are not well matched, especially using a small light camera, blur phenomenon occurs and leads to a deteriorated low-quality image. For a standard camera (a lens and a sensor), a real point is blur if it is not located between two planes, perpendicular to the optical axis, which define the depth of field. In a catadioptric system, virtual points -instead of real points- have to be in the depth of field of the camera to avoid blur. The distribution of all virtual points, called virtual image, is thus essential to be assessed to analyze blur -and other properties- in a panoramic image.

At first approximation (section 2), to any source point is associated a unique virtual point, defined by the intersection of two rays. This approximation is valid in practice, but in reality the image of a source point is a small curve. This curve is defined through the concept of caustic, whose geometric construction is exposed (section 3).

J. Blanc-Talon et al. (Eds.): ACIVS 2010, Part I, LNCS 6474, pp. 379–389, 2010.

Usually, in a catadioptric system, Single View Point (SVP) is a popular condition, useful for easy modeling and simulations, but it is not compulsory (and is also practically hard to follow). In most of the case [8] [10] [11] caustics are used to study non-SVP system properties (field of view, resolution, etc.) or camera calibration. Caustics are determined through the pinhole entrance pupil, which give one caustic to each studied mirror. Our approach is definitively different from already existing approaches. In this article, we associate caustics with virtual image (section 4).

Our catadioptric system (composed of a hyperbolic mirror and a small camera, called hypercatadioptric camera) is analyzed through the caustic approach to determine useful equations (section 4), which lead to applications (section 5) issued from our caustic analysis: depth of field, spatial resolution and image transformation.

2   First Approximation

For any optical system, one may define a source point (source of light), and an image point which is the image of the source point in a sensor (through an optical system, the lens). For any catadioptric system, one may add a virtual point, which can be considered as the real point if the mirror does not exist. The virtual point position usually depends on the camera position and the profile of the mirror.

Fig. 1-a shows the first approximation analysis. To the source point P_S is associated an image point P_I and a virtual point P_V. These two last points are defined from two special rays issued from the source point: the first ray is reflected on P_1 on the mirror surface, goes through the diaphragm D and the focus of the lens L, and is projected on the camera sensor; the second ray is reflected on P_2 on the mirror surface, goes through the lens center and is also projected on the camera sensor[1]. P_I is then defined by the two reflected rays. These two rays, going back, define the virtual point as seen from the camera if the mirror does not exist. In Fig.1-b, two vertical lines (one each side) of source points are used to analyze the virtual image, the result is shown by the red line.

The camera is obviously not a pin-hole camera (in which case there wouldn't have any blur problem). However, as the size of the diaphragm is very small, the approximation is correct in practice. The detail of this analysis has been done in [12].

Nevertheless, in a real case, to any source point is associated not a single point (where all rays seem to converge) but a small curve, built from all rays issued from the source, and limited by the diaphragm aperture. This curve is defined thanks to a geometric construction shown next section.

---

[1] For SVP models, the position of the camera has two options: the second focus of the hyperbola is located either on the center of the lens or on the focus of the lens. In this section, the second model is used; however, the first model is used in the next sections to simplify the calculations.

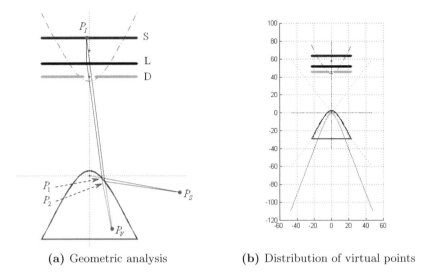

(a) Geometric analysis   **(b)** Distribution of virtual points

Fig. 1. Modeling of virtual image by two rays

3   Caustic Geometric Construction

The caustics [5] [3] [9] is an inevitable geometric distortion. It is built from
the envelope of light rays issued from a finite or infinite-located point after the
modification by an optical instrument: caustics by reflection (mirror) are called
catacaustics and caustics by refraction (through a glass for instance) are called
diacaustics. Before presenting our model, let us expose how to obtain a caustic
curve.

The caustic curve is built thanks to a geometric construction (see Fig.2).
From a given source point, one incident ray defines one point of the caustic. The
caustic curve is built from all incident rays issued from the source point. For
more details of this geometric construction, refer to [7] [4].

In Fig.2, the blue curve is the profile of the hyperbolic mirror, $P_S(x_S, y_S)$
is the source point, $P_H(x_H, y_H)$ is the intersection of any incident ray and the
hyperbolic mirror, $[P_R P_H]$ is the radius of curvature of the hyperbola at P_H, and
P_R is the center of the associated circle. P_A is obtained after two perpendicular
projections on $(P_S P_H)$ and $(P_R P_H)$ respectively. P_L is the projection of the
reflected ray on the plane of the lens. Finally, P_C is the intersection between
$(P_A P_S)$ and the reflected ray. Let us put this into equations.

Let $\mathcal{H}$ be the hyperbola[2] equation (the axis reference is located on the mirror
focus):

$$\mathcal{H} : \frac{(y_H - \frac{c}{2})^2}{a^2} - \frac{x_H^2}{b^2} = 1 \tag{1}$$

---

[2] a and b are the hyperbola parameters, $c = 2\sqrt{a^2 + b^2}$ is the distance between the
two focus of the hyperbola.

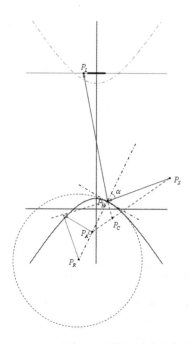

Fig. 2. Caustic obtained by a geometric method

First and second derivative of the hyperbola are used to calculate the radius of curvature r:

$$y' = -\frac{a}{b} \cdot \sqrt{\frac{x^2}{b^2 + x^2}} \tag{2}$$

$$y" = -ab(b^2 + x^2)^{-\frac{3}{2}} \tag{3}$$

$$r = |\frac{(1 + y'^2)^{\frac{3}{2}}}{y"}| \tag{4}$$

Next, one may calculate the incident angle α between the incident ray and the normal:

$$\alpha = arctan(y'_H) + \frac{\pi}{2} - arctan(\frac{y_S - y_H}{x_S - x_H}) \tag{5}$$

On this basis, we can calculate x_L:

$$x_L = (1 + \frac{2y'_H}{1 - y'^2_H} \cdot \frac{y_S - y_H}{x_S - x_H}) \cdot (c - y_H)/(\frac{2y'_H}{1 - y'^2_H} - \frac{y_S - y_H}{x_S - x_H}) + x_H \tag{6}$$

y_L being a constant (for a SVP-based model, $y_L = c$), the equation of the reflected ray $(P_L P_H)$ is known. Next, the radius of curvature and the incident angle are used to calculate the coordinates of P_A:

$$x_A = x_H - r \cdot cos^2\alpha\sqrt{\frac{y'^2_H}{1 + y'^2_H}} \tag{7}$$

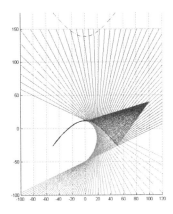 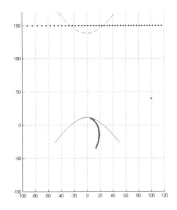

(a) Numerical simulation for caustic   **(b)** Caustic based on calculations

Fig. 3. Caustic curve of a source point

$$y_A = y_H - r \cdot \cos^2\alpha\sqrt{\frac{1}{1 + y_H'^2}} \tag{8}$$

Then P_A and P_S are used to define the equation of $(P_A P_S)$. Finally, the point of the caustic P_C is obtain through the intersection of $(P_A P_S)$ and $(P_L P_H)$:

$$x_C = \frac{\left(\frac{y_H x_L - c x_H}{x_L - x_H} \cdot (x_A - x_S) + x_S y_A - x_A y_S\right)}{\left(y_A - y_S + \frac{c - y_H}{x_L - x_H} \cdot (x_S - x_A)\right)} \tag{9}$$

$$y_C = \frac{c x_C - y_H x_C - c x_H + y_H x_L}{x_L - x_H} \tag{10}$$

Thanks to these results, one may build the caustic issued from a source point (Fig. 3-b), to be compared with a simple simulation of reflected rays (Fig. 3-a). The caustic curve corresponds perfectly to the envelop of reflected rays.

4   Caustic-Based Virtual Image Modeling

As seen earlier, our approach is definitively different from already existing approaches: caustics have never been used to define virtual images and, by extension, depth of field, image formation, etc. In [12], based on modeling of virtual image, the problem of blur can be analyzed and the best parameters of system can be obtained. Thanks to the caustic approach, a more complete and accurate model can be developed easily.

4.1   Image Formation from One Source Point

The (cata)caustic curve is obtained by using all the reflected rays that come from a light source and reflected on the mirror. But for real catadioptric camera,

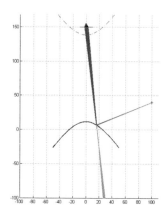

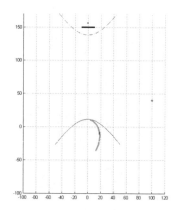

(a) Numerical simulation for virtual image

(b) Virtual image calculated with caustic equations

Fig. 4. Virtual image of a source point

few of reflected rays pass through the camera lens, that is to say that not all rays are useful for the image formation. These 'successful' rays (where P_L is located in the lens) define a useful section of the caustic curve (Fig. 4).

In Fig.4-b, the virtual image of a source point is part of the caustic curve (the red part), Fig.4-a is simulated to compare with Fig.4-b.

Since the virtual image of a given source point is not a point but a curve, the corresponding image (going through the lens) is also a curve (Fig. 5, where the lens is supposed to be ideal), corresponding to the image of the catacaustic with the classical (ideal) lens transformation.

In Fig.5-a, all reflected rays (still) don't intersect in a single point but (still) can be analyzed by the envelop (caustic) Fig.5-b (this curve is obtained from the previous equations and the ideal lens formula). This is another cause of blur in a catadioptric system. However, the real impact is very small as the red curve is also very small.

4.2   Image Formation from Multiple Source Points

The complete virtual image includes all source points, so the caustic has to be calculated for each of them. Actually, as seen previously, only the 'useful' part of the caustic can be taken into account. To obtain the whole virtual image, the source point has to be moved everywhere.

We here consider a vertical line of source points to simulate all points of the scene (as the distance from the focus as almost no impact [12]) and corresponding caustics with the equations previously elaborated.

A simplified model is used here, which considers only one incident ray from the source point. The considered ray is the one for which the reflected ray reaches the center of the lens (pin-hole camera model). In other words, to one source

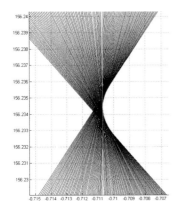

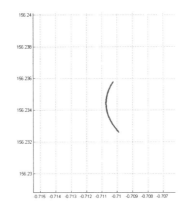

(a) Numerical simulation for real image

(b) Real image calculated with caustic equations

Fig. 5. Real image of a source point

point is associated only one point of the caustic. P_H is the associated point on the hyperbola. Considering the SVP model, we can associate the equation of the incident ray (that goes from the source point to the first focus of the hyperbola) to the equation of the hyperbola:

$$\frac{y_H}{x_H} = \frac{y_S}{x_S} \tag{11}$$

$$\frac{(y_H - \frac{c}{2})^2}{a^2} - \frac{x_H^2}{b^2} = 1 \tag{12}$$

Based on these two equations, we can obtain the coordinates of P_H:

$$x_H = \frac{\frac{y_S c}{a^2 x_S} - \sqrt{\frac{4 y_S^2}{a^2 x_S^2} + \frac{c^2}{a^2 b^2} - \frac{4}{b^2}}}{\frac{2 y_S^2}{a^2 x_S^2} - \frac{2}{b^2}} \tag{13}$$

$$y_H = \frac{y_S}{x_S} \cdot x_H \tag{14}$$

Even if the lens is not located at the second focus of hyperbola, *i.e.* not-SVP model, a similar method can be used to obtain the coordinates of P_H (calculus are slightly more complicated but the principle is the same).

Fig. 6-a shows the three caustics issued from three source points of the vertical line. As we can see, the green curve has moved, and as a consequence the useful part (red points) has also moved. Obviously, outside the simplified model, the distribution of virtual image of a vertical line is not a simple curve but a curved surface.

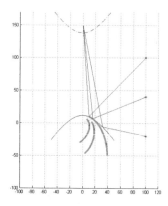
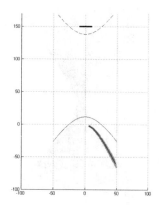

(a) Caustics calculations of three source points

(b) Virtual image of a vertical line

Fig. 6. Distribution of virtual image

Fig. 6-b shows, in green, the whole virtual image (*i.e.* the useful part of the caustics) of a vertical line and, in red, the points of the caustics considering the simplified model. As we can see, the simplified model is good enough to analyze properties of the catadioptric camera: depth of field, image formation, etc.

4.3   Comparison between the First Approximation and the Caustic Approach

The caustic approach has two main advantages compared with the first approximation:

- For each source point, we can use only one incident ray to obtain the position of virtual point; this simplified model can help us to analyze the image formation of many complicated optical systems, *e.g.* multi-mirror catadioptric system.
- With the limit of the size of the lens, we can use caustic to get the the complete and accurate model of virtual image; this model can help us to analyze deeply the image formation of catadioptric system.

5   Applications

5.1   Depth of Field of a Catadioptric System

In our simulations, blur has appeared due to the use of cheap cameras (with a relative large aperture) and the compactness of our system (short distance between the camera and the mirror).

The depth of field of a standard camera depends on the focal distance, the aperture and the distance in the scene. A point is seen blurred if it is located

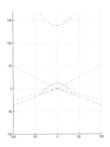

(a) Sharp zone around the mirror

(b) Sharp zone in the panoramic image

Fig. 7. Sharp zone of a catadioptric camera

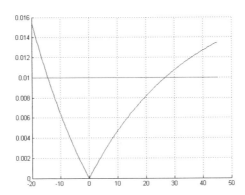

Fig. 8. Diameter of circle of confusion. x-axis represents the incident angle $(^o)$, y-axis represents the size of the circle of confusion (mm).

outside the depth of field. In a catadioptric system, a point of the scene is seen blurred if its virtual image is located outside the depth of field of the camera.

The depth of field of a standard camera being defined between two planes, which are perpendicular to the optical axis, the depth of field of a panoramic camera is limited by two cones. Each cone is defined by a circle and the focus of the mirror. The circles are the intersection between the planes and the mirror (Fig. 7).

Let us suppose that the sensor is located at the incident angle of 0° (between the incident ray and the perpendicular plan), we can obtain the relation between the circle of confusion and the incident angle (Fig.8). The definition of *blur* is relative, it must also consider the image size, resolution, distance from the observer, etc. Our definition is that a point is blurred if and only if the associated circle of confusion is greater than two pixels. This allow us to quantify the depth of field of the catadioptric camera.

Let us note that the term of 'depth of field' has a sense with a standard camera, as the sharpness is defined in the depth of the scene. Considering a catadioptric camera, it would be more accurate to use the term of 'sharpness angle', 'sharpness domain' or 'sharpness zone'.

5.2   Mirror Choice

Our caustic-based model allow us to understand and anticipate blur in a catadioptric camera. Considering a given camera with its own parameters (that we cannot change) and the assembling constraints (usually due to the application), our model is used to determinate the *best* parameters of the mirror. *'Best'* meaning here that the sharpness domain is the biggest possible one.

In our case, using a USB webcam (focus=$6mm$, lens diameter=$3mm$, sensor size=$4mm$, resolution=640×480, pixel size is $0.005mm$, and the distance mirror-camera is $150mm$) in a robotics application, the *best* parameters for a hyperbolic mirror have been defined: $a = 63.3866, b = 40.0892$.

5.3   Image Resolution and Image Transformation

Moreover, the virtual image can be used to analyze the resolution of the space in the panoramic image, and, in the same time, to transform the panoramic image from the circular model to rectangle model without radial distortion (Fig. 9).

The correspondence between the incident angle and the pixel location is obtained according to the distribution of the virtual image; the curve is shown in Fig. 9-a. In Fig. 9-b, we use a series of circles to represent incident angles, from the outside to inside, the angles are $-15^\circ, -5^\circ, -15^\circ, -25^\circ, -35^\circ, -45^\circ, -55^\circ$.

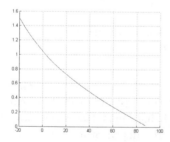

(a) Correspondence between angle (x-axis) and pixel location (y-axis)

(b) Spatial resolution in panoramic image

(c) Panoramic image in rectangle model

Fig. 9. Relation between space and image

Based on Fig. 9-a, the transformation of a panoramic image to a rectangular image can be easily done in order to keep a constant radial resolution (Fig.9-c).

6   Conclusion

In this article, we describe an optical method to calculate caustics, and we present a new method to obtain virtual image, based on caustics. This new method is more complete, more accurate and easier to compute with respect to existing methods. Our model can be used in every cases, not only with the SVP constraint in a catadioptric system. According to our model and the virtual image determination, we have defined several applications: the analysis of the catadioptric camera angle sharpness domain ('depth of field'), the determination of the best parameters of catadioptric system mirror to reduce the blur, and also the analysis of the relation between image and space. Since the caustic-based simplified model needs only one ray, it can be easily applied in more complicated optics system, *e.g.* multi-mirror catadioptric system.

References

1. Baker, S., Nayar, S.K.: A theory of single-viewpoint catadioptric image formation. International Journal of Computer Vision 35, 175–196 (1999)
2. Baker, S., Nayar, S.K.: Single viewpoint catadioptric cameras. In: Benosman, R., Kang, S.B. (eds.) Panoramic Vision: Sensors, Theory, Applications. Springer, Heidelberg (2001)
3. Born, M., Wolf, E.: Principles of Optics: Electromagnetic Theory of Propagation, Interference and Diffraction of Light, 7th edn. Cambridge University Press, Cambridge (October 1999)
4. Bruce, J.W., Giblin, P.J., Gibson, C.G.: On caustics of plane curves. The American Mathematical Monthly 88(9), 651–667 (1981)
5. Hamilton, W.R.: Theory of systems of rays. Transactions of the Royal Irish Academy 16, 69–174 (1828)
6. Hecht, E., Zajac, A.: Optics. Addison-Wesley, Reading (1974)
7. Ieng, S.H., Benosman, R.: Les surfaces caustiques par la géométrie, application aux capteurs catadioptriques. Traitement du Signal, Numéro spécial Vision Omnidirectionnelle 22(5) (2005)
8. Micusik, B., Pajdla, T.: Autocalibration & 3d reconstruction with non-central catadioptric cameras (2004)
9. Nye, J.: Natural Focusing and Fine Structure of Light: Caustics and Wave Dislocations, 1st edn. Taylor & Francis, Abington (January 1999)
10. Swaminathan, R., Grossberg, M., Nayar, S.K.: Caustics of catadioptric cameras. In: Proc. International Conference on Computer Vision, pp. 2–9 (2001)
11. Swaminathan, R., Grossberg, M.D., Nayar, S.K.: Non-single viewpoint catadioptric cameras: Geometry and analysis. International Journal of Computer Vision 66(3), 211–229 (2006)
12. Zhang, S., Zenou, E.: Optical approach of a hypercatadioptric system depth of field. In: 10th International Conference on Information Sciences, Signal Processing and their Applications (to appear 2010)

Projection Selection Algorithms for Discrete Tomography

László Varga*, Péter Balázs**, and Antal Nagy

Department of Image Processing and Computer Graphics
University of Szeged
Árpád tér 2, H-6720 Szeged, Hungary
{vargalg,pbalazs,nagya}@inf.u-szeged.hu

Abstract. In this paper we study how the choice of projection angles affect the quality of the discrete tomographic reconstruction of an object. We supply four different strategies for selecting projection angle sets and compare them by conducting experiments on a set of software phantoms. We also discuss some consequences of our observations. Furthermore, we introduce a possible application of the proposed angle selection algorithms as well.

Keywords: discrete tomography, reconstruction, adaptive projection acquisition, non-destructive testing.

1 Introduction

The main goal of tomographic reconstruction is to determine the inner structure of objects from their projections taken along a set of directions. This is usually done by exposing the objects to some electromagnetic or particle radiation on one side, measuring the amount of transmitted radiation on the other side, and reconstructing the inner densities of the objects by a suitable algorithm.

There are several appropriate algorithms for tomographic reconstruction capable of giving accurate results when sufficiently many projections are available. However the cost of acquiring projections can be extremely high, and the radiation can damage the objects of study, too. Due to these problems there is always a need to reduce the number of projections required for the reconstruction.

For this purpose, one can develop more accurate new algorithms by using some a priori information of the objects of interest, e.g., by assuming that the objects can only consist of a few different materials with known attenuation coefficients, and/or their shape fulfill some special property [3,4]. Another approach for reducing the number of required projections is to try to take the projections with

---

* Corresponding author.
** This research was partially supported by the TÁMOP-4.2.2/08/1/2008-0008 and TÁMOP-4.2.1/B-09/1/KONV-2010-0005 programs of the Hungarian National Development Agency and by the János Bolyai Research Scholarship of the Hungarian Academy of Sciences.

J. Blanc-Talon et al. (Eds.): ACIVS 2010, Part I, LNCS 6474, pp. 390–401, 2010.

the highest information content. Thus, a smaller set of projections can hold just enough information for a proper reconstruction. In [8] the authors showed that in the case of continuous reconstruction the number of required projections can be significantly reduced by choosing the right angles with some heuristic algorithms. It was also shown in [7,10] that the choice of the proper projection angles can particularly be crucial in the case of discrete tomography, when usually only a handful of projections are available for the reconstruction.

This paper focuses on examining the differences between the discrete tomographic reconstructions of the same object performed by the same algorithm but from different projection sets. We introduce several algorithms for finding the appropriate projection angles of given objects, and compare these approaches through experiments conducted on a set of software phantoms. We discuss a possible practical application of the proposed algorithms as well.

The structure of the paper is the following. In Section 2 we explain the central problem of discrete tomography and describe an algorithm for solving it. In Section 3 we introduce several methods to select proper angles for the reconstruction. In Section 4 we give the details of the frameset applied to compare our angle selection algorithms. In Section 5 we summarize the experimental results. In Section 6 we discuss a possible application of the proposed angle selection algorithms. Finally, in Section 7 we summarize our observations.

2   Discrete Tomographic Reconstruction

In a formulation of two dimensional transmission tomography the goal is to reconstruct an unknown $f(u, v)$ function from a set of its projections given by

$$[Rf](\alpha, t) = \int_{-\infty}^{\infty} f(t\cos(\alpha) - q\sin(\alpha), t\sin(\alpha) + q\cos(\alpha)) \, dq \qquad (1)$$

line integrals with different α angles and t distances from the origin. Although there is a thorough mathematical theory and an exact formula for continuous reconstruction when all the possible projections are available, in a practical application we can only handle a finite number of projections and the function itself must be also discretised. In the sequel we will assume that the function $f : \mathbb{R}^2 \to \{0, 1\}$ to be reconstructed is binary and takes a constant value on each unit square determined by the 2-dimensional integer lattice, that is

$$f(u + a, v + b) = f(u + c, v + d), \ u, v \in \mathbb{Z}, \ a, b, c, d \in [0, 1). \qquad (2)$$

We will further assume that the f function has a bounded support. With these restrictions the final task can be regarded as the reconstruction of a two dimensional binary image (where 0 stands for the background and 1 for the foreground) and the reconstruction problem can be represented by a system of equations

$$\mathbf{A}\mathbf{x} = \mathbf{b}, \quad \mathbf{A} = (a_{i,j})_{n \times m} \in \mathbb{R}^{n \times m}, \ \mathbf{x} \in \{0, 1\}^n, \ \mathbf{b} \in \mathbb{R}^m . \qquad (3)$$

Here, $\mathbf{x}$ is the vector of all n pixels of the unknown image to be reconstructed, $\mathbf{b}$ is the vector of the total of m measured projection values and $\mathbf{A}$ describes the

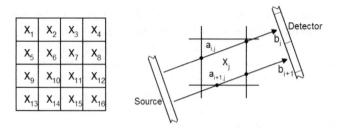

Fig. 1. Representation of the ordering of the pixels and the parallel beam geometry used

connection between the pixels and the projection beams by all $a_{i,j}$ giving the length of the line segment of the i-th ray through the j-th pixel. Figure 1 shows an example for the projection representation we used. Now, the task is to solve (3) which is usually performed by the different versions of the so-called algebraic reconstruction technique (see [1,3,5]).

In our case we used a slightly different approach that reformulates the reconstruction as an energy minimization problem. The algorithm given in [9] applies D.C. programming (a technique for minimizing the difference of convex functions) for minimizing the energy function given as

$$J_\mu(\mathbf{x}) := \|\mathbf{A}\mathbf{x} - \mathbf{b}\|_2^2 + \frac{\gamma}{2} \sum_{j=1}^{n} \sum_{l \in N_4(j)} (\mathbf{x}_j - \mathbf{x}_l)^2 - \mu\frac{1}{2}\langle \mathbf{x}, \mathbf{x} - \mathbf{e} \rangle, \quad \mathbf{x} \in [0, 1]^n , \quad (4)$$

where γ is a given constant controlling the weight of the smoothness term on the image, $N_4(j)$ is the set of pixels 4-connected to the j-th pixel, and $\mathbf{e}$ denotes the vector with all n^2 coordinates equal to 1. Minimizing the energy function (4) with the proper parameters and projections, results in an $\mathbf{x}$ vector which contains the pixel values of the reconstruction. The main advantage of this approach is that it can handle the possible inconsistency of the equation system (3) and it incorporates prior information into the model, too.

The basic operation of this algorithm starts out by looking for a continuous result by minimizing the $J_\mu(\mathbf{x})$ function omitting the last term (by setting $\mu = 0$). In the proceeding we iteratively increase μ with a $\mu_\Delta > 0$ value by which – as it can easily be proved – the algorithm will converge to a binary result. The exact description of the algorithm and its mathematical background can be found in [9]. In the sequel we will refer to this algorithm as "DC".

3   Angle Selection Algorithms

It has already been shown in [7,10] that the choice of projection angles can have a significant influence on the result of the reconstruction of certain objects. However, the previous studies dealt only with the case when the projections were taken equiangularly. Here, we extend those results to the case when the projections can be taken from arbitrary directions around the objects.

While conducting experiments with equiangular projection sets – as it was done in [10] – is relatively easy, we found that the problem becomes much more complex when we omit the assumption of equiangularity. Even if we restrict ourselves to angles of integer degrees between $0°$ and $179°$ the solution space can be too large to perform an exhaustive search in it. Therefore, we will use heuristic algorithms for finding not necessarily the best, but sufficiently good angle sets to the reconstruction.

In the following, $S(\alpha, p)$ will denote a set of angles defined as

$$S(\alpha, p) = \left\{ \alpha + i\frac{180°}{p} \mid i = 0, \dots, p - 1 \right\}, \tag{5}$$

for a p number of projections and a starting angle α. On the other hand, L will stand for an ordered list of angles $L = \langle \alpha_1, \alpha_2, \dots, \alpha_p \rangle$ with arbitrary α_i-s and arbitrary p. We will use the notations $\mathbf{x}_{S(\alpha,p)}$ and $\mathbf{x}_L$ for the reconstructions from the projections taken with $S(\alpha, p)$ and L angle sets, respectively, produced by the DC reconstruction algorithm. Finally, we will denote by $\mathbf{x}^*$ the vector of pixel values of the expected reconstruction (the image of the original object) and use $RME(\mathbf{x}^*, \mathbf{y})$ for measuring the relative mean error of a given $\mathbf{y}$ vector of reconstructed pixels, calculated as

$$RME(\mathbf{x}^*, \mathbf{y}) = \frac{\sum_{i=1}^{n} |x_i^* - y_i|}{\sum_{i=1}^{n} x_i^*}. \tag{6}$$

Informally, the RME value is the number of mistaken pixels in the reconstruction normalized with the number of object pixels of the original image.

We consider only integer angles between $0°$ and $179°$. In our notation $0°$ stands for the projection with vertical beams aimed from the bottom to the top of the image and increasing degrees of angles means a counterclockwise rotation.

We now present four different angle selection methods, two simple equiangular ones for a basic reference, and two more complex ones allowed to result in arbitrary angles from the defined possibilities.

Naive angle selection

The method we call **Naive** is a simple, picture independent angle set selection technique. For every image and a given projection number p we simply choose the appropriate equiangular projection set with $0°$ starting angle defined by $S(0°, p)$. Note that most applications use a similar approach for choosing angles.

Equiangular search

We can improve the results of the naive angle selection by trying to make a reconstruction of the phantoms from the $S(\alpha, p)$ projection sets with all integer α starting angles varying form $0°$ to $\lfloor \frac{180}{p} \rfloor°$ and selecting the projection set producing the smallest $RME(\mathbf{x}^*, \mathbf{x}_{S(\alpha,p)})$ value. This is exactly the same algorithm that was used in [10] for similar experiments. In the sequel we will simply call this algorithm **EquiAng**.

Greedy angle testing

One of our non-equiangular approaches for optimal angle selection is a greedy algorithm. The basic idea of this method is to start out with a projection angle set containing one single predetermined angle, and then to add new angles iteratively to the current set, based on a local decision. In every iterations we add the angle to the current set which causes the greatest improvement in the resulting reconstruction. The best angle is chosen by trying to add each unused projection angle to the original set, making a reconstruction with the new set, and keeping the angles belonging to the reconstruction with the smallest RME value. At the end of this algorithm the result is an ordered list of angles with decreasing significance.

Greedy: Greedy angle selection algorithm.
Input: $\mathbf{x}^*$ vector of image pixel values, $k \geq 2$ maximal number of angles, and
$\quad\quad \alpha_1$ predetermined angle.
Output: $L = \langle \alpha_1, \alpha_2, \ldots, \alpha_l \rangle$ angle list so that $l \leq k$.

Step 1. Set $L_1 = \langle \alpha_1 \rangle$, $i = 1$;
Step 2. Let $i \leftarrow i + 1$;
Step 3. Let $0° \leq \alpha^* \leq 179°$ be an integer angle for which $RME(\mathbf{x}^*, \mathbf{x}_{\langle L_{i-1}, \alpha^* \rangle})$
$\quad\quad$ is minimal;
Step 4. Let the next list of angles be $L_i = \langle L_{i-1}, \alpha^* \rangle$;
Step 5. If $i = k$ or $RME(\mathbf{x}^*, \mathbf{x}_{L_i}) = 0$ return with L_i otherwise go to **Step 2**

In addition to the image data and the maximal number of projection angles this method also requires an α_1 starting angle since our implementation of the DC reconstruction algorithm cannot produce a reasonable result with just one projection. In our experiments for each image this angle was given as an integer angle with minimal $\|\mathbf{x}^* - \mathbf{y}_\alpha\|_2^2$ value, where $\mathbf{y}_\alpha$ stands for the reconstruction of the image produced by the SIRT algorithm (described in [5]) from only one projection with α angle.

Altering angles with simulated annealing

This non-equiangular algorithm is based on the fact that the optimal angle searching problem can itself be represented as an energy minimization task. Having this in mind, the optimal L^* list of angles must satisfy

$$RME(\mathbf{x}^*, \mathbf{x}_{L^*}) = \min_L \ RME(\mathbf{x}^*, \mathbf{x}_L). \tag{7}$$

In this way we can reformulate the optimal angle searching problem as finding the minimal value of $RME(\mathbf{x}^*, \mathbf{x}_L)$ with varying L. Because of the complexity of the new energy function – as it contains the result of a reconstruction – we have chosen to do the minimization with simulated annealing [6].

AltAng: Angle selection with simulated annealing.

Input: $\mathbf{x}^*$ vector of image pixel values, $L_0 = \langle \alpha_1, \alpha_2, \ldots, \alpha_p \rangle$ starting angle list, T_0 starting temperature, $0 < h < 1$ cooling rate, N angle step range.

Output: $L = \langle \alpha'_1, \alpha'_2, \ldots, \alpha'_p \rangle$.

Step 1 Choose a random $i \in \{1, \ldots, p\}$ integer from a uniform distribution;

Step 2 Choose a random $\alpha'_i \in \{\alpha_i - N, \ldots, \alpha_i + N\} \setminus \{\alpha_i\}$ integer angle from a uniform distribution, and replace the i-th angle so that the new angle list is $L' = \langle \alpha_1, \ldots, \alpha_{i-1}, \alpha'_i, \alpha_{i+1}, \ldots, \alpha_p \rangle$;

Step 3 If $RME(\mathbf{x}^*, \mathbf{x}_{L'}) < RME(\mathbf{x}^*, \mathbf{x}_L)$ then $L \leftarrow L'$ and proceed with **Step 5**;

Step 4 Let $L \leftarrow L'$ with $e^{-\frac{RME(\mathbf{x}^*, \mathbf{x}_{L'}) - RME(\mathbf{x}^*, \mathbf{x}_L)}{T}}$ probability;

Step 5 If a stopping criteria is met then return with the current L angle set, otherwise let $T \leftarrow hT$ and start over from **Step 1**;

In a more informal description, this algorithm starts with a basic fixed-size angle list and in each iteration it tries to alter one of the angles changing it inside a predefined neighborhood. If the random change results in a better angle set then we accept the new angle. If the new angle is worse than the previous one we can accept it with a probability driven by the T temperature and the difference between the RME values of the two reconstructions with the different angle sets. We decrease the temperature in each iteration and – by this – the probability of accepting worse angles is also decreased.

4 Test Frameset and Phantom Images

To compare the performance of the given algorithms we performed experimental tests on a set of software phantoms. In this section we will give a description of the test frame set and provide more details on the algorithms given in Section 3.

We conducted the experiments with five software phantoms of different types, all of them were scaled to the same size of 256 by 256 pixels. These phantoms can be seen in Figure 2.

As described before we used parallel beam geometry with each measured value representing the projection of the image along one single line. In every projection we set the distance of the beams – or detector elements – to 1 pixel and used as many as needed to cover the whole image. The rotation center of the angles – or the origin of the coordinate system belonging to Equation (1) – was placed exactly into the center of the image. The distances of the projection lines from the origin were set $i + 1/2$ pixels with integer i values.

The reconstructions were performed by the DC algorithm implemented in C++ with GPU acceleration using the CUDA sdk (see [13]). In each reconstruction we set the parameters of the algorithm as described in [12] except the setting of Δ_μ directly to 0.1 instead of calculating it dynamically for every reconstruction. In this way we could perform one reconstruction in 10-30 seconds,

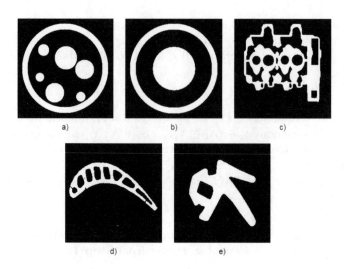

Fig. 2. Phantom images used in the experiments

depending on the complexity of the image to be reconstructed and the number of projections used.

For each phantom we used the angle selection algorithms for finding angle sets with 2 to 11 projections. In the case of the **Naive** and **EquiAng** algorithms this meant ten processes for each phantom with different p projection numbers. In the case of the **AltAng** algorithm we took the best angle set from five different runs for every phantom and number of projections. With the **Greedy** algorithm we only had to perform one process with a $p = 11$ value for each phantom. This made a total of 35320 reconstructions performed in about 200 hours on an Intel Core 2 CPU and an NVIDIA Geforce 8800 GT GPU.

The parameters of of the **AltAng** algorithm were set empirically. We set the values $T_0 = 0.02$ and $h = 0.95$. The neighborhood of the projection angles was determined depending on the projection number p as $N = (\lfloor 180/p \rfloor - 5)°$, that is, we decreases the neighborhood of the angles when there were more projections, in order to keep the probability of changing the order of the angles low. It is important to note that the search space of possible solutions is not reduced this way. For each image and p number of projections the starting angle set of this algorithm was the output of the **EquiAng** algorithm, i.e., the $S_{\alpha,p}$ angle set that produced the best reconstruction. Each time the stopping criteria for the process was reaching 200 iterations, or a perfect reconstruction. When the equiangular search already resulted in a projection set giving a perfect reconstruction we did not start the random search at all.

5   Numerical Results and Their Interpretation

After performing the tests we compared the angle sets produced by the four angle selection algorithms. Table 1 contains a summary of the results by giving the RME values of the reconstructions with the angle sets of the different algorithms. In addition, Figure 3 presents the same result graphically for the phantom of Figure 2c.

Our first consideration was to compare the results of the different angle selection algorithms on the same phantoms with the same numbers of projections. As it was already shown in [7,10] the **EquiAng** algorithm usually gives better – but never worse – results than the **Naive** method. This is not so surprising since the equiangular search includes the angle set of the **Naive** algorithm.

We can also make valuable observations on the results of the **Greedy** algorithm. For certain images the angles given by this method can be significantly better than the ones given by the **EquiAng** or the **Naive** approaches (see the results for Figures 2d-e). However, in the case of the rotation invariant phantoms the greedy search can result in a local minima of RME. From the entries of

Table 1. Numerical results giving the RME values of the reconstructions produced by the DC algorithm with the angle sets proposed by different angle selection strategies (columns indicate the numbers of projections, and rows give the applied angle selection algorithm). Tests belonging to blank cells were not performed for reasons given in Sections 3 and 4.

Proj.Num.	2	3	4	5	6	7	8	9	10	11
Figure 2a										
Naive	1.1218	0.7943	0.5549	0.2904	0.0087	0	0	0	0	0
EquiAng	0.9339	0.6926	0.4687	0.1687	0.0002	0	0	0	0	0
Greedy	0.8568	0.5888	0.4664	0.2650	0.0407	0				
AltAng	0.0842	0.5749	0.3856	0.1082	0					
Figure 2b										
Naive	0.6586	0.4162	0	0	0	0	0	0	0	0
EquiAng	0.6070	0.4119	0	0	0	0	0	0	0	0
Greedy	0.6357	0.4062	0.2665	0.0707	0					
AltAng	0.6051	0.2687								
Figure 2c										
Naive	0.7951	0.7245	0.5392	0.5546	0.3465	0.4596	0.2725	0.1650	0.0643	0.0926
EquiAng	0.7951	0.7245	0.5146	0.4438	0.3362	0.3517	0.2725	0.1643	0.0643	0.0409
Greedy	0.7435	0.5912	0.4513	0.3736	0.2929	0.2090	0.1544	0.1057	0.0318	0
AltAng	0.7380	0.5709	0.4432	0.3450	0.2785	0.1841	0.1009	0.0444	0.0071	0
Figure 2d										
Naive	1.0348	0.7544	0.6239	0.3900	0.1615	0.0019	0	0	0	0
EquiAng	1.0348	0.7153	0.5308	0.2709	0.0849	0	0	0	0	0
Greedy	1.0751	0.7440	0.3672	0.1239	0.0508	0.0005	0			
AltAng	0.8447	0.5974	0.4091	0.1128	0.0044					
Figure 2e										
Naive	0.7742	0.5836	0.4255	0.1512	0	0	0	0	0	0
EquiAng	0.5475	0.1691	0.0500	0.0001	0	0	0	0	0	0
Greedy	0.5756	0.1530	0.0117	0						
AltAng	0.5268	0.1617	0.0029	0						

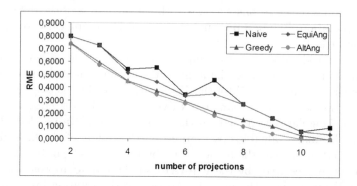

Fig. 3. *RME* values of the reconstructions of the phantom in Figure 2c with the angle sets provided by the four different angle selection algorithms

Table 1 we can also deduce that for the two phantoms with the rings (the ones in Figures 2a and 2b) the greedy search cannot yield a proper reconstruction from even the same number of projections sufficient for the **Naive** approach.

The final algorithm to compare is the simulated annealing based one. As we can deduce from Table 1, this approach gave in most of the cases better results than the others. Compared to the **Naive** or the **EquiAng** algorithms this behavior of algorithm **AltAng** is quite obvious since the base of the search in **AltAng** is given by those methods and the relatively small starting temperature does not allow acceptance of angle sets much worse than the previous ones. Even comparing the results to the ones of the **Greedy** algorithm, we can say that **AltAng** seems to give the best angle sets. The explanation of this is that this approach does not suffer from the defects of the other algorithms, i.e., it does not restrict the search to equiangular projections sets, and does not make unchangeable local decisions in the computation.

Despite the good results of the simulated annealing based strategy we must highlight that it has a serious drawback in making random searches. This process is greatly driven by fortune, and we cannot hope to get always such good results. This is why we decided here to take the best results from five different runs for each phantom and projection number. Naturally running the algorithm more times or allowing more iterations with a higher starting temperature could produce more stable results, probably closer to the optimal projection angle set.

As a summation of the comparison we can say that the result of a binary reconstruction can significantly depend on the angles chosen for creating projections of the objects of study. That is, we can get entirely different reconstruction results even if we use equiangular angle sets for the projections. If we allow the projections to be taken in arbitrary directions the difference can be even more significant. In a practical application this means that we can get acceptable results from fewer projections, and thus reduce the required number of projections – and with it the cost and the amount of radiation – by selecting the right angles. As a demonstration of our results Figure 4 shows an example with the

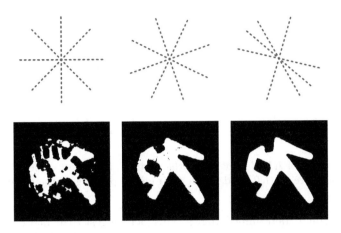

Fig. 4. Reconstructions of the phantom in Figure 2e with $S(0°, 4)$, $S(19°, 4)$ and $L = \langle 30°, 50°, 77°, 163° \rangle$ projection sets respectively. (Red dashed lines indicate the directions of the projections, images below are the corresponding reconstructions.)

reconstruction of the phantom of Figure 2e from three different projection sets with the same number of projections.

We can also come to further conclusions based on the data in Table 1. First, the result of a reconstruction can significantly be improved by choosing the angles in arbitrary directions. Another important consequence is that the accuracy of the discrete tomographic reconstruction algorithms can only be compared for fixed projection sets, and evaluations of reconstruction algorithms in the literature should also contain a detailed explanation of the applied projection geometry.

6   An Application of the Angle Selection Algorithms

Based on our results we can easily think of possible practical applications of the angle selection algorithms introduced in Section 3 as well. One such application has already been given in [10], by proposing to use a blueprint for determining the right angles to take projections from, in nondestructive testing (see [2]).

The paper [10] discussed only equiangular projections. Based on the results presented here further improvement can be achieved by allowing arbitrary angles to be used. Of course, we usually cannot put the object of study with the same exact direction into the scanner and acquire the desired projections. Thus the angles can slightly differ from the perfect ones. It can be useful to take a look on what happens if we alter the angles found by our algorithms. We conducted further experiments by rotating the best angle sets we found by angles $-90°, -89°, \ldots, 89°$. Some examples for the results can be seen graphically in Figure 5 for Figure 2d (left) and Figure 2e (right).

From Figure 5 we can deduce that – except a small noise – the curves are relatively smooth, but they increase with a high gradient when getting farther

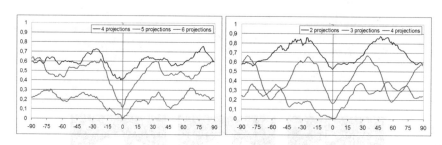

Fig. 5. The graph of RME values after the rotation of the best angle set around the phantoms in Figure 2d (left) and Figure 2e (right) depending on the angle of rotation

from the originally determined angles. This fact suggest that, in a real world application with non-equiangular projections, the objects of study must be placed into the scanner with high precision in order to get a good result without making additional projections. The explanation of this strictness in the angles can be that we developed our algorithms to try to find the angles giving the best reconstruction and altering those angles all at once can easily degrade the quality of the reconstructed image. Nevertheless, we may have a small freedom without getting unacceptable results.

Our observations show that the benefit of finding the right angles is the bigger if the object to be reconstructed is topologically simple. Our results show, that more complex objects – those require several projections for an acceptable reconstruction – are less dependent on the choice of projection angles. With an increasing number of projections, the differences between these projections get negligible and we can not get an improvement worth noting only by getting the better angles. Therefore we would advise applying the angle selection algorithm described in Section 3 for practical applications, in the case of simple objects.

7   Conclusion

In this paper we examined how the choice of the angles of projections can affect the result of binary tomographic reconstruction algorithms. We presented four different angle selection strategies and compared them through tests performed on a set of software phantoms. We found that the selection of angles can significantly affect the result of the DC tomographic reconstruction algorithm. We also showed that such results can lead to further conclusions and we also proposed a possible application for the presented algorithms, too.

In the future we plan to extend our studies to other reconstruction algorithms, and also the case when the measured data is affected by noise, which is the common situation in real applications.[1] In addition providing a more theoretical explanation of the problem would be a major breakthrough as well.

---

[1] By the time of reviewing the current paper we have already made efforts in this direction and submitted [11].

Acknowledgments

The authors would like to thank Joost Batenburg for providing test images (Figures 2c and 2d) for the studies. Phantom of Figure 2e was taken from the image database of the IAPR Technical Committee on Discrete Geometry (TC18).

References

1. Batenburg, K.J., Sijbers, J.: DART: a fast heuristic algebraic reconstruction algorithm for discrete tomography. In: IEEE Conference on Image Processing IV, pp. 133–136 (2007)
2. Baumann, J., Kiss, Z., Krimmel, S., Kuba, A., Nagy, A., Rodek, L., Schillinger, B., Stephan, J.: Discrete tomography methods for nondestructive testing. In: [4], ch. 14, pp. 303–331 (2007)
3. Herman, G.T., Kuba, A. (eds.): Discrete Tomography: Foundations, Algorithms and Applications. Birkhäuser, Basel (1999)
4. Herman, G.T., Kuba, A. (eds.): Advances in Discrete Tomography and Its Applications. Birkhäuser, Basel (2007)
5. Kak, A.C., Slaney, M.: Principles of Computerized Tomographic Imaging. IEEE Press, New York (1999)
6. Metropolis, N., Rosenbluth, A., Rosenbluth, M., Teller, A., Teller, E.: Equation of state calculation by fast computing machines. J. Chem. Phys. 21, 1087–1092 (1953)
7. Nagy, A., Kuba, A.: Reconstruction of binary matrices from fan-beam projections. Acta Cybernetica 17(2), 359–385 (2005)
8. Placidi, G., Alecci, M., Sotgiu, A.: Theory of adaptive acquisition method for image reconstruction from projections and application to EPR imaging. Journal of Magnetic Resonance, Series B, 50–57 (1995)
9. Schüle, T., Schnörr, C., Weber, S., Hornegger, J.: Discrete tomography by convex-concave regularization and D.C. programming. Discrete Applied Mathematics 151, 229–243 (2005)
10. Varga, L., Balázs, P., Nagy, A.: Direction-dependency of a binary tomographic reconstruction algorithm. In: Barneva, R.P., Brimkov, V.E., Hauptman, H.A., Natal Jorge, R.M., Tavares, J.M.R.S. (eds.) Computational Modeling of Objects Represented in Images. LNCS, vol. 6026, pp. 242–253. Springer, Heidelberg (2010)
11. Varga, L., Balázs, P., Nagy, A.: Direction-dependency of binary tomographic reconstruction algorithms. Submitted to Graphical Models (CompIMAGE 2010 special issue)
12. Weber, S., Nagy, A., Schüle, T., Schnörr, C., Kuba, A.: A benchmark evaluation of large-scale optimization approaches to binary tomography. In: Kuba, A., Nyúl, L.G., Palágyi, K. (eds.) DGCI 2006. LNCS, vol. 4245, pp. 146–156. Springer, Heidelberg (2006)
13. NVIDIA CUDA technology, web page (August 24, 2010), http://www.nvidia.co.uk/object/cuda_home_new_uk.html

Fast Mean Shift Algorithm Based on Discretisation and Interpolation

Eduard Sojka, Jan Gaura, Tomáš Fabián, and Michal Krumnikl

Technical University of Ostrava,
Faculty of Electrical Engineering and Informatics,
17. listopadu 15, 708 33 Ostrava-Poruba, Czech Republic
{eduard.sojka,jan.gaura,tomas.fabian,michal.krumnikl}@vsb.cz

Abstract. A fast mean shift algorithm for processing the image data is presented. Although it is based on the known basic principles of the original mean shift method, it improves the computational speed substantially. It is being assumed that the spatial image coordinates and range coordinates can be discretised by introducing a regular grid. Firstly, the algorithm precomputes the values of shifts at the grid points. The mean shift iterations are then carried out by making use of the grid values and trilinear interpolation. In the paper, it is shown that this can be done effectively. Measured by the order of complexity, the values at all grid points can be precomputed in the time that is equal to the time required, in the original method, for computing only one mean shift iteration for all image points. The interpolation step is computationally inexpensive. The experimental results confirming the theoretical expectations are presented. The use of the step kernel for computing the shifts (corresponding to the Epanechnikov kernel for estimating the densities), and the images with only a single value at each pixel are required.

1 Introduction

Mean shift (MS) is a density based clustering algorithm [9,4,6,7] that has recently attracted great attention and is now widely proposed for various imaging applications such as image segmentation [7], object tracking [8], and denoising [1]. One of the main problems, however, with applying the mean-shift based algorithms in practice is their high computational complexity. Several techniques have been reported to increase the speed of mean shift. For example, fast Gauss transform-based MS [13], locality sensitive hashing-based MS [10], multi-level hierarchy approach inspired by the Morse theory [11]. In [3], the number of iterations and the computational cost per iteration are mentioned as the bottlenecks of the Gaussian MS algorithm, and several accelerations strategies are presented. The efforts aiming at achieving a higher convergence rate is presented in [14]. In [2], the principle of the Gaussian blurring mean shift is revisited and it is shown how it can be used for image segmentation. The issues of computational complexity of the recently presented medoid-shift algorithm are discussed in [12].

Generally speaking, the speed up may be achieved as follows: (i) By faster performing the neighbourhood queries [10]; (ii) by faster evaluating the mean

J. Blanc-Talon et al. (Eds.): ACIVS 2010, Part I, LNCS 6474, pp. 402–413, 2010.

shift formula [13], (iii) by reducing the number of iterations [14]. Our approach follows the second technique. We exploit the basic theory of the original mean shift method and, as our own contribution, we present an algorithmic improvement leading to substantially shorter running times than are the times achieved by the usual implementation. We suppose that we deal with the points of the form (x, y, b), where (x, y) are the coordinates in image and b is a pixel value at (x, y), which is a real number (e.g., brightness). We introduce a discretization $\{(x_i, y_i, b_i)\}$ that has the form of a regular grid in which $\{(x_i, y_i)\}$ are the usual pixel positions in image, and $\{b_i\}$ is an equidistant quantisation introduced on the used range of intensity values. We firstly precompute the shifts at the grid points. Then we carry out the mean shift iterations by making use of these precomputed values and trilinear interpolation. Clearly, this approach requires that the shifts at the grid points are computed and stored effectively. The key observation on which the method is based is the following one (simply speaking): For the step kernel (it corresponds to the Epanechnikov shadow kernel for computing densities), the shifts for all $\{b_j\}$ at a certain (x_i, y_i) can be computed in the same time as is the time needed for computing one mean shift iteration at one point (x, y, b) in the original method. We present the algorithm how it can be done that is based on the sweeping technique known from computational geometry. Roughly speaking, if we neglect the times that are not theoretically important (e.g., the time for interpolation), the effect should be the same as if only one iteration in the original method were required for each point. The experiments show that the algorithm has the properties that were expected and that, moreover, it may have some other positive features that can be explained by certain filtering (introduced by discretisation) in the space of shift/density values. The following limitations should be stated on the other hand: (i) The step kernel is considered for computing the shifts; (ii) the images with only a single value at each pixel are required (the colour images must be transformed into one channel images).

We note that the method we propose differs from the spatial discretisation acceleration strategy presented in [3]. In that method, each pixel is subdivided into a grid of cells. If, during processing a certain image point, the projection (onto the image plane) of its iteration trajectory enters the cell that has already been visited, the iterations stop and the previously computed trajectory and attractor are used. The method is based on the assumption that exploring only the projection of trajectory is sufficient. Similar approach is also mentioned in [5]. According to our experience, the projection does not suffice. In real-life images, the situation is quite frequent that the trajectories intersecting in the projection may be very distant in reality since they substantially differ in intensities.

The paper is organised as follows. The overview of the original mean shift method is given in Section 2. Section 3 is devoted to the description of the method we propose (although we are aware of the fact that it is only an algorithmic improvement of the original method, we call it a *new method* from now on for brevity). The issues of effective implementation are discussed in Section 4. In Section 5, the experimental results are presented.

2   Review of the Mean Shift Algorithm

In this section, a review of the original mean shift algorithm is presented [6,7]. Generally, a set $\{x_i\}_{i=1}^n$, $x_i \in \mathbb{R}^d$ of points (feature vectors) is to be processed. In images, each pixel gives one such feature vector containing the pixel position and the grey level or colour. For $\{x_i\}$, the kernel density estimate (KDE) at x with the kernel $K(.)$ and with the half bandwidth (half window size) h is given by

$$\widehat{f}_K(x) = \frac{1}{nh^d} \sum_{i=1}^n K\left(\frac{x - x_i}{h}\right). \tag{1}$$

Since the mean shift procedure is based on finding the local maxima of KDE, the estimate of the gradient of KDE is of importance that is of the form

$$\widehat{\nabla f}_K(x) \equiv \nabla \widehat{f}_K(x) = \frac{1}{nh^d} \sum_{i=1}^n \nabla K\left(\frac{x - x_i}{h}\right). \tag{2}$$

Various kernels have been studied for the use in Eq. (1). The kernel yielding the minimum mean integrated square error of estimation is the Epanechnikov kernel

$$K_E(x) = \begin{cases} \frac{1}{2}c_d^{-1}(d+2)(1 - \|x\|^2) & \text{if} \quad \|x\| \leq 1 \\ 0 & \text{otherwise} \end{cases}, \tag{3}$$

where c_d is the volume of the unit d-dimensional sphere. Another popular kernel is a Gaussian kernel. Since we use the Epanechnikov kernel in our method, we restrict ourselves to this case also in the rest of this section. For the Epanechnikov kernel, the density gradient estimation from Eq. (2) can be expressed as follows

$$\widehat{\nabla f}_K(x) = \frac{1}{nh^d c_d} \frac{d+2}{h^2} \sum_{x_i \in S_h(x)} (x_i - x)$$

$$= \frac{n_x}{nh^d c_d} \frac{d+2}{h^2} \left[\frac{1}{n_x} \sum_{x_i \in S_h(x)} (x_i - x) \right], \tag{4}$$

where $S_h(x)$ is a hypersphere centered at x, having the radius of h, the volume of $h^d c_d$, and containing n_x points $x_i \in S_h(x)$. The quantity $n_x/(nh^d c_d) \equiv \widehat{f}_G(x)$ can be seen as a kernel density estimate computed with the uniform kernel over $S_h(x)$. In Eq. (4), the last term in the square brackets is the sample *mean shift*. The equation shows that the gradient is proportional to the mean shift. The steepest gradient ascent method may, therefore, be realised by using the mean shift instead of the whole gradient of KDE. From the rightmost term in Eq. (4), the new position of x that can be used when seeking for a local maximum of KDE is given by

$$x \leftarrow \frac{1}{n_x} \sum_{x_i \in S_h(x)} x_i \equiv M(x), \tag{5}$$

where $M(x)$ stands for the *new position* computed for x.

Let $M^2(x)$ stand for $M(M(x))$ and so on. For clustering on $\{x_i\}_{i=1}^n$, the iterations starting at each data point can be run that map each x_i to $M^\infty(x_i) \equiv a(x_i) \equiv a_i$. For a_i, we use the term *attractor* of x_i. Clearly, only a finite number of iterations can be done in practice. This process is a gradient ascent technique taking x_i and moving it to the place a_i with a locally maximal value of KDE. Since many points can be attracted to one KDE node, the algorithm may be used for clustering, e.g., for image segmentation. It has been proven that for convex kernels with monotonically decreasing profile, which is also the case of the Epanechnikov kernel, the sequences $\{M^k(x_i)\}$ and $\{\widehat{f}_K(M^k(x_i))\}$, $k = 1, 2, \ldots$ converge. Moreover, the latter is monotonically increasing [7].

In addition to segmentation, the mean shift algorithm can also be used for image filtering. For this purpose, the vectors x_i, a_i can be divided into their spatial (spatial image coordinates) and range parts (grey level or colour) $x_i = (x_i^s, x_i^r)$, $a_i = (a_i^s, a_i^r)$. Filtering is then carried out by computing the vectors (x_i^s, a_i^r) for all image points.

3   Proposed Method

Consider the 2D intensity images, e.g., greyscale images. In this case, we have the points $x = (x^s, x^r)$, $x^s \in \mathbb{R}^2$, $x^r \in \mathbb{R}$ (Section 2) defining a 2D manifold (alternatively, we could consider $x^s \in \mathbb{R}^3$ and $x^r \in \mathbb{R}$ for the 3D intensity images). Suppose that a cube $\Omega \subset \mathbb{R}^3$, $\Omega \equiv \Omega^s \times \Omega^r$ exists containing all the points. We introduce a sampling of the vector field of new positions, which is done in a regular grid $\{x_g\}$ of sample points in Ω. The grid of sample points in Ω^s typically corresponds to the grid structure of image. The sampling of intensity values may also be given by the images we deal with (e.g., the images with 256 levels of intensity may be processed) or some sampling technique may be used otherwise if necessary.

The overview of the algorithm we propose is the following. Firstly, we compute the values of new positions $\{M(x_g)\}$ at sample points. Theoretically, the computation is based on Eq. (5), similarly as in the original method, but we propose an algorithm that makes it possible to compute the new positions at the sample points quickly. Then, for every image point x_i, we carry out the iterations $\{M^k(x_i)\}$. For doing that, we do not use the formula from Eq. (5). Instead, for determining each new position, we repeatedly use the trilinear interpolation in the sampled vector field. In the rest of this section, we will show that this method is effective, i.e., that the whole computation can be done quickly. In Section 5, we will also show that the result obtained in this way is good, i.e., comparable with the result obtained from the original method.

The effectiveness of the method is based on the following observation. Consider an equidistant quantisation with N_b intensity values $\{b_j\}_{j=1}^{N_b}$ in the space of intensities; we may suppose that $\{b_j\}$ is an interval of integer numbers. For each grid node x_g, we have $x_g = (x_g^s, x_g^r)$, $x_g^r \in \{b_j\}$. Say that the values of new positions at a certain x_g^s should be computed. Let N_s stand for the number of points that must be considered in the neighborhood of each image point with respect to a chosen value of bandwidth (for accessing the neighbouring points, we exploit the grid structure of images). We claim that the time of $\max(\Theta(N_b), \Theta(N_s))$ is sufficient for computing the new positions for all N_b intensity values at x_g^s. For illustrating the importance of this claim, let us suppose that $N_b < N_s$, which is often the case. For example, we may have $N_b = 256$ levels of intensities. For $h = 10$, the bandwidth is $2 \times 10 + 1 = 21$, and $N_s = 21^2$ if the square neighbourhood is considered. The claim then says that, at the expense of the time complexity of computing one mean shift iteration by making use of Eq. (5) giving the move at only one single point, i.e., for one value of intensity, we can compute at x_g^s the new positions for all N_b intensity values. Since the claim is essential for our method, we present the algorithm how the computation can be done. The algorithm is then also directly used in practical implementation. The sweeping technique known from computational geometry is the main idea on which the algorithm is based.

Say that we want to carry out the computation for an image point whose coordinates are $x^s = (u, v)$. For computing the new position $M(u, v, b)$ for the intensity value of b, the points $x_i = (u_i, v_i, b_i)$ should be taken into account that satisfy the inequality

$$\frac{(u_i - u)^2}{h_s^2} + \frac{(v_i - v)^2}{h_s^2} + \frac{(b_i - b)^2}{h_r^2} < 1, \tag{6}$$

where h_s and h_r stand for the half bandwidth in the spatial and range domains, respectively (from now on, we will distinguish between these two values). In the algorithm, the new positions will be computed successively for increasing intensities. For given values of (u, v), the point (u_i, v_i, b_i) influences the result only for the intensities b lying in the range $b_{\min_i} < b < b_{\max_i}$. The values of $b_{\min_i}$ and $b_{\max_i}$ can be easily obtained from Eq. (6). We have

$$b_{\min_i, \max_i} = b_i \mp h_r \sqrt{1 - \frac{(u_i - u)^2}{h_s^2} - \frac{(v_i - v)^2}{h_s^2}}. \tag{7}$$

The sweeping algorithm for computing the new positions at a point for all intensity values may now be formulated as follows.

Algorithm 1. The algorithm for computing the new positions for (u, v) image grid coordinates and for all $b_1 \le b_j \le b_{N_b}$. *Input*: Source image, equidistant quantisation $\{b_j\}$, location (u, v). *Output*: The new positions $\{M(u, v, b_j)\}_{j=1,2,\ldots}$ with the same value as is the value obtained from Eq. (5). The following is done.

1. Take the image points that can influence the computation (let N_s be their number), i.e., the image points from a neighbourhood of (u, v). We may take, e.g., a square with $N_s = (2\lfloor h_s \rfloor + 1) \times (2\lfloor h_s \rfloor + 1)$ pixels. For each such point, compute the values $b_{\min_i, \max_i}$. If two different real values are obtained from Eq. (7), the point is further processed by inserting its data into two priority queues. Into the *insert-event queue*, the values of $(\lfloor b_{\min_i} \rfloor, u_i, v_i, b_i)$ are placed. The *delete-event queue* contains the values $(\lfloor b_{\max_i} \rfloor, u_i, v_i, b_i)$.

In the queues, the point records are kept sorted according to $\lfloor b_{\min_i} \rfloor$ and $\lfloor b_{\max_i} \rfloor$, respectively.

2. Clear the counter n_x of points falling into the sphere $S_h(u, v, b)$. Clear the counters computing the sums Σu_i, Σv_i, Σb_i of coordinates for the points falling into the sphere (Section 2, Eq. (5)).

3. Process all the intensity values b_j, $b_1 \leq b_j \leq b_{N_b}$ from the smallest to the largest. For each intensity b_j, do the following:

   (a) Take out the set of point data $\{(\lfloor b_{\min_k} \rfloor, u_k, v_k, b_k) : \lfloor b_{\min_k} \rfloor = b_j\}$ from the insert-event queue. For each point in this set, increment the counter n_x, and update the sums Σu_i, Σv_i, Σb_i by adding u_k, v_k, and b_k, respectively.

   (b) Take out the set of point data $\{(\lfloor b_{\max_k} \rfloor, u_k, v_k, b_k) : \lfloor b_{\max_k} \rfloor = b_j\}$ from the delete-event queue. For each point in this set, decrement the counter n_x, and update the sums Σu_i, Σv_i, Σb_i by subtracting u_k, v_k, and b_k, respectively.

   (c) Compute the values of the new position vector for b_k from the momentary values of the sums and the counter, i.e., $M(u, v, b_k) = (\Sigma u_i/n_x, \Sigma v_i/n_x, \Sigma b_i/n_x)$.

The time complexity of the algorithm, i.e., the time complexity of computing the new positions for a given (u, v) and for all N_b intensity values is the following: The time for computing the values $\lfloor b_{\min_i} \rfloor$, $\lfloor b_{\max_i} \rfloor$ including sorting them in the queues is linear in the number of points, i.e., $\Theta(N_s)$ (linear time of sorting is due to the fact that we deal here with integer numbers; it can be realised, e.g., by inserting into an array of lists of values). All the actions that are carried out in Step 3 can be done in the time that is linear in the number of points and in the number of intensity levels, i.e., $\Theta(N_s) + \Theta(N_b)$. It is due to the fact that each point is touched only two times (inserted and deleted) and due to the fact that the output values of new positions are computed for each value of intensity. It follows that the total running time required by the algorithm is $\Theta(N_s) + \Theta(N_b) = \max(\Theta(N_s), \Theta(N_b))$.

Similarly as in the original method, the iterations $\{M^k(x_i)\}$ are computed for all image points x_i. The difference rests in the use of trilinear interpolation instead of Eq. (5). For interpolation, the values of new positions are available at sample points $\{x_g\}$. Say that the value of new position for an arbitrary point $(u, v, b) \in \Omega$ is to be computed. The values, denoted by $M_1, \ldots, M_8$, in the eight neighbouring grid nodes are needed for that. Let ξ, η, μ be the fractional parts of u, v, and b, respectively. The new position for a general point (u, v, b) can be obtained, in a constant time, by making use of the equation

$$M(\xi, \eta, \mu) = [(1 - \xi)(1 - \eta)M_1 + \xi(1 - \eta)M_2 + (1 - \xi)\eta M_3 + \xi\eta M_4](1 - \mu)$$
$$+ [(1 - \xi)(1 - \eta)M_5 + \xi(1 - \eta)M_6 + (1 - \xi)\eta M_7 + \xi\eta M_8]\mu. \quad (8)$$

If we have $N_b < N_s$, and if the number of iterations is also expected to be less than N_s, we may conclude that for the whole image containing N_p pixels, the new algorithm will run in $\Theta(N_p N_s)$ time. The original algorithm, in contrast, runs in $\Theta(k N_p N_s)$ time, where k stands for the number of iterations.

4   Implementation Issues

In the algorithm, the values of new position at each image pixel are computed for all N_b values of intensity. We use the term *vector of new positions* (or simply a *vector*) for these N_b values associated with one pixel. The practical trouble is with storing these vectors for all pixels. For saving memory, we limit the number of vectors that can be stored simultaneously. It is expressed by the quantity denoted by M_s. If $M_s = 1$, it means that the vectors can be stored for all pixels. The value of $M_s = 0.1$, for example, tells that the vectors can be stored only for 10% of pixels. The vectors are not computed beforehand, but on demand during the interpolation. If a vector is required that has not been computed yet, it is computed. If the prescribed amount of memory is exhausted, the longest unused vector is forgotten. If a vector is forgotten and then required again, it is computed again. In Section 5, we show that this mechanism is efficient.

5   Experimental Results

During experimental evaluation, the following properties have been tested: (i) the compliance of the results of the new algorithm with the results given by the original mean shift method, (ii) the running time, (iii) the issues of memory consumption. Recall that, for describing the iterative process of finding the attractor of x_i in the original mean shift method, we have introduced (Section 2) the notation $M^\infty(x_i) \equiv a(x_i) \equiv a_i$; a_i may be divided into the spatial and the range part $a(x_i) \equiv (a^s(x_i), a^r(x_i))$. In a similar meaning, we now introduce $\widehat{a}_i \equiv \widehat{a}(x_i) \equiv (\widehat{a}^s(x_i), \widehat{a}^r(x_i))$ for the attractor of x_i obtained in the new method. For measuring the difference between the results of the original and new method, we can measure the distance between the attractors for all image points x_i. Let N_p be the number of image points. We introduce the following quantities

$$d_s^2 = \frac{1}{N_p} \sum_{i=1}^{N_p} \|\widehat{a}^s(x_i) - a^s(x_i)\|^2, \quad d_r^2 = \frac{1}{N_p} \sum_{i=1}^{N_p} \|\widehat{a}^r(x_i) - a^r(x_i)\|^2. \quad (9)$$

The first quantity measures the Euclidean distance between the spatial parts of corresponding attractors; the second measures the distance between the range parts. Introducing the second metric is motivated by the fact that the distance between the spatial parts need not necessarily be relevant. Consider, for example, a big (relatively to the value of h_s) area in image whose ideal intensity is constant, but a certain amount of noise is present. For image points from such an area, a lot of attractors (sometimes quite distant) are obtained by the original mean shift method. Their exact spatial position a_i^s is determined, in essence, only by noise, i.e., is less relevant. The position a_i^r in the intensity space, on the other hand, is relevant. We note that d_r measures the distance between the images obtained by the original and the modified mean shift image filtering, respectively (Section 2).

For presenting the results of testing, several greyscale images of size 1024×768 pixels are used (Fig. 1). The intensity levels are $[0, 1, \ldots, 255]$, i.e., $N_b = 256$.

Fig. 1. Source images for testing

The results of mean shift filtering obtained by making use of the new and original method, respectively, are shown in Fig. 2.

For judging the compliance of the results, various quantities are given in Table 1. In both methods, the iterations were stopped after the size of shift dropped below the value of 0.01. In the table, the values of the difference d_r introduced by Eq. (9) between the results of filtering should be seen relatively with respect to the size of the used intensity interval (256). As another clue that may help to understand the practical importance of the difference of a certain size, a quantity denoted by c_r is presented too. It is a difference obtained for the original method. In this case, the test image, and the test image modified by adding a small amount of Gaussian noise (zero mean, $\sigma = 1.0$) are now used for obtaining the values of $a^r(x_i)$ and $\hat{a}^r(x_i)$, respectively. From the values of d_r, we can see that the differences in the results are relatively small, typically below 1% of intensity range and are comparable with the differences that are caused by adding a small amount of noise to the input test images in the original method.

Further values that make it possible to judge the properties of the new method are stated in Table 1. The quantities D_n and D_o stand for the normalised density achieved by the new and the original method, respectively. By *normalised achieved density* we mean that for all image points x_i, the sum of the kernel density estimates at their attractors $a(x_i)$ is determined (the shadow Epanechnikov kernel is used that corresponds to the unit kernel used for shifting) and normalised to the value per one pixel. The quantities denoted by B_n and B_o express the *normalised length of boundaries* in the images filtered by the new and original method, respectively. If the intensity difference between two neighbouring pixels (we consider four-connectedness) is greater than a predefined value ε, the pixel pair contributes to the length of boundaries by one. The final total length of boundaries determined for all pixel pairs is then normalised by dividing by the square root of the number of image pixels. In the table, the values of B_n and B_o are presented for $\varepsilon = 3$. Finally, the mean square distances, denoted by Q_o and Q_n, between the intensities at corresponding pixels in the source and filtered test image are evaluated for the new and original method, respectively.

Fig. 2. The results of mean shift filtering obtained by the new algorithm (*the top row of images*) and the original algorithm (*bottom row of images*). Only a cutout is shown from each image for better visibility. $h_s = 10$, $h_r = 20$.

From the table, it can be seen that the new method always gives slightly higher values of the mean achieved normalised density and a shorter normalised boundary length (which may also be regarded as illustrating the quality of eventual segmentation). This must be clearly accompanied by slightly greater values of Q_n (greater than Q_o). This behaviour can be easily explained. The sampling in the new method seems to introduce a certain filtering in the space of densities. In the original method, it may happen that the iterative process will stop at an indistinctive local density maximum. The sampling may filter out such badly visible maxima. Thus, the new method may continue to the maximum that is more apparent.

For testing the running times, the original method was thoroughly implemented. Naturally, also in this case, the fact was taken into account that the image points are organised in a regular grid and, therefore, the relevant points are better accessible than in the case of general input. In the new method, the number of pixels in which the vectors of new positions can be precomputed was set to $M_s = 0.03$ (i.e., 3%, Section 4). The numbers of iterations, denoted by n_n and n_o, and the running times, denoted by T_n and T_o, achieved by the new and the original method, respectively, are given in Table 2 (Intel Core 2 Duo computer, 2.4 GHz, only one core used, Intel C++ compiler). Two sets of results are presented that were obtained for stopping the iterations after the size

Table 1. Testing the compliance of the results of the new and original method: The normalised differences (d_r) between the images filtered by the original and the new method, the normalised differences (c_r) caused in the original method by adding a small amount of noise (a clue for better understanding the values of d_r), the normalised achieved densities (D_n, D_o), the normalised achieved boundary lengths (B_n, B_o), and the mean square differences (Q_n, Q_o) between the image and the filtered image for the new and original method, respectively

	Test	d_r	c_r	D_n	D_o	B_n	B_o	Q_n	Q_o
1	Image 1 ($h_s = 10$, $h_r = 20$)	2.48	2.34	134.0	133.0	145.0	156.3	7.7	7.1
2	Image 2 ($h_s = 10$, $h_r = 20$)	2.67	2.31	140.7	139.1	101.0	107.7	8.4	7.7
3	Image 3 ($h_s = 10$, $h_r = 20$)	3.45	3.31	124.9	122.9	173.2	195.1	11.0	10.0
4	Image 1 ($h_s = 20$, $h_r = 40$)	2.32	3.14	545.6	544.4	90.3	93.1	13.3	13.1
5	Image 2 ($h_s = 20$, $h_r = 40$)	2.15	2.34	590.1	588.7	48.4	52.8	13.5	13.2
6	Image 3 ($h_s = 20$, $h_r = 40$)	2.59	3.52	531.2	529.6	96.5	102.3	18.0	17.7

of shift dropped below either the value of 0.1 or the value of 0.01. As can be seen, the values of the speed-up factor vary between 3 and 17 approximately. The behaviour of factor corresponds to the theoretical expectation (it should be proportional to the average number of iterations that are needed in the original method, Section 3). In the new method, the running times increase with the number of iterations slowly (only due to the computational cost of trilinear interpolation). The times seem to be longer than is the time of one iteration in the original method (2.5 times approximately), which is simply due to a bigger overhead of the more complicated algorithm. The $\Theta(N_b)$ time we have neglected in the theoretical estimations also plays the role, which is visible especially for smaller values of h_s.

The goal of the last test was to show that the speed-up factor may be significant even though a low memory consumption is required. For this reason, the running times were measured for various amounts of memory available for

Table 2. Testing the running times for various 1024×768 pixel images and various values of h_s, h_r. The numbers of iterations (n_n, n_o), running times in seconds (T_n, T_o) for the new and the original method, respectively, and the speed-up factors (T_o/T_n). The iterations had been stopped after the shift size dropped either below the value of 0.1 (*left table*) or 0.01 (*right table*).

	n_n	T_n [s]	n_o	T_o [s]	T_o/T_n		n_n	T_n [s]	n_o	T_o [s]	T_o/T_n
1	12.7	7.5	8.0	22.5	3.0	1	45.4	9.2	12.9	36.4	3.9
2	23.1	7.6	12.5	35.3	4.6	2	69.5	10.3	21.6	61.0	5.9
3	24.9	8.7	14.4	40.8	4.7	3	61.1	10.5	21.7	61.4	5.9
4	18.7	25.7	12.7	137.6	5.4	4	46.3	27.5	22.9	247.5	9.0
5	37.7	26.3	22.8	246.9	9.4	5	82.6	27.9	45.6	493.1	17.7
6	38.3	26.7	26.1	282.4	10.6	6	70.8	28.4	43.3	468.8	16.5

Table 3. The increase of running time of the new method with the decreasing amount (M_s) of available memory

	$M_s = 0.3$	0.1	0.03	0.01	0.003
1	1.09	1.08	1	1.11	3.73
2	1.08	1.03	1	1.15	3.79
3	1.12	1.02	1	1.20	4.45
4	1.04	1	1.04	2.01	
5	1.05	1	1.02	2.59	
6	1.09	1	1.08	2.98	

running the algorithm (Section 4). The shortest time for each image was taken as a base. The times achieved for other values of M_s are expressed relatively with respect to this base time in Table 3. The pixels were processed in rows, i.e., no special order was used. Clearly, the running times increase if only a small amount of memory is available. The fact that the large amount of memory does not lead to the absolute shortest time can be easily explained: The memory is only useful if it is necessary. Merely the overhead times for maintaining the memory increase otherwise. From the table, it seems that the new method may be useful even though the precomputed vectors of new positions can be stored for only 1% - 10% of pixels, i.e., if a relatively small amount of memory is available.

6   Conclusion

We have proposed a fast algorithm for computing the classical mean shift procedure with the finite support step kernel for computing the shifts. Measured by the order of complexity, the algorithm runs in the time that is equal to the time required for computing only a single mean shift iteration step (for each point) in the original method. We believe that this itself can be regarded as an interesting outcome since the methods striving to reduce the number of iterations can hardly be better for the mentioned kernel. The experiments have confirmed this result, although the practical running times on a real computer are a bit longer and correspond to approximately 2.5 iterations, which can be still regarded as acceptable. The speed-up factor we have achieved in the experiments was typically between 5 and 15. It is not as much as it was reported, for example, in [3] but, for achieving the speed-up, we use the full representation of iteration trajectories, i.e., we do not reduce them into their projections onto the image plane, which may lead to erroneously detected attractors in more confusing image areas. It also follows that the speed-up factor of the method increases as the original method requires more and more iterations.

On the other hand, the following limitations of the algorithm should be clearly mentioned: (i) For computing the shifts, the algorithm requires the unit kernel, which corresponds to the Epanechnikov shadow kernel for computing the densities (some authors prefer the use of Gaussian kernel); (ii) the images with a single value at each pixel are required (the multichannel images must be converted by making use of a suitable technique, e.g., PCA [11]); (iii) the number of intensity levels should not be too high since the memory consumption as well as the running time could increase otherwise.

Acknowledgements. This work was partially supported by the grant FR-TI1/262 of the Ministry of Industry and Trade of the Czech Republic.

References

1. Barash, D., Comaniciu, D.: A Common Framework for Nonlinear Diffusion, Adaptive Smoothing, Bilateral Filtering and Mean Shift. Image and Vision Computing 22, 73–81 (2004)
2. Carreira-Perpiñán, M.: Fast Nonparametric Clustering with Gaussian Blurring Mean-Shift. In: International Conference on Machine Learning, pp. 153–160 (2006)
3. Carreira-Perpiñán, M.: Acceleration Strategies for Gaussian Mean-Shift Image Segmentation. In: Conference on Computer Vision and Pattern Recognition, pp. 1160–1167 (2006)
4. Cheng, Y.: Mean Shift, Mode Seeking and Clustering. IEEE Transactions on Pattern Analysis and Machine Intelligence 17, 790–799 (1995)
5. Christoudias, C.M., Georgescu, B., Meer, P.: Synergism in Low Level Vision. In: International Conference on Pattern Recognition, pp. 150–155 (2002)
6. Comaniciu, D., Meer, P.: Mean Shift Analysis and Applications. In: International Conference on Computer Vision, pp. 1197–1203 (1999)
7. Comaniciu, D., Meer, P.: Mean Shift: A Robust Approach toward Feature Space Analysis. IEEE Transactions on Pattern Analysis and Machine Intelligence 24, 1–18 (2002)
8. Comaniciu, D., Ramesh, V., Meer, P.: Kernel-Based Object Tracking. IEEE Transactions on Pattern Analysis and Machine Intelligence 25, 564–575 (2003)
9. Fukunaga, K., Hostetler, L.D.: The Estimation of the Gradient of a Density Function, with Application in Pattern Recognition. IEEE Transactions on Information Theory 21, 32–40 (1975)
10. Georgescu, B., Shimshoni, I., Meer, P.: Mean Shift Based Clustering in High Dimensions: A Texture Classification Example. In: International Conference on Computer Vision, pp. 456–463 (2003)
11. Paris, S., Durand, F.: A Topological Approach to Hierarchical Segmentation Using Mean Shift. In: Conference on Computer Vision and Pattern Recognition, pp. 1–8 (2007)
12. Vedaldi, A., Soatto, S.: Quick Shift and Kernel Methods for Mode Seeking. In: Forsyth, D., Torr, P., Zisserman, A. (eds.) ECCV 2008, Part IV. LNCS, vol. 5305, pp. 705–718. Springer, Heidelberg (2008)
13. Yang, C., Duraiswami, R., Gumerov, N., Davis, L.: Improved Fast Gauss Transform and Efficient Kernel Density Estimation. In: International Conference on Computer Vision, pp. 464–471 (2003)
14. Yang, C., Duraiswami, R., Dementhon, D., Davis, L.: Mean-Shift Analysis Using Quasi-Newton Methods. In: International Conference on Image Processing, pp. 447–450 (2003)

Learning to Adapt: A Method for Automatic Tuning of Algorithm Parameters

Jamie Sherrah

DSTO Melbourne
506 Lorimer Street, Fishermans Bend, VIC 3207 Australia
jamie.sherrah@dsto.defence.gov.au

Abstract. Most computer vision algorithms have parameters that must be hand-selected using expert knowledge. These parameters hinder the use of large computer vision systems in real-world applications. In this work, a method is presented for automatically and continuously tuning the parameters of algorithms in a real-time modular vision system. In the training phase, a human expert teaches the system how to adapt the algorithm parameters based on training data. During operation, the system measures features from the inputs and outputs of each module and decides how to modify the parameters. Rather than learning good parameter values in absolute terms, *incremental* changes are modelled based on relationships between algorithm inputs and outputs. These increments are continuously applied online so that parameters stabilise to suitable values. The method is demonstrated on a three-module people-tracking system for video surveillance.

1 Introduction

Algorithm parameters are the bane of computer vision researchers and practitioners. Most algorithms have a set of parameters that must be set manually for a specific data set or environment. Example algorithm parameters are:

- The threshold in image binarisation.
- The number of clusters in k-means clustering (model complexity).
- The learning rate in statistical background modelling (temporal scale).
- The window size in KLT tracking (spatial scale).

Generally expert knowledge is required to set algorithm parameters properly. Often the expert has no guidance or automatic method to set the algorithm parameters, so a trial-and-error approach is taken.

While manual selection of algorithm parameters might be tolerable in the computer vision laboratory, it can be a stumbling block for deployment. A commercial vision system might be deployed on a variety of different data sets or environments, each requiring different parameter settings. A professional integrator could calibrate the system initially, but this would not help with seasonal variations, non-stationarities and unexpected changes to the system.

J. Blanc-Talon et al. (Eds.): ACIVS 2010, Part I, LNCS 6474, pp. 414–425, 2010.

To facilitate the use of computer vision systems in real-world applications, robust and adaptive algorithms are needed. One approach to making robust systems is to provide a more intuitive interface for the human operator to select parameters, for example see [8]. However operator feedback is not always available for real-time systems, and not practical for large-scale systems such as visual surveillance networks. In such cases, it would be desirable for the system to be *autonomic* [2]: self-managing with an automated parameter-tuning mechanism.

1.1 Related Work

The problem of automatic tuning of algorithm parameters has been approached previously with rigorous modelling [12], distributed self-regulating systems based on output quality measures [11,13] or on corrective feedback from a human operator [15,14], and reinforcement of consensus [9,10]. These approaches seem to lack generality, resulting in complicated hand-crafted solutions to specific applications. The burden of manually engineering relationships between parameters and quality measures can be relieved by machine learning based on ground truth training data. Good parameters have been learned as a function of the input space [1] and of the output space [5,7,6,3]. Whereas learning-based methods can be easier to apply to new systems, the ability of a trained system to generalise in previously-unseen conditions or environments is a key issue. In [7,6,3], a scene reference model is learned for a visual surveillance scenario based on hand-labelled training data. The distribution of "normal" output features is learned and subsequently used to compute the quality of an output based on how normal it is. The trained system's whole concept of quality is based on those scenarios present in the training set, which in general cannot cover all eventualities for a given scene. Furthermore this method relies on labour-intensive labelling of data by an expert *per deployment*, which is significantly more work than manually tuning the parameters.

1.2 A New Approach to Adapting Parameters

In this paper a novel method is presented for automatically tuning the parameters of a modular real-time computer vision system. The method is modelled on the way a human operator generally goes about adjusting algorithm parameters: the input and output of the algorithm are inspected, and expert knowledge is used to decide whether to increment or decrement the parameter or leave it alone. This automatic tuning is applied continuously to keep the parameters at values that produce good output. The novel aspects of the method are:

1. It is observed that the suitability of a parameter depends not just on the algorithm's output, but on the output *given the input*. For example when binarising an image, an all-zero output is appropriate when then input image is also all zeros, but not when the input contains significant intensities.
2. Rather than modelling the whole input/output space to determine quality, the *relationship* between input and output is modelled. This relationship is more generic and allows better generalisation from training data.

3. The method uses training data to learn *incremental* changes to parameters rather than absolute parameter values. For the binarisation example, when presented with the input and output images it is much easier to determine that the threshold needs to be increased or decreased than to prescribe an appropriate threshold for the input.
4. A new data labelling method is proposed that allows many training labels to be generated from only two hand-selected parameter values.

These ideas are demonstrated in a people-tracking system consisting of three modules: background modelling, foreground binarisation, and tracking. It is shown that the method can continuously adapt the parameters of the system for test sequences taken at a different time and view point from the training data. The parameters converge to approximately the same values from several different initial conditions.

2   Algorithm Parameters and Quality

Let us begin by discussing algorithm parameters[1] and why they are needed at all. Computer vision problems are problems of inference, and assumptions must be made to constrain the process of recovering information about the 3D world from 2D images. These assumptions provide a context for tractable algorithms. The parameter values given to an algorithm are an important means of specifying that context. While it is the aim of the researcher to create robust algorithms that have as few parameters as possible, eradicating parameters altogether is neither possible nor desirable. Another way of viewing algorithm parameters is by the chicken-egg principle. Often the algorithm parameters can only be directly computed from the estimated model parameters, which in turn must be computed given the algorithm parameters and input data.

Usually the researcher or operator provides contextual knowledge by setting the algorithm parameters manually. This process introduces a subjective notion of the *quality* of the parameter values. Consider an algorithm that has a single parameter θ to be a functional mapping from input X to output Y:

$$Y = \mathcal{F}(X; \theta) \tag{1}$$

Let $P(X)$ be the distribution over the input space. We can define a quality function $Q(\theta)$ to be a subjective measure of the quality of parameter values. $Q(\theta)$ exists entirely in the mind of the human algorithm developer or operator. The function is illustrated in Figure 1. $Q(\theta)$ quantifies the ability of the algorithm to generate desirable outputs given inputs sampled from $P(X)$. There is an optimal parameter value θ^* that maximises $Q(\theta)$. Since $Q(\theta)$ is subjective, so is θ^*: that is, the optimal parameters are the best values as chosen by the human operator.

---

[1] In this paper the term "algorithm parameter" refers to an ordinal constant given to an algorithm, as opposed to a parameter that is estimated by the algorithm from the input data. For example in k-means clustering, k is an algorithm parameter and the cluster centres are estimated parameters.

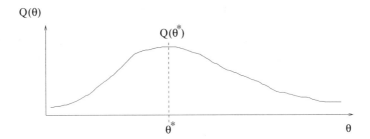

Fig. 1. The quality function $Q(\theta)$ quantifies the subjective goodness of an algorithm parameter value

When configuring a real-time system, the operator is often unable to directly produce the optimal parameter value. Rather he/she starts with the current value, looks at the system input and output, and decides whether the parameter is too high, too low or just right. The parameter is modified in a corrective manner and the process continues by trial-and-error until the results are satisfactory. This process is exemplified in Figure 2. The task is to select a threshold to binarise the foreground likelihood image from a background model shown in Figure 2(a). The operator does not immediately know that the best threshold is 55 grey values. From an initial threshold value and referring to the input image, it can be seen that there are too many foreground pixels (Figure 2(b)). The threshold is too low, so it is increased somewhat. Now the operator perceives that the foreground objects are broken and partially missing (Figure 2(c)), so the threshold must be too high. Finally the threshold is decreased a little bit, resulting in an acceptable segmentation (Figure 2(d)).

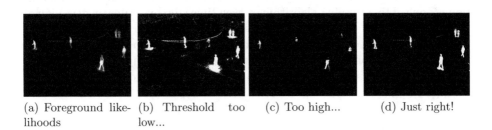

(a) Foreground likelihoods (b) Threshold too low... (c) Too high... (d) Just right!

Fig. 2. Example of different thresholds in foreground segmentation

If things were this simple then the algorithm developer could simply fix $\theta = \theta^*$ and be done with it. The problem is that $P(X)$ varies with different data sets, or in the case of real-time (online) systems it can be non-stationary. This causes $Q(\theta)$ and hence θ^* to vary with conditions also. For autonomous systems, a mechanism is required to update the parameters as the input distribution varies. Such a mechanism is proposed in the next section.

3   Estimating Optimal Parameters

The goal of this work is to develop a method to automatically adapt computer vision algorithm parameters in a similar manner to a human operator. The discussions here are confined to real-time video processing systems, such as those used for video surveillance analytics. In this case, the input space distribution could vary due to deployment in a new location (e.g. the camera moved), or due to non-stationarity (e.g. weather change, transition from a quiet to busy time of day). Since parameter quality is subjective, statistical learning from expert knowledge is a suitable approach.

Unlike previous efforts [1,7], the approach proposed here avoids the difficult task of modelling the whole input space. It is based on two key observations:

1. Manual tuning is often performed as a series of incremental changes to the parameter, requiring only the *gradient* of the quality function $dQ/d\theta$.
2. For many algorithms, there is a relationship between $dQ/d\theta$ and relative properties of the input and output. This relationship is much simpler to model than the input space, and is applicable for a wider range of $P(X)$ since it is more a property of the algorithm than of $P(X)$.

Using these observations an automatic method can be designed to mimic the way a human adapts algorithm parameters. The following two assumptions must first be made:

1. The algorithm parameter quality function is unimodal.
2. A non-stationary $P(X)$ changes slowly with time.

The first assumption means that the gradient of $Q(\theta)$ always points in the direction of θ^*. The second assumption means that the optimal value θ^* changes slowly with time so that an adaptive method can successfully track it. Adaptation is applied to a running algorithm at each time step by estimating the sign of the quality function gradient and adjusting the parameter in that direction. The direction is computed from the algorithm input and output using a function that is learned offline from human input. Over time θ_t should converge to its optimal value. In the following sections the details are given as to how this method can be applied in practice.

4   Example: People-Tracking System

For the remainder of this paper the parameter adaptation method is demonstrated using a very simple people-tracking system. The system operates on video from a fixed-view camera and consists of three modules, each possessing a single parameter. The system is depicted in Figure 3. First a statistical background model is used to compute the likelihood that each pixel is foreground:

$$f_t(x) = \left| \frac{I_t(x) - \mu_t(x)}{\sigma_t(x)} \right| \tag{2}$$

where $I_t(x)$ is the luminance input image, and $\mu_t(x)$ and $\sigma_t(x)$ are the parameters of a normal distribution learned recursively for each pixel:

$$\mu_{t+1}(x) = \alpha \cdot I_t(x) + (1 - \alpha) \cdot \mu_t(x) \tag{3}$$

$$\sigma_{t+1}^2(x) = \alpha \cdot (I_t(x) - \mu_t(x))^2 + (1 - \alpha) \cdot \sigma_t^2(x) \tag{4}$$

The single parameter for this module is the learning rate α. Second, these likelihoods are thresholded to compute a binary foreground mask using the threshold parameter T:

$$\phi_t(x) = \begin{cases} 1 \text{ if } f_t(x) \geq T \\ 0 \text{ otherwise} \end{cases} \tag{5}$$

Third, the connected components of the foreground mask are tracked over time. A set of states is maintained and matched to observations by nearest distance. The tracker has an algorithm parameter τ that is the time lag, measured in frames. When an observation is not matched by any tracker state, a new tracker state is created. This state is not *mature* until it has been observed for at least τ frames. If a state is ever unmatched while it is immature, then it is removed from the set. If a mature tracker state is unmatched for τ consecutive frames, it is also removed from the set.

Fig. 3. Diagram representing the three-module people-tracking system

While relatively simple, this system is interesting enough to show the flexibility of the approach. There is a diversity of input/output data types: images, masks, segmented regions and tracks. The background modelling and tracking modules both carry state, and the background model learning rate has a delayed effect on the output.

5   Learning to Adapt

This section presents the details of the automatic parameter tuning method. Each parameter of each algorithm is treated independently. Parameters are confined to a range and quantised, so that values come from an ordered set $\theta \in \{v_1, \ldots v_N\}$. The admissible parameter values for the people-tracking system are shown in Table 1. A parameter is adapted online by estimating the current optimal direction $\lambda_t(X, Y, \theta)$:

$$\lambda_t = \text{sign}(dQ_t/d\theta) = \begin{cases} +1 \text{ if } \theta_t < \theta_t^* \\ -1 \text{ if } \theta_t > \theta_t^* \\ 0 \quad \text{otherwise} \end{cases} \tag{6}$$

Table 1. Admissible values for the quantised algorithm parameters of the people-tracking system

Parameter	Description	Values
λ	background model learning rate	0.0001, 0.0003, 0.0010, 0.0032, 0.0100, 0.0316, 0.1000
T	foreground segmentation threshold	$0, 1, 2, \ldots 255$
τ	tracker time lag (frames)	$0, 2, 4, \ldots 100$

The parameter is updated for the next time step by adjusting it to the next quantised parameter value in the direction of λ_t:

$$\theta_{t+1} = v_k; \quad \theta_t = v_j, \ k = j + \lambda_t \tag{7}$$

λ_t is modelled as a function of the module input X_t and output Y_t:

$$\lambda_t = \mathcal{C}(X_t, Y_t) = \mathcal{C}(X_t, \mathcal{F}(X_t; \theta_t)) \tag{8}$$

Since λ_t is estimated from instantaneous data, it is implicitly assumed that $P(X) = \delta(X_t)$. The process of parameter adjustment proceeds in a continuous fashion. Because the background model and tracker carry state and parameter changes have a delayed effect, the following heuristic is used for these modules. The parameter is only allowed to change in the same direction as the previous change after a time delay has expired, where the delay is dictated by the estimated time for the current parameter to take effect.

The function $\mathcal{C}(.)$ is estimated offline from a training set $\{(X_i, Y_i, \theta_i)\}$ using supervised learning. The human operator teaches the system about the subjective parameter quality function by labelling the training data as described in the next section. Since λ_t is discrete, the function $\mathcal{C}(.)$ is approximated by a classifier trained on the labelled data. A three-class support vector machine is employed for this purpose. The classifier is trained on features extracted from the input and output of the algorithm module, as described later.

5.1   Labelling Training Data

The assumption that the parameter quality function is unimodal can be exploited to interactively label training data with minimal effort. The class labels that are to be assigned are essentially the sign of the gradient of the quality function that is depicted in Figure 1. Since the quality function is subjectively determined by a human, and a good algorithm should have stable performance for a broad range of parameter values, let us assume that the quality function is in reality coarsely quantised, as shown in Figure 4. The optimal parameter values span a broad peak in the unimodal quality function, bounded by θ_A^* and θ_B^*. Values $\theta \in [\theta_A^*, \theta_B^*]$ can be considered to be optimal parameter values, and the corresponding value of λ_t is zero since no change to the parameter is required. Similarly $\lambda_t = +1$ for $\theta < \theta_A^*$ and $\lambda_t = -1$ for $\theta > \theta_B^*$. Thus for a given X_t, if θ_A^* and θ_B^* are known then a training example $(X_t, Y_t(\theta), \lambda_t(\theta))$ can be computed automatically for

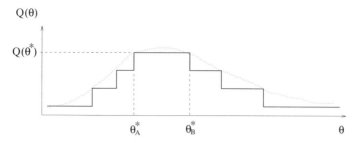

Fig. 4. The quantised quality function

each $\theta \in \{v_1, \ldots v_N\}$. In other words by manually providing two parameter values, N training examples are generated.

For each of the three people-tracking modules a graphical user interface (GUI) was constructed in Matlab that allows the developer to efficiently set θ_A^* and θ_B^* for each training input. An example is shown in Figure 5 for the foreground segmentation module. The left-most image is the original foreground likelihood image from the background model. The other two images show the result of thresholding using θ_A^* and θ_B^*. Using the sliders below, these thresholds can be very quickly set by the developer. The central slider is increased until the amount of clutter and speckle noise in the image above it is considered just acceptable. Similarly the right-most slider is decreased until all the scene objects are shown in the image above it. This process takes just seconds and generates 256 training examples. A similar approach was taken for the other two modules.

5.2   Features for Classification

If the classifier were trained on the raw input and output values from the algorithm it would not generalise well due to the high dimensionality of these spaces

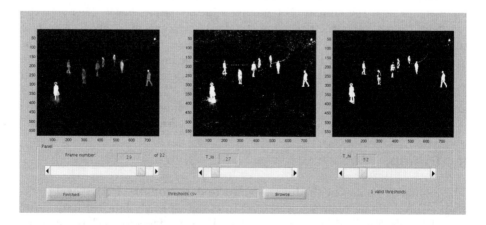

Fig. 5. The GUI used to label training data for the foreground segmentation module

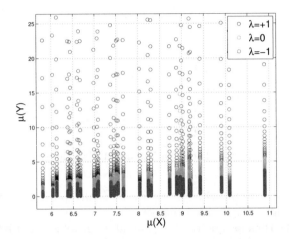

Fig. 6. Two of the features used for adaptation of the thresholding module, plotted versus each other for the whole training set. The three labelled classes are shown in different colours.

and the limited amount of training data. Consequently features must be computed that are sensitive to the quality gradient and invariant to other factors. Selection of features requires expert knowledge from the developer. However this knowledge needs only be applied once during algorithm development.

An algorithm can be seen as a transformation applied to its input to produce the output. The features extracted from input and output must facilitate modelling of the relationship between the parameter quality function gradient and the changes made by this transformation. For example in the foreground segmentation module, the developer observed that the number of pixels in the output mask relative to the number of bright pixels in the input image seems to give an indication of whether or not to increase or decrease the threshold. So the selected features should give some measure of the number of bright pixels in the input image, and the number of true pixels in the output mask. Therefore the four features used were the mean and standard deviations of all pixels in each of the input (f_t) and output (ϕ_t) images. Two of these, the input and output image means, are plotted in Figure 6 for each example in the training set, with the three labelled classes shown as different colours. A similar approach was taken for the other two modules, resulting in 10 features for the background model and 7 for the tracker. Note that the background model features were averaged over the last 10 frames to account for the delayed effect of the learning rate.

6   Results

The parameter tuning method was applied to data from the PETS 2009 workshop [4]. A training sequence was used to obtain sparsely labelled data using the GUI tools described in Section 5.1. The three classifiers for each of the modules were trained sequentially: first the background model, then the results from the background model were used as input to train the foreground segmentation, whose outputs were used to train the tracking module. The people-tracking system was then run on the training sequence in operational mode. For each module, the algorithm parameter was updated online using the trained classifier for that module. The parameter values over time are shown in Figure 7, one plot for each of the three modules. For each module three different initial conditions were used, shown in different colours on each plot. The method succeeded in tuning the parameters over time. A significant result is that for all modules the long-term tuning behaviour was largely independent of the initial conditions. This is remarkable given that the classifier outputs *changes* to parameter values and carries no temporal state.

Next, the system was run on two previously-unseen test sequences. The first was recorded from the same camera as the training sequence but at a different time of day (Figure 8), and the second from a different camera at the same time as the training sequence (Figure 9). These results are consistent with those from the training sequence, indicating that the method does have some ability to generalise to new conditions. Note that a bias in parameter values due to

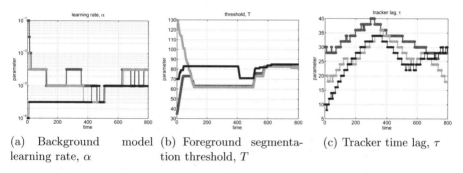

(a) Background model learning rate, α (b) Foreground segmentation threshold, T (c) Tracker time lag, τ

Fig. 7. Results from the training sequence. Parameter values are plotted as a function of time for three different initial values

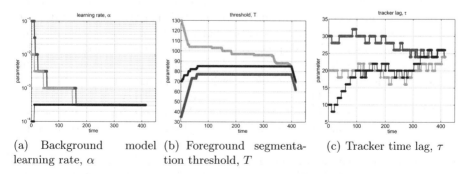

(a) Background model learning rate, α (b) Foreground segmentation threshold, T (c) Tracker time lag, τ

Fig. 8. Results from a sequence recorded at a different time from the training sequence. Parameter values are plotted as a function of time for three different initial values.

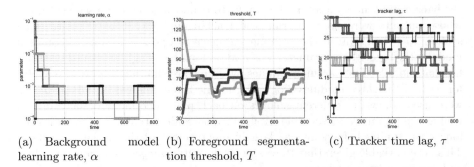

(a) Background   model (b) Foreground segmenta-   (c) Tracker time lag, τ
learning rate, α tion threshold, T

Fig. 9. Results from a sequence recorded from a different view but at the same time as the training sequence. Parameter values are plotted as a function of time for three different initial values.

initial conditions is not surprising since the system seeks a plateau of equally-good parameter values. In Figure 9 the tracker time lag τ is somewhat erratic, again due to the module's internal state and the non-linear dependence on the parameter. The limited amount of training data might be a contributing factor.

7   Discussion and Conclusion

A new method has been presented for automatically tuning the parameters of a real-time computer vision system. A human operator generates training examples of how to modify parameters to optimal values given the system input and output. A classifier is then trained to replicate this function. The classifier uses features that are hand-chosen to emphasise the differences between the system input and output that relate to the quality of the current parameters. Such a relation is easier to learn than mapping the whole input or output space, and more universal because it pertains to the algorithm rather than to the data.

A weak point of the method is the subjective selection of features for the classifier, more research is required in this area. Machine learning could be used to select appropriate features from a very large set. The experimental system in this paper addresses some difficult cases, in particular the background model learning rate which has a delayed effect when modified. How to handle such parameters in a more principled way needs to be investigated further. Speed of convergence needs to be improved by incorporating a variable step size into the method, i.e. the magnitude of $dQ/d\theta$ as well as the sign.

The generalisation ability of this adaptive method needs to be explored more carefully. Although the method attempts to model the transformation process of the algorithm independent of the data, it should not be expected to generalise to any possible input domain. This is because the concept of parameter quality is subjective, and may be different in different domains. For example if the task were to track high-speed vehicles or sports people then the most appropriate features and the mapping learned by the classifier might be quite different from the example given here.

References

1. Cai, X.C., Sowmya, A., Trinder, J.: Learning parameter tuning for object extraction. In: Asian Conf. on Computer Vision, pp. 868–877 (2006)
2. Crowley, J.L., Hall, D., Emonet, R.: Autonomic computer vision systems. In: Blanc-Talon (ed.) Advanced Concepts for Intell. Vision Systems (August 2007)
3. Crowley, J.L., Hall, D., Emonet, R.: An automatic approach for parameter selection in self-adaptive tracking. In: VISAPP, Portugal. Springer, Heidelberg (February 2006)
4. Ferryman, J., Shahrokni, A.: An overview of the PETS 2009 challenge. In: PETS Workshop, Miami, USA, pp. 25–30. IEEE Computer Society, Los Alamitos (June 2009)
5. Scotti, G., Marcenaro, L., Regazzoni, C.S.: SOM based algorithm for video surveillance system parameter optimal selection. In: AVSS, pp. 370–375 (2003)
6. Hall, D.: Automatic parameter regulation for a tracking system with an auto-critical function. In: CAMP Workshop, pp. 39–45 (July 2005)
7. Hall, D.: Automatic parameter regulation of perceptual systems. Image and Vision Computing 24(8), 870–881 (2006)
8. Huang, Y., Brown, M.S.: User-assisted ink-bleed correction for handwritten documents. In: Joint Conf. on Digital Libraries, pp. 263–271. ACM, New York (2008)
9. Marsico, M., Nappi, M., Riccio, D.: Multibiometric people identification: A self-tuning architecture. In: Int'l Conf. on Advances in Biometrics, pp. 980–989. Springer, Heidelberg (2009)
10. De Marsico, M., Nappi, M., Riccio, D.: A self-tuning people identification system from split face components. In: Wada, T., Huang, F., Lin, S. (eds.) PSIVT 2009. LNCS, vol. 5414, pp. 1–12. Springer, Heidelberg (2009)
11. Murino, V., Foresti, G.L., Regazzoni, C.S.: A distributed probabilistic system for adaptive regulation of image-processing parameters. IEEE Trans. Systems, Man and Cybernetics 26(1), 1–20 (1996)
12. Ramesh, V., Haralick, R.M., Zhang, X., Nadadur, D.C., Thornton, K.B.: Automatic selection of tuning parameters for feature extraction sequences. In: CVPR, pp. 672–677 (1994)
13. Robertson, P., Brady, M.: Adaptive image analysis for aerial surveillance. IEEE Intelligent Systems 14, 30–36 (1999)
14. Shekhar, C., Burlina, P., Moisan, S.: Design of self-tuning IU systems. In: Image Understanding Workshop, pp. 529–536 (1997)
15. Shekhar, C., Moisan, S., Vincent, R., Burlina, P., Chellappa, R.: Knowledge-based control of vision systems. Image and Vision Computing 17(9), 667–683 (1999)

Pseudo-morphological Image Diffusion Using the Counter-Harmonic Paradigm

Jesús Angulo

CMM-Centre de Morphologie Mathématique, Mathématiques et Systèmes, MINES
Paristech; 35, rue Saint Honoré, 77305 Fontainebleau Cedex, France
jesus.angulo@ensmp.fr

Abstract. Relationships between linear and morphological scale-spaces
have been considered by various previous works. The aim of this paper is
to study how to generalize the diffusion-based approaches in order to introduce nonlinear filters which effects mimic morphological dilation and
erosion. A methodology based on the counter-harmonic mean is adopted
here. Details of numerical implementation are discussed and results are
provided to illustrate the behaviour of various studied cases: isotropic,
nonlinear and coherence-enhanced diffusion. We also rediscover the classical link between Gaussian scale-space and dilation/erosion scale-spaces
based on quadratic structuring functions.

1 Introduction

Two fundamental paradigms of image filtering appear distinguished nowadays
in the state-of-the-art. On the one hand, differential methods inspired from
the (parabolic) heat equation, including isotropic diffusion [15], nonlinear diffusion [18,10], anisotropic diffusion [24], etc. The main properties of these techniques are the appropriateness to deal with the notion of scale-space of image
structures and the ability to process symmetrically the bright/dark image structures. Practical algorithms involve (local-adaptive) kernel convolution as well
as PDE-formulation and subsequent numerical solutions. The interested reader
should refer to basic references [12] and [23]. On the other hand, mathematical
morphology operators [20,21] which are formulated in terms of geometric notions
as well as in terms of complete lattice theory. Morphological filters entail mainly
the computation of supremum and infimum values in neighbourhoods (or structuring elements) which correspond respectively to the dilation and the erosion,
the two basic operators. Morphological operators present also good scale-space
properties [3] but, by the natural duality of complete lattices, most operators
appear by pairs and one acts on bright structures and the other one on dark
structures. This latter property of asymmetry is in fact an advantage which allows defining evolved operators by product of a pair of dual ones. For instance,
the opening (resp. closing) is obtained by the product of an erosion (resp. dilation) followed by a dilation (resp. erosion), then the product of openings and
closings leads to the alternate filters and other families of morphological filters [20,21]. Diffusion involves blurring image structures whereas morphological

J. Blanc-Talon et al. (Eds.): ACIVS 2010, Part I, LNCS 6474, pp. 426–437, 2010.

dilation and erosion involve enhancement of image structure transitions. In fact, morphological operators are related to geometric optics models and in particular to the (hyperbolic) eikonal equation. Hence, there exists also a well motivated formulation of morphological operators using PDEs [1,2,7,17]. This differential or continuous-scale morphology can be solved using numerical algorithms for curve evolution [19]. Thus multiscale flat dilation/erosion by disks as structuring elements (resp. unflat dilation/erosion by parabolic structuring functions) can be modelled in a continuous framework. Morphological operators using geometric structuring elements are today one of the most successful areas in image processing. However, it is obvious that the soundness and maturity of numerical methods to implement the different versions of image diffusion constitute an advantage against continuous morphology implementation, which requires more specific numerical schemas to achieve robust results [4,6].

The aim of this paper is to study how to generalize the diffusion-based approaches in order to introduce nonlinear filters which effects mimic morphological dilation and erosion. Or using other words, our goal is to propose a new approach of pseudo-morphological image diffusion based on standard numerical implementations.

Related work. Theoretical investigation of the relation between the scale-space concepts of linear and morphological scale spaces has been carried out by various studies. A parallelism between the role which plays the Fourier transform in the convolution with Gaussian kernels and the dilation using quadratic structuring function has been established using the notion of slope transform. More generally, the slope transform and its applications to morphological systems was developed independently and simultaneously by [11] and [16]. In [9] it was shown that the slope transform in the (max, +)-algebra corresponds to the logarithmic multivariate Laplace transform in the (+, ·)-algebra; and that the Cramer transform as the Legendre-Fenchel transform of the logarithmic Laplace transform. It was studied in [13] the structural similarities between linear and morphological processes in order to construct a one-parameter semi-linear process that incorporates Gaussian scale-space, and both types of morphological scale-spaces by quadratic structuring elements as limiting processes of a one-parameter transformation of grey-level values. More recently, it was proposed in [26] a morphological scale-space by deforming the algebraic operations related to Minkowski (or L^p) norms and generalised means, where the Gaussian scale-space is a limit case. We adopted here a different methodology in order to link diffusion-based image filtering and morphological image filtering. The starting point of our approach is the notion of counter-harmonic mean [8]. In fact, the idea of using the counter-harmonic mean for constructing robust morphological-like operators, without the notions of supremum and infimum, was proposed in [22]. Our purpose in this paper is to go further and to exploit the counter-harmonic mean to propose a more general framework which can be exploited for the various algorithms of image diffusion.

Paper organisation. The paper is organised as follows. In the next section we review the notion of counter-harmonic mean. The appropriateness of counter-harmonic mean to approximate flat dilation/erosion is considered in Section 3. Section 4 introduces the novel counter-harmonic Gaussian scale-space, or counter-harmonic isotropic diffusion, and the limit relationships with parabolic dilation/erosion are considered. Section 5 extends these investigations to the nonlinear diffusion, in particular to the Perona and Malik model and to the Weickert model of coherence-enhanced diffusion. The paper is concluded with a summary and perspectives in Section 6.

2 Counter-Harmonic Mean (CHM)

Let us start by presenting the basic notion of this paper. Proofs of the results given below as well as other properties can be found in [8].

Let $\mathbf{a} = (a_1, a_2, \cdots, a_n)$ and $\mathbf{w} = (w_1, w_2, \cdots, w_n)$ be real n−tuples, i.e., $\mathbf{a}, \mathbf{w} \in \mathbb{R}^n$. If $r \in \overline{\mathbb{R}}$ then the r−th *counter-harmonic mean* (CHM) of $\mathbf{a}$ with weight $\mathbf{w}$ is given by [8]

$$\mathfrak{K}^{[r]}(\mathbf{a}; \mathbf{w}) = \begin{cases} \frac{\sum_{i=1}^{n} w_i a_i^r}{\sum_{i=1}^{n} w_i a_i^{r-1}} & \text{if } r \in \mathbb{R} \\[2mm] \max(a_i) & \text{if } r = +\infty \\ \min(a_i) & \text{if } r = -\infty \end{cases} \tag{1}$$

It will be denoted $\mathfrak{K}^{[r]}(\mathbf{a})$ the equal weight case. We notice that $\mathfrak{K}^{[1]}(\mathbf{a}; \mathbf{w})$ is the weighted arithmetic mean and $\mathfrak{K}^{[0]}(\mathbf{a}; \mathbf{w})$ is the weighted harmonic mean.

Property 1. If $1 \leq r \leq +\infty$ then $\mathfrak{K}^{[r]}(\mathbf{a}; \mathbf{w}) \geq \mathfrak{M}^{[r]}(\mathbf{a}; \mathbf{w})$; and if $-\infty \leq r \leq 1$ then the following stronger results holds: $\mathfrak{K}^{[r]}(\mathbf{a}; \mathbf{w}) \leq \mathfrak{M}^{[r-1]}(\mathbf{a}; \mathbf{w})$; where $\mathfrak{M}^{[r]}(\mathbf{a}; \mathbf{w}) = \left(\frac{1}{W} \sum_{i=1}^{n} w_i a_i^r \right)^{1/r}$ is the r−th power-mean, or *Minkowski weighted mean of order* r, defined for $r \in \mathbb{R}^*$. Inequalities are strict unless $r = 1, +\infty$, $-\infty$ or $\mathbf{a}$ is constant.

Property 2. If $\mathbf{a}$ and $\mathbf{w}$ are n−tuples and if $-\infty \leq r \leq s \leq +\infty$ then $\mathfrak{K}^{[r]}(\mathbf{a}; \mathbf{w}) \leq \mathfrak{K}^{[s]}(\mathbf{a}; \mathbf{w})$, with equality if and only if $\mathbf{a}$ is constant.

3 Robust Pseudo-morphological Operators Using CHM

The CHM has been considered in the state-of-the-art of image processing as an appropriate filter to deal with salt and pepper noise [14]. More precisely, let $v = f(x, y)$ be a grey-level image: $f : \Omega \to \mathcal{V}$. Typically, for digital 2D images, $(x, y) \in E$ where $\Omega \subset \mathbb{Z}^2$ is the discrete support of the image. The pixel values are $v \in \mathcal{V} \subset \mathbb{Z}$ or $\mathbb{R}$, but for the sake of simplicity of our study, we consider that $\mathcal{V} = [0, 1]$. The CHM filter is obtained as

$$\kappa_B^P(f)(x, y) = \frac{\sum_{(s,t) \in B(x,y)} f(s,t)^{P+1}}{\sum_{(s,t) \in B(x,y)} f(s,t)^P} = \mathfrak{K}^{[P+1]}(\{f(s,t)\}_{(s,t) \in B(x,y)}) \qquad (2)$$

where $B(x, y)$ is the window of the filter, centered at point (x, y), i.e., the structuring element in the case of morphological operators. This filter is well suited for reducing the effect of pepper noise for $P > 0$ and of salt noise for $P < 0$.

In the pioneering paper [22], starting from the natural observation that morphological dilation and erosion are the limit cases of the CHM, i.e., $\lim_{P \to +\infty} \kappa_B^P(f)(x, y) = \sup_{(s,t) \in B(x,y)} (f(s,t)) = \delta_B(f)(x, y)$ and $\lim_{P \to -\infty} \kappa_B^P(f)(x, y) = \inf_{(s,t) \in B(x,y)} (f(s,t)) = \varepsilon_B(f)(x, y)$; it was proposed to use the CHM to calculate robust nonlinear operators which approach the morphological ones but without using max and min operators. In addition, these operators are more robust to outliers (i.e., to noise) and consequently they can be considered as an alternative to rank-based filters in the implementation of pseudo-morphological operators.

It is easy to see that for $P \gg 0$ ($P \ll 0$) the pixels with largest (smallest) values in the local neighbourhood B will dominate the result of the weighted sum. Of course, in practice, the range of P is limited due to the precision in the computation of the floating point operations. Property 1 of the previous section justifies theoretically the suitability of CHM with respect to the alternative approach by high-order Minkowski mean, as considered by Welk [26]. Let us illustrate empirically how both means converge to the supremum (resp. infimum) when positive P increases (negative P decreases). Fig. 1 depicts convergence with respect to the value of P for the erosion (in blue) and dilation (in red), using Minkowski mean in (a) and using CHM in (b). The convergence is measured as the average difference value between the CHM for each P and the exact dilation/erosion obtained by max and min. The curves correspond to the image

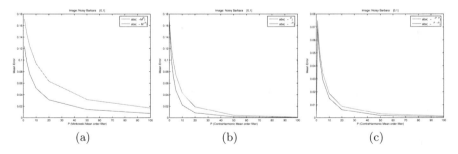

(a)   (b)   (c)

Fig. 1. Convergence with respect to P of nonlinear power means-based operators to morphological operators: (a) pseudo-dilation and pseudo-erosion using Minkowski mean, (b) pseudo-dilation and pseudo-erosion using Counter-Harmonic mean, (c) pseudo-opening and pseudo-closing using Counter-Harmonic mean

results provided on the website[1], which includes other comparative examples of the methods discussed in the present paper. The practical advantage of CHM to approach morphological operators is obvious: even for $P = 100$ (or $P = -100$) the dilation (resp. erosion) is not reached for Minkowski mean whereas the error in the results for CHM is already negligible for $P = 20$ (resp. $P = -20$). We notice also, as expected from Property 1, that the convergence to the erosion with $P \ll 0$ is faster than to the dilation with equivalent $P \gg 0$. The asymmetry involves that $\kappa_B^P(f)$ and $\kappa_B^{-P}(f)$ are not dual operators with respect to the complement, i.e., $\kappa_B^P(f) \neq \complement\kappa_B^{-P}(\complement f)$ with $\complement f = 1 - f$. In Fig. 1(c) are also given rates of convergence of CHM to the opening and closing using the product of $\kappa_B^P(f)$ and $\kappa_B^{-P}(f)$: results are extremely good already for values $P = 10$. As it was already pointed out in [22], the fundamental drawback of $\kappa_B^P(f)$ (resp. $\kappa_B^{-P}(f)$) is the fact that $f(x, y) \not\leq \kappa_B^P(f)(x, y)$ with $P > 0$ (resp. $f(x, y) \not\geq \kappa_B^{-P}(f)(x, y)$ with $P < 0$). Or in other words, the extensitivity (resp. anti-extensitivity) for $P > 0$ (resp. $P < 0$) is not guaranteed. However, according to Property 2, the following ordering relationship holds: $\kappa_B^P(f)(x, y) \leq \kappa_B^{-P}(f)(x, y)$.

4   Counter-Harmonic Gaussian Scale-Space

Canonic multiscale image analysis involves obtaining the multiscale linear convolutions of the original image $\psi(f)(x, y; t) = (f * K_\sigma)(x, y) = \int_\Omega f(u, v)K_\sigma(x - u, y - v)dudv$, where K_σ is the two-dimensional Gaussian function $K_\sigma(x, y) = \frac{1}{2\pi\sigma^2}\exp\left(\frac{-(x^2+y^2)}{2\sigma^2}\right)$, which variance (or width) σ^2 is proportional to the scale t; i.e., $\sigma^2 = 2t$. Larger values of t lead to simpler image representations. Hence, we can define the counter-harmonic Gaussian scale-space of order P as

$$\eta(f)(x, y; t; P) = \frac{(f^{P+1} * K_{\sqrt{2t}})(x, y)}{(f^P * K_{\sqrt{2t}})(x, y)} = \frac{\int_E f(u, v)^{P+1}K_{\sqrt{2t}}(x - u, y - v)dudv}{\int_E f(u, v)^P K_{\sqrt{2t}}(x - u, y - v)dudv}.$$

(3)

By choosing $P > 0$ (resp. $P < 0$), $\eta(f)(x, y; t; P)$ leads to a scale-space of pseudo-dilations (resp. pseudo-erosions), which filtering effects for a given scale t depend on the nonlinearity order of P, which skew the Gaussian weighted values towards the supremum or infimum value, see Fig. 2.

Limit statements. We know that $\eta(f)(x, y; t; +\infty) = \delta_B(f)(x, y)$, i.e., flat dilation where B is the square support of the kernel $\sigma = \sqrt{2t}$. Let us consider the limit case for $P \uparrow\uparrow$. By rewriting $f^P = \exp(P\log(f))$, taking first order Taylor expansion $\log(f) \approx f - 1$ and first order Taylor expansion of exponential function such that $N/D = \exp(\log(N/D)) \approx 1 + \log(N) - \log(D)$, we have: $\lim_{P\to+\infty} \eta(f)(x, y; t; P) = 1 + \log\int_\Omega \exp((P + 1)[f(x - u, y - v) - \frac{(u^2+v^2)}{2(P+1)(2t)} - 1])dudv - \log\int_\Omega \exp(P[f(x - u, y - v) - \frac{(u^2+v^2)}{2P(2t)} - 1])dudv$. Using now the standard result $\lim_{P\to+\infty}\{\int_\Omega g^P(x)dx\}^{1/P} = \sup_{x\in\Omega} g(x)$, which holds

---
[1] http://cmm.ensmp.fr/~angulo/research/examplesPseudoMorphoDiffusions/
examplesPseudoMorphoDiffusions.html

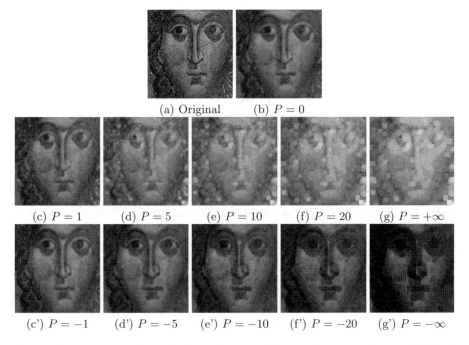

Fig. 2. Pseudo-morphological Gaussian convolution (isotropic linear diffusion) $\eta(f)(x, y; t; P)$ at scale $t = 5$: First row, original image and standard Gaussian filtered image ($P = 0$); middle row, counter-harmonic Gaussian pseudo-dilations ($P > 0$); bottom row, counter-harmonic Gaussian pseudo-erosions ($P < 0$)

for positive and bounded function g with support space Ω, and considering continuity and monotonicity of the log, we obtain: $\lim_{P \to +\infty} \eta(f)(x, y; t; P) = 1 + (P+1) \sup_{(u,v) \in \Omega} (f(x - u, y - v) - \frac{(u^2 + v^2)}{2(P+1)(2t)} - 1) - P \sup_{(u,v) \in \Omega} (f(x - u, y - v) - \frac{(u^2 + v^2)}{2P(2t)} - 1)$. By considering that both supremum operations gives closer values, we finally obtain:

$$\lim_{P \to +\infty} \eta(f)(x, y; t; P) = \sup_{(u,v) \in \Omega} \left(f(x - u, y - v) - \frac{(u^2 + v^2)}{2P(2t)} \right), \qquad (4)$$

which can be interpreted as the dilation of $f(x, y)$ with a quadratic structuring function $b(x, y; t; P) = \frac{(x^2 + y^2)}{2P(2t)}$, that is, the CHM framework involves a "normalization" by P of the original Gaussian kernel scale parameter during unlinearization. This result is perfectly coherent with those obtained from totally different paradigms [26,13]. We notice again that for $P = +\infty$ the structuring function becomes flat and hence we obtain the flat dilation.

Interpretation as CHM Linear Diffusion and iterative framework. A filtered image $u(x, y; t)$ of $f(x, y)$ is calculated by solving the diffusion equation with the original image as initial state, and reflecting boundary conditions:

$$\partial_t u = \operatorname{div}\left(c\nabla u\right) = c\Delta u = c\left(\frac{\partial^2 u}{\partial x^2} + \frac{\partial^2 u}{\partial y^2}\right) \tag{5}$$

$$u(x,y;0) = f(x,y)$$

$$\partial_{\mathbf{n}} u|_{\partial\Omega} = 0$$

where c is the conductivity and $\mathbf{n}$ denotes the normal to the image boundary $\partial\Omega$. The popularity of the Gaussian scale-space is due to its linearity and the fact that the multiscale function $\psi(f)(x,y;t)$ can be generated from the isotropic heat diffusion, i.e., $u(x,y;t) = (f * K_{\sqrt{2t}})(x,y) = \psi(f)(x,y;t)$, $t > 0$. The PDE can also be solved using finite differences in an explicit schema. Pixel i represents the location (x_i, y_i). Let h_l denote the grid size in the direction l (working on square grid, we assume 1 for horizonal and vertical directions and $\sqrt{2}$ for 45° and $-45°$ directions); and τ denote the time step size (to guarantee stability, the step size must satisfy [24]: $\tau = 1/(\sum_{l=1}^{m} 2/h_l^2)$), considering discrete times $t_k = k\tau$ (with k positive integer). By u_i^k we denote approximation to $u(x_i, y_i; t_k)$. The simplest discretization can be written in a compact way as [25]:

$$u_i^{k+1} = u_i^k + \tau\left(\sum_{l=1}^{m}\sum_{j\in\mathcal{N}_l(i)} \frac{c_j^k + c_i^k}{2h_l^2}(u_j^k - u_i^k)\right), \tag{6}$$

where $\mathcal{N}_l(i)$ consists of the two neighbours of pixel i along the l discretized direction. The conduction coefficients c_i^k are considered here as constant in time and space.

Thus, the pseudo-morphological isotropic diffusion of order P can be rewritten as

$$\eta(f)(x,y;t;P) = \frac{[u(x,y;t)]^{P+1}}{[u(x,y;t)]^{P}}, \tag{7}$$

where $[u(x,y;t)]^P$ is the solution of diffusion equation 6 with the initial condition $u(x,y;0) = f(x,y)^P$. But starting from the PDE numerical solution, it is also possible to define an iterative CHM-based isotropic diffusion, $\widehat{\eta}(f)(x,y;t;P)$, by a coupled evolution of both power terms, according to the following discretization:

$$u_i^{k+1} = \frac{(u_i^k)^{P+1} + \tau\left(\sum_{l=1}^{m}\sum_{j\in\mathcal{N}_l(i)}\frac{c_j^k+c_i^k}{2h_l^2}((u_j^k)^{P+1} - (u_i^k)^{P+1})\right)}{(u_i^k)^P + \tau\left(\sum_{l=1}^{m}\sum_{j\in\mathcal{N}_l(i)}\frac{c_j^k+c_i^k}{2h_l^2}((u_j^k)^P - (u_i^k)^P)\right)}. \tag{8}$$

As we can expect, the results of decoupled $\eta(f)(x,y;t;P)$ and coupled $\widehat{\eta}(f)(x,y;t;P)$ diffusions are different. We observed from the experiments, provided in the above mentioned website, that the effects of $\widehat{\eta}(f)(x,y;t;P)$ are more "morphological" for equivalent order P, with sharper transitions between structures. Fig. 5(f) and (g) corresponds just to a comparison of the pseudo-opening obtained by product of pseudo-erosion and pseudo-dilation $\widehat{\eta}\left(\widehat{\eta}(f)(x,y;t;-P)\right)(x,y;t;P)$ and the counterpart decoupled diffusion operators.

5 Counter-Harmonic Nonlinear Diffusion

Ideas introduced above are extended in this section to two well-known cases of evolved image diffusion.

Nonlinear diffusion. The big disadvantage of isotropic diffusion is the fact that linear smoothers do not only smooth the noise but also blur and shift structure edges, which are important image features in some applications, i.e., segmentation and object recognition. The pioneering idea introduced by Perona and Malik [18] to reduce these problems is to locally adapt the diffusivity, i.e., the value of the conductivity c, to the gradient of the image at each iteration. More precisely, this nonlinear diffusion involves replacing the diffusion equation 5 by the following model:

$$\partial_t u = \text{div} \left(g \left(\|\nabla u\|^2 \right) \nabla u \right). \tag{9}$$

In this model the diffusivity has to be such that $g\left(\|\nabla u\|^2\right) \to 0$ when $\|\nabla u\|^2 \to +\infty$ and $g\left(\|\nabla u\|^2\right) \to 1$ when $\|\nabla u\|^2 \to 0$. One of the diffusivities Perona and Malik proposed is the function $g(s^2) = 1/\left(1 + (s^2/\lambda^2)\right)$, $\lambda > 0$, where λ is a threshold parameter that separates forward and backward diffusion. This model accomplishes the aim of blurring small fluctuations (noise) while enhancing edges (by preventing excessive diffusion). To avoid some numerical and

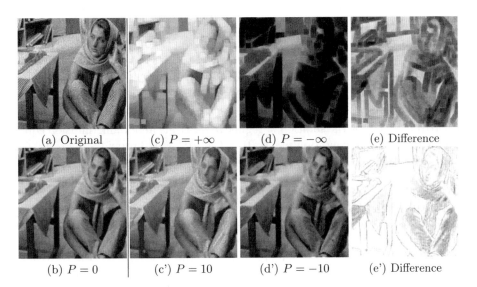

(a) Original   (c) $P = +\infty$ (d) $P = -\infty$ (e) Difference

(b) $P = 0$ (c') $P = 10$ (d') $P = -10$ (e') Difference

Fig. 3. Pseudo-morphological nonlinear diffusion $\xi(x, y; t)$ at scale $t = 5$ (regularization parameter $\sigma = 0.5$): (a) original image, (b) standard nonlinear diffusion, (c)/(d) standard dilation/(d) standard erosion, (e) image difference between dil./ero. (gradient), (c')/(d') pseudo-dilation/erosion by counter-harmonic nonlinear diffusion, (e') image difference between pseudo-dil./ero

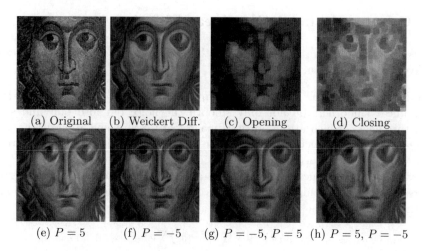

(a) Original   (b) Weickert Diff.   (c) Opening   (d) Closing

(e) $P = 5$ (f) $P = -5$ (g) $P = -5, P = 5$ (h) $P = 5, P = -5$

Fig. 4. Pseudo-morphological anisotropic diffusion $\chi(x, y; t; P)$ at scale $t = 10$ (with regularization parameters: local scale $\sigma = 1.5$, integration scale $\rho = 6$) : (a) original image, (b) standard anisotropic diffusion, (c)-(d) opening and closing of size equivalent to $t = 5$, (e)/(f) pseudo-dilation/erosion by counter-harmonic anisotropic diffusion, (g)/(h) pseudo-opening/closing by counter-harmonic anisotropic diffusion

theoretical drawbacks of this model, it was proposed in [10], a new version of Perona and Malik theory, based on replacing diffusivity $g\left(\|\nabla u\|^2\right)$ by a regularized version $g\left(\|\nabla u_\sigma\|^2\right)$ with $\nabla u_\sigma = \nabla\left(K_\sigma * u\right)$ where K_σ is a Gaussian kernel. This latter model is just used in our framework and the numerical solution can be obtained using the explicit scheme 6, where c_i^k is here the approximation to $g\left(\|\nabla u_\sigma(x_i, y_i; t_k)\|^2\right)$, with the gradient computed by central differences.

Similarly to the isotropic case, we can now define the pseudo-morphological counter-harmonic nonlinear diffusion of order P as $\xi(f)(x, y; t; P) = \frac{[u(x,y;t)]^{P+1}}{[u(x,y;t)]^P}$, where $[u(x, y; t)]^P$ is the solution of regularized Perona and Malik diffusion equation with the initial condition $u(x, y; 0) = f(x, y)^P$. Fig. 3 provides the results of pseudo-dilation and pseudo-erosion ($P = 10$ and $P = -10$) using the regularized Perona and Malik model on a noisy image. Comparing with respect to the standard filtering ($P = 0$), the good properties of denoising without blurring are conserved but in addition, an effect of dilation/erosion is obtained. This kind of pseudo-morphology is useful for instance to compute morphological gradient (i.e., $\xi(f)(x, y; t; P) - \xi(f)(x, y; t; -P)$) of noisy images or to construct filters as morphological openings (i.e., $\xi(\xi(f)(x, y; t; -P))(x, y; t; P)$), see Fig. 5(d) and (h) the comparison of the standard Perona and Malik diffusion and the corresponding pseudo-opening diffusion, which removes some small bright structures. It is also possible to define the coupled case by computing the counter-harmonic but this discussion is out of the paper scope. A critical point here is the choice of parameter λ, which is an ill-posed problem. Sophisticated approaches in the state-of-the-art are based on noise estimation. We have determined empirically that the value $\lambda = 1/m \left(\sum_{l=1}^{m} \text{Mean}(\nabla_l u(x,y;t)) \right)$ (which of course is different for P and $P+1$) leads to stable results.

Coherence-enhanced diffusion. Coherence-enhanced diffusion, or tensor-driven diffusion, was introduced by Weickert [24] in order to achieve an anisotropic diffusion filtering based on directionality information. The idea is to adapt the diffusion process to local image structure using the following non-linear diffusion equation:

$$\partial_t u = \text{div} \left(\mathbf{D} \nabla u \right). \tag{10}$$

where the conductivity function becomes a symmetric positive definite diffusion tensor $\mathbf{D}$, which is a function adapted to the structure tensor $\mathbf{J}_\rho(\nabla u_\sigma) = K_\rho * (\nabla u_\sigma \otimes \nabla u_\sigma)$. The eigenvectors of $\mathbf{J}_\rho$ are orthonormal and the eigenvalues are positive. The corresponding eigenvalues (let us call them $\mu_1 \geq \mu_2$) describe the local structure. Flat areas give $\mu_1 \approx \mu_2$, straight edges give $\mu_1 \gg \mu_2 = 0$ and corners give $\mu_1 \geq \mu_2 \gg 0$. In order to control the diffusion, $\mathbf{J}_\rho$ is not used directly, but tensor $\mathbf{D}$ has the same eigenvectors as $\mathbf{J}_\rho$, but different eigenvalues, thus controlling the diffusion in both directions. The eigenvalues are $\lambda_1 = \alpha$ and $\lambda_2 = \alpha + (1 - \alpha) \exp(-C/\kappa)$, where κ is the orientation coherence and $C > 0$ serves as a threshold parameter. Parameter $\alpha > 0$ is quite important and serves as a regularization parameter which keeps $\mathbf{D}$ uniformly positive definite. For this diffusion, we have used in our tests a numerical implementation using the additive operator splitting (AOS) scheme [24], which is particularly efficient and

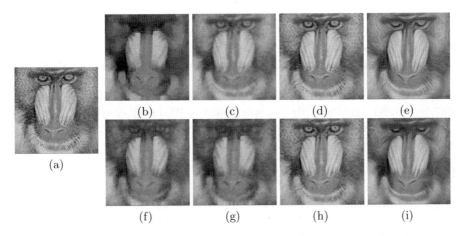

Fig. 5. Comparison of standard diffusions and pseudo-morphological openings: (a) original image, (b) standard opening using a square 11×11, (c) isotropic diffusion $t = 5$, (d) Perona and Malik diffusion $t = 5$, (e) Weickert diffusion $t = 10$, (f) pseudo-opening using isotropic diffusion $t = 5$, $P = 10, P = -10$, (g) pseudo-opening using coupled isotropic diffusion $t = 5$, $P = 10, P = -10$, (h) pseudo-opening using Perona and Malik diffusion $t = 5$, $P = 5, P = -5$, (i) pseudo-opening using Weickert diffusion $t = 10$, $P = 5, P = -5$

has the advantage of being rotationally invariant compared to their multiplicative counterparts.

As previously, the pseudo-morphological counter-harmonic coherence-enhanced diffusion of order P is defined as $\chi(f)(x,y;t;P) = \frac{[u(x,y;t)]^{P+1}}{[u(x,y;t)]^P}$, where $[u(x,y;t)]^P$ is the solution of Weickert diffusion equation 10 with the initial condition $u(x,y;0) = f(x,y)^P$. As in the previous case, we have to adapt the regularization parameter α to the dynamics of the power images $f(x,y)^P$ in order to have numerical stable results. Empirically, we have observed that $\alpha = 0.01|P|$ for $P \neq 0$ (with 0.005 for $P = 0$) leads to satisfactory results. In any case, a deeper study on the numerical implementation of counter-harmonic Weickert diffusion, in particular in the case of coupled diffusion, is required. Example of pseudo-morphological anisotropic diffusion are given in Fig. 4 and Fig. 5(e)-(i). Dark regions are anisotropically pronounced in pseudo-erosion schemes ($P < 0$) whereas bright regions are anisotropically emphasized in pseudo-dilation as well as in their products, respectively the pseudo-openings and pseudo-closings.

6   Conclusions and Perspectives

We have introduced pseudo-morphological image diffusion using the notion of counter-harmonic mean. In particular, we have studied the counter-harmonic Gaussian scale space and the corresponding generalization of Perona and Malik diffusion model as well as of Weickert model of coherence-enhanced diffusion. Preliminary results are quite promising however, a more detailed study on the interest of these evolved pseudo-morphological operators for real problems is necessary. We have given a first analysis about the limit statements, but a deeper study is still required about the behaviour of the counter-harmonic linear diffusion with respect to value of P. In particular, we believe that the relationship between our numerical framework and an hybrid evolutionary PDE such as $\partial_t u = \alpha \Delta u \pm \beta \|\nabla u\|^2$ (with variable coefficients α and β which determines the part of linear *versus* morphological smoothing w.r.t. P) should be explored. This hybrid equation was already mentioned in [7], considered in [13] and it is related also to Kuwahara-Nagao PDE introduced in [5] but, to our knowledge, it remains an open problem.

References

1. Alvarez, L., Guichard, F., Lions, P.-L., Morel, J.-M.: Axioms and fundamental equations of image processing. Arch. for Rational Mechanics 123(3), 199–257 (1993)
2. Arehart, A.B., Vincent, L., Kimia, B.B.: Mathematical morphology: The Hamilton-Jacobi connection. In: Proc. of IEEE 4th Inter. Conf. on Computer Vision (ICCV 1993), pp. 215–219 (1993)
3. van den Boomgaard, R., Dorst, L.: The morphological equivalent of Gaussian scale-space. In: Proc. of Gaussian Scale-Space Theory, pp. 203–220. Kluwer, Dordrecht (1997)
4. van den Boomgaard, R.: Numerical solution schemes for continuous-scale morphology. In: Nielsen, M., Johansen, P., Fogh Olsen, O., Weickert, J. (eds.) Scale-Space 1999. LNCS, vol. 1682, pp. 199–210. Springer, Heidelberg (1999)

5. van den Boomgaard, R.: Decomposition of the Kuwahara-Nagao operator in terms of a linear smoothing and a morphological sharpening. In: Proc. of ISMM 2002, pp. 283–292. CSIRO Publishing (2002)

6. Breuß, M., Weickert, J.: Highly accurate PDE-based morphology for general structuring elements. In: Tai, X.-C., Mørken, K., Lysaker, M., Lie, K.-A. (eds.) Scale Space and Variational Methods in Computer Vision. LNCS, vol. 5567, pp. 758–769. Springer, Heidelberg (2009)

7. Brockett, R.W., Maragos, P.: Evolution equations for continuous-scale morphology. IEEE Trans. on Signal Processing 42(12), 3377–3386 (1994)

8. Bullen, P.S.: Handbook of Means and Their Inequalities, 2nd edn. Springer, Heidelberg (1987)

9. Burgeth, B., Weickert, J.: An Explanation for the Logarithmic Connection between Linear and Morphological System Theory. International Journal of Computer Vision 64(2-3), 157–169 (2005)

10. Catte, F., Lions, P.-L., Morel, J.-M., Coll, T.: Image selective smoothing and edge detection by nonlinear diffusion. SIAM Journal on Numerical Analysis 29(1), 182–193 (1992)

11. Dorst, L., van den Boomgaard, R.: Morphological Signal Processing and the Slope Transform. Signal Processing 38, 79–98 (1994)

12. Florack, L.: Image Structure. Kluwer Academic Publishers, Dordrecht (1997)

13. Florack, L., Maas, R., Niessen, W.: Pseudo-Linear Scale-Space Theory. International Journal of Computer Vision 31(2-3), 1–13 (1999)

14. Gonzalez, R.C., Woods, R.E.: Digital Image Processing. Addison-Wesley, Boston (1992)

15. Lindeberg, T.: Scale-Space Theory in Computer Vision. Kluwer Academic Publishers, Dordrecht (1994)

16. Maragos, P.: Slope Transforms: Theory and Application to Nonlinear Signal Processing. IEEE Trans. on Signal Processing 43(4), 864–877 (1995)

17. Maragos, P.: Differential morphology and image processing. IEEE Transactions on Image Processing 5(1), 922–937 (1996)

18. Perona, P., Malik, J.: Scale-Space and Edge Detection Using Anisotropic Diffusion. IEEE Trans. Pattern Anal. Mach. Intell. 12(7), 629–639 (1990)

19. Sapiro, G., Kimmel, R., Shaked, D., Kimia, B.B., Bruckstein, A.M.: Implementing continuous-scale morphology via curve evolution. Pattern recognition 26(9), 1363–1372 (1993)

20. Serra, J.: Image Analysis and Mathematical Morphology. Vol I, and Image Analysis and Mathematical Morphology. Vol II: Theoretical Advances. Academic Press, London (1982/1988)

21. Soille, P.: Morphological Image Analysis. Springer, Berlin (1999)

22. van Vliet, L.J.: Robust Local Max-Min Filters by Normalized Power-Weighted Filtering. In: Proc. of IEEE 17th International Conference of the Pattern Recognition (ICPR 2004), vol. 1, pp. 696–699 (2004)

23. Weickert, J.: Anisotropic Diffusion in Image Processing. ECMI Series. Teubner-Verlag, Stuttgart (1998)

24. Weickert, J.: Coherence-Enhancing Diffusion Filtering. Int. J. Comput. Vision 31(2-3), 111–127 (1999)

25. Weickert, J.: Efficient image segmentation using partial differential equations and morphology. Pattern Recognition 31(9), 1813–1824 (2001)

26. Welk, M.: Families of generalised morphological scale spaces. In: Griffin, L.D., Lillholm, M. (eds.) Scale-Space 2003. LNCS, vol. 2695, pp. 770–784. Springer, Heidelberg (2003)

Non-maximum Suppression
Using Fewer than Two Comparisons per Pixel

Tuan Q. Pham

Canon Information Systems Research Australia (CiSRA)
1 Thomas Holt drive, North Ryde, NSW 2113, Australia
tuan.pham@cisra.canon.com.au
http://www.cisra.com.au

Abstract. Non-Maximum Suppression (NMS) is the task of finding all local maxima in an image. This is often solved using gray-scale image dilation, which requires at least 6 comparisons per pixel in 2-D. We present two solutions that use fewer than 2 comparisons per pixel with little memory overhead. The first algorithm locates 1-D peaks along the image's scan-line and compares each of these peaks against its 2-D neighborhood in a spiral scan order. The second algorithm selects local maximum candidates from the maxima of non-overlapping blocks of one-fourth the neighborhood size. Both algorithms run considerably faster than current best methods in the literature when applied to feature point detection. Matlab code of the proposed algorithms is provided for evaluation purposes.

1 Introduction

The term 'non-maximum suppression' first appeared in an edge detection context as a method to reduce thick edge responses to thin lines [1]. This type of directional NMS operates one-dimensionally (1-D) perpendicular to the edge. Kitchen and Rosenfeld [2] extended the concept to isotropic NMS to locate two-dimensional (2-D) feature points from an image. The feature points are selected as local maxima of a 'cornerness' image over some neighborhood. This NMS approach to corner detection was subsequently adopted by many interest point detectors [3–5]. This paper deals with the latter, isotropic, definition of NMS. We target efficient algorithms that require little extra memory use.

There are known NMS algorithms that require a fixed number of comparisons per pixel regardless of the suppression neighborhood size. One-dimensional max filter, for example, requires three comparisons per pixel [6, 7, 13]. By separable implementation, a two-dimensional max filter can be realized from only six comparisons per pixel. Recently, Neubeck and Van Gool (2006) [8] proposed a block-partitioning algorithm that reduces the number of comparisons down to 2.39 per pixel. However, they were unaware of a simple algorithm dated 20 years back by Förstner and Gülch (1987) [9] that has a similar level of computational complexity. Yet, all of these prior art methods require more than two comparisons per pixel. In this paper, we extend the algorithms in [8] and [9] to reduce the number of comparisons to fewer than two comparisons per pixel.

J. Blanc-Talon et al. (Eds.): ACIVS 2010, Part I, LNCS 6474, pp. 438–451, 2010.
© Springer-Verlag Berlin Heidelberg 2010

The remainder of the paper is organized as follows. Section 2 describes three previous NMS methods in the literature. Section 3 presents our scan-line algorithm for 3×3-neighborhood NMS. Section 4 extends the 3×3 algorithm to handle $(2n+1) \times (2n+1)$ neighborhood. It also presents a second solution for general 2-D NMS using block partitioning. Section 5 compares our algorithms with the prior art methods in terms of computational complexity and runtime under Matlab. A coarse-to-fine extension of our algorithms is presented in Section 6. Finally, Matlab code for the proposed algorithms is provided in the Appendix.

2   Previous Solutions

A straightforward approach to NMS over a rectangular neighborhood is described in Figure 1a. The input image pixels are visited in a raster scan order (from left to right, then from top to bottom). Each visited pixel is compared to other pixels in its neighborhood (5×5 in Figure 1) also in a raster scan order. The central pixel c is a non-maximum if a larger or equal neighbor is found. The algorithm then skips to the next pixel in the scan line.

The straightforward method is simple to implement but it can take a long time to process an image. For example, under a worst-case scenario of an increasing intensity trend that runs along the raster order, the straightforward method requires $\lceil (2n + 1)^2/2 \rceil^1$ comparisons per pixel for a $(2n + 1) \times (2n + 1)$ neighborhood. A best-case scenario happens when the intensity trend is reversed. The straightforward method then requires only one comparison per pixel. On average, however, the straightforward method requires $O(n)$ comparisons per pixel (according to the experimental result in Figure 7a).

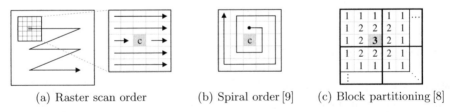

(a) Raster scan order   (b) Spiral order [9]   (c) Block partitioning [8]

Fig. 1. Previous solutions for 2-D non-maximum suppression (5×5 neighborhood)

It turns out that the complexity of a raster scan algorithm can be significantly reduced by visiting the neighboring pixels in a different order. Förstner and Gülch [9] presented such an algorithm with a local spiral order as shown in Figure 1b. By comparing with closer neighbors first, the central pixel is guaranteed to be a 3×3-neighborhood local maximum before it is tested against a larger neighborhood. Because the number of 3×3 local maxima in an image is usually small ($\leq 25\%$ of the total number of pixels), the spiral order algorithm quickly finds any non-maximum and skips to the next pixel. The number of

---

^{1} $\lceil x \rceil$ and $\lfloor x \rfloor$ rounds x to the nearest integer towards $+\infty$ and $-\infty$, respectively.

$(2n + 1) \times (2n + 1)$ local maxima also decreases rapidly as the neighborhood size increases. As a result, the computational complexity of this algorithm is roughly constant (≤ 5 comparisons per pixel to detect a 3×3 non-maximum) irrespective of the neighborhood size.

Recently, Neubeck and Van Gool [8] presented an efficient NMS algorithm that requires 2.39 comparisons per pixel on average and 4 comparisons per pixel in the worst-case. They observed that the maximum pixel of a $(2n+1) \times (2n+1)$ neighborhood is also the maximum of any $(n+1) \times (n+1)$ window that encloses the pixel. The input image is partitioned into non-overlapping blocks of size $(n + 1) \times (n + 1)$, and the local maximum of each block is detected (Figure 1c illustrates this for $n = 2$). The block maximum is then tested against its $(2n + 1) \times (2n + 1)$ neighborhood minus the enclosing $(n + 1) \times (n + 1)$ block. Using only one comparison per pixel, the block partitioning step reduces the number of local maximum candidates by a factor of $(n + 1)^2$. As a result, the Neubeck method is quite efficient for large neighborhood sizes.

For small to medium neighborhood sizes, the Neubeck method still has to process a large number of candidates: $MN/(n + 1)^2$ for an $M \times N$ image. Each of these candidates requires a maximum of $(2n + 1)^2 - (n + 1)^2 - 1$ comparisons with its neighbors. Although Neubeck and Van Gool have a solution to reduce the number of extra comparisons per candidate down to $2 + O(1/n)$, their solution increases the algorithm complexity and memory use significantly. We observe that when a block's candidate is not a $(2n+1) \times (2n+1)$-neighborhood maximum, most of the time it lies on the block boundary. This happens when the block's candidate lies on an intensity trend that extends into an adjacent block. A quick way to reject this candidate is therefore to check if it lies on a block boundary first, and if it does, compare it against three immediate neighbors on the adjacent block. This simple trick achieves a similar computational complexity as the improvement in Neubeck's method without using the extra memory.

3   3×3-Neighborhood Non-maximum Suppression

NMS for a 3×3 neighborhood is often solved by mathematical morphology [10], whereby the input image is compared against its gray-scale dilated version. Pixels where the two images are equal correspond to the local maxima. However, mathematical morphology does not return strict local maxima, where the center pixel is strictly greater than all neighboring pixels. Morphology is also inefficient. Even a separable implementation of a 3×3-neighborhood gray-scale image dilation requires six comparisons per pixel [6, 7].

In this section, we propose a scan-line algorithm for 3×3 NMS that requires at most 2 comparisons per pixel. The algorithm first searches for 1-D local maxima along the scan line. Each scan-line maximum is then compared against its neighbors in adjacent rows. A rolling buffer of two binary masks is kept for a current and a next scan line. As a new central pixel is processed, its future neighbors (i.e. unvisited neighbors) are masked out if they are smaller than the central pixel. Masked pixels will be skipped when it is their turns for processing.

Figure 2a illustrates part of our algorithm to find 1-D local maxima along the scan-line [8]. The arrow from one pixel to another denotes a comparison between the central pixel and its neighbor. At the beginning of the sequence [1, 2, 3, 4, 3, 2, 1, 2, 3], the intensities are on an increasing trend. As a result, only one forward comparison is needed before the current pixel is marked as a non-maximum. When the increasing trend stops at a local maximum (*circled* in Figure 2a), its right neighbor is masked out (shaded). The scan-line algorithm then continues with the next unmasked pixel which has a of value 2 in Figure 2a. This time, both a forward and a backward comparison are needed before the pixel is ruled out as a candidate. Again, the right neighbor of value 1 is masked out after being found smaller than the central pixel. In general, every second pixel on a decreasing trend is masked out. This 1-D non maximum suppression algorithm therefore requires one comparison per pixel.

(a) 1D non-maximum suppression   (b) raster scan order   (c) our scan order

Fig. 2. 3-neighborhood non-maximum suppression and 3×3-neighborhood scan order

When extending the 1-D NMS algorithm in [8] to 2-D, we found that the order in which the six neighbors on different rows are compared to the central pixel significantly influences the efficiency of the algorithm. A conventional method traverses a 3×3 neighborhood along a raster scan order as shown in Figure 2b. This results in a maximum of five comparisons per output pixel in a worst-case scenario of an intensity trend that runs along the raster scan. In this scenario, the central pixel is always greater than its four preceding neighbors. Hence, a fifth comparison with the immediate neighbor on the right is needed to reject the central pixel.

In our scan-line algorithm, the future neighbors on the row below are compared first, followed by the past neighbors on the row above (visit order shown in Figure 2c). worst-case scenario happens when the three future neighbors are smaller than the central pixel. However, this does not happen to every pixel in the image because the central pixel must be a strict maximum along the current scan-line. Furthermore, future neighbors can be masked out if found to be smaller than the current pixel. Masked out pixels will be skipped in the future, which saves computations. Similar to the 1-D NMS in Figure 2a, this pixel skipping trick helps reduce the effective cost of this inter-row comparison to one comparison per pixel. As a result, our 3×3-neighborhood NMS requires at most two comparisons per pixel.

Another reason to visit the future neighbors before the past neighbors is: because the current pixel was not masked out, it is either higher than the past neighbors, or the past neighbors were not processed. In the first case, comparison with the past neighbors is superfluous without triggering an early non-maximum detection. In the second case, since the past neighbors were previously skipped, they are likely to be small, which again reduces the chance of an early non-maximum detection of the current pixel.

4 $(2n+1)^2$-Neighborhood Non-maximum Suppression

Two algorithms for $(2n + 1) \times (2n + 1)$-neighborhood NMS are presented. The first algorithm extends the scan-line algorithm in Section 3, which use the spiral traverse order from Förstner and Gülch [9]. The second algorithm extends the block partitioning algorithm of Neubeck and Van Gool [8]. Both algorithms use fewer than two comparisons per pixel.

4.1 Scan-Line Algorithm

The scan-line algorithm for 3×3-neighborhoods in Section 3 can be extended to handle $(2n+1) \times (2n+1)$ neighborhoods for $n \geq 1$. First, $(2n+1)$-neighborhood maxima on the current scan-line are located (*circled pixels* in Figure 3b). These 1-D maxima serve as candidates for the 2-D maxima. Each candidate is then compared against its $(2n + 1) \times (2n + 1)$ neighborhood in a spiral order similar to that of Foerstner's method. Note that the neighbors on the same scan-line have already been compared and can therefore be skipped (*gray pixels* in Figure 3c). This results in a maximum of $2n(2n+1)$ neighbors to be compared per candidate. In practice, the average number of comparisons per candidate is much smaller thanks to the spiral traverse order (explained in Section 2).

The detection of the $(2n + 1)$-neighborhood maxima on a 1-D scan-line f is shown in detail in Figure 3a. If g is the sign of the finite difference of f, g is either -1, 0 or 1 depending on the local slope of f. g's finite difference h therefore equals -2 at local peaks, +2 at local troughs and 0 elsewhere. 1-D peak and trough detection therefore requires only one comparison per pixel. Next, each 1-D peak is compared against its $(2n+1)$-neighborhood with the knowledge of the extremum detector h. Neighboring pixels which are on a consecutive downward slope from

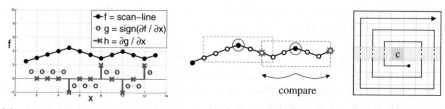

(a) 1D peak and trough detection   (b) 1D non-max suppression   (c) spiral traverse

Fig. 3. Scan-line algorithm for $(2n + 1) \times (2n + 1)$ non-maximum suppression ($n = 3$). In Figure 3b, *dashed windows* are the local neighborhoods of the *circled pixels*; *hollow pixels* are on a downward slope from the corresponding circled pixel, hence need not be re-compared; *star pixels*, on the other hand, are to be compared against the left circled pixel. In Figure 3c, *gray pixels* need not be re-compared against the central pixel c.

the local peak, i.e. $\{x|h(x) = 0\}$, are by definition smaller than the current peak, hence need not be re-compared. Only pixels outside the enclosing troughs of the current peak need extra comparison. The number of extra comparisons to obtain $(2n + 1)$-neighborhood maxima from an initial list of 3-neighborhood maxima is therefore very small for a smooth function f.

4.2   Quarter-Block Partitioning Algorithm

As described earlier in Section 2, Neubeck and Van Gool [8] partition an image into non-overlapping blocks of size $(n + 1) \times (n + 1)$ and use these blocks' maxima as candidates for the $(2n + 1) \times (2n + 1)$-neighborhood maximum detection. If this is loosely referred to as a half-block partitioning algorithm (because Neubeck's block size roughly equals half the neighborhood size), then a quarter-block partitioning algorithm can be described with reference to Figure 4 as follows. The $M \times N$ image in Figure 4a is partitioned into non-overlapping blocks of size $m \times m$ where $m = \lfloor (n + 1)/2 \rfloor$. The maximum of each block is extracted to form a $\lfloor M/m \rfloor \times \lfloor N/m \rfloor$ block maximum image in Figure 4b. 3×3 local maxima of this block maximum image are selected as candidates for the $(2n + 1) \times (2n + 1)$-neighborhood maxima detection (*gray pixel* in Figure 4b). Each candidate is finally compared to its $(2n+1) \times (2n+1)$ neighborhood minus the $3m \times 3m$ neighboring pixels already compared during the block-partitioning step (Figure 4c).

It can be shown that a $(2n + 1) \times (2n + 1)$ window always fully encloses 3×3 partitioned blocks of size $m \times m$ each. A $(2n + 1) \times (2n + 1)$-neighborhood maximum therefore is also a 3×3 local peak in the block maximum image. The quarter-block partitioning algorithm avoids Neubeck's inefficiency problem of having many false candidates lying on the block boundaries. Each of our candidates, on the other hand, lies well within the middle of a $3m \times 3m$ neighborhood. The number of candidates of our method is therefore significantly smaller than that of Neubeck. This is a key reason why our quarter-block method is considerably faster Neubeck's. Our algorithm also requires fewer comparisons to evaluate the full neighborhood of a candidate: $(2n + 1)^2 - 9\lfloor (n + 1)/2 \rfloor^2$ compared to $(2n + 1)^2 - (n + 1)^2$.

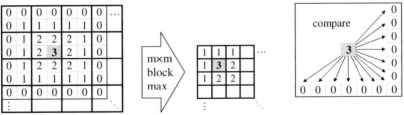

(a) input image with overlaid $m \times m$ blocks
(b) block maximum image
(c) comparison with the rest of the neighborhood

Fig. 4. Quarter-block partitioning algorithm for $(2n + 1)^2$ NMS ($n = 3$, $m = 2$)

5   Results

5.1   3×3-Neighborhood Non-maximum Suppression

We compared our 3×3 NMS algorithm in section 3 with two other algorithms: the straightforward and the gray-scale morphology algorithm [10]. Both ours and the straightforward method were implemented in *non-vectorized* Matlab code (see the Appendix). Matlab ®Image Processing Toolbox (R2008a) function `imregionalmax` was used for the morphology implementation.

Six gray-scale images were used in this experiment: `worst` and `best` are 256×256 images of worst and best-case scenarios for the straightforward algorithm (see section 2 for description). `noise` is a 256×256 image of uniformly distributed noise. 256^2, 512^2 and 1024^2 refer respectively to Harris cornerness [3] images of the `Cameraman`, `Lena` and `Pentagon` square image of the corresponding size. We used the following variant of the Harris cornerness function that does not require a tuning parameter:

$$C = \frac{\sum\limits_{S} I_x^2 \sum\limits_{S} I_y^2 - \left(\sum\limits_{S} I_x I_y\right)^2}{\sum\limits_{S} I_x^2 + \sum\limits_{S} I_y^2 + \varepsilon} \tag{1}$$

where I_x and I_y are Gaussian gradients ($\sigma = 1$) of the input image I along the $x-$ and $y-$direction, respectively; $\sum\limits_{S}$ is an average operator over a neighborhood S, which is a 11×11-pixel window in our experiments; and $\varepsilon = 2^{-52}$ is a small offset added to the denominator to avoid division by zero in flat image areas.

The number of intensity comparisons and the average runtime over 100 executions were recorded for each test image on an Intel 3.2 GHz system with 3.25 GB of RAM, the result of which is shown in Figure 5.

Figure 5a shows that our 3×3-neighborhood NMS method requires between 1 to 1.5 comparisons per input pixel. The complexity of the straightforward method varies more widely, ranging from one comparison in its best-case to five comparisons in its worst-case with an average of 2.5 comparisons per pixel. The morphology algorithm requires the most comparisons at eight per pixel. Note that the worst-case scenario of the straightforward method is actually the best-case scenario for ours and vice versa.

The execution time shown in Figure 5b is generally in agreement with the algorithm complexity in Figure 5a. On average, our method runs at a speed of $0.1\mu s$ per pixel. This is 25% faster than the straightforward method. The straightforward method is only faster than ours in its best-case scenario. When compared to morphology, our algorithm implemented in pure Matlab code is almost five-time faster than Matlab's built-in function `imregionalmax` written in C++. This demonstrates that simple *non-vectorised* Matlab code can run as fast as C code with the help of Matlab Just-In-Time (JIT) compiler. The execution time of our algorithm is quite stable over a wide range of image contents and sizes. It is also independent of the number of detected local maxima.

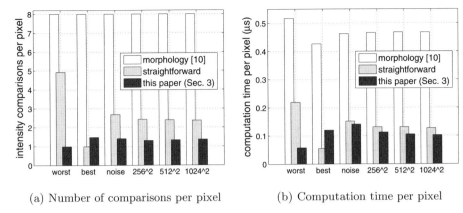

(a) Number of comparisons per pixel   (b) Computation time per pixel

Fig. 5. Comparison of different algorithms for 3×3 non-maximum suppression

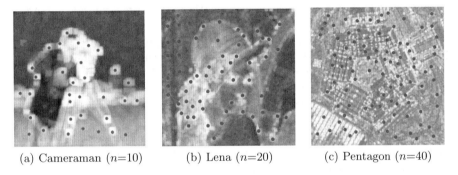

(a) Cameraman (n=10)   (b) Lena (n=20)   (c) Pentagon (n=40)

Fig. 6. Results of non-maximum suppression on several Harris cornerness images

5.2 (2n+1)×(2n+1)-Neighborhood Non-maximum Suppression

We compared two of our 2-D NMS algorithms in Section 4 with three prior art methods: straightforward, Förstner [9] and Neubeck [8]. The algorithms were used to detect Harris corners [3] from three images: **Cameraman** (256×256), **Lena** (512×512) and **Pentagon** (1024×1024). Examples of corners found from these images using different neighborhood size n are displayed in Figure 6. Larger neighborhood sizes were used for larger images to improve the corner separation. We have also tested the robustness of our algorithms by shifting the input images by several pixels in each direction and obtained the same set of corners. This confirms that our implementations of all NMS algorithms work correctly as expected.

To compare the complexity of different NMS algorithms, the number of pairwise intensity comparisons were counted for each test image. These numbers are then normalized by the number of pixels in each input image. Their average is finally plotted in Figure 7a for different values of neighborhood sidelength n. Figure 7a shows that the complexity of the straightforward method is linearly

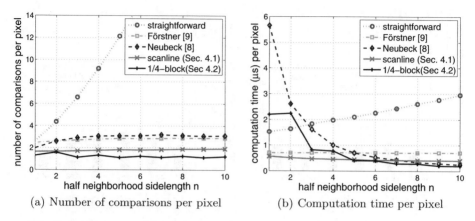

(a) Number of comparisons per pixel   (b) Computation time per pixel

Fig. 7. Performance of $(2n+1)\times(2n+1)$-neighborhood non-maximum suppression

proportional to the neighborhood sidelength n. All other methods, however, require a similar number of comparisons per pixel irrespective of the neighborhood size. Our scan-line method in Section 4.1, being an improvement of the Förstner method, requires 40% fewer comparisons than the Förstner method. Our quarter-block partitioning method in Section 4.2, being an improvement of the Neubeck method, requires 60% fewer comparisons than its predecessor. Both our methods use fewer than two comparisons per pixel. The quarter-block method is slightly cheaper than the scan-line method.

Average runtime of these five different algorithms on three test images are plotted in Figure 7b. The runtime of the straightforward method increases linearly with the neighborhood sidelength n as expected. For other methods, however, the run time does not always correspond to the complexity in Figure 7a. For small neighborhood sidelength ($n \leq 2$), the block partitioning methods (Neubeck and ours in Section 4.2) are even slower than the straightforward methods. This is because the block size is too small for any significant candidate pruning. The scan-line methods (Förstner and ours in Section 4.1), on the other hand, show stable runtime over a large range of neighborhood sizes. Both scan-line methods need less than 1 microsecond to process one pixel. Our scan-line algorithm is on average 60% faster than Förstner algorithm. As the neighborhood size gets larger ($n \geq 5$), the block partitioning methods start showing advantage over the scan-line methods. Our quarter-block partitioning algorithm is on average 40% faster than Neubeck algorithm.

6   Extensions and Applications

NMS algorithms usually require at least one comparison per pixel to process an image. This is because each pixel needs be compared to at least one larger neighbor before it is ruled out as a non-maximum. Even with our fastest NMS algorithms in Section 4, it still takes an order of one second to process a megapixel image in Matlab. Further speedup is therefore desirable.

Fortunately, NMS can be applied to a down-sampled image without substantial loss of detection accuracy. This is especially true when the neighborhood size is large and the input image is smooth. Harris corner detection, for example, often starts with a cornerness image that was previously low-pass filtered. NMS on a low-resolution image (e.g. by pixel binning) produces a small number of candidates. These candidates can then be compared against their full neighborhood in the original image.

Both algorithms described in this paper are extendable to N-D. The scan-line algorithm in Section 4.1 can be applied recursively: local maxima of an i-D slice of the input image over the first i dimensions are candidates to the $(i + 1)$-D local maxima over the first $(i + 1)$ dimensions. The block partitioning algorithm in Section 4.2 is dimension-dependent because an N-D image can be divided into a grid of N-D blocks.

NMS can be used to find distinctive feature points in an image. To improve the repeatability of a detected corner across multiple images, the corner is often selected as a local maximum whose cornerness is significantly higher than the close-by second highest peak [11]. NMS with a small neighborhood size can produce an oversupply of initial peaks. These peaks are then compared with other peaks in a larger neighborhood to retain strong ones only. The initial peaks can be sorted during NMS to facilitates the later pruning step.

For some applications such as multi-view image matching, an evenly distributed set of interest points for matching is desirable. An oversupplied set of NMS point features can be given to an adaptive non-maximal suppression process [12], which reduces cluttered corners to improve their spatial distribution.

7   Conclusion

We have described two new algorithms for non-maximum suppression of two-dimensional images. The scan-line algorithm improves upon a previous method by Förstner and Gülch [9] and it is 60% faster than [9]. The quarter-block partitioning algorithm improves upon the current best method in the prior art by Neubeck and Van Gool [8] and it is 40% faster than [8]. The scan-line method is the preferred method for small neighborhood sizes ($n < 5$), while the quarter-block algorithm runs faster for larger neighborhood sizes ($n \geq 5$). Both of our algorithms require fewer than two comparisons per input pixel while other algorithms in the literature require more than two. Runtime under Matlab on a 3.2 GHz Intel system consistently took less than 0.5 microsecond per pixel. These fast NMS algorithms require little memory overhead, which is desirable for many computer visions tasks such as object and corner detection. Our algorithms can also be extended to handle images of any dimension.

References

1. Rosenfeld, A., Kak, A.: Digital Picture Processing, 2nd edn. Academic Press, London (1976)
2. Kitchen, L., Rosenfeld, A.: Gray-level corner detection. Pattern Recognition Letters 1, 92–102 (1982)

3. Harris, C., Stephens, M.: A combined corner and edge detector. In: Proc. of the Fourth Alvey Vision Conference, pp. 147–151 (1988)
4. Lowe, D.: Distinctive image features from scale-invariant keypoints. IJCV 60, 91–110 (2004)
5. Mikolajczyk, K., Schmid, C.: Scale and affine invariant interest point detectors. IJCV 60, 63–86 (2004)
6. van Herk, M.: A fast algorithm for local minimum and maximum filters on rectangular and octagonal kernels. Pattern Recognition Letters 13, 517–521 (1992)
7. Gil, J., Werman, M.: Computing 2-d min, median, and max filters. IEEE Trans. on PAMI 15, 504–507 (1993)
8. Neubeck, A., Van Gool, L.: Efficient non-maximum suppression. In: Proc. of ICPR, vol. 3, pp. 850–855 (2006)
9. Förstner, W., Gülch, E.: A fast operator for detection and precise locations of distinct points, corners, and centres of circular features. In: Proc. of Intercommission Conf. on Fast Processing of Photogrammetric Data, pp. 281–305 (1987)
10. Soille, P.: Morphological Image Analysis: Principles and Applications. Springer, Heidelberg (1999)
11. Schmid, C., Mohr, R., Bauckhage, C.: Evaluation of interest point detectors. IJCV 37, 151–172 (2000)
12. Brown, M., Szeliski, R., Winder, S.: Multi-image matching using multi-scale oriented patches. In: Proc. of CVPR, vol. 1, pp. 510–517 (2005)
13. Coltuc, D., Bolon, P.: Fast computation of rank order statistics. In: Proc. of EUSIPCO, pp. 2425–2428 (2000)

A   Matlab Code

A.1   3 × 3 Non-maxima Suppression

Below is a non-vectorized Matlab implementation of the 3×3-neighborhood non-maxima suppression algorithm described in Section 3. This function produces the same output as `imregionalmax` from Matlab Image Processing Toolbox, only faster.

```
function mask = nonmaxsupp3x3(im)

[h w] = size(im);   mask = false([h w]);   % binary output image
skip = false(h,2);   cur = 1;   next = 2;   % scanline masks

for c=2:w-1
  r = 2;
  while r<h
    if skip(r,cur), r=r+1; continue; end   % skip current pixel

    if im(r,c)<=im(r+1,c)      % compare to pixel on the left
      r=r+1;

      while r<h && im(r,c)<=im(r+1,c),   r=r+1; end   % rising
      if r==h, break; end    % reach scanline's local maximum
```

```
    else                          % compare to pixel on the right
        if im(r,c)<=im(r-1,c),   r=r+1; continue; end
    end
    skip(r+1,cur) = 1;            % skip next pixel in the scanline

    % compare to 3 future then 3 past neighbors
    if im(r,c)<=im(r-1,c+1),   r=r+1; continue; end
    skip(r-1,next) = 1;        % skip future neighbors only
    if im(r,c)<=im(r  ,c+1),   r=r+1; continue; end
    skip(r  ,next) = 1;
    if im(r,c)<=im(r+1,c+1),   r=r+1; continue; end
    skip(r+1,next) = 1;
    if im(r,c)<=im(r-1,c-1),   r=r+1; continue; end
    if im(r,c)<=im(r  ,c-1),   r=r+1; continue; end
    if im(r,c)<=im(r+1,c-1),   r=r+1; continue; end

    mask(r,c) = 1;   r=r+1;   % a new local maximum is found
  end
  tmp = cur;   cur = next;   next = tmp;   % swap mask indices
  skip(:,next) = 0;                        % reset next scanline mask
end
```

A.2   Spiral Indexing of a Local $(2n + 1) \times (2n + 1)$ Neighborhood

The following function returns the row and column offsets of pixels in a local $(2n+1) \times (2n+1)$ neighborhood when traversed in a spiral order. Due to Matlab's column-major order, the traverse order is slightly different from the row-major spiral order in Figure 1b.

```
function [r,c] = spiralindex(n)
r = 0;   c = 0;   run = 0;
for ii=1:n
    run = run+1;
    dr=-1;   dc= 0;
    for jj=1:run,   r = [r; r(end)+dr]; c = [c; c(end)+dc]; end
    dr= 0;   dc= 1;
    for jj=1:run,   r = [r; r(end)+dr]; c = [c; c(end)+dc]; end
    run = run+1;
    dr= 1;   dc= 0;
    for jj=1:run,   r = [r; r(end)+dr]; c = [c; c(end)+dc]; end
    dr= 0;   dc=-1;
    for jj=1:run,   r = [r; r(end)+dr]; c = [c; c(end)+dc]; end
end
dr=-1; dc= 0;
for jj=1:run, r = [r; r(end)+dr]; c = [c; c(end)+dc]; end
```

A.3 Scan-Line Algorithm for $(2n + 1) \times (2n + 1)$ NMS

A non-vectorized Matlab implementation of the scan-line algorithm for $(2n+1) \times (2n + 1)$-neighborhood non-maximum suppression (Section 4.1) is given below.

```
function mask = nonmaxsupp_scanline(im,n)

[h w] = size(im);  mask = false([h w]);  % binary output image
scanline = zeros(h,1);  skip = false(h,1);    % scanline mask

[dr,dc] = spiralindex(n);  % index neighborhood in a spiral path
I = find(dc~=0);  dr = dr(I);  dc = dc(I);  % skip current line

for c=n+1:w-n
    scanline = im(:,c);  skip(:) = false;      % current scanline
    resp = [0; diff(sign(diff(scanline))); 0]; % discrete Hessian
    peaks = find(resp(n+1:end-n)==-2) + n;      % peak indices

    for ii=1:length(peaks)
        r = peaks(ii);
        if skip(r), continue; end          % skip current pixel

        curPix = scanline(r);  whoops = false;

        for jj=r+1:r+n, if resp(jj)~=0, break; end; end; %downhill
        for jj=jj:r+n
            if curPix <= scanline(jj), whoops=true; break; end
            skip(jj) = 1;     % skip future pixels if < current one
        end
        if whoops, continue; end      % skip to next scanline peak

        for jj=r-1:-1:r-n, if resp(jj)~=0, break; end; end;
        for jj=jj:-1:r-n
            if curPix <= scanline(jj), whoops=true; break; end
        end
        if whoops, continue; end      % skip to next scanline peak

        % if reach here, current pixel is a (2n+1)-maximum
        for jj=1:length(I)    % visit neighborhood in spiral order
            if im(r,c)<=im(r+dr(jj),c+dc(jj)),  break; end
        end
        if jj>=length(I) && im(r,c)>im(r+dr(jj),c+dc(jj))
            mask(r,c) = 1;    % a new (2n+1)x(2n+1)-maximum is found
        end
    end
end
```

A.4 $(2n+1) \times (2n+1)$ Quarter-Block Partitioning Algorithm

Below is a vectorized Matlab implementation of the quarter-block partitioning algorithm described in Section 4.2. Note that we actually compare a local maximum candidate with its full $(2n+1) \times (2n+1)$ neighborhood instead of with individual unvisited neighbors because vectorized code runs faster in this case.

```
function mask = nonmaxsupp_quarterblock(im,n)

[h w] = size(im); mask = false([h w]); m = floor((n+1)/2);
hh = floor(h/m);          % hh x ww = number of m x m blocks,
ww = floor(w/m);          % starting from (m,m) offset

%% vectorised code to compute local maxima of m—by—m blocks
val = im(1:hh*m,1:ww*m);
[val,R] = max(reshape(val,[m hh*ww*m]),[],1);
val = reshape(reshape(val,[hh ww*m])',[m ww hh]);
R = reshape(reshape(R   ,[hh ww*m])',[m ww*hh]);   % row indices &
[val,C] = max(val,[],1);          % column indices of local maxima
R = reshape(R(sub2ind([m ww*hh],C(:)',1:ww*hh)),[ww hh])';
val = squeeze(val)';  C = squeeze(C)';

%% compare each candidate to its (2n+1)x(2n+1) neighborhood
mask0 = nonmaxsupp3x3(val);     % local maxima of block max image
for I = find(mask0)'
   [ii,jj] = ind2sub([hh ww],I);
   r = (ii-1)*m + R(ii,jj);
   c = (jj-1)*m + C(ii,jj);
   if r<=n||c<=n||r>h-n||c>w-n, continue; end      % out of bound

   % compare to full (2n+1)x(2n+1) block for code simplicity
   if sum2(im(r+(-n:n),c+(-n:n))>=val(ii,jj))==1,
       mask(r,c) = 1;    % a new (2n+1)x(2n+1)—maximum is found
   end
end
```

Hit-or-Miss Transform in Multivariate Images

Santiago Velasco-Forero and Jesús Angulo

CMM-Centre de Morphologie Mathématique
Mathématiques et Systèmes, MINES ParisTech;
35, rue Saint-Honore, 77305 Fontainebleau cedex - France
{santiago.velasco,jesus.angulo}@mines-paristech.fr

Abstract. The Hit-or-Miss transform (HMT) is a well-known morphological operator for template matching in binary images. A novel approach for HMT for multivariate images is introduced in this paper. The generic framework is a generalization of binary case based on a h-supervised ordering formulation which leads to reduced orderings. In particular, in this paper we focus on the application of HMT for target detection on high-resolution images. The visual results of the experiments show the performance of proposed approach.

Keywords: Mathematical Morphology, Hyperspectral Imagery, Hit-or-Miss Transform, Remote Sensing, Colour Images.

1 Introduction

Since the first Landsat satellite was launched by the NASA in 1972, satellite remote sensing has become an important source of data for better understanding the earth's natural resources, and to increase the number of researchers in image processing with applications from international security system to archaeology. Depending on the sensor systems, civil and commercial satellites can produce several types of imagery data, including high-resolution RGB, panchromatic, multispectral, hyperspectral and radar, each of which have particular advantages and withdraws, depending on the specific requirements of the user. An efficient template matching operator to deal with automatic processing of these huge collections of images to extract spatial/spectral structures matching with a prototype or target is required in many applications. In the literature, template matching as testing under classical distribution assumptions, feature template matching in low-dimensional representation and matching points using Hausdorff Distance [1,2], are the most frequently alternatives to solve this problem. However, the extension to vectorial images is not evident or it requires strong theoretical assumptions. On the other hand, mathematical morphology (MM) offers several tools for image processing, including a template matching operator called the Hit-or-Miss Transform (HMT). This operation was devised by Matheron and Serra [3] in the mid-sixties, but unfortunately, there are not an unique extension to grey-level images [4,5,6], or multivariate images [7,8]. Our approach, it is inspired by ideas from [9] using supervised ordering to formulate a

J. Blanc-Talon et al. (Eds.): ACIVS 2010, Part I, LNCS 6474, pp. 452–463, 2010.

HMT for multiband images as a natural extension of the binary case to complete lattices.

2   Complete Lattices in $\mathbb{R}^p$

In this section, fundamentals of complete lattices for $\mathbb{R}^p$ are reviewed. For a detailed exposition on complete lattice theory refer to [10] and [11]. A space $\mathcal{L}$ endowed with a partial order $\leq$ is called a *complete lattice*, denoted $(\mathcal{L}, \leq)$ if every subset $\mathcal{H} \subseteq \mathcal{L}$ has both supremum (join) $\bigvee \mathcal{H}$ and infimum (meet) $\bigwedge \mathcal{H}$. A *minimum (smallest)* is an element of the lattice $\mathcal{H}$ such that if $l \in \mathcal{H} \Rightarrow n \leq l, \forall l$. We denote the minimum of $\mathcal{L}$ by $\bot$. Equivalently, we denote the maximum of $\mathcal{L}$ by $\top$. For $a, b \in \mathcal{L}$ such that $a \leq b$, the interval $[a, b]$ denotes the set $\{l \in \mathcal{L} : a \leq l \leq b\}$ corresponding to the hyperbox with lower vertex a and upper vertex b. If $a > b$, we set $[a, b] = \emptyset$. For $\mathcal{H} \subseteq \mathcal{L}$, we use the notation $box(\mathcal{H})$ to denote the smallest interval or hyperbox that contains $\mathcal{H}$. If $\mathcal{H} = \emptyset$ then $box(\mathcal{H}) = \emptyset$. Otherwise, $box(\mathcal{H})$ is given by $[\bigwedge \mathcal{H}, \bigvee \mathcal{H}]$. A nonempty subset $\mathcal{H}$ of $\mathcal{L}$ is a *chain* in $\mathcal{L}$ if $\mathcal{H}$ is totally ordered by $\leq$. A finite chain with n elements can be written in the form $c_1 \leq c_2 \leq \ldots \leq c_n$. Such a chain said to have length $n - 1$. Let $\mathcal{L}$ be a poset with no infinite chains. If $a \leq b$, then the *distance* $dist(a, b)$ from a to b is the maximum length of all the chains from a to b, if this maximum is finite. Otherwise the distance is infinite. Let R be a nonempty set and $\mathcal{L}$ a complete lattice. Furthermore, let $h : R \to \mathcal{L}$ be a surjective mapping. As it was defined in [12], we refer by $\leq_h$ as the *h-ordering* given by:

$$r \leq_h r' \Leftrightarrow h(r) \leq h(r'), \quad \forall r, r' \in R \tag{1}$$

Note that $\leq_h$ preserves reflexivity ($r \leq_h r$) and transitivity ($r_1 \leq_h r_2$ and $r_2 \leq_h r_3 \Rightarrow r_1 \leq_h r_3$) but is not a total ordering. Additionally, an equivalence class is defined by $\mathcal{L}[z] = \{r \in R | h(r) = z\}$. The notion of *h-supervised ordering* was defined by [9] for a nonempty set R based on the subsets $B, F \subset R$, such that $B \bigcap F = \emptyset$, as a h-ordering that satisfies the conditions: $h(\mathbf{b}) = \bot$, if $\mathbf{b} \in B$, and $h(\mathbf{f}) = \top$ if $\mathbf{f} \in F$. Equivalently, h is a supervised ordering if $box(h(R)) = [h(\mathbf{b}), h(\mathbf{f})]$ for some $\mathbf{b} \in B$ and $\mathbf{f} \in F$. A *h-supervised ordering* is denoted by $h_{\{B, F\}}$. Once this additional supervised restriction is imposed, an adequate vector ranking scheme can be formulated based on $\{B \cup F\}$. The main motivation of defining this new supervised ordering schema is to obtain maximum and minimum in the lattice $\mathcal{L}$ interpretable with respect to sets B and F. At this point, the problem is how to define an adequate ordering for a given vectorial space and, in the case of supervised ordering, that should include the information from the subsets $\{B, F\}$. An inherent difficulty in the multivariate data situation is the lack of a "natural" concept of rank. There is not an obvious and unambiguous method of fully ordering vectors. To extend univariate order concepts to multivariate data, four types of sub-ordering principles have been introduced [13] i.e., (marginal ordering, reduced ordering, partial ordering and conditional ordering). Different reported approaches are illustrated in figure 1. Figures 1(a-c) presents three different schemes to order the vectorial space, but they are not taking into consideration the information contained in the data. These orderings share the same minimum and maximum in the induced lattice, the vectors $\mathbf{0} = \perp$ and $\mathbf{1} = \top$, i.e., the vector with the minimum(maximum) value in each marginal ordering. Another approach is to use a dimensional reduction algorithm, for example, principal component analysis (PCA) [14] or some non-linear projections approach [15]. It considers the first projection to induce the ordering. The minimum and maximum induced for that ordering are a priori unknown. An example is illustrated in figure 1(d). In this case, the minimum or maximum can change including a new element in the set. In [16], the ordering is based on a reference spectrum exhibiting lattice where the minimum has been fixed. However, that maximum is associated with the "farthest" vector but that does not have a real interpretation. In [9], the supervised ordering is introduces. It brings forth an interesting observation, the lattice exploits the information carried directly by the vectors in $\{F, B\}$. Figures 1(e-f) show these two referenced ordering, but in advantage the supervised ordering induces a lattice with predefined minimum/maximum. The basic idea is deduce a prediction function from training data $\{B, F\}$ to induce the ordering. In this paper, we use the Support Vector Machines (SVMs) to calculate the supervised ordering [17]. SVMs constructs a set of hyperplanes in a high dimensional space, to separate in two classes, the vectors emanate from $\{F\}$ and $\{B\}$. Thus, the distance to that maximum-margin hyperplane can be employed as a supervised ordering.

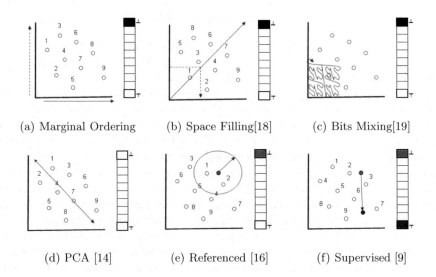

(a) Marginal Ordering   (b) Space Filling[18]   (c) Bits Mixing[19]

(d) PCA [14]   (e) Referenced [16]   (f) Supervised [9]

Fig. 1. Some vectorial ordering strategies proposed in the literature. The associated lattice is also illustrated.

3   Hit-or-Miss Transform in Multivariate Images

In this section, we briefly recall the definition of the Hit-or-Miss Transform before reviewing existing basic foundations of mathematical morphology for complete lattice. Finally we explain how these definitions can be applied to colour and multivariate images.

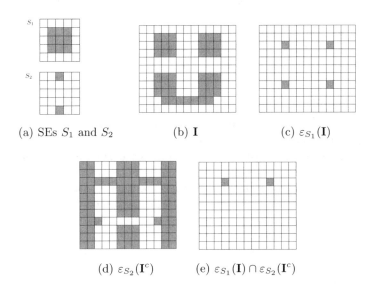

(a) SEs S_1 and S_2 (b) $\mathbf{I}$ (c) $\varepsilon_{S_1}(\mathbf{I})$

(d) $\varepsilon_{S_2}(\mathbf{I}^c)$ (e) $\varepsilon_{S_1}(\mathbf{I}) \cap \varepsilon_{S_2}(\mathbf{I}^c)$

Fig. 2. Illustrative example of Hit-or-Miss Transform in binary images: $HMT(\mathbf{I}; S_1, S_2)$

3.1   Hit-or-Miss Transform in Binary Images

Mathematical morphology is a nonlinear image processing methodology based on the application of lattice theory to spatial structures. For a general account on mathematical morphology the interested reader should refer to [20,21,4,22]. A pattern probe S called Structuring Element (SE) is involved in most of the morphological operators. In binary case, at it was presented by Soille in [4]: "the first question that may arise when we probe a set with a structuring element is: Does the structuring element fit the set? The eroded set is the locus of points where the answer to this question is affirmative." Thus the erosion of a set $\mathbf{I}$ by a structuring element S is denoted by $\varepsilon_S(\mathbf{I})$ and it is defined by:

$$\varepsilon_S(\mathbf{I}) = \bigcap_{s \in S} \mathbf{I}_{-s} \qquad (2)$$

The hit-or-miss transform (HMT) is a fundamental operation on binary images. In such images, this operator uses two disjoint structuring elements: the first has to match the foreground while the second has to match the background. Both matches are necessary in order the operator to give a positive matching response. HMT uses a pair (S_1, S_2) of SEs, and looks for all positions where S_1 can be fitted within a figure $\mathbf{I}$, and S_2 within the background $\mathbf{I}^c$, in other words, it is defined by:

$$HMT(X; S_1, S_2) = \varepsilon_{S_1}(\mathbf{I}) \cap \varepsilon_{S_2}(\mathbf{I}^c)$$
$$= \{x \in \Omega | \varepsilon_{S_1}(\mathbf{I}(x)) = \varepsilon_{S_2}(\mathbf{I}(x)^c) = 1\} \qquad (3)$$

One assumes that $S_1 \cap S_2 = \emptyset$, otherwise we always have $HMT(\mathbf{I}; S_1, S_2) = \emptyset$. One calls S_1 and S_2, respectively, the foreground and background SE. Figure 2(a-e) presents the binary HMT for a pedagogical example. We remark that HMT is simultaneously finding templates for the both pattern contained in the SEs, for the original image and its complementary dual.

3.2   Mathematical Morphology in Complete Lattices

The definition of morphological operators needs a complete lattice structure, i.e., the possibility of defining an ordering relationship between the points to be processed. During the last fifteen years, the extension of mathematical morphology to colour and vectorial images has been an active field and therefore many different approaches have been proposed. For a detailed state-of-the art on colour mathematical morphology the reader is referred to the papers [23,16]. Once the family of orderings have been established, the morphological vector operators are defined in the standard way. Different vectorial ordering were illustrate in figure 1. We limit here our developments to the flat operators, i.e., the structuring elements are planar shapes. Let $\mathbf{I} : \Omega \to \mathbb{R}^P$ be a vectorial image. According to the previous developments, we consider that there exists a mapping $h : \mathbb{R}^P \to \mathcal{L}$, such that by transforming to the intermediate image $h(\mathbf{I})$ we have a representation of the original vectorial image $\mathbf{I}$ in the lattice $\mathcal{L}$, i.e., $\mathbf{I} : \Omega \to \mathcal{L}$. The functions from Ω onto $\mathcal{L}$ are denoted by $\mathcal{F}(\Omega, \mathcal{L})$, where $\Omega \subset \mathbb{Z}^2$ is the support space of the image. The partial ordering in lattice $\mathcal{L}$ is denoted $\leq_{\mathcal{L}}$. If $\mathcal{L}$ is a complete lattice, then $\mathcal{F}(\Omega, \mathcal{L})$ is a complete lattice too. Let ψ be an operator on a complete lattice $\mathcal{F}(\Omega, \mathcal{L})$; ψ is increasing if $\forall \mathbf{I}, \mathbf{G} \in \mathcal{F}(\Omega, \mathcal{L})$, $\mathbf{I} \leq_{\mathcal{L}} \mathbf{G} \Rightarrow \psi(\mathbf{I}) \leq_{\mathcal{L}} \psi(\mathbf{I})$. It is anti-extensive if $\psi(\mathbf{I}) \leq_{\mathcal{L}} \mathbf{I}$ and it is extensive if $\mathbf{I} \leq_{\mathcal{L}} \psi(\mathbf{I})$. An operator is idempotent if it is verified that $\psi(\psi(\mathbf{I})) = \psi(\mathbf{I})$. As it was presented in [12] these properties are valid in particular using h-ordering, therefore also for h-supervised ordering.

The h-erosion, or erosion based on h-ordering, of an image $\mathbf{I} \in \mathcal{F}(\Omega, \mathcal{L})$ at pixel $x \in \Omega$ by the structuring element $S \subset \Omega$ of size n is given by $\varepsilon_{h,nS}(\mathbf{I})(x) = \{\mathbf{I}(y) : \mathbf{I}(y) = \wedge_h[\mathbf{I}(z)], z \in (nS)_x\}$, where $\wedge_h$ is the infimum according to the total ordering h. The corresponding h-dilation δ_h, is obtained by replacing the $\inf_h$ by the $\sup_h$, i.e., $\delta_{h,nS}(\mathbf{I})(x) = \{\mathbf{I}(y) : \mathbf{I}(y) = \vee_h[\mathbf{I}(z)], z \in (nS)_x\}$. The erosion and the dilation are increasing operators. Moreover, the erosion is anti-extensive and the dilation is extensive. It will be denoted by $\varepsilon_{\{B,F\}}$ the supervised erosion associated to the h-supervised ordering $h_{B,F}$. In the case of $h_{\{B,F\}}$, erosion shrinks the structures which have a spectrum close to F; "peaks of spectrum" thinner than the structuring element disappear by taking the spectrum of neighboring structures with a spectrum values close to B. As well, it

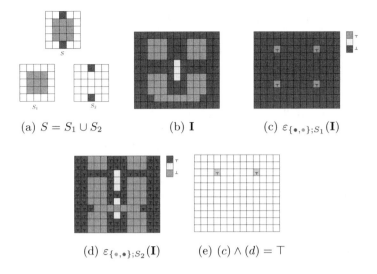

(a) $S = S_1 \cup S_2$ (b) $\mathbf{I}$ (c) $\varepsilon_{\{\bullet,\circ\};S_1}(\mathbf{I})$

(d) $\varepsilon_{\{\circ,\bullet\};S_2}(\mathbf{I})$ (e) $(c) \wedge (d) = \top$

Fig. 3. Comparison between binary HMT and the extension for multiband images. The lattice induced by the h-supervised ordering is presented in each case, using $\bot$ and $\top$ for minimum and maximum values respectively.

expands the structures which have a vector value close to background. Dilation using supervised ordering, produces the dual effects, enlarging the regions having a spectrum close to F and contracting those close to B and far from F.

3.3   Hit-or-Miss Transform in Complete Lattices

In the following a new approach will be presented. The proposal can be used to find an exact template matching in the original multivariate image $\mathbf{I}$ with the structuring element $S = S_1 \cup S_2$ with $S_1 \cap S_2 = \emptyset$ and $S_1, S_2 \in \Omega$, where Ω is the support space of the image. Our approach defines HMT using the h-supervised ordering presented in section 2, as a natural extension of the original HMT defined in the binary case. It is important to remark that expression 3 can be expressed in term of h-supervised ordering as follows,

$$HMT(\mathbf{I}; S_1, S_2) = \{x \in \Omega | h_{\{0,1\}}(\varepsilon_{\{0,1\};S_1}(\mathbf{I})) = \mathbf{1} \wedge h_{\{1,0\}}(\varepsilon_{\{1,0\};S_2}(\mathbf{I})) = \mathbf{0}\}$$

In the case that $\mathbf{I}$ and S are binary, then the natural order is $\{0 = \bot, 1 = \top\}$ and the complement inverses the order to $\{1 = \bot, 0 = \top\}$. In the h-supervised ordering the inverse ordering, associated to complementation can be induced interchanging the referenced set $\{B, F\}$ by $\{F, B\}$. Thus the expression 3 can be generalized using the h-supervised ordering as follows,

$$HMT(\mathbf{I}; \{B, F\}, S_1, S_2) = \{x \in \Omega | \forall i, h_i(\varepsilon_{h_i;S_i}(\mathbf{I}(x))) = \top_i\} \qquad (4)$$

where

$$h_i = \begin{cases} h_{\{B,F\}} | h(b) = \bot, h(f) = \top & \text{if} \quad i=1; \\ h_{\{F,B\}} | h(f) = \bot, h(b) = \top & \text{if} \quad i=2. \end{cases}$$

From 4, it easy to note that for each SE there are a set of vector value associated. Therefore, we formulate a *generalized* HMT based on the sets of couple $\{B_i, S_i\}_{i=1,...,k}$ such that $S_i \in \Omega, S_i \cap S_j = \emptyset, \forall i \neq j$, and $B_i \subset \mathbb{R}^n$, as follows,

$$HMT(\mathbf{I}; \{B_i, S_i\}) = \{x \in \Omega | \forall i, h_{\{B_i, B_{-i}\}}(\varepsilon_{\{B_i, B_{-i}\}; S_i}(\mathbf{I}(x))) = \top_i\} \quad (5)$$

where $B_{-i} = \bigcup_{j \neq i} B_j$, $\{S_i\}_{i=1...k}$ is the family of structuring elements and $\{B_i\}_{i=1...n}$ is the family of vectorial values associated with $\{S_i\}_{i=1...k}$. The expression 4 is a particular case when $i = 2$, $B_1 = B$ and $B_{-1} = F$.

For practical application the generalized HMT can be useful as a template matching technique, but it requires to be robust, noise insensitive and automatic. We refer keen readers to [7] for a comprehensive review of robust HMT in grey scale images. In our formulation a robust version includes a threshold in equation 5 to allow a degree of noise in the "detection" of each S_i related to B_i. Thus, the *HMT-ϵ* is defined as follows,

$$HMT_\epsilon(\mathbf{I}; \{B_i, S_i\}) = \{x \in \Omega | \forall i, dist(h_{\{B_i, B_{-i}\}}(\varepsilon_{\{B_i, B_{-i}\}; S_i}(\mathbf{I}(x))), \top_i) \leq \epsilon\} \quad (6)$$
$$= \{x \in \Omega | \forall i, h_{\{B_i, B_{-i}\}}(\varepsilon_{\{B_i, B_{-i}\}; S_i}(\mathbf{I}(x))) \in box(\top_i - \epsilon, \top_i)\}$$

Note that both definitions in 6 are equivalent. Clearly 4 is a particular case of 6 with $\epsilon = 0$. The parameter ϵ can be interpreted as the allowed maximum difference between each theoretical value $\top_i$ and the value detected for the operator HMT_ϵ.

4   Experiments

The template matching method proposed in this paper were applied to two different problems and here we present some of the obtained results.

4.1   Geometrical Pattern Problem

The proposed algorithm is tested using a colour image of size 448×322 with a "diamond pattern" of size 6×6 of different colours. In figure 4, the application of vectorial HMT to the original colour image (Figure (4(a)) is illustrated using two sets of template to match (Figure (4(b-c)). The intermediate steps (h-supervised erosions) are further exemplified in figure 4(d-e,g-h). The final detection maps are presented in figure 4(f,i). In this toy example, the detection is perfect, and it is according with the natural generalization from the binary case.

To analyze the robustness of our proposal, the original image is normalized to the interval $[0, 1]$ and then corrupted with white Gaussian noise with variance, $\Sigma = 0.05$. The results were recorded and plotted as Receiver Operating Characteristic (ROC) curves. In that case, HMT_ϵ have to be more accurate to avoid the false positives caused by inadequate parameters. In this experiment, the supervised ordering is calculated using SVMs with gaussian and polynomial kernels. Figure 5(a) shows that the low-degree polynomial kernel has a similar performance that a gaussian kernel with a adequate parameter σ. Additionally, ROC-curves are presented in 5(b) for different noisy versions of the image, with various values of Gaussian noise of variance Σ using a polynomial kernel of degree one.

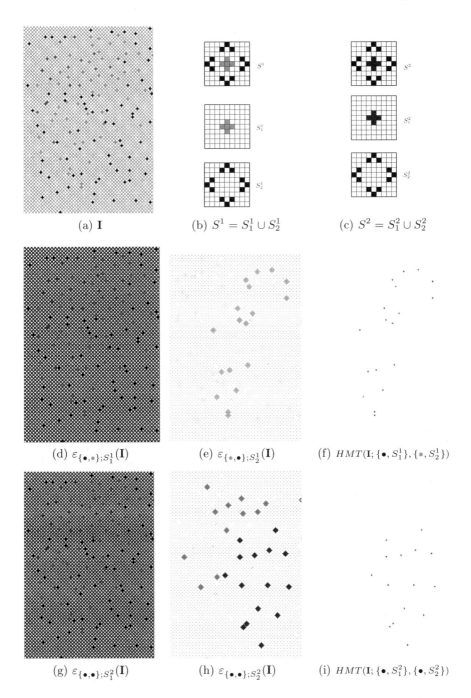

(a) $\mathbf{I}$

(b) $S^1 = S_1^1 \cup S_2^1$

(c) $S^2 = S_1^2 \cup S_2^2$

(d) $\varepsilon_{\{\bullet,\bullet\};S_1^1}(\mathbf{I})$

(e) $\varepsilon_{\{\bullet,\bullet\};S_2^1}(\mathbf{I})$

(f) $HMT(\mathbf{I}; \{\bullet, S_1^1\}, \{\bullet, S_2^1\})$

(g) $\varepsilon_{\{\bullet,\bullet\};S_1^2}(\mathbf{I})$

(h) $\varepsilon_{\{\bullet,\bullet\};S_2^2}(\mathbf{I})$

(i) $HMT(\mathbf{I}; \{\bullet, S_1^2\}, \{\bullet, S_2^2\})$

Fig. 4. Example of template matching using the proposal hit-or-miss transform for colour images

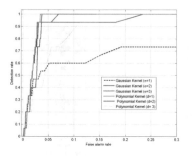 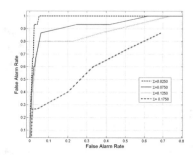

(a) HMT using gaussian and polyno- (b) HMT using polynomial kernel with
mial kernel with different parameters   different value of noise variance Σ with
                                        additive gaussian noise

Fig. 5. ROC-curves in the geometrical pattern problem

4.2 Ship Detection in High-Resolution RGB Images

To illustrate the performance of this operator in a real example, we compare
the proposed HMT in the extraction of image objects characterized by spectrum
and shape simultaneously. This is a natural colour, 50 centimeter high-resolution,
WorldView-2 satellite image featuring the village Samaheej, Bahrain in the Per-
sian Gulf, collected at January 28, 2010, and available in www.digitalglobe.com.
The original colour image is reduced to $[2326, 864, 3]$ pixels for improve the
visualization $(7(a))$. Our approach run over that test image for two sets of SEs.
The main goal is the extraction of ships using the colour information in $\{B_1, B_2\}$
and the shape information in S^1, S^2. In the first scenario we extract the bigger
ships using as S^1 a square of 47 pixels, such that $S^1 = S^1_1 \cup S^1_2$ as it is shown
in figures 6(a) and 6(b). The set of pixels background B and foreground F are
shown in figures 6(e)6(f). In the second scenario the smaller ships are extracted
using S^2 as a square of 28 pixels, such that $S^2 = S^2_1 \cup S^2_2$. S^2_1 and S^2_2 are

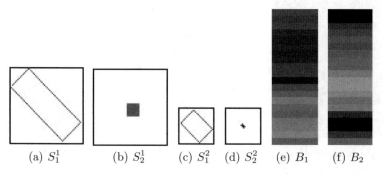

(a) S^1_1 (b) S^1_2 (c) S^2_1 (d) S^2_2 (e) B_1 (f) B_2

Fig. 6. SEs considered in the Bahrain Image. In both scenarios, the sets of pixels
background and foreground are the same.

(a) $\mathbf{I}$ (b) $HMT_\epsilon(\mathbf{I}, \{B_1, S_1^1\}, \{B_2, S_2^1\})$ (c) $HMT_\epsilon(\mathbf{I}, \{B_1, S_1^2\}, \{B_2, S_2^2\})$

(d) Zoomed in version (a)   (e) Enlarged results of (b)

Fig. 7. Ship detection in High-Resolution Samaheej Image using HMT_ϵ

presented in figures 6(c-d). The results are presented in figures 7 (b-c) for the two scenarios using the proposed robust HMT_ϵ. It is important to remark the sole large ship which is not detected correspond to one (botton-right 7(d)) presenting an orientation which involves that the background shape template (i.e. S_1^1) does no match in a suitable way. In the case of small ships, some false alarms are obtained, which correspond to objects on the sea and colour similar to the distribution B_1 in the shape S_2^2. Obviously, the results should be more robust using a more selective shape prototype of the ship shape as well as a better spectral resolution which would involve more selective values of B_1 and B_2. The values in the h-ordering were normalized between $[0, 1]$ and the parameter ϵ was fixed to 0.4. An optimal parameter selection can be done, however that is beyond the scope of this paper.

5 Conclusion and Perspectives

We have introduced a genuine extension of the classical binary Hit-or-miss transform based on h-supervised ordering for complete lattices in $\mathbb{R}^p$. Standard HMT involves a pair of disjoint structuring elements, one for the foreground and the other el background. Hence, our formulation of supervised h-orderings which requires training sets for the foreground and background is appropriate for the definition of generalized HMT. In addition, the natural duality by inverting foreground and background solves the complementation required for the HMT. More practically, the interest of the HMT transform for combined spatial/spectral image detection has been illustrated for multivariate images. The combination of prior information given by the shape of the structuring elements as well as the spectral values for the foreground and background is compatible with the current paradigm of structural target detection in remote sensing applications. We should remark also that our supervised morphological framework can simultaneously implementing HMT where templates have the same shape but different alternative values for the foreground/background. We have also studied the influence of the learning method (i.e., kernel parameters of SVM), used in the construction of the h-ordering, in the results of the HMT. This robustness as well as the good properties against noise of HMT entail promising perspectives for its application in many real problems. In ongoing research two issues should be considered in depth. On the one hand, to evaluate the interest of unflat erosions in the construction of HMT, which will allow to define more "fuzzy" structuring elements. On the other, to conceive different ways of parallelisation of the HMT for an efficient implementation of the generic case where a family of templates is associated to the target structure, e.g., group of rotations and scale transformation of the object shape.

References

1. Sim, D., Kwon, O., Park, R.: Object matching algorithms using robust hausdorff distance measures. IEEE Trans. Image Processing 8, 425–429 (1999)
2. Zhu, Z., Tang, M., Lu, H.: A new robust circular gabor based object matching by using weighted hausdorff distance. Pattern Recognition Letters 25, 515–523 (2004)
3. Serra, J.: Image Analysis and Mathematical Morphology. Academic Press, Inc., Orlando (1983)
4. Soille, P.: Morphological Image Analysis. Springer, Heidelberg (1999)
5. Naegel, B., Passat, N., Ronse, C.: Grey-level hit-or-miss transforms - Part I: Unified theory. Pattern Recognition 40, 635–647 (2007)
6. Ronse, C.: A lattice-theoretical morphological view on template extraction in images. Journal of Visual Comm. and Image Representation 7, 273–295 (1996)
7. Aptoula, E., Lefevre, S., Ronse, C.: A hit-or-miss transform for multivariate images. Pattern Recognition Letters 30, 760–764 (2009)
8. Weber, J., Lefevre, S.: A multivariate Hit-or-Miss transform for conjoint spatial and spectral template matching. In: Elmoataz, A., Lezoray, O., Nouboud, F., Mammass, D. (eds.) ICISP 2008. LNCS, vol. 5099, pp. 226–235. Springer, Heidelberg (2008)

9. Velasco-Forero, S., Angulo, J.: Morphological processing of hyperspectral images using kriging-based supervised ordering. In: ICIP (2010)
10. Roman, S.: Lattices and Ordered Sets. Springer, Heidelberg (2008)
11. Heijmans, H.: Theoretical aspects of gray-level morphology. IEEE Trans. Pattern Analysis and Machine Intelligence 13, 568–582 (1991)
12. Goutsias, J., Heijmans, H., Sivakumar, K.: Morphological operators for image sequences. Comput. Vis. Image Underst. 62, 326–346 (1995)
13. Barnett, V.: The ordering of multivariate data (with discussion). Journal of the Royal Statistical Society Series A 139, 318–354 (1976)
14. Jolliffe, I.T.: Principal Component Analysis. Springer, Heidelberg (1986)
15. Lezoray, O., Charrier, C., Elmoataz, A.: Learning complete lattices for manifold mathematical morphology. In: Proc. of the ISMM, pp. 1–4 (2009)
16. Angulo, J.: Morphological colour operators in totally ordered lattices based on distances: Application to image filtering, enhancement and analysis. Comput. Vis. Image Underst. 107, 56–73 (2007)
17. Cristianini, N., Shawe-Taylor, J.: An Introduction to support vector machines and other kernel based learning methods. Cambridge University Press, Cambridge (2000)
18. Regazzoni, C., Teschioni, A.: A new approach to vector median filtering based on space filling curves. IEEE Trans. Image Processing 6, 1025–1037 (1997)
19. Chanussot, J., Lambert, P.: Extending mathematical morphology to color image processing. In: Int. Conf. on Color in Graphics and Image Proc., pp. 158–163 (2000)
20. Serra, J.: Image Analysis and Mathematical Morphology. Academic Press, Inc., Orlando (1982)
21. Goutsias, J., Heijmans, H.: Mathematical Morphology. IOS Press, Amsterdam (2000)
22. Haralick, R., Sternberg, S., Zhuang, X.: Image analysis using mathematical morphology. IEEE Trans. Pattern Analysis and Machine Intelligence 9, 532–550 (1987)
23. Aptoula, E., Lefèvre, S.: A comparative study on multivariate mathematical morphology. Pattern Recognition 40, 2914–2929 (2007)

Topological SLAM Using Omnidirectional Images: Merging Feature Detectors and Graph-Matching

Anna Romero and Miguel Cazorla

Instituto Universitario Investigación en Informática;
P.O. Box. 99 03080 Alicante
aromero@dccia.ua.es,miguel.cazorla@ua.es

Abstract. Image feature extraction and matching is useful in many areas of robotics such as object and scene recognition, autonomous navigation, SLAM and so on. This paper describes a new approach to the problem of matching features and its application to scene recognition and topological SLAM. For that purpose we propose a prior image segmentation into regions in order to group the extracted features in a graph so that each graph defines a single region of the image. This image segmentation considers that the left part of the image is the continuation of the right part. The matching process will take into account the features and the structure (graph) using the GTM algorithm. Then, using this method of comparing images, we propose an algorithm for constructing topological maps. During the experimentation phase we will test the robustness of the method and its ability constructing topological maps. We have also introduced a new hysteresis behavior in order to solve some problems found in construction of the graph.

Keywords: Topological Mapping, Graph matching, Visual features.

1 Introduction

The extraction and matching of features is an important area of robotics since it allows, among other things, object and scene recognition and its application to object localization, autonomous navigation, obstacle avoidance, topological SLAM.

The SLAM (Simultaneous Localization And Mapping) problem consists of estimating the position of the robot while building the environment map. The problem is not trivial, since errors in position estimation affect the map and vice versa. In the literature, depending on the form to represent the robot environment, we can talk of two types of SLAM: the Metric SLAM and the Topological SLAM. In the first, the position is determined by a continuous space, *i.e.* we know exactly what position the robot has on the map (with an assumed error). It is easy to find solutions that include odometry, sonars and lasers ([20,22]). There are less solutions using vision since calculating the exact position is more complicated. In the second type, the different points where you can find the robot are represented by a list of positions, *i.e.* the map is a discrete set of locations which defines a small region on the environment. In this case there are plenty of solutions that use images for the calculations. In [26] they use the images captured

J. Blanc-Talon et al. (Eds.): ACIVS 2010, Part I, LNCS 6474, pp. 464–475, 2010.

by the AIBO robot to learn the topological map. We also find solutions using omni-directional images such as [27] and [23], [28] where a topological map is constructed using an incremental algorithm.

For both object and scene recognition we need methods of extracting features and/or regions from images. Several solutions in the literature use different methods for extracting the features. In [4], they use an over-segmentation algorithm to split the image into small regions. In [5], they combine the Harris corner detector with a SIFT descriptor. Many solutions in the literature are based on the combination of a segmentation algorithm with a feature extractor ([4], [11], [9]).

Object recognition requires a manually selected database to describe the objects that the robot must recognise. In the case of scene recognition we could require a scene database as in [10] where they introduce the concept of "Visual Place Categorization" (VPC) which consists of identifying the semantic category of one place/room using visual information. However, there are situations requiring no pre-existing database as it is constructed as the robot navigates through the environment ([11], [12]) such as in the SLAM problem.

Affine invariant feature detectors have been shown to be very useful in several computer vision applications, like object recognition and categorization, wide baseline stereo and robot localization. These detection algorithms extract visual features from images that are invariant to image transformations such as illumination change, rotation, scale and slight viewpoint change. High level vision tasks that rely on these visual features are more robust to these transformations and also to the presence of clutter and occlusions. A more detailed survey of the state of the art of visual feature detectors can be found in [6]. In this work, the authors assess the performance of different algorithms for the matching problem, with the Maximally Stable Extremal Regions algorithm (MSER) [7], the Harris affine and the Hessian affine [8] being best suited for that task.

Several methods are based on a combination of feature detectors (regions, contours and/or invariant points) to improve the matching and taking advantage of the extraction methods used, as well as eliminating some of the problems of the individual methods. However, it has not proposed the creation of structures from the extracted features to check the overall consistency of the matchings but the features are matched one by one without taking into account any possible neighborhood relationships. Some of those methods apply a matching consistency, eliminating cross-matches, those matches that intersects with others. In the case of omnidirectional images, this cannot be done, due to the circular nature of the images.

In this paper we propose a method for matching features and an algorithm to construct topological maps using this comparison method. For the image comparison method we propose image pre-processing in two steps: segmentation into regions (using JSEG) and invariant feature extraction (using MSER with SIFT descriptors). Each of the regions obtained in the first step will contain a list of invariant points inside its domain. For each region, our method will construct a graph with the invariant points considering that omnidirectional images have special characteristics. The feature matching is carried out by comparing the graph of each of the regions of the current image with the representative graph (built with all points of the image) of each of the previously captured images. This approach takes into account both the feature descriptors and the structure of those features within the region. We apply the image comparison method in our topological map algorithm in order to group images that are considered to belong to the same area.

The rest of the paper is organized as follows: Section 2 describes the pre-processing of the image (JSEG segmentation) and feature extraction (MSER). Section 3 explains the graph matching using the GTM algorithm. Then, in section 4 we describe the algorithm that constructs topological maps. In 5 we present the results obtained applying the combination of the image matching method and the two versions of the topological mapping algorithm. Finally in 6, we draw certain conclussions.

2   Image Processing

MSER (Maximally Stable Extremal Regions) [7] is an affine invariant shape descriptor. The MSER algorithm detects regions that are darker or brighter than their surroundings and can be scale invariant. The algorithm uses the SIFT descriptor to describe the detected regions. Due to the nature of the descriptors, it is possible to associate (match) an MSER region (feature) of an image with one that appears in another image using Euclidean distance in the matching process. Despite the robustness of the method we can find many cases where the feature matching has not been successful (false positives or outliers). To eliminate these false positives and thus obtain a more reliable and robust results in identifying scenes seen before, we propose to use a structure (graph) with which to compare (and match) images. To detect the different image regions (which eventually form the sub-graphs for comparison) we use the segmentation algorithm JSEG.

2.1   Segmentation

Feature detection and extraction methods find characteristics along the whole image. Our goal is to group features according to the image region to which they belong, so we need a segmentation algorithm to divide an image into regions. In our case we use the one proposed in [2] and known as JSEG algorithm.

Considering the special characteristics of omnidirectional images (the left is a neighbour of the far right of the image, *i.e.*, the image is circular) a piece of the initial part of the image has been added to the final of the image. This is to avoid that a region that has been cut during the capture of the image (a region part is on the left and the other part is on the right) is taken as two separate regions. In figure 1 we can see the original image with the initial part added to the final of the image and the result to apply the JSEG algorithm.

JSEG finds homogeneity of a particular color pattern and texture. It assumes that the image:

- Contains a set of regions with approximately the same color and texture.
- Color data in each region of the image can be represented with a small set of quantized colors.
- Colors between two neighboring regions are distinguishable from each other.

Fig. 1. Above: Image captured to which was added to the end a piece of the initial part of the image. Below: Result in applying JSEG. The region inside the ellipse is an example of a region that could have been cut.

In order to obtain different regions, JSEG performs segmentation in two steps: color quantization and spacial segmentation. In the first step of the algorithm, image colors are coarsely quantized without significantly degrading the image quality. This will extract a few representative colors that can be used as classes which separate regions of the image. For each image pixel, the algorithm find its class and replace its value, building an image of labels (class-map).

In the second step, a spatial segmentation is performed directly on the class-map without taking into account the color similarity of the corresponding pixel. This transforms the output from the previous step in a J-Image ([2]). Once this image is calculated, the algorithm uses a region growing method for image segmentation. Initially, the JSEG considers the image as one region, performs an initial segmentation with the scale and repeats the same process with the new regions and the next scale. Once the seed-growing step ends, the regions that have been over-segmented are merged using a grouping method. Finally we get two images, one where each pixel has the value of the region it belongs to and one with the real image which have overlapped the edges of each region.

An advantage of separating the segmentation into two steps yields an increase in the processing speed of each of the steps, which together do not exceed the time required for processing the whole problem. Furthermore, the process is not supervised and therefore there is no need for experiments to calculate thresholds, since the algorithm automatically determines them.

2.2   Feature Detection and Extraction

Once the different regions of the image have been determined, we proceed to extract image features. In our case we use the affine invariant shape descriptor MSER.

The algorithm described in [7] searches extremal regions, that is, regions in which all pixels are brighter or darker than all the pixels in their neighborhood. The image pixels are taken in intensity order, forming connected component regions that grow and merge, until all pixels have been selected. From all these connected components, or extremal regions, the algorithm selects those for which size remains constant during a given number of iterations. Finally, the selected Maximally Stable Extremal Regions, that can have any arbitrary shape, are transformed into ellipses.

For each image, the features of the entire image are acquired and stored to build a representative graph of the image. Furthermore, each feature is assigned to the region it belongs to (by using the position of the feature in the image and taking into account that the initial pixels and the final pixels of the image are neighbors), obtaining a set of invariant points for every region calculated in the segmentation step. Points that belong to the same region are those used to construct the various sub-graphs that describe the image, *i.e.* each region has its own graph, built with all the features in its domain. Note that it is possible that some regions not to have any feature associated or some points not to belong to any particular region, in this case the region (or points) is discarded because it does not contain any interesting data.

3   Matching with Graphs

The feature matching process could result in unwanted false positives. To eliminate these outliers we suggest the use of graphs as the structure for matching. The use of graphs allows us to check not only a single invariant point consistency, but also a set of points that have some relationship with each other.

The selected method for graph matching is GTM [3] (Graph Transformation Matching). This algorithm needs a list of the position of the matched points as input (x_1, y_1) (x_2, y_2). This list is calculated as follows:

- A $KD - Tree$ is built (this tree structure, $KD - tree$, allows relatively quick insertions and searches for a k-dimensional space (128 dimensions in our case, the SIFT descriptor dimension)) with all points of the base image (all points that forms the representative graph).
- For each region of the current image (image sub-graphs):
  - For each point in the region, the closest one in the $KD - Tree$ is found. If its Euclidean distance is below a threshold, we have found a match.

Once this step is completed, we have a list of matched points that describe a common region between the two images. As this matching may result in many false positives we use the GTM algorithm to compare the structure of the region in both images to eliminate those false positives in the matching.

GTM is a point matching algorithm based on attributed graphs [3] that uses information from the local structure (graph) for the treatment of outliers. The graph constructed for comparison is called K-Nearest-Neighbours which is built by adding an edge to the adjacency matrix for the pair (i, j) if node j is one of the k nearest neighbours of node i and if the Euclidean distance between the two points is also less than the average distance of all points on the graph. If a node has not k edges, it is disconnected until we finish graph construction.

Once the two graphs from the two images have been constructed, the algorithm eliminates iteratively the correspondences distorting neighborhood relations. To do this, what is considered an outlier is selected, the two nodes (invariant points) that form the match (false positive) are removed from their respective graphs and also the references to those nodes in the two adjacency matrices. Then, the two graphs are then recalculated again. The process continues until the residual matrix (the difference between the adjacency matrices of two graphs) is zero. At this point we consider that the algorithm has found a consensus graph. Once this is acquired, the disconnected nodes are eliminated of the initial matching, obtaining a match where the false positives are removed.

4   Topological Mapping

The results of the previous section allow let us know if two images can be seen as part of the same environmental region (they have been taken at nearby positions in the real world). Using this method for image comparison we have built an algorithm capable of creating topological maps from a sequence of images that form a path in the real world. Our algorithm does not require a database because it is created as a new image is captured.

The algorithm builds topological maps in the form of undirected graphs that can be used in applications of topological SLAM. The topological map consists of nodes representing a particular area of the environment and an adjacency matrix that shows the relationships between them. The nodes can consist of any number of images, but always have a representative image. This image is one that has more regions in common with the rest of images belonging to the node. In order to calculate the node representative and its minimum matching percentage, we use the formulas:

$$R = \arg \max_{i \epsilon I} (\min_{j \epsilon I, i \neq j} (C(i,j))) \tag{1}$$

$$N_R = \max_{i \epsilon I} (\min_{j \epsilon I, i \neq j} (C(i,j))) \tag{2}$$

These equations appeared in [23] and use the number of matched points in function $C(i,j)$. In order to use our previous method, we have modified this formula as follows:

$$C(i,j) = \frac{Number\ of\ matched\ points}{min(NP_i, NP_j)} \tag{3}$$

where NP_k is the number of points in image k. We select the image with the least number of points since it will match at most this number of points that otherwise could not reach 100% in the equation.

Unlike the algorithm proposed in [23], we added a second threshold (Th_{adj}). This threshold is lower than Th_{min} (used to compare the current image with the representative of the node) and it is used in comparing the adjacent nodes to the current node. In this way we can improve the creation of maps, as seen in figure 3.

The algorithm builds the topological map as follows:

1. When the robot captures a new image, it checks whether the image belongs to the region that defines the current node. For this, the new image is compared with

```
Topological Mapping Algorithm {
 TG ← φ //Topological graph
 for each i ∈ I //I = Dataset Image
   addIᵢ ← addInitialPartToImageFinal( Iᵢ )
   {JSEG} ← JSEGRegionSegmentation( addIᵢ )
   {MSER} ← MSERFeatureDetection( Iᵢ ) //features set
   GRᵢ ← {MSER} in KD-Tree structure //Img. Representat. Graph
   SGᵢ ← φ //Image sub-graph with a kd-tree structure
   for each j ∈ {JSEG}
     SGᵢ(j) ← {k} | k ∈ {MSER} ∧ (xₖ, yₖ) ∈ D(JSEGⱼ)
       where (xₖ, yₖ) = k feature coordenates
       and D(JSEGⱼ) =  JSEGⱼ domain
   end for each
   TG ←  addNewImage(TG, Iᵢ, GRᵢ, SGᵢ)
 end for each
}
topologicalGraph addNewImage(TG, Iᵢ, GRᵢ, SGᵢ) {
 distance ← calculateDistance(Iᵢ, nodeRepresentativeImage(currentNode))
 if (distance >= Th_min)
   currentNode ← Iᵢ
 else
   distanceAdjacent ← maximumAdjacentNodeDistance(Iᵢ, nodeRepresentative)
   adjacent ← maximumAdjacentIndexNode(Iᵢ, nodeRepresentative)
   if (distanceAdjacent >= Th_adj)
     currentNode ←= TG(adjacent)
     TG(adjacent) ← Iᵢ
   else
     distanceNodes ← maximumNoAdjacentNodeDistance(Iᵢ)
     noAdjacent ← maximumNoAdjacentIndexNode(Iᵢ)
     if(noAdjacent >= Th_min)
       currentNode ← noAdjacent
       TG(noAdjacent) ← Iᵢ
     else
       node ← newNode(Iᵢ)
       currentNode ← node
       TG ← node
     end if
   end if
 end if
}
```

Fig. 2. Topological Mapping Algorithm

the node representative and if the matching percentage passes a certain threshold (Th_{min}), it is added to the node.

2. If the image does not exceed the threshold, it is compared with all the node representatives, to find the node whose percentage is higher. To give priority (more weight) to the adjacent nodes to the current node we introduce a new threshold

(Th_{adj}) lower than the previous one ($Th_{adj} \leq Th_{min}$). If the image exceeds the matching adjacent node threshold (Th_{adj}) it is added to that adjacent node. If not, the image is compared to the other nodes and if it exceeds the minimum threshold ($Thmin$) it is added to the node with the highest matching percentage.

3. If no match is found we establish that we have seen a new node, so it creates it and add an edge between new node and the previous one.

4. In any case, if we add an image to an existing node, if $Th_{min} \leq C(i,j) \leq N_R$, the node representative is re-calculated.

Figure 2 shows the pseudo-code of the algorithm. The function $calculate Distance$ calculates the distance between two images. The $maximum Adjacent Node Distance$ calculates the maximum distance ($distance = 0$ means the images are not similar, $distance = 1$ means the images are equal) between the image and the adjacent nodes of the current node, and the function $maximum No Adjacent Node Distance$ calculates the maximum distance between the image and the no-adjacent nodes.

5   Results

This section shows the results of applying the whole algorithm on the set of images described in [1] which are available for download from the authors' website. The images are omnidirectional, with a resolution of 2048x618. The tests were conducted on the images for the first route, the first 3,000 of the data-set. Omnidirectional images have a special features not found in other images. When images covering an angle of 360° it is possible to find two images from the same scene containing objects in a different situation or objects that have been cut.

In a previous work [24] we compare the response of the graph-based matching algorithm using different feature detectors. In [25] we describe the topological mapping algorithm using only one threshold and without taking into account that two objects that appeared at the beginning and end of the image could actually be the same object (because of the omnidirectional image characteristics).

In figure 3 we have the graph representing the topological map created by our algorithm with two thresholds (green graph, middle image) and with two threshold and region omnidirectional-merge (blue map, below image). Due to the large number of images, they have been processed 1 of every 15. The circles in the image represent the positions of the node representative and the arcs are the relations between the nodes (the edges of the graph). The thresholds for considering a pair of images belong to same region has been estimated empirically.

As we can see, even though the path is composed by several laps in the environment, the topological map has not allocated different nodes for each of the laps made, but considers the existing loop-closure and combines images of the same area captured at different times in a single node. However, there are some situations in the middle image where the algorithm has created multiple nodes for the same area or there are many edges. In some cases it is because we have not taken pictures in a row, but in other cases is due to changes in light. In order to see how the new algorithm behaves in such situations in the region marked as "sample 1" (figure 4) images were taken 1 of every 2, looking at this two images, we can see that they do not have the same illumination

Fig. 3. The path taken is shown in the image above (from authors page [1]). Middle image: the topological graph generated using two thresholds. Below image: the topological graph generated using two thresholds and the merging of the cut regions.

and also in the second image the tree cover parts that could be useful for identification (occlusion of many points of interest). Something similar occurs in the tunnel area but in this case, images inside the tunnel have very dark regions so there is no detection of so many feature points in order to match them. In the below image we have fewer nodes because the regions that appear at the beginning and end of the image have been merged in a single region and the result of the comparison between a pair of images taken from a different angle improved significantly.

Fig. 4. From sample 1:tree. Above: image representative of node 2. Below: the one of node 28.

Moreover, the use of two thresholds in our algorithm has improved the topological map, getting less nodes (connecting more regions) and less edges (relations between nodes become clear).

6   Conclusions

In this paper we have presented a new method for creating topological maps. The method consists of the combination of image segmentation into regions and the extraction of feature detectors, and then the creation of a graph structure from those features. Thus, for the matching of two images we take into account both the extracted features and the structure (graph) formed by these features. Then, we construct the topological map using this comparison method (with two thresholds), obtaining a non-directed graph that divides the environment into regions and indicates the relationships between different areas.

During the experimentation phase we constructed a topological graph that describes the environment captured during a long path and with several loop-closures (several laps). As we have seen the environment is divided into several areas, most of them unique, that is, are described by a single node. In cases where more than one node has appeared, we have seen changes due to illumination and occlusions.

As future work, we plan to improve the algorithm in order to reduce the sensitivity to changes in illumination and occlusions. We also intend to make a more advanced study of the behavior of the algorithm using different features (SIFT, SURF, Harris-Affine, Hessian-Affine). We want also to extend our graphs in a circular way, in order to take into account the circular property of this kind of images in the construction of the K-Nearest-Neighbor graph at the GTM algorithm.

Acknowledgements

This work has been supported by grant DPI2009-07144 from Ministerio de Ciencia e Innovacion of the Spanish Government.

References

1. Smith, M., Baldwin, I., Churchill, W., Paul, R., Newman, P.: The New College Vision and Laser Data Set. I. J. Robotic Res. 28(5), 595–599 (2009)
2. Deng, Y., Manjunath, B.S.: Unsupervised Segmentation of Color-Texture Regions in Images and Video. IEEE Trans. Pattern Anal. Mach. Intell. 23(8), 800–810 (2001)
3. Aguilar, W., Frauel, Y., Escolano, F., Elena Martinez-Perez, M., Espinosa-Romero, A., Lozano, M.A.: A robust Graph Transformation Matching for non-rigid registration. Image Vis. Comput. 27(7), 897–910 (2009)
4. Joo, H., Jeong, Y., Duchenne, O., Ko, S.-Y., Kweon, I.-S.: Graph-based Robust Shape Matching for Robotic Application. In: IEEE Int. Conf. on Robotics and Automation, Kobe, Japan (May 2009)
5. Azad, P., Asfour, T., Dillmann, R.: Combining Harris Interest Points and the SIFT Descriptor for Fas Scale-Invariant Object Recognition. In: IEEE Int. Conf. on Intelligent Robots and Systems, St. Lois, USA (October 2009)
6. Mikolajczyk, K., Tuytelaars, T., Schmid, C., Zisserman, A., Matas, J., Schaffalitzky, F., Kadir, T., Van Gool, L.: A comparison of affine region detectors. IJCV 65(1/2), 43–72 (2005)
7. Matas, J., Chum, O., Urban, M., Pajdla, T.: Robust wide baseline stereo from maximally stable extremal regions. In: BMVC, pp. 384–393 (2002)
8. Mikolajczyk, K., Schmid, C.: Scale and Affine invariant interest point detectors. IJCV 60(1), 63–86 (2004)
9. Chen, X., Huang, Q., Hu, P., Li, M., Tian, Y., Li, C.: Rapid and Precise Object Detection based on Color Histograms and Adaptive Bandwidth Mean Shift. In: IEEE Int. Conf. on Intelligent Robots and Systems, St. Lois, USA (October 2009)
10. Wu, J., Christensen, H.I., Rehg, J.M.: Visual Place Categorization: Problem, Dataset, and Algoritm. In: IEEE Int. Conf. on Intelligent Robots and Systems, St. Lois, USA (October 2009)
11. Liu, M., Scaramuzza, D., Pradalier, C., Siegwart, R., Chen, Q.: Scene recognition with Omnidirectional Vision for Topological Map using Lightweight Adaptive Descriptors. In: IEEE Int. Conf. on Intelligent Robots and Systems, St. Lois, USA (October 2009)
12. Vaquez-Martin, R., Marfil, R., Bandera, A.: Affine image region detection and description. Journal of Physical Agents 4(1), 45–54 (2010)
13. Canny, J.F.: A computational approach to edge detection. IEEE Transaction on Pattern Analysis and Machine Intelligence 8(6), 679–698 (1986)
14. Smith, S.M., Brady, J.M.: SUSAN - A New Approach to Low Level Image Processing. International Journal of Computer Vision 23, 45–78 (1995)
15. Lowe, D.G.: Distinctive image features from scale-invariant keypoints. International Journal of Computer Vision 60(2), 91–110 (2004)
16. Bay, H., Tuytelaars, T., Gool, L.V.: Surf: Speeded up robust features. Computer Vision and Image Understanding (CVIU) 110(3), 346–359 (2008)
17. Smith, R.C., Cheeseman, P.: On the representation and estimation of spatial uncertainty. Int. J. of Robotics Research 5(4), 56–68 (1986)
18. Smith, R., Self, M., Cheeseman, P.: Estimating uncertain spatial relationships in robotics. In: Cox, I.J., Wilfong, G.T. (eds.) Autonomous Robot Vehicles, pp. 167–193. Springer, Heidelberg (1990)
19. Julier, S., Uhlmann, J.K.: A counter example to the theory of simultaneous localization and map buildin. In: ICRA, pp. 4238–4243. IEEE, Los Alamitos (2001)
20. Montemerlo, M., Thrun, S.: Simultaneous localization and mapping with unknown data association using FastSLAM. In: Proc. of Intl. Conf. on Robotics and Automation, Taiwan, vol. 2, pp. 1985–1991 (2003)

21. Montemerlo, M., Thrun, S., Koller, D., Wegbreit, B.: FastSLAM: A factored solution to the simultaneous localization and mapping problem. In: AAAI/IAAI, pp. 593–598 (2002)
22. Diosi, A., Kleeman, L.: Advanced Sonar and Laser Range Finder Fusion for Simultaneous Localization and Mapping. In: Proc. of Intl. Conf. on Intelligent Robots and Systems, Japan, vol. 2, pp. 1854–1859 (2004)
23. Valgren, C., Lilienthal, A.J., Duckett, T.: Incremental Topological Mapping Using Omnidirectional Vision. In: IROS, pp. 3441–3447. IEEE, Los Alamitos (2006)
24. Romero, A.M., Cazorla, M., Suau, P., Escolano, F.: Graph-Matching Based Method for scene recognition on Omnidirectional Images. In: IROS (2010) (in revision)
25. Romero, A.M., Cazorla, M.: Topological SLAM Using a Graph-Matching Based Method on Omnidirectional Images. In: X Workshop de Agentes Físicos, Valencia (2010)
26. Motard, E., Raducanu, B., Cadenat, V., Vitri Ă ă, J.: Incremental On-Line Topological Map Learning for A Visual Homing Application. In: ICRA, pp. 2049–2054. IEEE, Los Alamitos (2007)
27. Goedeme, T., Nuttin, M., Tuytelaars, T., Van Gool, L.J.: Omnidirectional Vision Based Topological Navigation. International Journal of Computer Vision 74(3), 219–236 (2007)
28. Valgren, C., Duckett, T., Lilienthal, A.J.: Incremental Spectral Clustering and Its Application To Topological Mapping. In: ICRA, pp. 4283–4288. IEEE, Los Alamitos (2007)

Constraint Optimisation for Robust Image Matching with Inhomogeneous Photometric Variations and Affine Noise

Al Shorin, Georgy Gimel'farb, Patrice Delmas, and Patricia Riddle

University of Auckland, Department of Computer Science
P.B. 92019, Auckland 1142, New Zealand
{al,ggim001,pdel016,pat}@cs.auckland.ac.nz

Abstract. While modelling spatially uniform or low-order polynomial contrast and offset changes is mostly a solved problem, there has been limited progress in models which could represent highly inhomogeneous photometric variations. A recent quadratic programming (QP) based matching allows for almost arbitrary photometric deviations. However this QP-based approach is deficient in one substantial respect: it can only assume that images are aligned geometrically as it knows nothing about geometry in general. This paper improves on the QP-based framework by extending it to include a robust rigid registration layer thus increasing both its generality and practical utility. The proposed method shows up to 4 times improvement in the quadratic matching score over a current state-of-the-art benchmark.

Keywords: Robust Image Matching, Robust Image Registration, Reweighted Iterative Least Squares, Affine Functions, Inhomogeneous Photometric Noise, QP, Hildreth-D'Esopo Algorithm.

1 Introduction

Digital images capture both *photometric* and *geometric* properties of a real world 3D scene (from this point forward, for brevity, these properties will be denoted by letters p and g respectively). Matching or registering semantically similar images has to account for their p- and g-dissimilarities or noise (not to be confused with independent random noise which is denoted here as residual noise). These dissimilarities can be caused by a great deal of factors but it is convenient to think of them as being either *intrinsic* or *extrinsic* to the scene. The examples of the former type of noise include scene shadows, changing illumination, or different object poses, while the latter are most commonly introduced after image acquisition, e.g. brightness or scale adjustments. The third dichotomy of noise introduced here can be used to describe the complexity of dissimilarity patterns between the target and template images: noise patterns can be either *homogeneous* (or smooth) or *inhomogeneous* (or non-smooth). The distinction between those is somewhat arbitrary, but in this paper it is assumed that patterns are homogeneous if they can be accurately modelled by slowly varying functions

J. Blanc-Talon et al. (Eds.): ACIVS 2010, Part I, LNCS 6474, pp. 476–487, 2010.

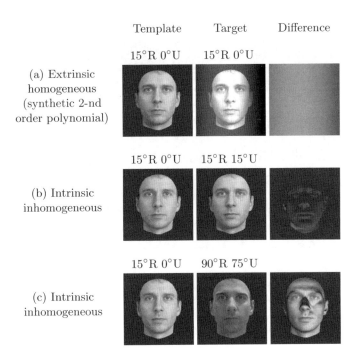

	Template	Target	Difference

(a) Extrinsic homogeneous (synthetic 2-nd order polynomial) — 15°R 0°U   15°R 0°U

(b) Intrinsic inhomogeneous — 15°R 0°U   15°R 15°U

(c) Intrinsic inhomogeneous — 15°R 0°U   90°R 75°U

Fig. 1. Homogeneous/extrinsic (a) and inhomogeneous/intrinsic (b,c) noise patterns for image 01 from Fig. 3. Notice significant effects of rotated illumination source (c). *The difference images are enhanced for visualisation purposes by the contrast factor of 1.8 and the offset of 30/255. The images are from the MIT database [9].*

of image coordinates such as low-order polynomials. Otherwise the pattern is non-smooth or inhomogeneous. The rationale for this distinction comes from the upper bound of modelling complexity of the current state-of-the-art and is further described in Section 2.

It is expected that *intrinsic p*-variations between the images of 2D objects on a frontal plane will be *homogeneous* in nature, while those of complex 3D objects will be highly *inhomogeneous*. Natural 3D scenes will almost certainly guarantee a great deal of inhomogeneity, for example, because variable illumination conditions will introduce complex shadow patterns on complex 3D surfaces. Figure 1 illustrates the notion of homogeneity: homogeneous *p*-variations (a) can be represented by a 2nd-order polynomial of image *xy*-coordinates, wherein the inhomogeneous patterns (b,c) arising from varying scene illumination are much more intricate. Noise complexity becomes more apparent under larger directional light changes (c).

A comprehensive set of inhomogeneous patterns arising from 18 different light source positions is given in Fig. 2. These images show absolute differences between two images of the same subject: one under fixed frontal illumination and the other under the light source which was rotated along horizontal and vertical axes. Cross-correlation $C = r^2$ for all the pairs provide a quantifiable statistical

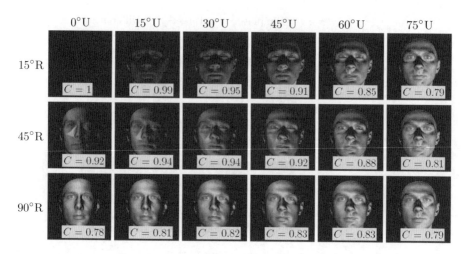

Fig. 2. The difference images between two identical faces taken under various illumination conditions: image 01 from Fig. 3 with frontal illumination vs. 18 of its variants taken under different horizontal (R) and vertical (U) lighting orientations. *The images were enhanced for visualisation purposes with the contrast factor of 1.8 and the offset of 30/255. Images are from the MIT database [9].*

measure of the magnitude of inhomogeneous template-target p-differences. The correlation values rapidly decrease for large changes in light source orientation.

Inhomogeneous p-variations pose a challenging problem to the state-of-the-art image matching as there is a notable paucity of sufficiently expressive models for representing such complex noise. Many popular algorithms [8,1] relate signal differences to low-order polynomial contrast factors and offsets. The residual is described by an independent random field of additive deviations with typically a centre-symmetric probability function. Clearly, the low-order polynomial is incapable of approximating complex natural p-noise patterns. Increasing the polynomial order past the quadratic complexity may not be appropriate as this will inevitably introduce numerical instability. An example of the practically established upper bound can be found in the recent 2nd-order polynomial model which only deals with 10 parameters [8].

While an adequately expressive p-noise model is required because inhomogeneous instrinsic noise is virtually unavoidable in practical applications, the situation is more manageable with g-variations as often it is possible to control the pose and other g-properties of the scene. Hence an-extrinsic-only g-noise model is frequently sufficient, and many g-variations encountered in practical problems can be closely approximated by planar rigid transformations.

Finally, because p- and g-noise is often modelled separately with quite different mathematical tools, combining them can be a challenging problem. Although many known methods derive and utilise a singular optimisation routine incorporating both components, it is not a trivial exercise for the algorithm presented in this paper: p- and g-parts involve totally different mathematical models

(QP vs. polynomial), different kernels (quadratic vs. robust), and the four orders of magnitude difference in their search space cardinalities respectively.

This paper presents a method which combines two disparate g- and p-models and proposes a novel framework for image matching under realistic image variations.

2   Previous Work

Image matching under realistic signal variations has been of interest for decades. At the early days, only zero-order polynomial models of spatially constant brightness and contrast have been used to derive various correlation-based matching methods [5]. The earlier work originates from the pioneering work in computer vision in the 1960s [6]. More recently, it was followed by a number of various quadratic-kernel, polynomial-based p-noise models [3].

In response to failures of non-robust techniques [3], matching methods based on Huber's statistics and second-order polynomial models of spatially variant brightness and contrast [7] constituted a step forward and later branched out into a family of related algorithms [2,16,15]. The latter replace the traditional squared-error kernel with a more robust, in the presence of large signal differences, M-estimator.

Robust matching algorithms often utilize numerical techniques such as gradient descent search for iterative suboptimal minimisation. The number of search parameters grows quadratically, as $(\nu + 1)(\nu + 2)$, with the polynomial order ν. In addition to numerical instability of higher-order polynomial functions, both the convergence rate and the speed of gradient search is notably affected as the number of parameters grows. This highlights the main dilemma of today's image matching — either the model expressiveness can be increased by incorporating a larger number of parameters to approximate natural p-noise patterns, or its robustness using a non-quadratic formulation, but not both. Methods based on polynomial p-noise models and robust estimators (matching error kernels) have to deal with computational instability and intractability should they try to increase their expressiveness to account for real-world noise patterns. In practice, these methods are forced to tackle only a small number of parameters that hinders adequate modelling of inhomogeneous noise.

As the global polynomial-based approach is not easily scalable, a number of alternative formulations have been explored in the literature. One robust approach avoids dealing with the entire N-dimensional space, where N is the image lattice cardinality, and instead uses selective heuristic sampling of the space [15]. Unfortunately, this method relies on manual crafting of a heuristic thus requiring human intervention. Additionally, most of the signal space is completely ignored. Another robust alternative is image preprocessing using edge and contour detection [16]. As with other approaches, it can only account for a low-order polynomial contrast and offset deviations, and hence it fails when realistic non-smooth variations appear.

Other methods try to avoid using robust statistics, employing the conventional least-squares approach. Unfortunately, they are equally unable to create the richer problem space. Several notable examples include correlation-based matching in the frequency domain [4], correlation-based stereo matching [1], employing correlation between local regions rather than individual pixels [14,17], divide-and-conquer matching in the pixel space by breaking down the entire image into smaller patches and evaluating localised scores [18], or even matching with a mixture model of global and local p-parameters where the local parameters describe specific signal relationships under illumination changes due to diffuse, ambient and specular reflections [10,13]. All these methods are restricted by a number of oversimplifications, have inadequately small parametric search spaces and, as a result, cannot capture the complexity of more general noise.

Recently, a promising new direction was explored wherein the problem of matching is looked at as the constraint optimisation problem [12]. This novel nonparametric quadratic programming based approach implements a model which is expressive enough to successfully capture complex intrinsic p-noise. Its large search space exploits $6N$ linear constraints in the immediate 2-neighbourhood of a pixel, while a fast QP algorithm is used to solve it. Despite showing a dramatic improvement over the state-of-the-art in terms of modelling power, it knows nothing about geometry and it assumes the perfect geometric alignment between the template and the target, thus seriously limiting its usefulness. To the best of our knowledge, a matching algorithm which can account for both affine g-noise and inhomogeneous p-noise has not been proposed yet.

3   The Proposed Matching Method

Suppose a greyscale image $\mathbf{s}$ is encoded as $\mathbf{s} : \mathcal{R} \rightarrow \mathcal{Q}$ where the lattice $\mathcal{R} = [(i,j) : i = 0, \ldots, m-1; j = 0, \ldots, n-1]$ has the total of $N = m \times n$ pixels, and where the grey level signal is defined by the finite set $\mathcal{Q} = \{0, 1, \ldots, Q-1\}$. Then, $s_{i,j}$ is the image grey level, i.e. intensity or brightness, at pixel (i,j). Let $\mathbf{t} : \mathcal{R} \rightarrow \mathcal{Q}$ denote the template $\mathbf{t}$ of the target $\mathbf{s}$.

The approach introduced in this paper merges two independent noise model layers: the p-model implementing the QP matching algorithm [12] and the g-model employing a classic robust affine registration algorithm [8].

P-model: QP-based image matching. The least-squares error kernel reduces the problem of image matching described below to a QP problem with $6N$ linear constraints sufficiently descriptive for a great range of inhomogeneous p-noise [12]. Admissible p-deviations in the target image $\mathbf{s}$ with respect to the template image $\mathbf{t}$ are represented by constraining changes of the neighbourhood signals to the predetermined range $E = [e_{\min}, e_{\max}]$ where $0 < e_{\min} < 1 < e_{\max}$. If the image $\hat{\mathbf{s}}$ is obtained by relaxing the neighbourhood relationships in $\mathbf{t}$ with the admissible multiplicative range E, then the local constraints on $\hat{\mathbf{s}}$ can be defined as

$$\Delta_{\min:i,i-1;j} \leq \hat{s}_{i;j} - \hat{s}_{i-1;j} \leq \Delta_{\max:i,i-1;j}$$
$$\Delta_{\min:i;j,j-1} \leq \hat{s}_{i;j} - \hat{s}_{i;j-1} \leq \Delta_{\max:i;j,j-1}$$
$$0 \quad\quad \leq \quad \hat{s}_{i;j} \quad \leq \quad Q-1$$

for all pixel pairs $((i,j); (i-1,j))$ and $((i,j); (i,j-1))$ in $\mathcal{R}$, where

$$
\begin{aligned}
\Delta_{\min:i,i-1;j} &= \min_{e \in E}\{e\ (t_{i,j} - t_{i-1,j})\} \\
\Delta_{\max:i,i-1;j} &= \max_{e \in E}\{e\ (t_{i,j} - t_{i-1,j})\} \\
\Delta_{\min:i;j,j-1} &= \min_{e \in E}\{e\ (t_{i,j} - t_{i,j-1})\} \\
\Delta_{\max:i;j,j-1} &= \max_{e \in E}\{e\ (t_{i,j} - t_{i,j-1})\}.
\end{aligned}
$$

The objective function of Eq. (1) assumes centre-symmetric residual noise. Its matching score is based on the Cartesian metric of the distance between $\hat{\mathbf{s}}$ and $\mathbf{t}$ under the constrained signal deviations of Eq. (1), and its minimiser is determined as

$$
\hat{\mathbf{s}} = \arg\min_{\hat{\mathbf{s}} \in \mathcal{H}(\mathbf{t};E)} \left\{ \sum_{(i,j) \in \mathcal{R}} (\hat{s}_{i;j} - s_{i;j})^2 \right\}, \tag{1}
$$

where $\mathcal{H}(\mathbf{t};E)$ describes all images $\hat{\mathbf{s}}$ which satisfy the constraints imposed by Eq. (1), i.e. all images with admissible deviations from $\mathbf{t}$. This QP problem is solved with the well-known Hildreth-d'Esopo algorithm thus guaranteeing the convergence of $\hat{\mathbf{s}}$ to a solution arbitrary close to the global minimiser. More details on the method including its derivation can be found in the literature [11].

G-model: Robust affine image registration. Let $\boldsymbol{\gamma} = [\gamma_0\ \gamma_1\ \gamma_2]^{\mathsf{T}}$ and $\boldsymbol{\delta} = [\delta_0\ \delta_1\ \delta_2]^{\mathsf{T}}$ denote six parameters $\boldsymbol{\theta} = (\boldsymbol{\gamma}, \boldsymbol{\delta})$ of the affine transform. Given the set of pixels $s_{i,j} \in \mathbf{s}$, $t_{i,j} \in \mathbf{t}$ where $(i,j) \in \mathcal{R}$, the transformation field $(\Delta i, \Delta j)$ is defined as

$$
\begin{aligned}
\Delta i &= \boldsymbol{\gamma}^{\mathsf{T}}\mathbf{v} = \gamma_0 + \gamma_1 i + \gamma_2 j \\
\Delta j &= \boldsymbol{\delta}^{\mathsf{T}}\mathbf{v} = \delta_0 + \delta_1 i + \delta_2 j,
\end{aligned} \tag{2}
$$

where $\mathbf{v} = [1\ i\ j]^{\mathsf{T}}$. The affine transformation expressed in terms of this transformation field $(\Delta i, \Delta j)$ can be rewritten as

$$
s_{i+\Delta i, j+\Delta j} = t_{i,j} + \epsilon_{i,j} \quad \text{for all } (i,j) \in \mathcal{R}, \tag{3}
$$

where ϵ is centre-symmetric p-noise due to the imprecise nature of the g-model.

Finding an estimate of the affine transformation field directly is hard. The truncated first-order Taylor series decomposition of $s_{i+\Delta i, j+\Delta j}$ can simplify the problem to

$$
s_{i,j} = t_{i-\Delta i, j-\Delta j} - \mathbf{v}^{\mathsf{T}}\left(\frac{ds}{di}\boldsymbol{\gamma} + \frac{ds}{dj}\boldsymbol{\delta}\right) + \epsilon_{i,j} \equiv t_{i-\Delta i, j-\Delta j} - \boldsymbol{\theta}^{\mathsf{T}}\mathbf{c}_{i,j} + \epsilon_{i,j}, \tag{4}
$$

where the gradients $\frac{ds}{di}$ and $\frac{ds}{dj}$ are approximated by differences between the pixel at location (i,j) and its two adjacent neighbours [7]. Zero gradient scalars are chosen for the border condition. Weights $\mathbf{c}_{i,j}$ in the linear combination of the affine parameters $\boldsymbol{\theta}$ in Eq. (4) can be computed from the respective gradient values and pixel coordinates.

The minimiser $\hat{\boldsymbol{\theta}}$ can be found by solving the robust function, leading to the formulation of robust affine registration

$$\hat{\boldsymbol{\theta}} = \underset{\gamma,\delta \in \boldsymbol{\theta}}{\arg \min} \sum_{i,j} \rho \left(s_{i,j} - t_{i-\Delta i, j-\Delta j} + \boldsymbol{\theta}^{\mathsf{T}} \boldsymbol{c}_{i,j} \right), \tag{5}$$

where an arbitrary M-estimator $\rho(\ldots)$, e.g. the Lorentzian $\rho(z) = \log \left(1 + \frac{z^2}{2} \right)$, can be employed. The cost function can be solved by any appropriate numerical procedure. In this paper, the re-weighted iterative least-squares method was implemented. The method uses the idea of W-estimation which is conditionally equivalent to the Gauss-Newton method as shown elsewhere [11]. The approximate solution offered by this method was previously shown to be satisfactory for image matching purposes [8].

4   Experimental Results

Dataset. All experiments are based on the MIT dataset [9]. It was selected due to consistency in scene poses for all images in the set, and a great deal of inhomogeneous intrinsic p-noise under strictly controlled and variant illumination as demonstrated in Fig. 2. The data base contains 360 images of 10 persons (36 per subject) captured with different vertical and horizontal orientation of two dominant illumination sources: the former changes from $0°$ (direct) to $75°$ (top), and the latter – from $15°$ (direct) to $90°$ (right). The additional ambient light source makes all facial features visible regardless of the dominant light source position. All the images have the same facial expression, geometry and backgrounds so that the experiments could be conducted in the controlled conditions. Images of all 10 subjects taken under the frontal illumination ($15°$R and $0°$U) are reproduced in Fig. 3.

Experiments. The proposed unified framework for image matching has been tested on a set of images subjected to appropriate p- and g-transformations

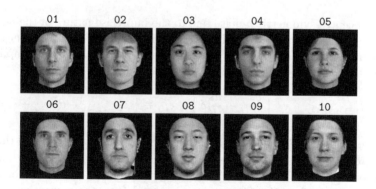

Fig. 3. All 10 images with frontal illumination $15°$R and $0°$U from the MIT dataset [9]

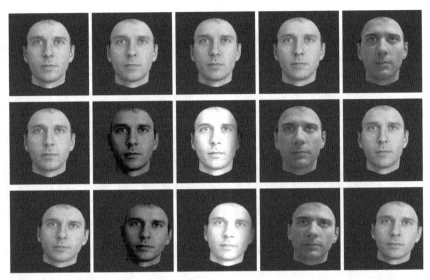

Fig. 4. A typical experimental setup for each of the five test cases. Images in vertical triplets show a template (top), the template with p-noise (centre), and the template with both p-noise and affine transformation (bottom). The bottom image is the target in the template-target pair. *Images are from the MIT dataset [9].*

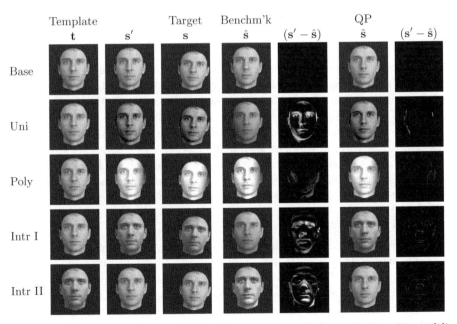

Fig. 5. Experimental results for all the five test cases (Subject 01 from Fig. 3 [9]). Residual differences of the model $\hat{\mathbf{s}}$ from the geometrically untransformed target $\mathbf{s}'$ are scaled up for visualisation purposes. The less, i.e. the darker, the residual, the better pixel-wise matching performs.

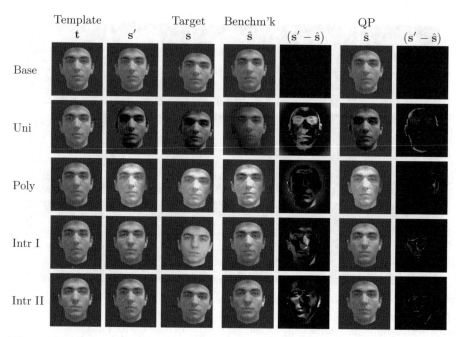

Fig. 6. Experimental results for all the five test cases (Subject **04** from Fig. 3 [9]). Residual differences of the model $\hat{s}$ from the geometrically untransformed target s' are scaled up for visualisation purposes. The less, i.e. the darker, the residual, the better pixel-wise matching performs.

forming five test cases described below. Introduced affine transformations combine translation, rotation, and scaling. A typical experimental setup for all five test cases is shown in Fig. 4 where the translation of $(40/200, 10/200)$, the rotation of $\frac{\pi}{36}$, and the vertical scaling of 0.92 was performed on the template image. The affine transformations were identical in all experiments and were largest possible to keep the face within the image lattice boundaries. In terms of p-variations, the test cases are identical to the ones defined for the QP-based approach [12]: all variables are the same including the dataset selected [9], the benchmark [8], the stopping rule and the multiplicative range E.

1. **Base Case:** Only affine noise is involved; no p-variations.
2. **Uniform Case:** A potentially lossy "darkening" p-transformation on low-value signals truncated to stay within the valid signal range $[0..255]$. The function of $f_{i,j} = 1.3t_{i,j} - 40/256$ was used to simulate uniform p-noise.
3. **Polynomial Case:** 2nd-order polynomial noise was introduced with the "brightening" function $f_{i,j} = (0.035i - 0.00021i^2)t_{i,j} + 28/256$. As with Case (2), transformed values outside $[0..255]$ were truncated.
4. **Intrinsic Case:** An image of the same subject taken under different p-conditions was chosen randomly.
5. **Intrinsic Swapped Case:** Same as above, but the images are swapped.

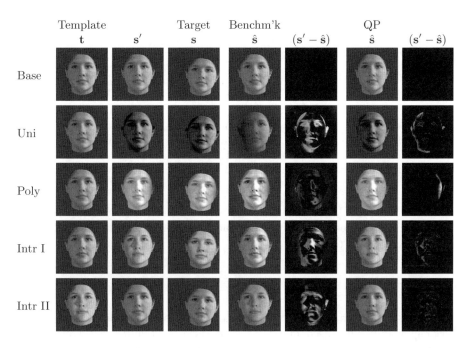

Fig. 7. Experimental results for all the five test scenarios (Subject 05 from Fig. 3 [9]). Residual differences of the model **ŝ** from the geometrically untransformed target **s′** are scaled up for visualisation purposes. The less, i.e. the darker, the residual, the better pixel-wise matching performs.

Out of all test cases, the most important ones are intrinsic Cases (4) and (5). This is because the degree of the algorithm's success needs to be judged on the matching task involving both inhomogeneous p-noise and affine g-variations. Recall that the current state-of-the-art would fail under these conditions either because intrinsic variations caused by, for example shadows, exceed the model complexity [8], or because geometry cannot be modelled at all [12]. Although, the proposed method outperforms the benchmark in all five cases, the improvements shown with Cases (4) and (5) are of greater theoretical significance.

The typical outcome of a five test case run and the comparison of the proposed method to the benchmark is demonstrated in Figs. 5-7. The results for 36 target–template pairs for each scenario are validated in Table 1.

The proposed method outperforms the benchmark in all implemented cases: the error means have been reduced by a factor ranging from 2.0 to 4.6. The improvement is statistically significant ($p < 0.0002$) in 4 out of 5 cases, while Base Case (1) still shows the satisfactory p value of 5.4%. Predictably, the highest registered mean errors were on the polynomial case. As was mentioned above, this is the result of the loss of signal depth due to value truncation. It should be also emphasized that the greatest improvement was achieved in terms of the

Table 1. Total squared differences $\|\hat{s} - s\|^2 \times 10^6$ for the experiments run. Note that κ and p-value denote the mean improvement ratios and the p-values for the one-tailed hypothesis $H_0 : \mu_{\text{benchmark}} > \mu_{\text{our algorithm}}$, respectively).

Test case	Benchmark		Our algorithm		Analysis	
	Mean	Std	Mean	Std	κ	p-value
Base	0.4	0.5	**0.2**	**0.3**	2.0	0.054
Uniform	13.0	11.3	**3.8**	**6.1**	3.4	< 0.0002
Poly	16.1	13.6	**6.9**	**6.1**	2.3	< 0.0002
Intrinsic	8.6	6.8	**1.8**	**2.5**	4.6	< 0.0002
Intrinsic Swapped	8.2	6.0	**2.1**	**2.5**	4.0	< 0.0002

mean error ratios in Cases (4) and (5). This shows that the point of the greatest theoretical interest has been successfully addressed here, and it constitutes the main contribution of this work.

5   Conclusions

The proposed new image matching algorithm successfully combines the recent photometric-only QP-based matching with the robust affine registration and achieves a marked performance improvement when dealing with inhomogeneous photometric noise caused, for example, by varying illumination of a 3D scene.

The proposed algorithm preserves the modularity of its p- and g-components. Individually, each component creates its own robust matching methodology that, when combined, improves the known state-of-the-art approach based on the low-order polynomial model or any other noise model that is limited by the upper bound of such a polynomial [14,13]. The proposed approach does not restrict the expressibility of the photometric noise model yet it remains robust.

References

1. Basri, R., Jacobs, D., Kemelmacher, I.: Photometric stereo with general, unknown lighting. International Journal of Computer Vision 72(3), 239–257 (2007)
2. Chen, J., Chen, C., Chen, Y.: Fast algorithm for robust template matching with M-estimators. IEEE Trans. on Signal Processing 51(1), 230–243 (2003)
3. Crowley, J., Martin, J.: Experimental comparison of correlation techniques. In: Proc. International Conference on Intelligent Autonomous Systems (IAS-4), Karlsruhe, Germany, March 27-30, pp. 86–93 (1995)
4. Fitch, A., Kadyrov, A., Christmas, W., Kittler, J.: Fast robust correlation. IEEE Trans. on Image Processing 14(8), 1063–1073 (2005)
5. Gruen, A.: Adaptive least squares correlation: a powerful image matching technique. South African Journal of Photogrammetry, Remote Sensing and Cartography 14(3), 175–187 (1985)
6. Kovalevsky, V.: The problem of character recognition from the point of view of mathematical statistics. In: Kovalevsky, V. (ed.) Character Readers and Pattern Recognition. Spartan, New York (1968)

7. Lai, S.: Robust image matching under partial occlusion and spatially varying illumination change. Computer Vision and Image Understanding 78(1), 84–98 (2000)
8. Lai, S., Fang, M.: Method for matching images using spatially-varying illumination change models, US patent 6,621,929 (September 2003)
9. M.I.T. face database (accessed August 24, 2006)
   http://vismod.media.mit.edu/pub/images
10. Pizarro, D., Peyras, J., Bartoli, A.: Light-invariant fitting of active appearance models. In: Proc. IEEE Conference on Computer Vision and Pattern Recognition, CVPR 2008, Anchorage, Alaska, pp. 1–6 (June 2008)
11. Shorin, A.: Modelling Inhomogeneous Noise and Large Occlusions for Robust Image Matching. Ph.D. thesis, University of Auckland (2010)
12. Shorin, A., Gimel'farb, G., Delmas, P., Morris, J.: Image matching with spatially variant contrast and offset: A quadratic programming approach. In: Kasparis, T., Kwok, J. (eds.) S+SSPR 2008. LNCS, vol. 5342, pp. 100–107. Springer, Heidelberg (2008)
13. Silveira, G., Malis, E.: Real-time visual tracking under arbitrary illumination changes. In: Proc. IEEE Conference on Computer Vision and Pattern Recognition, CVPR 2007, June 17-22, pp. 1–6 (2007)
14. Tombari, F., Di Stefano, L., Mattoccia, S.: A robust measure for visual correspondence. In: Proc. 14th Int. Conf. on Image Analysis and Processing (ICIAP), Modena, Italy, pp. 376–381 (September 2007)
15. Wei, S., Lai, S.: Robust and efficient image alignment based on relative gradient matching. IEEE Trans. on Image Processing 15(10), 2936–2943 (2006)
16. Yang, C., Lai, S., Chang, L.: Robust face image matching under illumination variations. Journal on Applied Signal Processing 2004(16), 2533–2543 (2004)
17. Zhu, G., Zhang, S., Chen, X., Wang, C.: Efficient illumination insensitive object tracking by normalized gradient matching. IEEE Signal Processing Letters 14(12), 944–947 (2007)
18. Zou, J., Ji, Q., Nagy, G.: A comparative study of local matching approach for face recognition. IEEE Trans. on Image Processing 16(10), 2617–2628 (2007)

Author Index

Printing: Mercedes-Druck, Berlin
Binding: Stein+Lehmann, Berlin